─── Temporary ───

Military Lodging

Around the World

by
L. Ann Crawford
Vice President, Military Marketing Services, Inc.
and Publisher, Military Living Publications
and
William "Roy" Crawford, Sr., Ph.D.
President, Military Marketing Services, Inc.
and Military Living Publications

Vice President - Marketing - R. J. Crawford

Editor - Donna L. Russell
Assistant Editors - Nicole Clark, Elizabeth Ksiazek, Kathie Russell,
and Margaret Volpe
Cover Design - Susan P. Druzak

Cover Photo Credits - Mologne House photo taken by R. J. Crawford, the Inn at Schofield, the Hale Koa and the Fort Myer photos taken by Ann Crawford. All other photos were furnished by the facility shown.

Chief of Staff - Timothy G. Brown, TSgt, USAF (Ret)

Office Staff:
John Camp, Beth Casteel, Nigel Fellers, Maureen Fleegal,
Irene Kearney, Lourdes Medina, Sandy Moore, Tin Ngo,
Karme Raggio, Joel Thomas, MSgt, USA (Ret),
Ricky Thomas, Larry Williamson.

Military Living Publications
P. O. Box 2347
Falls Church, Virginia 22042-0347
TEL: (703) 237-0203 - FAX: (703) 237-2233

NOTICE

The information in this book has been compiled and edited either from the activity/installation listed, its superior headquarters, or from other sources that may or may not be noted by the authors. Information about the facilities listed, including contact phone numbers and rate structures, could change. This book should be used as a guide to the listed facilities with this understanding. Please forward any corrections or additions to: **Military Living Publications, P.O. Box 2347, Falls Church, Virginia 22042-0347.** TEL: 703-237-0203, FAX: 703-237-2233.

This directory is published by Military Marketing Services, Inc. T/A Military Living Publications, a private business in no way connected with the U.S. Federal or any other government. This book is copyrighted by L. Ann and William Roy Crawford, Sr. Opinions expressed by the publisher and authors of this book are their own and are not to be considered an official expression by any government agency or official.

The information and statements contained in this directory have been compiled from sources believed to be reliable and to represent the best current opinion (at press time) on the subject. No warranty, guarantee, or representation is made by Military Marketing Services, Inc., as to the absolute correctness or sufficiency of any representation contained in this or other publications and we can assume no responsibility.

**Copyright 1997
L. Ann and William "Roy" Crawford
MILITARY MARKETING SERVICES, INC.,
(T/A MILITARY LIVING PUBLICATIONS)
First Printing - June 1997**

All rights reserved under International and Pan-American copyright conventions. No part of this book may be reproduced in any form without permission in writing from the publisher, except by a reviewer who wishes to quote briefly from listings in connection with a review written for inclusion in a magazine or newspaper, with source credit to **MILITARY LIVING'S *TEMPORARY MILITARY LODGING AROUND THE WORLD*.** A copy of the review, when published, should be sent to Military Living Publications, P.O. Box 2347, Falls Church, Virginia 22042-0347.

Library of Congress Cataloging-in-Publication Data

```
Crawford, Ann Caddell.
    Military living's temporary military lodging around the world / by
L. Ann Crawford and William "Roy" Crawford ; editor, Donna L.
Russell.
        p.   cm.
    Includes index.
    ISBN 0-914862-67-7
    1. United States--Armed Forces--Barracks and quarters-
-Directories.   2. Military bases, American--Directories.
I. Crawford, William Roy, 1932-     .  II. Russell, Donna L.
III. Title.
UC403.C72    1997
355.7'0973--dc21                                             97-17542
                                                                CIP
```

ISBN 0-914862-67-7

Printed in Canada

INTRODUCTION

This book will pay for itself many times over. All you have to do is use it! There are places to stay on military installations for as little as $5 or $8 per night. The most common charges we found quoted were in the $35-$50 price range for a family of five sharing one unit in a transient lodging facility, or $40-$55 for a Navy Lodge unit, many of which have sleeping space for five, wall-to-wall carpeting, color TV, kitchenette with all utensils, and more. Since our last edition, inflation has caused some military lodging prices to increase; however, they have not increased to the same degree or at the same rate as prices in the civilian sector. In some large cities, the commercial cost of lodging has risen to $200 per night, or more. Clearly, *Temporary Military Lodging Around the World* can greatly reduce the high cost of travel experienced by military families.

Before the first edition of this book was published in 1971, there was a big "catch" involved in getting to use temporary lodging facilities. The problem was finding out which installation had what. Military Living Publications has solved that problem by doing the leg work for you. Just glance through the hundreds of listings that follow and you will find out why this book is indispensable if you want to "travel on less per day...the military way!"™

HOW TO USE THIS DIRECTORY

Each listing has similar information, listed in the following order:

Official Name of Installation (AL01R2)
Temporary Military Lodging Mailing Address
Scheduled to close month/day/year (if applicable)

Location Identifier: Example: (AL01R2). The first two characters (letters) are state or country abbreviations used in Military Living's books. The next two-character set is a random number (00-99) assigned to a specific location. The fifth character, an R, stands for Region. The sixth character indicates the location of the region.

TELEPHONE NUMBER INFORMATION: C- This is the commercial telephone service for the installation's main or information/operator assistance number. The designation has also been used for other commercial numbers in this directory, including the number to be called for billeting reservations. Within the North American Area Code System, the first three digits are the area code. For foreign country locations, we have provided full telephone numbers for dialing from the U.S. and in-country. The first two to three digits, after direct dial long distance (011), are the Country Code, the next one to four digits are the city code, if used (consult your local directory or operator for specific dialing instructions). The next three digits are the area telephone exchange/switch number. For foreign countries, the exchange number can be either fewer or more digits than in the U.S. system. The last four digits are usually the information or operator assistance number or the individual telephone line number. In the United Kingdom (UK), dialing instructions are given from the telephone exchange serving the installation. These numbers are different for each location in the UK from which you are dialing. Consult the local directory or operator for specific dialing instructions.

D- This is the Department of Defense, worldwide, Defense Switched Network (DSN). We have, at the request of our readers, included the DSN prefix (area voice codes) with most numbers in each listing. In most cases, the number given is for information/operator assistance.

DSN-E: (Defense Switched Network - Europe) which replaced the European Telephone System (ETS). See standard DSN-E emergency and service numbers listed in Appendix D.

FAX: Telefax numbers are listed for reservations when available.

LOCATION: Here you'll find specific driving instructions to the Temporary Military Lodging location from local major cities, interstate/country highways and routes. More than one routing may be provided. **USMRA**: Coordinates in *Military Living's UNITED STATES MILITARY ROAD ATLAS* which are given for each CONUS and US Possession location. **NMC**: is the nearest major city. Distance in miles and directions from the temporary military lodging (TML) location to the nearest major city are provided.

Lodging Office: In most cases the lodging/billeting address is the address we have provided at the beginning of the listing. In those cases that it is not at the beginning of the listing, it will be listed here. The building number, street address, etc., are listed to provide you the physical location of the lodging office. The C-, D-, and/or FTS telephone numbers and FAX numbers of the billeting office are given when provided

iii

to us. **We have "bolded" (darkened) reservation numbers for the convenience of our readers - this should help, particularly when making expensive overseas calls.** Hours of operation of the billeting office, main desk, or contact office are listed. Check in/check out points and times are given. Use of TML by government civilian employees on duty is specified. Other helpful general billeting information is detailed. E-mail addresses, when available, are listed at the end of each lodging office text.

TML: (Temporary Military Lodging) Each category of TML, i.e., Guest House, Hotel, Army/Navy/Air Force/Marine Corps Lodge, and so on, is listed separately in most cases. The category of occupancy, i.e., all ranks, specific grades, officer, enlisted, male, female, is given. Occupancy by leave or duty status is given. Reservation requirements and some contact telephone numbers are listed. The accommodations (bedroom, two bedroom, three bedroom, separate bedroom, suite), and number of each category of accommodation is given last in parenthesis. Appointments, services and supporting facilities such as kitchens, utensils, television, air conditioning, maid service, cribs, cots, washer/dryer, ice, vending machines, handicapped facilities, etc., are given where they were provided to us. Where there is a charge for services it is noted, otherwise it is free. Whether the structure is older or modern, its condition, and if renovations or improvements have taken place since 1990 are specified. The per day rates are listed for each category of occupant. Please note that rates can change often. Priorities and restrictions on occupancy are listed. **NOTE:** Pets are not allowed in temporary lodging facilities unless otherwise noted, but for the convenience of our readers we have noted where kennel facilities are available. Also, all facilities are open to men and women unless otherwise noted.

DV/VIP: (Distinguished Visitor/Very Important Person) The contact office or person, building, room and telephone number for DV/VIP lodging and other support is given where available. The grade/status for DV/VIPs at the installation is specified. The use of DV/VIP facilities/services by retirees and lower grades is indicated.

TML Availability: The best and most difficult times for TML are listed as reported. If possible, call, FAX or write regarding availability before you travel or take your chances on space-available use.

Points of Interest for visitors are indicated and are bolded near the bottom of the installation listing. Some listings carry military information of interest to visitors such as famous units stationed, or on post/base military museums. Post/base/station locator, medical emergency and police telephone numbers are provided where available. Other Military Living publications carry many support facility telephone numbers used on listings that are closing or expanding in some manner, "inside information" may also be included here.

Please review Appendix A, General Abbreviations, Appendix C, Billeting Regulations and Navy Lodge Polocies. Also see Appendix B, Temporary Military Lodging Questions and Answers about TML Regulations that supplement the basic TML listings and Appendix D, Telephone Information.

BASE CLOSURES

The 1995 Defence Base Closure and Realignment Commission's Report was accepted by Congress and became Public Law on 28 September 1995.

The 1995 law, along with previous directed closures and realignments in the basic law in 1988, 1990, 1991 and 1993, complete the base closure and realignments which have been approved by Congress. These directed closures have been noted at the beginning of each listing affected with the DoD estimated date of final closure. Some bases have already closed and consequently have been deleted from this edition.

It should also be noted that final closure dates will be established for each installation. These dates could change as the DoD completes the final closure plans and as funding becomes available to effedt the closures. Support facilities on the affected bases will normally decrease gradually; therefore, it is best to check with each military installation scheduled for closure or realignment before you go. Some bases scheduled for closure or realignment do not have temporary lodging and, consequently, are not listed in this book.

We have noted in the title of each listing scheduled for closure the planned closure of the temporary lodging.

Lastly, it should be noted that the 1995 Defense Base Closure and Realignment Law along with previous base closure laws only apply to domestic United States Bases and United States Bases located in U.S. possessions. The Secretary of Defense, acting within his authority, announced on 1 July 1993 and 24 February 1994, the further reduction or realignment of the United States Military Sites Overseas (in Foriegn countries). In early 1997 the Secretary of Defense announced the closing of Augsberg, GE Community and related realignments.

Some Words About Our Changing World

The military is undergoing sweeping changes which have made this book both challenging and interesting to publish. Some installations are closing, and others are realigning. We have included the dates of expected closure as provided to us at the beginning of each listing. Installations which will close prior to 30 September 1997 have been excluded from this book. The information in this book is as accurate as we can make it. The information in this book has been provided by billeting facilities worldwide. However, as with all directories, there are changes that happen daily that cause inaccuracies. **Military Living Publications** has always relied on its readers to write or call when information has become outdated. It is the secret of our success. Please do not hesitate to let us know when information is incorrect, or if we have missed a lodging opportunity for your fellow travelers. Enjoy.

EDITOR'S NOTE: Most installations that replied to our request have furnished FAX numbers for reservations and/or which credit cards are accepted at their lodging facilities. If you come across a listing which does not have either FAX numbers or credit cards listed, it is suggested that you phone before you go as there is a good chance that this installation did not respond to our request for information. If you do stay at a facility which did not respond to our request, we would appreciate it if you could forward any information on that facility to us at:

Military Living Publications
ATTN: Editor - TML
P.O. Box 2347
Falls Church, VA 22042-0347

CENTRAL RESERVATION SYSTEMS

ARMY LODGING RESERVATIONS
1-800-GO-ARMY-1

The United States Army and the United States Navy of the Uniformed Services have established central reservation systems for temporary military lodging, operating through 1-800 toll free telephone service. At press time, the other Uniformed Services had not established central reservation service for temporary military lodging. The following information is provided for these Uniformed Services systems:

United States Army Lodging Reservations: The Army Central Reservation Center (ACRC), located at Redstone Arsenal, AL is an ongoing Army "Quality of Life" initiative of the US Army Community and Family Support Center, Hospitality Directorate. The ACRC is not a new service, but has been expanded and improved. The original toll-free reservation service began in 1994. In October 1994, ACRC absorbed the Lodging Success Program, which gives travelers the opportunity to make reservations at conveniently located, high-quality, economically priced commercial (off-post) hotels in the National Capital Region (Washington, D.C. area).

This is how the ACRC operates: When you call the toll-free number **1-800-GO-ARMY-1 (1-800-462-7691)** you will hear two choices:

Dial 1: to make reservations for on-post lodging in a temporary duty or permanent change of station status, to make Lodging Success Program reservations, to obtain information about on-post leisure accommodations, or to make reservations for Armed Forces Recreation Center hotels in Europe.

Dial 2: to make leisure travel (vacation) reservations at commercial hotels off post anywhere in the United States through Carlson Wagonlit Travel. (A percentage of the Carlson Wagonlit Travel commission from room bookings is returned to Army MWR for reinvestment in soldier and family programs). **The ACRC agents do not make reservations at AFRC Shades of Green™ on Walt Disney World® Resorts, call the resorts directly; Tel: C: 1-407-824-3600 or Fax: C: 1-407-824-3540.**

Once you make your choice, you will be connected to a reservations agent ready to help you book your rooms.

Who can use the ACRC?

* Military personnel and DoD civilians on official travel
* Soldiers and families on permanent change of station orders
* Soldiers and families traveling space-A to Army installations
* Army Reservists and families
* Military retirees and families

The ACRC agents are on duty Monday through Friday from 0600 to 2100; Saturdays, Sundays and holidays, 0800 to 1800, Eastern Standard or Daylight Time.

Travelers from outside the CONUS can use ACRC by dialing DSN D-312-897-2790. Reservations may also be faxed to C-205-876-6870 or D-312-746-6870. Reservations at AFRC Europe and The Inn at Schofield Barracks, HI can be booked through ACRC 1-800-Go-Army-1. Patrons for all other overseas locations must dial direct (please see each listing in this book for dialing numbers from CONUS/ Overseas). Some individual Army Lodging Locations in CONUS have toll-free, 1-800 numbers which are contained in each listing.

NAVY LODGING RESERVATIONS

BACHELOR QUARTERS
CENTRAL RESERVATION SYSTEM (BQCRS)

UNITED STATES NAVY 1-800-576-9327 (SATO)

The Navy has achieved its goal of providing Navy-wide Bachelor Quarters Central Reservation System (BQCRS) coverage for convenient, one-stop travel services. The Navy Bachelor Quarters at each base are connected on line through the BQCRS. All Navy military and many civilian personnel on official temporary duty travel are required to make lodging reservations through BQCRS when they make transportation arrangements. Personnel who are traveling by personally owned vehicles or those who require reservations for lodging only should call **SATO at 1-800-576-9327.**

Personnel on leave, vacation or leisure time travel (Not on Government funded orders in connection with PCS, TAD or TDY) must call each Navy BEQ/BOQ directly for information and reservations. Please see the reservations telephone and telefax numbers in each Navy listing in **Temporary Military Lodging Around The World**. Most lodging for leave personnel is on a space-A basis only.

NAVY LODGE PROGRAM

FOR TOLL-FREE RESERVATIONS: 1-800-NAVY INN (1-800-628-9466)

Reservations and all other information such as Rates and Hours of Operation can be obtained by calling 1-800 NAVY-INN (1-800-628-9466). **All Navy Lodges located in foreign countries (listed in this book) must be called directly for reservations (except personnel on PCS orders). The complete telephone dialing instructions from CONUS are in each Navy Lodge listing.** Rates, hours of operation and other information is available at the 1-800-NAVY INN (1-800-628-9466) number.

From Overseas (in Foreign Countries) to make Navy Lodge Reservations call: **Japan-0031-11-3313; Spain-900-93-1123; United Kingdom-0500-893652 and Italy-1678-70740.**

At press time there were 39 Navy Lodges operating worldwide. Three additional lodges are planned in the near future at: Annapolis NS, MD-Fall 1997; Dam Neck Fleet Combat Training Center, Atlantic, Virginia Beach, VA-Late 1997 and Monterey Naval Postgraduate School, CA-Fall 1998.

Many Temporary Lodging Facilities worldwide have E-mail addresses from which you can make reservations and request information. We have listed each E-mail address which we have in the text of each listing contained in this book.

There are no central reservation systems for the USMC, USCG and USAF. Reservations for lodging facilities operated by these Uniformed Services must be coordinated directly with each lodging facility. Postal mail and E-mail addresses along with commercial and defense telephone and telefax numbers are published in each lodging listing in this book.

Military Living's Travel Club ID Number ML3009

For Worldwide Reservations, Call Your Professional Travel Agent or Dollar Rent A Car

Important Dollar Rent A Car Telephone Numbers

1-800-800-4000	Worldwide Reservations
1-800-800-6000	EuroDollar® Reservations
1-800-235-9393	Emergency Roadside Service
1-800-800-5252	Customer Center

www.dollarcar.com

★★★★★★★★★★★★★★★★★★★★★★★★★★★★★★★★★★★

A National Patriotic Organization of American Military Officers of All Uniformed Services
Active, Reserve, Retired, Former and their Descendants

The Military Order of the World Wars

77 Years of Selfless Service to the Nation
Serving America's Future Through Support of JROTC, ROTC and Youth Leadership Conferences
We Stand To Stimulate Love of Country and Flag • Maintain Law and Order
• Promote Patriotic Education • Defend the Honor and Supremacy of the National Government
• Foster Fraternal Relations Between the Services
Members include: Pershing, MacArthur, Marshall, Truman, Westmoreland, Mundy, Sullivan and

"Take Time To Serve Your Country"

Name_____ Rank/Status_____
Address_____ City_____ State____ Zip_____
Service Branch_____ Telephone (___)_____

__Regular Annual $30   __*Regular Perpetual $250 (Four Installments of $62.50)
__Hereditary Annual $30 __*Hereditary Perpetual $250 (Four Installments of $62.50)
__Former Member $30   __*Hereditary Perpetual (Under 21) $125 (Four Installments of $31.25)

Membership includes subscription to *Officer Review*.
* Perpetual memberships are a one time cost.

Detach and remit to: MOWW, 435 North Lee Street, Alexandria, VA 22314
Phone (703) 683-4911 • Fax (703) 683-4501
E-Mail: MOWWHQ@aol.com • Homepage: moww.org

There's A New House *near* The White House

We welcome Active Duty Military, Retirees, Guard & Reserve and Active and Retired Government Civilians for Official Duty or Leisure Travel. Eligible Family Members, to include Unaccompanied and Visitors of Patients, are also welcome.

- ★ The Army's Newest Hotel
- ★ 200 Luxury Rooms and Suites
- ★ Restaurant
- ★ Meeting & Banquet Space
- ★ State-of-the-Art Security
- ★ 15 Minutes to Downtown Attractions
- ★ 5 Minutes to Metro
- ★ Courtesy Van
- ★ 50% Handicap Accessible

- ★ Free Parking
- ★ Total Convention Services
- ★ Weddings
- ★ Meetings from 2-200
- ★ Outdoor Recreation Facilities for Picnics, Athletics, etc.
- ★ Total Business Center Support
- ★ Adjacent to Chapel
- ★ Fitness Center Access

Walter Reed Army Medical Center, Washington, D.C.

P.O. Box 59728, Washington D.C. 20012
Phone: 202-726-8700 • **Fax: 202-782-4665**

CONTENTS

UNITED STATES

LOCATION IDENTIFIER	INSTALLATION	PAGE

ALABAMA

AL07R2	Dauphin Island Coast Guard Recreational Facility	1
AL01R2	Fort McClellan	1
AL02R2	Fort Rucker	2
AL04R2	Gunter Annex/Maxwell Air Force Base	3
AL03R2	Maxwell Air Force Base	4
AL06R2	Redstone Arsenal	5

ALASKA

AK18R5	Clear Air Force Station	6
AK15R5	Eielson Air Force Base	7
AK09R5	Elmendorf Air Force Base	7
AK10R5	Fort Greely	8
AK03R5	Fort Richardson	9
AK07R5	Fort Wainwright	10
AK08R5	Kodiak Coast Guard Support Center	11
AK25R5	Sitka Coast Guard Air Station	12

ARIZONA

AZ01R4	Davis-Monthan Air Force Base	13
AZ02R4	Fort Huachuca	14
AZ16R4	Gila Bend Air Force Auxiliary Field	15
AZ03R4	Luke Air Force Base	15
AZ05R4	Yuma Army Proving Ground	17
AZ04R4	Yuma Marine Corps Air Station	17

ARKANSAS

AR04R2	Fort Chaffee	18
AR02R2	Little Rock Air Force Base	19
AR03R2	Pine Bluff Arsenal	19
	Other Installations in Arkansas	
AR07R2	Camp Joseph T. Robinson	20

CALIFORNIA

CA13R4	Barstow Marine Corps Logistics Base	20
CA47R4	Beale Air Force Base	21
CA30R4	Camp Pendleton Marine Corps Base	22
CA83R4	Camp San Luis Obispo	23
CA34R4	China Lake Naval Air Warfare Systems Center, Weapons Division	24
CA38R4	Coronado Naval Amphibious Base	25
CA03R4	Del Mar Beach Cottages	26
CA48R4	Edwards Air Force Base	27
CA09R4	El Centro Naval Air Facility	27
CA22R4	El Toro Marine Corps Air Station	28
CA37R4	Fort Hunter Liggett	29
CA01R4	Fort Irwin National Training Center	30
CA46R4	Fort MacArthur	31
CA45R4	Fort Mason Officers' Club	31
CA06R4	Lemoore Naval Air Station	32

ix

CALIFORNIA, continued

CA39R4	Los Alamitos Armed Forces Reserve Center	33
CA25R4	Los Angeles/Long Beach Coast Guard Eleventh Reseerve Coast Guard District	34
CA08R4	March Air Base	34
CA20R4	Marines' Memorial Club	35
CA35R4	McClellan Air Force Base	37
CA14R4	Miramar Naval Air Station	37
CA15R4	Moffett Federal Air Field	38
CA16R4	Monterey Naval Postgraduate School	39
CA43R4	North Island Naval Air Station	40
CA18R4	Oakland Army Base	41
CA23R4	Petaluma Coast Guard Training Center	42
CA40R4	Point Mugu Naval Air Weapons Station	42
CA32R4	Port Hueneme Naval Construction Battalion Center	44
CA74R4	Presidio of Monterey	45
CA53R4	San Clemente Island Naval Auxiliary Landing Field	45
CA57R4	San Diego Marine Corps Recruit Depot	46
CA26R4	San Diego Naval Station	47
CA79R4	San Diego Naval Submarine Base	48
CA54R4	San Diego Naval Training Center	49
CX01R4	San Diego YMCA Inns	49
CA44R4	Sierra Army Depot	50
CA50R4	Travis Air Force Base	51
CA86R4	Tustin Marine Corps Air Station	52
CA27R4	Twentynine Palms Marine Corps Air/Ground Combat Center	52
CA29R4	Vandenberg Air Force Base	53

Other Installations in California

CA98R4	Camp Roberts	54
CA24R4	Lake Tahoe Coast Guard Recreation Facilities	54
CA59R4	San Diego Naval Medical Center	54

COLORADO

CO10R3	Fitzsimons US Army Garrison	54
CO02R3	Fort Carson	55
CO06R3	Peterson Air Force Base	56
CO07R3	United States Air Force Academy	57

Other Installations in Colorado

CO01R3	Farish Recreation Area	58

CONNECTICUT

CT05R1	Camp Rowland	58
CT01R1	New London Naval Submarine Base	59
CT02R1	United States Coast Guard Academy	60

DELAWARE

DE01R1	Dover Air Force Base	60

DISTRICT OF COLUMBIA

DC02R1	Anacostia Naval Station	61
DC01R1	Bolling Air Force Base	62
DC05R1	Fort Lesley J. McNair	63
DC03R1	Walter Reed Army Medical Center	64
DC12R1	Washington Navy Lodge	65

FLORIDA

FL42R1	Camp Blanding Training Site	65
FL06R1	Cecil Field Naval Air Station	66
FL19R1	Corry Naval Technical Training Center	67
FL27R1	Eglin Air Force Base	67
FL17R1	Homestead Air Reserve Base	68
FL18R1	Hurlburt Field	69
FL08R1	Jacksonville Naval Air Station	69
FL15R1	Key West Naval Air Station	70
FL02R1	MacDill Air Force Base	72
FL28R1	Marathon Recreation Cottages	72
FL13R1	Mayport Naval Station	73
FL09R1	Oak Grove Park	74
FL11R1	Orlando Naval Training Center	74
FL35R1	Panama City Naval Coastal Systems Station Naval Surface Warfare Center	75
FL03R1	Patrick Air Force Base	76
FL14R1	Pensacola Naval Air Station	77
FL49R1	Shades of Green™ on Walt Disney World® Resort	79
FL04R1	Tyndall Air Force Base	80
FL05R1	Whiting Field Naval Air Station	80

GEORGIA

GA17R1	Albany Marine Corps Logistics Base	81
GA12R1	Athens Navy Supply Corps School	82
GA16R1	Atlanta Naval Air Station	83
GA23R1	Camp Frank D. Merrill	84
GA13R1	Dobbins Air Reserve Base	84
GA11R1	Fort Benning	85
GA21R1	Fort Gillem	86
GA09R1	Fort Gordon	87
GA08R1	Fort McPherson	88
GA15R1	Fort Stewart	89
GA10R1	Hunter Army Airfield	90
GA03R1	Kings Bay Naval Submarine Base	90
GA02R1	Moody Air Force Base	92
GA14R1	Robins Air Force Base	93

HAWAII

HI10R6	Barbers Point Naval Air Station	94
HI01R6	Barbers Point Recreation Area	94
HI04R6	Barking Sands Pacific Missile Range Facility	95
HI02R6	Bellows Recreation Area	96
HI09R6	Fort Shafter	97
HI08R6	Hale Koa Hotel AFRC	97
HI11R6	Hickam Air Force Base	99
HI12R6	Kaneohe Bay Beach Cottages	100
HI12R6	Kaneohe Marine Corps Base	101
HI17R6	Kilauea Military Camp AFRC	101
HI23R6	Lualualei Naval Magazine	102
HI19R6	Pearl Harbor Naval Submarine Base	103
HI20R6	Pearl Harbor Naval Station	103
HI13R6	Schofield Barracks	104
HI03R6	Tripler Army Medical Center	105
HI05R6	Waianae Army Recreation Center	105

IDAHO

ID04R4	Gowen Field	106
ID01R4	Mountain Home Air Force Base	107

ILLINOIS

IL04R2	Charles Melvin Price Support Center	107
IL07R2	Great Lakes Naval Training Center	108
IL08R2	Rock Island Arsenal	109
IL02R2	Scott Air Force Base	110

INDIANA

IN07R2	Camp Atterbury	111
IN03R2	Crane Division Naval Surface Warfare Center	111
IIN01R2	Grissom Air Reserve Base	112

IOWA

IA02R2	Camp Dodge	114

KANSAS

KS04R3	Fort Leavenworth	115
KS02R3	Fort Riley	115
KS03R3	McConnell Air Force Base	116

KENTUCKY

KY02R2	Fort Campbell	118
KY01R2	Fort Knox	118

LOUISIANA

LA01R2	Barksdale Air Force Base	120
LA12R2	Camp Beauregard ARNG Training Site	121
LA07R2	Fort Polk	121
LA13R2	Jackson Barracks	122
LA11R2	New Orleans Naval Air Station/Joint Reserve Base	123
LA06R2	New Orleans Naval Support Activity	124

MAINE

ME10R1	Bangor Air National Guard Base	125
ME07R1	Brunswick Naval Air Station	125
ME08R1	Cutler Naval Computer and Telecommunications Station	126
ME09R1	Winter Harbor Naval Security Group Activity	127

MARYLAND

MD11R1	Aberdeen Proving Ground	128
MD02R1	Andrews Air Force Base	129
MD06R1	Bethesda National Naval Medical Center	130
MD01R1	Curtis Bay Coast Guard Yard	131
MD07R1	Fort Detrick	132
MD08R1	Fort George G. Meade	133
MD13R1	Fort Ritchie	134
MD04R1	Indian Head Naval Surface Warfare Center	134
MD09R1	Patuxent River Naval Air Warfare Center	135
MD05R1	Solomons Navy Recreation Center	136

MARYLAND, continued

MD10R1	United States Naval Academy/Annapolis Naval Station	137
MD22R1	Washington Naval Air Facility	137

MASSACHUSETTS

MA16R1	Armed Services YMCA of Boston	138
MA07R1	Boston Coast Guard Integrated Support Command	139
MA10R1	Cape Cod Coast Guard Air Station	139
MA09R1	Devens Inn and Conference Center	140
MA02R1	Fourth Cliff Family Recreation Area	141
MA06R1	Hanscom Air Force Base	141
MA03R1	Westover Air Reserve Base	142

MICHIGAN

MI10R2	Camp Grayling	143
MI01R2	Selfridge US Army Garrison	144
	Other Installations in Michigan	
MI04R2	Point Betsie Recreation Cottage	144

MINNESOTA

MN02R2	Camp Riley National Guard Training Center	145
MN01R2	Minneapolis-St. Paul IAP/Air Reserve Station	145

MISSISSIPPI

MS01R2	Columbus Air Force Base	146
MS03R2	Gulfport Naval Construction Battalion Center	147
MS02R2	Keesler Air Force Base	148
MS04R2	Meridian Naval Air Station	149
MS06R2	Pascagoula Naval Station	150
	Other Installations in Mississippi	
MS07R2	Camp Shelby Training Site	151

MISSOURI

MO03R2	Fort Leonard Wood	151
MO01R2	Lake of the Ozarks Recreation Area	152
MO02R2	Marine Corps Support Activity at Richards-Gebaur Airport	153
MO04R2	Whiteman Air Force Base	153

MONTANA

MT03R3	Malmstrom Air Force Base	154

NEBRASKA

NE02R3	Offutt Air Force Base	155

NEVADA

NV02R4	Fallon Naval Air Station	157
NV03R4	Indian Springs Air Force Auxiliary Field	158
NV01R4	Nellis Air Force Base	158

NEW HAMPSHIRE

NH02R1	Portsmouth Naval Shipyard	159

NEW JERSEY

NJ01R1	Armament Research, Development and Engineering Center	160
NJ10R1	Bayonne Military Ocean Terminal	161
NJ13R1	Cape May Coast Guard Training Center	162
NJ11R1	Earle Naval Weapons Station	162
NJ03R1	Fort Dix Army Training Center	163
NJ05R1	Fort Monmouth	164
NJ08R1	Lakehurst Naval Air Engineering Station	164
NJ09R1	McGuire Air Force Base	165

NEW MEXICO

NM02R3	Cannon Air Force Base	166
NM05R3	Holloman Air Force Base	167
NM03R3	Kirtland Air Force Base	168
NM04R3	White Sands Missile Range	169

NEW YORK

NY06R1	Fort Drum	170
NY02R1	Fort Hamilton	170
NY12R1	Niagara Falls Air Reserve Station	171
NY17R1	Soldiers', Sailors', Marines', and Airmen's Club	172
NY07R1	Staten Island Navy Lodge	173
NY09R1	Stewart Army Sub-Post	173
NY16R1	United States Military Academy, West Point	174

NORTH CAROLINA

NC10R1	Camp Lejeune Marine Corps Base	175
NC09R1	Cape Hatteras Recreational Quarters	176
NC02R1	Cherry Point Marine Corps Air Station	176
NC03R1	Elizabeth City Coast Guard Support Center	177
NC05R1	Fort Bragg	178
NC13R1	Fort Fisher Air Force Recreation Area	179
NC06R1	New River Marine Corps Air Station	180
NC01R1	Pope Air Force Base	180
NC11R1	Seymour Johnson Air Force Base	181

NORTH DAKOTA

ND03R3	Camp Gilbert C. Grafton	183
ND04R3	Grand Forks Air Force Base	184
ND02R3	Minot Air Force Base	185

OHIO

OH06R2	Camp Perry Clubhouse	186
OH05R2	Defense Supply Center	186
OH01R2	Wright-Patterson Air Force Base	187

Other Installations in Ohio

OH13R2	Gentile Air Force Station	188
OH11R2	Youngstown Air Reserve Station	188

OKLAHOMA

OK02R3	Altus Air Force Base	188
OK03R3	Camp Gruber Training Site	189
OK01R3	Fort Sill	190

OKLAHOMA, *continued*

OK04R3	Tinker Air Force Base	191
OK05R3	Vance Air Force Base	192

OREGON

OR03R4	Kingsley Field	193
OR07R4	Rilea Armed Forces Training Center	193

PENNSYLVANIA

PA08R1	Carlisle Barracks	194
PA06R1	Defense Distribution Region East	195
PA04R1	Fort Indiantown Gap	195
PA03R1	Letterkenny Army Depot	196
PA15R1	Pittsburgh Air Reserve Station	197
PA05R1	Tobyhanna Army Depot	197
PA01R1	Willow Grove Naval Air Station/Joint Reserve Base	198

RHODE ISLAND

RI01R1	Newport Naval Education & Training Center	199

SOUTH CAROLINA

SC01R1	Beaufort Marine Corps Air Station	200
SC07R1	Beaufort Naval Hospital	201
SC06R1	Charleston Air Force Base	201
SC11R1	Charleston Naval Weapons Station	202
SC09R1	Fort Jackson	202
SC08R1	Parris Island Marine Corps Recruit Depot	203
SC10R1	Shaw Air Force Base	205
SC02R1	Short Stay	206

SOUTH DAKOTA

SD01R3	Ellsworth Air Force Base	206

TENNESSEE

TN02R2	Arnold Air Force Station	207
TN01R2	Memphis Naval Support Activity	208

TEXAS

TX50R3	Armed Services YMCA	209
TX07R3	Belton Lake Recreation Area	210
TX26R3	Brooks Air Force Base	210
TX10R3	Corpus Christi Naval Air Station	211
TX12R3	Dallas Naval Air Station	212
TX14R3	Dyess Air Force Base	213
TX06R3	Fort Bliss	214
TX02R3	Fort Hood	215
TX18R3	Fort Sam Houston	216
TX21R3	Fort Worth Naval Air Station/Joint Reserve Base	217
TX24R3	Goodfellow Air Force Base	217
TX30R3	Ingleside Naval Station	218
TX03R3	Kelly Air Force Base	219
TX22R3	Kingsville Naval Air Station	220
TX25R3	Lackland Air Force Base	220

TEXAS, continued

TX05R3	Laughlin Air Force Base	221
TX19R3	Randolph Air Force Base	222
TX09R3	Red River Army Depot	223
TX37R3	Sheppard Air Force Base	224

UTAH

UT11R4	Camp Williams	225
UT04R4	Dugway Proving Ground	226
UT02R4	Hill Air Force Base	226
UT05R4	Tooele Army Depot	228

VIRGINIA

VA50R1	Camp Pendleton Virginia National Guard	228
VA02R1	Cheatham Annex Fleet and Industrial Supply Center	229
VA06R1	Dahlgren Naval Surface Warfare Center	230
VA25R1	Dam Neck Fleet Combat Training Center Atlantic	231
VA30R1	Defense Supply Center Richmond	231
VA17R1	Fort A. P. Hill	232
VA12R1	Fort Belvoir	233
VA10R1	Fort Eustis	234
VA15R1	Fort Lee	235
VA13R1	Fort Monroe	236
VA24R1	Fort Myer	237
VA16R1	Fort Pickett	237
VA08R1	Fort Story	238
VA01R1	Judge Advocate General's School	240
VA07R1	Langley Air Force Base	240
VA19R1	Little Creek Naval Amphibious Base	241
VA18R1	Norfolk Naval Base	243
VA26R1	Norfolk Naval Shipyard	244
VA09R1	Oceana Naval Air Station	245
VA11R1	Quantico Marine Corps Base	245
VA46R1	Wallops Island AEGIS Combat Systems Center	246
VA14R1	Yorktown Naval Weapons Station	247

Other Installations in Virginia

VA28R1	Yorktown Coast Guard Reserve Training Center	248

WASHINGTON

WA08R4	Bangor Naval Submarine Base	248
WA10R4	Everett Naval Station	249
WA02R4	Fairchild Air Force Base	250
WA09R4	Fort Lewis	251
WA15R4	Madigan Army Medical Center	252
WA05R4	McChord Air Force Base	252
WA16R4	Pacific Beach Resort and Conference Center	253
WA11R4	Puget Sound Naval Shipyard	254
WA06R4	Whidbey Island Naval Air Station	255

Other Installations in Washington

WA25R4	Bremerton Naval Hospital	256
WA07R4	Jim Creek Regional Outdoor Recreation Area	256

WEST VIRGINIA

WV03R1	Camp Dawson Army Training Site	257
WV06R1	Sugar Grove Naval Security Group Activity	258

Other Installations in West Virginia
WV02R1   Eastern West Virginia Regional Airport.................................... 259

WISCONSIN

WI02R2   Fort McCoy 259
Other Installations in Wisconsin
WY03R2   Sherwood Point Cottage... 260

WYOMING

WY01R4   Francis E. Warren Air Force Base.. 260
Other Installations in Wyoming
WY06R4   Grant's Village, Yellowstone National Park............................... 261

UNITED STATES POSSESSIONS

GUAM

GU01R8   Andersen Air Force Base 262
GU05R8   Guam Naval Computer & Telecommunications Area Master Station, WESTPAC 263
GU02R8   Guam Naval Station 263

PUERTO RICO

PR03R1   Borinquen Coast Guard Air Station 264
PR01R1   Fort Buchanan 265
PR02R1   Roosevelt Roads Naval Station... 265
PR04R1   Sabana Seca Naval Security Group Activity 266

FOREIGN COUNTRIES

BAHRAIN

BA01R9   Bahrain Naval Support Unit 267

BELGIUM

BE01R7   NATO/SHAPE Support Group (US).. 268
BE02R7   Tri-Mission Association 269
Other Installations in Belgium
BE01R7   SHAPE/Chievres Air Base Community 269

CANADA

CN04R1   8th Wing Trenton 269

CUBA

CU01R1   Guantanamo Bay Naval Station.. 270

DENMARK

Other Installations in Denmark
DN02R7   Thule Air Base (Greenland)... 271

FRANCE

FR01R7	Cercle Des Armées	271
FR02R7	United Service Organizaitons (USO) - Paris	273

GERMANY

GE60R7	Ansbach Base Support Battalion	274
GE39R7	Augsburg Base Support Battalion	275
GE90R7	Babenhausen Kaserne	275
GE91R7	Bad Aibling Station	276
GE01R7	Bad Kreuznach Community	277
GE34R7	Bamberg Base Support Battalion	277
GE54R7	Baumholder Annex (Bieuenfeld)	278
GE03R7	Baumholder Base Support Battalion	279
GE08R7	Chiemsee AFRC	280
GE37R7	Darmstadt Base Support Battalion	280
GE68R7	Freidberg Community	281
GE10R7	Garmisch AFRC	282
GE62R7	Garmisch Community	283
GE23R7	Giessen Base Support Battalion	283
GE11R7	Grafenwöhr Community	284
GE13R7	Hanau Community	285
GE33R7	Heidelberg Community	286
GE71R7	Hohenfels Community	286
GE72R7	Illesheim Community	287
GE30R7	Kaiserslautern Community, Ramstein Air Base	287
GE75R7	Kitzingen Community	288
GE40R7	Landstuhl Medical Center	289
GE43R7	Mannheim Base Support Battalion	290
GE36R7	Oberammergau Community	290
GE24R7	Ramstein Air Base	291
GE16R7	Rhein Main Air Base	293
GE48R7	Schweinfurt Base Support Battalion	293
GE18R7	Sembach Air Base, Annex (Ramstein Air Base)	294
GE19R7	Spangdahlem Air Base	295
GE20R7	Stuttgart Community	296
GE85R7	Vilseck Base Support Battalion	297
GE27R7	Wiesbaden Base Support Battalion	298
GE31R7	Worms Community	299
GE21R7	Wuerzburg Community	299

Other Installations in Germany

GE46R9	Geilenkirchen Air Base	300

GREECE

Other Installations in Greece

GR05R9	Souda Bay Naval Support Activity/Air Facility (Crete)	300

HONG KONG

HK02R8	Hong Kong Community	300

ICELAND

IC01R7	Keflavik Naval Station	301

ITALY

IT03R7	Admiral Carney Park	302
IT04R7	Aviano Air Base	303
IT10R7	Camp Darby	303
IT13R7	La Maddalena Naval Support Activity	304
IT05R7	Naples Naval Support Activity	305
IT01R7	Sigonella Naval Air Station	306
IT06R7	Vicenza Community	307

Other Installations in Italy

IT16R7	Gaeta Naval Support Activity	308

JAPAN

JA14R8	Atsugi Naval Air Facility	308
JA07R8	Camp S. D. Butler Marine Corps Base	310
JA06R8	Camp Zama	311
JA12R8	Iwakuni Marine Corps Air Station	312
JA08R8	Kadena Air Base	313
JA03R8	Misawa Air Base	314
JA01R8	New Sanno US Forces Center	315
JA09R8	The Okuma Joint Services Rec Facility - Okinawa	317
JA15R8	Sasebo Fleet Activities	317
JA10R8	Tama Outdoor Recreation Area	319
JA02R8	Tokyo Administration Facility	319
JA11R8	Torii Station	320
JA05R8	Yokosuka Fleet Activities	320
JA04R8	Yokota Air Base	322

KOREA

RK01R8	Camp Casey	323
RK02R8	Camp Henry	323
RK10R8	Camp Hialeah	324
RK08R8	Camp Humphreys	324
RK03R8	Camp Page	325
RK06R8	Chinhae Fleet Activities	325
RK09R8	Dragon Hill Lodge	326
RK05R8	Kunsan Air Base	327
RK04R8	Osan Air Base	327
RK11R8	Seoul House	328
RK07R8	Yongsan Army Garrison	329

Other Installations in Korea

RK12R8	Camp Carroll	329
RK11R8	Cheju-Do Airport	329

NETHERLANDS

NT02R7	Brunssum International Inn	330

PANAMA

PN02R3	Fort Clayton	330
PN01R3	Howard Air Force Base	331
PN09R3	Panama Canal (Rodman) Naval Station	332

PORTUGAL

PO01R7	Lajes Field, (Azores)	333

SAUDI ARABIA

Other Installations in Saudi Arabia
SA01R9 Dhahran Community 334
SA03R9 Riyadh Community 334

SINGAPORE

SI01R1 Sembawang 334

SPAIN

SP01R7 Moron Air Base 335
SP02R7 Rota Naval Air Station 336

TURKEY

TU03R9 Incirlik Air Base 337
TU04R9 Izmir Air Station 338

UNITED KINGDOM

UK01R7 RAF Alconbury 339
UK05R7 Diego Garcia Atoll, U.S. Navy Support Facility 339
UK11R7 RAF Fairford 340
UK07R7 RAF Lakenheath 341
UK13R7 London Service Clubs 342
UK08R7 RAF Mildenhall 344
UK10R7 Portsmouth Royal Sailors' Home Club 345
UK14R7 Royal Fleet Club 345
Other Installations in the United Kingdom
UK13R7 London Naval Activity 346
UK22R7 Menwith Hill Station 346
UK09R7 RAF Croughton 346
UK25R7 St Mawgan Joint Maritime Facility 346

APPENDICES

APPENDIX A - General Abbreviations 347
APPENDIX B - Temporary Military Lodging Questions & Answers 349
APPENDIX C - Billeting Regulations and Navy Lodge Information 352
APPENDIX D - Telephone Information 362

UNITED STATES

ALABAMA

Dauphin Island Coast Guard Recreational Facility (AL07R2)
P.O. Box 436, Mobile Coast Guard Group
Dauphin Island, AL 36628-0436

TELEPHONE NUMBER INFORMATION: Main installation numbers: C-334-861-7113.

Location: Off base. On the Gulf of Mexico approximately 40 miles south of Mobile. I-10 to AL-193 (Exit 17). South approximately 35 miles to Dauphin Island. Left at dead end to east end of island. Follow signs to complex. NMI: Mobile CGG, 40 miles north. *USMRA: Page 36 (B-10).* NMC: Mobile, 40 miles north.

Lodging Office: None. Reservations required, by application only, with advance payment. Up to 60 days in advance for active CG; up to 45 days, all other active branches and reserve; up to 30 days, all others. C-205-861-7113.

TML: TLF. Three-bedroom cottages, private bath (13). Bedding and linens provided. Seven day maximum stay for cottages during summer. Rates: weekend (Fri-Sun) $100-$120; weekly (Sun-Fri) $140-$160; weekly (Sun-Sun or Fri-Fri) $240-$280. Reservations as outlined above.

Gulf beaches, visits to historic Fort Gaines and Mobile, serious bird watching, wading for flounder and crab at night, or deep sea fishing are all a part of the simple, unhurried relaxation that is Dauphin Island.

Fort McClellan (AL01R2)
Bldg 3295
14th Street and Summerall Road
Fort McClellan, AL 36205-5000
Scheduled to close September 1999.

TELEPHONE NUMBER INFORMATION: Main installation numbers: C-205-848-4611, D-312-865-1110.

Location: Nine miles north of I-20. Take AL-21 North to fort. Also located 25 miles southeast of I-59. Take US-431 to fort. *USMRA: Page 36 (F-3).* NMC: Anniston, three miles southeast.

Lodging Office: Bldg 3295, Welcome Center, 14th Street and Summerall Road, 24 hours. **C-205-848-4338/3546, D-312-865-4338/3546,** Fax: C-205-848-4920, D-312-865-4920. Check in billeting 1400 hours, check out 1100 hours daily.

TML: Fort McClellan Lodge. Bldg 3127, all ranks, leave or official duty. Check in at lodge. Handicapped accessible. C-205-848-4916, D-312-865-4916. Rooms, two double beds/queen size sofa sleeper, private bath (50). A/C, cribs, essentials, ice vending, kitchenette, complete utensils, housekeeping service, special facilities for DAVs, color TV in room and lounge, coin washer/dryer. New structure. Rates: $35.75 per night. Maximum six persons. DAVs (hospital patients) and dependents, and PCS can make reservations, others Space-A.

ALABAMA
Fort McClellan, continued

TML: VEQ. Bldgs 269, 940, 941, 943-946, enlisted, all ranks, official duty only. C-205-848-4338/3546. Rooms, private and semi-private baths (640); 3-bedroom cottage (E9 only), private bath (1). A/C, ice vending, housekeeping service, refrigerator, color TV, washer/dryer. Modern structures. Rates: $10.50 per night, cottage $25 per night.

TML: VOQ. Bldgs 2275-2277, 3136, 3137, officers all ranks, official duty only, C-848-4338/3546. Bedroom, private bath (179); bedroom, semi-private bath (177). A/C, community kitchen, essentials, refrigerator, kitchenette (some units), color TV in room and lounge, washer/dryer, ice vending. Older structures. Renovated 1990. Rates: $10.50 per night.

TML: DV/VIP. Bldgs 57, 300, 900, 1026, leave or official duty, officers O6+. Bedroom, private bath (4); two bedroom, private bath (5); 3-bedroom cottages, private bath (3). A/C, essentials, ice vending, kitchenette, complete utensils, housekeeping service, refrigerator, color TV, washer/dryer. Older structures, remodeled. Rates: Building 57 $20.50 per night, Buildings 1026, 300, 900 $25 per night. Additional person $4 per day. Duty can make reservations Mon-Fri C-205-848-5616. Retirees, lower ranks Space-A.

DV/VIP: Protocol, USACML+MPCEN+FM, C-205-848-5616, O6+, GS-13+. Retirees and lower ranks Space-A.

TML Availability: Best, Nov-Dec. Difficult, other times.

CREDIT CARDS ACCEPTED: Visa, MasterCard and American Express.

For military history buffs, trace the history of women in the Army in Bldg 1077, the role of chemical and biological weapons in Bldg 2299, and the history of the military police corps in Bldg 3182.

Locator 848-3795   Medical 848-2345   Police 848-5555

Fort Rucker (AL02R2)
Billeting Branch
Bldg 308, 6th Ave
Fort Rucker, AL 36362-5000

TELEPHONE NUMBER INFORMATION: Main installation numbers: C-334-255-1030, D-312-558-1030.

Location: Ninety miles southeast of Montgomery, midway between the capital city and Florida Gulf Coast, and seven miles south of Ozark, off US-231 on AL-249. Clearly marked. *USMRA: Page 36 (F,G-8)*. NMC: Dothan, 22 miles south.

Lodging Office: Bldg 308, 6th Ave. **C-334-598-5216, D-312-558-2626,** Fax: C-334-598-1242, 24 hours. All travelers report to billeting. Check in between 1400-1800hours, check out 1100 hours daily.

TML: VOQ/VEQ/DVQ. Bldg 308, for all ranks on TDY. Efficiency suites, family suites, kitchen and non-kitchen rooms, and six lake cottages. Rates: $20, $14, $12 and $10. Reservations 60 days in advance for TDY, 21 days for AD, others seven days in advance.

Temporary Military Lodging Around the World - 3

ALABAMA
Fort Rucker, continued

TML: Guest House. Bldg 124, all ranks, leave or official duty, C-334-598-6352, D-312-558-2888, 0645-2200 hours daily. Two double beds, sofa bed, private bath (38). A/C, kitchen, housekeeping service, color TV, washer/dryer, ice machine. Rates: $30. Reservations 60 days in advance for TDY, 21 days for active duty, others seven days in advance.

DV/VIP: ATTN: Protocol, Bldg 114 (Post HQ), C-334-255-3100, D-312-558-3100. O6/GS-15+. Retirees and lower ranks one night only.

TML Availability: Best, Oct-Apr. Limited, May-Sep.

CREDIT CARDS ACCEPTED: Visa, MasterCard and American Express can be used to secure/confirm room.

"**Dixie's Heartland**" is sprinkled with fine fresh water fishing. Landmark Park has sixty acres of shady nature trails and boardwalks, picnic sites and historic restorations. Waterworld in Dothan is good family entertainment.

Locator 255-1030   Medical 255-7900   Police 255-2222

Gunter Annex, Maxwell Air Force Base (AL04R2)
University Inn-Gunter Lodging
100 S. Turner Blvd
Gunter Annex, AL 36114-3011

TELEPHONE NUMBER INFORMATION: Main installation numbers: C-334-416-3360/4611, D-312-596-3360.

Location: Take I-65 to northern bypass, six miles to exit on AL-231, continue west one mile to AFB. Coming from the opposite direction, from I-85, follow signs and take eastern bypass north one mile to AL-231. Then west one mile to AFB. *USMRA: Page 36 (E,F-6)*. NMC: Montgomery, two miles southwest.

Lodging Office: Bldg 100 S. Turner Blvd. **C-334-416-3360/4611,** Fax: C-334-416-3945, D-312-596-3945. Check in 1400 hours daily.

TML: VAQ. Bldgs 545 and 610, enlisted all ranks, leave or official duty. Check in at Lodging Office. Separate bedroom, semi-private bath (247); bedroom, private bath (250); chief suites, private bath (6). Refrigerator, A/C, color TV, housekeeping service, washer/dryer. DAV facilities, modern structure. Check out 1200 hours daily. Rates: $7 per person, $9.50 per couple; suites $16. Duty can make reservations, others Space-A.

TML: VOQ. Bldgs 50, 51, 215, 235, 565, 610, 650 and 660, officers all ranks, leave or official duty. handicap accessible. Suites with private bath (37); rooms, semi-private bath (enlisted use this facility) (69); rooms, private bath (40). Refrigerator, A/C, color TV, housekeeping service, cribs and cots, washer/dryer, DAV facilities, older buildings. Check out 1200 hours daily. Rates: $8 per person, $11-two people; suites $16. Duty can make reservations, others Space-A.

TML: TLF. Bldg 90, all ranks, leave or official duty. Two-bedroom, private bath (3); 3-bedroom apartment, private bath (1). Kitchen, utensils, A/C, color TV, housekeeping service, cribs, washer/dryer. Modern structure. Check out 1200 hours daily. Rates: 3-bedroom, E1-E6, $20, E7-O10, $24; 2-bedroom, E1-E6, $18, E7-O10, $22. Duty can make reservations, others Space-A.

ALABAMA
Gunter Annex, Maxwell Air Force Base, continued

DV/VIP: Bldgs 50, 215, 235. O6+, leave or official duty. Separate bedroom, private bath, kitchenette (17). Rates: $16.

TML Availability: Good, except for enlisted quarters (SNCOA expansion).

CREDIT CARDS ACCEPTED: Visa, MasterCard and American Express.

Visit Oak Park's W.A. Gayle Planetarium, the Montgomery Zoo, and the state capital building where Jefferson Davis took the oath of office as President of the Confederate States of America.

Locator 270-4000   Medical 416-5816   Police 416-4250

Maxwell Air Force Base (AL03R2)
Services SQ SVML
352 West Drive
Maxwell AFB, AL 36112-6024

TELEPHONE NUMBER INFORMATION: Main installation numbers: C-334-953-1110, D-312-493-1110.

Location: Take I-85 S to I-65, exit on Day Street which leads to main gate of base. *USMRA: Page 36 (E-6).* NMC: Montgomery, 1.5 miles southeast.

Lodging Office: Bldg 157, 351 West Drive. **C-334-953-2055, D-312-493-2055,** Fax: C-334-953-2618, D-312-493-2618, 24 hours. Check in billeting 1400 hours, check out 1200 hours daily. Government civilian employee billeting for official duty only.

TML: TLF. Bldgs 305, 371, 409, and 410, all ranks, leave or official duty. Bedroom apartments, private bath (30). Kitchen, limited utensils, A/C, color TV, housekeeping service, cribs/cots, washer/dryer, soda/snack vending, ice vending. Modern structure. Rates: E-1-E-6 $18; E7+ $22 per apartment. Maximum five per unit. Duty can make reservations any time, Space-A can make reservations 24 hours in advance.

TML: VAQ. Bldg 221, enlisted all ranks, leave or official duty. SNCO suites, private bath (6); single rooms, shared bath (56). Soda/snack vending. Rates: suites $16 per person, maximum $23; single rooms $7 per person, maximum $9.50.

TML: VOQ. Bldgs 10, 20, 50 and 51 (Chestnut Street), 51 (E. Sycamore Street), 505, 510, 520, 530, 540, 550, 554, 605, 620, 630, 640, all ranks, leave or official duty. Bedroom, semi-private bath (563); bedroom, private bath, kitchenette (78); suites with kitchenette, private bath (97); bedroom, private bath (103). Kitchen, A/C, color TV, housekeeping service, cribs/cots, washer/dryer, soda/snack vending, ice vending. Modern and older structures. Rates: $8 per person, maximum $11. Duty can make reservations any time, Space-A can make reservations 24 hours in advance..

TML: Chief Suites. Bldg 121, E-7 to E-9, leave or official duty. Separate bedrooms, private bath (5). A/C, essentials, soda/snack vending, ice vending, housekeeping service, refrigerator, color TV, washer/dryer, wet bar, microwave. Renovated. Rates: $16 per person, maximum $23. Maximum three per unit. Duty can make reservations any time, Space-A can make reservations 24 hours in advance.

TML: DVQ. Bldgs 51, 330, 340, 356, 380. Sitting room, bedroom, private bath, soda/snack vending stocked bar, exercise room. Rates: $16 per person, maximum $23.

ALABAMA
Maxwell Air Force Base, continued

DV/VIP: Protocol Office, Bldg 800. C-334-953-2095. O7+. Retirees Space-A.

TML Availability: Extremely limited, year-round.

CREDIT CARDS ACCEPTED: Visa, MasterCard and American express.

Transportation: On Base taxi 953-5038 (official duty only), car rental agencies located in lobby.

While here be sure to visit the Civil Rights Memorial, Montgomery Zoo, W.A. Gayle Planetarium, Executive Mansion, State Capitol Archives and History Museum, and the first White House of the Confederacy.

Locator 953-5027   Medical 953-2333   Police 953-7222

Redstone Arsenal (AL06R2)
ATTN: AMSRI-RA-DPW-HM-BF
Bldg 244, Goss Road
Redstone Arsenal, AL 35808-5099

TELEPHONE NUMBER INFORMATION: Main installation numbers: C-205-876-2151, D-312-746-0011.

Location: Off US-231 West on Martin Road to main gate with visitor control. For uniformed personnel, Gate 8 is on Drake Ave. Take US-72 East to Jordan Lane, south to Drake. Drake becomes Goss Road at the Arsenal. *USMRA: Page 36 (E-1)*. NMC: Huntsville, adjacent north and east sides. Huntsville International Airport off I-565 is just 10 miles from Redstone Arsenal.

Lodging Office: Bldg 244, Goss Rd. **C-205-876-5713/8028,** Fax: C-205-876-2929, D-312-246-2929, 24 hours. Check in facility, check out 1100 hours daily. Government civilian employee billeting.

TML: The Trail Blazer. Bldg 244, all ranks, leave or official duty, C-205-837-4130. Bedroom, private bath (17); bedroom, kitchen, private bath (4). Refrigerator, community kitchen, limited utensils, A/C, color TV, housekeeping service, cribs, coin washer/dryer, ice vending. Modern structure, redecorated. Bldgs 238 and 239 accommodate those traveling with pets. Rates: $22 per person. Duty can make reservations, others Space-A.

TML: VOQ. Bldgs 55, 60, 62, 131, 132, 135 all ranks, official duty only. Bedrooms, private bath (25); 2-bedroom, semi-private bath (86); 3-bedroom cottages fully equipped (3). All units have color TV, A/C and housekeeping service, other amenities. Rates: $24.50 per person. Duty can make reservations. Duty on leave Space-A. Check with billeting for availability.

TML: DVQ. Bldgs 56, 58. Field grade and General Officers. Decorated and fully equipped 3 bedroom cottages. Rates: sponsor $24.50, each additional person $5, maximum $34.50 per family. Duty can make reservations, others Space-A.

DV/VIP: Contact billeting office. O6+. Retirees and lower ranks Space-A.

TML Availability: Very good, Nov-Feb. Difficult, other times.

6 - *Temporary Military Lodging Around the World*

ALABAMA
Redstone Arsenal, continued

CREDIT CARDS ACCEPTED: Visa, MasterCard and American Express.

Visit the Alabama Space and Rocket Center, I-565 West of Huntsville.

Locator 876-3331   Medical 876-8621   Police 876-2222

ALASKA

Clear Air Force Station (AK18R5)
13 SWS/MAFS
P.O. Box 40145
Clear AS, AK 99704-0013

TELEPHONE NUMBER INFORMATION: Main installation numbers: C-907-585-1110, D-317-585-1110.

Location: Seventy-eight miles south of Fairbanks, 35 miles north of Healy, on the Parks Hwy. Road is on the right as you travel south. Watch for the sign. *USMRA: Page 128 (F-4)*. NMC: Fairbanks, 78 miles northeast.

Lodging Office: Bldg 200. **C-907-585-6425, D-317-585-6425,** Fax: C-907-585-6549, D-317-585-6549, 0800-1700 hours Mon-Fri, other times Duty Manager, C-907-585-6351. Check in billeting, check out 1200 hours daily. Reservations required. Government civilian employee billeting.

TML: BOQ, BEQ. Bldgs 202, 204. Officers and enlisted all ranks, official duty. Bedroom, private bath (8); bedroom, common bath (12). Community kitchen, limited utensils, refrigerator, color TV in room and lounge, housekeeping service, washer/dryer, soda/snack vending. Exercise room available. Barracks, renovated. Bldg 204 has (2) DV/VIP suites for O6+. Rates: $10-$20. Reservations required.

TML: TLQ. Bldg 3, officers and enlisted all ranks, official duty, C-907-585-6425/6487, D-307-585-6576, 0730-1630 hours, after hours report to consolidated club, Bldg 209. Check out 1100 hours. Bedrooms, shared bath (10); separate bedroom, private bath (2). Community kitchen, limited utensils, color TV in room and lounge, housekeeping service, washer/dryer, soda/snack vending, ice vending. Exercise room available. Wood frame building. Rates: not provided. Reservations required.

TML Availability: Extremely limited, May-Sep.

CREDIT CARDS ACCEPTED: Visa and MasterCard.

Transportation: On Base Shuttle/Bus.

This facility is in the heart of Alaska, very near to Denali (Mount McKinley) National Park and has wonderful fishing, hunting and many other outdoor activities. The last weekend of July is the Bluegrass Festival in the nearby town of Anderson.

Locator 585-1110   Medical 585-6414   Police 585-6313

ALASKA

Eielson Air Force Base (AK15R5)
354 SVS/SVML
3112 Broadway Ave, Suite 4
Eielson AFB, AK 99702-1870

TELEPHONE NUMBER INFORMATION: Main installation numbers: C-907-377-1110, D-317-377-1110.

Location: On the Richardson Hwy (AK-2), AFB is clearly marked. *USMRA: Page 128 (F,G-4)*. NMC: Fairbanks, 26 miles northwest.

Lodging Office: Gold Rush Inn, Bldg 2270, Central Ave. **C-907-377-1844, D-317-377-1844,** Fax: C-907-377-2559, 24 hours. Check in billeting, check out 1100 hours daily. Government civilian employee billeting.

TML: TLF. Bldg 3305, all ranks, leave or official duty. Separate bedrooms, private bath (living room has sleeper sofa and chair) (40). Kitchen, complete utensils, color TV, housekeeping service, cribs, washer/dryer, VCR, microwave, handicap accessible. Modern structure. Rates: $35 per room. Maximum five per room. Duty can make reservations, others Space-A.

TML: VOQ/VAQ. Bldgs 2270-2272. All ranks in respective quarters. Leave or official duty. All buildings, handicap accessible. One-bedroom, private bath (VOQ) (207). One-bedroom, private bath (VAQ) (179). Refrigerator, microwave, VCR, cribs, essentials, ice vending, color TV in room and lounge, housekeeping service, washer/dryer. New three story structures. Rates: $12 per person. Duty can make reservations, others Space-A.

DV/VIP: Protocol Office, 354 FW/CCP, Bldg 3112, room 5, C-907-377-7686. E9/O6+. Retirees Space-A. Rates: $27.

TML Availability: Good, Sep-Apr. Note: Space-A May-Aug limited to non-existent.

CREDIT CARDS ACCEPTED: Visa, MasterCard and American Express.

Enjoy Denali National Park, historical Fairbanks, hunting, fishing and skiing in season. All outdoor activities are available both on and off base.

Locator 377-1841   Medical 377-2296   Police 377-5130

Elmendorf Air Force Base (AK09R5)
North Star Inn
Bldg 31-250, Acacia Street
Elmendorf AFB, AK 99506-3565

TELEPHONE NUMBER INFORMATION: Main installation numbers: C-907-552-1110, D-317-552-1110.

Location: Off Glenn Hwy. Take Muldoon Gate, Boniface Gate, Post Road Gate or Government Hill Gate exits. The AFB is next to Fort Richardson. *USMRA: Page 128 (F-5) and Page 131 (B,C,D,E-1)*. NMC: Anchorage, two miles southwest.

ALASKA
Elmendorf Air Force Base, continued

Lodging Office: North Star Inn, Bldg 31-250, Acacia Street. **C-907-552-2454, D-317-552-2454,** Fax: C-907-552-8276, 24 hours. Check in facility, check out 1200 hours daily.

TML: TLF. Bldgs 21-400 and 2-700 areas, all ranks, TDY or official duty. 21-400: 1-bedroom, private bath (100). Sofa rollaway bed, fully equipped kitchen, refrigerator, microwave, color TV, housekeeping service, washer/dryer. 2-700: 3-bedroom, private bath, fully equipped kitchen, refrigerator, microwave, color TV, housekeeping service, washer/dryer. Older structures. Rates: $35 per unit. Personnel on orders can make reservations, others Space-A.

TML: VOQ. Officer all ranks, TDY or official duty. Bedroom, private bath (87); bedroom, private bath, kitchenette (20). Rates: single $12; double $17. Personnel on orders can make reservations, others Space-A.

TML: VAQ. Enlisted all ranks, TDY or official duty. (E1-E3) Shared bedroom and bath (258 rooms 464 beds); E4 and above single room, shared bath (15); DV suites (9). Lounge, reading room, exercise room, conference room. Rates: single $12; double $17. Personnel on orders can make reservations, others Space-A.

DV/VIP: Protocol Office. Reservations for O6+. C-907-552-3210, D-317-552-3210.

TML Availability: Fairly good. Best, Nov-Jan. Extremely limited, May-Sep.

CREDIT CARDS ACCEPTED: Visa, MasterCard and American Express.

Alaska's largest city boasts many cultural events, museums, sporting events (the Anchorage Bowl is a world class ski resort), and restaurants in a spectacular setting. Outdoor activities abound.

Locator 552-4860   Medical 552-5555   Police 552-3421

Fort Greely (AK10R5)
Billeting Office
P.O. Box 1023
Delta Junction, AK 99737-5000
Scheduled to close 2001.

TELEPHONE NUMBER INFORMATION: Main installation numbers: C-907-873-4113, D-317-873-4113.

Location: Off AK-4, five miles south of junction of AK-2 and AK-4. Five miles south of Delta Junction. *USMRA: Page 128 (F,G-4)*. NMC: Fairbanks, 105 miles northwest.

Lodging Office: ATTN: Billeting. Bldg 663, First Street. **C-907-873-3285, D-317-873-3285,** Fax: C-907-873-3003, D-317-873-3003, 0730-1530 hours Mon, Tue, Thur, Fri, 0730-1130 hours Wed. Others hours, call or report to SDO, Bldg 501, C-907-873-4720. Check in 1300 hours, check out 1100 hours daily. Government civilian employee billeting.

Temporary Military Lodging Around the World - 9

ALASKA
Fort Greely, continued

TML: VOQ. Bldg 702, 801, all ranks, leave or official duty. Bldg 702: Sitting room, double bed, (14); family quarters, two single beds, one double, separate bedrooms, (5). All with microfridge, telephone, color CATV, private bath, housekeeping service (Mon-Fri), cribs/cots, washer/dryer. Bldg 801: Sitting room, double bed, kitchenette, (12); single bed, kitchenette (4); DVQ has queen bed, sitting room, full kitchen, microwave, mini-bar (4). All with private bath, telephone, color cable TV, housekeeping service (Mon-Fri), cribs/cots, washer/dryer, snack vending. Rates: Bldg 702, $20 first occupant; Bldg 801, $22 first occupant; DVQ, $32 first occupant. Bldgs 702 and 801 each additional person $7. Pets allowed, $2 per pet/per day, limit 2 pets. TDY or PCS may make reservations 120 days in advance; unofficial, seven days. Unofficial rates same as official. Contractor rate, $60.

TML Availability: Good. Best, Apr-May and Sep-Dec. Difficult, Jan-Feb and Jul-Aug.

CREDIT CARDS ACCEPTED: Visa, MasterCard, American Express and Discover.

Hunting, fishing, all summer and winter sports are part of living in Alaska. A visit to nearby Delta Junction and Fairbanks, farther north, will give a visitor a taste of life on "the last frontier."

Locator 873-3255   Medical 873-4498   Police 873-1111

Fort Richardson (AK03R5)
P.O. Box 240373, ATTN: APVR-RPW-HB
Fort Richardson, AK 99505-0373

TELEPHONE NUMBER INFORMATION: Main installation numbers: C-907-384-1110, D-317-384-1110.

Location: Main gate is on Glenn Hwy, five miles south of Eagle River. *USMRA: Page 128 (F-5) and Page 131 (E-1).* NMC: Anchorage, eight miles northeast.

Lodging Office: Bldg 600, Room 105A, 5th Street and Richardson Drive. **C-907-384-0436, D-317-384-0436,** Fax: C-907-384-0470, 0600-2230 hours Mon-Fri, 1000-1730 hours Sat-Sun. Other times SDO, Bldg 1, C-907-384-2000. Check in billeting, check out 1100 hours daily. (Summer hours may vary.) Reservations check in after 1300. Government civilian employee billeting in VOQ/DV/VIP.

TML: VOQ. Bldgs 55, 57, 58, 345, 347, 1107, 1113, 1114, officers and enlisted all ranks, leave or official duty. Separate bedroom, private bath (111). Kitchen (some), refrigerator, microwave, CATV, housekeeping service, cribs/cots, washer/dryer, ice vending. Older structure, renovated. Rates: $13-17, each additional person $4. Reservation 120 days in advance for official PCS, TDY or ADT, seven days in advance for Space-A.

TML: DV/VIP. **The Igloo,** Bldg 53. Officers O5+, leave or official duty, C-907-384-1586. Separate bedroom suites, private bath (14); bedroom, kitchen, private bath apartments (2). Refrigerator, limited utensils, color TV, housekeeping service, cribs/cots, washer/dryer, ice vending. Older structure, renovated. Rates: Apartments $25, each additional person $4; suites $20, each additional person $4. Reservation policy same as VOQ.

10 - Temporary Military Lodging Around the World

ALASKA
Fort Richardson, continued

DoD Conference Center

TML: Seward Resort, C-907-224-5559, 800-770-1858, D-317-384-FISH (3474)/LINE (5463). Premier Cabin (2), sleeps six, one bedroom, sleeper sofa, loft, furnished, linens, kitchen, fireplace, use of boat. Rates: $300-$400. Deluxe Cabin (2), sleeps six, one bedroom, sleeper sofa, loft, furnished, linens, kitchen, fireplace. Rates: $124-164. Cabin (10), sleeps six, one bedroom, sleeper sofa, loft, furnished, linens, kitchen. Rates: $99-$139. Motel: Bedroom (56), sleeps four, two double beds, full bath, linens, microwave, micro refrigerator. Meeting/conference room available. Rates: $59-$89 daily. See *Military Living's Military RV, Camping and Rec Areas Around the World* for additional information and directions.

DV/VIP: ATTN: APVR-CS-P, Protocol Office, Bldg 1, Room 111, C-907-384-2067, O6+. Retirees and lower ranks Space-A seven days in advance.

TML Availability: Good, Oct-Apr. Difficult, other times.

CREDIT CARDS ACCEPTED: Visa, MasterCard, American Express and Novus.

Visit the Fish and Wildlife Museum in Bldg 600. The Earthquake Park in Anchorage commemorates the violence of the far North, while towering mountains, wildlife parks, the Cook Inlet and great downhill skiing welcome visitors nearby.

Locator 384-0306   Medical 552-5555   Police 384-0823

Fort Wainwright (AK07R5)
Fort Wainwright Billeting
P.O. Box 35086
Fort Wainwright, AK 99703-0086

TELEPHONE NUMBER INFORMATION: Main installation numbers: C-907-353-6113/7500, D-317-353-6113/7500.

Location: From Fairbanks, take Airport Way East which leads to the main gate of the post. *USMRA: Page 128 (F-4)*. NMC: Fairbanks, 3.5 miles west.

Lodging Office: Bldg 1045 (**Murphy Hall**), Gaffney Road. **C-907-353-7291/6294**, 0630-2230 hours Mon-Fri, 1030-1730 hours Sat-Sun. Other hours SDO, Bldg 1555, C-907-353-7500. Check in billeting 1300 hours, check out 1200 hours daily.

TML: VEQ/VOQ. Bldg 4056, enlisted and officer all ranks, leave or official duty. Bedroom, private bath (27, 12 suites). Refrigerator, microwave, color TV, housekeeping service, cribs/cots, washer/dryer, soda/snack vending, ice vending. Older structure. Rates: sponsor, singles $10; suites $13, each additional person $4. Duty, TDY can make reservations 120 days in advance, others three days.

TML: VEQ/VOQ. Bldg 4063, enlisted and officer all ranks, leave or official duty. Two-bedroom, private bath (4); single bedroom, private bath (4); bedroom, private bath (16) (12 suites). Refrigerator, microwave, color TV, housekeeping service, cribs/cots, washer/dryer, ice vending. Rates: sponsor, singles $10; suites $13, each additional person $4. Duty, TDY can make reservations 120 days in advance.

Temporary Military Lodging Around the World - 11

ALASKA
Fort Wainwright, continued

TML: VEQ/VOQ. Bldgs 4064, enlisted and officers all ranks, leave or official duty. Two-bedroom, private bath (8); bedroom, private bath (8). Refrigerator, color TV, housekeeping service, essentials, cribs/cots, washer/dryer, food/ice vending. Older structures. Rates: sponsor $13, each additional person $4. Duty, TDY can make reservations 120 days in advance, others three days.

TML: VEQ/VOQ. Bldg 1045, enlisted and officers, all ranks. Leave or official duty. Bedroom, private bath (26). Refrigerator, microwave, color TV, housekeeping service, cribs/roll away, washer/dryer, food/ice vending. Rates: sponsor $13, each additional person $4. Duty, TDY can make reservations 120 days in advance, others three days.

TML: VEQ/VOQ. Building 1063 and 4062, enlisted and officers, all ranks. Leave or official duty. Bedroom, private bath (35). Kitchenette, refrigerator, microwave, color TV, housekeeping service, cribs/rollaway, washer/dryer, food/ice vending. Rates: sponsor $15, each additional person $4. Duty, TDY can make reservations 120 days in advance, others three days.

DV/VIP: Bldg 1045. Officers O6+, leave or official duty. Protocol C-907-353-6671. Bedroom deluxe suite (4). Refrigerator, microwave, color TV, housekeeping service, cribs/rollaway, washer/dryer, food/ice vending. Rates: sponsor $20 and $25, each additional person $4. Duty, TDY can make reservations 120 days in advance, others three days.

TML Availability: Difficult, year round.

In summer Fairbanks hosts Midnight Sun baseball games, in winter (Feb-Mar) the North American Championship Sled Dog Race (and others), University of Alaska Eskimo Olympics. New shopping malls belie wilderness nearby.

Locator 353-6815   Medical 353-5143/5172   Police 353-7535

Kodiak Coast Guard Support Center (AK08R5)
MWR, P.O. Box 195027
Kodiak, AK 99619-5027

TELEPHONE NUMBER INFORMATION: Main installation numbers: C-907-487-5267, D-317-487-5267.

Location: From city of Kodiak, take main road southwest for seven miles. Base is on the left side. *USMRA: Page 128 (E-7).* NMC: Kodiak, seven miles northeast.

Lodging Office: Guest House, Bldg N-30. **C-907-487-5446,** Fax: C-907-487-5075, 24 Hours. Check in at facility 1400 hours, check out 1200 hours daily.

TML: Guest House. Bldg N-30, all ranks, leave or official duty. Bedroom, private bath (2); bedroom, shared bath (39); family suites, shared bath (2); suite with sitting room, private bath(1). Community kitchen, freezer, CATV, housekeeping service, cribs, washer/dryer, ice vending, children's play area. Meeting/conference rooms, exercise room with pool and mini-mart close by. Older structure, three floors. Rates: single $40; double $50; triple $60; family suite $80; suite with sitting room $60 . PCS have priority, others Space-A. **Golden Anchor Restaurant and Bar, Family Pizza and Fun Center, and All Hands Dining Facility located within one mile.**

TML: BEQ. Rooms (10), 19 beds, all ranks, leave or official duty, C-907-487-5260. Rates: no charge.

12 - Temporary Military Lodging Around the World

ALASKA
Kodiak Coast Guard Support Center, continued

TML: DV/VIP. Guesthouse. Officer O5, E9, GS15+, official duty, others Space-A. Reservations accepted. VIP suites (3), two interconnecting by bath, C-907-487-5446, same facilities and rates as Guest House above. Rate: $70.

TML Availability: Good, Oct-Apr. Difficult, May-Sep.

CREDIT CARDS ACCEPTED: Visa, MasterCard and American Express.

Transportation: On Base shuttle/bus, Mon-Sat; Off Base Taxi, AAA Ace Mecca C-907-486-3211, A&B Taxicabs C-907-486-4343; Car Rental Agencies: Avis Rent-A-Car 907-487-2264, Budget Rent a Car 907-487-2220, Kodiak Auto Rental 907-487-2272, Rent-A-Heap 907-487-4001.

Kodiak is known for its big bears (the biggest in the world), which are tourist attractions in themselves, great scenery, wonderful king crab and salmon, which is not so threatening, and more tasty.

Locator 487-5267   Medical 487-57577   Police 487-5266

Sitka Coast Guard Air Station (AK25R5)
611 Airport Road
Sitka, AK 99835-6500

TELEPHONE NUMBER INFORMATION: Main installation numbers: C-907-966-5420, D-none.

Location: At end of Airport Road. on Jponski Island, .5 miles north. of airport terminal. *USMRA: Page 128 (I-7).* NMC: Juneau, 90 miles northeast by air.

Lodging Office: 611 Airport Road. **C-907-966-5591,** 0800-1600 hours Mon-Fri. Other times SDO, C-907-966-5420. Check in at facility, check out 0800-1600 hours daily. Other hours, SDO in Flight Operations Center. Government civilian employee billeting.

TML: BEQ. Enlisted all ranks, official duty. Bedrooms, semi-private bath (2). Color TV, washer/dryer. Rates: $6. Maximum two persons per unit. CATV, washer/dryer. Modern structure. Reservations for active duty on orders and reservists and National Guard on orders, others Space-A. No pets.

DV/VIP: Public Affairs office, USCG Air Station, Sitka, AK 99835, C-907-966-5423.

TML Availability: Extremely limited. Best, fall to spring. Difficult, summer.

This small island community has an abundance of sport fishing and hunting. Sitka Historical Park, totem poles and the Sitka shoreline are picturesque. Visit the Russian Bishop's House; St. Michaels Russian Orthodox Church, and Castle Hill, site of the 1867 transfer of Alaska Territory to the US.

Locator 966-5420   Medical 966-5555   Police 747-3245

ARIZONA

Davis-Monthan Air Force Base (AZ01R4)
Inn on Davis-Monthan
355 SVS/SVML
3375 S. Tenth Street
Davis-Monthan AFB, AZ 85707-4237

TELEPHONE NUMBER INFORMATION: Main installation numbers: C-520-228-3900, D-312-228-1110.

Location: Exit Alvernon Way #265 off I-10, proceed left at traffic light. Alvernon Way eventually becomes Golf Links Road. After about two miles you will turn right on Craycroft road and proceed to main gate. *USMRA: Page 108 (F-9).* NMC: Tucson, three miles southwest.

Lodging Office: Inn on Davis-Monthan, Bldg 2350, 3375 S. Tenth Street, ATTN: Inn on Davis Monthan, P.O. Box 15013. **C-520-228-1500 ext 1, or C-520-228-3309, D-312-228-3309**, 24 hours. Check in billeting after 1300, check out 1100 hours daily except TLFs check out 1000 hours. Government civilian employee billeting.

TML: TLF. Various buildings, all ranks, official duty, C-520-228-3309/3230. Two-bedroom, private bath (15); 4 bedroom, private bath (1). Kitchen, complete utensils, A/C, color TV, housekeeping service, cribs/cots, washer/dryer. Modern structure. Rates: E1, E2-01 $15.50; E3+ $24. PCS in/out can make reservations, others Space-A.

TML: VAQ. Bldgs 3511, 4210, enlisted E1-E6, official duty, C-520-228-3309/3230. Bedroom, double occupancy, common bath (139); SNCO suites (4), kitchen, private bath; separate bedroom, private bath (E7-E9) (4). Refrigerator, A/C, color TV, housekeeping service, washer/dryer, ice machine. Modern structure. Rates: suites $10 per person, $4 second person. Official duty can make reservations, others Space-A.

TML: VOQ. Bldgs 2350, 2550, 4065, officer all ranks, Enlisted E7-E9, leave or official duty, C-520-228-3309/3230. Bedroom, shared kitchen, private bath (144); two room suites, separate bedroom, kitchen, private bath (24); 2-bedroom, living room, kitchen, private bath (8). SNCO suites, kitchen, private bath, separate bedroom, E7-E9 (4). Refrigerator, microwave, A/C, CATV, housekeeping service, washer/dryer, ice machine. Modern structure. Rates: rooms $8 per person, maximum $16 per family; NCO suites $14 per person, maximum $28 per family. Official duty can make reservation, others Space-A.

TML: DV/VIP. Bldg 4065, officer O6+, leave or official duty, C-520-228-3600. Two bedroom suites, O6+, private bath (6); One bedroom deluxe suites (two special for general/flag officers). Refrigerator, microwave, complete utensils, A/C, CATV, stocked bar/refrigerator, housekeeping service, ice vending. Modern structure. Rates: $16 per person, each additional person $7. Maximum $28 per family. All categories can make reservations. Protocol may cancel reservations for non-AD if AD requires space.

DV/VIP: 355th WG Protocol. C-520-228-3600. O6+. Retirees Space-A.

TML Availability: Difficult. Best, Aug-Dec.

CREDIT CARDS ACCEPTED: Visa, MasterCard and American Express.

14 - Temporary Military Lodging Around the World

ARIZONA
Davis-Monthan Air Force Base, continued

Visit Old Tucson, Reid Park and Zoo, Arizona-Sonora Desert and Pima Air Museum. Nearby Mt Lemmon is the site of local snow sports in winter.

Locator 228-3347   Medical 228-3878   Police 228-3200

Fort Huachuca (AZ02R4)
Billeting Office
P.O. Box 12775
Fort Huachuca, AZ 85670-2775

TELEPHONE NUMBER INFORMATION: Main installation numbers: C-520-538-7111, D-312-879-0111.

Location: From I-10 take AZ-90 S to Sierra Vista and main gate of fort. *USMRA: Page 108 (F,G-9,10).* NMC: Tucson, 75 miles northwest.

Lodging Office: Bldg 43083, Service Road. **C-520-533-2222/5361, D-312-821-2222/5361,** Fax: C-520-458-0459, 24 hours. Check in 1400 hours, check out 1100 hours. Military and government civilian employee billeting.

TML: Guest House. Bldgs 42017, 52054, all ranks, leave or official duty. Bedroom, two double beds, private bath (21); separate bedroom, double bed, private bath (6); 2-bedroom, double beds, private bath (3); 3-bedroom, double beds, private bath (3). Community kitchen, refrigerator, A/C, color TV, housekeeping service, cribs, washer/dryer. Modern structure. Rates: $32-$36.50 per unit. Maximum eight persons in 42017, five persons in 52054. Duty can make reservations, others Space-A. Pets OK first night only. Must be boarded by second day. On-post kennels usually available.

TML: DVQ. Bldg 22104, officers O4+, official duty. Suites - separate bedroom, private bath (6); two bedroom, private bath (2). Kitchen, A/C, color TV, housekeeping service, cribs, washer/dryer. Older structure. Rates: sponsor $37.50, each additional person $5. Duty can make reservations, others Space-A.

TML: VOQ/VEQ. Bldgs 43083-43086, all ranks. Bedroom, private bath or semi-private bath (210). Kitchen and refrigerator in most units, A/C, color TV, housekeeping service, washer/dryer. Modern structure. Rates: VOQ $18.50, VEQ $16.50, $5 for spouse. Active duty can make reservations, others Space-A.

TML Availability: Best, Dec. Difficult, other times

CREDIT CARDS ACCEPTED: Visa, MasterCard, American Express and Discover.

Visit historic Bisbee and Tombstone, the "Town too tough to die". The ITR office on post is the information office on local activities. Hunting and fishing are good. How about a picnic on Reservoir Hill with a view of 100 miles!

Locator 538-7111   Medical 533-9200   Police 533-2181

ARIZONA

Gila Bend Air Force Auxiliary Field (AZ16R4)
HC01 Box 22
Gila Bend AFAF, AZ 85337-5000

TELEPHONE NUMBER INFORMATION: Main installation numbers: C-520-683-6200, D-312-896-5200 (Security Police).

Location: From Phoenix, take I-10 W to SR-85 S to Gila Bend. The field is four miles out of town. Also off I-8 between Yuma and Casa Grande. *USMRA: Page 108 (C-7,8).* NMC: Phoenix, 65 miles northeast.

Lodging Office: ATTN: **Desert Hideaway Inn**, Bldg 4300, Gila Bend AFAF, AZ 85337. **C-520-683-6238, D-312-896-5238,** Fax: C-520-683-6121, D-312-896-5121, hours of operation 0700-1600 or 0700-2000 hours Mon-Fri (depending on occupancy). After hours check in at Security Bldg 300. Check out 1200 hours.

TML: VAQ. Bldg 4300, enlisted, all ranks, leave or official duty. Private bedroom, private bath (50); semi-private bath (5). A/C, refrigerator, microwave, CATV. Laundry facility and fitness room available. Rates: single $8.50; double $11.75. Duty can make reservations, others Space-A.

TML: VOQ. Bldgs 2358 A, B, C, D, officer, all ranks. 2-bedroom, semi-private bath (4). A/C, fully equipped kitchen, CATV in living room. Rates: single $8.50; double $11.75. Duty can make reservations, others Space-A.

TML Availability: Very good. Difficult, Oct-Jan.

CREDIT CARDS ACCEPTED: Visa, MasterCard and American Express.

Hunting, fishing, boating, and trips to Tucson, the Organ Pipe National Monument, and Rocky Point Mexico are favorite activities in this area.

Locator 683-6200   **Medical** 683-6200   **Police** 683-6200

Luke Air Force Base (AZ03R4)
Fighter Country Inn
7012 N. Bong Lane
Luke AFB, AZ 85309-1534

TELEPHONE NUMBER INFORMATION: Main installation numbers: C-602-856-7411, D-312-853-0111.

Location: From Phoenix, west on I-10 to Litchfield Road, north on Litchfield Road approximately five miles. Also, from Phoenix, on I-17 to Glendale Ave, west on Glendale Ave to intersection of Glendale Ave and Litchfield Road, approximately 16 miles. *USMRA: Page 108 (D-6,7).* NMC: Phoenix, 20 miles southeast.

Lodging Office: ATTN: **Fighter Country Inn**, 7012 N. Bong Lane. **C-602-935-2641, D-312-896-3941.** Fax: C-602-856-3332, 24 hours. Check in lodging office 1400 hours daily, check out 1200 hours daily.

16 - Temporary Military Lodging Around the World

ARIZONA
Luke Air Force Base, continued

TML: VOQ. Five buildings, officers all ranks, leave or official duty. Bedroom, private bath (68); shared suites, private bath (28). Kitchen, refrigerator, A/C, color TV, housekeeping service. Modern structure. Rates: $8.50 per person per night.

TML: TLF. Four buildings, all ranks, leave or official duty. Bedroom, private bath (40). Kitchen, utensils, A/C, color TV, housekeeping service, washer/dryer. Modern structure. Rates: $22 per night.

TML: VAQ. Two buildings, enlisted all ranks, leave or official duty. Bedroom, private bath (6); two bedroom, semi-private bath (70). Kitchen, utensils, A/C, color TV, housekeeping service, washer/dryer. Older structure. Rates: Maximum $8.50 per person per night.

TML: Fort Tuthill Recreation Area. Write to: Fort Tuthill Recreation Area, Highway Contract 30, Box 5, Flagstaff, AZ 86001-8701. C-602-856-3401, C-520-774-8893, C-800-552-6268, D-312-896-3401, Fax: C-602-856-7990, D-312-896-7990; 24 hours. All ranks, leave or official duty. Chalet (1), 3-bedroom, furnished; A-Frames (11), 2-bedroom, furnished; Cabins (11), studio, furnished; Hotel (20 rooms): double, occupancy four (8); queen, occupancy two (8); queen, handicap accessible, occupancy two; queen, kitchenette, occupancy two (2). Refrigerator, kitchenette (some), utensils, TV (lounge and room), housekeeping service, cribs/cots, washer/dryer, ice vending, soda/snack vending. Meeting/conference room and mini-mart available. Recently renovated. Check in front desk Reservations accepted. **See *Military Living's Military RV, Camping and Rec Areas Around the World* for additional information and directions.**

TML: DV/VIP. Two buildings, officer O7+, leave or official duty. Two-bedroom house, private bath (2). Kitchen, utensils, A/C, color TV, housekeeping service. Rates: $16 per person per night. Duty can make reservations, others Space-A.

DV/VIP: Protocol Officer, 58th FW, C-602-856-5851, ranks O6+. Retirees and lower ranks Space-A on a day-by-day basis.

TML Availability: Best, Oct-Apr. Difficult, other times.

CREDIT CARDS ACCEPTED: Fort Tuthill Recreation Area accepts Visa, MasterCard, American Express and AF Club Card.

See Phoenix State Capital Building murals, the Desert Botanical Garden in Papago Park. Pioneer Arizona, a living history museum, and the Phoenix Zoo are worth a visit. Also, the Grand Canyon is 90 miles away.

Locator 856-6405   Medical 856-7506   Police 856-6349

1-800-552-6268
- **Closest military location to the Grand Canyon**
- Programmed trips - rafting on Colorado River, backpacking and mountain biking in the Grand Canyon, bus tours etc.
- Near Flagstaff Airport with shuttle bus
- Located at 7,000 feet in Ponderosa Pine Forest
- Winter Nordic & Alpine skiing

* Please see Fort. Tuthill's listing above for more info.

Temporary Military Lodging Around the World - 17

ARIZONA

Yuma Army Proving Ground (AZ05R4)
ATTN: STEYP-EH-H
Bldg 1000, Cactus Street
Yuma, AZ 85365-9100

TELEPHONE NUMBER INFORMATION: Main installation numbers: C-520-328-2151, D-312-899-2151.

Location: Northeast of I-8 turn right on US-95. Southwest of I-10 turn left on US-95. US-95 is north/south route which bisects APG. *USMRA: Page 108 (A-6,7,8; B-7,8).* NMC: Yuma, 27 miles southwest.

Lodging Office: Bldg 1000, Cactus Street. **C-520-328-2129/2127**, 0630-1700 hours Mon-Fri. Check in 1400, after hours Bldg 611, check out 1100 hours daily. Government civilian employee billeting.

TML: Guest House. Bldg 538, all ranks, leave or official duty. Bedroom, private bath (10). Kitchen, utensils, A/C, color TV in room and lounge, housekeeping service, cribs/cots, washer/dryer, ice vending. Modern structure. Rates: sponsor $18, each additional person $3. Maximum four per room. Reservations required. One room handicap accessible.

TML: VOQ. Bldg 1004, all ranks, official duty only. Suites, private bath (10); Bedroom, semi-private bath (10). Community kitchen, A/C, color TV in room and lounge, housekeeping service, washer/dryer, ice vending. Modern structure. Rates: sponsor $23, each additional person $4. All categories can make reservations.

TML: DV/VIP. Bldg 944 A/B, officer O6+, official duty. Suites, private bath (2). Refrigerator, community kitchen, A/C, color TV, housekeeping service, cribs/cots, washer/dryer, ice vending, coffee machine, beverages. Older structure. Rates: sponsor $25, each additional person $4. O6/GS-15+.

TML Availability: Good, Apr-Dec. Difficult, Jan-Mar.

CREDIT CARDS ACCEPTED: American Express.

Visit the Century House Museum for local history, Fort Yuma and the St Thomas Mission, Yuma Territorial Prison and Museum, and the Quechan Indian Museum in Old Fort Yuma to get a taste of this pre-old west town.

Locator 328-2151   Medical 328-2911   Police 328-2720

Yuma Marine Corps Air Station (AZ04R4)
MCAS Yuma Billeting Fund
Box 12776 MCAS Yuma
Yuma, AZ 85369-9100

TELEPHONE NUMBER INFORMATION: Main installation numbers: C-520-341-2011, D-312-951-2011.

Location: From I-8 take Ave 3E south for one mile to MCAS on the right. Adjacent to Yuma IAP. *USMRA: Page 108 (A-8).* NMC: Yuma, three miles northwest.

18 - Temporary Military Lodging Around the World

ARIZONA
Yuma Marine Corps Air Station, continued

Lodging Office: Bldg 1020. **C-520-341-2262, D-312-951-2262**, 24 hours. Check in billeting, check out 1000 hours.

TML: TLQ. **Hostess House**, Bldg 1020, all ranks, leave or official duty, C-520-341-2262. Separate bedroom, private bath (13). Refrigerator, community kitchen, A/C, color TV, housekeeping service, cribs/cots, ice vending. Older structure. Rates: $25. Seven day limit, then daily. All categories can make reservations. *Note: Closed as of 4 May 1997 for six months due to renovations.*

TML Availability: Extremely limited.

Located on the Colorado River, fine water recreation is available, as well as hunting, golf, and trips to nearby Mexico for shopping, festivals and restaurants.

Locator 726-2011   **Medical 726-2772**   **Police 726-2361**

ARKANSAS

Fort Chaffee (AR04R2)
ATTN: Billeting Office
Bldg 1370, Fort Smith Blvd
Fort Chaffee, AR 72905-5000
Lodging transferred to Army National Guard 1 April 1997.

TELEPHONE NUMBER INFORMATION: Main installation numbers: C-501-484-2141, D-312-962-2111. Police 484-2666.

Location: From I-40, take the I-540 spur to Fort Smith. From I-540, exit at Fort Chaffee exit sign. Take state Hwy 59 S across Arkansas River to Hwy 22. It goes past Fort Chaffee main gate. Five to six miles total. *USMRA: Page 76 (A,B-4,5)*. NMC: Fort Smith, six miles southwest.

Lodging Office: Bldg 1370, Fort Smith Blvd. **C-501-484-2252, D-312-962-2252,** 0700-1530 Mon-Thu, 0700-2000 Fri, 0700-1600 Sat-Sun. Closed on Federal holidays.

TML: VEQ/VOQ. Various buildings. All ranks, TDY have priority, limited Space-A. Bedrooms, private/shared baths; suites, private bath. A/C, refrigerator, kitchen, in-room telephones (suites), washer/dryer, color TV, housekeeping service. Older structures, some renovated. Rates $6-$25. No pets. Reservations accepted two weeks in advance.

TML: DVQ. Cottages (9). All ranks, TDY have priority, limited Space-A. A/C, kitchen (2), refrigerator, telephones, washer/dryer, color TV, housekeeping service. Older structures, some renovated. Rates: single $25; married $35. No Pets. Reservations accepted two weeks in advance.

TML Availability: Difficult, summer.

CREDIT CARDS ACCEPTED: Visa, MasterCard, American Express, Diners Club and Discover.

ARKANSAS
Fort Chaffee, continued

Historic Fort Smith, on the Arkansas River, five miles. Gateway to the Ozarks. Fayetteville - University of Arkansas is an opportunity for sporting events. Wildlife management area, excellent hunting and fishing.

Medical 494-2488   Police 911

Little Rock Air Force Base (AR02R2)
P.O. Box 1192
Little Rock AFB, AR 72099-0001

TELEPHONE NUMBER INFORMATION: Main installation numbers: C-501-988-3131, D-312-731-1110.

Location: Use US-67/167 to Jacksonville, take AFB exit to main gate. *USMRA: Page 76 (D,E-5).* NMC: Little Rock, 18 miles southwest.

Lodging Office: Bldg 1024, Cannon Circle. **C-501-988-6753/1141** 24 hours, **D-312-731-6753** during normal duty hours, Fax: C-501-988-7769, after duty hours C-501-988-6200, D-312-731-7769. Check in billeting, check out 1200 hours daily.
TML: VOQ/VAQ. **Razorback Inn,** Bldg 1024, all ranks, official duty, C-501-988-6652. Spaces available (290). No TLF. Refrigerator, A/C, color TV, housekeeping service, washer/dryer, ice vending. Modern structure, remodeled. Rates: VAQ/VOQ $10, DV $16-$27. Children not authorized. Duty can make reservations, others Space-A.

DV/VIP: 314 AW/CCE. C-501-988-6828/3588. O6+. TDY to base only. Retirees and Space-A call lodging direct for availability.

TML Availability: Extremely limited. Best, Dec. 20-31.

CREDIT CARDS ACCEPTED: Visa, MasterCard and American Express.

See War Memorial Park, Arkansas Traveller's Baseball, Burns Park, and Governor's Mansion.

Locator 988-6025   Medical 988-7333   Police 988-3221

Pine Bluff Arsenal (AR03R2)
ATTN: SIOPB-PWH
Bldg 15-330, Kabrich Circle
Pine Bluff Arsenal, AR 71601-9500

TELEPHONE NUMBER INFORMATION: Main installation numbers: C-501-540-3000, D-312-966-3000.

Location: Off US-65 NW of Pine Bluff. Take AR-256, cross AR-365 into main gate of Arsenal. Or south on US-65 from Little Rock, 35 miles, follow signs. *USMRA: Page 76 (E-6).* NMC: Pine Bluff, eight miles southeast.

Lodging Office: Bldg 15-330, Room 6, Sibert Road. **C-501-540-3008**, 0730-1600 hours daily. Other hours OD, C-501-540-2700. Check in billeting, check out 1200 hours daily. Government civilian employee billeting.

ARKANSAS
Pine Bluff Arsenal, continued

TML: TQ and BOQ. Bldgs 15-330, 15-350, all ranks, leave or official duty. Bedroom, private bath (6); separate bedroom, private bath (14); two bedroom, private bath (1). Refrigerator, community kitchen, utensils, A/C, color CATV, housekeeping service, iron/ironing board, washer/dryer. Older structure, Rates: sponsor $20; DV/VIP $25; adults $1, children (12+) $1, under 12 free. Duty can make reservations, others Space-A.

TML Availability: Extremely limited.

CREDIT CARDS ACCEPTED: Visa, MasterCard and American Express.

Great hunting and fishing. Also a nine hole golf course and a recreation area.

Locator 540-3000   Medical 540-3409   Police 540-3506

Note: Effective 1 October 1997 Area Code will change to 870.

Other Installations in Arkansas

Camp Joseph T. Robinson, Post Billeting BOQ, Bldg 7400, North Little Rock, AR 72119-9600, **C-501-212-5100**, Fax C-501-212-5271. Rates: $4-$12.

CALIFORNIA

Barstow Marine Corps Logistics Base (CA13R4)
Food & Hospitality Branch
Bldg. 44
Barstow MCLB, CA 92311-5047

TELEPHONE NUMBER INFORMATION: Main installation numbers: C-619-577-6211, D-312-282-6611/6612.

Location: On I-40, 1.5 miles east of Barstow. Take I-15 NE from San Bernardino, or west from Las Vegas, NV. Signs mark direction to MCLB. *USMRA: Page 111 (G-12,13).* NMC: San Bernardino, 75 miles southwest.

Lodging Office: Bldg 44. **C-619-577-6418, D-312-282-6418,** Fax: 619-577-6542, 0800-1600 hours daily. Other hours OD, Bldg 30, Room 8, C-619-577-6611. Check in/out at billeting.

TML: TLF. **Oasis Lodge.** Bldg 114, all ranks, leave or official duty. Food and Hospitality Branch, Bldg 44, C-619-577-6418. Bedroom, private bath, (2); 2-bedroom, private bath (2). Kitchen, utensils, A/C, color TV. Older structure. Reservations accepted. Rates: $25. Check out 1100 hours daily. All categories can make reservations in advance.

TML: VIP. Bldg 11-A, 06+, leave or official duty. C-619-577-6555, D- 312-282-6555. Two bedroom, private bath (1). Kitchen, utensils, A/C, color TV, housekeeping service, washer/dryer. Older structure. Rates: $35 per unit. All categories can make reservations. Check out 1100 hours daily.

CALIFORNIA
Barstow Marine Corps Logistics Base, continued

DV/VIP: Commanding General, Bldg 15, C-619-577-6555, D-312-282-6555, FAX: 619-577-6058. O6+. Retired & lower ranks Space-A. Rates: $35 per unit.

TML Availability: Good, Aug.-Apr. Difficult, other times.

CREDIT CARDS ACCEPTED: (normal working hours only) Visa, MasterCard, Discover and American Express (government card only.).

Visit Calico Ghost Town, eight miles east. Lake Delores is 13 miles east for water recreation. Southern California is an easy reach, and Las Vegas not too far east..

Locator 577-6211   **Medical 577-6591**   **Police 911**

Beale Air Force Base (CA47R4)
Gold Country Inn
9 SVS/SVML
Bldg 24112, A Street
Beale AFB, CA 95903-1615

TELEPHONE NUMBER INFORMATION: Main installation numbers: C-916-634-3000, D-312-368-3000.

Location: From CA-70 N exit south of Marysville to North Beale Road, continue for 10 miles to main gate of AFB. *USMRA: Page 110 (C,D-5,6)*. NMC: Sacramento, 40 miles south.

Lodging Office: Gold Country Inn. Bldg 24112, B Street. **C-916-634-2953, D-312-368-2953,** Fax: C-916-634-3674, D-312-368-3674, 24 hours. Check in billeting, check out 1200 hours daily. Government civilian employee billeting.

TML: TLF. Bldgs 5109-5112, all ranks, official duty, Space-A. Two-bedroom, private bath (3); 3-bedroom, private bath (6); 4-bedroom, private bath (8). Kitchen, complete utensils, A/C, color TV in room and lounge, housekeeping service, cribs/cots, washer/dryer, microwave. Older structure. Rates: Range from $14-$24 for 2-bedroom, 3-bedroom, 4-bedroom. All Space-A is $24. All must make reservations.

TML: VOQ. Bldgs 2350-2360, officer all ranks, official duty, Space-A. Bedroom, private bath (47). Kitchen, A/C, limited utensils, color TV in room and lounge, housekeeping service, cribs/cots, washer/dryer, microwave. Older structure. Rates: $10 per person, $14 per couple

TML: VAQ. Bldg 18000, enlisted all ranks, official duty, Space-A. Bedroom, semi-private bath, (18); Two bedrooms, semi-private bath (34); SNCO suites, private bath (3). Refrigerator, A/C, color TV in room and lounge, housekeeping service, cribs/cots, washer/dryer, ice vending, microwave. Older structure, remodeled. Rates: $1 per person, $14 per couple. SNCO rates: $16 per person, $23 per couple. Reservations accepted.

DV/VIP: Protocol Office, C-916-634-2954, O6+, retirees. Reservations required.

TML Availability: Good, Sep-May. Difficult, other times.

CALIFORNIA
Beale Air Force Base, continued

CREDIT CARDS ACCEPTED: Visa, MasterCard and American Express.

In the center of historic California gold rush country, east of Marysville and north of Sacramento. Outdoor sports are popular.

Locator 634-2960   Medical 634-4444   Police 634-2000

Note: A new area code, 650, will be added on 1 August 1997 to the current 415 and 916 areas. There will be a six month grace period for those numbers that are effected.

Camp Pendleton Marine Corps Base (CA30R4)
Billeting/Bachelor Housing Office
Bldg 1341, Box 555013
Camp Pendleton MCB, CA 92055-5013

TELEPHONE NUMBER INFORMATION: Main installation numbers: C-619-725-4111, D-312-365-4111.

Location: On I-5 which is adjacent to main gate. Take Camp Pendleton off ramp from I-5 at Oceanside. *USMRA: Page 111 (F-14,15).* NMC: Oceanside, adjacent to base.

Lodging Office: Bldg 1341, **C-619-725-3718/3451/3732,** 24 hours. Check in as indicated, check out 1200 hours daily. Government civilian employee billeting.

TML: TOQ. Bldgs 1341, 1342, Mainside, officers all ranks, WO1-O6. Check in at billeting. Bedroom, single occupancy, semi-private bath (20); separate bedrooms, queen bed, private bath (18). Refrigerator, microwave, coffee maker, color CATV, AM/FM radio, community kitchen, washer/dryer. Older structure, renovated. Rates: Bldg 1341 TAD/TDY $18, others $22; Bldg 1342 TAD/TDY $20, others $28, each additional person $5. TAD/TDY and PCS in/out can make reservations, others Space-A.

TML: TOQ. Bldg 210440 (Del Mar). From main gate, one block, left to fire station, left to stop sign, left to TOQ on the left. Check in at facility. Call for reservations. Officers, WO1-O6, leave or official duty. Suites, queen bed, kitchenette with utensils, private bath (6); studio, private bath, club facilities with limited dining (15); bedroom, shared living room, private bath (72). Refrigerator, microwave, coffee maker, color CATV, AM/FM radio, washer/dryer. New structure. Rates: TAD/TDY $17-$20, others $19-$27, each additional person $5. Duty can make reservations, others Space-A.

TML: TEQ. Bldg 16146, enlisted all ranks, leave or official duty. Check out 1200 hours. Bedroom, queen bed, community bath (42). Refrigerator, microwave, coffee maker, color CATV, AM/FM radio, washer/dryer. Older structure. Rates: TAD/TDY, $17-$20, others $18-$22, $5 each additional person. Duty can make reservations, others Space-A.

TML: BEQ. Camp Pendleton Naval Hospital. E1-E4, C-619-725-1383. Bedroom, sleeps three, iron/ironing boards. Check in after 1200, check out 1100.

TML: DVQ/VIP. Bldg 1342, 1751. Officer O6+, leave or official duty, C-619-725-5080/5830 (Joint Protocol Officer). Two-bedroom, kitchen, living room, dining room, den, 1.5 baths (3); DVQ bedroom, queen bed, living room, refrigerator, utensils, service bar, private bath (2). Microwave,

CALIFORNIA
Camp Pendleton Marine Corps Base, continued

coffee maker, color CATV, AM/FM radio, base phone, washer/dryer. Older structure, Rates: TAD/TDY $20-$30, others $27-$52, each additional person $5. Maximum six per suite. TAD/TDY can make reservations, others Space-A. General/Flag rank have priority.

DV/VIP: ATTN: Joint Protocol Officer, Bldg 1160, C-619-725-5780. O6+. Retirees and lower ranks Space-A.

TML: Guest House, MWR. **Ward Lodge.** Fifteen miles from main gate. Bldg 1310, all ranks, leave or official duty. Reservations accepted, C-619-725-5304. Check in at facility. Bedroom, private bath (64). Kitchen (36 units), limited utensils, A/C, color TV in room and lounge, VCR, housekeeping service, cribs ($1), cots ($1), coin washer/dryer, ice vending, facilities for DAVs, swimming pool. Modern structure. Rates for PCS/leave personnel: $30 with kitchen, $25 without kitchen. All categories can make reservations.

TML: San Onofre Recreation Beach. C-619-725-7629. Mobile homes/Cottages, 1-3 bedrooms (36). Rates: $35-50 daily. See *Military Living's Military RV, Camping and Rec Areas Around the World* for additional information and directions.

TML: Club Del Cottages, (Camp Del Mar Beach) mobile homes, reservations by phone or in person, C-619-725-2134. Leave or official duty. Cottages, one bedroom, private bath (48); two bedroom mobile homes, two sets bunk beds, sleeps six, private bath (14); four bedroom mobile homes, double wide, sleeps 16, private bath (1). Full kitchen, no housekeeping service, bring bed linens, blankets, pillows, towels, etc. Recreation area with many amenities, ITT Office has tickets to Southern California attractions. Summer package, minimum stay seven days. Mon-Thu, leave Fri; Fri-Sun, leave Mon. Rates: cottages $30 daily; 2-bedroom mobile home $30; 4 bedroom mobile home $60. Winter rates available. No pets. All categories can make reservations. **Note: See complete lodging listing in this book under Club Del Cottages, and also in** *Military RV, Camping and Rec Areas Around the World.*

TML Availability: Fairly good, Oct-Mar. Difficult, other times.

CREDIT CARDS ACCEPTED: Visa, MasterCard and American Express.

Beaches, all forms of water recreation, Mission San Luis Rey, and 72 golf courses are within easy reach of Camp Pendleton.

Locator 725-4111   **Medical 725-6308**   **Police 911**

Camp San Luis Obispo (CA83R4)
ATTN: Billeting Manager
P.O. Box 4360
San Luis Obispo, CA 93403-4360

TELEPHONE NUMBER INFORMATION: Main installation numbers: C-805-594-6200, D-312-630-6200.

Location: Take Hwy 1 five miles northwest of the city of San Luis Obispo. *USMRA: Page 111 (C-11).* NMC: San Luis Obispo, five miles southeast.

24 - Temporary Military Lodging Around the World

CALIFORNIA
Camp San Luis Obispo, continued

Lodging Office: Bldg 738, San Joaquin Ave. **C-805-594-6500, D-312-630-6500**, 0800-1630 Tue-Sun, 0800-1330 Mon. Check in 0800-1630, check out 1200 hours. Government civilian employee billeting.

TML: BOQ. Transient housing. Rooms, apartments, cottages, all ranks, leave or official duty. Bedroom, community bath (101); bedroom, hall bath (39); 2-bedroom, private bath (8); three bedroom, private bath (3); various bedroom/bath combinations (4). Refrigerator, kitchen (some units), limited utensils, color TV, housekeeping service. Older structure, redecorated. Rates: leave/official duty, sponsor: duty $14, leave $15; $15 each additional person, maximum charge $45, up to 5 people; $60 over 6 people. Maximum varies per unit. Duty can make reservations, Space-A tentative reservations up to one month in advance. No pets allowed.

DV/VIP: No separate office, call billeting, O6+. Retirees, lower ranks Space-A.

TML Availability: Fairly good. Best, Sept-Mar. Difficult other times.

There is a small aircraft museum on this California Army National Guard Post. Don't miss local state beaches. Visit local wineries, Hearst Castle, San Luis Obispo Mission Plaza and Farmers Market.

Locator 594-6500   **Medical 911**   **Police 911**

China Lake Naval Air Warfare Systems Center, Weapons Division (CA34R4)
Central Billeting, Bldg 1395
China Lake NWC, CA 93555-6100

TELEPHONE NUMBER INFORMATION: Main installation numbers: C-619-939-9011, D-312-437-9011

Location: From US-395 or CA-14, take CA-178 E to Ridgecrest and the main gate. *USMRA: Page 111 (G-10,11,12; H-11)*. NMC: Los Angeles, 150 miles southwest.

Lodging Office: Bldg 1395. **C-619-939-3146**, Fax C-619-939-2789, 24 hours. Check in after 1500, check out 1200 hours daily. Government civilian employee billeting.

TML: Transient House. Ten buildings, all ranks, leave or official duty. Three-bedroom, private bath, kitchen (utensils on request). A/C, CATV, housekeeping service, telephone, washer/dryer. Rates: Depends on rank. Duty can make reservations, others Space-A.

TML: BOQ. 00496, 00499, officers all ranks, leave or official duty. Bedroom, private bath (24). Refrigerator, central cooling, color TV, CATV in lounge, individual heaters, hall phones, housekeeping service. Older structure. Rates: $24 per room, maximum 2 people. No children allowed. Personnel on orders can make reservations, others Space-A.

TML: BEQ. Bldg 1395, E7-E-9, leave or official duty. Bedroom, shared bath (12). A/C, color TV, CATV in lounge, housekeeping service, washer/dryer. Older structure. Rates: $12 per person. Unaccompanied personnel only. Duty can make reservations, others Space-A.

CALIFORNIA
China Lake Naval Air Warfare Systems Center, Weapons Division, continued

TML: DV/VIP. Bldgs 00662, 00663, officers O6/GS-15+, leave or official duty. Three bedroom suites, private bath (4). Kitchen, utensils, A/C, CATV, housekeeping service. Older structure. Rates: $34 per day. Duty can make reservations, others Space-A.

DV/VIP: Protocol Office, C-619-939-2383/3039, D-314-437-2383/3039, O6+. Retirees and lower ranks Space-A.

TML Availability: Good.

Four wheelers enjoy hundreds of trails nearby, while popular mountain areas (Mammoth, June and the Greenhorn Mountains) draw other enthusiasts year round. Visit Red Rock Canyon, and Fossil Falls.

Locator 939-2303   Medical 939-2911   Police 939-3323

Coronado Naval Amphibious Base (CA38R4)
Combined Bachelor Quarters
BOQ Bldg #500
San Diego, CA 92155-5000

TELEPHONE NUMBER INFORMATION: Main installation numbers: C-619-437-2011, D-312-577-2011.

Location: From San Diego, I-5 S to Palm Ave (CA-75) W 10 miles. Follow signs to Naval Amphibious Base, Coronado. *USMRA: Page 118 (C,D-7,8).* NMC: San Diego, five miles north.

Lodging Office: Bldg 504, Tulagi Street. **C-619-437-3860, D-312-577-3860,** Fax: C-619-437-3475 (BOQ); Bldg 302, **C-619-437-3494, D-312-577-3494,** Fax: C-619-437-2556 (BEQ), 24 hours. Check in billeting 1500, check out 1200 hours daily. For group reservations call C-619-437-5268, D-312-577-5268.

TML: BOQ. Bldg 504, officers all ranks, leave or official duty. Accessible to handicapped. Bedroom units, private bath (374); separate bedroom, private bath (90). Refrigerator, color TV, housekeeping service, washer/dryer, ice vending, soda/snack vending. Exercise room available. Modern structure. Rates: sponsor $11, guests $2.75. Duty can make reservations, others Space-A reservations 24 hours in advance.

TML: BEQ. Bldg 302, enlisted all ranks, leave or official duty. handicap accessible. DV suite private bath (4), DV suite, common bath (2), E7-E9 common bath (10), E5-E6 common bath (87), E1-E4 common bath (36). Housekeeping service, refrigerator, color TV, washer/dryer, soda/snack vending. Exercise room available. Rates: DV $12 per person, E1-E9 $6 per person. Duty can make reservations, others Space-A after 1800 hours.

TML: DV/VIP. Bldg 504. Officers O6-10, leave or official duty. Separate bedroom suites, private bath (20). Refrigerator, color TV, housekeeping service, washer/dryer, ice vending. Modern structure. Rates: Sponsor $29, each guest $7.25. Duty can make reservations, others Space-A 24 hours in advance.

DV/VIP: Reservations: C-619-437-3860, O6+/civilian equivalent. Retirees Space-A.

CALIFORNIA
Coronado Naval Amphibious Base, continued

TML Availability: Good most of the year.

CREDIT CARDS ACCEPTED: Visa, MasterCard and American Express.

Transportation: Off Base Shuttle/Bus, Off Base Taxi, Car Rental Agencies.

Coronado Bay and the Pacific Ocean offer all water sports; Seaport Village and Sea World are good family fun. There are a multitude of attractions in San Diego.

Locator 437-2011   Medical 437-2375/2376   Police 437-3432

Del Mar Beach Cottages (CA03R4)
Lodging Office, Bldg 210595
Camp Pendleton, CA 92055-5018

TELEPHONE NUMBER INFORMATION: Main installation numbers: C-619-725-7935, D-312-365-2463.

Location: Exit I-5 on Harbor Drive/Camp Pendleton. Enter either the Del Mar Gate or the Main Gate on Camp Pendleton. Approximately 2.5 miles from either gate. *USMRA: Page 111 (F-14,15)*. NMC: Oceanside, one mile south.

Lodging Office: Bldg 210595. **C-619-725-2134**, 0800-2200 hours. Check in facility 1400-1630 hours daily. Late arrival should be pre-arranged. Check out 1200 hours daily. No government civilian employees billeting.

TML: Club Del, mobile homes, officer, enlisted E6+, leave or official duty. Two-bedroom, private bath, beach front, sleeps six (12). Four bunk beds, one double, full bath, living room, kitchen with refrigerator, microwave, stove, coffee maker, cooking utensils, TV. Number seven is doublewide, 4 bedrooms, sleeps 16 with eight beds, four sleeper couches, 2 baths, fully equipped kitchen. One bedroom, double bed and sleeper couch sleeps 4 (47). Fully equipped kitchen and bath. Housecleaning aids furnished, bring bed linens, pillows, dish soap, towels, food and firewood, ice vending, washer/dryer. Rates: $30, winter/summer, 1-2 bedroom units; $30, four-bedroom units $60. Trailer #9/E9 only, #10/O6 only, #11/O7 only. If checkout occurs during non-working hours, patron forfeits the right to be present for inspection. Reservations all categories, must be paid 4 weeks prior to occupancy. Duty and Reservists, Camp Pendleton, can make reservations 12 weeks in advance, duty and Reservists (other stations) 10 weeks, retirees, 8 weeks. No bumping, mail in reservations not accepted. Call 619-725-2134 for further information. No Pets.

TML Availability: Good, Oct-Apr. Difficult, other times.

CREDIT CARDS ACCEPTED: Visa, Mastercard and Discover.

All ocean activities available in the area, a 26 mile Ocean shoreline. Oceanside, San Clemente, and Carlsbad nearby.

Locator 725-4111   Medical 725-6308   Police 911

Temporary Military Lodging Around the World - 27

CALIFORNIA

Edwards Air Force Base (CA48R4)
95 SVS/SVMH
115 Methusa Avenue
Edwards AFB, CA 93524-1031

TELEPHONE NUMBER INFORMATION: Main installation numbers: C-805-277-1110, D-312-527-1110

Location: Off CA-14, 18 miles east of Rosamond and 30 miles northeast of Lancaster. Also, off CA-58, 10 miles southwest of Boron. *USMRA: Page 111 (F,G-12)*. NMC: Los Angles, 90 miles southwest.

Lodging Office: Bldg 5602. **C-805-277-4101/3394,** Fax: C-805-277-2517, D-312-527-2517, 24 hours. Check in 1400, check out 1200 hours daily.

TML: VOQ. Bldgs 5601, 5603, officers all ranks, leave or official duty. Bedroom, living room, private bath (36). Fully furnished, A/C, color TV, housekeeping service, washer/dryer, ice vending. Older structure, newly furnished. Rates: $16 per person. Duty can make reservations, others Space-A.

TML: VAQ. Bldgs 5602, 5603, 5604, all ranks, leave or official duty. Bldg 5602: Rooms (48). Bldg 5603: SNCO suites (8). Bldg 5604: Share Bath. A/C, color TV, housekeeping service, washer/dryer. Older structure. Rates: $10 per person. Duty can make reservations, others Space-A.

TML: TLF. Bldgs 7022-7031, all ranks. One bedroom suite/family quarters, private bath (51). Double and single bed, sleeper couch in living room, A/C, color TV, washer/dryer, kitchen. Rates: $21. PCS personnel can make reservations, others Space-A.

TML: DV/VIP. Bldg 5601, officer O6+. One bedroom suites, private bath (10). A/C, color TV, housekeeping service. Older structure. Rates: $16 per person. Duty can make reservations, others Space-A.

DV/VIP: Protocol, ATTN: AFFTC/CCP, Bldg 2650, room 200, C-805-277-3326. O7+/SES.

TML Availability: Good, all year.

CREDIT CARDS ACCEPTED: Visa, MasterCard and American Express.

Los Angeles, 90 miles southwest, many Southern California attractions are nearby.

Locator 277-2777   Medical 277-4427   Police 277-3340

El Centro Naval Air Facility (CA09R4)
Bldg 401
El Centro NAF, CA 92243-5001

TELEPHONE NUMBER INFORMATION: Main installation numbers: C-619-339-2524, D-312-958-4645/4646.

28 - Temporary Military Lodging Around the World

CALIFORNIA
El Centro Naval Air Facility, continued

Location: Take I-8, two miles west of El Centro, to Forrester Road exit, 1.5 miles to Evan Hewes Hwy left west for four miles, right on Bennet Road to main gate. *USMRA: Page 111 (H-15,16).* NMC: El Centro, seven miles east.

Lodging Office: Bldg 401. **C-619-337-4645/4918, D-312-958-4645/4918.** Fax: C-619-337-4936, 24 hours. Check in billeting, check out 1100 hours daily. Government civilian employees on orders billeted.

TML: Navy Lodge. Bldg 388, 392 all ranks, leave or official duty. Reservations: **1-800-NAVY-INN.** Lodge number is C-619-339-2478, Fax: C-619-351-4914. Check in 1500-1800, check out 1200 hours daily. Two-bedroom trailers, one queen, one double, private bath (5), one handicap accessible unit. Kitchenette, utensils, microwave, coffee/tea, A/C, CATV, housekeeping service, cribs, mini-mart, free washer/dryer, picnic grounds, playground. Rates: $40 per unit. All categories can make reservations.

TML: BOQ. Bldg 270, officers, leave or official duty. Bedroom, two beds, private bath (36); separate bedrooms, private bath (2); bedroom suite, private bath (DV/VIP) (2). Refrigerator, limited utensils, A/C, color TV in room and lounge, housekeeping service, ice vending. Older structure, remodeled. Rates: $8 per person, $18 VIP. Duty can make reservations, others Space-A. Also TVQ rooms ($4). Inquire.

TML: BEQ. Bldg 4001. Enlisted, all ranks, leave or official duty. Bedroom, two beds, shared bath (48); suites, private bath E7+ (6); single bed, shared bath (24). Refrigerator, CATV, A/C, housekeeping services, Mon-Sat, TV lounge, arcade games, snack vending, non smoking lounge. New structure Rates: $4-$8. Duty, reservists on orders, retired Space-A.

DV/VIP: Contact billeting, O6+, retirees Space-A. C-619-339-8535.

TML Availability: Fair. Difficult, Sep-Jun.

CREDIT CARDS ACCEPTED: Visa, MasterCard and American Express. The Navy Lodge accepts Visa, MasterCard, American Express and Discover.

Hunting, fishing, golfing, tennis, hiking and camping are all available in the Imperial Valley, it is also the winter home (Jan-Mar) of the "Blue Angels."

Locator 339-2555   Medical 339-2675/2666   Police 339-2525

El Toro Marine Corps Air Station (CA22R4)
Lodging Office, Bldg 58
El Toro MCAS, CA 92709-5001
Scheduled to close December 1999.

TELEPHONE NUMBER INFORMATION: Main installation numbers: C-714-726-3011, D-312-997-3011.

Location: Off I-5, take the Sand Canyon Road exit. Follow signs to MCAS. *USMRA: Page 111 (F-14): Page 117 (G,H-7,8).* NMC: Los Angeles, 40 miles northwest.

Temporary Military Lodging Around the World - 29

CALIFORNIA
El Toro Marine Corps Air Station, continued

Lodging Office: Bldg 58. C-714-726-3500/2084, D-312-997-3500/2084, Fax: C-714-726-3308, 0700-2400 hours daily. Check in facility, check out 1200 hours daily. Government civilian employee billeting.

TML: TLF. Bldg 823, four blocks from main gate. All ranks, leave or official duty, C-714-726-3500/2084, 0700-2000 hours daily. Suites, sitting room, bedroom, queen size bed, sofa bed (24). Kitchen, complete utensils, A/C, color TV in room and lounge, housekeeping service, coin washer/dryer, soda/snack vending, ice vending, facility for DAVs. Modern structure. Close to exchange, seven day store and commissary. Rates: $35 per unit. Maximum 4 per unit. Duty can make reservations, others Space-A.

TML: TOQ/DVQ. Bldgs 33, 35, 248, 249, 250 (DVQ), 375 officers all ranks, leave or official duty, C-714-726-3001. Bedroom, shared bath; separate bedrooms, private bath (17); 2-bedroom suite, private bath (2); 3-bedroom suite, private bath (3). Kitchen (five units), refrigerator, A/C, color TV in room and lounge, housekeeping service, cots, washer/dryer, soda/snack vending, ice vending. Rates: common bathrooms $6.50; private bathrooms, $9.50, each additional guest $4; civilians $7; suites $15, each additional guest $4; DVQ rooms $20, each additional guest $5, maximum $30.

TML: TEQ, EFQ. Bldgs 660, 668. Bedroom, queen bed, private bath (E6+) (28); bedroom, shared bath (to E5, four persons per room); EFQ bedrooms, private bath (43). Refrigerator, microwave, cooking facilities, washer/dryer, housekeeping service, color TV in room (EFQ in lounge). Rates: TEQ $7, each additional guest $4; EFQ $4-$5 .

TML: Big Bear Recreation Area. Write to: The Lodge, Bldg 823, MCAS El Toro, Santa Ana, CA 92709, C-714-726-2626/2572, D-312-997-2626/2572. All ranks, leave or official duty. Chalets, 1-bedroom, sofa bed, living room, loft (two double beds) (8). Kitchen, microwave, utensils, fireplace, color TV, bring personal items, many recreational facilities. All categories may make reservations, active duty MCAS El Toro and Tustin have priority. *Note: This facility will continue to operate under Miramar MCAS (what Miramar NAS will become) after El Toro MCAS closes in 1999.* See *Military Living's Military RV, Camping and Rec Areas Around the World* **for additional information and directions.**

DV/VIP: Bldg 250, C-714-726-3624, O6+. Retirees and lower ranks Space-A.

TML Availability: Good, winter months. Difficult, summer months.

CREDIT CARDS ACCEPTED: Visa, MasterCard and American Express.

Orange County, Mission Viejo, Laguna Hills, Laguna Niguel and San Juan Capistrano Mission are all nearby.

Locator 726-2100   Medical 911   Police 726-3527/8

Fort Hunter Liggett (CA37R4)
ATTN: AFRC-FMH-PWH
P.O. Box 631
Jolon, CA 93928-7000

TELEPHONE NUMBER INFORMATION: Main installation numbers: C-408-386-5000, D-312-949-2291.

30 - *Temporary Military Lodging Around the World*

CALIFORNIA
Fort Hunter Liggett, *continued*

Location: From US-101 S exit at King City to CA-G-14, south to main gate. *USMRA: Page 111 (C-10).* NMC: San Luis Obispo, 60 miles south.

Lodging Office: Bldg 205. **C-408-386-2511, D-312-686-2511,** Fax: C-408-386-2209, D-312-686-2209, 0800-1630 hours duty days. Other hours SDO, Bldg 205, C-408-386-2511. Check in 1200, check out 1000 hours daily. Government civilian employee billeting.

TML: VOQ/VEQ. Bldg T-128, officers and enlisted all ranks. Separate bedrooms, private bath (30). Share kitchen with adjoining room, refrigerator, A/C, color CATV, housekeeping service. Modern structure. Rates: officers, $22.50 per room, each additional person $5. Reservations accepted duty only, others Space-A.

TML Availability: Good, most of the year.

CREDIT CARDS ACCEPTED: Visa, MasterCard, American Express, and Diners' Club.

Famous for the yearly return of the swallows—just like Capistrano. Nearby is Mission San Antonio de Padua. Hunting and fishing available on post in season.

Locator 386-2533/2520   Medical 386-2570   Police 386-2613

Fort Irwin National Training Center (CA01R4)
Lodging Office, Bldg 109
Fort Irwin, CA 92310-0041

TELEPHONE NUMBER INFORMATION: Main installation numbers: C-619-380-4111, D-312-470-4111.

Location: Take I-15 E from Los Angeles for 125 miles or I-15 W from Las Vegas, NV, for 150 miles. Fort is north of I-15 near Barstow, watch for signs. *USMRA: Page 111 (G,H-11,12).* NMC: San Bernardino, 60 miles southwest.

Lodging Office: Bldg 109, Langford Lake Road. **C-619-380-4599**, 24 hours. Check in 1400-1800 hours, check out 1200 hours daily.

TML: Tiefort Lodge. All ranks, leave or official duty. One bedroom, private bath (20). Mobile homes. Three-bedroom, two private baths (8). Kitchen, utensils, A/C, color TV, housekeeping service, washer/dryer. Reservations accepted. Rates: $26 lodge, $20 mobile homes. Maximum six per unit. All categories eligible, early reservations suggested.

TML: VOQ. Bldg 98. All ranks, leave or official duty. Single and double bedrooms, shared bath (30). Rates: $30 single, $35 double. Call for more information.

TML: DVQ. Bldg 28 and mobile home, officers O6+, C-619-380-4223. Bedroom, private bath (8). Refrigerator, A/C, color TV, housekeeping service, mini bar. Modern structure. Rates:$30-$35. Maximum capacity per unit, one to three. Reservations required.

DV/VIP: Protocol, Bldg 151, C-619-380-4223, O6+. Lower ranks Space-A.

TML Availability: Good, winter. Difficult, summer.

Temporary Military Lodging Around the World - 31

CALIFORNIA
Fort Irwin National Training Center, continued

Visit NASA's Goldstone Deep Space Tracking Station for a group tour. Rainbow Basin has many interesting fossils (<u>not</u> collectable!), and Park Moabi Marina in a quiet cove off the Colorado river are of interest to visitors.

Locator 380-3369   Medical 380-3242   Police 380-4444

Fort MacArthur (CA46R4)
Fort MacArthur Inn
2400 South Pacific Ave, Bldg 37
San Pedro, CA 90731-2960

TELEPHONE NUMBER INFORMATION: Main installation numbers: C-310-363-8296, D-312-833-8296.

Location: At the end of Harbor 110 Freeway S, left on Gaffey Ave to 22nd Street, left to Pacific Ave, right two blocks, left to gate. *USMRA: Page 117 (C-7)*. NMC: Los Angeles, 18 miles north.

Lodging Office: Fort MacArthur Inn, Bldg 37, South Pacific Ave, **C-310-363-8296,** 0600-2200 Mon-Fri, 0600-2100 hours Sat-Sun. Check in 1400 hours, check out 1100 hours.

TML: TLF. Bldg 40, all ranks, leave or official duty. Reservations only for official duty, others Space-A. Separate bedrooms, private bath (22). Sofa becomes double bed; chair, single bed. Kitchen, utensils, color TV, HBO, housekeeping service, cribs/cots, washer/dryer, ice vending. Older structure. Renovated 1992. Rates: based on rank, $24 per night. Maximum capacity per room, three to five.

TML: VOQ/VAQ. Bldg 36, all ranks. Bedroom, private bath (27). Microwave, complete utensils, color TV, HBO, housekeeping service, cribs/cots, washer/dryer, ice vending. Older structure. Rates: $10 per person, maximum $14. Reservations only for official duty, others Space-A.

TML: DV/VIP. Cottages 14-17, officers O7+, leave or official duty. Two-bedroom units, private bath (2); bedroom, private bath (2). Kitchen, utensils, color TV, housekeeping service, cribs/cots, washer/dryer. Older structure, renovated. Rates: sponsor $16, maximum $23 per family. Maximum four per cottage. Must make reservations through Protocol C-310-363-2030.

COTTAGES: 14-16 available to O6+ on Space A.

TML Availability: Best, Nov-Apr. Difficult, other times.

Locator 363-1876   Medical 363-8301   Police 363-8385

Fort Mason Officers' Club (CA45R4)
Bldg #1, Bay and Franklin Streets
San Francisco, CA 94123-5000

TELEPHONE NUMBER INFORMATION: Main installation numbers: C-415-441-7700.

Location: Entrance on Bay and Franklin Streets, three blocks north of US-101 (Lombard Street). *USMRA: Page 119 (C-5)*. NMC: San Francisco, in the city.

32 - *Temporary Military Lodging Around the World*

CALIFORNIA
Fort Mason Officers' Club, continued

Lodging Office: Reservation Office: Bldg #1, Bay and Franklin Streets. **C-415-441-7700.** Fax: C-415-441-2680, 0900-1700 hours Tue.-Sat. Check in 1400 hours, checkout 1100 hours daily.

TML: Guest Quarters, officers all ranks, active duty, reservist, retirees or GS-7 DOD employees. Reservations accepted up to 60 days in advance. Suites, private bath (2); bedroom, private bath (3); CATV, telephone, refrigerator, bar, housekeeping service, ice available, continental breakfast, morning paper and other amenities. Lunch and dinner available on scheduled days. Older Victorian structure, remodeled 1990. Rates: Single or double, 1 bedroom $65; suites $75; each additional guest $15 extra, deposit required.

TML Availability: Difficult, all year. Reservations accepted up to 60 days in advance.

Fort Mason is a National Park. It offers a magnificent view of Alcatraz Island and San Francisco Bay. Close to North Beach, Fisherman's Wharf and Chinatown. Convenient location, good public transportation. On 1 October 1997, Presidio of Monterey will take over operations.

Note: A new area code, 650, will be added on 1 August 1997 to the current 415 and 916 areas. There will be a six month grace period for those numbers that are effected.

Lemoore Naval Air Station (CA06R4)
CBQ Billeting Fund
Bldg 852 (Code 4400)
Lemoore, CA 93246-5001

TELEPHONE NUMBER INFORMATION: Main installation numbers: C-209-998-0100, D-312-949-1110.

Location: On CA-198, 24 miles east of I-5, 30 miles west of CA-99 in the south central part of the state. *USMRA: Page 111 (D-10).* NMC: Fresno, 40 miles north northeast.

Lodging Office: BEQ , Bldg 880, **C-209-998-4784.** Fax: C-209-998-2637, 24 hours. BOQ , Bldg 800, **C-209-998-4609.** Fax: C-209-998-2542, 24 hours.

NAVY LODGE

TML: Navy Lodge. Bldg 908/909, all ranks, leave or official duty. Reservations: 1-800-NAVY-INN. Lodge number is C-209-998-5791, D-312-949-4861, Fax: C-209-998-6149. Check in 1500-1800, check out 1200 hours daily. Efficiency rooms, private bath, two queen beds (38), one queen bed and one sofa (2), handicap accessible (2). Kitchenette, complete utensils, A/C, CATV, housekeeping service, coin washer/dryer, ice vending. Rates: sponsor $36. Maximum five per room. All categories can make reservations. Military member may sponsor guest. Non smoking rooms available.

TML: BEQ. Bldg 880, enlisted all ranks, leave or official duty. Check in/out (1200 hours daily) at billeting office. Rooms (44), two persons per room. Refrigerator, microwave, A/C, CATV, VCRs, housekeeping service, ice vending, washer/dryer, sauna, jacuzzi, weight room, library, BBQ area, soda/snack vending. Meeting/conference room, exercise room, and mini-mart available. Modern structure. Rates: Sponsor $5. Duty can make reservations, retirees and DAVs Space-A.

Temporary Military Lodging Around the World - 33

CALIFORNIA
Lemoore Naval Air Station, continued

TML: BOQ. Bldg 800, officers all ranks and E7+, leave or official duty, C-209-998-4760. Check in/out (1200 hours daily) front desk of facility. Rooms, private bath (60). Refrigerator, microwave, A/C, CATV, VCRs, housekeeping service, washer/dryer, ice vending, 50" TV in lounge, sauna, jacuzzi, weight room, library, BBQ area. Modern structure. Rates: On orders $9. Retirees, DAVs, reservists Space-A, others can make reservations.

DV/VIP: Commanding Officer, C-209-998-3344, O6+. Retirees Space-A.

TML Availability: Good all year.

CREDIT CARDS ACCEPTED: Visa, MasterCard and American Express. The Navy Lodge accepts Visa, MasterCard, American Express and Discover.

Transportation: On Base Shuttle/Bus.

In the San Joaquin Valley, near Sequoia and Yosemite National Parks, two hours from the coast or mountains, and three hours from Los Angeles and San Francisco. Excellent base facilities.

Locator 998-3789   Medical 998-4435   Police 998-4749

Los Alamitos Armed Forces Reserve Center (CA39R4)
Bldg 19, 11200 Lexington Drive
Los Alamitos, CA 90720-5001

TELEPHONE NUMBER INFORMATION: Main installation numbers: C-310-795-2000, D-312-972-2000. Police 795-2100.

Location: Take I-605 N from I-405 N or S. Exit at Katella and follow signs. Clearly marked. *USMRA: Page 117 (E-6,7).* NMC: Los Angeles, 35 miles northwest.

Lodging Office: Bldg 19, Armed Forces Reserve Center. **C-310-795-2124, D-312-972-2124,** Fax: C-310-795-2125 0800-1630 hours daily. Check in facility 0800-1630 Sat-Thur, 0800-1630 Fri, check out 1200 hours daily. After duty hours pick up key at Security, Bldg 57.

TML: TLF. All ranks, leave or official duty. Two-bedroom shared, shared bath (female) (10); 2-bedroom shared bath (enlisted) (198); 2-bedroom shared, hall bath (officers) (37); bedroom, private bath (O6+) (10); suites, private bath (O7+) (5). Amenities: After 1300 on Sunday, any authorized soldier/retiree/Federal or Civil employee may reserve a VIP and/or O6 quarters for their use until Friday. E1-O5 share quarters. Meeting/conference rooms and exercise room available. Duty can make reservations, others Space-A. Rates: $11-$20, depending on rank, $6 each additional person.

TML Availability: Limited, particularly on weekends, call ahead.

CREDIT CARDS ACCEPTED: Visa, MasterCard and American Express.

Los Alamitos is used extensively for reserve training, but Anaheim (Disneyland!) and Orange County, including great beach cities are nearby.

Locator 795-2000   Medical 911   Police 795-2100

CALIFORNIA

Los Angeles/Long Beach Coast Guard
Eleventh Coast Guard District (CA25R4)
USCG LHA LA/LB P.O. Box 8
Terminal Island Station
San Pedro, CA 90731-0208

TELEPHONE NUMBER INFORMATION: Main installation numbers: C-310-732-7564/7560.

Location: Take Gaffey Street exit off Hwy 110. Take Gaffey until road ends. Co-located with PT Fermin Lighthouse on Coast Guard Base, Terminal Island, San Pedro, CA, 13 miles west of Long Beach. *USMRA: Page 117 (C-7).* NMC: Long Beach, 11 miles east.

Lodging Office: Local Housing Authority, Integrated Support Command, 1001 S. Seaside Ave, Terminal Island. **C-310-514-6450,** 0700-1600 hours Mon-Fri.

TML: Guest House. **Point Fermin.** All ranks, leave or official duty. Two-bedroom, private bath (2). Kitchen, complete utensils, color TV, washer/dryer. Outstanding View. Rates: vary by rank. Active Duty, Reservists and retirees can make reservations on a priority, Space-A basis.

TML: BEQ. Bldg 20, all ranks leave or official duty. Two-bedroom, private bath, small refrigerator, laundry facilities, soda/snack vending, lounge.

TML Availability: Good year round, but very busy Jun-Sep and holidays and weekends.

Close to beach cities, Los Angeles harbor, and all that Southern California has to offer.

March Air Reserve Base (CA08R4)
The March Inn
655 M Street, Suite 4
March ARB, CA 92518-2113

TELEPHONE NUMBER INFORMATION: Main installation numbers: C-909-655-1110, D-312-947-1110.

Location: Off CA-60 and on I-215 which bisects ARB. *USMRA: Page 111 (G-14).* NMC: Riverside, 11 miles southwest.

Lodging Office: 655 M Street, Suite 4, **The March Inn.** **C-909-655-5241,** Fax: C-909-655-4574, D-312-947-4574, 24 hours. Check in lodging office, check out 1100 hours daily.

TML: VOQ/VAQ. Bldgs 100, 102, 311, 400, 2418, 2419, 2420, 2421, all ranks, leave or official duty. Rooms and suites (385+ beds). Refrigerator, kitchenette (except for Bldgs 311, 400, and 2418), A/C, color TV room and lounge, housekeeping service, cots, washer/dryer, ice vending. All rooms are stocked with snacks and beverages. Meeting/conference rooms available. Modern structures. "McBride Suites" (VOQ). Recent VAQ renovation. Rates: VOQ, sponsor $10; VAQ, sponsor $10; suites $16. Duty can make reservations, others Space-A.

DV/VIP: March ARB, C-909-655-3060, O6+ duty or on leave. DVQ rate: $16. Lower ranks Space-A.

CALIFORNIA
March Air Reserve Base, continued

TML Availability: Good, Oct-Feb. Difficult, Apr-Sep.

CREDIT CARDS ACCEPTED: Visa, MasterCard and American Express.

This Inn has more than 385 bedspaces, serving 60,000 visitors a year with a staff of about 65, lots of recent improvements, a good place to stay. See nearby Riverside, the Mission Inn, Castle Park. Disneyland is less than one hour away.

Locator 655-1110   **Medical 7-911**   **Police 7-911**

Marines' Memorial Club (CA20R4)
609 Sutter Street
San Francisco, CA 94102-5000

TELEPHONE NUMBER INFORMATION: Main installation numbers: C-415-673-6672, Fax: C-415-441-3649. Reservations: **1-800-5-MARINE** or **415-673-6604 (direct).**

Location: Use CA-101 or CA-580. Take CA-580 N to San Francisco, cross the Bay Bridge. Take 5th Street exit, up 5th Street to O'Farrell. Turn right and go to Powell Street. Turn left, go to Sutter Street, turn left. Corner of Sutter and Mason. *USMRA: Page 119 (C-5).* **Author's Note:** This is NOT "military lodging" in the sense that we list other military installations in this book. The Marines' Memorial Club is a club/hotel exclusively for uniformed services personnel, active duty and retirees and their guests. Any former member of the Armed Forces of the United States with an Honorable discharge may join the club. Call 1-800-5-MARINE for information. The club is not a part of the government but is a private, non-profit organization and is completely self-supporting. This club/hotel is a living memorial to Marines who lost their lives in the Pacific during WWII. It opened on the Marine Corps' Birthday, 10 Nov 1946, and chose as its motto "A tribute to those Marines who have gone before; and a service to those who carry on."

Lodging Office: Check in and out at lobby desk. Check out 1200 hours daily. Occupancy limited to two weeks except when vacancies exist, 24 hours. For brochure or more info write to the above ATTN: Club Secretary, or call C-415-673-6672.

TML: Hotel, all ranks, leave or official duty. Guest rooms (137); deluxe suites (11); family suites (3). Reservations required. Courtesy coffee/tea in room, ice, soft drinks vending, room service, large closets. Rates: average room $75-100, average suite $175. Rates higher for guests of members. All active duty military services, PHS and NOOA considered as members. Retirees membership fee tax deductible. Club facilities include theater, library/museum, swimming pool, gym, coin-operated launderette, valet, exchange store, package store, rooms for private parties, and a dining room and lounge in the Skyroom on the 12th floor, overlooking San Francisco. Convenience store/news stand and coffee shop outside hotel adjacent to entrance. Hotel discount parking on Sutter Street. Ask at desk.

TML Availability: Best, winter months. Make reservations well in advance.

CREDIT CARDS ACCEPTED: Visa, MasterCard, American Express and Diners' Club.

CALIFORNIA
Marines' Memorial Club, continued

In the heart of San Francisco, within walking distance of Cable Cars, many major attractions.

Locator 673-6672   Medical 911   Police 553-0123

Note: A new area code, 650, will be added on 1 August 1997 to the current 415 and 916 areas. There will be a six month grace period for those numbers that are effected.

****

ATTENTION!
THERE IS A FIRST CLASS HOTEL WITH LOW RATES IN THE HEART OF DOWNTOWN SAN FRANCISCO!

Why not enjoy the very best in America's favorite city? Only one block from Union Square, cable cars, theaters and great shopping.

MARINES' MEMORIAL CLUB

Our first class rooms are from $70 and luxurious Suites from $100. You'll enjoy fine dining in our Skyroom Dining Room and Lounge. Our facilities also include Banquet and Meeting Rooms and a Health Club and pool.

609 Sutter Street - San Francisco, CA 94102   Phone (415) 673-6672

For Reservations and Membership Information Call

1-800-5-MARINE

*Membership in this unique organization is available to former and retired members of all branches of the U.S. Armed Services.

****

CALIFORNIA

McClellan Air Force Base (CA35R4)
77 SPTG/SVML
5405 O'Malley Ave
McClellan AFB, CA 95652-1003
Scheduled to close July 2001.

TELEPHONE NUMBER INFORMATION: Main installation numbers: C-916-643-4113, D-312-633-1110.

Location: Off I-80 East. From I-80 take Madison Ave exit. Clearly marked. *USMRA: Page 110 (C-6).* NMC: Sacramento, 10 miles southwest.

Lodging Office: Bldg 89, 5405 O'Malley Ave, Palm Gate. **C-916-643-3267, C-916-643-6223, D-312-633-6223,** Fax: C-916-643-6222. Check in billeting 24 hours, check out 1200 hours daily. Government civilian billeting.

TML: Guest House. Bldg 1430, all ranks, leave or official duty. One and 2-bedroom available, private bath (20). Kitchen, utensils, A/C, color TV, cribs/cots, washer/dryer. Modern structure. Rates: $24 per unit. Duty can make reservations, others Space-A. Also, VOQ/VAQ available for single occupancy only. $10 person, $14 couple, suites $16 person, $23 couple.

DV/VIP: Protocol, Bldg 200, C-916-643-2845. O6+. Retirees/lower ranks Space-A.

TML Availability: Good, winter months. Difficult, summer through fall months.

CREDIT CARDS ACCEPTED: Visa, MasterCard, American Express and Diners' Club.

Northern Californian skiing, water sports, and Sacramento cosmopolitan activities make McClellan a good choice for a stopover.

Base Information 643-4113   Medical 643-4733   Police 643-6160

Note: A new area code, 650, will be added on 1 August 1997 to the current 415 and 916 areas. There will be a six month grace period for those numbers that are effected.

Miramar Naval Air Station (CA14R4)
BQ MGR, Code 193A/Bldg M312
19920 Polaris Ave
San Diego, CA 92145-5399
Scheduled to realign to Miramar Marine Corps Air Station 1 October 1997.

TELEPHONE NUMBER INFORMATION: Main installation numbers: C-619-537-1011, D-312-577-1011.

Location: Fifteen miles north of San Diego, off I-15. Take Miramar Way exit or Miramar Road exit. *USMRA: Page 118 (C,D-2,3,4; E,F-2,3).* NMC: San Diego, 15 miles southwest.

Lodging Office: Bldg M-312. Check in facility, check out 1200 hours daily. **C-619-537-4235, D-312-577-4235,** Fax: C-619-537-4243, D-312-577-4243. Desk C-619-537-4233, D-312-577-4233.

38 - Temporary Military Lodging Around the World

CALIFORNIA
Miramar Naval Air Station, continued

NAVY LODGE **TML:** Navy Lodge. Bldg 516, all ranks, leave, official duty or retirees. Reservations: **1-800-NAVY-INN**. Lodge number is C-619-271-7111, D-312-577-4855, Fax: C-619-695-7371, 24 hours. Check in 1500-1800 hours, check out 1200 hours. Units, two double beds (40), queen (4), king (16), double with sofa bed (28), handicap accessible rooms (2), all with private bath. Seventy non smoking. Kitchenette, microwave, stovetop, refrigerator, toaster, complete utensils, A/C, CATV, coffee/tea, phones, cribs, rollaways, coin washer/dryer, housekeeping service, mini-mart. Modern structure. Rates: $42 per unit. All categories can make reservations. Kennels near lodge on base.

TML: BEQ. Bldg 639, 640, enlisted, leave or official duty only, 24 hours. Shared room, private bath (104). CATV, washer/dryer. Older structure. Rates: $6.50 per person. Duty on orders can make reservations, others Space-A.

TML: BOQ. Bldg M-312, M-325, all officer ranks, leave or official duty, 24 hours. Bedrooms and suites, private and shared baths. Color TV, housekeeping service, washer/dryer. Older structure. Rates: $12 per person. Duty on orders can make reservations, others Space-A.

DV/VIP: C-619-537-1221, O6+. Retirees Space-A.

TML Availability: Good, Nov-Dec. Difficult, summer.

CREDIT CARDS ACCEPTED: Visa, MasterCard and Navy Travel Card. Navy Lodge accepts Visa, MasterCard, American Express and Discover.

San Diego's Old Town, Shelter and Harbor Islands, Sea World, and Balboa Park downtown are all not to be missed. Water sports, golf, tennis, and nearby Mexico will keep visitors from ever being bored in this lovely city.

Locator 537-1011   **Medical 537-4655**   **Police 537-1213**

Moffett Federal Air Field (CA15R4)
Moffett, CA 94043-0128
This installation has been converted to a NASA and other Federal agency base.

TELEPHONE NUMBER INFORMATION: Main installation numbers: C-415-604-5000, D-312-359-5000.

Location: On Bayshore Freeway, US-101, 35 miles south of San Francisco, CA. *USMRA: Page 119 (F-9).* NMC: San Jose, seven miles south.

Lodging Office: Bldg 20, **C-415-603-9503**, D-312-359-9503, Fax C-415-603-7896, 24 hours. Reservations: C-415-603-9805. Check in 1300 at lodging office, check out 1200 hours daily.

NAVY LODGE **TML:** Navy Lodge, Bldg 593, Vernon Ave, Mountain View CA 94013. All ranks, leave or official duty, reservists, retirees. Reservations: **C-1-800-NAVY-INN**, Lodge number is C-415-962-1542, Fax: C-415-694-7538, 0700-2300 hours

Temporary Military Lodging Around the World - 39

CALIFORNIA
Moffett Federal Air Field, continued

daily. Check in 1500-1800, check out 1200 hours daily. Bedroom, two double beds, kitchenette, microwave, private bath (50). Housekeeping service, washer/dryer, ice vending. Modern structure. Rates: $44 per unit. All categories can make reservations.

TML Availability: Limited.

CREDIT CARDS ACCEPTED: Visa, MasterCard and American Express are accepted at the Navy Lodge.

Visit historic Hangar One for a trip into Naval Aviation. Carmel by the sea and Pebble Beach are nearby.

Locator 604-5000   Medical 603-8251   Police 604-5461

Note: A new area code, 650, will be added on 1 August 1997 to the current 415 and 916 areas. There will be a six month grace period for those numbers that are effected.

Monterey Naval Postgraduate School (CA16R4)
Combined Bachelor Quarters
1 University Circle, Room 118a
Monterey, CA 93943-5007

TELEPHONE NUMBER INFORMATION: Main installation numbers: C-408-656-2441/2/3, D-312-878-2441/2/3.

Location: Take CA-1 North to central Monterey exit, right at light onto Camino Aguajito. Immediate, very sharp, right onto Tenth Street, left onto Sloat Ave and into Main Gate. Or South on CA-1, take Aguajito Road exit to Mark Thomas Drive, left on Sloat Ave, turn right into Main Gate. *USMRA: Page 111 (B-9).* NMC: Monterey, in city limits.

Lodging Office: Bldg 220, **Herrmann Hall,** 1 University Circle. **C-408-656-2060/69, D-312-878-2060/69,** Fax: C-408-656-3024, D-312-878-3024, 24 hours. Check in billeting 1500 hours with reservation, 1600 hours for Space-A, check out 1100 hours daily. Write to: CBQ, Monterey, CA 93943. Government Civilian employee billeting (BOQ). Duty billets available during school vacations.

TML: BOQ. Bldgs 220, 221, 222, officers all ranks, official duty and Space-A. Bedroom, private bath (181); 2-room suites (VIP) (4); single room suites (VIP) (4). Microwave, refrigerator, TV, VCR, telephone, housekeeping service, cots/cribs washer/dryer, soda/snack vending, ice vending, pool table. Older structure. Rates: standard room $10 per day per person, each additional guest $2.50; single VIP suite $20, $5 each additional guest, 2-room suite ($25), each additional guest $6 per day. Duty can make reservations. No pets.

TML: BEQ. Bldgs 205, 259 enlisted E1-E9, on official duty. Check out 1100 hours. Three (3) Bedrooms, (6 spaces for males, 3 spaces for females). Refrigerator (in room), TV/VCP, washer/dryer, soda/snack vending, and exercise equipment in lounge. Unaccompanied personnel only. No pets.

DV/VIP: Bldg 220, officers O6+, official duty, and Space-A can make reservations at C-408-656-2511/2/3/4.

40 - Temporary Military Lodging Around the World

CALIFORNIA
Monterey Naval Postgraduate School, continued

TML Availability: Best, Christmas during school vacation. Extremely limited other times. Call for availability.

CREDIT CARDS ACCEPTED: Visa, MasterCard and American Express.

Transportation: Off Base Taxi 646-1234.

In the heart of one of the most prestigious areas of California, The BOQ (Herrmann Hall) began life as the Hotel Del Monte. Nearby are Pebble Beach, 17 mile drive, Steinbeck's Cannery Row, the Monterey Bay Aquarium, Fisherman's Wharf and Carmel Mission.

Locator 656-2441   Medical 656-2333   Police 656-2555

North Island Naval Air Station (CA43R4)
Lodging Office, Bldg I
North Island NAS, CA 92135-5220

TELEPHONE NUMBER INFORMATION: Main installation numbers: C-619-545-1011, D-312-735-0444.

Location: From I-5 N or S exit at Coronado Bridge (toll). Also, from CA-75 N to CA-282 to base. In Coronado. *USMRA: Page 118 (B,C-6,7).* NMC: San Diego, 4 miles northeast.

Lodging Office: Bldg I for officers. **C-619-545-7545/7492**, Fax: C-619-545-7546. Bldg 1500 for enlisted, C-619-545-9551, 24 hours. Check in facility (between 1500-1800 hours for confirmed reservations), check out 1200 hours daily. Government civilian employee with order billeting available at BOQ.

NAVY LODGE — **TML:** Navy Lodge. Bldg 1401A, Naval Air Station, North Island, San Diego, CA 92135, all ranks, leave, official duty, retirees. Directions: From I-S north or south, exit at Coronado Bridge. Continue past toll plaza to Alameda Blvd, turn left. Right lane directs you to main gate (McCain Blvd). From main gate go 1/4 mile to Rogers Road, turn left. Follow two miles, lodge is on left. Reservations: **C-1-800-NAVY-INN**. Lodge number is C-619-435-0191 or 619-545-6940, Fax-619-522-7455, 24 hours. Check in 1500-1800 hours, check out 1200 hours daily. Bedroom, two queen beds, private bath, kitchenette, limited utensils (90). Bedroom, two queen beds, private bath refrigerator, microwave, coffee maker, no utensils (100). A/C, color CATV, housekeeping service, cribs, coin washer/dryer, soda/snack vending, ice vending and mini-mart. Modern structure on ocean front, all rooms renovated in 1993. Call for rates. All categories can make reservations.

DV/VIP: PAO. C-619-545-8167. O6+. Retirees and lower ranks if approved by commander.

TML Availability: Good, except Apr-Sep.

CREDIT CARDS ACCEPTED: Visa, MasterCard, American Express and Discover accepted at Navy Lodge.

Transportation: On base shuttle/bus 545-1011, off base taxi available, car rental agency: Admiral 435-1478.

Temporary Military Lodging Around the World - 41

CALIFORNIA
North Island Naval Air Station, continued

North Island is the birthplace of Naval aviation. The San Diego Trolley connects to downtown and bus routes. See Mission Valley, the zoo, Balboa Park. 100 additional Navy Lodge units available November 1996.

Locator 545-1011   Medical 545-4306   Police 545-7423

Oakland Army Base (CA18R4)
Jacobs Hall Guest Facility
Bldg 650, Oakland Army Base
Oakland, CA 94626-5015
Schedule to close September 1999.

TELEPHONE NUMBER INFORMATION: Main installation numbers: C-510-466-9111, D-312-859-9111.

Location: Near junction of I-80, I-580, and CA-880, south of the San Francisco Oakland Bay Bridge. *USMRA: Page 119 (D-5).* NMC: Oakland, two miles southeast.

Lodging Office: Jacobs Hall, Bldg 650. **C-510-444-8107, D-312-858-3113,** Fax: C-510-466-2997, D-312-859-2997, 24 hours. Check in front desk, check out 1100 hours daily. Government civilian employee billeting.

TML: Guest House, Bldg 650, all ranks, leave or official duty. Bedroom, double beds, private bath (23); 2-room suites, queen-size bed, living room, sofa bed, private bath (25); 3-room suites with bedroom, living room, den with sofa bed, private bath (4). All have refrigerator, color CATV, HBO, Video movie rentals, ice vending, soda/snack vending, housekeeping service, iron/ironing board, complimentary coffee, some non-smoking rooms. Meeting/conference room available. Modern structure. Rates: Standard $35-$45, 2-room suite $45-$55, 3-room suites $55-$65. All categories can make reservations.

TML: Two 3-bedroom condos (both sleep 10). **Keys Waterfront Condo:** two baths, two sun decks, fireplace, fully equipped kitchen. Also, indoor and outdoor swimming pool, tennis courts, private beach, sauna, and nearby children's playground. **Tahoe City Condo:** 2.5 baths, patio deck, fully equipped kitchen. Also, two outdoor swimming pools, jacuzzi/sauna, golf course, tennis courts, volleyball courts, nearby children's playground, and boat ramp. Rates: $70 daily (2-5 night stay, Sun-Thur), $80 daily (Sun-Thur), $95 daily (Fri, Sat, and holidays), $500 7-day package. See *Military Living's Military RV, Camping and Rec Areas Around the World* for additional information and directions.

TML Availability: Good.

CREDIT CARDS ACCEPTED: Visa, MasterCard, American Express, Diners' Club and Discover.

Lake Merritt, Lakeside Park, the Oakland Museum, Jack London Square in Oakland are of interest to visitors. Marine World Africa USA Theme Park in Vallejo, Paramount Great America Theme Park in Santa Clara and a host of several professional sports teams. Across the bay is San Francisco itself; just north is the wine country and the Redwoods, both treasures.

Locator 466-9111   Medical 466-2918   Police 466-2424

CALIFORNIA

Petaluma Coast Guard Training Center (CA23R4)
MWR Guest Housing
299 Tomales Road
Petaluma, CA 94952-5000

TELEPHONE NUMBER INFORMATION: Main installation numbers: C-707-765-7215.

Location: Exit US-101 N to East Washington Ave West. Follow Washington Ave nine miles west to Coast Guard Training Center. *USMRA: Page 110 (B-6,7)*. NMC: San Francisco, 49 miles south.

Lodging Office: 599 Tomales Road, Petaluma, CA 94952 (office is located in the Consolidated Club on Nevada Street). **C-707-765-7248,** 0900-1800 hours daily. Check in at facility, check out time discussed with manager. Government civilian employee billeting, maximum stay two weeks. Reservations accepted 0800-1800 hours Mon-Fri.

TML: TLQ. Bldg 134, all ranks, leave or official duty. Bedroom, private bath (8); Four person unit, semi-private bath (1). Refrigerator, color TV, cribs, washer/dryer, ice vending, soda/snack vending, microwave. Meeting/conference room, exercise room, and mini-mart available. Older structure. Rates: $25 per room, semi-private rooms $14. All categories can make reservations. PCS have priority. No pets.

DV/VIP: One VIP suite in Harrison Hall (O6+), leave or official duty. Private bath, refrigerator, color TV, housekeeping service. Rate: $35 per night. Retirees Space-A. Call CO's office for reservations, C-707-765-7248. No pets.

TML Availability: Generally good. Difficult, summer months.

The Petaluma area is saturated with historical lore and legend. Early California missions, a Russian fort (Fort Ross), Sonoma County wineries, and Russian River swimming, fishing and canoeing will all draw visitors.

Locator 765-7215   **Medical 765-7200**   **Police 765-7215**

Point Mugu Naval Air Weapons Station (CA40R4)
The Missile Inn, CBQ
Point Mugu NAWC, CA 93042-5001

TELEPHONE NUMBER INFORMATION: Main installation numbers: C-805-989-1110, D-312-351-1110.

Location: Eight miles south of Oxnard and 40 miles north of Santa Monica, on Coast Hwy, CA-1. *USMRA: Page 111 (E-13)*. NMC: Los Angeles, 50 miles southeast.

Lodging Office: The Missile Inn, CBQ, Bldg 27, D Street, between Sixth and Seventh Streets. **C-805-989-8255/8235, D-312-351-8255,** Fax: C-805-989-7470, D-312-351-7470, 24 hours. Check in facility, check out 1000 hours daily. Government civilian employee billeting.

TML: BOQ. Various buildings, some cottages. Officers all ranks, leave or official duty. Bedroom, two beds, private bath, (46). Refrigerator, color TV/VCR, housekeeping service, roll-away beds, washer/dryer, essentials, soda/snack vending, ice vending. Meeting/conference rooms, exercise room,

CALIFORNIA
Point Mugu Naval Air Weapons Station, continued

and mini-mart available. Older structure, renovated. Rates: $10 per person per room; suites $15. Duty and civilians on orders can make reservations, others Space-A.

TML: BEQ. Enlisted E1-E6, leave or official duty. Bedrooms, common bath. Refrigerator, color TV/VCR, housekeeping service, essentials, soda/snack vending, washer/dryer. Meeting/conference rooms, exercise room, and mini-mart available. Older structure, renovated. Rates: E1-E4 $6 per person, E5-E6 $8, E7-E9 $12, O1-O5 $10 room and $12 suite. Duty only can make reservations, unaccompanied retirees Space-A. No dependents.

TML: TVEQ. Enlisted E7-E9, leave or official duty. Suites, private bath (9). Refrigerator, color TV/VCR, housekeeping service, essentials, soda/snack vending, ice vending, washer/dryer. Meeting/conference rooms, exercise room, and mini-mart available. Older structure, renovated. Rates: Suites $15 per person. Eligibility same as BEQ.

TML: DV/VIP. Bldg 170, officers O6+, leave or official duty. Bedroom suites, private bath (8). Kitchenette, above amenities. Older structure, renovated. Rates: Room $15 and suite $25. Duty can make reservations, others Space-A.

TML: Recreational Motel: **The Mugu Lagoon Beach Motel.** C-805-989-8407, D-312-351-8407. All ranks, leave or official duty. Check in at facility, 24 hours. Check out 1100 hours. Late check out call front desk. Bedroom, two beds, private bath (24); suites, two beds, private bath (2). Kitchenette, limited utensils, color TV, housekeeping service, essentials, cribs/cots, coin washer/dryer, handicap accessible, soda/snack vending, ice vending. Meeting/conference rooms, exercise room, and mini-mart available. Rates: $40-50, each additional person $4; suites $57-$65, each additional person $4. All categories may make reservations.

TML: Beach Cabins, on one of the finest surfing and swimming beaches in California. All ranks, retired, DoD civilians, base contractors, family members and guests. C-805-989-8407. D-312-351-8407. Bedrooms, two rooms, one double bed, one hideaway, private bath (6); Kitchen, utensils, CATV, fenced in porch, housekeeping service, barbecue, pets at an additional fee. Rates: $40 for military, $45 for civilian, each additional person $4. All categories may make reservations.

DV/VIP: Command Protocol, Bldg 36, C-805-989-8672, O6+.

TML Availability: Fair. Difficult, Mar-Sep. Recreational motel good year round, most difficult in Jun, Jul and Aug.

CREDIT CARDS ACCEPTED: Visa, MasterCard and American Express.

This facility is on the Pacific Ocean, close to the great shopping in Santa Monica, and within reach of coastal range recreation as well as the famous beaches of Southern California. Full range of support facilities on base.

Locator 989-7209   **Medical 989-8875**   **Police 989-7670**

CALIFORNIA

Port Hueneme Naval Construction Battalion Center (CA32R4)
Bldg 1435, Pacific Road
Port Hueneme NCBC, CA 93043-4301

TELEPHONE NUMBER INFORMATION: Main installation numbers: C-805-982-4711, D-312-360-4711.

Location: Seven miles west of US-101. Take Victoria Ave exit in Ventura to Channel Islands Blvd, left to Ventura Road, right to Sunkist Road, turn right and enter at Sunkist Gate. *USMRA: Page 111 (D,E-13)*. NMC: Santa Barbara, 25 miles north.

Lodging Office: Bldg 1435, Pacific Road. **C-805-982-4497**, 0730-1700 hours. Check in at facility. Government civilian employee no billeting.

NAVY LODGE

TML: Navy Lodge. Bldg 1172, all ranks, leave or official duty. Reservations required. Reservations: C-1-800-NAVY-INN. Lodge number is C-805-985-2624, Fax: C-805-984-7364. Check in 1500-1800, check out 1200. Two double beds, private bath, kitchenette, (21); queen size bed, sleeper chair, private bath (21); two double beds, private bath (6). Microwave, coffee/tea, color TV, housekeeping service, phones, cribs/cots, coin washer/dryer, mini-mart, picnic grounds, playground, ice vending, Western Union. Modern structure, remodeled. Rates: Single $47; double $53. Maximum four persons. Duty and retirees can make reservations, others Space-A.

TML: BEQ: Duty only, Bldg 1435, C-805-982-4497, D-312-551-4115, Fax: C-805-982-4849, D-312-551-4948. Private room, shared/private bath, non-smoking rooms, microwave, irons, hair dryers, coffee/tea, color TV, housekeeping service, phones, coin washer/dryer, fitness center, lounge, ice vending, soda/snack vending. Rates: E1-E6 $14 per person; E7-E9 $29 per person.

TML: BOQ: Bldg 1164, C-805-982-5785, Fax: C-805-982-5662. Officer rooms: double bed, private bath, non-smoking rooms, microwave, irons, hair dryers, coffee/tea, color TV, housekeeping service, phones, coin washer/dryer, fitness center, lounge, ice vending, soda/snack vending. Officer suites: above plus kitchenettes, living room. Rates: $14 per person for a room, $17 per person for a suite.

TML: DV/VIP: Guest House, Bldgs 39, 1435, officers O6+, leave or official duty. Reservations required, call protocol C-802-985-4741, check in Bldg 1164. Bldg 39, one cottage (Doll House), private bath. Kitchen, utensils, color TV, housekeeping service. Older structure (1925), patio. Active Duty can make reservations, others Space-A.

DV/VIP: Officers O6+, leave or official duty, call C-805-982-5785 for reservations. Enlisted, E9+, leave or official duty, call C-805-982-4497/4115 for reservations.

TML Availability: Good, winter months. Difficult, summer months.

CREDIT CARDS ACCEPTED: Visa, MasterCard and American Express. Visa, MasterCard, American Express, Diners' Club and Discover are accepted at the Navy Lodge.

Temporary Military Lodging Around the World - 45

CALIFORNIA
Port Hueneme Naval Construction Battalion Center, continued

In easy access of metropolitan Los Angeles, coastal Ventura County boasts wonderful weather. This is the home of the famous Seabees, a bustling complex of 10,000 military and civilians, and more than 1600 acres.

Locator 982-4711   Medical 982-6301   Police 982-4591

Presidio of Monterey (CA74R4)
Bldg 366, Room 8
Presidio of Monterey, CA 93944-5006

TELEPHONE NUMBER INFORMATION: Main installation numbers: C-408-647-5184/5104, D-312-878-5184/5104.

Location: From San Francisco, south for 100 miles on US 101, CA Hwy 156 W for five miles, CA Hwy 1 S for ten miles. Take Pacific Grove/Del Monte Hwy exit. Go two miles, bear right through tunnel. Turn left into Presidio of Monterey. *USMRA: Page 111 (B-9)*. NMC: Monterey, in city limits.

Lodging Office: Bldg 366, Room 8. **C-408-242-5091, D-312-878-5091,** Fax -408-242-5298. 0600-1900 Mon-Fri, 0700-1600 Sat-Sun. After hours check in at SDO in Bldg 614.

TML: TQ, all ranks, leave or official duty. Bedroom, shared bath (40). Rates: $25, $2 each additional person. Two-bedroom, private bath (7). Rates: $25, $2 each additional person. Bedroom, private bath (34). Rates: $30, $2 each additional person. Two-bedroom cottages (7). Rates: $40, $2 each additional person. Three-bedroom cottage (1). Rates: $45, $2 each additional person. All above have refrigerator, microwave, CATV, cribs, iron, coffee, housekeeping, laundry facilities. Some units and all cottages have full kitchens, utensils, and cookware. No pets; kennels available. Official Duty may make reservations 60 days in advance, others Space-A.

TML: DVQ, O6+. Protocol C-408-242-5336/5302, D-312-878-5336/5302.

TML Availability: Good. Limited family units, especially in summer

Within minutes of many famous Monterey Peninsula tourist attractions: Monterey Bay Aquarium, Fisherman's Wharf, Cannery Row, Pebble Beach golf courses, Seventeen Mie Drive, Point Lobos, Carmel, and Big Sur.

Locator 242-5000   Medical 242-5234   Police 242-5634

San Clemente Island Naval Auxiliary Landing Field (CA53R4)
P.O. Box 357054
San Diego, CA 92135-7054

TELEPHONE NUMBER INFORMATION: Main installation numbers: C-619-524-9127.

Location: Eighty miles off of the coast. Visitors must be sponsored by military stationed on the island. *USMRA: Page 111 (E-15)*. NMC: Los Angeles, 50 miles east.

Lodging Office: Bldg 60196. **C-619-524-9202,** Fax: C-619-524-9203, 0700-1600 hours Mon-Fri.

46 - Temporary Military Lodging Around the World

CALIFORNIA
San Clemente Island Naval Auxiliary Landing Field, continued

TML: BEQ/BOQ. Bldgs 60105 ,60112, 60121, 60152, 60196, all ranks, active and official duty. Check in lodging office, after hours call, C-619-524-9214. Bedrooms, refrigerator, kitchenette, color TV, washer/dryer, soda/snack vending. Exercise and mini-mart available. Renovated; new carpeting. Rates: $10 per night. Reservations accepted for those eligible.

TML Availability: Extremely limited.

Transportation: On base shuttle/bus 524-9227.

Locator 524-9202   Medical 524-9356   Police 524-9214

San Diego Marine Corps Recruit Depot (CA57R4)
MCRD Billeting
Bldg 625, 3800 Chosin Ave
San Diego, CA 92140-5196

TELEPHONE NUMBER INFORMATION: Main installation numbers: C-619-524-1011, D-312-524-1720.

Location: From airport, Pacific Coast Hwy to MCRD exit. From I-5 south take Old Town exit, turn right at second light to Gate 4. *USMRA: Page 118 (C-6).* In the city.

Lodging Office: Bldg 625. **C-619-524-4401,** Fax C-619-524-0617, 24 hours daily. Lodging available for DoD civilians on official duty.

TML: TOQ. Bldg 312, officers, all ranks, leave or official duty. Check in billeting 24 hours. Check out 1200 hours. Suites with separate bedroom, private bath (10). Kitchenettes in suites, others common kitchen, micro-refrigerators, coffee pots and essentials, color TV, telephones, housekeeping service, washer/dryer, cribs, new carpeting, recently remodeled modern structure. handicap accessible. Rates: sponsor $20, additional adult $2. Maximum $22 per family. Maximum 3 persons per room. Military on orders have priority, others Space-A. No pets.

TML: TEQ. Bldgs 619, 625, enlisted all ranks, leave or official duty. Check in billeting 2400 hours daily, check out 1200 hours. Room with two beds, private bath (39); suites, separate bedroom, private bath (2); units with shared bath (178). Micro-refrigerator, coffee pots, essentials, housekeeping service, color TV, washer/dryer, cribs. Modern structure, new carpeting, satellite service, telephones, new furniture in each room. handicap accessible. No pets. Rates: sponsor $8, additional adult $7. Maximum $15 per family. Maximum two per room. Military on orders have priority, others Space-A.

TML: DV/VIP. Bldg 31, room 238. Protocol officer, D-619-524-8710, O6+. Active duty and retirees, DoD civilians: TOQ and TEQ available. Others Space-A.

TML Availability: Good to very good. Best, Jan-May, Sep-Dec. Difficult, Jun-Aug.

CREDIT CARDS ACCEPTED: Visa, MasterCard, American Express and Discover.

This is the Marine Corps' oldest operating installation on the West coast, and is a short distance from downtown San Diego. Check out San Diego Zoo, Seaworld, beaches, fishing, and bargain shopping in nearby Tijuana, Mexico.

CALIFORNIA
San Diego Marine Corps Recruit Depot, continued

Locator 524-1728   Medical 524-4079   Police 524-4202

San Diego Naval Station (CA26R4)
Combined Bachelor's Housing
Naval Station Box 368145, Code 84
2450 McHugh Street, Suite 1
San Diego, CA 92136-5395

TELEPHONE NUMBER INFORMATION: Main installation numbers: C-619-556-1011, D-312-526-1011.

Location: Off I-5, seven miles south of San Diego Airport. Take 28th Street exit. Naval Station is at 28th and Main Streets. *USMRA: Page 118 (D-7,8).* NMC: San Diego, 7 miles south.

Lodging Office: Bldg 3362 (BEQ), Bldg 3144 (BOQ). **C-619-556-8672**, Fax: C-619-556-7263, 0730-1630 hours daily. Other hours, Watch Section/Central Assignments, Bldg 3362. Check in facility, check out 1200 hours daily. Government civilian employees billeting.

NAVY LODGE TML: Navy Lodge. Bldg 3191, 3526, all ranks, leave or official duty. Reservations: **C-1-800-NAVY-INN**. Lodge number is C-619-234-6142, Fax: C-619-238-2704, 24 hours. Check in 1500 hours, check out 1200 hours. 143 total units, two double beds, private bath (82); King size bed, private bath (8); One double bed, private bath (48). Five handicap accessible, 105 non-smoking. Kitchenette, utensils, microwave, coffee, A/C, CATV, clocks, phones, cribs, rollaways, coin washer/dryer, ice vending, vending machine, playground, heated swimming pool, housekeeping service. Rates: $44-$50. Government civilian employees billeting with ID and orders. All categories can make reservations.

TML: BEQ. Bldg 3362, enlisted all ranks, official duty only. Beds, semi-private bath (E7+ private bath) (3500). Telephone, TV lounge, housekeeping service, washer/dryer, ice vending, soda/snack vending. Meeting/conference rooms and mini-mart available. Rates: E1-E6 $10 per person, E7-E9 $10-$12 per person, (4) DoD civilian VIP rooms available at $12. Dependents not authorized. Reservations required.

TML: BEQ. Bldg 3203, E7-E9, official duty only. Bedroom, private bath (75); separate bedrooms, private bath (57). Telephones, refrigerator, color TV, housekeeping service, washer/ dryer, ice vending soda/snack vending. Meeting/conference rooms and mini-mart available. Rates: $10 per person. Maximum two per room. Children not authorized. Duty can make reservations, others Space-A.

TML: BOQ. Bldg 3144, officers all ranks, official duty only. Bedroom, private bath (77), two room suite with kitchenette (8). All rooms have telephones, CATV, microwave, refrigerator, coffee, housekeeping service, washer/dryer, ice vending soda/snack vending. Meeting/conference rooms and mini-mart available. Rates: $10-$18 per person. Children not authorized. Duty can make reservations, others Space-A.

TML: Fisher House. Located at San Diego Naval Medical Center. Note: Appendix B has the definition of this facility. C-619-532-9055.

CALIFORNIA
San Diego Marine Corps Recruit Depot, continued

TML Availability: Good, except PCS rotations, summer months.

CREDIT CARDS ACCEPTED: Visa, MasterCard, and American Express. The Navy Lodge accepts Visa, MasterCard, American Express, Diners' Club and Discover.

Transportation: Off base shuttle/bus 1-800-789-5254, off base taxi 291-333.

America's Finest City welcomes you to vacation paradise! Visit the world famous San Diego Zoo, Wild Animal Park, Sea World, Seaport Village, Old Town, Balboa Park and much more. Enjoy the best year-round climate in the U.S.

Locator 556-1011   Medical 556-8082   Police 556-1526

San Diego Naval Submarine Base (CA79R4)
Dolphin Lodge and Inn
140 Sylvester Road, Bldg 601
San Diego NSB, CA 92106-3521

TELEPHONE NUMBER INFORMATION: Main installation numbers: C-619-553-1011, D-312-933-1011.

Location: From I-5 take Rosecrans West onto base. *USMRA: Page 118 (B-6).* NMC: San Diego, in city limits.

Lodging Office: Dolphin Lodge and Inn. BOQ. Bldg 601, Sylvester Road. **C-619-553-9381, D-312-553-9381**, Fax: C-619-553-0613. BEQ. Bldg 300. **C-619-553-7533**. Check in facility. Check out 1200 hours.

TML: BOQ. Bldg 601. Officers, all ranks, official duty or leave. Bedroom, private bath (58); separate bedrooms, kitchenette, private bath, roll away beds, ice vending, utensils, housekeeping service, refrigerator, microwave, telephones, voice-mail, CATV, washer/dryer, weight room, jacuzzi, two catering facilities. Modern structure. Rates: sponsor $18, each additional person $4; VIP suites $28, each additional person $7.

TML: BOQ. Bldg 501. Officers, all ranks, official duty or leave. Bedroom, private bath (77); separate bedrooms, private bath, roll away beds, ice vending, utensils, microwave, refrigerator, telephones, voice-mail, CATV, washer/dryer, jacuzzi, two catering facilities. Modern structure. Rates: sponsor $13, each additional person $3; VIP suites $24, each additional person $4.

TML: BEQ. Bldg 300, enlisted, E1-E6, official duty or leave. Rooms with various bath combinations; MCPO suites (2). Snack vending, ice vending, housekeeping service, refrigerator, telephones, voice-mail, CATV, washer/dryer. Modern structure. Rates: sponsor $6; MCPO suites $20. Duty can make reservations, others Space-A.

TML Availability: Fairly good. Best, Oct-Dec. Difficult, May-Aug.

CREDIT CARDS ACCEPTED: Visa, MasterCard and American Express.

Temporary Military Lodging Around the World - 49

CALIFORNIA
San Diego Naval Submarine Base, continued

Located on beautiful Point Loma, with a spectacular view of San Diego Harbor, and the city, this facility is on the bus line close to beaches, Old Town, Sea World, the San Diego Zoo, and many other recreational delights.

Locator 553-1011   Police 553-7070   Medical 532-6400

San Diego Naval Training Center (CA54R4)
Lodging Office, Bldg 82
San Diego, CA 92133-1449
Scheduled to close December 1998.

TELEPHONE NUMBER INFORMATION: Main installation numbers: C-619-524-0557, D-312-524-0557.

Location: From I-8 W take Rosecrans exit to Nimitz Street, left on Nimitz to Harbor Drive, turn left on Harbor Drive (Gate 1). From I-5 N take Rosecrans exit to Nimitz Street, left on Nimitz to Harbor Drive, turn left on Harbor Drive (Gate 1). *USMRA: Page 118 (B,C-6).* NMC: San Diego, four miles east.

Lodging Office: Bldg 584. **C-619-524-4788,** D-312-524-4788, 0630-1530 hours Mon-Fri.

TML: BEQ. Bldg 584. Rates: Single $4, others $2 each.

TML: BOQ. **Admiral Kidd Inn**, Bldg 82, officers all ranks, leave or official duty, C-619-524-5382, D-312-524-5382, Fax 619-524-0754. Separate bedroom, private bath. Refrigerator, microwave, CATV. Rates: $16.50-$21.60, each additional person $4.

TML: DV/VIP. Officers, C-619-524-0557. Rates: $20-$29.60, each additional person $5.

See Mission Valley, the zoo, and Balboa Park.

Locator 524-1935   Medical 524-4929   Police 524-5796

San Diego YMCA Inns (CX01R4)
500 West Broadway
San Diego, CA 92101-5000

TELEPHONE NUMBER INFORMATION: Main installation numbers: Reservations: **C-619-234-5252,** Fax: C-619-234-5272.

Location: Take CA-5 South to CA-8 East to 163 South; 163 turns into 10th Ave. Turn right on Broadway, to 500 West Broadway. *USMRA: Page 118 (C-6).*

Author's Note: This is NOT military owned or operated lodging. This lodging is provided by the Armed Services Young Mens Christian Association (YMCA). The Downtown Armed Services YMCA reopened this hotel under new management as "The Inn at the YMCA" February 1, 1993. It will continue to offer quality accommodations for budget travelers, students and the military. It is accessible to the harbor, the Greyhound Bus station, Amtrak, and trolley stations as well as being minutes from the airport. Also, Horton Plaza, The Gaslamp Quarter, Seaport Village, Little Italy, the

CALIFORNIA
San Diego YMCA Inns, continued

San Diego Convention Center, Coronado Island, and the Santa Fe Train depot are close by. Services include a full-service restaurant, fitness facilities, indoor pool and hot tub, a large military lounge and recreation area, laundry and dry cleaning, a barber shop and 24 hour desk service. It is available to all military personnel, whether on duty or on leave, retirees and their guests at reduced rates as well as budget travelers and students.

Office: Check in and out at lobby desk, 24 hours. Check out 1100 hours daily. For a brochure or more info write to: The Inn at the YMCA, 500 West Broadway, San Diego, CA 92101, or call the above number.

TML: Hotel, all ranks, leave or official duty. Guest rooms (268). Reservations required. Color TV in lounge and in room, housekeeping service, coin operated washer/dryer, handicap accessible units, snack vending (restaurant on premises). Rates: $19.95 per person per night, $84.50 per week, ($55 deposit for weekly/monthly guests). Cash, travelers checks, money orders and government issued checks. No pets.

TML Availability: Good. Best, winter months. Make reservations well in advance.

In the heart of San Diego, and within walking distance of a trolley system that can take you to famous Southern California beaches, a world class zoo, and Mexico!

Sierra Army Depot (CA44R4)
Lodging Office, Bldg P144
Herlong, CA 96113-9999

TELEPHONE NUMBER INFORMATION: Main installation numbers: C-916-827-2111, D-312-855-4910.

Location: 55 miles north of Reno, NV, off US-395. Right on CA-A26 from Reno. When traveling south on US-395, left on CA-A25. *USMRA: Page 110 (E-4)*. NMC: Reno, 55 miles southeast.

Lodging Office: Bldg P144, **C-916-827-4544, D-312-855-4544**, Fax: C-916-827-5360, D-312-855-5360, duty hours. Other hours, Sec Radio Room, Bldg P-100, C-916-827-4345. Check in facility, check out 1100 hours daily. Government civilian employee billeting.

TML: Guest House, Bldg P144, (Club), all ranks, leave or official duty. Bedroom, private bath (15). Microwaves (in five apartments), refrigerator, limited utensils, housekeeping service, cribs/cots, TV, VCR, washer/dryer. New structure. Rates: $38-$53. PCS/TDY can make reservations, all others Space-A. Discounts during specified seasons. Please call.

DV/VIP: PAO, C-916-827-4544. Determined by Commander.

TML Availability: Good, winter. Difficult, summer.

CREDIT CARDS ACCEPTED: Visa, MasterCard and American Express.

Water sports, hiking, skiing, and most outdoor activities are popular in this Northern California paradise. Lassen Volcanic National Park, the Eagle Lake Marina, and the Reno/Tahoe areas have rich recreational opportunities.

Temporary Military Lodging Around the World - 51

CALIFORNIA
Sierra Army Depot, continued

Locator 827-4328   **Police 827-4345**

Note: An area code change will occur on 1 November 1997. 530 will replace 916.

Travis Air Force Base (CA50R4)
530 Sevedge Drive, Bldg 404
Travis AFB, CA 94535-2216

TELEPHONE NUMBER INFORMATION: Main installation numbers: C-707-424-1110/5000, D-312-837-1110.

Location: Off I-80 North, take Air Base Parkway exit. *USMRA: Page 110 (C-7).* NMC: San Francisco, 45 miles southwest.

Lodging Office: Bldg 404, Sevedge Drive. **C-707-424-4779, D-312-837-4779,** Fax: C-707-424-5489, D-312-837-5489, 24 hours. Check in facility, check out 1200 hours daily. Government civilian employee billeting.

TML: TLQ. Bldg 404, all ranks, leave or official duty. Studio apartments and two-bedroom apartments, private bath (79). Kitchen, color TV, A/C, soda vending, housekeeping service, telephone. Fitness, recreation and dining facilities within walking distance. Modern structure. Rates: $24 per unit. Duty can make reservations, others Space-A.

TML: VOQ. Bldg 404, officers all ranks, leave or official duty. Bedroom, semi-private bath (201). Refrigerator, A/C, TV, soda vending, housekeeping service. Fitness, recreation and dining facilities within walking distance. Older structure. Rates: $10 first person, $14 for two. Duty can make reservations, others Space-A.

TML: VAQ. Bldg 404, enlisted all ranks, leave or official duty. Reservations accepted. Rooms with various bath combinations (645). Same as VOQ above.

TML: DV/VIP. Bldg 404, officer O6+, leave or official duty. D-312-837-3185. Suites, private bath (23). A/C, color TV, soda vending, housekeeping service. Fitness, recreation and dining facilities within walking distance. Older structure. Rates: $16 first person, $23 for two. Duty can make reservations, others Space-A.

TML: Fisher House. Note: Appendix B has the definition of this facility. C-707-423-7267.

DV/VIP: DV lounge at Air Terminal, D-312-837-3185, O6+. Retirees Space-A.

TML Availability: Very limited, summer. Good, other times.

CREDIT CARDS ACCEPTED: Visa, MasterCard and American Express.

San Francisco, almost unlimited cultural and recreational opportunities. California beach towns and wine country, the capital city of Sacramento, and the Sierra Nevada mountains are all within reach of Travis.

Locator 424-2026   **Medical 423-3462**   **Police 438-2011**

52 - Temporary Military Lodging Around the World

CALIFORNIA

Tustin Marine Corps Air Station (CA86R4)
Tustin MCAS, CA 92710-5001
Scheduled to close December 1997.

TELEPHONE NUMBER INFORMATION: Main installation numbers: C-714-726-3011, D-312-977-3011.

Location: Near the I-5 and 55 interchange, take Red Hill Ave exit. West 1.5 miles to main gate (Valencia is the cross street). *USMRA: Page 117 (G-7).* NMC: Irvine/Tustin, Los Angeles, 45 miles northwest.

Lodging Office: Billeting Office, Bldg 20A, Moffett/Cross Streets, **C-714-726-7984/7336, D-312-997-7984/7336,** 0700-1530 hours daily. After duty hours SDO, Bldg 4, C-714-726-7324. Check in, check out at billeting.

TML: DV/VIP "Quarters C" (**Hideaway**). O6+, leave or official duty. Commanding Officer, MCAS Tustin. C-714-726-7301.

TML Availability: Difficult to extremely limited.

Located near Disneyland, Newport Beach, and Laguna, there is no shortage of entertainment nearby, if you can stay here.

Locator 726-3736   Medical 726-9911   Police 726-9911

Twentynine Palms Marine Corps Air/Ground Combat Center (CA27R4)
Billeting Fund
P.O. Box X-15
Twentynine Palms, CA 92278-5006

TELEPHONE NUMBER INFORMATION: Main installation numbers: C-760-830-6000, D-312-957-6000.

Location: From west on I-10 exit on CA-62 NE to base. From east on I-40 exit south at Amboy. *USMRA: Page 111 (H,I-13,14).* NMC: Palm Springs, 60 miles southwest.

Lodging Office: Bldg 1565, 5th Street near Desert View, Conference Center. **C-760-830-7375, D-312-957-7375,** Fax: C-760-830-5980, D-312-957-5980, 24 hours. Check in facility 1400, check out 1100 hours daily. Government civilian employee billeting.

TML: BOQ/BEQ, all ranks, leave or official duty. VIP Quarters O4/GS-10+ (5); three CG guest house rooms; 16 rooms (O4+); 69 rooms (O1-O3); 40 SNCO rooms. Community kitchen, A/C, color TV, microwave in room and lounge, housekeeping service, washer/dryer, ice vending. Older structure. Rates: Adults $13, $20, $22. Duty can make reservations, except in guest house, others Space-A. No pets. No smoking rooms are available.

TML: TLF. Bldg 690, two miles from main gate. C-760-830-6573/6583, Fax C-760-830-4709. One-bedroom family units, trundle beds, private bath (24). Kitchen, washer/dryer, BBQ, playground.

CALIFORNIA
Twentynine Palms Marine Corps Air/Ground Combat Center, continued

Walking distance to commissary, seven day store, Burger King and Child Development Center. Recreation equipment check out center available. Rates: $33 single AD, $35 family AD, visitors $38. Maximum six per room. All ranks may make reservations. No pets.

DV/VIP: Protocol Office, C-760-830-6109, O4+. Retirees and lower ranks Space-A.

TML Availability: Good, winter months. Difficult, summer months.

CREDIT CARDS ACCEPTED: Visa, MasterCard, American Express and Diners' Club.

Five miles from Joshua Tree National Monument where the low Colorado and the high Mojave deserts come together. Many come from miles around to see the desert blooming with wild flowers.

Locator 830-6853   Medical 830-7254   Police 830-6800

Vandenberg Air Force Base (CA29R4)
Vandenberg Lodge
P.O. Box 5579
Vandenberg AFB, CA 93437-5079

TELEPHONE NUMBER INFORMATION: Main installation numbers: C-805-734-8232, D-312-276-8232.

Location: From south on US-101, west on CA-246, north on CA-S20 to AFB. From north on US-101, west on US-1 from Gaviota, north on CA-S20 to AFB. *USMRA: Page 111 (C-12)*. NMC: Santa Maria, 22 miles north.

Lodging Office: ATTN: **Vandenberg Lodge**, Bldg 13005, Oregon at L Street. **C-805-734-8232, ext 6-2245**, Fax: D-312-276-0720, 24 hours. Check in billeting 1500 hours, check out 1200 hours daily. Government civilian employee billeting.

TML: TLF. All ranks, leave or official duty. handicap accessible. One- or four-bedroom, private bath (26). Kitchen, complete utensils, CATV, housekeeping service, cribs/cots, washer/dryer, essentials. Modern structure. Rates: $16-$21 per room. Maximum five per room. Duty can make reservations. Retirees can make reservations for medical appointments only, others Space-A.

TML: VAQ. Bldg 13140A, enlisted all ranks, leave or official duty. Private bedroom, shared bath (61); SNCO quarters, E7+ (10), bedroom/private bath, living room with sofa bed. Vending machines, essentials. Rates: $9 per person; SNCO $12 per person. Also have (4) E9+ quarters at $16 per person. Duty can make reservations, others Space-A.

TML: VOQ. 11000 area. Officers all ranks, leave or official duty. handicap accessible. Bedroom, private bath (77); Essentials, ice vending. Modern structure. Rates: $12 per person. Maximum two persons per unit. Duty can make reservations, others Space-A.

TML: VOQ. Bldg 13800 area. Officers all ranks, leave or official duty. Private bedroom, private bath (96). Rooms arranged in quads, full kitchen, living room and washer/dryer are shared. Rates: $12 per person. Duty can make reservations, others Space-A.

54 - Temporary Military Lodging Around the World

CALIFORNIA
Vandenberg Air Force Base, continued

TML: DV/VIP. **Marshallia Ranch**, Bldg 1338, officers O7/GS-16+, leave or official duty, C-805-734-3711. Four-bedroom, private and semi-private bath, suites (4). Kitchen, utensils, A/C, color satellite TV, housekeeping service, washer/dryer, ice vending. Historic structure. Rates: $16 per person. All categories can make reservations.

DV/VIP: For reservations 30 SPW/CCP. C-805-734-3711. O6+.

TML Availability: Best, Nov-Jan. Difficult, Apr-Oct.

CREDIT CARDS ACCEPTED: Visa, MasterCard and American Express.

Transportation: On base taxi 734 8232 ext 6-1843, off base taxi 736-3636.

Central Coastal California is a treasure trove for visitors. Visitors should see Solvang ("little Denmark"), Gaviota Beach, Santa Barbara and the Hearst Castle (San Simeon), to name only a few attractions within reach of Vandenberg.

Locator 6-1841   Medical 6-1847   Police 6-3911

Other Installations in California

Camp Roberts, San Roberts, CA 93451-5000. **C-805-238-8312.** BOQ/BEQ, $13.50 duty, $16.50 per person.
Lake Tahoe Coast Guard Recreation Facilities. PO Box 882, Tahoe City, CA 96145-0882. C-916-583-7438. Two A-frame cottages, each with two apartments, heat fully furnished, private bath, CATV. Two-bedroom apartment, sleeps nine. Rates: $30-$45. One-bedroom apartment, sleeps seven. Rates: $15-$30. See *Military Living's Military RV, Camping and Rec Areas Around the World* for additional information and directions.
San Diego Naval Medical Center, Bldg 26, San Diego, CA 92134-5000. **C-619-532-6272/6273,** Fax: C-619-532-5195. Exit from I-5 to Pershing Drive and west on Florida Canyon Drive to entrance. BEQ, On-bedroom, shared bath, sleeps two. Rates: $0. Extremely limited.

COLORADO

Fitzsimons US Army Garrison (CO10R3)
Fitzsimons Lodge
P.O. Box 6388
Aurora, CO 80045-6388
Scheduled to close July 1999.

TELEPHONE NUMBER INFORMATION: Main installation numbers: C-303-361-8241, D-312-943-8241.

Location: From I-70 take Peoria Ave (281), exit south on Peoria Ave, about one mile to Colfax Ave, Turn left (east) to first traffic light. Left again to enter main gate. From I-25 take I-225 N to Colfax Ave, west on Colfax Ave to third traffic light. Right at light to enter main gate. *USMRA: Page 116 (C-3).* NMC: Denver, eight miles west.

COLORADO
Fitzsimons US Army Garrison, continued

Lodging Office: Bldg 400, Charlie Kelly Blvd. **C-303-361-8903**, D-312-943-8903, Fax: C-303-361-9066, 0700-2200 hours Mon-Fri. Reservations accepted 0800-1500 hours Mon-Fri. Check in/out at facility.

TML: VOQ/VEQ: Bldg 400, all ranks, leave or official duty. Check out 1100 hours daily. Bedroom, private bath, one person (115); bedroom, private bath, two persons (75). CATV, refrigerator, telephone with wake-up service/private voice-mail, coffee makers, cribs, rollaways, housekeeping service, washer/dryer, ice machine. No pets, kennels near installation. Rates: $18-$23. TDY military and DoD civilian, PCS military, reservists on individual orders, military family members on medical TDY orders and attendants to patients in hospital can make confirmed reservations, others Space-A.

TML: Fisher House. Located at Denver VA Medical Center. Note: Please see Appendix B for a definition of this facility. C-303-361-4259.

DV/VIP: Commander's office, C-303-361-8824, D-312-942-8824, O6+. Reservations made through lodging, C-303-361-8903. Retirees Space-A.

TML Availability: Good, Oct-Dec. Difficult, other times.

CREDIT CARDS ACCEPTED: Visa, MasterCard and American Express.

Outdoor activities abound in two national parks, four national monuments, and eleven national forests. Denver visitors must see the state capital complex, US Mint, Larimer Square, and the Denver Museum of Art.

Locator 361-8241   Medical 361-8181   Police 361-3791

Fort Carson (CO02R3)
Colorado Inn
Bldg 7301, Woodfill Road
Colorado Springs, CO 80913-5023

TELEPHONE NUMBER INFORMATION: Main installation numbers: C-719-526-3431, D-312-691-3431.

Location: From Colorado Springs, take I-25 or CO-115 S. Clearly marked. *USMRA: Page 109 (F,G-5,6) and Page 115 (C,D-6,7)*. NMC: Colorado Springs, six miles north.

Lodging Office: Colorado Inn, Bldg 7301, Woodfill Road. **C-719-526-4832**, Fax: C-719-526-5239, 24 hours. Check in facility 1400 hours, check out 1100 hours daily. Government civilian employee billeting. Phones in all rooms. **Reservations 60 days in advance.** No pets. Smoking and non-smoking rooms available.

TML: DV/VIP. Bldg 7305, officers O5+, enlisted E9, leave or official duty. One- and two-bedroom, private bath (8). A/C, kitchen, housekeeping service, CATV, washer/dryer. Older structure, renovated in 1993. Rates: sponsor $28, adult $13, child under 16 free. Reservations through Protocol Office.

TML: VOQ/VEQ. Bldgs 7302, 7304, all ranks, leave or official duty. Bedroom, private baths (156). Shared kitchenette, A/C, CATV, washer/dryer. Rates: sponsor $23, adult $10, child under 16 free.

COLORADO
Fort Carson, continued

TML: VEQ. Bldgs 7301, all ranks, leave or official duty. Bedroom, private bath (19). Shared kitchenette, A/C, CATV, washer/dryer. Rates: sponsor $20, adult $5.

DV/VIP: Protocol Office, Bldg 1430, C-719-526-5811, O5+. Retirees, lower ranks Space-A.

TML Availability: Difficult. Best, Nov-Apr.

CREDIT CARDS ACCEPTED: Visa, MasterCard and American Express.

Don't miss a visit to historic Pikes Peak, see the Royal Gorge and early mining towns, gambling casinos, and Cripple Creek, which lured thousands to the "golden west".

Locator 526-0227   Medical 526-7000   Police 526-2333

Peterson Air Force Base (CO06R3)
Bldg 1042, Stewart Avenue
Peterson AFB, CO 80914-1294

TELEPHONE NUMBER INFORMATION: Main installation numbers: C-719-556-7321, D-312-834-7321.

Location: Off US-24 (Platte Ave), east of Colorado Springs. Clearly marked. *USMRA: Page 109 (G-5) and Page 115 (D,E-5,6)*. NMC: Colorado Springs, four miles west.

Lodging Office: Bldg 1042, Stewart Ave, **C-719-556-7851, D-312-834-7851**. Reservations: C-719-597-2010, Fax: C-719-556-7852, 24 hours. Check in facility, check out 1100 hours daily. Government civilian employee lodging.

TML: TLQ. Bldgs 1091-1094, all ranks, leave or official duty. handicap accessible. Bedroom, private bath (40). Refrigerator, kitchen, complete utensils, color TV, A/C, housekeeping service, cribs, washer/dryer, ice vending. Older structure, redecorated. Rates: $24 per unit, sleeps four persons. Duty can make reservations, others Space-A. Space-A policies same as VOQ below.

TML: VOQ. Bldgs 1026, 1030. Officers all ranks, leave or official duty. handicap accessible. Bedroom, private bath (32); bedroom suites, private bath (DV/VIP) (33). Kitchen, essentials, ice vending, refrigerator, A/C, color TV, housekeeping service, washer/dryer. Modern structures. Rates: sponsor/adult, Bldg 1026 $10 per person, Bldg 1030 $16 per person. Maximum two persons per unit. Maximum charge $14 (Bldg 1026), $23 (Bldg 1030). No children, no infants. Duty can make reservations, others Space-A. Space-A released when rooms clean and available. First come, first served. Non-smoking facility. Unaccompanied dependents may be Space-A with active duty or retired sign in.

TML: VAQ. Bldg 1143, enlisted E1 to E6, leave or official duty. Bedroom, double occupancy, semi-private bath, (64); bedroom, single occupancy, shared bath (18); SNCO suites, private bath (7). A/C, color TV in room and lounge, refrigerator, housekeeping service, washer/dryer, snack vending, ice vending, essentials. Modern structure. Rates: VAQ, sponsor/adult, $9 per person. No children, no infants. Maximum two persons per unit. Maximum charge $13. Rates: SNCO suites, sponsor/adult, $16 per person. Maximum two persons per unit. Maximum charge $23. No children, no infants. Duty can make reservations, others Space-A. Space-A policies same as VOQ above.

CALIFORNIA
Peterson Air Force Base, continued

TML: DV/VIP. Bldgs 999, 1026, 1030, officer O7+. Bedroom, private bath (10). A/C, essentials, ice vending, kitchen with complete utensils, housekeeping service, refrigerator, color TV, washer/dryer. Bldgs 999, 1026 and 1030. Rates: sponsor/adult, $16 per person. Maximum two persons per unit. Maximum charge $23 on leave, $16 active duty. No children, no infants. Rooms for protocol reservations. Lower ranks Space-A except 999.

DV/VIP: Protocol, Bldg 1, C-719-554-3012, O7+. Retirees Space-A. VOQ Space-A policies.

TML Availability: Difficult. Best, Dec-Feb.

CREDIT CARDS ACCEPTED: Visa, MasterCard and American Express.

Area skiing and camping are some of the finest in the US; this is the home of NORAD, Space Command HQ. Visit historic Pikes Peak and USAF Academy.

Locator 556-4020   Medical 556-4333   Police 556-4000

United States Air Force Academy (CO07R3)
10 Service Squadron/SVML Bldg 3130
Academy Drive, Suite 100
Colorado Springs, CO 80840-4980

TELEPHONE NUMBER INFORMATION: Main installation numbers: C-719-333-1818, D-312-259-3110.

Location: West of I-25 N from Colorado Springs. Two gates, about five miles apart, provide access from I-25 and are clearly marked. *USMRA: Page 109 (F-4,5) and Page 115 (A,B,C-1,2,3).* NMC: Colorado Springs, five miles south.

Lodging Office: Bldg 3130, Academy Drive. **C-719-472-3060**, Fax: C-719-333-4936, 24 hours. Check in facility, check out 1100 hours daily. Government civilian employee lodging.

TML: DVQ. Bldg 3130, officers O7+, leave or official duty. Bedroom, private bath (8). Kitchen, study, living room, refrigerator, utensils, color TV, housekeeping service, washer/dryer, cribs/cots, ice vending, handicap accessible. Modern structure, renovated. Rates: sponsor $14, adult $14. Maximum two per family. Most reservations handled through protocol office for O7+ and equivalent.

TML: VOQ. Bldg 3130/3134, officers all ranks, leave or official duty. Bedroom, private bath (10); separate bedrooms, semi-private bath (14); 2-bedroom, semi-private bath (16). Refrigerator, color TV in lounge, housekeeping service, cribs/cots, washer/dryer, ice vending, handicap accessible. Modern structures. Rates: sponsor $8, adult $8, child $8, infant up to two years free. Maximum capacity depends on type of room. Duty can make reservations, others Space-A, will accept three days prior to arrival for non-confirmed Space-A reservation.

TML: TLF. Bldg 4700/02, all ranks, official duty or leave. Three-bedroom houses (26). Kitchen, complete utensils, color TV, housekeeping service, cribs/cots, washer/dryer. Modern structures. Rates: $24 per night. Family quarters intended primarily for use by PCS personnel in/out. Others Space-A on day-to-day basis.

DV/VIP: Protocol Office, Harmon Hall, Bldg 2304, room 328, C-719-333-3540, O7+.

58 - Temporary Military Lodging Around the World

COLORADO
United States Air Force Academy, *continued*

TML Availability: Best, Jan-Apr. Difficult, other times.

CREDIT CARDS ACCEPTED: Visa, MasterCard and American Express.

At the foot of the Rocky Mountains, near skiing and mountain resorts. New visitor's center, gift shop and exhibits. Guided tours, 18 hole golf courses. Cadet Wing holds 1300 hours formation, visitors watch from the chapel wall.

Locator 472-4262   Medical 472-5000   Police 472-2000

Other Installations in Colorado

Farish Recreation Area. PO Box 146, Woodland Park, CO 80866-0146. C-719-687-9098/9306, Fax: C-719-686-1437. Two-bedroom cottage, sleeps eight, linens, utensils. Four-bedroom lodge, sleeps 17, linens, utensils. Rates: $35-$65 daily. See *Military Living's Military RV, Camping and Rec Areas Around the World* for additional information and directions.

CONNECTICUT

Camp Rowland (CT05R1)
Bldg 805
Niantic, CT 06357-2597

TELEPHONE NUMBER INFORMATION: Main installation numbers: C-860-691-6000, D-312-636-6000.

Location: From I-95, exit 74, follow Route 161 towards Niantic Center to Smith Street. Follow signs. *USMRA: Page 16 (F,G-9).* NMC: New London, 15 miles east.

Lodging Office: Bldg 805. **C-860-691-6001,** Fax: C-860-691-6065, 0800-1600 hours Mon-Fri. Check in at lodging office.

TML: BOQ. Bldgs 9, 201, all ranks, leave or official duty. Bedroom, refrigerator, color TV in lounge, housekeeping service, soda/snack vending, other essentials. Meeting/Conference rooms and mini-mart available. Being renovated 1997/1998. Reservations accepted. Rates: $6-$8. No pets.

TML: BEQ. Bldgs 57, 61, E7-E9, leave or official duty. Bedroom, refrigerator, color TV in lounge, housekeeping service, soda/snack vending, other essentials. Meeting/Conference rooms and mini-mart available. Reservations accepted. Rates: $6-$8. No pets.

TML: DV/VIP. Bldgs 53, 68. O6+, C-860-691-6001.

TML Availability: Good. Best, Sept-Apr.

Locator 691-6000   Medical 911   Police 911

Temporary Military Lodging Around the World - 59

CONNECTICUT

New London Naval Submarine Base (CT01R1)
ATTN: CO/Lodging
Groton, CT 06349-5044

TELEPHONE NUMBER INFORMATION: Main installation numbers: C-860-449-3011, D-312-241-3011.

Location: From I-95 north take exit 86 to CT-12. Go left on Crystal Lane, right on to main gate. Base clearly marked. *USMRA: Page 16 (H-8) and Page 25 (C,D-1).* NMC: Hartford, 50 miles northwest.

Lodging Office: None. Call BOQ and BEQ for reservations and Space-A information (listed below).

NAVY LODGE — **TML:** Navy Lodge, **off main base, from CT-12 South, right on Pleasant Valley Road, right on Lestertown Road, right on Dewey Ave.** 77 Dewey Ave, Groton, CT 06340, Bldg CT-380, all ranks, leave or official duty. Check in 1500-1800 hours daily, check out 1200. Reservations: **1-800-NAVY-INN**. Lodge number is C-860-446-1160, Fax: C-860-449-9093. Bedroom, two double beds, private bath (49); bedroom, queen bed and studio couch, private bath (18). Twenty-four interconnecting, two handicap accessible, 34 non-smoking. Kitchenette, microwave, utensils, A/C, CATV, clocks, coffee/tea, cribs, phones, housekeeping service, coin washer/dryer, picnic grounds, playgrounds, snack vending. Modern structure, renovated. Rates: $42 per unit. Maximum four persons. All categories can make reservations.

TML: BOQ. Bldgs 379 officers, all ranks, enlisted E7+, leave or official duty, C-860-449-3416. Check in 1500 hours, check out 1100 hours daily. Bedroom, private bath (105); DVQ bedroom, private bath (7). A/C, kitchen, in room phones, CATV, housekeeping service, ice machine, coffee machines, essentials, washer/dryer. Newly renovated 1993. Bar/night club in BOQ 1993. Rates: $17 per person. DVQ bedroom $21.

TML: TQ. Chalet Susse International Hotel. E1 hotel on New London NSB. Check in 1500 hours, check out 1100 hours. C-above number. Bedroom, private bath (150). A/C, refrigerator, CATV, telephones, laundry area, housekeeping service. Rates: $60.27 per night, higher rates for personnel on leave.

DV/VIP: Suites in BOQ and Swiss Chalet. Call above number.

TML Availability: Fairly good. Navy Lodge, all year.

CREDIT CARDS ACCEPTED: Visa, MasterCard and American Express. Visa, MasterCard, American Express and Discover are accepted at the Navy Lodge.

Visit Mystic seaport for history, USCG Academy, USS Nautilus Memorial/Submarine Force Library and Museum for a view of the modern Navy. Try a game of chance at Foxwood Casino.

Locator 449-3082   Medical 449-3666   Police 445-9721

CONNECTICUT

United States Coast Guard Academy (CT02R1)
15 Mohegan Ave, Chase Hall
New London, CT 06320-4135

TELEPHONE NUMBER INFORMATION: Main installation number: C-860-444-8444.

Location: From New York City and New Haven take I-95 S to exit 83, left at traffic light at end of ramp, follow signs to academy. From Hartford, take Route 24 east to Route 2 E, take exit 28 S to 395 S, take left exit 78 to Route 32 S, follow signs to academy. Clearly marked. *USMRA: Page 16 (H-8), 25 (C-2)*. NMC: Hartford, 50 miles north.

Lodging Office: Chase Hall. C-860-444-8484, Fax: C-860-444-8455, 0730-1600 hours Mon-Fri. Check in facility, check out 1000 hours daily. After duty hours, check in Monro Hall-OOD office. E-mail: becker@dcseq.vscga.edu.

TML: BOQ, **Guest Quarters**, Chase Hall, all ranks, active, leave or official duty. Bedrooms with common bath (39). Refrigerator, color TV in room and lounge, cribs/rollaways available ($3 per night) washer/dryer, housekeeping services, soda/snack vending, mini mart. Older structure. Rates: $17 per person, $29 for double, $32 for triple. Maximum three per room. Duty can make reservations, all others Space-A only.

TML Availability: Good, Jan-Feb and Aug-Dec. Difficult, Mar-Jul.

CREDIT CARDS ACCEPTED: Visa, MasterCard, American Express and Discover.

Fifteen miles from Mohegan Sun Casinos. Several major cities within 150 mile radius, good for shopping and sight seeing.

Medical 444-8401   **Police 444-8597**

DELAWARE

Dover Air Force Base (DE01R1)
Lodging Manager
Bldg 805, 14th Street
Dover AFB, DE 19902-7219

TELEPHONE NUMBER INFORMATION: Main installation numbers: C-302-677-3000, D-312-445-3000.

Location: Off US-113. Clearly marked. *USMRA: Page 42 (I-3)*. NMC: Dover, five miles northwest.

Lodging Office: Bldg 846, corner of Summer Street. **C-302-677-2841, D-312-445-2841**, Fax: C-302-677-2936, D-312-445-2936, 24 hours. Check out 1100 hours daily.

TML: TLF. Bldg 803, all ranks, leave or official duty. TLF: bedroom family suites, private bath (14); VOQ: bedroom, double beds, shared bath (27). Kitchenette, sofa sleeper (TLF) refrigerator, A/C, color TV, housekeeping service, cribs/cots, washer/dryer, ice vending. Older structure. Rates:$24. PCS/TDY can make reservations, others Space-A.

DELAWARE
Dover Air Force Base, continued

TML: VOQ/DV. Bldg 806, officers O4+, enlisted SNCOs, leave or official duty. Suites, private bath (DV) (10); suites, private bath (SNCO) (5). Refrigerator, A/C, color TV, housekeeping service, washer/dryer. Modern structure. Rates: $16 per person, $23 couple. Maximum two per room. (Arnold Suite by Protocol 677-4366). Scheduled for renovation October 1997.

TML: VAQ. Bldgs 481, 482, enlisted E1-E4, leave or official duty. Bedrooms, single beds, common bath (92). A/C, color TV, refrigerator, housekeeping service, clock radio, coffee makers. Rates: $10.

TML: VAQ. Bldg 801 (removed from inventory December 1997), all ranks, leave or official duty. Bedrooms, single beds, shared bath (55). A/C, refrigerator, color TV, housekeeping service, telephones, clock radio, coffee maker. Rates: $10.

TML: VAQ. Bldg 802 (under renovation-available September 1997), enlisted aircrew members, TDY, SNCOs. Bedrooms, single beds, shared bath (55). A/C, refrigerator, color TV, housekeeping service, telephones, clock radio, coffee maker. Rates $10.

TML: VAQ.Bldgs 410,411 and 412 (102). Bedrooms, single bed, private bath (available June 1997) Rates: $10.

TML: VOQ. Bldg 804 (removed from inventory November 1997) all ranks, leave or official duty. Bldg 805, official aircrew members. Bedrooms, double bed, shared bath (27); 805 bedrooms, double bed, shared bath (44). Rates: $10.

TML Availability: Very good, Oct-Apr. Very limited May-Sep. *Note: May be limited until 10 September 1997 due to construction. The project will include a new VOQ. Keep up to date with more information through Military Living's R&R Space-A Report®.*

Dover is the jumping off point for many Space-A flights to Europe and beyond. See *Military Space-A Air Opportunities Around the World*, and *Military Space-A Air Basic Training* for information on this money saver for the military.

Locator 677-3000　　　　**Medical 735-2600**　　　　**Police 677-6664**

DISTRICT OF COLUMBIA

Anacostia Naval Station (DC02R1)
Billeting, Bldg 74
2701 S Capitol Street SW
Washington, DC 20374-5061

TELEPHONE NUMBER INFORMATION: Main installation numbers: C-202-545- 6700, D-312- 222-6700.

Location: I-395 N, exit South Capitol Street, main entrance is on right. *USMRA: Page 54 (F,G-5)*. NMC: Washington, DC, in southeast section.

62 - *Temporary Military Lodging Around the World*

DISTRICT OF COLUMBIA
Anacostia Naval Station, *continued*

Lodging Office: Bldg 93, **C-202-433-2007/2006**, 0600-2200 Mon-Fri, 0900-2100 Sat-Sun, C-202-433-2193. Check in 1500-1800, check out 1200 hours daily. Write to BOQ, Bldg 93, Anacostia Naval Station, Washington, D.C. 20374-0001. This office is for permanent party only.

TML: VFQ. Bldg 2, officers, O7+ official duty or leave. Reservations: C-202-433-4052. Bedroom suites, private bath (9). Kitchenette (some), microwave, A/C, color TV, housekeeping service. Rates: $30, $5 family members. No pets. Reservations, 30 days in advance. PCS, TDY have priority, others Space-A.

TML: BOQ. Exit from I-295 North, take Naval Station Exit, (1 exit past Bolling AFB). Turn right at traffic light to gate. From Defense Blvd on left, past Reserve Center, turn right to BOQ. Bldg 93. Officers, official duty or leave. C-202-433-2006, Fax C-202-433-8819. Check in 1200 hours, check out 1100 hours daily. Government civilian employees GS-7+. Bedroom (twin beds), private bath (22), bedroom, shared bath (4). A/C, CATV, housekeeping service, refrigerator, microwave, washer/dryer. Active duty on orders and government civilian employees, GS7+ may make reservations, others are Space-A.

TML: BEQ. Enlisted billeting, active duty, on orders only, one week stay only. Bedroom, private bath (2) (one male, one female), in the barracks. C-202-767-4455 for reservations.

TML Availability: Good, Dec-Apr. Difficult, other times.

For military history buffs, visit the Navy Memorial Museum, the Display Ship Barry (DD-933), the Marine Corps Museum (with famous flags raised over Mt. Suribachi and Iwo Jima), and the Combat Art Gallery.

Locator 703-545-6700   Medical 433-3757   Police 433-2411

Bolling Air Force Base (DC01R1)
11 SPTG/SVML
Bldg 602, 52 Thiesen Street
Bolling AFB, DC 20332-5100

TELEPHONE NUMBER INFORMATION: Main installation numbers: C-202-767-6700, D-312-297-0101.

Location: Take I-95 (east portion of Capital Beltway, I-495) N or S, exit to I-295 N, exit 1, right onto Overlook Ave at the light, and continue to South Gate. I-295 S, exit 1 to first light. Right at the light to the South Gate. From South Capitol Street, south past Main Gate and bear right onto Overlook Ave to South Gate. Clearly marked. *USMRA: Page 54 (F-6)*. NMC: Washington, in southeast section of the city.

Lodging Office: Bolling Inn. Bldg 602, 52 Thiesen Street, 11 SPTG/SVML. **C-202-767-5316**, Fax: C-202-767-5878, 24 hours. Check in billeting 1400, check out 1200 daily.

TML: TLF. Apartments, all ranks, leave or official duty. Separate bedrooms, private bath (49). Kitchen, A/C, color TV in room and lounge, housekeeping service, washer/dryer, ice vending. Older structure. Rates: $24 per room. Maximum four per room. Unaccompanied dependents not authorized. Reservations TDY, others Space-A.

District of Columbia
Bolling Air Force Base, continued

TML: VOQ. Officer O1-O6, leave or official duty. Suites, private bath (55); Refrigerator, A/C, color TV in room and lounge, housekeeping service, washer/dryer, ice vending. Rates: first person $16, each additional person, $7. Reservations TDY personnel only, others Space-A.

TML: VAQ. Enlisted E1-E6. Bedroom, shared bath (44); Refrigerator, CATV, housekeeping service, washer/dryer. Older structure. Rates: $10 per night. Reservations TDY, others Space-A.

TML: VIP. O7+. Suites, private bath (23). Refrigerator, A/C, color TV, housekeeping service, washer/dryer. Older structure. Rates: $27 per person. Duty can make reservations. Also SNCO quarters, $16 per person, reservations via Protocol. Others Space-A.

DV/VIP: Protocol Office, Bldg P-20, C-202-767-5584, O7+. Retirees Space-A. Rates: $25 per night.

TML Availability: Difficult. Better during winter months.

CREDIT CARDS ACCEPTED: Visa, MasterCard and American Express.

On the Potomac, across from historic Alexandria, and in sight of the Capitol and famous monuments. Bolling is headquarters for the Air Force District of Washington.

Locator 767-4522   Medical 767-5233   Police 767-5000

Fort Lesley J. McNair (DC05R1)
Bldg 50, Johnson Lane
Washington, D.C. 20593-5050

TELEPHONE NUMBER INFORMATION: Main installation numbers: C-202-433-4073, D-312-288-4073.

Location: At confluence of Anacostia River and Washington Channel, SW. Enter on P Street SW. Take Maine Ave SW, to right on 4th Street SW, to dead end at P Street. Left then immediate right to main gate. *USMRA: Page 54 (F-5) and Page 55 (E-4).* NMC: Washington DC, in SW section of city.

Lodging Office: Bldg 50, 318 Jackson Ave, Fort Myer, VA, 22211-5050, 24 hours, **C-703-696-3576/77, D-312-226-3576/77,** Fax C-703-696-3490. Check in 1400 hours, check out 1200 hours daily. Late check out C-703-697-7051. Key pick up is at Fort Myer billeting office; advance payment required. Key drop off, drop box in lounge at Fort McNair.

TML: VOQ/VEQ. Bldg 54, Fort McNair (historic building), all ranks, leave or official duty. Reservation, check in and out at Bldg 50, Fort Myer, VA. Suites, two beds, private bath (2); bedroom, private bath (25). Refrigerator, A/C, color TV in room and lounge, housekeeping service, washer/dryer. Rates: sponsor $25, each additional person $5, suites: sponsor $30, each additional person $5. Maximum two per unit. TDY, PCS can make reservations, field grade Space-A. No pets.

TML Availability: Very Good. Difficult, Apr-Nov.

CREDIT CARDS ACCEPTED: Visa, MasterCard and American Express.

Transportation: On base shuttle/bus 475-2004, off base shuttle/bus 475-2004, off base taxi 522-2222, car rental agency 524-1863.

64 - Temporary Military Lodging Around the World

District of Columbia
Fort Lesley J. McNair, continued

Included in the original plans for the District of Columbia, Fort McNair is nearly 200 years old. Site of the trial and execution of President Lincoln's conspirators and where Walter Reed did his research work. Home of the National Defense University, National War College, Industrial college of the Armed Forces and the Inter-American Defense College. See the Washington waterfront, restaurants, seafood markets, monuments and the scenic Potomac River nearby.

Locator 545-6700   **Medical 475-1829**   **Police 475-2004**

Walter Reed Army Medical Center (DC03R1)
6900 Georgia Ave
Washington, DC 20307-5001

DoD Conference Center

TELEPHONE NUMBER INFORMATION: Main installation numbers: C-202-782-3501/02, D-312-662-3501/02.

Location: 6900 Georgia Ave NW. From I-495 (Capital Beltway) take Georgia Ave/Silver Spring exit, follow Georgia Ave approximately four miles to Walter Reed Army Medical Center's Elder Street gate on right (this gate is open 24 hours). To reach the Forest Glen support facilities from Georgia Ave, south, right turn on to Linden Lane, cross over B&O railroad bridge, support facility on left (.75 miles from Georgia Ave). *USMRA: Page 54 (F-2)*. NMC: Washington, DC, in city limits.

Lodging Office: Bldg 6825, Georgia Ave (at Butternut Street). **C-202-782-2096/2076**, 0800-1530 hours daily. Check in facility, check out 1100 hours daily. No government civilian employee billeting.

TML: Mologne House Hotel, P.O. Box 59728, C-202-782-4600, D-312-662-4600, 24 hours, all ranks, leave or official duty. Bedrooms, private bath; studio with kitchenette, private bath; suite with kitchenette (200). Refrigerator, A/C, color TV, utensils, housekeeping service, ice vending, cribs/cots, coin washer/dryer, handicap accessible (100). Meeting/conference rooms, fitness center, commissary, restaurant and gift shop available. New modern structure. Rates: $58 single, $70 suite. Reservations required. No pets.

TML: Guest House. Bldg 17, all ranks, leave or official duty, C-202-782-3044, D-312-291-3044. Bedroom, common baths, semi-private bath, private bath (62). A/C, CATV, housekeeping service, cribs/cots, coin washer/dryer, ice vending, facilities for DAVs. Older structure. Rates: $30-$38 per night. Maximum three per unit. Priority to PCS, members of immediate family of seriously ill patients and MEDEVAC/AIRVAC personnel. Out-patients may make reservations, others Space-A.

TML: Fisher House. Located at Forest Glen Annex. Note: Appendix B has the definition of this facility. C-301-295-7374. There is a second Fisher House at WRAMC. The second can be reached at C-301-295-7374.

TML: Walter Reed Inn. Georgia Ave at Butternut Street, C-202-782-7076/7096. Bedrooms, private bath (51); suites (3). Rates: $38-$45 per night. Call for more information and to make reservations.

TML: VOQ. Bldg 18, all ranks, leave or official duty, C-782-2076/2096. Check out 1100 hours daily. Bedroom, private bath (54) (three with kitchen); separate bedrooms, private bath (5). Kitchen, complete utensils, A/C, CATV, housekeeping service, cots, coin washer/dryer, ice vending. Modern structure, remodeled 1992. Rates: $34, $40 suites with kitchen (O6+TDY). Maximum three per room. Duty can make reservations, others Space-A.

CALIFORNIA
Walter Reed Army Medical Center, continued

TML: DVQ. Bldg 18, C-202-782-7076/7096, all ranks, leave or official duty. Potomac & Chesapeake Suite. Rates: $50 per night. Call for more information or reservations.

DV/VIP: Chief of Staff, C-202-782-3117, 3 units available.

TML Availability: Best, Mar-Apr and Sep-Oct. Difficult, others times.

Walter Reed is in D.C. near the National Zoo and National Cathedral, both star attractions for visitors. Other monuments are within 30 minute drive.

Locator 782-1150 (mil)   Medical 782-3501   Police-782-3325
        782-0546 (civ)

Washington Navy Lodge (DC12R1)
Bldg 4412 Beyer Road
Bellevue Housing Community
Washington, DC 20032-5000

Location: Take I-95 (east section of Capital Beltway, I-495) north or south, exit to I-295 N, exit 1, onto Overlook Avenue, right at the light. Left at next light into Bellevue Housing Community on Magazine Road. Left on Beyer Road to Navy Lodge.

NAVY LODGE

TML: Navy Lodge, Bldg 4412, 112 Bowline Green SW, Washington, DC 20032-5000. All ranks, leave or official duty. Reservations: **1-800-NAVY-INN**. Lodge number is C-202-563-6950, Fax: C-202-563-2970, 24 hours. Check in 1500-1800 hours, check out 1200 hours daily. Bedroom, private bath (50). Kitchen, utensils, A/C, color TV, cribs, high chairs, soda/snack vending, ironing boards, dining/living room areas, sleeps up to four persons (two double beds). Two handicap accessible rooms available. Modern structure. Rates: $52 per unit. PCS on orders may make reservations anytime, active duty may make reservations 60 days in advance, others 30 days in advance.

Bolling Air Force Base is 1/2 mile away. Public transportation located outside the entrance gate. All attractions of Washington, DC, Alexandria, Annapolis and Baltimore are nearby.

FLORIDA

Camp Blanding Training Site (FL42R1)
Billeting Office
Route 1, Box 465
Starke, FL 32091-9703

TELEPHONE NUMBER INFORMATION: Main installation numbers: C-904-533-2268, D-312-960-2268.

FLORIDA
Camp Blanding Training Site, continued

Location: From Jacksonville, take SR21 (Blanding Blvd) 15 miles south to SR 215. Take SR 215 until you reach SR 16. Turn west and proceed one mile to main gate. *USMRA: Page 38 (F-4).* NMC: Jacksonville, 30 miles north.

Lodging Office: Bldg 2392, **Finegan Lodge**. **C-904-533-3381, D-312-960-3381,** Fax: C-904-533-3540, 0800-1630 hours Mon-Sat. After duty hours report to MP at Main Gate. Check in 1300 hours, check out 1100 hours. Government civilian employee billeting.

TML: TLF. Bldg 2392, **Finegan Lodge**. All ranks, leave or official duty. Bedroom, semi-private bath (98). CATV, housekeeping service, coin washer/dryer, soda/snack vending, ice vending. Rates: Active duty PCS/TDY$10, all others $10.56. Reservations can be made by AD, others Space-A.

DV/VIP: Contact Training Site Manager at C-904-533-3357, D-312-960-3357. O6+, retirees and lower ranks Space-A.

TML Availability: Good, Nov-Feb.

CREDIT CARDS ACCEPTED: Visa, MasterCard and American Express.

Under one hour drive to Gainesville, Jacksonville and St. Augustine. Three hours to Walt Disney World and the Orlando area.

Locator 533-2268   Medical 533-3105   Police 533-3462

Cecil Field Naval Air Station (FL06R1)
Combined Bachelor's Quarters
P.O. Box 117, Bldg 331
NAS Cecil Field, FL 32215-0117
Scheduled to close August 1999.

TELEPHONE NUMBER INFORMATION: Main installation numbers: C-904-778-5626, D-312-860-5626.

Location: Take Normandy exit west off I-295 and follow Normandy (FL-228) to main gate. *USMRA: Page 38 (G-3).* NMC: Jacksonville, 20 miles east.

Lodging Office: Bldg 331, D Ave and 4th Street. **C-904-778-5255, D-312-860-5255/5258,** Fax: C-904-778-6730, 24 hours. Check in facility, check out 1100 hours daily.

TML: BOQ. Bldg 331, officers all ranks, leave or official duty. Bedroom, private bath (50); separate bedroom, private bath (61); bedroom, shared bath (20). Refrigerator, A/C, essentials, color TV, housekeeping service, cribs/cots, washer/dryer, snack vending, ice vending. Modern structure. Rates: sponsor on leave $8, sponsor on duty $4, adult $4, child $4. Duty can make reservations, others Space-A. Also bedrooms, shared bath (10) for E7-E9 on official duty.

TML: BEQ. Bldg 902, enlisted E1-E6 on official duty. Check out 1100 hours. Bedroom, private bath (6). Bedrooms, private bath, two beds in room (16). A/C, essentials, food vending, housekeeping service, color TV, washer/dryer. Older structure, renovated. Rates: $4.

Temporary Military Lodging Around the World - 67

FLORIDA
Cecil Field Naval Air Station

DV/VIP: BOQ, Bldg 331, C-904-778-0641, D-312-860-5255/8. O6+. Retirees and lower ranks Space-A. Rates: sponsor $16, guest $5. Building 904, bedroom (2). E8-E9 sponsor $16, guest $3.

TML Availability: Good, Nov-Jan. Difficult, other times.

CREDIT CARDS ACCEPTED: Visa, MasterCard and American Express.

St. Augustine is 45 miles south. Check out the beaches and the Jacksonville seaport.

Locator 778-5240   Medical 778-5508/5378   Police 778-5381

Corry Naval Technical Training Center (FL19R1)
640 Roberts Avenue, Room 112
NTTC/Corry Station, Pensacola, FL 32511-5138

TELEPHONE NUMBER INFORMATION: Main installation number: C-904-452-6512/13, D-312-922-0111.

Location: Off US-98, three miles north of Pensacola NAS. *USMRA: Page 39 (A,B-13), Page 53 (B-4).* NMC: Pensacola, five miles northeast.

Lodging Office: C-904-452-6541, D-312-922-6609, Fax C-904-452-6685, D-312-922-6685, 24 hours.

TML: Quarry Station. Enlisted, leave or official duty. E1-E4 double room, private bath (48); E5-E9 private room, private bath (106). Microfridge, clock radio, hair dryer, iron/ironing board, color TV/VCP, coffee maker. Rates: E1-E4 $8.50; E5-E9 $11, $2.50 each additional person. Duty can make reservation, others Space-A.

TML: Barracks. Triple room, shared bath. Call for more information.

DV/VIP: E5+, Family suite: two bedroom, two bath, sleep sofa (20). Stereo, color TV/VCP, microfridge, coffee pot, phone. Rates: $20 first, $2.50 each additional person. Maximum capacity 5 people per unit. Duty can make reservations, others Space-A.

TML Availability: Difficult due to current renovation processes; more rooms added after August 1997. Call for more information.

Locator 452-6512   Medical 911   Police 452-6130

Eglin Air Force Base (FL27R1)
96 SVS/SVML
Eglin AFB, FL 32542-5498

TELEPHONE NUMBER INFORMATION: Main installation numbers: C-904-882-1110, D-312-872-1110.

Location: Exit I-10 at Crestview, and follow posted signs to Niceville and Valparaiso (Eglin AFB). *USMRA: Page 39 (B,C,D-13) and Page 53 (E,F,G,H-1,2,3,4).* NMC: Fort Walton Beach, 14 miles west.

FLORIDA
Eglin Air Force Base, continued

Lodging Office: Eglin Inn, Bldg 11001, Boatner Road. **C-904-882-4534/0312, D-312-872-4534,** Fax: C-904-882-2708, D-312-872-2708, 24 hours. Check in billeting 1400 hours, check out 1100 hours daily.

TML: VAQ. All ranks, leave or official duty. Suite (SNCOQ) (18); bedroom, private bath (89); bedroom, shared bath (54). Rates: $10-$16 per person, payment due upon check in. TLF. Bedroom, private bath (33); 2-bedroom, private bath (32); 3-bedroom, private bath (1); separate bedroom, private bath (1). Rates: $20-$24. VOQ. Bedrooms, private bath (112); suites (several). Rates: $10-$16 per person, payment due upon check in. Refrigerator, microwave, coffee maker, A/C, color TV/VCR, housekeeping service, snack vending, ice vending, exercise room. Duty can make reservations, others Space-A.

TML: Duke Field, 919 MSS/MSRH, 506 Drone Street, Suite 6, Eglin AFB, Field 3, FL 32542-5000. C-904-883-6390. 0715-1545 Mon-Fri. Bedroom (175), two twin beds, refrigerator, housekeeping service. Rates: $10 daily.

DV/VIP: HQ AFDTC/CCP, Bldg 1 (Command Section), C-904-882-3011/3238.

TML Availability: Very good, Nov-Jan. Difficult, other times.

CREDIT CARDS ACCEPTED: Visa, MasterCard and American Express.

Transportation: On base shuttle/bus 882-3791, off base taxi Airport Taxi Service 651-0404, car rental agencies: Avis 651-0822, National 651-1113, Hertz 651-0612, Guardian 243-5515.

Eglin Inn recently won the 1996 Air Force Innkeeper Award in the large base category. Their exemplary customer service, facilities, equipment, and procedures won Eglin Inn the award for the second year in a row. Phone Natural Resources on Eglin for information on the wonderful outdoor activities on Eglin Reserve. Don't miss Fort Walton Beach's Miracle Strip, deep sea fishing off Destin, and visit historic Pensacola, 50 miles west.

Locator 882-1113   **Medical 882-7227**   **Police 882-2502**

Homestead Air Reserve Base (FL17R1)
29050 Coral Sea Blvd
Homestead ARB, FL 33039-1299

TELEPHONE NUMBER INFORMATION: Main installation numbers: C-305-224-7000, D-312-791-7000.

Location: Exit 6 off FL Tnpk. Left at bottom of ramp, approximately half of a mile to the traffic light at 288th Street SW. Turn left into main gate. *USMRA: Page 39 (I-14) and Page 51 (A,B-10).* NMC: Miami, 40 miles northeast.

Lodging Office: Homestead Inn, 29050 Coral Sea Blvd. **C-305-224-7168, D-312-791-7168,** Fax C-305-224-7290, D-312-224-7290, 0700-2100 daily, 0900-1800 holidays.

TML: Bedroom, private bath (200); Suites, full bath, stocked bar, microwave, refrigerator, color TV, telephone (5). Rates: VOQ $10 first person, $14 two people, VAQ $7 first person, $9.50 two people, DV $16 first person, $23 two people.

Temporary Military Lodging Around the World - 69

FLORIDA
Homestead Air Reserve Base, continued

Locator 224-7000   **Medical 911**   **Police 224-7115**

Hurlburt Field (FL18R1)
16 SVS/SVML
301 Tully Street
Hurlburt Field, FL 32544-5844

TELEPHONE NUMBER INFORMATION: Main installation numbers: C-904-884-1110, D-312-579-1110.

Location: Off US-98, five miles west of Fort Walton Beach. Clearly marked. *USMRA: Page 39 (C-13) and Page 53 (H-4).* NMC: Pensacola, 40 miles west.

Lodging Office: Bldg 90509, Simpson Street. **C-904-884-6245, C-904-581-1627, D-312-579-6245,** Fax: C-904-884-5043, 24 hours. Check in billeting, check out 1200 hours daily. Government civilian employee billeting.

TML: VAQ/VOQ. Bldgs 90344-90346, 90507, 90508, all ranks, leave or official duty. handicap accessible. Bedroom, private and semi-private bath (179); separate bedrooms, private bath (29). Kitchen, limited utensils, A/C, color TV, housekeeping service, cribs/cots, essentials, washer/dryer, ice vending, VOQ stocked wet bar. Older structure. Rates: VAQ, sponsor, $9, 2 people $12.50; VOQ, sponsor $10, 2 people $14; DV Suites, $16, 2 people $23. Maximum two persons per unit. Duty can make reservations, others Space-A. See Eglin AFB listing for other TML.

TML: TLF. Units (24). Rates: $20 per night.

DV/VIP: Protocol Office, Bldg 1, C-904-884-2308. O6+. Retirees and lower ranks Space-A.

TML Availability: Difficult. Best, Dec-Feb.

CREDIT CARDS ACCEPTED: Visa, MasterCard and American Express.

The catching and eating of fish is a big deal here! "The World's Luckiest Fishing Village" caters to all fishing needs. Numerous fine restaurants. Various facilities will be under renovation from 1995 to 1997.

Locator 884-6333   **Medical 884-7882**   **Police 884-6423**

Jacksonville Naval Air Station (FL08R1)
CBQ, Box 11
Jacksonville, FL 32212-5000

TELEPHONE NUMBER INFORMATION: Main installation numbers: C-904-542-2345, D-312-942-2345.

Location: Access from US-17 South (Roosevelt Blvd). On the St. Johns River. *USMRA: Page 38 (G-3) and Page 50 (B,C-6,7).* NMC: Jacksonville, nine miles northeast.

70 - Temporary Military Lodging Around the World

FLORIDA
Jacksonville Naval Air Station, continued

Lodging Office: Bldg 11. BOQ: **C-904-542-3138/3139**, Fax C-904-542-5002, BEQ: **C-904-542-3537/4052**, Fax C-904-542-4053, 24 hours. Check in facility after 1200 hours, check out 1200 hours daily. Government civilian employee billeting.

NAVY LODGE

TML: Navy Lodge. All ranks, leave or official duty. Reservations: **1-800-NAVY-INN**. Lodge number is C-904-542-6000, Fax: 904-777-1736, 24 hours. Check in 1500-1800, check out 1200 daily. Bedroom, two double beds, private bath (50). twelve interconnecting, two handicap accessible, 40 non-smoking. Kitchenette, microwave, utensils, A/C, CATV, HBO, clocks, coffee/tea, cribs/cots, phones, iron/ironing board, housekeeping service, coin washer/dryer, snack vending, ice vending, picnic grounds, playground, rollaways. Modern structure. Rates: $40 per unit. Active duty can make reservations 60 days in advance, retired, 30 days.

TML: BOQ. Bldgs 11, 845, officers all ranks, leave or official duty. Bedroom, private bath (110); bedroom, shared bath (8); separate bedroom, private bath (96). Refrigerator, telephones, TV in room and lobby, one large, two small conference rooms, housekeeping service, washer/dryer, snack vending, ice vending, sauna, fishing dock. Bldg 11, older structure. Rates: TAD $12 per person, dependents 12 years+ $3 (one charge). Rates based on room assignments: $9, $14, $17, $25 VIP. GS up to $45. Civilians $17 and $25. Retirees Space-A, $17 and $25. Reservations taken 45 days in advance for transient personnel. No pets. Call billeting for more information. Geographical bachelors on Space-A basis in inadequate quarters only.

TML: BEQ. E1-3: two/three to a room, shared bath; E4: two to a room, shared bath; E5-6: private or two to a room, private bath; E7-9: private room, private bath. Call billeting for more information.

DV/VIP: PAO, C-904-542-3147/3138. O6/GS-15+. Retirees and Space-A only after 1800 hours.

TML Availability: Fair. Difficult, summer months.

CREDIT CARDS ACCEPTED: Visa and MasterCard.

Don't miss boating and water sports on over 74 square miles of inland waters, golf courses, wonderful beaches that are among Florida's finest. Also visit museums, symphony, St. Augustine, and Cypress Gardens.

Locator 542-2340   Medical 777-7300   Police 542-2661/2662

Key West Naval Air Station (FL15R1)
Trumbo Point Annex
Key West, FL 33040-9001

TELEPHONE NUMBER INFORMATION: Main installation numbers: C-305-293-3700, D-312-483-3700.

Location: For Trumbo Point Annex, take Florida Turnpike, US-1 S, turn right at Key West. At intersection of Palm turn right. Next traffic light, look for six story, white building. Boca Chica Key is seven miles north of Key West. *USMRA: Page 39 (G-16)*. NMC: Miami, 150 miles north.

FLORIDA
Key West Naval Air Station, continued

Lodging Office: No central billeting office. CBQ at Trumbo Point Annex, Bldg C2076. **C-305-293-4100/4305**, Fax C-305-293-4302, 24 hours daily. Check in facility after 1200, check out 1100 hours daily. Government civilian employee billeting, GS 1+ (on orders only).

TML: BOQ. Officers, all ranks, leave or official duty. handicap accessible. Reservations required for personnel on orders. BOQ: bedroom, private bath (260); DVOQ Suites: separate bedroom, private bath (18); DVOQ single (12). Community kitchen, snack vending, ice vending, housekeeping service, refrigerator, color TV in rooms and lounge, washer/dryer. Rates: single rooms $10, $18 & $24, each additional person $2.50, $4 & $6. DVOQ Suites $30, each additional guest $7, Townhouses $45, each additional guest $9. Maximum 3 persons per unit.

TML: BEQ Boca Chica, E1-E9, Bldg 648/649. Single, private bath (42); Double, private bath (49); Senior Enlisted Suites, private bath (2). Kitchen, ice vending, soda/snack vending, washer/dryers, telephone, micro-fridge, cable TV/VCPs, movie service. Bldg 639, substandard rooms. Single, shared bath (69). Ice vending, washer/dryers, pool/video room, cable TV, housekeeping service. Call for rates and more information.

TML: BOQ. Truman Annex, E1-E6. Substandard, Bldg 438 and 439. C-305-293-5264, D-312-483-5264. Single, shared bath (16); double, shared bath (127). Common kitchen, washer/dryers, ice vending, soda/snack vending, cable TV, pool/video room, fitness center. Rates: Single $18, Double $10, $2.50 each additional person.

TML: Navy Lodge. Bldg 4114, Sigsbee Park, six miles south of NAS in Key West, on the bay. Reservations: **1-800-NAVY-INN**. Lodge number is C-305-292-7556, Fax: C-305-296-4309. All ranks, leave or official duty. Check in 1500-1800 hours, check out 1200 hours. Bedrooms, two double beds, private bath (26). Two units handicap accessible. Kitchenette, microwave, utensils, hair dryer, ice, iron/ironing board, A/C, cribs/cots, phones, coin operated washer/dryer, ice vending. Rates: $48 per day October to May, $62 per day May to Oct, $48 PCS year round with proof of orders. MWR Sunset Lounge, community center with tickets, commissary and exchange across the road. MWR marina boat and snorkel rental gear. Modern structure. All categories may make reservations.

TML: MWR Trailers. Near Old Town Key West. C-305-293-4431, D-312-483-3144. Office closed Sun, Mon and Holidays (arrivals for these days will be arranged). MWR Dept, Box 9027, NAS Key West 33040. Duty or retired, DoD civilians, dependents. Two-bedroom, double beds, private bath (12). A/C, kitchen, complete utensils, dining room, microwave, linens provided, limited housekeeping service, within walking distance of Old Key West. Rates: $48 per night May-Dec, $55 Jun-Apr. All categories can make reservations three to four months in advance.

TML: DV/VIP. Quarters Guest house, Truman Annex, O6+. Three-bedroom beach house (1). A/C, kitchen, all amenities. Rates: $36, guests $9. Call CO Secretary, NAS Key West, FL 33040. Reservations required, others Space-A.

TML Availability: Extremely limited. Best, summer.

Here is the place to kick back and relax by the ocean.

Locator 292-2256   **Medical 292-4444**   **Police-292-2531**

FLORIDA

MacDill Air Force Base (FL02R1)
MacDill Inn
6SVS/SVML/Lodging
P.O. Box 6826
MacDill AFB, FL 33608-5502

TELEPHONE NUMBER INFORMATION: Main installation numbers: C-813-828-1110, D-312-968-1110.

Location: Take I-75 S to I-275 S. Exit at Dale Mabry west, five miles south to MacDill AFB main gate. *USMRA: Page 38 (E,F-8) and Page 54 (E,F-3,4).* NMC: Tampa, five miles north.

Lodging Office: MacDill Inn, Bldg 411, corner Hangar Loop Road and Tampa Blvd. **C-813-828-2661,** Fax: C-813-828-2660, 24 hours. Check in lodging, check out 1100 hours daily. Government civilian employee billeting.

TML: TLF. Bldgs 893, 905, 906, all ranks, PCS families are Priority 1, all others are Priority 2. handicap accessible. Bedroom, private bath (24). Kitchen, refrigerator, utensils, A/C, color TV/VCR, cots/cribs, housekeeping service, essentials, washer/dryer, snacks at front desk, ice vending. Exercise and conference rooms available. Rates: $24 per family. Maximum five per unit. Duty can make reservations, others Space-A.

TML: VAQ. Bldg 372, enlisted E1-E6, leave or official duty. Bedroom, shared bath (62). Refrigerator, A/C, color TV, housekeeping service, washer/dryer. Older structure. Rates: $10, each additional person $4. Maximum two per unit. Duty can make reservations, others Space-A.

TML: VOQ. Bldgs 312, 366, 390, 411, officers all ranks, leave or official duty. Bedroom, private bath (117); bedroom, semi-private bath (44). A/C, color TV, housekeeping service, washer/dryer, ice vending. Modern structure. Rates: sponsor $8 per person. Maximum two per unit. No children. Duty can make reservations, others Space-A.

DV/VIP: 6th ARW/CCP, C-813-828-2056. O6+.

TML Availability: Extremely limited, Jan-Mar. Limited, Apr-Sep. Best, Oct-Dec.

CREDIT CARDS ACCEPTED: Visa, MasterCard and American Express.

Local attractions include Busch Gardens, Tampa Aquarium, Epcot Center, Disney World, Sea World - this is an area with lots of interesting things to see.

Locator 828-2444   Medical 828-2334   Police 828-3322

Marathon Recreation Cottages (FL28R1)
7th Coast Guard District
Miami, FL 33131-3050

TELEPHONE NUMBER INFORMATION: Main installation numbers: C-305-536-5850.

Location: On base. In the Florida Keys on US-1 (Overseas Highway) at mile marker 48 in Marathon. Enter recreation area from US-1. *USMRA: Page 39 (H-15).* NMC: Miami, 111 miles northeast.

FLORIDA
Marathon Recreation Cottages, continued

Lodging Office: None. Reservations required, by application only, with payment at least eight weeks in advance. Credit cards are not accepted. **C-305-743-3549.**

TML: TLF. One bedroom cottage, private bath (4). One double bed, two single sofa beds, one rollaway bed (sleeps five), fully furnished, utensils, AC, TV. Rates: $20-$35 per day depending on rank. Reservations as outlined above.

Situated on Marathon Key in the heart of the Florida Keys. Beaches on Atlantic and Gulf sides. Activities available include fishing, swimming, boating, hiking, and bicycling.

Mayport Naval Station (FL13R1)
Lodging Office
Bldg 425, P.O. Box 20098
Mayport, FL 32228-0098

TELEPHONE NUMBER INFORMATION: Main installation numbers: C-904-270-5011, D-312-960-5011.

Location: From Jacksonville, FL on Atlantic Blvd (FL-10) E to Mayport Road (FL-A1A) left (north) to Naval Station. *USMRA: Page 38 (H-3) and Page 50 (F-3).* NMC: Jacksonville, 10 miles west.

Lodging Office: No central billeting office. Check in facility, check out 1200 daily. Government civilian employee billeting.

TML: BOQ. Bldg 425, officers all ranks, leave or non-Navy personnel on orders, C-904-270-5567, official Navy duty (SATO) 1-800-576-9327. Kitchenette, CATV, refrigerator, A/C, housekeeping service, washer/dryer, ice vending. Modern structure. Rates: $15, VIP $22, DV $30. Duty on orders to Mayport can make reservations, others Space-A.

TML: BEQ. Bldg 1586, enlisted all ranks, leave or non-Navy personnel on orders, C-904-270-5575, official Navy duty (SATO) 1-800-576-9327. Bedroom, hall and private baths (244); separate bedroom (1). DV/VIP with kitchen. Rates: DV/VIP $21, E1-6 $6.25, E7-9 $10.25. Duty on orders to Mayport can make reservations, others Space-A.

TML: Navy Lodge. All ranks, leave or official duty. Reservations call **1-800-NAVY-INN.** Lodge number is C-904-270-5554, Fax: C-904-270-6153. Check in 1400-1600 hours, check out 1200 hours daily. Two-bedroom mobile homes, private bath (19). Kitchen, complete utensils, A/C, color TV, cribs, housekeeping service, coin washer/dryer. Rates: $50. All categories can make reservations. **New 52 unit lodge,** two queen-size beds, private baths, kitchenette, microwave and refrigerator (32). Rate: $54. One queen-size bed, private bath, microwave and refrigerator (20). Rate: $47. *Runner-up of the 1996 Edward E. Carlson Award for Navy Lodge excellence in the large category.*

DV/VIP: Commander/DO, C-904-270-4501. E9, O7+.

TML Availability: Very good, Nov-Mar. Difficult, other times.

FLORIDA
Mayport Naval Station, continued

CREDIT CARDS ACCEPTED: Visa, MasterCard and American Express. The Navy Lodge accepts Visa, MasterCard, American Express and Discover.

Near Jacksonville, historic St. Augustine. Deep sea fishing, and famous Florida beaches - shark's teeth are picked up on local beaches.

Locator 270-5401   Medical 270-5303   Police 270-5583

Oak Grove Park (FL09R1)
MWR Dept
Pensacola NAS, FL 32508-5000

TELEPHONE NUMBER INFORMATION: Main installation numbers: C-904-452-0111, D-312-922-0111.

Location: From I-10 to US-29, S Pensacola. Take Navy Blvd to front gate. *USMRA: Page 39 (A,B-13) and Page 53 (A,B-4,5).* NMC: Pensacola, eight miles east.

Lodging Office: None.

TML: Recreational Cabins, officer and enlisted, all ranks, leave or official duty, **C-904-452-2535, D-312-922-2535.** Check in 1200-1630 hours, check out 0730-1000 hours. Handicap accessible. One bedroom cabins, private bath (12). A/C, kitchen, complete utensils, refrigerator. Modern structures. Rates: $35 per day. All categories can make reservations up to three months in advance.

DV/VIP: No Protocol Office.

TML Availability: Best, Oct-Apr. Difficult, other times.

CREDIT CARDS ACCEPTED: Visa, MasterCard and American Express.

Coastal Florida, near Pensacola is known for water recreation, fishing.

Locator 452-0111   Medical 452-4256   Police 452-2353

Orlando Naval Training Center (FL11R1)
Navy Orlando Inn
1200 Leahy Street, Bldg 375
Orlando NTC, FL 32813-5005
Scheduled to close December 1998.

TELEPHONE NUMBER INFORMATION: Main installation numbers: C-407-646-4111, D-312-791-4111.

Location: On Bennet Road, .5 miles north of FL-50 (Colonial Drive). Bennet Road is about three miles from I-4 on FL-50. *USMRA: Page 38 (H-7).* NMC: Orlando, in city limits.

Lodging Office: Bldg 375, 1200 Leahy Street. **C-407-646-5614,** Fax: C-407-646-4855, 24 hours. Check in facility. Government civilian employee billeting (GS1+).

Temporary Military Lodging Around the World - 75

FLORIDA
Orlando Naval Training Center, continued

TML: BEQ/BOQ. Bldg 375, officer, enlisted all ranks, official duty, C-407-646-5614. Check out 1000 hours daily. Bedroom, one to three beds (depending on paygrade), private bath (130). A/C, color TV lounge, washer/dryer. Modern structure. Rates: $7.25 per person. Official orders Space-A. Bedroom, private bath (28); bedroom, private bath (22); 2-bedroom cottage, private bath (VIPs/Flag Officers). Refrigerator, microwave, A/C, color TV/VCR, housekeeping service, cots, washer/dryer. Older structure, renovated. Rates $8-$25. Duty can make reservations, others Space-A.

TML Availability: Best, Aug-Nov and Jan-Apr.

CREDIT CARDS ACCEPTED: Visa, MasterCard and American Express.

Don't miss Disney World, Cypress Gardens, Universal Studios, Sea World.

Locator 646-5340   **Medical 646-5322**   **Police 646-4340**

Panama City Naval Coastal Systems Station
Naval Surface Warfare Center (FL35R1)
484 Vernon Ave, Bldg 484
Panama City, FL 32407-7001

TELEPHONE NUMBER INFORMATION: Main installation numbers: C-904-234-4011, D-312-436-4011.

Location: In the Northwest section of Florida. Exit I-10 (N&S) to Hwy 231 (N&S) to Florida Hwy 98 (N&S). The facility is located off Hwy 98. *USMRA: Page 39 (E-14)*. NMC: Pensacola 100 miles west and Tallahassee 100 miles east.

Lodging Office: BEQ 484 Vernon Ave. Bldg 484; BOQ 349 Solomon Dr. Bldg 349, 24 hours. **C-904-234-7798 ext 2000, D-312-436-4991,** Fax:C-904-234-4991. Reservations: C-904-234-4217, D-312-436-4217.

TML: BOQ. **Seashore Inn.** Bldg 349, officers, W1+, leave or official duty. Suites (30); senior suites (12); VIP suites (5). Some handicap accessible. All rooms have private bath, kitchenette, A/C, phones, limited utensils, color CATV. Washer/dryers, jacuzzi, snack vending, ice vending, mini mart. Fully remodeled facility. Rates: DV suites $20 (member), $5 (guest); Senior suites $14 (member) $3.50 (guest); suite $10 (member), $2.50 (guest). Limit two to three persons per room. DV/VIP suites, 06+ GM/GS 15 and above. Reservations required for official duty, all others Space-A. C-904-234-4217/4556, D-312-436-4217/4556, Fax: C-904-234-4991. Check in 1600 hours, check out 1100 hours. No children under 16. No pets.

TML: All ranks. BEQ Bldg 484. Private bedroom with sofa sleeper, private bath (40). A/C, snack vending, ice vending, microwaves, refrigerators, color CATV/VCP, free movies, weight room, washer/dryer. Modern building with recent remodeling. E7/E9 suites $7.50; E6/E5 private room, shared bath $7.50; E1-E4 shared rooms, shared bath $4. No overnight guests allowed in Bldg 484.

TML: BEQ Bldg 304 Bedrooms with private baths $7.50 (member) $2.50 (guest) Color CATV, washer/dryer, microwaves, refrigerators, snack vending, ice vending. Very limited family lodging.

TML Availability: Good, Oct-Feb. Difficult, Mar-Sep.

FLORIDA
Panama City Naval Coastal Systems Station Naval Surface Warfare Center, continued

CREDIT CARDS ACCEPTED: Visa, MasterCard, and American Express.

Transportation: Off-base taxi 904-233-8299.

Visit the Armament Museum, beautiful sandy white beaches and enjoy Florida sport fishing.

Locator 234-4011   Medical 234-4177   Police 234-4332

MWR first for fun

Coastal Systems Station Panama City, Fl

Luxury Accommodations
on the
World's Most Beautiful Beaches

Condos on the Beach

These spacious fully equipped three bedroom, two bath units sleep up to eight. Watch the sun set over the Gulf from your private balcony.

Park Model Trailers

Comfortable attractive mobile homes. Located on base at the CSS Marina and Outdoor Recreation Area. Enjoy MWR's wide variety of rental boats and equipment.,

For Condo information and a copy of our color brochure
call 904-234-4556
For Park Model Trailers call 904-234-4402
Morale, Recreation and Welfare -Coastal Systems Station
6703 West Highway 98, Panama City, Fl 32407-7001

Patrick Air Force Base (FL03R1)
Space Coast Inn
45 SVS/SVML
P.O. Box 5005
Patrick AFB, FL 32925-3223

TELEPHONE NUMBER INFORMATION: Main installation numbers: C-407-494-1110, D-312-854-1110.

Location: Take I-95 S to exit 73 (Wickham Road), three miles to State Road 404 (Pineda Causeway), six miles, left on A1A, three miles to Patrick AFB. *USMRA: Page 38 (I-8)*. NMC: Cocoa Beach, two miles north.

Temporary Military Lodging Around the World - 77

FLORIDA
Patrick Air Force Base, continued

Lodging Office: Space Coast Inn, Bldgs 720, 820 Falcon Ave. **C-407-494-6590, D-312-854-6590,** Fax: C-407-494-7597, D-312-854-7597, 24 hours. Check in lodging 1500 hours, check out 1100 hours daily. Government/Military civilian employee lodging.

TML: TLF. Bldgs 1030, 1034, 1036, 1038, 1042, 1046, 1048, 1050, 1056, 1058, 1060, 1061, all ranks, leave or official duty. Two-bedroom, private bath (31); three-bedroom, private bath (20). Kitchen, living room, utensils, A/C, color TV, housekeeping service, cribs, washer/dryer. Older structure, renovated. Rates: $24.50 per unit. PCS duty families can make reservations, others Space-A.

TML: VAQ. Bldgs 501, 556, 727, enlisted E1-E8, leave or official duty. Bedroom, living room, private bath (28); bedroom, private bath (16); bedroom, shared bath (132). A/C, color TV, refrigerator, microwave, housekeeping service, washer/dryer, ice vending. Older structure, renovated. Rates: $10 and $14 per person. Duty can make reservations, others Space-A.

TML: VOQ. Bldgs 264, 265, 404, officers all ranks, leave or official duty. Two-bedroom, shared bath, living room (94); suites, private baths (11). A/C, color TV, refrigerator, microwave, housekeeping service, washer/dryer, ice vending. Renovated. Rates: $14.50 and $16 per person. Duty can make reservations, others Space-A.

TML: DV/VIP. Bldgs 250, 251, 253, officers O6+, leave or official duty. Bedroom suite, private bath (2); two-bedroom suite, private bath (1); four-bedroom house (1). AC, color TV, refrigerator, full kitchen with utensils, washer/dryer, housekeeping service. Older structure, renovated. Rates: $16 per person. Bldg 255, enlisted E9, leave or official duty. Bedroom suite, private bath (3). A/C, color TV, kitchen with utensils, washer/dryer, housekeeping service. Older structure, renovated. Rates: $16 per person. Reservations: PROTOCOL 407-494-4511. Duty can make reservations, others Space-A.

TML: Manatee Cove Recreational Lodging, C-407-494-4787, D-312-854-4787. Three-bedroom beach houses, 3 full baths (3); sleeps eight, furnished, kitchen, cable TV/VCR, washer/dryer, linens, and garage. Rates: $125-150 per day, $800-1000 per week. See *Military Living's Military RV, Camping and Rec Areas Around the World* for additional information and directions.

TML Availability: Good, Nov-Jan. Limited, other times.

CREDIT CARDS ACCEPTED: Visa, MasterCard and American Express.

Transportation: Car rental agency 783-2424.

Florida's "Space Coast" includes US Air Force Space Museum, Kennedy Center, Disney World, Sea World, Epcot Center, Cypress Gardens.

Locator 494-4542   **Medical** 494-8133   **Police** 494-2008

Pensacola Naval Air Station (FL14R1)
Basis BEQ, Bldg 3474
Pensacola NAS, FL 32508-5217

TELEPHONE NUMBER INFORMATION: Main installation numbers: C-904-452-0111, D-312-922-0111.

FLORIDA
Pensacola Naval Air Station, continued

Location: Off US-98, four miles south of I-10. Take Navy Blvd from US-98 or US-29 directly to NAS. *USMRA: Page 39 (A,B-13) and Page 53 (A,B-4,5).* NMC: Pensacola, eight miles north.

Lodging Office: Billeting office, Bldg 3472. **C-904-452-7077/4609, D-312-922-7077**, Reservations C-904-452-7077, D-312-922-7077, Fax: C-904-452-6483, D-312-922-7784, 24 hours.

NAVY LODGE

TML: Navy Lodge. Bldg 3875, all ranks, leave or official duty. Reservations: **1-800-NAVY-INN**. Lodge number is C-904-456-8676, Fax: 904-457-7151. Check in 1500 hours, check out 1200 hours daily. Bedroom, two queen beds, kitchenette (22). Rates: $37 per night. Two-bedroom, living room, kitchen, private bath mobile home (12). Rates: $37 per night. A new 52 unit beachside lodge has opened at Lighthouse Point, Bldg 3875. Kitchen, microwave, utensils, A/C, color TV, coffee/tea, housekeeping service, cribs/cots, phones, coin washer/dryer, snack vending, ice vending, picnic grounds, playground. Modern structure. Rates: $44 single queen and $55 two queens. All categories can make reservations. *Runner-up of the 1996 Edward E. Carlson Award for Navy Lodge excellence in the large category.*

TML: BOQ. Bldg 600, officers all ranks, leave or official duty, C-904-452-2755, Fax: C-904-452-3188, 24 hours. Check in 24 hours, out 1100 hours. Bedrooms, private bath (52); VIP rooms, private bath (O6+) (38); flag officer suites, private bath (5). CATV, microwave, coffee pots, etc. Renovated. Rates: $10, VIP $15, Flag $25. Duty, authorized civilians, can make reservations.

TML: BEQ. Bayshores. Bldg 3472, enlisted E1-E9. C-904-452-3438/4609, D-312-922-3438/4609, 24 hours. E5-E9, bedroom, private bath (1 man) (48); VIP suites, living room, kitchenette E7-E9, private bath (2); E1-E4, shared room, shared bath (112). CATV, coffee pots, microwave, refrigerator. Rates: E5-E6 $9.60, E7+ $25, E1-E4 $5.60, VIP $16.60, guest $2. Personnel assigned to NAS/no family check with BEQ on Space-A. Duty, TAD, reservists (orders) make reservations, retired and leave personnel Space-A.

TML: BEQ Bayshores. Bldg 3474, enlisted E1-E9, leave or official duty, C-904-452-7077, D-312-922-7077, Fax: D-312-922-7784. Rates: Mini-Apartment E7-E9 $25, bed/living room E5-E6 NATTC C school students $15.00, single room E5-E6 $9.60, shared room E1/E4 $5, guest $2. Personnel assigned to NAS/no family check with BEQ on Space-A. Duty, TAD, reservists (orders) make reservations, retired and leave personnel Space-A one day at a time.

TML Availability: Limited due to ongoing renovations for the next two years.

CREDIT CARDS ACCEPTED: Visa, MasterCard and American Express.

See miles of sugar-white sand beaches, fishing, etc.; Saenger Theater of performing arts in Pensacola; the Blue Angels; the USS Lexington.

Locator 452-4693   Medical 452-4138   Police 452-2653

FLORIDA

Shades of Green™ on WALT DISNEY WORLD® Resort (FL49R1)
P.O. Box 22789
Lake Buena Vista, FL 32830-2789

TELEPHONE NUMBER INFORMATION: Main installation numbers: C-407-824-3400, Fax: C-407-824-3460.

Location: From Orlando take I-4 W, exit 26B, Walt Disney World, follow Magic Kingdom Resort signs, go through Magic Kingdom toll booth, stay in far right lane following signs to Resort and hotels, at first light turn left, Seven Seas Drive past Polynesian Resort, come to three way stop, turn right on Floridian Way, driveway is first road to the left, Magnolia Palm Drive. *USMRA: Page 38 (G,H-7) and Page 53 (A-2,3).* NMC: Orlando, 15 miles northeast.

Description of Area: The newest addition to Armed Forces Recreation Centers is Shades of Green on Walt Disney World Resort. The former Disney Inn, Shades of Green is situated almost in the heart of the Magic Kingdom, nestled between two championship golf courses and a 9-hole executive course which are all part of Walt Disney World Resort. There are 287 rooms, two swimming pools, a toddler pool, two tennis courts, a small fitness center, and a children's play area. There are two restaurants with lounges nearby to relax and enjoy great food and the beverage of your choice. The hotel also offers an AAFES gift shop, a video arcade center, and laundry facilities. Free transportation: to all of Walt Disney World Resorts and Attractions is included for all Shades of Green guests. Discount tickets are available for most Orlando area attractions.

Season of Operation: Year round.

Reservations: Required. Military personnel, active, retired, Guard and Reserve, family members and DoD employees may make reservations by calling **C-407-824-3600**, Fax: C-407-824-3665. Write for reservations and information packet: Shades of Green on Walt Disney World Resort, P.O. Box 22789, Lake Buena Vista, FL 32830-2789.

RATES: *(effective 1 Oct 1996):* E1-E5, $57; E6-E9, O1-O3, WO1-CW3, GS 1-GS10, NF1-NF3, $81; O4-O6, CW4-CW5, GS 11-GS15, NF4-NF5, $89; O7-O10, Foreign Military, Retired DoD Civilians, NF6 $98. Rates are for double occupancy. Single room subtract $2. There will be an added charge of $10 per additional adult above two per room.

A vacation dream come true, a visit to Walt Disney World, Epcot Center, Disney MGM Studios Theme Park, and Blizzard Beach. Other attractions within an hour's drive are Busch Gardens, Cypress Gardens, hot air balloon rides, deep sea fishing Daytona and Cocoa Beach and Cape Canaveral where you can visit the Space Museum and if you're lucky, watch the space shuttle launch. If this is not enough to keep you busy, there is golf, swimming, and tennis all without leaving the resort.

80 - Temporary Military Lodging Around the World

FLORIDA

Tyndall Air Force Base (FL04R1)
325 SVS/SVML/Lodging
Bldg 1332
Tyndall AFB, FL 32403-5541

TELEPHONE NUMBER INFORMATION: Main installation numbers: C-904-283-1110, D-312-523-1110.

Location: Take I-10, exit US-231 S to US-98 E, signs mark the AFB. *USMRA: Page 39 (E-14).* NMC: Panama City, 10 miles northwest.

Lodging Office: P.O. Box 40040, Bldg 1332, Suwannee and Oak Drive. **C-904-283-4210 ext 0, D-312-523-4210,** Fax: C-904-283-4800, D-312-523-4800, 24 hours. Check in billeting 1400 hours, check out 1200 hours Mon-Fri, 1000 hours Sat-Sun. Government civilian employee lodging.

TML: VAQ/VOQ/DV/TLF. **Sand Dollar Inn.** All ranks, leave or official duty. VOQ: separate bedrooms, kitchen, private bath (200); VAQ: shared bedroom and shared bath(144); DV Suites: Private bedroom and bath (19); SRNCOQ: bedroom, private bath (24); NCO; efficiency apartments, private bath (40), sleeps four, cribs/rollaways available (TLF). A/C, color CATV in room and lounge, housekeeping service, washer/dryer, ice vending. Modern structure. Rates: E1-E6, $18 per first unit, $9 per second unit. E7 and Officer, $22 per first unit, $11 per second unit. VOQ, $8.50 per person, $11.75 per couple. VAQ, $8.50 per person, $11.75 per couple. DV and SRNCOQ, $16 per person, $23 per couple. Official duty should make reservations, others Space-A.

Note: Tyndall Fam-Camp has 2-bedroom cottages (3). Rates: $60 per day, $300 per week. Call C-904-283-2798 for more information and reservations.

DV/VIP: HQ, Bldg 647, C-904-283-2232. O6+. Retirees and lower ranks Space-A.

TML Availability: Very good, Jan-Feb. Fair, other times.

CREDIT CARDS ACCEPTED: Visa, MasterCard and American Express.

Beautiful white sand beaches, water sports, fishing, and small friendly communities.

Locator 283-2138   Medical 283-7523   Police 283-4124

Whiting Field Naval Air Station (FL05R1)
Consolidated Bachelor Quarters
7426 USS Lexington Circle
Milton, FL 32570-1655

TELEPHONE NUMBER INFORMATION: Main installation numbers: C-904-623-7011, D-312-868-7011.

Location: From Pensacola or Mobile take I-10 E, exit 7, US-90 to FL-89-7 N for seven miles, take FL-8 for seven more miles to NAS. *USMRA: Page 39 (B-13).* NMC: Pensacola, 25 miles southwest.

Lodging Office: Wings Inn. Bldg 2942, Lexington Circle. **C-904-623-7606, D-312-868-7606,** Fax: C-904-623-7238, 24 hours. Check in 1500 hours, check out 1200 hours daily. Government civilian employee billeting.

FLORIDA
Whiting Field Naval Air Station, continued

TML: BOQ. Bldg 2957. Family style 2-bedroom units (8). Single bedroom units (42). Lounge, kitchenette with some utensils, private bath, A/C, TV/VCR, sand volleyball court, fitness equipment, sauna, game room, picnic tables, grills. Rates: $8 per room, $10 per suite.

TML: BEQ. Bldg 2958, Family style 2-bedroom suites, private bath (70). Lounge, kitchenette with some utensils, A/C, TV/VCR. Some rooms have a twin bed. Rates: $8. AD can make reservations, others Space-A.

DV/VIP: Admiral's Office, Bldg 1401. C-904-623-7201. BOQ 05+, BEQ E9+ (no children under 10). Rates: $30. Retirees Space-A.

TML Availability: Good.

CREDIT CARDS ACCEPTED: Visa, MasterCard and American Express.

Small growing community, 25 miles northeast of Pensacola, 18 hole golf course, swimming pools, bowling alley, clubs, commissary and exchange. Stop in and see the new Whiting Field.

Locator 623-7011   Medical 623-7584   Police 623-7378

GEORGIA

Albany Marine Corps Logistics Base (GA17R1)
Live Oak Lodge Billeting
9201 Williams Blvd
Albany, GA 31705-1003

TELEPHONE NUMBER INFORMATION: Main installation numbers: C-912-439-5000, D-312-567-5000.

Location: Approximately three miles southeast of Albany. Accessible from US-82, US-300, and US-19. Follow the signs. *USMRA: Page 37 (C-8)*. NMC: Albany, three miles west.

Lodging Office: Live Oak Lodge. Bldg 9201. **C-912-439-5614, D-312-567-5614,** Fax: C-912-439-5690, D-312-567-5690, 0730-1600 hours Mon-Fri. After hours, contact DO, Bldg 3500. Check out 1130 hours.

TML: Family Transient Quarters. Bldgs 9251, 9253, 9255. Separate houses, three bedrooms, two baths. All facilities and amenities - housekeeping service, kitchen, washer/dryer, iron/ironing board, dishes, utensils, color TV. All ranks, primarily for AD military on PCS. Rates: $20 per night. Maximum six adults or children per unit. Military on leave, retirees, Space-A. No smoking. No pets.

TML: TEQ. Bldg 7966. One bedroom, private bath units for E6+, equivalent graded government employees on official orders. Rate: $9 per night. Maximum two adults, two children per unit. Retired military, Space-A. No smoking. No pets.

GEORGIA
Albany Marine Corps Logistics Base, continued

TML: Enlisted quarters available for E5 and below. No charge, call for information. No housekeeping service. No smoking. No pets.

TML: TOQ. Bldgs 10201, 10202, officers all ranks, leave or official duty. Equivalent government employees on official duty. One, three, and four-bedroom suites with kitchenettes. Handicap accessible suite available. Renovated. Rates: $12-$24 per unit. Retired military Space-A. No smoking. No pets.

TML: DV/VIP. Bldg 10300, officer O6+, leave or official duty. Two-bedroom, completely furnished detached house, private bath. All facilities and amenities. Housekeeping service, color TV, washer/dryer. Modern structure. Rates: $25. Official duty, leave and retirees, Space-A. No smoking. No pets.

DV/VIP: Contact Live Oak Billeting Office, O5+. Retirees and lower ranks Space-A.

TML Availability: Fairly good. Best Nov-Mar.

CREDIT CARDS ACCEPTED: American Express and Diners' Club.

Swimming at beautiful Radium Springs, south of Albany, outdoor sports, local Concert Association, Little Theater. Albany is a trade and distribution center for Southwest Georgia.

Locator 439-5000/5103   Medical 435-0806   Police 439-5181

Athens Navy Supply Corps School (GA12R1)
The Oaks
1425 Prince Avenue
Athens NSCS, GA 30606-2205

TELEPHONE NUMBER INFORMATION: Main installation numbers: C-706-354-1500, D-312-588-1500.

Location: From Athens take bypass, exit on Prince Ave, continue one mile to base at intersection of Prince and Oglethorpe Avenues. *USMRA: Page 37 (D-3)*. NMC: Atlanta, 70 miles west.

Lodging Office: The Oaks. 1425 Prince Avenue. **C-706-543-3033, D-312-588-7360,** 0800-0100 hours daily, Fax: C-706-354-7370, D-312-588-7370. Check in Brown Hall after 1400 hours, check out 1300 hours daily. Reservations 180 days in advance for those on orders to NSCS. All others Space-A. No pets.

TML: Brown Hall. All ranks, leave or official duty. Two-room suites, private bath (35). Some units have sofa bed, micro-refrigerator, A/C, color TV/VCP, coffee pot, iron/ironing board, washer/dryer, housekeeping service, soda/snack vending, ice vending, video rental. Rates: sponsor $22, guest $5.50. Maximum two per room. No pets.

TML: Wright Hall. All ranks, leave or official duty. One-room suites, private bath (72). Micro-refrigerator (in some rooms), A/C, color TV/VCP, coffee pot, iron/ironing board, washer/dryer, housekeeping service, soda/snack vending, ice vending, video rental. Rates: sponsor $9, guest $2.50. Maximum two per room. No pets.

GEORGIA
Athens Navy Supply Corps School, continued

TML: CBQ. C-706-543-3033, Fax C-706-354-7370. Check in between 0800-1300 hours, check out 1300 hours daily. Bedroom, private bath. A/C, color TV/VCR, coffee pot, micro-fridge, clock radio, housekeeping service. Call for more information.

TML Availability: Dependent on student/class loading.

The Oaks is the recipient of Chief Naval Education and Training "Innkeeper of the Year" for 1993, 1994, 1995, 1996. Admiral Elmo R. Zumwait Award for Excellence in BQ Management for 1994, 1995, and presented with a "Four Star" rating in bachelor quarters from Commander, naval Facility Engineering Command in 1996 and 1997. Athens has museums, restaurants, shopping, and the University of Georgia; the state botanical garden, and the Chattahoochee National Forest nearby. Atlanta 70 miles away...lots to do and see.

Locator 354-1500   **Medical 354-7321**   **Police 354-1500**

Atlanta Naval Air Station (GA16R1)
Combined Bachelor's Quarters
Bldg 54, Room 120
Marietta, GA 30060-5099

TELEPHONE NUMBER INFORMATION: Main installation numbers: C-770-421-6392, D-312-925-6392.

Location: From I-75, exit to GA-280, W to GA-3, south to main gate, adjacent to Dobbins AFB on the west. *USMRA: Page 37 (B-3) and Page 49 (A-1)*. NMC: Atlanta, 15 miles southeast.

Lodging Office: Bldg 54. **C-770-919-6393, D-312-925-6393,** Fax: C-770-919-6263, 24 hours. Check in billeting 1200 hours, check out 1200 hours daily. Government civilian employees billeting (orders).

TML: BOQ. Bldg 53, officers, all ranks, leave or official duty. Suites, private bath (5). A/C, microwave, housekeeping service, washer/dryer, telephones, CATV. Modern structure. No pets. Rates: $6 per night. Reservations required for those on orders, others Space-A.

TML: BEQ. Bldg 54, 63, enlisted, all ranks, leave or official duty. Bedroom, shared bath (23). Bedroom, private bath (1). A/C, microwave, housekeeping service, CATV, washer/dryer. Modern structure. No pets. Rates: $6 per night. Reservations required, others Space-A.

TML: World Famous Navy Lake Site. C-770-974-6309. Cabins: One to four-bedrooms (9), A/C, furnished, color TV, microwave, dishes, pots and pans, linens. Rates: $38-59. See *Military Living's Military RV, Camping and Rec Areas Around the World* for additional information and directions.

TML Availability: Very good during the week, difficult on weekends.

CREDIT CARDS ACCEPTED: Visa, MasterCard and American Express.

Stone Mountain State Park, with hiking, fishing and other outdoor activities, Six Flags over Georgia.

GEORGIA
Atlanta Naval Air Station, continued

Locator 919-5392   Medical 919-5300   Police 919-5394

Camp Frank D. Merrill (GA23R1)
5th Ranger Training Battalion
Dahlonega, GA 30533-9499

TELEPHONE NUMBER INFORMATION: Main installation numbers: C-706-864-3327/3367, D-312-797-5770.

Location: From Atlanta, take I-85 N to GA-400 N. GA-400 ends at J.B. Jones intersection, turn left on Hwy 19/60 N to Dahlonega, five miles. Left at light in town; follow signs. *USMRA: Page 37 (C-2)*. NMC: Atlanta, 60 miles southwest.

Lodging Office: Bldg 23, **C-706-864-0486, D-312-797-5770 ext 203,** Fax: C-706-864-0145, 0800-1200 hours, 1300-1700 hours Mon-Fri. Reservations required, advance payment. Credit Cards are not accepted. HP: http://www.home.msn.com.

TML: TLQ. Bldg 1, all ranks, leave or official duty. Five-bedroom cottage (2), sleeps six. Refrigerator, kitchenette, utensils, TV, cribs/cots, soda/snack vending. Fitness Center and Mini-mart available. Completely renovated 1988/1989. Rates: $35.00 first night, $20.00 each additional night.

DV/VIP: C-706-864-0486. O6+. Space-A only.

TML Availability: Good, Nov-Mar. Difficult, Apr-Oct.

Camp Merrill and Dahlonega are located in the North Georgia Mountains. Beautiful mountain views.

Locator 864-3327   Medical ext 189/190   Police 911

Dobbins Air Reserve Base (GA13R1)
Dobbins Inn
1295 Barracks Court, Bldg 800
Dobbins ARB, GA 30069-4821

TELEPHONE NUMBER INFORMATION: Main installation numbers: C-770-919-5000, D-312-925-5000.

Location: From I-75 N exit to GA-280 W (exit 111) to ARB. Clearly marked. *USMRA: Page 37 (B-3) and Page 49 (A-1)*. NMC: Atlanta, 17 miles southeast.

Lodging Office: Dobbins Inn. Bldg 800, 1295 Barracks Court. **C-770-919-4745, D-312-925-4745,** Fax: C-770-919-5185, 24 hours. Check in facility, check out 1200 hours daily. Government civilian employee lodging.

TML: VAQ. Bldg 801, enlisted, E1-E6, leave or official duty. Bedroom, semi-private bath (75). Refrigerator, A/C, cribs, essentials, color TV, washer/dryer, ice vending. Older structure, renovated 1990. Rates: $8 per person, $3 each additional person, maximum two per unit. Duty can make reservations, others Space-A 24 hours in advance.

GEORGIA
Dobbins Air Reserve Base, continued

TML: DV/VIP. Bldg 401, officer O6+, available to lower ranks Space-A, leave or official duty. Bedroom suites, private bath and sitting room (5). bedrooms (44). Refrigerator, A/C, cribs, essentials, ice vending, housekeeping service, color TV, washer/dryer. VOQ renovated 1992. Rates: DV rooms $12 per person, $5 each additional person; other rooms $8 per person, $3 each additional person. Maximum two per unit. Duty can make reservations, others Space-A 24 hours in advance.

TML: SNCO. Bldg 800, E7-E9. Two-room suites (4). Rate: $12 per person per night, $5 each additional person. Other SNCO rooms (40) single occupancy, share bath. SNCO rooms renovated 1992. Rate: $8 per person per night, $3 each additional person.

DV/VIP: PAO, C-770-919-4520. O7+. Retirees and lower ranks Space-A 24 hours in advance.

TML Availability: Good, Nov-Mar. Difficult, Apr-Oct.

CREDIT CARDS ACCEPTED: Visa, MasterCard and American Express.

Excellent fishing and boating in the Metro Atlanta area at Lake Altoona and Lake Lanier. Visit underground Atlanta, the Cyclorama, Stone Mountain Park and the Jimmy Carter Presidential Library.

Locator 919-5000   **Medical 919-5305**   **Police 919-4907**

Fort Benning (GA11R1)
Lodging Office
Bldg 399 Gillespie Street
Fort Benning, GA 31905-5122

TELEPHONE NUMBER INFORMATION: Main installation numbers: C-706-545-0110, D-312-835-0110.

Location: Borders South Columbus off I-185. Can be reached from US-80 and US-280. *USMRA: Page 37 (B-6)*. NMC: Columbus, five miles northwest.

Lodging Office: Bldg 399, Gillespie Street. **C-706-689-0067** (Auto Attendant), **D-312-835-3146/47**, Fax: C-706-682-9842, 24 hours. Check in facility, check out 1200 hours. All ranks, dependents (Space-A), reservists, and government civilian employees on TDY orders. Fee charged for late checkouts. No pets. No children.

TML: Guest House. Bldgs 36-38, and 96, C-706-689-1142, all ranks. Priority PCS personnel, others Space-A. Bedrooms, private bath, refrigerator, A/C, color TV, housekeeping service (Mon-Fri), living room sofa bed. Older structures, New Structure (Bldg 96), includes kitchenettes. Call for rates. Check out 1100 hours. (Fee equal to room).

TML: VOQ/VEQ. Bldgs 75, 83, 399, C-706-689-2505, all ranks, primarily for TDY students, may have Space-A for transients. Check out 1200 hours. Call for complete rates, $15 single. No children.

TML: MWR Destin Army Infantry Recreation Area, 557 Calhoun Ave, Destin, Fl 32541, C-1-800-642-0466, 904-837-2725. All ranks, leave or official duty, retirees, Fort Benning personnel. Motel: bedrooms, two double beds, private bath (54); duplex, two-bedroom, private bath (17); three-bedroom, private bath (5). Refrigerator, CATV, coffee pot, towels, linens, recreation rental equipment

GEORGIA
Fort Benning, continued

(large fishing and party vessels), close to Hurlburt field support. Rates: based on rank, motel $38-$49 per day; cottages $44-$65 per day. Additional fee for non ID card holders. No pets. **Note: see** *Military RV, Camping and Rec Areas Around the World* **for additional information.**

TML: MWR, Uchee Creek Army Campground and Marina. Located south of Columbus, easy access from US-80, I-185, US-280, US-431 and AL165. Bldg 0007. Reservations: C-706-545-7238/4055, D-312-835-7238/4053. Write: Community Recreation Division, P.O. Box 53323, ATTN: Uchee Creek Army campground/marina, Fort Benning, GA 31905-5226. Visa and MasterCard. Check in at facility, check out 1100 hours. All ranks, family members, government civilian employees. Secluded cabins, largest sleeps six, private bath (4); medium, sleeps four, private bath (10); small, sleeps four, no bath or kitchen facilities (comfort station on site). Large and medium cabins have microwave, stove, refrigerator, utensils, TV/VCR, A/C, heat. Guests furnish linen and towels, blankets and pillows provided. Recreation and rental equipment, country store, RV pads, marina, playground, fishing, and pool on campground. No pets. Availability: best on weekdays, worst on weekends, holidays and in summer; Winter, good all season.

TML: DV/VIP. McIver Street. Officer O6+. Protocol RSVP C-706-545-5724, D-312-835-5724. Check out 1100 (fee of $15 for late check out) Suite, private bath. Refrigerator, A/C, color TV, housekeeping service (Mon-Fri). Older structure. Rates $23, each additional person $10. Retired and lower ranks Space-A.

TML Availability: Best, Dec. Difficult, Jun-Sep.

CREDIT CARDS ACCEPTED: Visa, MasterCard, American Express and Discover.

For those interested in military history, visit the Infantry museum, the Infantry Hall of Fame and a number of other Fort Benning points of interest. See more about Camp Uchee in Military Living's *Military RV, Camping and Rec Areas Around the World.*

Locator 545-5217   Medical 544-2041   Police 545-5222

Fort Gillem (GA21R1)
Billeting
AFZK-PWH
Bldg 816 Fort Gillem
Forest Park, GA 30050-5000

TELEPHONE NUMBER INFORMATION: Main installation numbers: C-404-363-5000, D-312-797-1001.

Location: From I-75, east on I-285 to US-54 (Jonesboro Road), south for three miles to the main gate. Fort is five miles from Hartsfield IAP. *USMRA: Page 37 (C-4) and Page 49 (C-4).* NMC: Atlanta, 10 miles northwest.

Lodging Office: Bldg 816, Hood Ave. **C-404-363-5810,** 0730-1600 hours Mon-Fri. Check in facility, check out 1000 hours daily. No government civilian employee billeting. This is a sub-post of Fort McPherson.

GEORGIA
Fort Gillem, continued

TML: VOQ/VEQ. Bldgs 131, 134, all ranks, leave or official duty. Bedrooms, private bath (7); bedroom, private bath, (7). Kitchen, utensils, A/C, color TV, housekeeping service, washer/dryer, ice vending. Older structure. Rates: $23-$25 per apartment. Duty can make reservations, others Space-A.

DV/VIP: Billeting Office, C-404-363-5431. O6/GS-15+. Retirees and lower ranks Space-A.

TML Availability: Extremely limited.

CREDIT CARDS ACCEPTED: Visa, MasterCard and American Express.

"Gone with the Wind" country, and historic Atlanta attractions, combine with seashore, flatlands and mountains to make this area a joy to visit.

Locator 363-5000   Police 363-5982   Medical 752-3711

Fort Gordon (GA09R1)
HQDA, USASC&FC (ATZH-DIH-B)
Fort Gordon Billeting NAFI
Bldg 250, Griffith Hall
Fort Gordon, GA 30905-5040

TELEPHONE NUMBER INFORMATION: Main installation numbers: C-706-791-0110, D-312-780-0110.

Location: Between US-78/278 and US-1. Gates are on both US-78 and US-1. *USMRA: Page 37 (F-4)*. NMC: Augusta, 12 miles northeast.

Lodging Office: Griffith Hall, Bldg 250, Chamberlain Ave. Reservations: **C-706-791-2277, D-312-780-2277,** Fax: C-706-796-6595, 24 hours. Check in facility 1400 hours, check out 1100 hours daily.

TML: Stinson Guest House. Bldgs 37300, 37302, 18404, all ranks, leave or official duty, C-706-793-7160, D-312-780-7183, 24 hours. Check in 1300 to 1800 hours, check out 1100 hours daily, one hour additional on request. Bedrooms, private bath (103); handicap accessible rooms, private bath (3); kitchenettes (12). Refrigerator, microwave, A/C, color TV, cribs/rollaways ($2), washer/dryer, playground, BBQ grills, park area, video rental service, coffee service twice daily. Modern structure. Rates: $27/$29/$31 per unit. PCS/hospital visitors can make reservations 30 days in advance, others seven days in advance. Reservations held until 6 p.m. unless prepaid with cash or credit card. Pets must be boarded off post prior to check-in. Boarding information available at front desk.

TML: Guest House. Bldg 18404, all ranks, leave or official duty. Two-bedroom apartments, private bath (2). Kitchen, utensils, A/C, color TV. Modern structure. Rate: $35 per unit. PCS and hospital visitors can make reservations 30 days in advance, others seven days in advance. Pets must be boarded off post prior to check-in. Boarding information available at front desk.

TML: VOQ/VEQ. Bldgs 250, 36700, Military TDY all ranks, leave or official duty. Check in billeting. Bedroom, private bath (444). Refrigerator, microwave, A/C, color TV in room and lounge, housekeeping service, washer/dryer, ice vending, soda/snack vending. Modern structure. Rates: single $15, each additional person $2. Maximum two per room. Children authorized in Guest Housing only. Duty can make reservations, others Space-A. Pets must be boarded off post prior to check-in.

GEORGIA
Fort Gordon, continued

TML: DVQ. Bldgs 250, 36700, 34503/04/06, 34601/05, and quarters 6, officers O3+. Separate bedrooms, private bath (19). Kitchen, complete utensils, A/C, color TV, housekeeping service, cots. Bldg 250 and 36700 modern structures, others older structures. Rates: $21 single, $2 each additional person. Duty can make reservations, others, including lesser ranks, Space-A. Pets must be boarded off post prior to check-in.

TML: Gordon Recreation Area, C-706-541-1057, Fax: C-706-541-1936. Cabins (9) and mobile homes (8), 3-bedroom, furnished. Rates: $45-$60 daily. **See *Military Living's Military RV, Camping and Rec Areas Around the World*** for additional information and directions.

TML: Fisher House. Note: See appendix C for a definition of this facility. C-706-787-7100.

DV/VIP: Protocol Office, 10th floor, Signal Towers, C-706-791-5376/0022. O6+. Retirees and lower ranks (O3+) Space-A.

TML Availability: Good.

CREDIT CARDS ACCEPTED: Visa, MasterCard, American Express and Discover.

Transportation: On/off base shuttle/bus 722-6603, On/off base taxi 722-5588, on/off base bus 793-0026, car rental agency 1-800-227-7368.

Locator 791-4675   **Medical** 787-6686   **Police** 791-4537/2681

Fort McPherson (GA08R1)
Billeting Office
1496 Walker Avenue
Fort McPherson, GA 30330-1001

TELEPHONE NUMBER INFORMATION: Main installation numbers: C-404-464-3113, D-312-367-1110.

Location: Off I-75 take Lakewood Freeway (GA-166), exit to US-29 (Main St exit). Main gate is at Main Street exit. *USMRA: Page 49 (B-3).* NMC: Atlanta, in city limits.

Lodging Office: Bldg T-22. **C-404-464-3833/2253**, Fax: C-404-464-3376, D-312-367-3376, 0600-2330 hours daily. Other hours, SDO, Bldg 65, C-404-464-2980. Check in facility 1400 hours, check out 1000 hours daily. Government civilian employee billeting.

TML: VOQ/VEQ. Bldg T-22 (**Chateau**), all ranks, leave or official duty. One-bedroom, private bath (20). Refrigerator, microwave, community kitchen, individual telephone, A/C, color TV, lounge, housekeeping service, washer/dryer, ice vending. Older structure. Same rates as above.

TML: VOQ/VEQ. Bldg 168 (**Hardee Hall**), all ranks, leave or official duty. Eight suites, nine single rooms, private bath, refrigerator/microwave, color TV, individual telephones, common area kitchen. Modern structure. Duty can make reservations.

TML: DV/VIP. Lee Hall, officer O6+, leave or official duty, C-404-464-5388. Various size suites, private bath (8). Refrigerator, community kitchen, A/C, color TV in room and lounge, housekeeping service, ice vending. Historic structure. Rates: $30. Duty can make reservations, others Space-A.

GEORGIA
Fort McPherson, continued

TML: Lake Allatoona Army Recreation Area, C-770-974-3413/9420, Fax: C-770-974-1278. Apartment, 3-bedroom (3); Cabin, 2-bedroom/deluxe (5); Cabin, 2-bedroom (12); Cabin, 1-bedroom (8), A/C, furnished, microwave, CATV, bed linens, pots and pans, dishes, utensils. Bring towels, extra blankets, can opener, soap, detergent, sharpened knives. Several 2-bedroom cabins and 3-bedroom apartments are handicap accessible. Rates: $48-$63 for cabins and $75 for apartments daily. **See Military Living's Military RV, Camping and Rec Areas Around the World for additional information and directions.**

DV/VIP: Protocol Office, Bldg 200, C-404-464-538. O6+. Retirees and lower ranks Space-A.

TML Availability: Good. Best, Dec-Feb.

CREDIT CARDS ACCEPTED: Visa, MasterCard and American Express.

Fort McPherson is steeped in history, and surrounded by the vibrant city of Atlanta.

Locator 464-2743/4174   Medical 464-3711   Police 464-2281

Fort Stewart (GA15R1)
Fort Stewart Guest House
4951 Coe Ave
Fort Stewart, GA 31313-5000

TELEPHONE NUMBER INFORMATION: Main installation numbers: C-912-767-1110, D-312-870-1110.

Location: Accessible from US-17 or I-95. Also GA-119 or GA-144 crosses the Post. *USMRA: Page 37 (G,H-7).* NMC: Savannah, 35 miles northeast.

Lodging Office: ATTN: AFZP-DPW-B. Bldg 4951. **C-912-368-4184, D-312-870-8384,** Fax: C- 912-876-7469, 0730-2345 hours daily. Other hours, SDO, Bldg 01, C-912-767-8666. Check in billeting 1400 hours, check out 1100 hours daily. Government civilian employees billeting TDY, PCS.

TML: Guest House. Bldg 4951, all ranks, leave or official duty, C-912-767-8384/368-4184. Bedroom, dining room, private bath (sleeps six) (70). Kitchen, A/C, CATV, housekeeping service, cribs/cots, essentials, handicap accessible, washer/dryer, ice vending. Modern structure. Rates: $24 per room per night. Duty and DAVs can make reservations, others Space-A.

TML: BOQ/VOQ. Bldg 4950, C-912-368-4184, officers all ranks, official duty only. Reservations accepted (VOQ), not taken (BOQ). Bedroom, private bath (45). Kitchen, A/C, color TV, housekeeping service, washer/dryer, ice vending. Modern structure. Rates: $24 per room per night. BOQ rooms, inquire at above number. Maximum one per room, bonafide bachelor only, E7+.

TML: DVQ. Officer O6+, leave or official duty, C-912-767-8610. Two-bedroom cottages, private bath (2). A/C, cots/cribs, essentials, ice vending, kitchen, complete utensils, housekeeping service, handicap accessible, color TV, washer/dryer. Rate: $24-TDY, $24-PCS. Active and retirees can make reservations, others Space-A.

DV/VIP: Protocol, Bldg 01, C-912-767-8610. O6+. Retirees and lower ranks Space-A.

GEORGIA
Fort Stewart, *continued*

TML Availability: Fairly good. Best, Nov-Apr. Difficult, other times.

CREDIT CARDS ACCEPTED: Visa, MasterCard, American Express, Discover and Espirit.

Local recreational activities are hunting, fishing, tennis and golf. Ocean beaches are within driving distance, and historic Savannah is 40 miles northeast with many attractions.

Locator 767-2862   Medical 767-6666   Police 767-2822

Hunter Army Airfield (GA10R1)
Hunter Billeting Office
Bldg 6010
Hunter Army Airfield, GA 31409-5206

TELEPHONE NUMBER INFORMATION: Main installation numbers: C-912-352-6521, D-312-971-1110.

Location: From I-95 to GA-204 E for 13 miles to Savannah. Turn left onto Stephenson Ave, proceed straight into Wilson Ave Gate to installation. *USMRA: Page 37 (H-7)*. NMC: Savannah, in southwest part of city.

Lodging Office: Bldg 6010, Duncan and Leonard Streets. **C-912-352-5910/5834, C-912-355-1060**, Fax: C-912-352-6864, D-312-971-6864, 0600-2400 hours Mon-Sun. After hours, SDO, Bldg 1201, C-912-352-5140. Check in 1400 hours, check out 1100 hours daily. Government civilian employee billeting.

TML: Guest House/VOQ/VEQ. Bldgs 6005, 6010, all ranks, leave or official duty. Two-bedroom suites, private bath (32); bedroom, semi-private bath (9). Kitchen, complete utensils, essentials, A/C, color TV in room and lounge, housekeeping service, cribs/cots, washer/dryer, snack vending, ice vending, handicap accessible. Older structures. Renovated and remodeled. Rates: $20-$40 per family. All categories can make reservations. PCS and TDY have priority.

DV/VIP: Commander, 24th Inf Div, ATTN: AFZP-CS-P, Bldg 1, C-912-767-7742, D-312-971-8610. O5+. Retirees Space-A.

TML Availability: Very good, all times.

CREDIT CARDS ACCEPTED: Visa, MasterCard, American Express and Discover.

Near historic Savannah. Hunting, fishing, coastal Georgian beaches.

Locator 767-2862   Medical 352-5551   Police 352-6133

Kings Bay Naval Submarine Base (GA03R1)
Bachelor Housing Office, Bldg 1056
952 James Madison Road
Kings Bay, GA 31547-5015

TELEPHONE NUMBER INFORMATION: Main installation numbers: C-912-673-2000, D-312-860-2111.

GEORGIA
Kings Bay Naval Submarine Base, continued

Location: Off I-95 N of GA/FL border. Take exit 1 which leads right into base, or exits 2A or 2B, east to Kings Bay and follow road north to base. *USMRA: Page 37 (G-9).* NMC: Jacksonville, 40 miles south.

Lodging Office: ATTN: Housing Office QL31, Bldg 1056, 952 James Madison Road. **C-912-673-2165,** 0800-1630 hours Mon-Fri. Check in billeting, check out 1200 daily.

TML: Navy Lodge. Bldg 0158, all ranks, leave or official duty. Reservations: **1-800-NAVY-INN**. Lodge number is C-912-882-6868, Fax: 912-882-6800. Check in 1500-1800 hours, check out 1200 hours daily. Bedroom, two double beds, private bath (26). Four sets interconnecting, two handicap accessible, non-smoking. Kitchenette, microwave, utensils, A/C, CATV, housekeeping service, playground, cribs, coin washer/dryer, soda/snack vending, ice vending. Meeting/conference rooms and exercise room available. Modern structure. Rates: $36 per room. Maximum four per room. Fifteen VCPs - tape rental at desk. Duty and retirees can make reservations.

TML: BEQ. Bldg 1041, enlisted all ranks, leave or official duty, C-912-673-2163/2164. Bedroom, private bath (142). Refrigerator, A/C, color TV, cots, essentials, soda/snack vending, ice vending, housekeeping service, washer/dryer, microwave, coffee pot. Meeting/conference rooms and exercise room available. Modern structure. Rates: VIP $16 for one person or two, $21 for three or more; all others $10 for one person or two, $13 for three or more. Maximum VIP and family suite $21, maximum for bedrooms $13. Maximum four per unit. Duty can make reservations, others Space-A.

TML: BOQ. Bldg 1056, officers, all ranks, leave or official duty, C-912-673-2165/2169. handicap accessible. Bedroom, private bath (38); separate bedroom, private bath (98). A/C, cots, essentials, soda/snack vending, ice vending, housekeeping service, color TV in room, washer/dryer. Meeting/conference rooms and exercise room available. Modern structure. Rates: $10-$23 per person, maximum $13-$30. Maximum four per unit. Duty can make reservations, others Space-A.

TML Availability: Good. Best, Oct-Dec. Difficult, Jun-Sep.

CREDIT CARDS ACCEPTED: Visa, MasterCard and American Express. Navy Lodge accepts Visa, MasterCard, American Express and Discover.

Transportation: Off base shuttle/bus: 673-6900, on base taxi ext 8294, off base taxi 673-6900, car rental agency 261-1050.

Winner of the 1996 Elmo R. Zumwalt Award for Excellence in Housing. From the beauty and history of old Savannah to the beaches of the Golden Isles near Brunswick and the Cumberland Island National Seashore, coastal Georgia offers everything from sightseeing to fishing and hunting.

Locator 673-2000   Medical 673-2001 ext 4221   Police 673-2001 ext 2147

GEORGIA

Moody Air Force Base (GA02R1)
347 SVS/SVML
3131 Cooney Street
Moody AFB, GA 31699-1511

TELEPHONE NUMBER INFORMATION: Main installation numbers: C-912-257-4211, D-312-460-4211.

Location: On GA 125, 12 miles north of Valdosta. Also, can be reached from I-75 Exit 6 via US-41 and Inner Perimeter Road as well as I-75 via GA-122. *USMRA: Page 37 (D,E-9)*. NMC: Valdosta, 10 miles south.

Lodging Office: Bldg 3131, Cooney Street. **C-912-257-3893**, Fax: C-912-257-4971, D-312-460-4971, 24 hours. Check in lodging at 1400 hours, check out 1200 hours.

TML: TLF. Bldg 3080, enlisted all ranks, leave or official duty. Two-bedroom, private bath (12). Kitchen, A/C, color TV, housekeeping service, cribs/cots, washer/dryer. Community motel design. Rates: E1, E2 and O1, $13; E3-E6, $19.50; E7 and up, $24. PCS in/out, permissive TDY with family or PCS, retirement, separation, out patients, friends, relatives of patients, all others Space-A.

TML: VAQ. Bldg 3080, enlisted all ranks, leave or official duty. Units, private bath (17). Refrigerator, A/C, color TV, housekeeping service, washer/dryer. Community motel design. Rates: $10 per person, $14 per couple. PCS in/out, TDY can make reservations 24 hours a day, Space-A may make reservations 24 hours in advance of their arrival date.

TML: VOQ. Bldg 3132, officers all ranks, leave or official duty. Bedroom, private bath (29). Kitchen, refrigerator, A/C, color TV, housekeeping service, washer/dryer. Community motel design. Rates: $10 per person, $14 per couple. PCS in/out, TDY can make reservations 24 hours a day, Space-A may make reservations 24 hours in advance of their arrival date.

TML: DV. Bldgs 3132/3080, officers O6+, E8-E9, leave or official duty. Bedroom suites, private bath (officer) (5); bedroom suites, private bath (E8-E9). Kitchen, A/C, color TV, housekeeping service, washer/dryer. Community motel design. Rates: $16 per person, $23 per couple. PCS in/out, TDY can make reservations 24 hours a day, Space-A may make reservations 24 hours in advance of their arrival date.

TML: Grassy Pond Recreation Area, C-912-559-5840, D-312-460-1110 ext 559-5840. Cabins: sleeps six (6); sleeps nine (7), private bath, kitchen, linens, dishes, pots and pans. Bring bath and kitchen towels, wash cloths, paper towels, dish detergent. Rates: $25-$35 daily. See *Military Living's Military RV, Camping and Rec Areas Around the World* for additional information and directions.

DV/VIP: Protocol Office, 347 WG/CCP, Bldg 5113, C-912-257-4144, O6+, E9, retirees and lower ranks Space-A.

TML Availability: Good, May, Sep, Dec. Difficult, Jun-Aug.

CREDIT CARDS ACCEPTED: Visa, MasterCard and American Express.

GEORGIA
Moody Air Force Base, continued

Visit the mansion Crescent, in Valdosta, for tours, particularly during Azalea season. There are many freshwater lakes for fishing and water sports. Dove, quail, turkey and other wild game hunting in season is also popular.

Locator 257-3585   Medical 257-3232   Police 257-3108

Robins Air Force Base (GA14R1)
78 SPTG/SVML
755 Warner Robbins Street
Robins AFB, GA 31098-1469

TELEPHONE NUMBER INFORMATION: Main installation numbers: C-912-926-1113, D-312-468-1001.

Location: Off US-129 on GA-247 at Warner Robins. Access from I-75 S. *USMRA: Page 37 (D-6)*. NMC: Macon, 18 miles northwest.

Lodging Office: Pine Oaks Lodge, Bldg 557, Club Drive. **C-912-926-2100, D-312-468-2100**, Fax: C-912-926-0977, 24 hours. Check in facility.

TML: TLF. Bldg 1180-1183, all ranks, leave or official duty. Check out 1000 hours. Bedroom, private bath (40). Kitchen, complete utensils, A/C, color TV, housekeeping service, cots/cribs, ice vending, washer/dryer. Older structure. Rates: $18. Maximum five per unit. Duty may make reservations, others Space-A.

TML: VOQ. Bldgs 551, 553, 557, officers all ranks, leave or official duty. handicap accessible. Check out 1200 hours. DV Suites (5); Sr Officer suites (5). Bedroom, private bath (40); Private bedroom, semi-private bath (4); 2-bedroom, semi-private bath (40). A/C, refrigerator, color TV, housekeeping service, cribs/cots, washer/dryer. Older structure. Rates: DV Suites $16; other rooms $10 per person, maximum family rate $28. Maximum four per unit. Duty may make reservations, others Space-A.

TML: VAQ. Bldg 755, enlisted all ranks, leave or official duty. Check out 1200 hours. Private bedroom, shared bath (24); shared bedroom, shared bath (2); 2-bedroom, shared bath (40); E9 suites, private bath (6). Refrigerator, A/C, color TV, housekeeping service, washer/dryer, ice vending. Older structure. Rates: $6 per person. Chief suites $16. Duty may make reservations, others Space-A.

DV/VIP: Bldg 215, C-912-926-2761 Mon-Fri. O6+.

TML Availability: Good, Oct-May. Difficult, other times.

CREDIT CARDS ACCEPTED: Visa, MasterCard and American Express.

Transportation: On base shuttle/bus available.

Macon, 18 miles northwest, is the geographic center of Georgia, where shopping, parks (this is the Cherry Blossom Capital of the World) welcome visitors with true Southern hospitality. Also visit the Museum of Aviation, home of the Georgia Aviation Hall of Fame.

Locator 926-6027   Medical 926-3845   Police 926-2187

94 - Temporary Military Lodging Around the World

HAWAII

Barbers Point Naval Air Station (HI10R6)
CBQ, Bldg 77
Barbers Point, HI 96862-5050
Scheduled to close July 1999.

TELEPHONE NUMBER INFORMATION: Main installation numbers: C-808-471-7110, D-315-484-6266.

Location: Take HI-1 W (toward Waianee) to NAS/Makakilo exit, south for 2.5 miles to main gate. *USMRA: Page 129 (C-7).* NMC: Honolulu, 12 miles east.

Lodging Office: C-808-684-3191/682-1327, D-315-484-9146, Fax: C-808-684-0704, D-315-484-0704, 24 hours. Active duty check in 0700 hours, check out 1200 hours, Space-A check in 1600 hours, check out 1000 hours.

TML: BOQ. Bldg 77, Hornet Street, officers all ranks, leave or official duty. Bedroom, living room private bath (77). Refrigerator, microwave, coffee makers, A/C, color TV/VCR in room and lounge, hair dryers, housekeeping service, washer/dryer, soda/snack vending, ice vending. VHS movies available for no charge - sign out at front desk. Meeting/conference rooms and exercise room available. Rates: Adult $10. No children. Maximum two persons per room. Senior officer suites (12), $25 per person. Duty can make reservations, others Space-A.

TML: BEQ. Bldg 1788, enlisted all ranks, leave or official duty. E1-E4 shared room, shared bath (53); E7-E9 bedroom, shared bath (32); E5-E9 private room, private bath (14); E7-E9 senior enlisted suites, private room, private bath (4). Refrigerator, microwave, coffee makers, A/C, color TV in room and lounge, telephone system, housekeeping service, washer/dryer, soda/snack vending. Golf clubs and carts, tennis racquets and balls. Meeting/conference rooms and exercise room available. Modern structure, renovated 1992. Rates: $8-$10 per person. No children. Duty can make reservations, others Space-A.

DV/VIP: Twelve rooms available. O5+. Rates: $25; E7-E9 $10. Renovated 1993.

TML Availability: Good, winter months. Difficult, summer months.

CREDIT CARDS ACCEPTED: Visa, MasterCard and American Express.

Transportation: On base shuttlebus 684-2153, off base taxi 422-2222, car rental agency 671-5399.

Easy access to commissary and exchange facilities. The southwestern coast of Oahu, known for its beautiful beaches. Check Barbers Point Rec Area listing for more lodging.

Locator 684-7395   Medical 684-4300   Police 684-6620

Barbers Point Recreation Area (HI01R6)
Morale Welfare Recreation Dept
Naval Air Station
Barbers Point, HI 96862-5050
Scheduled to close September 1997.

HAWAII
Barbers Point Recreation Area, continued

TELEPHONE NUMBER INFORMATION: Main installation numbers: C-808-684-6266, D-315-484-6266.

Location: Take HI-1 W to Barbers Point/Makakilo exit. Left at sign then go through main gate. Turn right on Saratoga, 2nd building on left, Bldg 1924. *USMRA: Page 129 (C-7).* NMC: Pearl Harbor, 10 miles northeast.

Lodging Office: Morale, Welfare, Recreation Dept, **Beach Cottages,** Barbers Point NAS, HI 96862-5050. **C-808-682-2019, D-315-430-0111/2019,** Fax: C-808-682-4235, 0900-1700 hours Mon, Wed, Fri 0900-1400 Tue, Thur. Reservations 60 days in advance via written request. Priority system in effect. Call for information. Confirmation four weeks in advance. Mail applications to MWR Cottage Reservations, Naval Air Station, Barbers Point, HI 96862-5050. Reservations for three days Fri-Mon, four days Mon-Fri, seven days Mon-Mon or Fri-Fri. Check in at area 1400 hours daily, check out 0900 hours daily. Cottages cannot be used as party facility. Operates year round.

TML: Rec Cottages, all ranks. Two bedroom enlisted cottages (14); 2-bedroom officer cottages (6), VIP cottages (O6+) (2). Kitchen, complete utensils, color TV (VIP only), cribs/cots, BBQ grills. Meeting/conference rooms, exercise room, mini-mart available. Rates: enlisted $35 per unit; officer $50 per unit; VIP $65 per unit. Maximum six persons.

DV/VIP: Administration Office, Bldg 1, C-808-474-4103. O7/GS-16+. Retirees and lower ranks Space-A. Flag Officer Cottages 1760 and 1775 (Space-A to O6+). Reservations: C-808-474-2101, D-315-430-0111, 315-474/1181, Fax: C-808-474-8751.

TML Availability: Good, Jan-Apr and Oct-Nov. Difficult, other times.

CREDIT CARDS ACCEPTED: Visa, MasterCard and American Express.

Complete beach recreation area. Check with Special Services, Ticket Office for tourist/island activities. Complete support facility at NAS. For full details see Military Living's *Military RV, Camping and Rec Areas Around The World.*

Locator 684-7395   Medical 684-4300   Police 684-6620

Barking Sands Pacific Missile Range Facility (HI04R6)
MWR, P.O. Box 128
Kehaha, Kauai, HI 96752-0128

TELEPHONE NUMBER INFORMATION: Main installation numbers: C-808-335-4111, D-315-471-6111.

Location: From the airport, take Hwy 50 W about 30 miles. *USMRA: Page 129 (B-2).* NMC: Waimea, eight miles south.

Lodging Office: BEQ Bldg 1261. **C-808-335-4383, D-315-471-6383,** Fax: C-808-335-4194, D-315-471-6194, 0630-1500 hours, Mon-Fri for reservations, after hours leave message. For information on MWR Beach Cottages call C-808-335-4752, D-315-471-67569. Reservations are made by application only. You may call or write to: MWR Department, Beach Cottage Reservations PMRF, Barking Sands, P.O. Box 128, Kehaha, HI 96752-0128.

HAWAII
Barking Sands Pacific Missile Range Facility, continued

TML: MWR Beach Cottages. All ranks, leave or official duty. Two-bedrooms, private bath, sofabed, sleeps six (9). Handicap Accessible. Kitchen, utensils, microwave, refrigerator, color TV, washer/dryer, iron/ironing board, outdoor BBQ, balcony, ceiling fans. All Hands Club, Shenanigans, Fatty's galley/mess hall Menehune Inn. Indoor/Outdoor gear rentals, fitness gym, craft center, pool, theater. Rates: couple $50, each additional person $4. All categories may make reservations up to 60 days in advance. Check in at Recreation Center (Bldg 1264), 1400-2100 hours, after 2100 hours check in at BEQ office (Bldg 1261), check out 1000 hours. A late checkout will be charged one (1) days rental fee, unless prior notice is made to reservationist.

TML: TQ. One-bedroom (15). Duty must make reservations 30 days in advance, others Space-A. Rooms offered at no charge.

DV/VIP: Two cottages set aside for O6+. Reservations made by application only, C-808-335-4752, D-315-471-6752, Fax: C-808-335-4769, D-315-471-6769, or write to: MWR Department Beach Cottages Reservations, PMRF Barking Sands, PO Box 128, Kekaha, HI 96752-0128.

TML Availability: Very good, Sep-Feb. Difficult, Mar-Aug.

This is truly the Navy's "Best Kept Secret In Paradise!!" Captain Cook's historic landing place, and Waimea Canyon, "the Grand Canyon of Hawaii" and a seven mile strip of white sandy beach are nearby.

Locator 335-4111   Medical 335-4203   Police 335-4523

Bellows Recreation Area (HI02R6)
Reservation Office
P.O. Box 220
Bellows AFS, HI 96853-5000

TELEPHONE NUMBER INFORMATION: Main installation numbers: C-1-800-437-2607, D-315-259-8841.

Location: From Honolulu Airport or Hickam AFB, take H1 East to exit 21A (Pali Hwy). Go north on Pali Hwy (Hwy 61). Turn right onto Kalanlanaole Hwy (Hwy 72). Clearly marked. *USMRA: Page 129 (E-7)*. NMC: Kailua, nine miles northwest.

Lodging Office: Write to: Bellows Reservation Office, P.O. Box 220, Tinker Road, Waimanalo, HI 96795-5000. **C-1-800-437-2607** from US Mainland**, All Others C-808-259-8841.** Priorities: active duty 90 days in advance, in summer and December holiday time frames, others 75 days in advance. Other times reservations taken up to 1 year in advance. Maximum 14 day occupancy, sponsor or family member may register. Deposit (one night's rent) required 10 days after reservations made, (MasterCard, Visa, checks, and cash accepted) cancellations 14 days prior to occupancy. Note: When reservation period includes a Friday, Saturday or Federal Holiday - the beginning date of a reservation may not be canceled without canceling the entire reservation. Reservation office open 24 hours. Check in 1400 hours, check out 1200 hours.

TML: Two-bedroom cottages. All ranks, leave only. See above. Cottages, private bath, 2-bedroom configurations (105) (single and duplex units), 50 for officers, 55 for enlisted. Kitchen, complete utensils, CATV, ceiling fans, cribs, dishes, linens, towels, bedding all furniture. Rates: Back row $47, ocean view $52.

HAWAII
Bellows Recreation Area, continued

TML Availability: Good, Oct-Apr. Difficult, other times.

CREDIT CARDS ACCEPTED: Visa and MasterCard.

On Oahu's northwest coast, about 16 miles from downtown Waikiki, turquoise waters and gorgeous beaches await your arrival! Beach front recreation center. For camping see *Military RV, Camping and Rec Areas Around The World.*

Locator (Mgr) 259-5428   Medical 257-3133   Police-259-5955

Fort Shafter (HI09R6)
U.S. Army Garrison Hawaii
Fort Shafter, HI 96858-5100

TELEPHONE NUMBER INFORMATION: Main installation numbers: C-808-471-7110, D-315-430-0111.

Location: Take HI-1 W exit at Fort Shafter, clearly marked. *USMRA: Page 129 (D-7) and Page 131 (D-2; E-1, 2).* NMC: Honolulu, seven miles east.

Lodging: Billeting, Bldg 228-B, Jarrett White Road, Tripler AMC, HI 96859-5000. **C-808-839-2336**, 0630-2200 hours daily. Write to: TAMC Billeting Fund, Tripler Army Medical Center, Tripler AMC, HI 96859-5000. Check in billeting or facility, check out 1100 hours daily.

TML: Cottages. All ranks, leave or official duty. Two bedroom, private bath (8); three bedroom, private bath (4). Kitchen (some) others refrigerator and microwave, complete utensils, color TV, housekeeping service, cribs/cots, washer/dryer. Older structure. Rates: 2-bedroom cottage $35; 3-bedroom cottage $40, each additional person $6. Children under twelve, free. Maximum seven per unit. PCS can make reservations and have priority; PCS out seven days maximum, reservation in advance, PCS in 10 days, others Space-A.

TML Availability: Fair, most of the year.

The oldest army post in Hawaii, part of the post is a National Historic Place. Visit the Bishop Museum in Honolulu, the Honolulu Academy of Arts, Mission Houses Museum, and don't miss the beach!

Locator 438-1904   Medical 433-6620   Police 438-2885

Hale Koa Hotel AFRC (HI08R6)
2055 Kalia Road
Honolulu, HI 96815-1998

DoD Conference Center

TELEPHONE NUMBER INFORMATION: Main installation numbers: **C-808-955-0555** (24 hours), reservations: **1-800-367-6027, D-315-438-6739** (official travel), Fax: C-1-800-425-3329 (24 hours, except holidays).

HAWAII
Hale Koa Hotel AFRC, continued

Location: At 2055 Kalia Road, Waikiki Beach, Honolulu, HI. Fort DeRussy, is on Waikiki Beach, between the Ala Moana Blvd, Kalakaua Ave and Saratoga Road, about nine miles east of Honolulu International Airport. *USMRA: Page 129 (D-7), Page 131 (F-4).* NMC: Honolulu, inside city limits.

Description of Area: This morale-boosting, all ranks hotel, was opened in October 1975. Fourteen stories with 814 guest rooms with views of the Pacific Ocean and Koolau Mountains. All rooms identical in size, with private bath, lanai, color TVs, room-controlled air-conditioning, refrigerators. Some rooms handicap accessible. Coin-operated washers and dryers available. Beautifully landscaped gardens, famous Waikiki Beach, swimming pool, and recreational activities: tennis, snorkeling, swimming, volleyball and racquet ball. Casual or fine dining: Pool side Snack Bar, Happy's Self-Service Snack Bar, Snack Shack, Koko Cafe, Bibas Restaurant, or the Hale Koa Room, the hotel's signature restaurant. Private banquets, meetings, and conferences arranged through the hotel's catering services. Live entertainment and dancing in the Warriors Lounge, pool side drinks at the Barefoot Bar. Fitness center with sauna and locker rooms, Post Exchange, jewelry store, barber and beauty shops, car rental desk and tour and travel desk. Three dinner shows each week: Hale Koa Luau, Tama's Polynesian Revue, and Tuesday Night Magic. The Hale Koa is a complete resort. Dress: aloha-wear at all times.

Rates: The 1997 double rates quoted below. For single occupancy, deduct $2 from double rate. For more than two occupants, add $10 per person to double rate (maximum of four persons permitted). Children under 12 are free in parents' room if no additional beds are required. Cribs available at $4 a night. Most rooms have two double beds. Ocean front rooms have king beds only. Daily rates based on room location (generally the higher floors reflect increased rates).

1997 Double Occupancy Rates per night Effective 1 October 1996

CATEGORIES Active, Retired, Reserve & NG Enlisted Grades Officer Grades DoD Civilians Others	I Leave/Pass E1-E5*	II Leave/Pass E6-E9 W01-CW3 O1-O3 Up to GS10/NF3 Widows/DAV**	III Leave/Pass CW4-CW5 O4-O6 GS11-GM15	IV Official Travel All Grades TDY/PCS(TLA) Leave/Pass O7-O10 SES Civilians Retired DoD Civilians Foreign Services
Standard	$53	$66	$75	$78
Moderate	$60	$74	$85	$87
Superior	$66	$81	$92	$96
Partial Ocean View	$70	$86	$98	$102
Ocean View	$77	$95	$108	$112
Deluxe Ocean View	$83	$102	$116	$121
Ocean Front	$91	$112	$127	$132
Deluxe Ocean Front	$97	$120	$136	$142

Rates are subject to change on or before Oct. 1, 1997
*Rooms for sponsored guests of E1-E5 will be charged at Category II rates. **100% DAVs with DD-1173.

Season of Operation: Year round.

HAWAII
Hale Koa Hotel AFRC, continued

Reservations: Required. Reservations will not be accepted more than 365 days in advance of arrival date of requested stay. Reservations may be made for a maximum of 30 days. Extensions permitted on Space-A basis. Write for reservation and information packet: 2055 Kalia Road, Honolulu, HI 96815-1998. **C-1-800-367-6027, D-315-438-6739** (official travel) or Fax: C-808-425-3329 0800-1600 hours daily HI time,.

Eligibility: Active duty, retired military (DD form 2 Ret-gray or blue), Reserve and National Guard (DD form 2 Reserve-pink/red), dependents (DD-1173 or authorized dependent card for Reserve & Guard), DoD civilians (current employee I.D. card) and all foreign military with orders to U.S.

Hale Koa Luau on Mon and Thu, $27.95 adults, $17.95 children under 12. Tama's Polynesian Revue Dinner Show Wed night in the Banyan Tree Showroom, $17.95 adults and $9.50 children under 12. The Tuesday Night Magic Show Mexican/Italian dinner buffet $18.95 adults and $9.50 children under 12. ID cardholders may sponsor guests.

Check out the Army Museum, Diamond Head, Honolulu Zoo, Waikiki Aquarium, and Ala Moana Center, not to mention Downtown Honolulu.

Hickam Air Force Base (HI11R6)
Hickam Lodging
15 SVS/SVML
15 G Street, Bldg 1153
Hickam AFB, HI 96853-5328

TELEPHONE NUMBER INFORMATION: Main installation numbers: C-808-471-7110, D-315-471-7110.

Location: Adjacent to the Honolulu IAP. Accessible from HI-1 or HI-92. Clearly marked. *USMRA: Page 129 (D-7) and Page 131 (B,C-3,4).* NMC: Honolulu, six miles east.

Lodging Office: ATTN: 15 SVS/SVML, Bldg 1153. **C-808-449-2603, D-315-449-2603,** Fax: C-808-449-3572, 24 hours. Check in facility, check out 1200 hours daily. Government civilian employee billeting.

TML: VOQ. Nine buildings adjacent to O'Club. Officers all ranks, leave or official duty. Bedroom, private bath (34); 2-bedroom apartments, living room, private bath (88). Kitchen, microwave TV, housekeeping service. Older structure. Rates: $12 per person, maximum $24 per family. Duty can make reservations, others Space-A.

TML: VAQ. Bldgs 470, 471, senior enlisted E7+, leave or official duty. Two-bedroom apartments, private bath (16) kitchen, microwave, TV; single rooms, private bath (24). Housekeeping service. Older structure. Rates: $12 per person, maximum $24 per family. Duty can make reservations, others Space-A.

TML: VAQ. Bldg 1153 (female); Bldgs 1166, 1168 (male), enlisted E1-E6, leave or official duty. Bedroom, communal bath (33). Housekeeping service. Older structure. Rates: $12 per person. Maximum two persons per room Duty can make reservations, others Space-A.

HAWAII
Hickam Air Force Base, continued

TML: DV/VIP. Bldg 728, officers O9+, leave or official duty. Bldgs 725, 922, 934, one and 2-bedroom apartments, living room, private bath (26). Kitchen, microwave, TV, housekeeping service. Older structure. Rates: $27 per person, maximum $54 per family. Duty can make reservations, others Space-A.

DV/VIP: PACAF Protocol Office, O7+, C-808-449-4526. Bldg 1153, C-808-449-2603.

TML Availability: Difficult, most of the year.

CREDIT CARDS ACCEPTED: Visa, MasterCard and American Express.

Waikiki, Pearl Harbor's historic war memorial, shopping and sightseeing in Honolulu, hikes in local parks that put you in touch with Oahu's natural wonders. Whether you want relaxation or excitement, it's all here.

Locator 449-0165   Medical 449-6194   Police 449-7114

Kaneohe Bay Beach Cottages (HI12R6)
Morale, Welfare and Recreation
TLF Bldg 3038, P.O. Box 63073
Kaneohe Bay MCB, HI 96863-3037

TELEPHONE NUMBER INFORMATION: Main installation numbers: C-808-471-7110, D-315-430-0110.

Location: Take H-3 to MCAS. Cottages are across from the airstrip along the coast line, near Pyramid Rock overlooking Kaneohe Bay. *USMRA: Page 129 (E-6).* NMC: Honolulu, 14 miles southwest.

Lodging Office: TLF. Bldg 3038. Reservation priority list available on request. Waiting list. For reservations for cottages call **C-808-254-2716/2806**, Fax: C-808-254-2716. Check in after 1400 hours, before 1800 hours. Check out no later than 1000 hours. After hours check in call C-808-254-2663 or C-808-261-5196. Closed Thanksgiving, Christmas and New Years Day.

TML: Beach Cottages, 2-bedroom, living room, dining areas, private bath (11); Studio units (24), including two handicap accessible. Rates: cottages $60 per day; studio units $55 per day. All categories can make reservations. No pets.

TML Availability: Fairly good.

CREDIT CARDS ACCEPTED: Visa, MasterCard and Discover.

MCB full support facilities. (For details see Military Living's *Military RV, Camping and Rec Areas Around The World*). Beaches, boating, or just plain relaxing. You won't regret your stay at Kaneohe.

Locator 257-1294   Medical 257-3133   Police 257-2123

Temporary Military Lodging Around the World - 101

HAWAII

Kaneohe Marine Corps Base (HI12R6)
Custodian Billeting Fund/Facilities Department
P.O. Box 63062, MCBH
Kaneohe MCB, HI 96863-5001

TELEPHONE NUMBER INFORMATION: Main installation numbers: C-808-471-7110, D-315-430-0110.

Location: At end of H-3 on the windward side of Oahu. Off Makapu Blvd and Kaneohe Bay Drive. Clearly marked. *USMRA: Page 129 (E-6)*. NMC: Honolulu, 14 miles southwest.

Lodging Office: Bldg 503. **C-808-257-2409**, 0700-2330 hours daily, holidays 0800-2030 hours. Check in facility 1400 hours, check out 1000 hours daily. Closed Christmas and Thanksgiving.

TML: Hostess House, Bldg 3038, 1/4 mile from main gate. All ranks leave or official duty. C-808-254-2716, all ranks, leave or official duty. Bedrooms, private bath, kitchens (24). One mile from Subway, Cajun Chicken, package store and enlisted club. One mile from commissary exchange and 7 day store. Rates: $40 per day, $65 with temporary living allowance. Maximum six persons per unit. Older structure. Duty can make reservations, others Space-A.

TML: BOQ. Bldg 503. Officers all ranks, leave or official duty, C-808-257-2409, D-315-457-2409. Suites, private bath (36). Refrigerator, community kitchen, color TV in room and lounge, housekeeping service, washer/dryer, ice vending, spa/jacuzzi and conference room available. Older structure. Rates: sponsor $19.50, maximum $6 each dependent. Maximum four per suite. Duty can make reservations, others Space-A.

TML: Bldg 386. SNCO bedroom shared bath (6), one VIP suite.

DV/VIP: FMF PAC Protocol, Kaneohe MCB, HI 96863-5001, C-808-257-2378. O6+. Retirees Space-A.

TML Availability: Good. Best, Nov-Jan. Difficult, May-Jun.

See Kaneohe Bay Beach Cottages listing.

Locator 257-2008 **Medical 257-2505** **Police 257-2123**

Kilauea Military Camp AFRC (HI17R6)
ATTN: Reservations Office
Hawaii Volcanoes National Park, HI 96718-5000

TELEPHONE NUMBER INFORMATION: Main installation numbers: C-808-967-88333/8343.

Location: On island of Hawaii, 216 air miles southeast of Honolulu, 32 miles from Hilo IAP. Scheduled bus transport to Camp, reservations required Hilo to KMC. *USMRA: Page 129 (I,J-6,7)*. NMC: Hilo, 32 miles northwest.

Lodging Office: ATTN: Reservations Office, Hawaii Volcanoes National Park, HI 96718-5000. **C-808-967-8333/8343**, Fax: C-808-967-8343, Oahu C-808-438-6707 reservations required. First come, first served basis regardless of rank one year prior to the requested arrival date during non-peak

HAWAII
Kilauea Military Camp AFRC, continued

periods. Include name, rank, service, status and list children and guest(s) when applying for reservation. Priority I, AD, call 90 days in advance or write 120 days in advance; priority II, retirees, 60 days in advance; priority III, DoD civilian and other authorized personnel, 45 days in advance. Reservations Office, 0800-1600 hours daily. Check in 1500 hours, check out 1100 hours daily. From Oahu, call toll free above number 0800-1600 hours daily. Others call direct.

TML: Apartments and Cabins (62, all with fireplaces). One-bedroom, private bath; 2-bedroom with kitchen, private bath; 2-bedroom, private bath; 3-bedroom, private bath; 4-bedroom cabin, private bath; two dormitories with common baths and showers for large groups. Refrigerator or kitchen, CATV, housekeeping service, cribs ($1.25 per night), rollaways ($1.25), coin laundry. Rec lodge, 18 hole golf course, deep sea fishing and helicopter charters, bus tours. Rates: E1-E5 $15-$51; E6-E9, W1-W3, O1-O3 $36-$63; W4, O4-O10, DoD Civilian $46.50-$72.25, up to two person occupancy, each additional person $5.25. No charge under age 5. Dormitories $5.25-$7.75 per night.

TML Availability: Good, fall, winter, spring. Difficult, summer.

CREDIT CARDS ACCEPTED: Visa, MasterCard and American Express.

On the rim of Kilauea Crater at 4,000 feet, temperature 50-65 degrees, quiet guest cottages, hiking, lectures, movies, support facilities, this is the place to get away from it all. For more details see Military Living's *Military RV, Camping and Rec Areas Around the World.*

Locator 967-7315   Medical 967-8367   Police 967-8378

Lualualei Naval Magazine (HI23R6)
3 Constellation Street
Waianae, HI 96782-4301

TELEPHONE NUMBER INFORMATION: Main installation numbers: C-808-474-4340, D-312-474-4340.

Location: Follow H-1 Freeway W towards Waianae to Ewa exit. Follow for Weaver Road south to Iroquois Point Road. Turn left and travel to West Loch Branch gate. *USMRA: Page 129 (B,C-7) and Page 131 (A-3).* NMC: Honolulu, 20 miles southeast.

Lodging Office: Bldg 600. **C-808-474-7908/7909, D-312-474-7908/7909,** Fax: C-808-474-7922, D-312-474-7922, 0600-2200 hours (after hours call C-808-474-4341/1832).

TML: BEQ. Bldgs 601, 602, enlisted E1-E6 AD on orders to Lualualei Naval Magazine and its tenants only. Two-person bedroom, shared bath (91). Refrigerator, A/C, TV in lounge, washer/dryer, snack vending, ice vending.

TML Availability: Extremely limited. No Space-A.

Locator 474-4330   Medical 471-9541   Police 668-3261

HAWAII

Pearl Harbor Naval Submarine Base (HI19R6)
Commanding Officer
Pearl Harbor, HI 96860-6500

TELEPHONE NUMBER INFORMATION: Main installation numbers: C-808-471-7110, D-315-430-0111.

Location: Off H-1, adjacent to Honolulu IAP. Clearly marked. *USMRA: Page 129 (C-7) and Page 131 (A-1,2,3; B-2,3; C-2).* NMC: Honolulu, five miles east.

Lodging Office: Smallwood Hall, Bldg 1723, **Lockwood Hall**, Bldg 662. **C-808-471-9188, D-315-430-9188,** Fax: C-808-471-2944, 24 hours. Check in billeting office. E-mail: c44tepearl harbor.navy.mil, HP: http:\\www.pearlharbor.navy.mil\BQ\,.

TML: BEQ/BOQ/VOQ/DV/VIP. All ranks, leave or official duty. Rooms and suites (18). Refrigerator, kitchenette, utensils, color TV in rooms and lounge, housekeeping service, essentials, washer/dryer, ice vending, soda/snack vending. Meeting/conference room, exercise room and mini mart available. Modern structure, renovated. Rates: $9 per person per night, maximum charge per family $16. Maximum four per unit. Duty can make reservations, others Space-A.

DV/VIP: O6+. C-808-402-8300 ext 1000.

TML Availability: Very Good, Nov-Jan. Difficult, Jun-July.

CREDIT CARDS ACCEPTED: Visa.

Honolulu is a short drive away.

Locator 471-7110   Medical 471-9541   Police 471-7114

Pearl Harbor Naval Station (HI20R6)
Bldg 1623, Barracks Road
Pearl Harbor NS, HI 96860-6000

TELEPHONE NUMBER INFORMATION: Main installation numbers: C-808-471-8053, D-315-474-5210.

Location: Off H-1 adjacent to Honolulu International Airport. Clearly marked. *USMRA: Page 129 (C-7).* NMC: Honolulu, five miles east.

Lodging Office: BOQ/BEQ, **C-808-474-5210,** Fax C-808-423-1704, 24 hours. Check in after 1500 hours, check out 1300 hours daily. Government civilian employee billeting BOQ.

TML: BOQ. Bldg 662, C-808-471-1201, officers all ranks, leave or official duty. Bedroom, private bath (192); Makalapa VIP suites (6). A/C, refrigerator, color TV, housekeeping service, washer/dryer, snack vending, ice vending, room telephones. Modern structure. Rates: sponsor $20, adult $4. Maximum two persons. Duty can make reservations, others Space-A. No children.

TML: BEQ. Bldg 1623, 808-471-8053 enlisted all ranks, leave or official duty. Singles only. Bedroom (84). Refrigerator, color TV, housekeeping service, washer/dryer, snack vending, ice

HAWAII
Pearl Harbor Naval Station, *continued*

vending. Modern structure. Rates: E1-E6 $9 per person. Bldg 1507, E7-E9 only. Bedroom, private bath (15), rates $16. Duty can make reservations, others Space-A. No dependents.

DV/VIP: CINCPACFLT Protocol, C-808-474-7256, O7+. Only O6 Space-A. Rates: $50.

TML Availability: Difficult. Best, Nov-Feb.

Visit the Bishop Museum and Planetarium to see what old Hawaii was like, Pier 9 at the foot of Fort Street Mall has spectacular views of Honolulu and the harbor from the Aloha Tower. Don't forget the Arizona Memorial and USS Bowfin.

Locator 474-6249   Medical 471-9541   Police 474-1237

Schofield Barracks (HI13R6)
Inn at Schofield Barracks
563 Kolekole Avenue
Wahiawa, HI 96786-6000

TELEPHONE NUMBER INFORMATION: Main installation numbers: C-808-655-4930, D-315-455-4930.

Location: From the airport take H-1 W until you see exit for H-2, Wahiawa/Mililani exit (right side). Stay on H-2 until it ends at a divided highway. At first light turn left on Kunia Road. Turn right through Foote Gate, left on Road A until it merges right onto Lyman Road. On Lyman take right onto Humphrey's. At stop sign turn left onto Kolekole Ave, inn is the next right. *USMRA: Page 129 (C-6).* NMC: Honolulu, 20 miles southeast.

Lodging Office: Inn at Schofield Barracks, 563 Kolekole Ave., Wahiawa, HI 96786. **C-808-624-9650, 1-800-490-9638**, Fax: C-808-624-5606, Check in 1500 hours, check out 1200 hours. E-Mail: theinn@innatschofield.com.

TML: Inn at Schofield Barracks. All ranks, leave or official duty. The inn has 192 rooms with private bath. A/C, color TV/VCR, microwave, refrigerator, coin washer/dryer, ice vending. Deli and mini mart available. Rates: One bed or two beds per room, single $68.50, double $95. One-bed with sofa sleeper $100. Reservations, PCS one year prior, all others 45 days in advance. No pets.

DV/VIP: Protocol Office, Fort Shafter, Bldg T-100, C-808-438-1577. O6+. Retirees and lower ranks Space-A. Primarily for TDY personnel.

TML Availability: Good. Most difficult summer.

CREDIT CARDS ACCEPTED: Visa, MasterCard, American Express, Diners' Club and Discover.

Transportation: On base shuttle 655-2248, on base taxi 655-4944, off base shuttle/bus 848-4400, off base taxi 422-2222, car rental agency 624-2324: Enterprise 622-0024.

In winter don't miss Major surfing meets held in Haleiwa on the north shore, just nine miles away, golf at Kalakaua, the post museum, and recreation equipment rental.

HAWAII
Schofield Barracks, continued

Locator 655-2299   Medical 655-4747   Police 655-7114

Tripler Army Medical Center (HI03R6)
Billeting
Bldg 228B, Jarrett White Road
Tripler AMC, HI 96859-5000

TELEPHONE NUMBER INFORMATION: Main installation numbers: C-808-433-6661, D-315-433-6661.

Location: Take H-1 W from Honolulu to Tripler exit. Turn right on Jarrett White Road to Tripler AMC. *USMRA: Page 129 (D-7) and Page 131 (D-1,2)*. NMC: Honolulu, three miles southeast.

Lodging Office: TAMC Billeting, Bldg 228B, Jarrett White Road adjacent to the Community Club, **C-808-839-2336**, (TDY-433-6905) 0700-2200 Mon-Fri, 0800-2200 Sat-Sun. Check in billeting 1300 hours, check out 1100 hours daily. Government civilian employee billeting.

TML: Guest House. Bldg 228B, 226E, 222C, 220D, all ranks, leave or official duty. Recently renovated, all rooms have private bath (69). Color TV, refrigerator, microwave, community kitchenette on each floor, housekeeping service, cribs/cots, washer/dryer, snack vending, ice vending. Older structure, renovated. Rates: $47, each additional person $6. No pets. Reservations accepted for TDY only. All others Space-A on day of arrival after 1400 hours.

TML: Fisher House. Note: Appendix B has the definition of this facility. C-808-839-2336.

TML Availability: Difficult. Best, winter.

Hawaii's rare and endangered plant life may be better appreciated at Haiku Gardens, Kaneohe, Foster Garden botanical park, and Paradise Park in Manoa Valley. Don't forget the Honolulu Zoo, in Kapiolani Park.

Locator 433-6661   Medical 433-6620   Police 438-7116

Waianae Army Recreation Center (HI05R6)
Bldg 4070, 85-010 Army Street
Waianae, HI 96858-5000

TELEPHONE NUMBER INFORMATION: Main installation numbers: C-808-668-3636.

Location: Located on west coast of Oahu. Take I-H1 W to HI-93 (Farrington Hwy) W to Waianae. Look for Aloha Gas Station on your left, turn left on Army St. *USMRA: Page 129 (B-6)*. NMC: Honolulu, 35 miles southeast.

Lodging Office: Rest Camp, Bldg 4070, 85-010 Army Street. **C-1-800-333-4158 (mainland) 1-800-847-6771 (outer island) 696-4158 (Oahu)**, 0900-1600 hours Mon-Fri. AD Army 90 days in advance. Other military personnel/retirees 80 days in advance. Reservist/DoD civilian 60 days in advance. Other federal employees 30 days. Deposit required. Twenty-one (21) day occupancy limit in a 60 day period. Year round operation. Check in 1630-1930, check out 1200 hours.

HAWAII
Waianae Army Recreation Center, continued

TML: Cabins. Leave, official duty, retirees. Two-bedroom cabins with kitchen (25); studio cabins with kitchen (5); deluxe cabins, 2-bedroom (9); deluxe cabins 3-bedroom (3). A/C, ceiling fans, refrigerator, color TV, deck, BBQ and picnic facilities, housekeeping service. Deluxe rooms have carpeting and VCRs. Utensils, dishes, bedding, tableware all furnished. Bring personal items and beach towels. Cribs (one time $5 charge), rollaways ($10 per night). No pets. Rates: deluxe 2-bedroom $65-$80 daily, 3-bedroom deluxe $75-$85 daily; standard 2-bedroom, with kitchen $50-$65 daily, studio with kitchen $40-$50. Three cabins constructed for handicap. Reservations in advance. AD Army 90 days, other duty and retired 80 days, reservists and DoD employees 60 days.

TML Availability: Good all year.

CREDIT CARDS ACCEPTED: Visa and MasterCard.

On the "Leeward" western side of Oahu, with the look of old Hawaii, and Waianae Mountain Range at 4,000 feet. The heart of "Pokai Bay" has one of the best beaches, snorkeling, surfing, swimming. Rentals, catering and meeting facilities. See Military Living's *Military RV, Camping and Rec Areas Around the World* for more information.

Locator 696-4158   Medical 911   Police 696-2811

IDAHO

Gowen Field (ID04R4)
Post Billeting
4200 W Ellsworth Street
Boise, ID 83705-8033

TELEPHONE NUMBER INFORMATION: Main installation numbers: C-208-422-5011/5366, D-312-422-5011/5366.

Location: From I-84, take Orchard Exit south, follow road approximately 1.5 miles to gate driveway. *USMRA: Page 98, (B-8).* NMC: Boise, two miles north.

Lodging Office: Bldg 669. C-208-422-4451, D-312-422-4451, Fax: C-208-422-4452, D-312-422-4452, 0730-1630 hours Mon-Fri.

TML Available: Army Lodge, BEQ, BOQ, CFQ, FEQ. Call lodging office or rates and accommodations. Exercise room and mini-mart available.

TML Availability: Good, Nov-Mar. Difficult, May-Jul.

DV/VIP: Office of the Adjutant General, Command Group Protocol, 4040 Guard Street, C-208-422-6179, O6+.

CREDIT CARDS ACCEPTED: Visa, MasterCard and American Express.

Locator 422-5011   Medical 911   Police 422-5366/5536

Temporary Military Lodging Around the World - 107

IDAHO

Mountain Home Air Force Base (ID01R4)
Sagebrush Hotel
445 Falcon Street
Mountain Home AFB, ID 83648-5000

TELEPHONE NUMBER INFORMATION: Main installation numbers: C-208-828-2111, D-312-728-1110.

Location: From Boise, take I-84 SE, 40 miles to Mountain Home exit, follow road through town to Airbase Road, 10 miles to main gate. *USMRA: Page 98 (C-9)*. NMC: Boise, 51 miles northwest.

Lodging Office: Sagebrush Hotel. 455 Falcon Street. **C-208-832-4661, D-312-728-6451,** Fax: C-208-828-4797, D-312-278-4797, 24 hours. Check in facility, check out 1200 hours daily. DoD civilians on orders are eligible.

TML: Hotel VOQ/VAQ, all ranks, leave or official duty. Bedroom, semi-private bath (90). Rates: $10 per person, $14 per couple. Refrigerator, community kitchen, microwave, A/C, CATV, HBO, housekeeping service, cribs/cots, washer/dryer, ice vending. Older structure. No pets.

TML: TLF. Sixteen houses with two, three or four bedrooms. PCS in/out, some Space-A. Private units with fully equipped kitchen, housekeeping. Rates: Airman Basic/2ndLt $12.00; Airman First Class/TSgt $19.00; MSgt+ $24.

DV/VIP: 366 WG/CCP, Bldg 1506, C-208-828-4536, O6+. Retirees Space-A. AD can make reservations, Space-A can reserve non-confirmed 72 hours prior to arrival. Units designated. Rates: $16.00 per night, $23 couple.

TML Availability: Very good, winter. Difficult, Jun-Aug.

CREDIT CARDS ACCEPTED: Visa, MasterCard, American Express and Optima.

| Locator 828-2111 | Medical 828-2319 | Police 828-2256 |

ILLINOIS

Charles Melvin Price Support Center (IL04R2)
SATAS-JH-C
Housing Dept, Bldg 102
Granite City, IL 62040-1801

TELEPHONE NUMBER INFORMATION: Main installation numbers: C-618-452-4211, D-312-892-4211.

Location: From I-70 take McKinley Bridge exit, cross Mississippi River, follow signs to Center. From I-270, cross river bridges and take first Granite City exit (IL-3) south to Center. *USMRA: Page 64 (C,D-7)*. NMC: St. Louis, seven miles west.

ILLINOIS
Charles Melvin Price Support Center, continued

Lodging Office: Bldg 102, Niedringhaus Ave. **C-618-452-4287,** 0730-1615 hours daily. Other hours, Security Office, Bldg 221, C-618-452-4224. Check in facility 1400 hours, check out 1000 hours daily.

TML: Guest House. Bldgs 101, 116, all ranks, leave or official duty, C-618-452-4287. Separate bedrooms, private bath (5); 2-bedroom, private bath, kitchen (2). Microwave, refrigerator, limited utensils, toaster, coffee pot, A/C, color TV, housekeeping service Mon-Fri, cots, washer/dryer. Older structure. Rates: sponsor $24, maximum $29-$34 per family. PCS reservations 90 days in advance, 30 day in advance.

TML Availability: Good, Nov-Mar. Difficult, May-Aug.

CREDIT CARDS ACCEPTED: Visa, MasterCard and American Express.

Nearby St Louis, with its cultural offerings, provides the excitement while small middle American communities make visitors feel right at home.

Locator 452-4211   Medical 331-4851   Police 452-4224

Great Lakes Naval Training Center (IL07R2)
Bldg 62
2701 Sheridan Road
Great Lakes NTC, IL 60088-5000

TELEPHONE NUMBER INFORMATION: Main installation numbers: C-847-688-3500, D-312-792-2002.

Location: From I-94 N or US-41 N to IL-137 (Buckley Road) to NTC. Clearly marked. *USMRA: Page 64 (G-1).* NMC: Chicago, 30 miles south.

Lodging Office: BOQ. Bldg 62. **C-847-688-3777, D-312-792-3777,** Fax: C-847-688-5815. BEQ. Bldg 834. **C-847-688-2170, D-312-792-2170,** 24 hours. Check in facility, check out 1300 hours. Government civilian employee billeting (if on official duty).

NAVY LODGE

TML: Navy Lodge. Bldg 2500, Meridian Drive, **C-1-800-NAVY-INN.** Lodge number is C-847-689-1485, Fax: C-847-689-1489, all ranks, leave or official duty. Check in 1500-1800 hours, check out 1200 hours. Bedroom, two double beds, private bath (50). Four sets interconnecting, two handicap accessible, 25 non-smoking. Kitchenette, utensils, A/C, color TV, phones, housekeeping service, coin washer/dryer, soda/snack vending, ice vending. Renovated July 1996. Bedroom, two double beds, private bath (100). Microwave, coffee, A/C, color TV, phones, housekeeping service, coin washer/dryer, soda/snack vending, ice vending. Rates: $48 per room (50 rooms for long term guests), $49.50 per room (100 rooms for short term guests). Maximum five per room. No pets. All categories can make reservations.

TML: BOQ. Bldg 62, ATTN: BQ, Bldg 62, NTC, Great Lakes, IL 60088-5121, Fax: C-847-688-5815. Officers all ranks, leave or official duty. Government civilians, all grades, official duty. Bedroom, sitting room, shared private bath (54); bedroom, private bath (1); suites, separate bedroom/sitting room, private bath (112); DV/VIP cottage, private bath (1). Refrigerator (kitchenette in cottage), microwave, iron/ironing board, color TV/VCR in room and lounge, game room, exercise

ILLINOIS
Great Lakes Naval Training Center, continued

room, washers/dryers, cribs/cots, soda/snack vending, ice vending, A/C, housekeeping service, essentials. Brick barracks structure. No pets. Rates: sponsor $23, each additional over age five $5.75; VIP $29, each additional $7.25. Maximum five per unit. Duty, Reservists, National Guard on orders and Medal of Honor recipients can make reservations, others Space-A. No pets.

TML: BEQ. Bldg 833, 834, Fax: C-847-688-4736, enlisted all ranks, leave or official duty. Bldg 833, E5-E9, bedroom, private bath (62); bedroom, private bath (76). Bldg 834, E6 and below, bedroom, private bath (214). Refrigerator, microwave, A/C, color TV in room and lounge, housekeeping service, essentials, coffee/tea, washer/dryer, snack vending. Brick barracks structure, renovated. Rates: E1-E6 $8; E7-E9 $13; VIP $29. Duty, Reservists and National Guard on orders can make reservations, others Space-A. DVEQs E7-E9. Retirees and lower ranks Space-A. Reservations required, call the Command Master Chief at C-847-688-3569. No pets.

DV/VIP: Commander, Bldg 1, C-847-688-3400. O6+. DVEQ Space-A E9+. Retirees and lower ranks Space-A. Check with commander, Bldg 1. Rates: sponsor $37, each additional person over age six $9. Maximum five per unit.

TML Availability: Good, Sept-Feb. Difficult, Jun-Aug.

CREDIT CARDS ACCEPTED: Visa, MasterCard and American Express. Navy Lodge accepts Visa, MasterCard, American Express and Discover.

Transportation: Off base shuttle/bus 1-800-654-7871, off base taxi 689-1050/473-5470, car rental agencies: Enterprise 1-800-325-8007, Hertz 1-800-654-3131.

Boating, swimming and all water sports are available through the marina Beach House. An 18 hole golf course, bowling center, and extensive other support facilities are available on base.

Locator 688-3500   Medical 688-4560   Police 688-3333/3340

Rock Island Arsenal (IL08R2)
SIORI-PW (Housing)
Bldg 102
Rock Island, IL 61299-7630

TELEPHONE NUMBER INFORMATION: Main installation numbers: C-309-782-6001, D-312-793-6001.

Location: From I-74 N in Moline exit to 3rd Ave W and follow signs to Arsenal Island located in middle of Mississippi River. *USMRA: Page 64 (C-2).* NMC: Quad cities of Rock Island and Molne IL and Davenport and Bettendorf in IA.

Lodging Office: Bldg 102. **C-309-782-2376, D-312-793-2376,** Fax: C-309-782-0133, D-312-793-0133. 0715-1545 hours daily, after hours report to police (Bldg 225). Check in housing office, check out 0900 hours daily.

TML: Bldg 60, all ranks, leave or official duty. (1) Fully equipped apartment ; bedroom (two beds), bath, kitchen, refrigerator, microwave, dinning area, TV, A/C, housekeeping service, washer/dryer.

CREDIT CARDS ACCEPTED: American Express.

ILLINOIS
Rock Island Arsenal, continued

While here visit the Rock Island Arsenal Museum, national Cemetery, Confederate Cemetery, and the Colonel Davenport House.

Locator 782-6002　　　　Medical 782-0801　　　　Police 782-5507

Scott Air Force Base (IL02R2)
The Scott Inn
375 SVS/SVML
Scott AFB, IL 62225-5000

TELEPHONE NUMBER INFORMATION: Main installation numbers: C-618-256-1110, D-312-576-1110.

Location: Off I-64 E or W, exit 19A west to IL-158 S, two miles and watch for signs to AFB entry. *USMRA: Page 64 (D-8).* NMC: St Louis, 25 miles west.

Lodging Office: The Scott Inn, Bldg 1510, F Street, **C-618-744-1200, D-312-576-1844** (front desk), Fax: D-312-576-6638 (for duty reservations only, no Space-A reservations), 24 hours. Check in lodging office, check out 1200 hours daily. Government civilian employee billeting in VOQ/VAQ.

TML: TLF. Bldgs 1550-1551, all ranks, leave or official duty. Separate bedroom, private bath, sleeps five (36). Exercise room, A/C, microwave, refrigerator, color TV, housekeeping service, washer/dryer, soda/snack vending, ice vending, beverages, snacks, stocked bar. Rates: $24. PCS to Scott can make reservations, others Space-A. No pets.

TML: DVQ. Bldg 150. **Essex House.** O6+, leave or official duty. Suites, private bath (10). A/C, refrigerator, microwave, color TV, housekeeping service, washer/dryer, ice vending, beverages, snacks, stocked bar. Rates: $14 per person per night, maximum $28. TDY can make reservations, other O6+ Space-A. Reservations made through Protocol, below number. No pets.

TML: VOQ. Bldg 1508. Officers, all ranks, leave or official duty. Bedroom, private bath (32); separate bedroom suites (2). Same amenities as above. Rates: $14, maximum $28. Bldg 1509 A,B. Bedroom, private bath (39); separate bedroom suites, private bath (8). Amenities as above. Rates: $12, maximum $24; suites $14, maximum $28. Bldg 1510 A. Bedroom, private bath (41); suites, private bath (7). Amenities as above. Rates: $8, maximum $16; suites $14, maximum $28. Bldg 1510B. Bedroom, private bath (37); bedroom, shared bath (14). Amenities as above, no stocked bar. Rates: $8, maximum $16. TDY can make reservations, others Space-A. No children under 18, no pets.

TML: VAQ. Bldg 1512. Enlisted, all ranks, leave or official duty. Bedroom, private bath, sleeps two (47); suites, private bath (9). Same amenities as above, except for stocked bar and snacks. Suites have officer amenities. Bldg 1513. Bedroom, private bath, sleeps two (44); bedroom, shared bath (4). Rates: $8, maximum $16. Amenities as above, no stocked bar, snacks. TDY can make reservations, others Space-A. No children under 18, no pets.

DV/VIP: AMC protocol, C-618-256-5555, D-312-576-5555. O6+. Retirees Space-A.

TML Availability: Fairly Good, Nov-Jan. Difficult, other times.

CREDIT CARDS ACCEPTED: Visa, MasterCard and American Express.

Temporary Military Lodging Around the World - 111

ILLINOIS
Scott Air Force Base, continued

Near the "Gateway to the West", visitors enjoy the cultural, sporting, and outdoor activities St Louis affords. Nearby small communities reflect the stability and warmth of middle America.

Locator 256-1841   Medical 256-1847   Police 256-2223

INDIANA

Camp Atterbury (IN07R2)
Bldg 506
Edinburgh, IN 46124-1096

TELEPHONE NUMBER INFORMATION: Main installation numbers: C-812-526-9711, D-312-786-2499.

Location: From I-65, take exit 76 (31N), left at Hospital Road. Enter post on Kings Drive at guard shack. *USMRA: Page 65 (E-6,7)*. NMC: Indianapolis, 45 miles north.

Lodging Office: Bldg 506. **C-812-526-1128** (phone and fax), 0730-1600 hours Mon-Thur and Sat-Sun, 0730-1900 hours Fri. Check in at lodging office.

TML: BOQ/BEQ. Bldgs 220, 221, all ranks, leave or official duty. Suites (4); bedrooms (170). Refrigerator, kitchenette, color TV (in some rooms), housekeeping service, washer/dryer, handicap accessible, ice vending, soda/snack vending. Meeting/Conference rooms, exercise room, and mini-mart available. Rates: $6-$10. Reservations required.

TML Availability: Very good.

Locator 526-1128   Medical 379-4441   Police 526-9711

Crane Division Naval Surface Warfare Center (IN03R2)
Combined Bachelor Quarters
Crane NSWC, IN 47522-5001

TELEPHONE NUMBER INFORMATION: Main installation numbers: C-812-854-1225, D-312-482-1225.

Location: From US-231 N or S exit to IN-45 or IN-645 to enter the center from the west. *USMRA: Page 65 (D-8)*. NMC: Bloomington, 22 miles northeast.

Lodging Office: Bldg 2682. **C-812-854-1176, D-312-482-1176,** Fax: C-812-854-4416, 0730-1500 hours. After duty hours, C-812-854-1225/1222, Bldg 1. Check in billeting.

TML: BOQ/VIP. Bldg 2681, officers, all ranks, leave or official duty. Bedroom, private bath (14); separate bedrooms, private bath, central kitchen, living room (VIP) (2). A/C, snack vending, refrigerator, microwave, housekeeping service, CATV in room and lounge. Older structure, remodeled. Rates: $11 per night; VIP suites $26 per night. Maximum two persons. All categories can make reservations.

INDIANA
Crane Division Naval Surface Warfare Center, continued

TML: BEQ. Bldg 2682, enlisted, all ranks, leave or official duty. Bedrooms, semi-private bath. A/C, essentials, snack vending, housekeeping service, refrigerator, CATV in room/lounge, washer/dryer. Modern structure, renovated. All categories can make reservations. Rates: single $11, each additional person $6.

DV/VIP: Bldg 1, C-812-854-1210. O6+. Retirees (Space-A same day reservation, for one night only on weekends).

TML Availability: Very good, all year.

CREDIT CARDS ACCEPTED: American Express.

Sportsman's paradise, 22,500 acres for hunting, fishing, boating. Camping available through the Marina. Nine hole golf course. Approximately one mile of nature trails.

Locator 854-2511   Medical 854-1220   Police 854-3300

Grissom Air Reserve Base (IN01R2)
Grissom Inn, Bldg 550
434 SVML
Grissom ARB, IN 46971-5000

TELEPHONE NUMBER INFORMATION: Main installation numbers: C-317-688-5211, D-317-928-5211.

Location: Off US-31, seven miles southwest of Peru, 65 miles north of Indianapolis. *USMRA: Page 65 (E-3)*. NMC: Indianapolis, 65 miles south.

Lodging Office: Grissom Inn, Bldg 333, Matador Street. **C-317-688-2596**, Fax: C-317-688-8751, D-312-928-8751, 16 hours daily, except training weekends, closed holidays. Check in facility, check out 1200 hours daily.

TML: VAQ. Bldgs 328, 329, 331, 332, enlisted all ranks, leave or official duty. Bed spaces (300). Refrigerator, A/C, color TV in room, housekeeping service, washer/dryer, snack vending, ice vending. Modern structure. Rates: $9. Duty can make reservations, others Space-A. No pets.

TML: VOQ. Bldgs 327-333, officers all ranks, 76 rooms. Rate: $10. No pets.

DV/VIP: CSG/ESO, Bldg 551, C-317-688-2844. O6+. Retirees Space-A. VOQ suites (2) VAQ suites (2). Rates: $14. No pets.

TML Availability: Good, Aug-April. Difficult, May-July.

CREDIT CARDS ACCEPTED: Visa, MasterCard and American Express.

If the Indianapolis 500 isn't excitement enough, try the historic Union Railroad Station, the Indiana Repertory Theater, the Bluegrass Music Festival, walking tours of Victorian Mansions, and Independence Day in Evansville.

Locator 688-5211   Medical 688-3353   Police 688-2503

NAUS

National Association for Uniformed Services

Let NAUS Represent Your Interests in Washington!

The ONLY Military/Veterans Association to Represent
- **ALL Grades**
- **ALL Ranks**
- **ALL Services**

Officer and Enlisted! Active, Reserve, National Guard, Retired, Other Veterans - Families and Survivors!

NAUS PAC

Our Political Action Committee.
Your Defense Fund for Military/Veterans Concerns!

Aggressive lobbying for military/veterans concerns is what we do best!

Join Today!

National Association for Uniformed Services
5535 Hempstead Way • Springfield, VA 22151-4094
TEL: 703/750-1342 or 800-842-3451• (FAX) 703/354-4380
E-Mail: NAUS@IX.Netcom.com
http://www.penfed.org/naus/home.htm

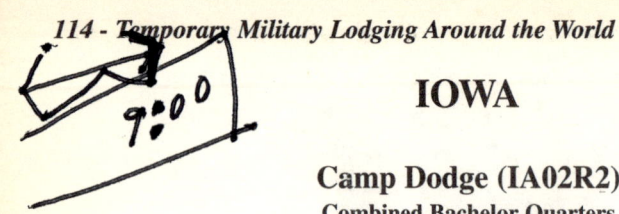

IOWA

Camp Dodge (IA02R2)
Combined Bachelor Quarters
7700 Northwest Beaver Drive
Johnston, IA 50131-1902

TELEPHONE NUMBER INFORMATION: Main installation numbers: C-515-252-4000 or 1-800-294-6607, D-312-946-2000.

Location: From I-35/I-80, take Merle Hay/Camp Dodge exit (exit 131); N on Iowa 401 approximately four miles to camp. *USMRA: Page 77 (E-5).* NMC: Des Moines, five miles southeast.

Lodging Office: Bldg A-8, 7th Street and Des Moines Ave. **C-515-252-4238 or 1-800-2946607 ext 4010, D-312-946-2238,** Fax: C-515-252-4092, D-312-946-2092, 0730-1700 hours daily. Check in Billeting Office, check out 0800 hours daily (late checkout call C-515-252-4238).

TML: TLF. Bldg A-5, all ranks, leave or official duty. Bedrooms, private bath (6), bedrooms, semi-private bath (4). Refrigerator, TV, housekeeping service, washer/dryer. Rates: AD $8, others $14. AD/reservists on orders can make reservations, others Space-A. No pets.

TML: BEQ. Bldg B-30, E7-E9, leave or official duty. Bedroom, hallway bath (6). Refrigerator, TV, A/C, housekeeping service. Renovated structure. Rates: AD $8, others $14. AD/reservists on orders can make reservations, others Space-A. No pets.

TML: BOQ. Bldg M-1, O1-O3 (male only), leave or official duty. Bedroom, hallway bath (13). Refrigerator, TV, housekeeping service. Rates: AD $8, others $14. AD/reservists on orders can make reservations, others Space-A. No pets.

TML: BOQ. Bldg M-3, O4-O5, leave or official duty. Bedroom, hallway bath (13), bedrooms, semi-private bath (4). Refrigerator, TV, housekeeping service. Rates: AD $8, others $14. AD/reservists on orders can make reservations, others Space-A. No pets.

DV/VIP: Bldgs A-2, A-4, A-7, A-18, A-62; O6+, leave or official duty. Bedroom, private bath (5). Refrigerator, microwave, TV, housekeeping service. Rates: AD $8, others $14. AD/reservists on orders can make reservations, others Space-A. No pets.

TML Availability: Good.

While here visit Adventureland Theme Park, White Water University Park, aquarium, zoo, and State Fairgrounds.

Locator 252-4000   **Medical 252-4235**   **Police 911**

… 115

KANSAS

Fort Leavenworth (KS04R3)
Lodging Operation
214 Grant Ave
Fort Leavenworth, KS 66027-1231

TELEPHONE NUMBER INFORMATION: Main installation numbers: C-913-684-4021, D-312-552-4021.

Location: From I-70 take US-73 N to Leavenworth. Fort is adjacent to city of Leavenworth. *USMRA: Page 78 (J-3)*. NMC: Kansas City, 30 miles southeast.

Lodging Office: Bldg 695, 115 Grant Ave. **C-913-684-4091 or 1-800-854-8627**, Fax: C-913-684-4397, 24 hours. Check in lodging after 1400 hours, check out 1000 hours daily. No pets.

TML: Guest House. Bldg 427, all ranks, leave or official duty, C-913-684-4091, D-312-552-4091. Two and 3-bedroom, private bath (12). Kitchen, complete utensils, A/C, color TV, housekeeping service, cribs/cots, room telephones, soda/snack vending, ice vending, washer/dryer. Meeting/conference rooms and exercise room available. Older structure, renovated. Rates: E1-E6 $25; E7+ $35. PCS can make reservations 30 days in advance, others Space-A.

TML: VOQ. **Hoge Barracks**, Truesdell Hall, Root and Schofield Hall. Officers/enlisted, all ranks, leave or official duty. Units (704), private and semi-private bath. Kitchen (some), A/C, color TV, housekeeping service, room telephones, soda/snack vending, ice vending, washer/dryer. Meeting/conference rooms and exercise room available. Rates: $16 (semi-private bath), $20 (private bath), each additional persons $5. TDY can make reservations, others Space-A.

TML: DV/VIP. Bldg 22 (**Cooke Hall**), Bldg 3 (**Thomas Custer House**), Bldg 213 (**Otis Hall**). Officers O6+, leave or official duty. Bedroom, private bath (8); Kitchen (some), refrigerator, utensils, A/C, TV, housekeeping service, room telephones, soda/snack vending, ice vending, washer/dryer. Meeting/conference rooms and exercise room available. Older structure. Rates: sponsor $20, each additional person $5. TDY can make reservations, others Space-A.

DV/VIP: Executive Services, C-913-684-4064. O6+. Retirees and others Space-A.

TML Availability: Difficult. Best, Dec. Limited, other times.

CREDIT CARDS ACCEPTED: Visa, MasterCard and American Express.

Transportation: Off base taxi 682-1229, car rental agency 727-2222.

Locator 684-3651/4021   **Medical** 684-6000   **Police** 684-2111

Fort Riley (KS02R3)
Lodging Office
45 Barry Ave
Fort Riley, KS 66442-5921

TELEPHONE NUMBER INFORMATION: Main installation numbers: C-913-239-1110, D-312-856-1110.

KANSAS
Fort Riley, continued

Location: On KS-18 and off I-70 in the central part of the state. Junction City, five miles southwest and Manhattan, 10 miles northeast. *USMRA: Page 78 (G,H-3,4)*. NMC: Topeka, 64 miles east.

Lodging Office: Billeting office, Bldg 45, Barry Ave, **C-913-239-2830/3525, 1-800-643-8991,** Fax: C-913-239-8882, 24 hours. Check in billeting office 1500 hours daily, check out 1100 hours daily. E-mail: allenl@riley-emn1army.mil.

TML: Guest House. Bldg 170, all ranks, leave or official duty. Bedroom, living room, kitchen, private bath (6); 2-bedroom, living room, kitchen, private bath (2). Older structure. Rates: $30-$35 per unit. Duty on PCS orders can make reservations, others Space-A.

TML: Guest House. Bldg 5309, all ranks, leave or official duty. Two-room suites, private bath (27); single rooms, private bath (3). Community kitchen, cribs, washer/dryer, soda/snack vending. Exercise room available. Older structure. Rates: suites $26, rooms $16. PCS can make reservations, others Space-A.

TML: VOQ/VEQ. Bldgs 45, 470, 471, 541, 542, 620, 621, all ranks, leave or official duty. Two-room suites, private bath, kitchenette (24); 2-bedroom, private bath, living room, kitchen (24); 1-bedroom, private bath, living room, kitchen (2); single rooms, kitchenette (61). Color TV, washer/dryer, soda/snack vending. Exercise room available. Older structures. Rates: $20-$35 per unit. Pet fee (Bldg 620 only) $10 per night. Duty on PCS/TDY can make reservations, others Space-A.

TML: DV/VIP. **Grimes Hall**, Bldg 510. **Bacon Hall**, Bldg 28. Officer O4+, leave or official duty. Bacon Hall is a 3-bedroom house for $40 per night; Grimes Hall offers Custer Suite for $30 per night; Stuart Suite for $25 per night; 1-bedroom suites for $20 per night (5). Kitchen, washer/dryer, soda/snack vending. Exercise room available. Older structure, all categories O5+ can make reservations by calling Protocol, C-913-239-8843.

TML Availability: Limited.

CREDIT CARDS ACCEPTED: Visa, MasterCard, American Express, Discover and Espirit.

Transportation: On base shuttle/bus 239-2636, on base taxi 239-2636, off base taxi 238-6161/6122/6131, car rental agencies 539-6261: Hertz 1-800-654-3131, Avis 1-800-831-2847, TC Auto Rentals 238-8133.

Don't miss the US Cavalry Museum, in Bldg 205, which traces the history of this illustrious post, the battle of the Little Big Horn, Wounded Knee, and then tour the Custer House.

Locator 239-9867   Medical 239-7777   Police 239-3053/MPMP

McConnell Air Force Base (KS03R3)
22 SVS/SVML
53050 Glen Elder, Suite 1
McConnell AFB, KS 67221-3504

TELEPHONE NUMBER INFORMATION: Main installation numbers: C-316-652-3840, D-312-743-3840.

Temporary Military Lodging Around the World - 117

KANSAS
McConnell Air Force Base, continued

Location: From the north, take I-35 (the Kansas Turnpike, which is a toll road) S to Wichita, exit at Kellogg Street (US-54) W to Rock Road, south to McConnell AFB. From the south, take I-35 (the Kansas Turnpike, which is a toll road) N to 47th Street, east to Rock Road, north to McConnell AFB. *USMRA: Page 78 (G-6).* NMC: Wichita, six miles northwest.

Lodging Office: Bldg 196, 53050 Glen Elder, Suite 1. **C-316-683-7711, D-312-743-6500,** Fax: C-316-652-4190, D-312-743-4190, 24 hours. Check in 1500 hours, check out 1100 hours daily.

TML: TLF (Bldg 193). Forty-five 1-bedroom suites. Fully furnished, equipped kitchen, A/C CATV, telephones. Housekeeping, washer/dryer, snack vending in Bldg 193. Rates: $24 PCS in/out may make reservations, others Space-A.

TML: VOQ. Bldgs 202, civilians and officers, leave or official duty. Suites, private bath (10). Kitchenette with refrigerator, microwave, A/C, CATV, telephones, housekeeping, washer/dryer, ice vending, sundries on sale in room. Rates: $10 per person, maximum $14. Official duty may make reservations, others Space-A.

TML: VOQ. Bldg 196. Civilians and officers, leave or official duty. Single rooms, private bath (20); suites (8). Kitchenette with refrigerator, microwave, A/C, CATV, telephones, housekeeping, washer/dryer, ice vending, sundries on sale at desk. Rates: singles $10 per person, maximum $14; suites $8 per person, maximum $16. Official duty may make reservations, others Space-A.

TML: VAQ. Bldg 319. Enlisted personnel, leave or official duty. Suites (38); private bath (6). Game room with pool tables, (snack vending, pinball, video games), fitness center, A/C, CATV, telephones, ice, washer/dryer, housekeeping, refrigerators, microwaves. Rates: $10 per person, maximum $14. Duty can make reservations, others Space-A.

TML: VAQ. Bldgs 202,. SNCOs, leave or official duty. Chief Suites (4). A/C, CATV, telephones, housekeeping, washer/dryer, refrigerator, microwave, ice vending, sundries on sale in room. Rates: $16 per person, maximum $23. Official duty may make reservations, others Space-A.

TML: DV/VIP. Bldg 202, officer O6+, leave or official duty. One-bedroom suites, private bath (4); 2-bedroom suites, private bath (2). A/C, CATV, telephones, housekeeping, washer/dryer, refrigerator, microwave, ice vending, sundries on sale in suites. Rates: $16 per person, maximum $23. Duty can make reservations, others Space-A through Protocol C-316-652-3110, D-312-743-3110.

TML: DV/VIP. Bldg 185, officers O7+, leave or official duty. Two-bedroom house, fully furnished, two private baths, kitchen (and utensils), washer/dryer, garage, refrigerator, microwave, CATV, A/C, housekeeping, telephones, sundries on sale in room. Rates $16 per person, maximum $23. Official duty may make reservations, others Space-A through Protocol C-316-652-3110, D-312-743-3110.

DV/VIP: HQ, C-316-683-6500, O6+. Retirees and lower ranks Space-A.

TML Availability: Good, Nov-Feb. Difficult, other times.

CREDIT CARDS ACCEPTED: Visa, MasterCard and American Express.

Visit Charles Russell, and others in the Wichita Art Museum, and Wyatt Earp in the Old Cowtown Museum. Stroll through one of the 80 municipal parks available to you, still restless? There are more than 600 nightclubs in Wichita.

Locator 652-3555   **Medical 652-3555**   **Police 652-3975**

KENTUCKY

Fort Campbell (KY02R2)
Billeting Office
Bldg 1581, Lee Road
Fort Campbell, KY 42223-5130

TELEPHONE NUMBER INFORMATION: Main installation numbers: C-502-798-2151, D-312-635-2151.

Location: In the southwest part of KY, four miles south of intersection of US-41A and I-24. ten miles northwest of Clarksville, TN. *USMRA: Page 40 (E,F-6,7).* NMC: Hopkinsville, 15 miles north.

Lodging Office: Bldg 1581, Lee Road. **C-502-798-5618, D-312-635-5618**, Fax: C-502-798-0602, D-312-635-0602, 0730-2100 hours daily. Check in facility 1400 hours, check out 1000 hours daily. Government civilian employee billeting. **NOTE: Ask about TDY/PCS/visitor billeting in this building.**

TML: Guest House. **Clifford C. Sims Guest House**, 26th and Indiana, Bldg 2601, C-502-798-2865, D-635-2865, all ranks, leave or official duty. Handicap accessible. Bedroom, two double beds, private bath (74). Community kitchen, refrigerator, A/C, color TV in room and lounge, housekeeping service, cribs/cots, washer/dryer, soda/snack vending, ice vending. Modern structure. Rates: double occupancy $32. All categories can make reservations.

DV/VIP: Protocol Office, Bldg T-39, C-502-431-8924. O6+.

TML Availability: Difficult.

CREDIT CARDS ACCEPTED: Visa, MasterCard, American Express and Discover.

Stroll Clarksville's Public Square and architectural district for turn-of-the-century buildings. Visit local watershed lakes for fishing and picnicking.

Locator 798-7196   Medical 798-8401   Police 798-2677

Fort Knox (KY01R2)
P.O. Box 1171
Fort Knox, KY 40121-5000

TELEPHONE NUMBER INFORMATION: Main installation numbers: C-502-624-1151, D-312-464-0111.

Location: From I-65 N in Louisville, exit Jefferson Freeway, 841 W to 31 W. Go south to Fort Knox. From I-64, exit I-264 W (Waterson) to I-65 S, to Jefferson Fort Knox to US-31 W south to Fort Knox. From I-71, exit I-65 S to exit Jefferson Freeway 841, west to 31 W then south to Fort Knox. Four entrances, look for main gate. *USMRA: Page 40,41 (H,I-3,4).* NMC: Louisville, 25 miles north.

Lodging Office: ATTN: ATZK-PWH, Bldg 4770 (**Newgarden Tower**), Dixie Hwy 31 W. **C-502-943-1000, D-312-464-3491,** Fax: C-502-942-8752, 24 hours. Check in/out as indicated. Government civilian employee billeting.

KENTUCKY
Fort Knox, continued

TML: Wickam Guest House. Bldg 6597, all ranks, leave or official duty, qualified family members and DoD civilians, C-502-942-0490, 24 hours. Check out 1200 hours. Bedroom, two beds, (50); bedroom, three beds, (24). Private bath, A/C, telephones, refrigerator, TV, cribs and microwaves available, washer/dryer, ice vending, soda/snack vending. Meeting/conference rooms, exercise room, and mini-mart available. Modern structure. Rates: single $15.50, double $35.50, each additional guest $3. All categories can make reservations.

TML: Guest House. Loriann Annex I. Bldgs 6625, all ranks, PCS only, C-502-942-0490. Check out 1200 hours. Two-bedrooms (16); five have private bath, others shared bedroom (1). Refrigerator, TV, pay phone in lounge, A/C in lounge, housekeeping service, washer/dryer, soda/snack vending, cribs, community kitchen. Meeting/conference room, exercise room and mini-mart available. Older structure. Rates: $10, no charge for additional occupant. PCS may make reservations, others Space-A.

TML: Guest House. Loriann Annex II. Bldg 6631, all ranks, PCS only, C-502-942-0490, 24 hours. Check out 1200 hours. Bedroom, two beds, shared bath (15); bedroom, one bed, shared bath (1). Refrigerator, TV, pay phone and AC in lounge, community kitchen. housekeeping service, washer/dryer, ice vending, soda/snack vending. Meeting/conference rooms, exercise room and mini-mart available. Modern structure. Rates: sponsor $10, no charge additional person. PCS may make reservations, others Space-A.

TML: DVQ. Bldg 1120, **Henry House**. Officers O7+, leave or official duty, C-502-624-6951, D-312-464-6951. Check out 1200 hours. Four-bedroom house (1). Kitchen, color TV, housekeeping service, washer/dryer, soda/snack vending. Meeting/conference rooms, exercise room and mini-mart available. Older structure. Rates: $27.50, each additional person $5. Duty can make reservations, others Space-A.

TML: DVQ. Bldg 1117, **Yeomans Hall**. Officers O6+, leave or official duty, C-502-624-6951. D-312-464-6951. Check out 1200 hours daily. Bedroom suites, private bath (10). A/C, color TV, refreshment center, housekeeping service, soda/snack vending. Meeting/conference rooms, exercise room and mini-mart available. Older structure. Rates: $27.50, each additional person $5. Duty can make reservations, others Space-A.

TML Availability: Good. Best, Nov-Mar. Difficult, other times.

CREDIT CARDS ACCEPTED: Visa, MasterCard, and American Express.

Transportation: Off base shuttle/bus and taxi 351-7373.

Visit the Patton Museum of Calvary and Armor, the US Bullion Depository, and Louisville, home of the Kentucky Derby and historic points of interest.

Locator 624-1141   **Medical 624-0911**   **Police 624-0911**

120 - *Temporary Military Lodging Around the World*

LOUISIANA

Barksdale Air Force Base (LA01R2)
Bldg 5155, 555 Davis Avenue
Barksdale AFB, LA 71110-2270

TELEPHONE NUMBER INFORMATION: Main installation numbers: C-318-456-2252, D-312-781-1000.

Location: Exit I-20 at Airline Drive, go south to Old Minden Road (.24 mile), left on Old Minden Road (1 block), then right on North Gate Drive (1 mile) to North Gate of AFB. *USMRA: Page 79 (B-2)*. NMC: Shreveport, one mile west. Co-located with Bossier City and Shreveport.

Lodging Office: Bldg 5155, 555 Davis Ave, second building on left after entering North Gate on Davis Ave. **C-318-747-4708, D-312-781-3091,** Fax: C-318-456-2267/1263, D-312-781-2267, 24 hours daily. Check in facility, check out 1200 hours daily.

TML: VAQ. **Barksdale Inn.** Bldg 5155, 4359, enlisted, leave or official duty. Handicap accessible. Separate bedroom, private bath (SNCO) (26); separate bedroom, shared bath (E-1-E-6) (74). Refrigerator, A/C, color TV, housekeeping service, cribs, washer/dryer, ice vending. Older structure, renovated. Rates: $10 per person, maximum $14 per day. Duty can make reservations, others Space-A.

TML: VOQ. Bldgs 5123, 5167, 5224, 2914, officers all ranks, leave or official duty. Separate bedroom, private bath (114); Bldg 5224, separate bedroom, private bath (O4+) (8); Refrigerator, A/C, color TV in room, housekeeping service, washer/dryer, ice vending. Older structure, renovated. Rates: Bldg 5167, $10 per person, maximum $14 per day; Bldg 5123 $10 per person, maximum $14 per day; Bldg 5224, $16 per person, maximum $23 per day. Duty can make reservations, others Space-A.

TML: TLF. Bldg 5243, all ranks, leave or official duty. Large family units (sleeps five) (16); small units (sleeps 4) (8). Kitchen, complete utensils, refrigerator, A/C, color TV, cribs, housekeeping service, washer/dryer, ice vending. Older structure, renovated. Rates: $24 per day maximum. Duty can make reservations, others Space-A.

TML: DV/VIP. Officer O6+, leave or official duty. Three-bedroom house, fully furnished, duty O7+ only, no retirees; one-bedroom suites, private bath (12); two-bedroom, private bath (4). Refrigerator, kitchen, complete utensils, A/C, color TV, housekeeping service, washer/dryer, ice vending. Older structure, renovated. Rates: $16 per person, maximum $23 per day; house $27 per person, maximum $39.5 per day. Duty can make reservations, others Space-A.

DV/VIP: PAO, 2nd Wing, C-318-456-4228. O6+. Retirees Space-A.

TML Availability: Good, all year.

Visit Barnwell Garden and Art Center, and the Shreveport-Bossier City American Rose Center, located in a 118 acre wooded park. Hunting and fishing in season on Barksdale, call Base Forestry C-318-456-2231/3353.

Locator 456-2252   Medical 456-4051   Police 456-2551

Temporary Military Lodging Around the World - 121

LOUISIANA

Camp Beauregard ARNG Training Site (LA12R2)
1111 F Street
Pineville, LA 71360-3737

TELEPHONE NUMBER INFORMATION: Main installation numbers: C-318-640-2080, D-312-485-8222/8223.

Location: Exit I49 at Alexandria, proceed north of US 165, turn right onto LA 116. Front gate located at first curve of LA 116. *USMRA: Page 79 (D-4)*. NMC: Alexandria, 5 miles S.

Lodging Office: Bldg 1111 F Street, **C-318-641-8269/8302.** Fax: C-318-641-8302, 0730-1600 Mon-Fri. Check in billeting, after hours Bldg 409.

TML: BOQ. Bldg 1101, all ranks, official duty only. Bedroom, shared bath (11); refrigerator, color TV in lounge. Meeting/Conference room, exercise room, snack vending machines available. Duty can make reservations. No pets allowed.

TML: BEQ. Bldg 1250, E6-E9, official duty only. Bedroom, private bath (9). Duty can make reservations. Meeting/Conference room, exercise room, snack vending machines available. No pets allowed.

TML: BEQ. Bldg 607, 608. Barracks facility, shared bath (20). Meeting/Conference room, exercise room, snack vending machines available. Duty, Reservists and National Guard can make reservations. No pets allowed.

DV/VIP: Contact Office of Chief of Staff, HQ Bldg, Jackson Barracks, New Orleans, LA 70146. C-504-278-8243. BC+.

TML Availability: Best, Sept-Apr. More difficult, May-Aug.

Locator 640-2080   **Medical ext 258**   **Police 641-8266**

Fort Polk (LA07R2)
Magnolia House
Bldg 522, Utah Avenue
Fort Polk, LA 71459-5000

TELEPHONE NUMBER INFORMATION: Main installation numbers: C-318-531-2911, D-312-863-1110.

Location: Off US-171 nine miles south Leesville. *USMRA: Page 79 (C-4)*. NMC: Alexandria, 45 miles east of Leesville.

Lodging Office: Magnolia House, Bldg 522, Utah Ave. **C-318-531-2941 or 318-537-9591, D-312-863-2941/4822,** 24 hours. Check in Magnolia House, check out 1100 hours daily. Government civilian employee billeting.

TML: Guest House. Bldg 522, Magnolia House. All ranks, leave or official duty. Bedroom, sleep sofa, private bath (70). Kitchen, microwave, color TV, housekeeping service, washer/dryer, snack vending. Rates: $27 all units. AD on PCS, visiting relatives and guests of patients in the hospital, and

LOUISIANA
Fort Polk, continued

active and retired military receiving outpatient care can make reservations, others Space-A. No pets in rooms, pet kennels Space-A.

TML: VOQ. Bldg 350, Woodfill Hall. Rooms (22); Bldg 331, 332, Cypress Inn Complex (two conference rooms with fax and computer ($10)). Rooms (58). Rates: first person $20, each additional person $5; cottages $20 first person, each additional person $5. Inquire about reservations. No pets.

TML: DV/VIP. Bldgs 8-12, 15, 17, 18, 426, 5674, officers O6+, DoD civilian GS-15+, and Sergeant Major of the Army. Official duty only. One-, two-, three- and four-bedrooms, private bath. Kitchen, complete utensils, A/C, color TV, housekeeping service. Older structure, renovated. Rates: first person $20, each additional person $5. Bldgs 11, 12 and 426 are $20 per bedroom and $5 each additional person. Upon request, personnel in grades O5+, on PCS in/out, may be given tentative, unconfirmed reservations. No pets.

TML Availability: Good, Oct-Mar. Difficult, other times.

CREDIT CARDS ACCEPTED: Visa, MasterCard, American Express, Discover and Espirit.

Best known for its outdoor recreation, the area is a paradise for hunters, and fishermen. Early Indian sites, a history that reads like a who's who of American legendary characters, and Lake Charles festivals are all of interest.

Locator 531-1272/3   Medical 531-3368/9   Police 531-2677

Jackson Barracks (LA13R2)
Military Dept, State of Louisiana
Bldg 57, Jackson Barracks
New Orleans, LA 70146-0330

TELEPHONE NUMBER INFORMATION: Main installation numbers: C-504-278-8364, D-312-485-8207.

Location: From I-10 to Claiborne exit to Jackson Barracks. USMRA: Page 90 (F-3,4). NMC: New Orleans, in city limits.

Lodging Office: Bldg 57, **C-504-278-8364, D-312-485-6207,** Fax: C-504-278-8715, Mon-Fri 0730-1600, after hours report to Security (Bldg 57). Check in 1500 at Billeting Office, check out 1100 hours.

TML: BOQ. Bldg 27, O1-O4, leave or official duty. Bedrooms, private bath (4), bedrooms, hall bath (12). Kitchenette, utensils, TV, washer/dryer Bldg 212. Rates: $10-$15 per person, maximum $20. Reservations required. No pets.

TML: BEQ. Bldg 209, E6-O4, leave or official duty. Apartments, bedroom (1 bed), sofa sleeper, private bath (1); bedroom (2 beds), private bath (2). Handicap accessible. Kitchenette, utensils, TV, washer/dryer. Rates: $20 per person, maximum $25. Reservations. No pets.

TML: BEQ. Bldg 214, E1-E5, leave or official duty. Bedroom, hall bath (11). Refrigerator, TV, washer/dryer in Bldg 212. Bldg 301, E1-E4, open bay barracks, male and female separate sides, 70 beds, TV in lounge, washer/dryer. Rates: Bldg 214, $8 per person, maximum $16; Bldg 301, $5. Reservations required.

LOUISIANA
Jackson Barracks, continued

DV/VIP: Bldg 24, 30, 49, 50, O5+, leave or official duty. Bldg 24, bedroom, private bath (2); Bldg 30, bedroom, private bath (1); Bldg 49, apartment (1); Bldg 50, apartment (2). Kitchenette, utensils, TV available. Rates: Bldgs 24 and 30, $30 per person, maximum $40; Bldgs 49 and 50, $25 per person, maximum $35. Reservations required. No pets.

TML Availability: Fairly good Jan-May and Sept-Dec. Most difficult Jun-Aug.

Locator 278-8364   **Medical 278-8011**   **Police 278-8460**

New Orleans Naval Air Station/Joint Reserve Base (LA11R2)
Bldg 40, Rinerd Road
Bell Chase, LA 70143-1001

TELEPHONE NUMBER INFORMATION: Main installation numbers: C-504-678-3011, D-312-363-3011.

Location: Off LA-23 in Belle Chase. Clearly marked. *USMRA: Page 79 (H-7) and Page 90 (F-6).* NMC: New Orleans, 13 miles north.

Lodging Office: BOQ/BEQ, Bldg 40, 4th Street, **C-504-678-3841**, Fax: C-504-392-1959 (BOQ/BEQ), 24 hours. Check in facility 1400, check out 1300 hours daily. Government civilian employee billeting.

TML: BOQ/BEQ. Bedrooms with shared or private bath (BOQ). Double room, shared bath (BEQ) Refrigerator, A/C, color TV in room and lounge, housekeeping service, ice vending, washer/dryer. Older structure-renovations planned 1998. Facilities available for all ranks, leave or official duty. Rates: $8 per person per night (BOQ); $4 per person per night (BEQ). Duty can make reservations, others Space-A.

TML: MWR Campground, C-504-678-3448/3142, D-312-363-3448/3142, Fax: C-504-678-3552, D-312-363-3552. Mobile home (1); 2-bedroom, linens, fully equipped kitchen. Rates: $30 daily. **See** *Military Living's Military RV, Camping and Rec Areas Around the World* **for additional information and directions.**

DV/VIP: CO, Bldg 46, C-504-678-3202, O6+. Retirees Space-A.

TML Availability: Good, except on drill weekends.

CREDIT CARDS ACCEPTED: Visa, MasterCard and American Express.

Should you be unable to get lodging here, don't forget there is a Navy Lodge at the Naval Support Activity nearby, call **1-800-NAVY-INN.**

Locator 678-3253   **Medical 678-3663**   **Police-678-3265**

124 - Temporary Military Lodging Around the World

LOUISIANA

New Orleans Naval Support Activity (LA06R2)
BEQ, Bldg 703 / BOQ Bldg 700
New Orleans, LA 70142-5007

TELEPHONE NUMBER INFORMATION: Main installation numbers: C-504-678-2655/6, D-312-485-2655/6.

Location: On the west bank of Mississippi River. From east, from I-10 east, take exit 235 B (right) to Cleveland Ave, to Claiborne Ave, right to Claiborne Center Lane ahead 3 stop lights to I-10, follow Business District/Westbank, Gretna signs (90W) across Mississippi River, take first exit (right) off bridge and follow Gen DeGaulle signs to left. Left turn on Shirley Drive and follow to end. Base is on Gen Meyer Ave at foot of Shirley Drive. Take Gen DeGaulle east exit after passing over bridge and turn left at Shirley Drive which leads to NSA. *USMRA: Page 90 (E,F-3,4).* NMC: New Orleans, 5 miles east.

Lodging Office: None.

TML: BOQ/BEQ. Bldgs 700, 703, 705, 710. All ranks, leave or official duty. BOQ **C-504-678-2264, D-312-678-2264**, Fax: C-504-678-2318, D-312-678-2318; BEQ **C-504-678-2252/2220, D-312-485-2252/2220,** Fax: C-504-678-2781, D-312-678-2781, 24 hours. Check in at facility, check out 1200 hours. Government civilian employee lodging. Bedroom, private bath (255); suites, private bath (12); VIP (2), reservations 45 days in advance. A/C, color TV, housekeeping service, essentials, washer/dryer, ice vending, soda/snack vending, minimart. Meeting/conference rooms and exercise room available. Barracks structure, renovated. Rates: BEQ $6; BOQ $10;. Duty, Reservists and National Guard on orders may make reservations, leave and retirees Space-A. No pets.

DV/VIP: BOQ VIP $10, **C-504-678-2104**; BEQ VIP $23, **504-678-2208**. O6+; E7+, lower ranks Space-A. No retirees.

NAVY LODGE
TML: Navy Lodge. Bldg 702, 2300 General Meyer Ave, New Orleans, LA 70142-5060, 0700-2000 hours daily. Check in 1500-1800, check out 1200 hours. All ranks, leave or official duty. Reservations: 1-800-NAVY-INN. Lodge number is C-504-366-3266, Fax: C-504-362-3752. Bedroom, 2 double beds, private bath (22) (recently remodeled). Three sets interconnecting, 11 non-smoking. Kitchen, microwave, utensils, A/C, CATV, VCP, clocks, coffee/tea, housekeeping service, cribs, high chairs, irons/ironing board, soda/snack vending, rollaways, safety deposit box, playground, ice vending, coin washer/dryer, ramps for DAVs. Modern structure, remodeled. Smoking and non-smoking rooms available. Rates: $42 per unit. Maximum four per unit. All categories can make reservations.

TML Availability: Good, Nov-Jan. Difficult, Apr-Sep.

CREDIT CARDS ACCEPTED: BOQ accepts Visa and Master card. BEQ accepts American Express. The Navy Lodge accepts Visa, MasterCard, American Express and Discover.

Transportation: Off base taxi.

Visit stately old homes, take a paddle-wheel boat dinner cruise, visit the new zoo, and the Aquarium of the Americas. Take in the Garden District and Bourbon Street. The French Quarter is made for strolling. One half block to Special Services and tickets!

Locator 678-3011   Medical 911   Police 678-2570

MAINE

Bangor Air National Guard Base (ME10R1)
Pine Tree Inn, Bldg 346
22 Cleveland Ave
Bangor ANGB, ME 04401-3099

TELEPHONE NUMBER INFORMATION: Main installation numbers: C-207-990-7700, D-312-698-7700.

Location: Located in Bangor city limits. Northbound on I-95 take exit 45B (West on Route 2). Turn right at Odlin Road (first set traffic lights). One mile, Cleveland Street on the right. Up the hill, Pine Tree Inn is located in Bldg 346, 22 Cleveland Ave. *USMRA: Page 18 (E-6,7)*. NMC: Bangor, in city limits.

Lodging Office: Pine Tree Inn, Bldg 346, 22 Cleveland Avenue, **C-207-942-2081**.

TML: The Army National Guard operates Pine Tree Inn for military members, retirees, and their families, C-207-942-2081. Check out 1200 hours. Bedroom, semi-private bath (46). Community kitchen, essentials, housekeeping service, refrigerator, color TV lounge, washer/dryer. Rates: official users $6 per night, non-official $11. Duty can make reservations, others Space-A.

DV/VIP: No Protocol Office.

TML Availability: Fairly good any time.

| Locator 990-7700 | Medical 911 | Police 911 |

Freeport Maine, home of millions of outlet shoppers, is an easy drive from Bangor ANGB. Don't miss this opportunity to go broke saving money!

Brunswick Naval Air Station (ME07R1)
351 Sewall Street
NAS Brunswick, ME 04011-5000

TELEPHONE NUMBER INFORMATION: Main installation numbers: C-207-921-1110, D-312-476-1110.

Location: From I-95 north exit US-1 north to Brunswick, Old Bath Road (Route 24) to main gate of NAS. *USMRA: Page 18 (C-9)*. NMC: Portland, 30 miles southwest.

Lodging Office: Bldg 220, **C-207-921-2245**, Fax: (BEQ) C-207-729-0232, (BOQ) C-207-921-2492, 24 hours. Check in facility (Space-A check in at 1800), check out 1100 hours. No government civilian employee billeting.

NAVY LODGE TML: .Navy Lodge. Bldg 364. **Topsham Annex, off base, call lodge for directions.** All ranks, leave or official duty. Reservations call **1-800-NAVY-INN**. Lodge C-207-725-6268, Fax: 207-721-9028, 0800-2000 hours. Check in 1500-1800, check out 1200 hours. Other hours OD, C-207-921-2214. Fax: C-207-721-9028.

MAINE
Brunswick Naval Air Station, continued

Livingroom, bedroom, double bed, private bath (12); bedroom, double bed, private bath (2). Kitchenette, microwave, utensils, CATV (HBO), VCPs, clocks, cots, cribs, snack vending, iron/ironing board, mini-mart, playground, rollaways, housekeeping service, coin washer/dryer. Older structure. Rates: $37-$40 per unit. All categories can make reservations.

TML: BOQ/BEQ, All ranks, leave or official duty. BOQ, bedroom, private bath, living area, refrigerator, community kitchen, limited utensils, color TV, VCP, video rentals, housekeeping services, cots, washer/dryer, ice vending, picnic tables, tennis, sauna, gym. Older structure. BEQ, single, double rooms, private bath, refrigerators, microwaves, coffee pots, color TV, housekeeping services, cots, washer/dryer, picnic tables, tennis courts, gym. Older Structure. Rates: BOQ: Transient and PCS $12; suites $24. BEQ, single $8; double $6; suites $16. Families authorized on space available only. Duty can make reservations.

DV/VIP: Brunswick NAS, Bldg 512, C-207-921-2568/2386/2214, O5+, retirees Space-A.

TML Availability: Good, Sep-Jan. Difficult, Apr-Aug.

CREDIT CARDS ACCEPTED: Visa, MasterCard and American Express. The Navy Lodge accepts Visa, MasterCard, American Express and Discover.

Fishing and hunting are considered "tops" here, 60 ski areas, including Sugarloaf (it has a 9,000 foot gondola line) make winter skiing here a favorite. But if you've never tasted shrimp and lobster, do it here! Freeport (home of L.L. Bean) is just 15 minutes south.

Locator 921-1110   **Medical 921-2610**   **Police 921-2585**

Cutler Naval Computer and Telecommunications Station (ME08R1)
Morale Welfare and Recreation
HC 69, Box 1198
Cutler, ME 04626-9603

TELEPHONE NUMBER INFORMATION: Main installation numbers: C-207-259-8203, D-312-476-7203.

Location: Take Hwy 95 to Bangor; 395 around Bangor; Routes 1A and 1 to East Machias; 191 to base (7 miles off route 1). *USMRA: Page 18 (G,H-7).* NMC: Bangor, 90 miles west.

Lodging Office: None. **C-207-259-8284/8201.** Check in MWR Hobby Shop, 0730-1600 hours daily. Check out 1200. After duty hours, Quarterdeck, Bldg 500.

TML: Rustic cabins (1), at Sprague's Neck, all ranks, leave or official duty. No electricity. Gas lights, wood stove, running water and indoor toilet. Kitchenette and utensils. Pets allowed. Call for further information and rates. All categories can make reservations (available Apr through Sep only).

TML Availability: Extremely limited, best Apr to Sep.

A real rustic get away for hiking, fishing, swimming, canoeing, or enjoying friendly "down east folks".

MAINE
Cutler Naval Computer and Telecommunications Station, continued

Locator 259-8229   Medical 259-8209   Police 259-8267

Winter Harbor Naval Security Group Activity (ME09R1)
10 Fabbri Green, Suite 84
Winter Harbor, ME 04693-0900

TELEPHONE NUMBER INFORMATION: Main installation numbers: C-207-963-5534, D-312-476-9011.

Location: From Ellsworth, take US-1 north to ME-186 east to Acadia National Park. Naval Security Station is on Schoodic Point in the park. *USMRA: Page 18 (F-8).* NMC: Bangor, 45 miles northwest.

Lodging Office: Combined billeting office in Bldg 84, **C-207-963-5534 ext 223/203, D-312-476-9223 ext 223/203,** 24 hours. Check in billeting, check out 1300 hours daily. Government civilian employee billeting.

TML: BEQ. Bldg 84, enlisted, leave or official duty. Bedroom, shared bath (E1-E6) (12); bedroom, shared bath (24); bedroom, shared bath (E7-E9) (6). Refrigerator, community kitchen, CATV/VCR in room and lounge, housekeeping service washer/dryer. Modern structure, new 1991. Rates: $4.

TML: BOQ. Bldg 192, officers all ranks, leave or official duty. Bedroom, private bath (4). Kitchen, limited utensils, CATV, housekeeping service, washer/dryer. Modern structure. Rates: $8 per person. Maximum two per room. Duty can make reservations, others Space-A.

TML: MWR cabins and house trailers, **Winter Harbor Recreation Area**. All ranks, leave or official duty, retirees, family members, **C-207-963-5537.** Cabins, 3-bedroom, private bath, fully furnished, sleep 5 (6). Each cabin has a gas fireplace and a TV/VCR. One of the cabins (Knox) is handicap accessible; house trailers, new, 70 by 14 feet, 3-bedroom, 1.5 baths, full size living room, fully equipped kitchen, washer dryer (5). Pets allowed in trailers for additional $10 fee. Full range of recreational opportunities, both summer and winter available. Close to base support activities. Rates: $50, May-Oct. All categories may make reservations 90 days in advance.

TML Availability: Good, Nov-Mar. Difficult, May-Sep.

CREDIT CARDS ACCEPTED: Visa, MasterCard, American Express and Diners' Club.

Located in Schoodic Point section of Acadia National Park, this is a favorite with hunters, fishermen, snow and water skiers. For additional information on the rec area, read *Military RV, Camping and Rec Areas Around the World.*

Locator 963-5534/5535   Medical ext 297/298   Police ext 2020

MARYLAND

Note: As of 1 May 1997, Maryland's telephone system went to a 10-digit dialing system. Regardless of the originating location, all phone calls must include the area code. Later in 1997 two new area codes (443, to work within the 410 area code and 240 to work within the 301 area code) will be added. Keep up to date on these and other changes with Military Living's R&R Space-A Report®.

Aberdeen Proving Ground (MD11R1)
2201 Aberdeen Blvd
Aberdeen PG, MD 21005-5001

TELEPHONE NUMBER INFORMATION: Main installation numbers: (Aberdeen Area) C-410-278-5201,(Aberdeen Area) D-312-298-1110, (Edgewood Area) C-410-671-5201, (Edgewood Area) D-312-584-1110.

Location: Aberdeen Area: take exit 85 east from I-95 north on MD-22 east for 2 miles to main gate. Also, from US-40 north to right on Maryland Blvd, entrance to main gate. NMC: Baltimore, 23 miles southwest. Edgewood Area: take exit 77 from I-95 north on MD-24 east for 2 miles to main gate. Also, from US-40 right on MD-24 to main gate. *USMRA: Page 42 (G-2,3).* NMC: Baltimore, 13 miles southwest.

Lodging Office: Bldg 2207, Bel Air Street, 24 hours. **C-410-278-5148/5149, D-312-298-4373/5148,** Fax: C-410-273-6500 ext 7310, E-mail: kthurma@apg-9army.mil. Check in 1300 hours, check out 1100 hours.

TML: Guest House, check in at front desk, Bldg 3322, all ranks, leave or official duty, C-410-278-3856, D-312-298-3856. Bedroom, 2 double beds, private bath (37); one to four bedroom apartments, private bath (18). Refrigerator, microwave, A/C, color TV in room and lounge, housekeeping service, cribs, cots, washer/dryer, ice vending, soda/snack vending. Meeting/conference room and exercise room available. Modern structure. Rates: E1-E4 $22; E5-E7, W1, O1-O2 $28; E8-E9, O3+ $31.50. Maximum five per room. TDY, permanent party, and PCS-in/out can make reservations, others Space-A.

TML: VOQ/VEQ. Several buildings, all ranks; official duty, C-410-278-5148/49. Check out 1100 hours. Bedroom, private bath (214); separate bedroom, semi-private bath (120). Essentials, kitchenette, A/C, color TV in room and lounge, housekeeping service, washer/dryer, soda/snack vending. Meeting/conference room and exercise room available. Older structure, recently remodeled. Rates: $31.50 per night. Maximum one per room. No pets allowed. Active duty, reservists and national guard can make reservations.

TML: DV/VIP. Bldg 30 officers O6+, GS-15 and above, leave or official duty, C-410-278-5156. Two separate bedrooms, private bath (2); two bedroom, private bath (4); three bedrooms, private bath (2). Kitchen, complete utensils, A/C, color TV, housekeeping service, cribs/cots, soda/snack vending. Meeting/conference room and exercise room available. Check out 1300 hours daily. Older structure. Rates: $45 per night. Duty can make reservations, others Space-A.

DV/VIP: TECOM Protocol, Ryan Building, C-410-278-1038. Or USAOC&S Protocol, Bldg 3071, C-410-278-1038, O6+, retirees Space-A.

TML Availability: Good, Nov-Jan. Difficult, other times.

MARYLAND
Aberdeen Proving Ground, continued

CREDIT CARDS ACCEPTED: Visa, MasterCard, and American Express.

Transportation: Off base taxi 272-0880.

On the Chesapeake Bay. Hunting, fishing, boating, three golf courses, two swimming pools, theater, bowling alley, fitness center. Baltimore is 30 miles south, DC 75 miles south, and Philadelphia 92 miles north. Lots to do here.

Locator 410-278-5201   Medical 410-272-2557   Police 410-278-5291

Andrews Air Force Base (MD02R1)
Gateway Inn
86th SVS/SVML
1375 Arkansas Rd
Andrews AFB, MD 20331-7002

TELEPHONE NUMBER INFORMATION: Main installation numbers: C-301-981-1110, D-312-858-1110.

Location: From I-95 (east portion of Capital Beltway, I-495) north or south, exit 9, first traffic light after leaving exit ramp turn left, go to main gate of AFB. Clearly marked. USMRA: Page *42 (E-5)* and *Page 55 (I,J-6,7)*. NMC: Washington, DC, 6 miles northwest.

Lodging Office: Gateway Inn, 1375, Arkansas Road, **C-301-981-4614, D-312-858-4614,** Fax: C-301-981-7997, D-312-858-7997, 24 hours. Reservations Fax: C-301-981-9277. Check in 1500 hours, check out 1200 hours daily. All guests are required to pay in advance. Government civilian employee billeting.

TML: TLF. Bldgs 1801-1804, 1328, 1330, all ranks, leave or official duty. Separate bedrooms, private bath (68). Kitchen, utensils, A/C, color TV, housekeeping service, cribs, washer/dryer, ice vending, iron/ironing board. Modern structure. Rates: $24. Maximum five per room. PCS to Andrews can make reservations, others Space-A (can make reservations 24 hours prior to arrival up to three days).

TML: VAQ. Bldgs 1373, 1376, 1580, 1629. Suites, private bath (5); Chief suites (1); rooms, shared bath (65). Refrigerator, microwave, A/C, color TV, VCR, soda/snack vending, iron/ironing board. Rates: suites $16; rooms $10 per person. Reservations required.

TML: VOQ. Bldgs 1349, 1360-1371. Officers, all ranks, leave or official duty. Bedrooms, private bath (30); suites, private bath (60). Refrigerator, microwave, A/C, color TV, VCR, iron/ironing board. Rates: suites $16; rooms $10 per person. Reservations required.

TML: DV/VIP. Bldg 1349. Officers O7+, leave or official duty. Bedrooms, private bath (31), DV suites, private bath (8). Kitchen, A/C, color TV, housekeeping service, washer/dryer, iron/ironing board. Rates: suites $16; rooms $10 per person per night. Official travellers can make reservations, others Space-A (can make reservations 24 hours prior to arrival up to three days).

TML: Fisher House. Note: Appendix B has the definition of this facility. C-301-981-1243.

MARYLAND
Andrews Air Force Base, continued

DV/VIP: Protocol, 89 AW/CCP, C-301-981-4525, O7+. Retirees Space-A.

TML Availability: Best, Dec-Feb. Difficult, Mar-Nov.

CREDIT CARDS ACCEPTED: Visa, MasterCard and American Express.

Transportation: On base shuttle.

Andrews is the military aerial gateway to Washington, DC for most overseas VIPs, and the home of "Air Force One", the President's aircraft. If you're lucky you can witness "important people" coming and going here.

Locator 301-981-1110   Medical 301-981-6250   Police 301-981-2500

Bethesda National Naval Medical Center (MD06R1)
Lodging Office, Bldg 60
Bethesda, MD 20889-5600

TELEPHONE NUMBER INFORMATION: Main installation numbers: C-301-295-5385, D-312-295-4611 (Hospital Information).

Location: From I-495 (Capital Beltway) take exit 34, Wisconsin Ave (MD-355, Rockville Pike) south for 1 mile to Naval Medical Center on left. Enter first gate, Wood Road S, for support facility. Also, can enter the center from Jones Bridge Road, off Wisconsin Ave. *USMRA: Page 55 (D,E-1).* NMC: Washington, DC 1 mile southeast.

Lodging Office: CBQ Billeting Office for BOQ/BEQ, Bldg 60. Check in facility, check out 1200 hours daily. Government civilian employee lodging. **C-301-295-5855/56,** Fax: C-301-295-0172. No government employee billeting. Duty Office - main hospital (central figure for problems) **C-301-295-4611.**

TML: Navy Lodge, Bldg 52, 8901 Wisconsin Ave, Bethesda, MD 20814-5000, all ranks, medical and PCS have priority. Reservations: 1-800-NAVY-INN. Lodge number is C-301-654-1795, 24 hours, Fax: C-301-654-9373. Check in 1500-1800, check out 1200. There are 72 units (15 smoking, 57 non-smoking). Bedroom, 2 double beds, private bath. Single rooms w/queen bed (does not include entire kitchenette facility). Four sets interconnecting units. Kitchenette, microwave, A/C, color CATV/VCP with Showtime and video rental, housekeeping service, cribs, phone/fax service, high chairs, rollaways, soda/snack vending, ice vending, coin washer/dryer, iron/ironing board, lounge, playground, exercise room. Mini-mart close by. Modern structure. Rates: single $52.50; double $62.50. AD may make reservations 60 days in advance, retirees/reservists 30 days in advance, PCS/patients anytime in advance.

TML: BOQ. Bldg 11, currently under renovation with completion slated for September 1998. DV/VIP suites available (2). Rates: $24 per night. Reservations required; contact the Billeting Office.

TML: BEQ. Bldg 60, officers, all ranks, official duty. Reservations required. Bedroom, common bath (43); separate bedrooms, private bath, kitchen (1) (CPOVIP); family rooms, kitchen, private bath (5). Rates: $12, $15 and $18, each additional person $2. Refrigerator, microwave, coffee maker, community kitchen, utensils, A/C, alarm clocks, portable blowdryers (mounted) CATV/VCR in

MARYLAND
Bethesda National Naval Medical Center, continued

lounge, housekeeping service, cribs/rollaways (upon request), washer/dryer, soda/snack vending, ice vending, exercise room, arcade and video rental. Mini-mart close by. Older structure. Quarters are inadequate and substandard.

TML: Fisher House. Note: Appendix B has the definition of this facility. C-301-295-5334. There are two houses at the NNMC.

DV/VIP: Cmdr, NATNAVMEDCEN, Bldg 1, room 5156A, C-301-295-5800, O6+. Retirees Space-A.

TML Availability: Very limited.

CREDIT CARDS ACCEPTED: The Navy Lodge accepts Visa, MasterCard, American Express and Discover.

Transportation: On/off base shuttle/bus, off base taxi and car rental agencies available.

Bethesda is located just north of Washington DC, shopping, and the Metro are close by.

Locator 301-295-4611   Medical 301-295-0999   Police 301-295-0999

Curtis Bay Coast Guard Yard (MD01R1)
Coast Guard MWR
Bldg 28A
Baltimore, MD 21226-1997

TELEPHONE NUMBER INFORMATION: Main installation numbers: C-410-636-4194.

Location: Take I-695 to exit 1, bear to your right, right on Hawkins Point Road, left into Coast Guard Yard. *USMRA: Page 42 (F-3) and Page 49 (C-4).* NMC: Baltimore, 5 miles northwest.

Lodging Office: Central billeting office. BQ Manager, Bldg 28A (BOQ), **C-410-636-7373**, Fax 410-636-7785, E-mail: tml/yard25@internet.uscg.mil, 0830-1500 Mon-Fri. Family Transient Lodging, Bldg 84. Reservations required. After duty hours, JOOD, Bldg 33, C-410-636-3993 (if reservations made). Check in facility after 1400 hours, check out 1100 hours daily. No government civilian employee billeting.

TML: TLF. Bldg 84. All ranks, leave or official duty. One, two and three bedroom suites, private bath (5). Kitchen, complete utensils, A/C, color TV, cribs, washer/dryer, playground. Handicap accessible. Exercise room with soda/snack vending and mini-mart available. Older structure. Rates available.upon request. Maximum 8 per family. All categories except widows and unaccompanied dependents can make reservations. PCS in/out have priority.

TML: BOQ. Bldg 28A, officer all ranks, official duty only. Reservations required. C-410-636-7373, 0830-1500. Bedroom, 2 beds, private bath (5). A/C, color TV/VCR, microwave, refrigerator, pool table in lounge, washer/dryer. Modern structure. Rates available upon request. Maximum 2 persons per unit.

TML Availability: Good, Oct-Apr. More difficult, other times.

MARYLAND
Curtis Bay Coast Guard Yard, continued

Southeast of Baltimore, a city rich in history and entertainment, where the Inner Harbor buzzes with shopping, dining and recreational opportunities.

Locator 410-636-7383   Medical 410-636-3144   Police 410-636-3993

Fort Detrick (MD07R1)
Billeting Office Manger/MCHD-PCH
810 Schreider Street, Suite 400
Frederick, MD 21702-5033

TELEPHONE NUMBER INFORMATION: Main installation numbers: C-301-619-8000, D-312-343-1110.

Location: From Washington, DC, take I-270 north to US-15 north. From Baltimore, take I-70 west to US-15 north. From US-15 north, in Frederick, exit Seventh Street. Clearly marked to post. *USMRA: Page 42 (D-2).* NMC: Baltimore, 50 miles east and Washington, DC, 50 miles southeast.

Lodging Office: 810 Schreider Street, Suite 400. **C-301-619-2154**, Fax: C-301-619-2010, 0800-1600 hours Mon-Fri. Check out 1000 hours daily. Government civilian employee billeting.

TML: Guest House. Bldgs 800-801, all ranks, leave or official duty. Two bedroom, private bath (1); three bedroom, private bath (3). Kitchen, utensils, microwave, dishwashers, telephones, housekeeping service, CATV, iron/ironing board, sofa bed, A/C, color TV, washer/dryer, soda/snack vending. Completely modernized. Rates: $24 per unit. PCS can make reservations, others Space-A. No pets.

TML: VOQ. Bldg 660, all ranks, leave or official duty. Bedroom suites, double beds, private bath (16). Kitchen, microwave, limited utensils, A/C, sofa bed, iron/ironing board, color TV, CATV, housekeeper service, washer/dryer, soda/snack vending, phone. Older structure, remodeled. Rates: $13 per room. TDY can make reservations, others Space-A. No pets.

TML: DVQ. Bldg 715, officers, leave or official duty. Suite, queen bed, private bath (1). Kitchen, microwave, limited utensils, A/C, CATV, color TV, iron/ironing board, telephone, housekeeping service, soda/snack vending. Older structure, remodeled. Rates: $18 per night. TDY can make reservations, others Space-A. No Pets.

DV/VIP: HQ Fort Detrick. C-301-619-2154. O6+. Retirees and lower ranks Space-A.

TML Availability: Good, Oct-Mar. Difficult, Jun-Aug.

CREDIT CARDS ACCEPTED: Visa, MasterCard, American Express, and MOST (debit).

Historic Frederick County offers visitors a variety of cultural, sports and recreational options. Both Baltimore and Washington, DC are nearby.

Locator 301-619-2233   Medical 301-619-7175   Police 301-619-7114

MARYLAND

Fort George G. Meade (MD08R1)
Post Lodging
P.O. Box 1069
Fort George G. Meade, MD 20755-5115

TELEPHONE NUMBER INFORMATION: Main installation numbers: C-410-677-6261, D-312-923-6261.

Location: Off Baltimore-Washington Parkway, I-295, exit MD-198 east which is Fort Meade Road. Clearly marked. *USMRA: Page 42 (E,F-4)*. NMC: Baltimore and Washington, DC, 30 miles from each city.

Lodging Office: Brett Hall, Post Billeting Fund, Bldg 4707, Ruffner Road, **C-410-677-6529/5884, D-312-923-5884,** 24 hours. Check in billeting, check out 1200 hours daily. Government civilian employee billeting.

TML: Guest House. Bldg 2793, **Abrams Hall**, all ranks, leave or official duty. Handicap accessible, C-410-677-2045. Check in 24 hours. Bedrooms with 2 beds, private bath (54). Refrigerator, community kitchen, A/C, essentials, color TV room and lounge, housekeeping service, cribs, washer/dryer, snack vending, ice vending, CATV, in-room telephone, microwaves. Older structure, completely renovated 1993-1994. Has a new $50,000 playground. Rates: PCS in/out $24.75-$28.75 per room. Priorities: PCS, hospital visitors, visitors of active duty assigned, TDY may stay 30 days. Reservations 30 days in advance, 1 night confirmed stay. (This does not pertain to personnel who are PCS, hospital visitors, active duty assigned, TDY, etc.)

TML: VOQ. Bldgs 4703, 4704, 4707, 4709, officers all ranks, leave or official duty. Bedroom, semi-private bath (142); one bedroom, private bath (4); separate bedroom suites, private bath (16). Kitchen (14 units), refrigerator, A/C, CATV, housekeeping service, washer/dryer, ice vending. Older structures, bathrooms renovated. Rates: $29 per room. TDY room confirmation duration of stay, confirmed 60 days in advance.

TML: SEBQ. Bldg 4705, enlisted E7-E9, official duty. Separate bedroom, private bath (30). Modern structure. Rates: No charge. For SNCO on PCS to Fort Meade only.

TML: BOQ. Bldg 4717, 4720, 4721, officers all ranks, official duty. Separate bedrooms, private bath (62). Rates: No charge. PCS to Fort Meade only.

TML: DVQ. Bldg 4415, officer O5+, TDY, PCS, leave or official duty. Separate bedrooms, private bath (5); two bedroom, private bath (2). Kitchen, limited utensils, A/C, color TV, housekeeping service, washer/dryer. Older structure, renovated. Rates: $29-$45 per room. Duty can make reservations, Protocol Office, others Space-A. Reservations 60 days in advance, one night confirmed stay for "others."

TML Availability: Good. Best months, Oct-Mar.

CREDIT CARDS ACCEPTED: Visa, MasterCard, American Express and Diners' Club.

Visit Baltimore's Fort McHenry National Monument, and new Inner Harbor, or see Annapolis' quaint shopping areas. Washington, DC is also a short drive from Fort Meade.

Locator 410-677-6261   Medical 410-677-2570   Police 410-677-6622

134 - Temporary Military Lodging Around the World

MARYLAND

Fort Ritchie (MD13R1)
Fort Ritchie Guest House
Bldg 520, Cushman Ave
Fort Ritchie, MD 21719-5010
Scheduled to close September 1998.

TELEPHONE NUMBER INFORMATION: Main installation numbers: C-301-878-1300, D-312-277-1300.

Location: From US-15 north exit at Thurmont, to MD-550 north for 7 miles to Cascade and main gate. From Hagerstown, take MD-64 east to MD-491, north to MD-550 and north to Cascade and main gate. *USMRA: Page 42 (C,D-1).* NMC: Hagerstown, 16 miles southwest, Baltimore, 50 miles southeast, Washington, DC, 55 miles southeast.

Lodging Office: Guesthouse, Bldg 520, Cushman Ave., **C-301-878-5171, D-312-277-5171**, Fax: C-301-241-4585, 0800-1630 Mon-Fri, 0800-1200 Sat-Sun, holidays. Other hours, MP Desk, Bldg 123. Check in facility, check out before 1130 hours daily. Government civilian employee billeting.

TML: Guest House. Bldg 520, all ranks, leave or official duty. Bedroom, private bath (21). Kitchen (9 units), refrigerator (12 units), complete utensils, VCR, CATV with HBO, housekeeping service, cribs/cots, coin washer/dryer, ice vending. Modern structure. Rates: PCS without kitchen $24, with kitchen $26. Maximum five per room. PCS can make reservations, others Space-A.

TML: VOQ/VEQ. Bldg 800, officers all ranks, enlisted E7-E9, leave or official duty. Bedroom, private bath (11); bedroom suite (DV)(1). (VQ) refrigerator, community kitchen, VCR, CATV with HBO in room and lounge, housekeeping service, washer/dryer. Rates: VQ $17.50; DVQ $24, each additional person $6. TDY can make reservations, others Space-A.

TML: Lakeside Hall. Bldg 11, C-301-878-4361, all ranks, leave or official duty. Bedroom, private bath, small living area w/pull-out couch (6); apartments with kitchenettes (2); Ritchie Suite (VIP)(1). Rates: non-members. Overlooking lake, lakeside activities include swimming, paddle boating, fishing, newly renovated, color TV, telephones in room, fax machine. Laundry service available.

DV/VIP: HQ 7th SIG, Bldg 307, C-301-878-5171, O6+. Retirees, Space-A.

TML Availability: Good, most of the year. Best, Mar-Jun.

CREDIT CARDS ACCEPTED: Visa, MasterCard, American Express and Discover.

Beautiful scenic small post. Great location for ski resorts in the area, swimming, fishing, golf and Gettysburg National Park.

Locator 301-878-5685   Medical 301-878-4132   Police 301-878-4228

Indian Head Naval Surface Warfare Center (MD04R1)
CBQ (Code 115), Indian Head Division
Indian Head, MD 20640-5000

TELEPHONE NUMBER INFORMATION: Main installation numbers: C-301-743-4000, D-312-354-4000.

MARYLAND
Indian Head Naval Surface Warfare Center, continued

Location: Take I-495 (Capital Beltway) east, exit to MD-210 south for 25 miles to station. *USMRA: Page 42 (D-5,6)*. NMC: Washington, DC, 25 miles north.

Lodging Office: Bldg 902, **C-301-743-4845, D-312-354-4845,** Fax: C-301-743-4486, 24 hours. Reservations are highly recommended.

TML: BOQ. Bldg 1542, all ranks, leave or official duty, 24 hours. Officer/enlisted rooms, private bath; A/C, color TV/VCR, housekeeping service, washer/dryer, snack vending. Rates: transient $8.75. Duty can make reservations, others Space-A. No Space-A for families or dependents.

TML: BEQ. Bldg 1752, 902, all ranks, leave or official duty, C-301-743-4845, 24 hours. Bedroom with 1 bed, semi-private bath (108). A/C, color TV, housekeeping service, washer/dryer, snack vending. Rates: $4.50 per day. Duty can make reservations, others Space-A. No Space-A for families or dependents. All Hands dinning facility located in Bldg 902.

DV/VIP: PAO. Bldg 20, C-301-743-4627. Inquire about qualifying rank. Lodging considered substandard by Navy standards. Retirees Space-A.

TML Availability: Fair, Jan-May, Sept-Dec. Difficult, other times.

CREDIT CARDS ACCEPTED: Visa, MasterCard and American Express.

Only 25 miles from Washington, DC makes this place within "shouting distance" of the many cultural and sporting events available to the area. The nearby Potomac River also provides recreational opportunities.

Locator 301-743-4303   Medical 301-743-4601   Police 301-743-4381

Patuxent River Naval Air Warfare Center (MD09R1)
Lodging Office, Bldg 406
Patuxent River NAWC, MD 20670-5199

TELEPHONE NUMBER INFORMATION: Main installation numbers: C-301-342-9343, D-312-342-3601.

Location: From I-95 (east portion of Capital Beltway, I-495) exit 7A to Branch Ave (MD-5) south. Follow MD-5 until it turns into MD-235 near Oraville, on to Lexington Park, and the NAS. Main gate is on MD-235 and MD-246 (Cedar Point Road). *USMRA: Page 42 (F-6,7)*. NMC: Washington, DC, 65 miles west.

Lodging Office: Bldg 406. **C-301-342-9343, D-312-342-3601,** Fax: C-301-342-1015, check in facility, check out 1200 hours daily

TML: BOQ. Bldg 406, officers all ranks, leave or official duty, C-301-342-9343. Rooms/suites, private baths (60). Kitchen, refrigerator, A/C, color TV/VCR, housekeeping service, cots, washer/dryer, ice vending, telephone. Two rooms handicap accessible. Rates: $15 per person, $8 additional person. No children. Reservations only from persons on TAD orders, retirees Space-A.

TML: DV/VIP. C-301-342-1108, one bedroom, king-size bed suites, dining room, living room, private bath, kitchen (2).

136 - Temporary Military Lodging Around the World

MARYLAND
Patuxent River Naval Air Warfare Center, continued

TML: DV/VIP. **Crowe's Nest** (located at Officers' Club). 1 suite, private bath. Ask about Gull Cottage. For reservations contact C-301-342-1180.

DV/VIP: PAO. C-301-342-7503, O7+, retirees Space-A.

TML Availability: Fairly good, winter. More difficult, Jun-Aug.

CREDIT CARDS ACCEPTED: BOQ accepts American Express.

The Special Interest Coordinator's office in Bldg 423 (C-301-863-3510) has discount tickets to Kings Dominion, Wild World, Busch Gardens, Hershey Park, local ski resorts, Colonial Williamsburg, sporting events.

Locator 301-342-3000   Medical 301-342-1422   Police 301-342-3911

Solomons Navy Recreation Center (MD05R1)
P.O. Box 147
Solomons, MD 20688-0147

TELEPHONE NUMBER INFORMATION: Main installation numbers: C-410-326-5000.

Location: Off base, on Patuxent River. From US-301, take MD-4 southeast to Solomons; or take MD-5 southeast to MD-235, then MD-4 northeast to Solomons. *USMRA: Page 42 (F-6)*. NMC: Washington, DC, 65 miles northwest.

Lodging Office: Bldg 411, **C-410-326-1260, DC Area 1-800-NAVY-230,** Fax: C-410-326-4280, 0900-2200 daily (summer), 0800-1800 off season. Late check-in if arranged in advance. All ranks, leave or official duty. Check in billeting, check out 1100 hours daily.

TML: Units are apartments, bungalows, and cottages. Two bedroom, private bath (1); three bedroom, private bath (25); four and five bedroom, private bath (2 and 9). Kitchen, limited utensils, rental linens, A/C, cribs (fee), coin washer/dryer, soda/snack vending, ice vending. Meeting/conference rooms available Older structures, some renovated. Rates: cottages E1-E5 $40-$56; E6-E9 $48.50-$64; Officers $59-$75; DoD civilians $75-$90; bungalows E1-E5 $38.50-$42.50; E6-E9 $47-$51; Officers $57-$61; DoD civilians $72.50-$77. All rates per night. Maximum 6 persons per cabin, three persons per bedroom. All categories except unaccompanied dependents can make reservations. Call for information about lottery reservation system.

TML Availability: Good, Oct-Apr. Difficult, other times.

CREDIT CARDS ACCEPTED: Visa, MasterCard and American Express.

Complete river recreational/camping area. Full support facility available at nearby Patuxent River NAWC. St. Maries City, Calvert Cliffs, Calvert Marine Museum, Farmers' Market, charter fishing, Point Lookout State Park. For complete details see *Military RV, Camping and Rec Areas Around The World*.

Locator 410-326-1260   Medical 911   Police 410-320-2436

MARYLAND

United States Naval Academy/ Annapolis Naval Station (MD10R1)
BOQ
2 Truxton Road
Annapolis, MD 21402-5071

TELEPHONE NUMBER INFORMATION: Main installation numbers: C-410-293-1000, D-312-281-0111.

Location: Two miles off US-50/301. Two exits to the Academy, clearly marked. Main gate is on King George Street, in Annapolis. Naval Station is across Severn River off US-50/301 east, first exit. Clearly marked. *USMRA: Page 42 (F-4) and Page 48 (D,E,F,G-1,2,3).* NMC: Annapolis, in city.

Lodging Office: Billeting Office, 2nd floor, **Officers' and Faculty Club,** C-410-293-3906, D-312-281-3906, Fax: C-410-293-2444, D-312-281-2444, Daily 0800-1600 0900-1400. Check in 1300 at billeting, check out 1100 at billeting. Government civilian employee billeting.

TML: O and F Club, second and third deck, officers all ranks, equivalent government employees, leave or official duty. Suites, private bath, sleeps to 5 persons (14). A/C, color TV, washer/dryer, housekeeping service. Older historic structure, remodeled. Rates: $10, each additional person $2. PCS, TAD/TDY have priority, others Space-A.

DV/VIP: O and F Club, third deck, reservations through Superintendent's Protocol Office: C-410-293-2403, O6+. VIP suites, private bath, coffee bar, honor bar with kitchenette (2). Rates: suites w/ kitchenette $20, each additional person $5; guest suite $15, each additional person $3. Retirees Space-A.

TML Availability: Best, Oct-Apr. Difficult, summer months.

CREDIT CARDS ACCEPTED: American Express.

Don't miss a visit to the waterfront shopping and restaurant area, where dreaming over yachts is "SOP". Visit the Naval Academy Chapel and historic buildings, and walk around historic Maryland's capital.

Locator 410-293-1000   Medical 410-293-3333   Police 410-293-4444

Washington Naval Air Facility (MD22R1)
Supply Officer, Naval Air Facility, Attn: Code 76
Bldg 3148, 1 San Diego Loop
Andrews AFB, MD 20762-5518

TELEPHONE NUMBER INFORMATION: Main installation numbers: C-301-981-2750, D-858-2750, Fax: C-301-981-3588, D-858-3588.

Location: From I-95 (east part of Capital Beltway, I-495) N or S, Exit 9. At first traffic light after leaving exit ramp, turn right into main gate of Andrews AFB. Also, from I-395 N, exit south Capital Street, cross Anacostia River on South Capital Street, bear left to Suitland Parkway E, exit Parkway at Morningside on Suitland Road east to main gate of Andrews AFB. Follow signs to east side of

MARYLAND
Washington Naval Air Facility, continued

Andrews AFB Clearly marked. *USMRA: Page 42 (E-5); Page 55 (I,J-6,7).* NMC: Washington DC, six miles northwest.

Lodging Office: C-301-981-2750, Fax: C-301-981-3588, 24 hours.

TML: BEQ. Bldg 1675, 1687. BOQ. Bldg 1384, 1385. No family quarters available. CATV, coffee maker, housekeeping services, soda/snack vending. Rates: enlisted $4; officer $8. Personnel on official orders may make reservations, others Space-A.

DV/VIP: Controlled by NAF Washington, DC Commanding Officer. Reservations must by made through the CO for VIP suites.

TML Availability: Limited, weekdays and reservist drill weekends.

CREDIT CARDS ACCEPTED: Visa, MasterCard and American Express.

Transportation: On base shuttle/bus.

Locator 981-2750   Medical 981-7511   Police 981-2001

MASSACHUSETTS

Armed Services YMCA of Boston (MA16R1)
150 Second Ave
Charlestown Navy Yard
Charleston MA 02129-5000
(This is not U.S. Government/Military Lodging.)

TELEPHONE NUMBER INFORMATION: Main installation numbers: C-617-241-8400, Fax: C-617-241-2856.

Location: From the Massachusetts Turnpike to Boston; JFK Expressway exit #25 and follow signs to USS Constitution; from North I-93 to Sullivan Square Exit, follow signs to USS Constitution. *USMRA: Page 24 (E-5).* NMC: Boston, in the city.

Lodging Office: C-800-495-9622, 617-241-8400, Fax: C-617-241-2856, 24 hours. Check in facility, check out 1130 hours daily. Government civilian employee billeting.

TML: All ranks, leave or official duty. Single and family accommodations. Write to: 150 Second Ave., Charlestown, MA 02129. Bedroom, two beds, private bath; adjoining rooms; suites, private bath (DV/VIP). A/C, kitchenette (must provide own cooking and eating utensils). DV/VIP, CATV, housekeeping service, coin washer/dryer, YMCA space rentals (meetings, gym, pool, function room) available. Rates: Military $40 and up, Civilian $60 and up. All categories may make reservations. Rates subject to change.

TML Availability: Very good.

MASSACHUSETTS
Armed Services YMCA of Boston, continued

CREDIT CARDS ACCEPTED: Visa, MasterCard and American Express.

Boston is one of America's most "walkable" cities - see bustling Faneuil Hall Marketplace and waterfront areas, the shops of Back Bay and picturesque squares of Beacon Hill. The Hub's many athletic and cultural events are only a few minutes away by car or Boston's rapid transit system, the "T".

Locator 241-8400   Medical 911   Police 911

Boston Coast Guard Integrated Support Command (MA07R1)
ATTN: MAA
427 Commercial Street
Boston, MA 02109-1027

TELEPHONE NUMBER INFORMATION: Main installation number: C-617-223-3313.

Location: Take Atlantic Ave exit off of I-93, turn onto Commercial Street. Located at corner of Commercial and Hanover. *USMRA: Page 24 (E-4,5)*. NMC: In heart of downtown Boston.

Lodging Office: 427 Commercial Street, Bldg 1. **C-617-223-3171**, Fax: C-617-723-3166, 0700-1530 hours, Mon-Fri. Check in billeting, check out 1100.

TML: BOQ/BEQ. All ranks, official duty. Handicap accessible units. Shared rooms, shared bath (15). TV in lounge area, washer/dryer, snack vending, ice vending. Rates: Were not furnished, please call for rates.

TML: Cuttyhunk Island Recreational Housing Facility, **C-617-223-8047/8375**. Three-bedroom apartment (1), sleeps eight, private bath, furnished, kitchen. Two-bedroom apartment (1), private bath, furnished, kitchen. Rates: $285-$500 weekly. See *Military Living's Military RV, Camping and Rec Areas Around the World* for additional information and directions.

TML Availability: Fairly good. Best, Oct-Feb, difficult, Mar-Sep.

Boston is one of America's most "walkable" cities - see bustling Faneuil Hall Marketplace and waterfront areas, the shops of Back Bay and picturesque squares of Beacon Hill. The Hub's many athletic and cultural events are only a few minutes away by car or Boston's rapid transit system, the "T".

Locator 223-3313   Medical 223-3250   Police 223-3313

Cape Cod Coast Guard Air Station (MA10R1)
ATTN: Temporary Quarters, Bldg 5204
USCG Air Station - Cape Cod
Otis ANGB, MA 02542-5024

TELEPHONE NUMBER INFORMATION: Main installation numbers: C-508-968-1000, D-312-557-4401, National Guard Base. Coast Guard Air Station, C-508-968-6300, D-312-557-6300.

MASSACHUSETTS
Cape Cod Coast Guard Air Station, continued

Location: Take MA Military Reservation exit off MA-28, south on Connley Ave approximately 2 miles to Bourne Gate. *USMRA: Page 17 (M-7).* NMC: Boston, 50 miles northwest.

Lodging Office: ATTN: Temporary Quarters, Bldg 5204, **C-508-968-6461**, 0800-1600 hours Mon-Fri 0900-1400 hours Sat and Sun. Check in billeting. Check out 1000 hours.

TML: TLF/BOQ. All ranks. Leave or official duty. Accessible to handicap. Advance payment required. Bedrooms with kitchen, private bath (4); two bedroom town houses, private bath (10); bedroom, private bath (BOQ) (19); bedroom efficiency apartments, private bath (16). Cots/cribs, essentials, soda vending, coffee in lounge, housekeeping service, refrigerator, color TV in lounge and room, utensils, coin washer/dryer, small child's playroom. Older structure, remodeled. Rates: moderate, PCS determined by rank. Reservations: PCS 90 days in advance, others 30 days. In summer vacationers, TDY 2 weeks in advance.

TML: Cape Cod Vacation Apartments, C-508-968-6461, D-312-557-6461. Townhouse apartments (12); 2-bedroom, sleeps six, one double bed, two twin beds, sleeper sofa, TV, kitchen, furnished. Rates: $21-$60 daily. Suites (18); 1-bedroom, sleeps five, two double beds, sleeper sofa, microwave, refrigerator, dinette. Rates: $21-$55 daily. Single quarters (2); private bath, furnished. Rates: $18-$50 daily. **See** *Military Living's Military RV, Camping and Rec Areas Around the World* **for additional information and directions.**

TML Availability: Good. Best Oct-Apr.

CREDIT CARDS ACCEPTED: Visa, MasterCard, American Express, Diners' Club and Discover.

Otis has 9-hole golf course and driving range. Newport mansions, beaches, Martha's Vineyard, and Nantucket Islands nearby make this a special place to visit.

Locator 968-1000   Medical 968-6570   Police 968-4010

Devens Inn and Conference Center (MA09R1)
22 10th Mountain Division Road (Bldg 2002)
Devens, MA 01432-5000

TELEPHONE NUMBER INFORMATION: Main installation numbers: C-508-772-4300/0188

Location: Take Route 2 (west from Route 495, or east from Leominster) to Devens/Jackson Road exit, to end of Jackson Road, right onto Givry, left onto MacArthur, take MacArthur to a right turn onto 10th Mountain Division Road. *USMRA: Page 17 (I-2,3).* NMC: Boston, 35 miles southeast.

Lodging Office: 22 10th Mountain Division Road, Bldg 2002 **C-508-772-4300/0188,** Fax: C-508-772-4903, 24 hours. Check in McGrath Guest House, check out 1100 hours daily. Government civilian employee billeting.

TML: Guest House. Bldg 2002, (located behind Burger King), **McGrath Guest House**, all ranks, official duty. Separate bedrooms, private bath (58). Full kitchen facilities, refrigerator, color TV, housekeeping service, cribs, snack vending. Rates: $50.

TML Availability: Good, Dec-Mar. Very difficult, summer.

MASSACHUSETTS
Devens Inn and Conference Center, continued

CREDIT CARDS ACCEPTED: Visa, MasterCard, American Express and Diners' Club.

Locator 772-4300/0188   Medical 777-8870   Police 772-6600

Fourth Cliff Family Recreation Area (MA02R1)
P.O. Box 479
Humarock, MA 01731-5001

TELEPHONE NUMBER INFORMATION: Main installation numbers: C-617-377-4441, D-312-478-4441.

LOCATION: Off base. I-95 or I-93 to MA-3, approximately 30 miles south of Boston; south to exit 12; MA-139 east to Marshfield. 1.5 miles to Furnace Street; turn left. Continue to "T" intersection; turn left on Ferry Street. Stay on Ferry Street to Sea Street; right over South River Bridge; left on Central Ave and proceed to gate. Check in at Bldg 7. *USMRA: Page 17 (M-4)*. NMC: Boston, 30 miles north.

Lodging Office: None. Reservations required. Confirmation w/credit card/cash/check within 5 days. Ask for map. **C-617-837-9269 (0800-1630 Mon-Fri)** or **1-800-468-9547**. Rec area open Memorial Day through Columbus Day. Cabins open year round.

TML: One- to three- bedroom cottages (3), 2-bedroom townhouses (2), 2-bedroom chalets (11) all ranks, leave or official duty. Rates: $45-$75 daily. All categories can make reservations. Pets not allowed in cabins but may be leashed in other areas. RV Camping available *(Check out Military Living's RV Camping and Rec Areas Around the World for more info)*.

TML Availability: Limited. Book early.

Easy access to Boston, Cape Cod, Martha's Vineyard and Nantucket Islands, and located high on a cliff overlooking the Atlantic and scenic North River, this is a superb location for a summer or winter vacation.

Locator 377-4441   Medical 911   Police 911

Hanscom Air Force Base (MA06R1)
Hanscom Inn
66 SVS/SVML
1427 Kirtland Street
Hanscom AFB, MA 01731-5000

TELEPHONE NUMBER INFORMATION: Main installation numbers: C-617-377-4441, D-312-478-4441.

Location: From I-95 north take exit 31A, MA-2A west for 2 miles to right on Hartwell Road which bisects the AFB. *USMRA: Page 17 (J-3) and Page 24 (A-2)*. NMC: Boston, 17 miles southeast.

Lodging Office: Hanscom Inn. Bldg 1427, **C-617-377-2112**, Fax: C-617-377-4961, D-312-478-4961, 24 hours. Check in 1400 hours, check out 1100 hours.

MASSACHUSETTS
Hanscom Air Force Base, continued

TML: TLF. Bldgs 1412, 1423, all ranks, official duty. C-617-377-2044. Handicap accessible. Bldg 1423, single bedroom, sofa bed, private bath, full kitchen, A/C, housekeeping service, cribs, washer/dryer in building. Rates for TLF $24 per night. TLF is used for PCS in/out. 30 days PCS in, 7 days PCS out. Space-A guests first come first served. Call for details.

TML: VQ. Bldg 1412, 1426, all ranks, official duty. Bldg 1426, bedroom, semi-private bath, A/C, housekeeping service, washer/dryer in building. Rates: $13.75 per person per night. TDY personnel have priority. Space-A requests accepted year round, confirmed 24 hours prior to arrival. Bldg 1412, all ranks, single bedroom, private bath, washer/dryer in building. Rates: $13.75 per person per night.

DV/VIP: Protocol Office, Bldg 1606, C-617-377-5151. O7+, retirees Space-A.

TML Availability: Fair. Best in Nov-Mar.

CREDIT CARDS ACCEPTED: Visa, MasterCard and American Express.

Delve into U.S. history by visiting Minute Man National Historical Park, Battle Road near Fiske Hill in Lexington, the Wayside Unit, home of the Alcotts, Nathaniel Hawthorne and others, and Lexington Green.

Locator 377-5111   **Medical 377-2333**   **Police 377-7100**

Westover Air Reserve Base (MA03R1)
650 Airlift Drive, Bldg 2201
Chicopee, MA 01022-1309

TELEPHONE NUMBER INFORMATION: Main installation numbers: C-413-557-1110, D-312-589-1110, 1-800-367-1110 ask for ext 2700 (base lodging).

Location: Take exit 5 off I-90 (MA Turnpike) in Chicopee. Westover is on MA-33. Signs mark way to base. *USMRA: Page 16 (F-4)*. NMC: Springfield, 8 miles south.

Lodging Office: Flyers Inn, Bldg 2201, 650 Airlift Drive. VOQ/VAQ: **C-413-557-2700, D-312-589-2700**, Fax: C-413-557-2835, D-312-589-2835, weekends only. Space Available check in 1700 hour, check out 1100 hours daily. Government civilian employee billeting.

TML: VOQ. Bldgs 2200, 2201. Officers, all ranks, leave or official duty. Bedroom, semi-private bath (10); two bedroom suites, semi-private bath (29). A/C, essentials, color TV/VCR rental, housekeeping service, ice vending. Older structure, remodeled. Rates: $8 per person; DV Suites $10 per person. Maximum four persons. Maximum depends on number per family. Duty can make reservations, others Space-A.

TML: VAQ. Bldgs 5101-5105, enlisted, E1-E8, leave or official duty. Rooms, shared bath (250); SNCO suites, private bath (32). Snack vending, ice vending, housekeeping service, refrigerator, color TV, washer/dryer. Older structures, 5101, 2 renovated. Rates: $8 per person; SNCO suites $8. Maximum two per unit. Duty can make reservations.

DV/VIP: Bldg 2200. C-413-557-5421, O5+ or unit commander. Rates: $8 per person, maximum two per unit. Retirees and lower ranks Space-A.

MASSACHUSETTS
Westover Air Reserve Base, continued

TML Availability: Good, except Jun-Sep.

Museums, parks, ski areas, Basketball Hall of Fame, professional stage and Symphony Hall in Springfield, are of interest to visitors. Several golf courses. Visit Forest Park Zoo, and the Naismith Memorial Hall of Fame.

Locator 557-3874   Medical 557-3565   Police 557-3557

MICHIGAN

Camp Grayling (MI10R2)
Housing Management Office, Bldg 560
Camp Grayling, MI 49739-0001

TELEPHONE NUMBER INFORMATION: Main installation numbers: C-517-348-7621, D-312-623-7621.

Location: On I-75 take Grayling exit. Camp Grayling is four miles west of Grayling. *USMRA: Page 66 (D-5)*. NMC: Traverse City, 60 miles west.

Lodging Office: Housing - Bldg 560, **C-517-348-3661, D-312-623-3661,** Fax: C-517-348-3844, D-312-623-3844. Check in by 1600 on a duty day, check out 1000. O'Club - Bldg 311, **C-517-348-9033**. Check out 1000.

TML: Run by Housing: Billeting for those on official duty. Individual rooms with centrally located restroom. Most buildings are unheated and consequently closed during colder months.

TML: Run by Housing: CTQ - all ranks, official duty and retirees. Reservations are a first come basis. Single bed, double occupancy (16)Housekeeping service, microwave, kitchenettes, TVs, VCRs, radio alarm clocks. Exchange, snack bar, and clubs available. Rates: official duty $13; unofficial duty $33; each additional person $23.

TML: Run by O'Club: Lake front cottages (4) and lake front mobile homes (2) available for officers. Fully furnished and equipped, can accommodate up to six people. Exchange, snack bar, and clubs available. Rates: $35 (minimum two night stay), $200 weekly. Open mid-Apr-mid-Oct.

TML: Run by O'Club: Rooms (unheated) (10) available with two to four beds in each for officers. Rates: $7. Open May-Sept.

TML: Run by O'Club: Campground space available to all active and retired National Guard Soldiers. Reservations required. Rates: $9. See Military Living's *Military RV, Camping and Rec Areas Around the World* for detailed information. Open mid-May-mid-Sept.

TML Availability: Limited, especially during colder months.

CREDIT CARDS ACCEPTED: O'Club accepts Visa, MasterCard and Discover. The Housing Management Office accepts cash or check.

144 - Temporary Military Lodging Around the World

MICHIGAN
Camp Grayling, continued

Hunting, camping, fishing and winter sports are available on this Limited on post support facilities. Commercial airlines available in Traverse City. Excellent local community canoeing. Watch for signs for "Sweet Talk" - a live on stage entertainment with a wide variety of popular music at the Speak Easy Saloon Lounge.

Selfridge US Army Garrison (MI01R2)
ATTN: AMSTA-CY-E
Bldg 410, 410 George Ave
Selfridge US Army Garrison, MI 48045-5016

TELEPHONE NUMBER INFORMATION: Main installation numbers: C-810-307-4011, D-312-273-4011.

Location: Take I-94 north from Detroit, to Selfridge exit, then east on MI-59 to main gate of base. *USMRA: Page 66 (G-9) and Page 70 (G-1).* NMC: Detroit, 25 miles southwest.

Lodging Office: Bldg 410, ATTN: AMSTA-CY-E, 410George Ave. Operated by U.S. Army, **C-810-307-4062**, Fax: C-810-307-6116, E-mail: philages@cc.tacom.army.mil, 24 hours. Check in billeting, check out 1100 hours daily. Government civilian employee billeting.

TML: Guest House. Bldg 916, all ranks, leave or official duty. Two bedroom, living room, dining room, private bath (7); bedroom, living room, dining room, private bath (8). Kitchen, utensils, color TV, cribs, soda/snack vending, washer/dryer. Meeting/conference rooms and exercise room available. Older structure. Rates: 1-bedroom $16; 2-bedroom $19. Maximum three in one bedroom, five in two bedroom. Duty can make reservations, others Space-A. Pets $3 per day.

TML: VOQ/VEQ. Bldg 410, all ranks, leave or official duty. Separate bedrooms, private bath (27). Microfridges, color TV, housekeeping service, soda/snack vending, washer/dryer. Meeting/conference rooms and exercise room available. Older structure, renovated. Rates: $22.50; VIP Suites $33. DV on TDY can make reservations, others call one day in advance Space-A.

TML Availability: Fairly good.

CREDIT CARDS ACCEPTED: Visa, MasterCard and American Express.

Transportation: Car rental agency: 1-800-RENTACAR.

Camping, hunting, fishing, boating, golfing and water sports are available in the many parks and recreational areas. Visit Museums, the Detroit Zoo, and don't forget Canada across Lake St. Clair or cross the border at Port Huron.

Locator 307-4011   Medical 307-4650   Police 307-4673

Other Installations in Michigan

Point Betsie Recreation Cottage, Coast Guard Group, MI 49417-5000. C-616-847-4510. Two-bedroom cottage (1), private bath, sleeps seven, furnished, gas grill, utensils, linens. Rates: $20-$25 daily. See *Military Living's Military RV, Camping and Rec Areas Around the World* for additional information and directions.

MINNESOTA

Camp Riley National Guard Training Center (MN02R2)
ATTN: Billeting
P.O. Box 150
Little Falls, MN 56345-0150

TELEPHONE NUMBER INFORMATION: Main installation numbers: C-320-632-7000, D-312-871-7000.

Location: From I-94 W to Clearwater exit, right on Hwy 24, N on Hwy 10, right to Route 371, left on Hwy 115, follow signs to front gate. USMRA: Page 80, (C,D-6). NMC: St. Cloud, 30 miles south.

Lodging Office: 6-76 Education Center, **C-320-632-7378, D-312-871-7378**, Fax C-320-632-7787, D-312-871-7787, E-mail: paycerl@tmg2.dma.state.mn.us, HP: www.dma.state.us/. 0700-2000 winter months, 0700-2300 summer months. Check in billeting, after hours check in main gate.

TML: TLQ. Bldg 7-171, 7-71, 10-73A, 10-173, all ranks, leave and official duty. 155 rooms. Handicap accessible rooms available. Refrigerator, color TV in unit and lounge, housekeeping service, washer/dryer, microwave in building, soda/snack vending. Meeting/conference rooms available. Rates: $13 leave/vacation; $10 PCS/TDY. Maximum one per unit. Duty can make reservations, others Space-A.

TML: DV/VIP. Bldg 8-71, 8-72, 18-71, 19-71, 19-73, O6+, active duty. Cottages (6). Refrigerator, kitchenette, color TV in lounge and unit, housekeeping service, washer/dryer, microwave in building. Rates: $18 per person per night; $15 PCS/TDY. Maximum capacity per unit 4 to 8. Duty is encouraged to make reservations, others Space-A.

DV/VIP: Personnel & Community Activities, P.O. Box 150, Little Falls, MN 56345-0150. C-320-632-7296. O6+.

TML Availability: Good, Oct-Apr. Difficult, Jun-Aug.

CREDIT CARDS ACCEPTED: Visa, MasterCard and American Express.

Minneapolis-St. Paul IAP/Air Reserve Station (MN01R2)
North Country Inn
934 SPTG/SVML - Bldg 711
760 Military Highway
Minneapolis, MN 55450-2000

TELEPHONE NUMBER INFORMATION: Main installation numbers: C-612-726-9440, D-312-783-1983/4.

Location: From I-35 north to crosstown MN-62 west to 34th Ave entrance. Follow signs to ARS. *USMRA: Page 89 (C-3).* NMC: Minneapolis-St Paul, in the city.

Lodging Office: The North Country Inn. 934 SPTG/SVML, Bldg 711, **C-612-713-1978**, Fax: C-612-713-1966, D-312-783-1966, 0700-2400 hours. Check in billeting 1430, check out 1000 hours.

MINNESOTA
Minneapolis-St. Paul IAP/Air Reserve Station, continued

Active duty, reservist, retired military, authorized dependents and duty government civilian employee billeting.

TML: VOQ. Bldg 711, officers, civilians, females (regardless of rank), SNCO (E7+), leave or official duty. Bedroom, private and semi-private baths. Officers (96); SNCO suites (3); DV suites (7). Refrigerator, A/C, color TV in room, housekeeping service, washer/dryer, ice vending. Older structure. Rates: first person $8, couple $11; suites first person $10, couple $14. Maximum two per room. Duty can make reservations any time, Space-A may make reservations 24 hours in advance.

TML: VAQ. Bldg 716, enlisted males (E6 and below). Private room, community bathroom (90). Refrigerator, A/C, color TV, housekeeping service, washer/dryer, ice vending. Older structure, to be renovated 1994. Rates: $8 single occupancy. Duty can make reservations, others Space-A.

TML Availability: Good, except Fri and Sat during Air Force (934th and 133AW) UTA drill weekends. Very scarce in summer.

CREDIT CARDS ACCEPTED: Visa, MasterCard and American Express.

While you're here check out the Mall of America, the Minnesota Zoo, various art museums and theaters. Also stop by the Metrodome to see either the Twins or Vikings play.

Locator 713-1000   **Medical 911**   **Police 713-1-911/1102**

MISSISSIPPI

Columbus Air Force Base (MS01R2)
Magnolia Inn, Bldg 956
14 SVS/SVML
179 F Street, Suite 6107
Columbus AFB, MS 39710-5000

TELEPHONE NUMBER INFORMATION: Main installation numbers: C-601-434-7322, D-312-742-7322.

Location: Off US-45 north, 60 miles west of Tuscaloosa, via US-82. *USMRA: Page 43 (G-3)*. NMC: Columbus, 10 miles south.

Lodging Office: Magnolia Inn, ATTN: 14th SVS/SVML, Bldg 956, F Street, **C-601-434-2548**, Fax: C-601-434-2777, D-312-742-2777, 24 hours. Check in billeting, check out 1200 hours daily. Government civilian employee billeting.

TML: TLF. Bldg 955, all ranks, leave or official duty. Bedrooms, private bath (20). Kitchen, utensils, A/C, color TV, housekeeping service, cribs/rollaway, washer/dryer, snack vending, ice vending, facilities for DAVs. Modern structure. Rate: E1-E6 $18 per unit; E7+ $22. Duty can make reservations, others Space-A.

MISSISSIPPI
Columbus Air Force Base, continued

TML: VOQ. Bldg 954, 956, officers all ranks, leave or official duty. Bedroom private bath (73); bedroom, private bath, kitchenette (58). Color TV, housekeeping service, washer/dryer, snack vending, ice vending. Older structure. Rates: first person $8.50, two people $11.75. Duty can make reservations, others Space-A.

TML: VAQ. Bldg 956, enlisted all ranks, leave or official duty. Spaces, semi-private bath (40); SNCO suites, private bath (3). Color TV, housekeeping service, washer/dryer, snack vending, ice vending. Older structure. Rates: first person $8.50, two people $11.75. Duty can make reservations, others Space-A.

DV/VIP: WG Exec, Bldg 724, C-601-434-7002 (active duty O6+ only). SNCO contact WG SEA at C-601-434-7005.

TML Availability: Good, Nov-Feb. Difficult, other times.

CREDIT CARDS ACCEPTED: American Express.

Columbus, with many antebellum structures never destroyed during the Civil War, is of interest to visitors. The area also hosts excellent fishing, boating and hunting along the Tennessee Tombigbee Waterway.

Locator 434-2841   Medical 434-2244   Police 434-7129

Gulfport Naval Construction Battalion Center (MS03R2)
BQ Director/Code 540
5200 CBC 2nd Street
Gulfport NCBC, MS 39501-5000

TELEPHONE NUMBER INFORMATION: Main installation numbers: C-601-871-2555, D-312-868-2121.

Location: Take US-49 south to Gulfport, follow signs to Center, from US-90 exit to US-49 (Broad Ave), from I-10 exit to US-49. *USMRA: Page 43 (F-10)*. NMC: New Orleans, LA, 70 miles west.

Lodging Office: ATTN: Commanding Officer, Code 540 BQ Director, 5200 CBC 2nd Street, Gulfport, MS 39501-5001. Reservations BEQ/BOQ: **C-601-871-2505**. Check in facility, check out 1300 hours daily. Government civilian employee billeting.

NAVY LODGE

TML: Navy Lodge. Bldg 331. All ranks, leave, retired or official duty. Reservations call **1-800-NAVY-INN.** Lodge number is C-601-864-3101, Fax: C-601-868-7392, check in 1500-2000 hours, check out 1200 hours daily. Bedroom, private bath (15). Two interconnecting units, 1 handicap accessible, 8 non-smoking. Kitchenette, microwave, utensils, A/C, CATV, VCR, clocks, coffee/tea (in office), cribs, rollaways, phones, hair dryers, high chairs, soda/snack vending, ice vending, iron/ironing board, housekeeping service, coin washer/dryer and playground. Modern structure. Rates: $42 (Oct-May); $50 (May to Oct) per unit. Maximum 5 per room. All categories can make reservations. *Runner-up of the 1996 Edward E. Carlson Award for Navy Lodge excellence in the small category.*

MISSISSIPPI
Gulfport Naval Construction Battalion Center, continued

TML: BOQ. Bldg 300, officers all ranks, leave or official duty, C-601-871-2226. Bedroom, private bath (36), (2 VIP rooms). Kitchen, A/C, color TV in room and lounge, housekeeping service, cribs/cots, washer/dryer, ice vending. Modern structure. Rates: $12 per person. Maximum three persons. Duty can make reservations C-601-871-2505.

TML: BEQ. Bldg 314, enlisted all ranks, leave, retired or official duty, C-601-871-2506. Bedroom, shared bath (90). A/C, color TV in room and lounge, telephone, housekeeping service, washer/dryer. Modern structure. Rates: $8 per person. Duty can make reservations, others Space-A.

DV/VIP: CO's Guest House. Bldg 102, C-601-871-2202, O6+. Rates: $22-$28. Retirees and lower ranks Space-A.

TML Availability: Good, Sep-Mar. Difficult, other times.

CREDIT CARDS ACCEPTED: Visa, MasterCard, American Express and Discover.

Transportation: Off base shuttle/bus Coast Linear Trans 432-2649, car rental agencies Thrifty 864-0762, Budget 864-5181, Hertz 863-276, off base taxi Yellow Cab 863-1511, Sun Cab 863-8002, City Cab 436-4655.

Swimming, fishing, sailing, windsurfing, sunning and beach combing in summer are popular. There are also casinos in the area. Visit Beauvoir (Confederate President Jefferson Davis' home), Gulf Islands National Seashore, Shearwater Pottery showroom.

Locator 871-2555   Medical 871-2807/2808   Police 871-2361

Keesler Air Force Base (MS02R2)
81 SVS/SVML
509 Larcher Blvd
Keesler AFB, MS 39534-2346

TELEPHONE NUMBER INFORMATION: Main installation numbers: C-601-377-1110, D-312-597-1110.

Location: From I-10 exit 46, follow signs to base. From US-90, north on White Ave to main gate. *USMRA: Page 43 (F-10).* NMC: Biloxi, in the city.

Lodging Office: Consolidated Front Desk for the **Inns of Keesler**: Bldg 2101, **Muse Manor** (C-601-377-2420), **C-601-377-2631/3663, D-312-597-2631/3663/3774,** Fax: C-601-597-3588 or C-601-377-0021, Mon-Fri. Check in facility, check out 1200 hours. Government civilian employee billeting.

TML: Guest House. Bldg 0470, all ranks, leave or official duty. Two bedroom, living room, dining room, semi-private bath (21). Refrigerator, housekeeping service, cribs, washer/dryer, ice vending. Rates: E7+ $22 single; E6 and below $18. Primarily for hospital patients and families of patients.

TML: VAQ. Bldgs 2101, 2002, 5025, enlisted all ranks, leave or official duty, C-601-377-2631. Bedroom, 2 beds, semi-private bath (638); separate bedrooms, semi-private bath for E7+ (8); bedroom, 1 bed, semi-private bath for E7+ (112). Refrigerator, A/C, color TV, housekeeping service, washer/dryer, snack vending, ice vending. Modern structure, renovated. Rates: enlisted $7, each additional person $2.50. Maximum two per room. Duty can make reservations, others Space-A.

MISSISSIPPI
Keesler Air Force Base, continued

TML: TLF. 0300 block, all ranks, leave or official duty. Separate bedrooms, private bath (40). Kitchen, utensils, A/C, color TV in room and lounge, housekeeping service, essentials, washer/dryer, snack vending, ice vending, playground rear of facility. Modern structure, renovated. Rates:E1-E6 $18; E7+ $22. Maximum five persons. Duty can make reservations, others Space-A.

TML: VOQ. Bldg 3821, 3823, 0470, 2004, officers all ranks, leave or official duty. Bedroom, private bath (224); bedroom, semi-private bath (328); two bedroom, semi-private bath (12); DV suites, private bath (6). Kitchen (98 rooms), A/C, color TV, housekeeping service, washer/dryer, ice vending. Modern structure. Rates: officers $8, each additional person $3; suites $10 per person, maximum $20 per suite. Duty can make reservations, others Space-A.

TML: Fisher House. Note: Appendix B has the definition of this facility. C-601-377-8264.

DV/VIP: KTTC/CCP, C-601-377-3359, E9+ and O6+, retirees and lower ranks Space-A.

TML Availability: Fairly good, all year. Best, Dec-Jan.

CREDIT CARDS ACCEPTED: Visa, MasterCard and American Express.

Biloxi is rich in history: eight flags have flown over the city. Visit the Old French House off Hwy 90, Ship Island, 12 miles offshore, the Jefferson Davis Shrine. White sand beaches, golf, fishing, boating and sailing are available.

Locator 377-2798   Medical 377-6555   Police 377-3720

Meridian Naval Air Station (MS04R2)
CBQ Manager
Bldg 218 (CBQ), Fuller Road
Meridian NAS, MS 39309-5003

TELEPHONE NUMBER INFORMATION: Main installation numbers: C-601-679-2211, D-312-367-2211.

Location: Take I-20 to Hwy 39 north from Meridian for 12 miles to 4-lane access road, clearly marked. Right for three miles to NAS main gate. *USMRA: Page 43 (G-6)*. NMC: Meridian, 15 miles southwest.

Lodging Office: Bldg 218 (CBQ), Fuller Road, **C-601-679-2186**, Fax: C-601-679-2745, 24 hours. Enter at main gate, go straight to flashing red light, turn left and proceed approximately .5 miles. Turn left at large complex (first building past Lake Helen), enter First Deck Central Complex. Check in facility, check out 1300 hours daily. Government civilian employee billeting.

TML: Family Quarters. Bldg 208, enlisted all ranks, leave or official duty. Separate bedrooms, private bath (25). Refrigerator, community kitchen, A/C, color TV, movie rental, housekeeping service, cribs/rollaways $1, washer/dryer, soda/snack vending. Meeting/conference room, exercise room, and mini-mart available. Older structure, renovated in 1988. Rates: $13 per room per night first three persons, each additional person $1. Maximum five per room. Duty can make reservations, others Space-A.

MISSISSIPPI
Meridian Naval Air Station, continued

TML: BEQ. Bldgs 218, enlisted all ranks, leave or official duty, handicap accessible. Bedroom, semi-private bath (12); bedroom, private bath (17). Refrigerator, community kitchen, A/C, color TV, movie rental, housekeeping service, washer/dryer, ice vending, soda/snack vending. Meeting/conference room, exercise room, and mini-mart available. Older structure, remodeled. Rates: E1-E9 $6. Maximum two per room. Duty can make reservations, others Space-A.

TML: VOQ. Bldg 218, officers all ranks, leave or official duty. Handicap accessible. Separate bedrooms, private bath (40). Community kitchen, A/C, color TV, movie rental, housekeeping service, cribs/rollaways $1, washer/dryer, ice vending, soda/snack vending. Meeting/conference room, exercise room, and mini-mart available.. Older structure, remodeled. Rates: single $10 per night, $15 per night up to three persons, each additional person $1. Maximum five per room.

TML: DV/VIP. Bldg 218, officer O6+, leave or official duty, handicap accessible. Two bedroom, private bath (6). Two units have kitchen, all have refrigerators. Community kitchen, limited utensils, A/C, color TV and VCR, movie rental, housekeeping service, cribs/rollaways $1, washer/dryer, ice vending, soda/snack vending. Meeting/conference room, exercise room, and mini-mart available.. Older structure, remodeled. Rates: $18 per room, maximum $18. Maximum three per room. Duty can make reservations, others Space-A.

TML Availability: Excellent year-round.

CREDIT CARDS ACCEPTED: Visa, MasterCard and American Express.

Transportation: Off base shuttle/bus, off base taxi.

Take a driving tour of the historic Natchez Trace, a local flea market, nearby Flora's Petrified Forest, and the Choctaw Fair for American Indian life and lore. ITT (in MWR) has information on theatrical, sports, special events tickets. Horseback riding, fishing, rollerblading, jogging trails, and bowling alley are all on base.

Locator 679-2528   Medical 679-2633   Police 679-2958

Pascagoula Naval Station (MS06R2)
100 Singing River Island, Bldg 63
Pascagoula, MS 39567-5000

TELEPHONE NUMBER INFORMATION: Main installation numbers: C-601-761-2181, D-312-358-2181.

Location: From I-10 E, exit 69, 4 miles south to Hwy 90, 4 miles west to Ingalls Access Road, 1 mile to Naval Station Causeway, three miles to gate. *USMRA: Page 43 (G-10)*. NMC: Pascagoula 2 miles east.

Lodging Office: Bldg 63, Singing River Island, **C-601-761-2182, D-312-358-2182,** Fax: C-601-761-2179, D-312-358-2179, 24 hours. Check in, check out 1200 hours daily, for late check out call C-601-761-2179. Government civilian employee billeting.

TML: TLF. Bldg 63, all ranks, leave or official duty. Handicap accessible. Separate bedrooms, semi-private bath (3), bedrooms, semi-private bath (12). Refrigerator, A/C, color TV, housekeeping service, washer/dryer, snack vending, ice vending. Fast food on base. Older structure. Rates: $5-$23 depending upon room. Active duty/reservists may make reservations, other Space-A.

Temporary Military Lodging Around the World - 151

MISSISSIPPI
Pascagoula Naval Station, continued

TML Availability: Very Good. (Reduced during remodeling, approximately 18 months beginning 1 July 1997).

CREDIT CARDS ACCEPTED: Visa, MasterCard and American Express.

Take a driving tour of the historic Natchez Trace, a local flea market, nearby Flora's Petrified Forest, and the Choctaw Fair for American Indian life and lore. ITT (in MWR) has information on theatrical, sports, special events tickets.

Medical 761-2363   Police 761-3333

Other Installations in Mississippi

Camp Shelby Training Site, Camp Shelby, MS 39047-5500. BEQ/BOQ **C-601-558-2540**, Fax C-601-558-2339.

MISSOURI

Fort Leonard Wood (MO03R2)
Billeting Manager
Bldg 470, Room 1201, Replacement Ave
Fort Leonard Wood, MO 65473-5000

TELEPHONE NUMBER INFORMATION: Main installation numbers: C-573-596-0131, D-312-581-0110.

Location: Two miles south of I-44, adjacent to Street Robert and Waynesville, at Fort Leonard Wood exit. *USMRA: Page 81 (E-6)*. NMC: Springfield, 85 miles southwest.

Lodging Office: Bldg 470, room 1201, Replacement Ave, **C-1-800-677-8356**, 24 hours. Check in billeting, check out 1200 hours daily. Government civilian employee billeting for TDY.

TML: Guest House. Many buildings, all ranks, leave or official duty. Handicap accessible (4). Separate bedroom, private bath (79). Refrigerator, microwave, stove top burners, utensils, iron/ironing board, A/C, color TV, housekeeping service, cribs/cots, washer/dryers, playroom. Rates: active duty by grade; retirees $24, each additional person $1; all others $36, each additional person $1. Pets allowed in four units at $3 per day. Reservations accepted for PCS in/out, persons with hospital appointments, and families of graduating soldiers, others Space-A.

TML: TDY. Eleven buildings, all ranks, official duty only. Bedroom, private bath (500). A/C, essentials, snack vending, ice vending, kitchen, limited utensils, housekeeping service, refrigerator, color TV, washer/dryer. Modern structure. Rates: sponsor $9, each additional person $3.50. Maximum two persons. Duty can make reservations, others Space-A.

TML: VOQ. Bldgs 4102, 4104, officers all ranks. TDY only. Bedroom, private bath (74); separate bedroom suites, private bath (8). Kitchen (47 units), refrigerator (74 units), A/C, color TV, housekeeping service, washer/dryer, ice vending, coffee makers, iron/ironing board. Modern

MISSOURI
Fort Leonard Wood, continued

structure, remodeled. Rates: sponsor $9, each additional person $3.50. Maximum two per room. Duty can make reservations, others Space-A.

TML: DV/VIP. Bldg 4104, officer O6+, official duty. Separate bedroom suites, private bath (8); three bedroom suite, private bath (1). Kitchen, utensils, A/C, color TV, housekeeping service. Modern structure. Rates: sponsor $13, each additional person $3.50. Maximum two per room. Duty can make reservations, others Space-A.

DV/VIP: Protocol Office, C-513-596-6183, O6/GS-15+. Retirees and lower ranks Space-A.

TML Availability: Good. Best Dec. Difficult May-Oct.

CREDIT CARDS ACCEPTED: Visa, MasterCard, American Express and Discover.

Crystal clear rivers and streams provide fishing, float trips, canoeing. Campers, hikers, hunters and horseback riders find the Ozarks a paradise. Guided tours through caves, and all levels of spelunking are available.

Locator 596-0677   Medical 596-0496   Police 596-6141

Lake of the Ozarks Recreation Area (MO01R2)
Route 1, Box 380
Linn Creek, MO 65052-5000

TELEPHONE NUMBER INFORMATION: Main installation numbers: C-573-596-0131, D-312-581-0110.

Location: From I-70 at Columbia, take Hwy 63 to Jefferson City, then take US-54 southwest to Linn Creek area, left at County Road A for 6 miles. Left on Lake Road (county sign A33) for 4.7 miles to travel camp. From I-44 northeast of Springfield, MO-7 northwest to Richland, right on State Road A and travel 19.8 miles to Freedom, right on Lake Road A33, approximately 5 miles to travel camp. *USMRA: Page 81 (D-6).* NMC: Jefferson City, 40 miles northeast.

Lodging Office: Bldg 528, Fort Leonard Wood, MO. Reservations required by phone, **C-573-346-5640** or in person, (3 Mar-23May 0900-1700 Mon-Wed; 24 May-1 Sep 0900-1700 Mon-Fri) No mail reservations. Call 30-45 days in advance. Full advance payment. Full service Memorial Day weekend-Labor Day weekend. Fri-Sun operations, Apr/May and Sep/Oct. Check in facility 1500 hours, check out 1100 hours day of departure. Active/Retiree/Reserve/National Guard/DoD Civilians are eligible.

TML: Mobile homes (27), cabins (3), duplexes (2). Two and three bedroom, A/C, kitchen, private bath, color TV, sofa bed.. Furnished except cleaning supplies. Linens, including towels, in duplexes and cabins. .Linens, but NO towels, in mobile homes. Rates: two-bedroom duplexes $49-$76/night, cabins $46-$72, three-bedroom deluxe mobile homes $41-$66, three-bedroom regular mobile homes $33-$59 per night, two-bedroom mobile homes $25-$48. A/C, kitchen, dishes and utensils, some cleaning supplies, color TV, no linens provided (except lake view mobile homes, duplexes). Rates applicable for active and retired personnel.

TML Availability: Fairly good, in season. Very good, off season.

MISSOURI
Lake of the Ozarks Recreation Area, continued

CREDIT CARDS ACCEPTED: Visa, MasterCard, American Express and Discover.

New Lake front trailers, cabins, duplexes, rustic and hookup campsites, rental office, and a 20 bay berthing dock for private boat storage. Jet Skis are available. This is a large and fully equipped recreational area, see Military Living's *Military RV, Camping and Rec Areas Around the World*.

Locator 596-0131   Medical 596-9331   Police 346-3693

Marine Corps Support Activity at Richards-Gebaur Airport (MO02R2)
15820 Elmwood Ave
Kansas City, MO 64147-1400

TELEPHONE NUMBER INFORMATION: Main installation numbers: C-816-843-3800.

Location: From Kansas City take US-71 south to 155th Street exit for Richards-Gebaur Memorial Airport. Between Granview and Belton. *USMRA: Page 81 (B-5), Page 89 (B-5)*. NMC: Kansas City, 17 miles north.

Lodging Office: Bldg 250, C-816-843-3850/1/2, D-312-894-3850/51, Fax C-816-843-3857, 0630-2345 Mon-Fri, 0730-2345 Sat-Sun, 0730-1600 holidays. Check in lodging office 1300 hours, check out 1100 hours daily.

TML: Bldg 250, 252. (102) Bedroom, shared bath; bedroom, private bath; family suites (4). DV suites (4). Bldg 250 modern structure, renovated. Bldg 252 modern structure, under renovation at press time. Refrigerator, telephones, housekeeping service, washer/dryer. Small exchange, community club and MWR office available. Rates: single $15; double shared bath $20; single $20, double private bath $25; family suites $22; single $25, double DV suites $35. Duty can make reservations, all others Space-A.

TML Availability: Good.

CREDIT CARDS ACCEPTED: Visa, MasterCard and American Express.

Many do not know this lodging still exists because the old Richards-Gebaur AFB is closed.

Whiteman Air Force Base (MO04R2)
Whiteman Inn
P.O. Box 5032
Whiteman AFB, MO 65305-5097

TELEPHONE NUMBER INFORMATION: Main installation numbers: C-816-687-1110, D-312-975-1110.

Location: From I-70 south exit to US-13 to US-50 east for 10 miles, then right on MO-132 which leads to AFB. *USMRA: Page 81 (C-5)*. NMC: Kansas City, MO 60 miles west.

MISSOURI
Whiteman Air Force Base, continued

Lodging Office: The Whiteman Inn. Bldg 325, Mitchell Ave, **C-816-687-1844**, Fax: C-816-687-3052, D-312-975-3052, 24 hours. Check in lodging 1600-1800, check out 1100 hours daily.

TML: TLF. Bldgs 3003, 3201/3/5 and 6 all ranks, leave or official duty. Three bedroom apartments, private bath (2); Bedroom, private bath (29). Kitchen, complete utensils, A/C, essentials, refrigerator, color TV, housekeeping service, cribs/cots, washer/dryer, ice vending. Handicap accessible (1). New and older structure, renovated. Rates: E1-E4, O1 $12; E5-E6 $19; E7+ and Space-A $24. PCS in/out can make reservations (60 days in advance recommended), others Space-A.

TML: Military Hospital. All ranks, leave or official duty, check in facility. Bedroom, semi-private bath (25). A/C, black/white TV, facilities for DAVs. Modern structure. Rates: $6.50 per person. Duty can make reservations, others Space-A.

TML: VOQ. Bldg 3200, officers all ranks, leave or official duty. Bedroom, living room, private bath (52), DV Suites (9). Refrigerator, microwave, A/C, essentials, color TV, housekeeping service, cribs/cots, washer/dryer. Modern structure. Rates: first person $10, two or more persons $14; DV Suites $16 and $23. Maximum two per room. Duty can make reservations, others Space-A.

TML: TAQ/VAQ. Bldg 1551, enlisted all ranks, leave or official duty. Separate bedrooms, semi-private bath (50); suites, semi-private bath (6). Refrigerator, A/C, essentials, CATV in room and lounge, housekeeping service, cots/cribs, ice vending, washer/dryer. Handicap accessible. Modern structure. Rates: suites, sponsor $10, adult maximum $14. Maximum two per suite. Duty can make reservations, others Space-A.

TML: DV/VIP. Bldgs 3001 (Truman House), 119 Travis Lane (Century House), 115 Travis Lane (Travis House) officers O6+, leave or official duty. Three bedroom house, 2 baths, (2); two bedroom house, private bath (1). Kitchen, all amenities. Rates: first person $27, two people $39.50. Duty can make reservations, others Space-A.

DV/VIP: Protocol: 509 SMW/CCP, C-816-687-7144, O6+. Retirees and lower ranks if other quarters are full.

TML Availability: Good all year except late July because of State Fair. Best, winter.

CREDIT CARDS ACCEPTED: Visa, MasterCard and American Express.

Locator 687-1841   Medical 687-3733   Police 687-3700

MONTANA

Malmstrom Air Force Base (MT03R3)
Malmstrom Inns
341 SVS/SVML
7028 4th Ave N
Malmstrom AFB, MT 59402-6835

TELEPHONE NUMBER INFORMATION: Main installation numbers: C-406-731-1110, D-312-632-1110.

MONTANA
Malmstrom Air Force Base, continued

Location: From I-15 north or south take 10th Ave south exit to AFB. From east take Malmstrom exit off US-87/89 to AFB. Clearly marked. *USMRA: Page 99 (D,E-4).* NMC: Great Falls, 1 mile west.

Lodging Office: Malmstrom Inns. 7028 4th Ave N, Bldg 1680, **C-406-727-8600/731-3394, D-312-632-3394,** Fax: C-406-731-3848, D-312-632-3848, 24 hours. Check in lodging, check out 1200 hours daily.

TML: TLF. Bldgs 1210, 1212, 1214, 1216. One mile from billeting office. All ranks, leave or official duty. Separate bedrooms, private bath (39). Kitchen, utensils, A/C, color TV, housekeeping service, cribs/cots, washer/dryer, ice vending. Older structure, renovated. Rates: $24. Maximum five per unit. Duty can make reservations, others Space-A.

TML: VOQ. Bldg 1620, officers all ranks, leave or official duty. Bedroom, private bath (22); separate bedroom suites, private bath (4); separate bedroom suites, private bath (DV/VIP) (4). Refrigerator, wet bar, microwave, color TV, housekeeping service, washer/dryer, ice vending. Older structure, renovated 1994. Rates: leave/duty $10 per room, each additional person $4; suites $16; double $23. Children not authorized. Duty can make reservations, others Space-A.

TML: VAQ. Bldg 1680, enlisted all ranks, leave or official duty. Bedroom, semi-private bath (27). Private rooms (2), separate bedroom suites (4). Refrigerator, microwave, color TV, ice vending, washer/dryer. Rates: single $10; double $14; suite $16; double suite $23. Maximum 2 persons. No children. Duty can make reservations, others Space-A.

DV/VIP: Protocol Office. 341 MW/CCP, Bldg 500, C-406-731-3430, O6+. Retirees Space-A.

TML Availability: Good, winter. Difficult, May-Sep.

CREDIT CARDS ACCEPTED: Visa, MasterCard and American Express.

This facility won the Air Force Innkeeper Award for 1996. It is one of Space Command's certified (four star) facilities in the command. Visit the Malmstrom Museum on base.

Locator 731-4121   **Medical 731-3424**   **Police 731-3895**

NEBRASKA

Offutt Air Force Base (NE02R3)
Offutt Inns
105 Grants Pass Street
Offutt AFB, NE 68113-2084

TELEPHONE NUMBER INFORMATION: Main installation numbers: C-402-294-1110, D-312-271-1110.

Location: From south-bound I-29/east or west-bound I-80, exit to US-75, then south 6.5 miles to AFB entrance. From north-bound I-29, exit to US-370, west 5.5 miles to Lincoln Street, then south .25 miles to AFB gate. *USMRA: Page 82 (I,J-5).* NMC: Omaha, north 8 miles.

NEBRASKA
Offutt Air Force Base, continued

Lodging Office: Guest Reception Center, Bldg 44, Grants Pass Street, **C-402-294-9000, D-312-271-3671,** Fax: C-402-294-3199, 24 hours. Check in 1500 hours, check out 1200 hours daily. Government civilian employee lodging. Reservations accepted on first-call, first-served basis. Duty personnel encouraged to re-confirm three days prior to arrival. Space-A confirmed/non-confirmed 24 hours prior to arrival.

TML: DVQ. Fort Crook House, quarters 13 (non-smoking), officers O6+, official duty or leave. Two bedroom, private bath (2). Full kitchen, microwave, A/C, color TV, housekeeping service, essentials. Historic Bldg - 1900, renovated. Rates: single $16, double $23. Maximum two persons per unit.

TML: VOQ. Fort Crook House, quarters 13 (non-smoking), officers/senior enlisted, official duty or leave. Separate bedroom suite, private bath (6); separate bedroom suite, shared bath (2). Kitchen, refrigerator, microwave, utensils, A/C, color TV, washer/dryer, housekeeping service, essentials. Historic Bldg -1900, renovated. Rates: single $16, double $23. Maximum four per unit.

TML: VOQ/SNCOQ. Malmstrom Inn, Bldg 432 (non-smoking), officers all ranks, SNCO (E7+), official duty or leave. Separate bedroom suite, private bath (28) SNCOQ (8). Refrigerator, microwave, A/C, color TV, housekeeping service, washer/dryer, ice vending, essentials. Older structure, renovated. Rates: SNCOQ single $16, double $23; VOQ single $8, double $16. Maximum two per unit.

TML: VOQ/VAQ. O'Malley Inn, Bldg 436 (non-smoking). Officer/enlisted, all ranks, official duty or leave. Bedroom, private bath (79). One handicap accessible unit. Refrigerator, microwave, A/C, color TV, housekeeping service, washer/dryer, ice vending. Modern structure. Rates: single $10, double $14. Maximum two per unit.

TML: DVQ. Offutt Inn, Bldg 479 (smoking), officer O6+, official duty or leave. Separate bedroom suites, private bath (5). Refrigerator, microwave, A/C, color TV, housekeeping service, washer/dryer, ice vending, essentials. Older structure, renovated. Rates: single $16, double $23. Maximum two per suite.

TML: VOQ/VAQ. Offutt Inn, Bldg 479, (smoking), officer/enlisted all ranks, official duty or leave. Bedroom, private bath (39). Older structure, renovated; two units handicap accessible. Refrigerator, microwave, A/C, color TV, washer/dryer, ice vending, housekeeping service, essentials. Older Structure - Renovated. Rates: VOQ single $10, double $14; VAQ single $10, double $14. Maximum two per room.

TML: VOQ. Bellevue/Papillion Lodges, Bldgs 5791/2. Officer/enlisted; large family; official duty or leave. Three bedroom, private bath (2). Complete kitchen, microwave, A/C, color TV, washer/dryer, housekeeping service, essentials. Older Structure - Renovated. Rates. single $16, double $23. Maximum six per unit.

TML: TLF. Platte River Lodge, Bldgs 5089-5093, all ranks, official duty or leave. Two room, private bath cottage (60). Complete kitchen, microwave, A/C, color TV, VCR, crib, highchair, washer/dryer, ice machines, housekeeping service, essentials. Older structure, renovated. Rates: E1, E2 O1 $14; E3-E6 $20.50; E7+ $24. Maximum six per unit.

DV/VIP: USSTRATCOM Protocol, Bldg: 500, C-402-294-4212, O7+. Retirees, Space-A.

Temporary Military Lodging Around the World - 157

NEBRASKA
Offutt Air Force Base, continued

TML Availability: Good. Best, Dec-Jan. More difficult, other times.

CREDIT CARDS ACCEPTED: Visa, MasterCard and American Express.

Try nearby Omaha's Old Town for shopping and dining, Fontenelle Park for hiking and the historic Southern Railroad Depot for getting in touch with this interesting area. Don't miss the Joslyn Art Museum. The Henry Dooly Zoo is located next to Rosenblatt Stadium, which hosts the College World Series in June.

Locator 294-5125   **Medical 294-7432**   **Police 294-5677**

NEVADA

Fallon Naval Air Station (NV02R4)
CBQ, Bldg 304
Fallon NAS, NV 89496-5000

TELEPHONE NUMBER INFORMATION: Main installation numbers: C-702-426-5161, D-312-890-2110.

Location: From US-50 exit to US-95 south at Fallon, for 5 miles to left on Union Street to NAS. *USMRA: Page 113 (C-4)*. NMC: Reno, 61 miles west.

Lodging Office: BEQ, **C-702-428-3003, D-312-890-2378,** BOQ **C-702-428-3000/3198,** Fax: C-702-426-2908, D-312-830-2908, open 24 hours. Reservations: C-702-426-2859, D-312-890-2859 BOQ check in facility, check out 1000 hours. Government civilian employee billeting.

TML: BEQ. Barracks 3, 5, 6, 7, 10, 11, 12, enlisted all ranks, leave or official duty. Total 587 units. Bedroom, shared bath; bedroom, 2 beds, shared bath; VIP rooms (10). Refrigerator, A/C, color TV w/VCR, housekeeping service, washer/dryer, ice vending. Exercise, conference rooms, mini-mart available. Modern structure. Rates: $6-$15. VIP. Duty can make reservations, retired and leave, Space-A.

TML: BOQ. Bldg 468, officers all ranks, leave or official duty. Bedroom, semi-private bath; separate bedrooms, private bath; DV/VIP suites, private bath (8). DVQ Suites w/fullsize kitchen (2). Kitchen (114 units), refrigerator, A/C, color TV, housekeeping service, washer/dryer, ice vending. Modern structure. Rates: sponsor $15, each additional person $3; DV/VIP $20. Duty can make reservations, others Space-A.

NAVY LODGE **TML:** Navy Lodge. Near Exchange Mall. **C-1-800-NAVY-INN.** C-702-426-2818, Fax: 702-426-2944. Large Double rooms, private bath, Kitchen (6). Rates: $38 per unit per night. Check in and out at main exchange. Check in by 1700.

DV/VIP: BOQ billeting C-702 426-2859. D 312 890-2859.

TML Availability: Impossible during CVW deployments - excellent rest of the time.

158 - Temporary Military Lodging Around the World

NEVADA
Fallon Naval Air Station, continued

CREDIT CARDS ACCEPTED: Visa, American Express.

Transportation: On base shuttle, car rental available.

The Carson River and Lake Lahontan fishing, boating, swimming, water skiing and local rock collecting are of interest. Call MWR for special rates to Reno, ghost towns, Virginia City, and other points of interest.

Locator 426-2709   Medical 426-3110   Police 426-2803

Indian Springs Air Force Auxiliary Field (NV03R4)
Lodging Office, Bldg 65
Indian Springs, NV 89018-7001

TELEPHONE NUMBER INFORMATION: Main installation numbers: C-702-652-0401, D-312-682-0401.

Location: On US 95, 45 miles North of Las Vegas. Clearly marked. *USMRA: Page 113 (F-8)*. NMC: Las Vegas, 4 miles south.

Lodging Office: Bldg 65, **C-702-652-0401, D-312-682-0401,** 0730-1630 hours daily. Check in billeting, check out 1100 hours daily. Write to: P.O. Box 569, Indian Springs, NV, 89018.

TML: VOQ. Bldg 37, officers, O6+. Bedroom, 2 beds, hall bath (1); separate bedroom suite, private bath (1). Kitchen, utensils, color TV, VCR, housekeeping service, essentials, washer/dryer.

TML: VAQ/VOQ. Bldgs 4-8, 24,127. All ranks, leave or official duty. Bedroom, 2 beds, private bath (107). Kitchenette (Bldg 127), utensils on request, refrigerator, color TV in lounge and room, housekeeping service, toiletries, washer/dryer, ice machine (Bldg 24), snack vending. Rates: enlisted $7; officer $9. All categories may make reservations 24 hours in advance of arrival. No pets.

TML Availability: Fairly good. Best winter months, more difficult, summer.

There is a casino off base with gaming available here, and the Las Vegas area offers many other activities. But the desert also attracts rock hounds, and would-be archeologist who look at Indian drawings among the red rock formations.

Locator 652-0401   Medical 118   Police 116

Nellis Air Force Base (NV01R4)
554 SVS/SVML
5990 Fitzgerald Blvd
Nellis AFB, NV 89191-6514

TELEPHONE NUMBER INFORMATION: Main installation numbers: C-702-652-1110, D-312-682-1110.

Location: Off I-15 north of Las Vegas. Also accessible from US-91/93. Clearly marked. *USMRA: Page 113 (G-9)*. NMC: Las Vegas, 8 miles southwest.

NEVADA
Nellis Air Force Base, continued

Lodging Office: Bldg 780, 5990 Fitzgerald Blvd, **C-702-643-2710, D-312-682-2711**, Fax: C-702-652-9172, D-312-682-9172 (**Fax numbers for those on official orders only**), 24 hours. Check in billeting, check out 1200 hours daily. Government civilian employee billeting. Note: there is additional lodging at Indian Springs, call C-702-652-0401 for information.

TML: TLF. 2900s (9 buildings). All ranks, leave or official duty. Handicap accessible. Bedroom, private bath (60). Wall beds in all living rooms. A/C, refrigerator, kitchen, complete utensils, color TV with VCR, housekeeping service, cribs/cots, playground for children, washer/dryer, snack vending, ice vending. Modern structure, remodeled. Rates: $20-$24. Maximum five per unit. Duty can make reservations, Space-A reservations one day prior to arrival.

TML: VAQ. Bldgs 536 and 552, enlisted, all ranks. Bedroom, semi-private bath (258). SNCO rooms, private bath (5). Chief's suite, private bath (1). Single rooms (1 double bed), shared bath (8). Refrigerator, A/C, color TV (with VCR, Bldg 552), housekeeping service, washer/dryer, essentials, snack vending, ice vending, microwave, room telephone, clock radio. Modern structure, remodeled. Rates: $10 per person; Chief's suite $9. Maximum two persons per unit. Children not allowed during deployments. Duty can make reservations, Space-A reservations one day prior to arrival..

TML: VOQ. Bldgs 523, 538, 540, 545, officers all ranks, leave or official duty. Bedroom, private bath (153). VIP suites, private bath (5). Kitchen, utensils only in suites, essentials, refrigerator, A/C, color TV with VCR, housekeeping service, washer/dryer, microwave, room telephone, clock radio, iron/ironing board. Modern structures. Rates: $10 per person, $14 per person VIP suites, all other VOQ rooms $8. Maximum two persons per unit. No children. Duty can make reservations, Space-A reservations one day prior to arrival.

DV/VIP: Protocol Office, Bldg 620, room 112, C-702-643-2987, D-312-682-2987.

TML Availability: Extremely limited. Best, spring and Nov-Dec. Difficult other times.

CREDIT CARDS ACCEPTED: Visa, MasterCard and American Express.

The Las Vegas area offers Lake Mead for boating and swimming, Mt Charleston for snow skiing, Red Rock Canyon for scenic hiking, and Hoover Dam for sheer wonderment. Of course, Las Vegas is noted for night life and gaming!

Locator 652-1841   Medical 653-2343   Police 652-2311

NEW HAMPSHIRE

Portsmouth Naval Shipyard (NH02R1)
CBQ/H-23
Portsmouth, NH 03804-5000

TELEPHONE NUMBER INFORMATION: Main installation numbers: C-207-438-1000, FAX 207-438-3580.

160 - Temporary Military Lodging Around the World

NEW HAMPSHIRE
Portsmouth Naval Shipyard, continued

Location: From I-95 north take Maine exit #2 to Route 236, approximately 1.5 miles to gate #2. Located on an island on Piscataqua River between Portsmouth and Kittery, ME. *USMRA: Page 23 (H-9)*. NMC: Boston, 60 miles south.

Lodging Office: Bldg H-23, Central registration **C-207-438-1513/2015**, Fax: C-207-438-3580, D-315-685-1513, 24 hours. Check in after 1400, check out 1200 hours.

TML: BOQ/BEQ/DVOQ All ranks, leave (space available) or official duty (may make reservations 30 days in advance), handicap accessible. Fitness center, hot tub with sauna available. Color TV-VCR in rooms, video rental at front desk. Housekeeping service daily. Hairdryer, amenities basket, refrigerator/microwave, large screen TV in lounge, washer/dryer, available Sunday sales include frozen pizza, dinners, soda, chips candy, burritos & personal items. No pets. Rates: BOQ Suite $15.75, each additional person $3.75; BOQ single $8.25, each additional person $2; DVOQ $19 per room, each additional person $4; BEQ E5-E9 $8.25 per room, each additional guest $2; BEQ E1-E4 $4.75 per guest. Maximum three per room. No pets. Duty can make reservations, others Space-A.

TML: Family quarters. Eight two-room suites with the above amenities. Rates: $15.75 per room, $4 per additional guest. Children under five free. Due to room size, families with more than five persons must rent two rooms. No Pets.

TML Availability: Fairly good. Depends on number of ships in overhaul.

CREDIT CARDS ACCEPTED: American Express.

Local skiing at White Mountain, outlet shopping in nearby Kittery, and trips to Boston are some of the favorite pursuits in this area.

Locator 438-1000   **Medical** 438-2555   **Police** 438-2351

NEW JERSEY

Armament Research, Development and Engineering Center (NJ01R1)
US Army ARDEC
ATTN: AMSTA-AR-PWH, Bldg 34N
Picatinny Arsenal, NJ 07806-5000

TELEPHONE NUMBER INFORMATION: Main installation numbers: C-201-724-4021, D-312-880-4012.

Location: Take I-80 west, exit 34B, follow signs to Center, 1 mile north. From I-80 east, exit 33 follow signs to Center. *USMRA: Page 19 (E-2)*. NMC: Newark, 30 miles east.

Lodging Office: ATTN: AMSTA-AR-PWH, Bldg 34N, **C-201-724-3506/2190**, Fax: C-201-724-6801, D-312-880-6801, 0800-1630 Mon-Fri. Check in billeting 1500, check out 1100 hours daily. After hours, persons with reservations may check in with Desk Sgt for key, Bldg 173, C-201-724-6666. Government civilian employee billeting.

NEW JERSEY
Armament Research, Development and Engineering Center, continued

TML: Guest House/VIP. Bldg 110, all ranks, leave or official duty. Four room, three bed VIP suite, kitchen, living room, dining area, private bath (1); three room apartments, private bath (1). Community kitchen, refrigerator, A/C, color TV in room and lounge, housekeeping service, cribs/cots, washer/dryer. Older structure, renovated. Rates: Guest House, single $18, double $24; child 3-12 $2, 13+ $6; each additional person $7; VIP single $30, double $38, children 3-12 $3, 13+ $8.

TML Availability: Fairly good, Oct-Apr. Difficult, other times.

CREDIT CARDS ACCEPTED: American Express.

Visit the Village Green in Morristown for shopping and Rockaway Townsquare Mall with its 100+ stores and foodcourt, enjoy local restaurants specializing in German, French, Italian, Spanish and Greek food. Don't miss the New Jersey Shakespeare Festival at Drew University.

Locator 724-2852   Medical 724-2113   Police 724-6666

Bayonne Military Ocean Terminal (NJ10R1)
Liberty Lodge
Bldg 51A, Military Ocean Terminal
Bayonne, NJ 07002-5302
Scheduled to close July 2001.

TELEPHONE NUMBER INFORMATION: Main installation numbers: C-201-823-5111, D-312-247-0111.

Location: From New Jersey Turnpike, exit 14A to NJ-169 east to main gate. Follow green and white signs. *USMRA: Page 26 (C-5,6).* NMC New York City, 10 miles northeast.

Lodging Office: None.

Guest House: Liberty Lodge. C-201-823-8700, D-312-247-5666, Fax: C-201-823-5664 for reservations and information,0630-2330. Bedrooms, with two double beds, private bath (40). TV, telephone, individually controlled heating and A/C. Rates: room $50 per night, with kitchenette $55. All ranks, retirees, DoD Civilians, family and friends Space-A basis.

TML Availability: Fair.

CREDIT CARDS ACCEPTED: Visa, MasterCard, American Express and Diners' Club.

Inexpensive day: take the ferry from Staten Island to Battery Park. From there you can visit the Statue of Liberty, (by taking another ferry), or walk to the World Trade Center, Wall Street, or Chinatown, (Canal St, from the Park subway).

Locator 823-5111   Medical 823-7371   Police 823-6666/6000

162 - Temporary Military Lodging Around the World

NEW JERSEY

Cape May Coast Guard Training Center (NJ13R1)
MWR Office
1 Munroe Ave
Cape May, NJ, 08204-5002

TELEPHONE NUMBER INFORMATION: Main installation numbers: C-609-898-6900, D-312-898-6900.

Location: From the Garden State Parkway south, Parkway turns into Lafayette. Go over 2 bridges and turn left onto Sidney Ave, left on Washington, then take the first right and follow to Pittsburgh. Follow sign to Training Center entrance. *USMRA: Page 19 (D-10)*. NMC: Wildwood, 8 miles north.

Lodging Office: MWR Office, Bldg 269. 0800 to 1630 Mon-Fri. No after hours, Sat, Sun or holiday. **C-609-898-6922,** Check in, out at MWR Office. Government civilian employee billeting.

TML: TLQ. Officers and enlisted all ranks. Cottages, 2 bedrooms, private bath (6). Refrigerator, kitchenette, utensils, CATV, cribs/cots. Wood frame buildings. PCS and TDY have priority, others Space-A. Rates equivalent to BAQ and VHA per day.

DV/VIP: MWR Office. C-609-898-6922. O6+. Retirees and lower ranks Space-A.

TML Availability: Lodging in the TLQ on a Space-A basis is quite rare year round, according to officials at Cape May.

Townsends Inlet Recreation Facility is located 15 miles north, call C-609-263-3722 for activities. Resort Area. Fishing Boating, beaches. Museums, and parks abound.

Locator 898-6900   Medical 898-6959   Police 911

Earle Naval Weapons Station (NJ11R1)
Quality of Life Department
201 Hwy 34 S
Colts Neck, NJ 07722-5020

TELEPHONE NUMBER INFORMATION: Main installation numbers: C-908-866-2000, D-312-449-2000.

Location: From Garden State Parkway, south, exit 100-B, Route 33 West to Route 34 North. *USMRA: Page 19 (F,G-5)*. NMC: Newark, 50 miles north.

Lodging Office: ITT Office, NWS Earle, 201 Hwy 34 S. C-29, **C-908-866-2103, D-312-449-2103,** Fax: C-908-866-1042, 0830-1600 Mon-Fri. Check in facility. No civilian employee billeting, primarily for PCS use.

TML: BEQ, BOQ, TLQ. Active duty, PCS or active assigned at Earle only. Mobile homes, private bath (4). No pets. Refrigerator, color CATV, kitchen with utensils. Rates $20-$40 per night, depending on rank. Maximum six per unit.

TML Availability: Difficult. Best winter.

Temporary Military Lodging Around the World - 163

NEW JERSEY
Earle Naval Weapons Station, continued

Seven miles from the New Jersey shore, where sport fishing, swimming and boating are available. One hour from New York City.

Locator 724-2345   Medical 866-2300   Police 866-2291

Fort Dix Army Training Center (NJ03R1)
AFZT-EH-H, Billeting Branch
P.O. Box 419
Fort Dix, NJ 08640-5523

TELEPHONE NUMBER INFORMATION: Main installation numbers: C-609-562-1011, D-312-944-1110.

Location: From NJ Turnpike (I-95), exit 7, right onto NJ-206, short distance left on NJ-68 and continue to General Circle and main gate. *USMRA: Page 19 (E,F-6)*. NMC: Trenton, 17 miles northwest.

Lodging Office: ATTN: ATZD-EH-H, Bldg 5255, Maryland Ave and First Street, **C-609-562-3188**, Fax: C-609-562-3752, 24 hours. Check in facility, check out 1100 hours daily.

TML: Doughboy Inn. Guest House, Bldg 5997, C-609-723-5579, Fax: C-609-562-3367, all ranks, leave or official duty, C-609-562-6663. Bedroom, 2 double beds, private bath (76). Community kitchen, A/C, color TV, telephone, housekeeping service, cribs/cots ($2.50 per night), coin washer/dryer, ice vending, soda/snack vending. Mini-mart available. Modern structure. Rates: TDY double $35; three persons $40; four or more $45. All categories can make reservations.

TML: VOQ/VEQ. Bldg 5255, all ranks, leave or official duty. Bedroom, semi-private bath (VEQ) (65); separate bedrooms, private bath (VOQ) (10). Refrigerator, A/C, color TV in room and lounge, housekeeping service, cribs/cots, washer/dryer, ice vending, soda/snack vending. Mini-mart available. Older structure, renovated. Rates: TDY $21 per night, each additional person $5. All categories can make reservations.

TML: DVQ. Bldg 5256, officers O6+, leave or official duty. Bedroom suites, private bath (4); two bedroom apartments, private bath (4). Kitchen (apartments), refrigerator (suites), utensils, A/C, color TV in room and lounge, housekeeping service, cribs/cots, washer/dryer, ice vending, soda/snack vending. Mini-mart available. Modern structure. Rates: $21, each additional person $5. All categories can make reservations.

DV/VIP: HQ USATC and Fort Dix, ATTN: Office of The Secretary General Staff, C-609-562-5059/6293, O6+/civilian equivalent. Retirees Space-A.

TML Availability: Good, Oct-Mar. Difficult, other times.

CREDIT CARDS ACCEPTED: Visa, MasterCard and American Express.

Nearby Brindle Lake, a 30 acre lake surrounded by about 2,000 acres of pine forest provides rental boats (no power boats), camping, picnic and barbecue facilities. Visit Trenton and its historic sites 17 miles northwest.

Locator 562-1011   Medical 562-2695   Police 562-6001

NEW JERSEY

Fort Monmouth (NJ05R1)
Lodging Office
Bldg 270, Allen Ave
Fort Monmouth, NJ 07703-5108

TELEPHONE NUMBER INFORMATION: Main installation numbers: C-908-532-9000, D-312-992-9000.

Location: Take NJ Turnpike to I-95, exit 7A (Shore Points); east to Garden State Parkway; north to exit 105 for Eatontown and Fort Monmouth. *USMRA: Page 19 (G-5).* NMC: New Brunswick, 23 miles northwest.

Lodging Office: Bldg 270, Allen Ave, **C-908-532-1635/1092**, Fax: C-908-532-8996, 0745-2345 hours daily. Other hours, Work Center Office, Bldg 166, C-908-532-1122. Check in lodging office, check out 1100 hours daily. Government civilian employee billeting on official business.

TML: Guest House. Bldg 365, all ranks, leave, or official duty. Suites bedroom/sitting room, private bath (90). All have kitchen, microwave, color TV, housekeeping service, sleeper couch, cots, washer/dryer, ice vending. Conference rooms available. Five units handicap accessible. Rates: E1-E7, O1 single $21, two or more persons $27; E8+, O2+ single $30, two or more persons $35; unofficial business single $40, two or more persons $45. All categories can make reservations Space-A. No pets.

TML: VOQ. Bldgs 270, 360, 363, 364, 1202, officers, TDY civilians, enlisted, senior NCOs on official duty. Inquire about rooms and services. Rates: $38 per night, $48 for two or more persons. No children. Duty can make reservations, others Space-A. No pets.

TML: DVQ. Bldg 259, **Blair Hall**, officers O6+, leave or official duty. Inquire about rooms and services available. Modern structure, renovated. Rates: $38 per night, two or more persons $48. Duty can make reservations, others Space-A. No pets.

TML Availability: Good.

CREDIT CARDS ACCEPTED: Visa, MasterCard and American Express.

Transportation: On-base shuttle, off-base taxi available.

Within 5 miles of the ocean, the area also has two race tracks for thoroughbreds and trotters. Atlantic City 1 1/2 hours south, New York City, 1 hour north. Nearby Garden State Art Center for ballet has concerts year round.

Locator 532-1492/2540   Medical 532-2789   Police 532-1112

Lakehurst Naval Air Engineering Station (NJ08R1)
Combined Bachelor's Quarters
NAWC Bldg 481
Lakehurst, NJ 08733-5041

TELEPHONE NUMBER INFORMATION: Main installation numbers: C-908-323-2011, D-312-624-1110.

NEW JERSEY
Lakehurst Naval Air Engineering Station, continued

Location: Take Garden State Parkway south to NJ-70 west to junction of NJ-547 right and proceed 1 mile to base. *USMRA: Page 19 (F-6)*. NMC: Trenton, 30 miles northwest.

Lodging Office: Bldg 481, **C-908-323-2266, D-312-624-2266,** Fax: C-908-323-2269, D-312-624-2269, 24 hours. Check in facility, check out 1100 hours daily. Government civilian employee billeting.

TML: BOQ. Bldg 33, officers, O3 and below, official duty. Bedroom suites, private bath (16). A/C, microfridge, essentials, ice vending, housekeeping service, color TV, washer/dryer. Rates: $8 per night. Older structure. AD, retirees may make reservations at above number, or write to: CBQ, NAWC Lakehurst, NJ, 08733.

TML: BEQ. Bldg 480, **Casey Hall,** enlisted, E-4 and below, official duty. Bldg 481, 481, **Maloney Hall**, enlisted, all ranks, official duty. Bedrooms, hall bath (62); VIP bedrooms (E-7+), private bath (3). Essentials, ice vending, housekeeping service, color TV, washer/dryer, sauna, jacuzzi, exercise room. Rates: E4 and below (students) $2; E4 and below $4; E5+ $4. Older structure. Active duty, retirees may make reservations at above number, or write to: CBQ, NAWC Lakehurst, NJ, 08733.

TML: DV Quarters. Cottages, private bath (6). Kitchenette, complete utensils, essentials, housekeeping service, color TV, washer/dryer (available in Bldg 481). Older structure, renovated 1991. Rates: DV $27 per night; VIP $15. Maximum 4 per unit. No pets. All categories may make reservations at above number and address.

TML: DV/VIP: Guest House, O6+. Contact Exec's Office, C-908-323-2369.

TML Availability: Very good, all year.

CREDIT CARDS ACCEPTED: Visa, MasterCard and American Express.

This is the site of the crash of the Airship Hindenburg. On base golf course and driving range and club house, biking, boating, fishing and hunting in season. There is a nearby Lakehurst conservation area.

Locator 323-2582   **Medical 323-2231**   **Police 323-2332**

McGuire Air Force Base (NJ09R1)
All American Inn, Bldg 2717
SVS/SVML
McGuire AFB, NJ 08641-5012

TELEPHONE NUMBER INFORMATION: Main installation numbers: C-609-724-1100, D-312-440-0111.

Location: From New Jersey Turnpike, exit 7 to 206 south to NJ-68 southeast to AFB. Adjacent to Fort Dix. Clearly marked. *USMRA: Page 19 (E-6)*. NMC: Trenton, 18 miles northwest.

Lodging Office: All-American Inn SVS/SVML, Bldg 2717, **C-609-724-2954, D-312-440-2954,** Fax: C-609-724-2035, 24 hours. Check in facility by 1700, check out 1100 hours daily. Government civilian employee billeting. **Note: As of 1 April 1997, all rooms are smoke and tobacco free.**

166 - Temporary Military Lodging Around the World

NEW JERSEY
McGuire Air Force Base, continued

TML: TLQ. All ranks, leave or official duty. C-609-724-3336/7 0745-1600 hours Mon-Fri. Other hours, C-609-724-2340. One bedroom with foldout couch, private bath (30). Kitchen, A/C, housekeeping service, washer/dryer. Older structure. Rates: O1 $23.50; E1-E2 $19.50; all others $24 per unit. PCS have priority, others Space-A up to 24 hours in advance.

TML: VOQ/VAQ. All ranks, leave or official duty. Bedroom, semi-private bath (VOQ) (100); bedroom, semi-private bath (VAQ) (359). A/C, color TV, housekeeping service. Older structure. Rates: $10 per person. Duty can make reservations, Space-A up to 24 hours in advance.

TML: DV/VIP. Officers O6+ and E-9 leave or official duty. C-609-724-2954. Bedroom suites, private bath (17). A/C, color TV, housekeeping service. Rates: $16 per person.

DV/VIP: Protocol Office, C-609-724-2954, O6+ and E-9.

TML Availability: Good, Oct-Apr. Difficult, other times.

CREDIT CARDS ACCEPTED: Visa, MasterCard and American Express.

New Jersey coastal fishing is popular here. Trenton, the state capital, has many historic sites and an excellent Cultural Center. Miles of roads and trails show off a number of well kept state forests. Atlantic City, New York and Philadelphia are nearby.

Locator 724-1100   **Medical 562-4061**   **Police 911**

NEW MEXICO

Cannon Air Force Base (NM02R3)
Caprock Inn
401 S. Olympic Blvd
Cannon AFB, NM 88103-5328

TELEPHONE NUMBER INFORMATION: Main installation numbers: C-505-784-3311, D-312-681-1110.

Location: From Clovis west on US-60/84 to AFB. From NM-467 enter the Portales Gate. *USMRA: Page 114 (H-5)*. NMC: Clovis, 7 miles east.

Lodging Office: Caprock Inn. 401 S. Olympic Blvd, **C-505-784-2918/2919, D-312-681-2918/2919**, Fax: C-505-784-4833, D-312-681-4833, 24 hours. Check in billeting, check out 1200 hours daily. Government civilian employee billeting.

TML: TLF. Bldgs 1812, 1818, 1819. All ranks. Leave or official duty. Family units (44); Kitchen, utensils, A/C, color TV, housekeeping service, washer/dryer, ice vending. Older structure. Rates: $24 per room. PCS in/out can make reservations, others Space-A. List of kennels available.

TML: VOQ, VAQ. Bldg 1800B. Officer all ranks, DoD civilians. Leave or official duty. VOQ units (20); VAQ units (32). Rooms share community living area and kitchen. A/C, color TV in room and

Temporary Military Lodging Around the World - 167

NEW MEXICO
Cannon Air Force Base, continued

lounge, housekeeping service, washer/dryer, ice vending. Older structure. Rates: $10. Duty can make reservations, others Space-A.

TML: DV/VIP. Protocol, Bldgs 1800A and 1812. C-505-784-2727. E-9 and officer O6+. Leave or official duty. Separate bedroom suites, private bath (6). Kitchen, utensils, color TV, housekeeping service, washer/dryer, ice vending. Older structure. Rates: $10 per person, maximum charge $16. Duty can make reservations, others Space-A.

DV/VIP: Protocol Office, 27TFW/CCEP, Bldg 1, C-505-784-2727, O6+. Retirees Space-A.

TML Availability: Good, Nov-Feb. Difficult, other times.

CREDIT CARDS ACCEPTED: Visa, MasterCard and American Express.

Visit the Blackwater Draw Museum, Roosevelt County Museum, or the Oasis State Park outside Portales for fishing, hiking, picnics and camping. Local lakes offer good fishing.

Locator 784-2424   **Medical 784-4033**   **Police 784-4111**

Holloman Air Force Base (NM05R3)
1040 New Mexico Ave
Holloman AFB, NM 88310-8159

TELEPHONE NUMBER INFORMATION: Main installation numbers: C-505-475-6511, D-312-867-1110.

Location: Exit US-70/82, 8 miles southwest of Alamogordo. Clearly marked. *USMRA: Page 114 (D,E-7)*. NMC: La Cruces, 50 miles southwest, El Paso, TX 65 miles southeast.

Lodging Office: Bldg 583, 1040 New Mexico Ave, **C-505-475-3311, D-312-867-6123,** Fax: C-505-475-7753, D-312-867-7753, 24 hours. Check in facility, check out 1200 hours daily. Government civilian employee billeting.

TML: TLF. Bldgs 590, 591, 592, 593, 594, all ranks, leave or official duty. Bedroom, private bath, sofa and chair sleepers (50). Kitchen, complete utensils, A/C, color TV, housekeeping service, cribs/cots/hi-chairs, washer/dryer, ice vending. Rates: $12-$24. PCS in/out can make reservation, others Space-A. No pets.

TML: VAQ/VOQ. Bldg 342, enlisted all ranks, leave or official duty. Bedroom, semi-private bath (128); Refrigerator, microwave, coffee makers, A/C, color TV, housekeeping service, washer/dryer, ice vending. New facility 1993. Rates: $10 per person. Maximum 2 per room. TDY, PCS in/out can make reservations, others Space-A. No pets.

TML: VOQ. Bldgs 582, 583, 584-587, officers all ranks, leave or official duty. Bedroom, private bath (30); separate bedrooms, private bath (130); two bedroom, semi-private bath (24). Kitchen, microwave, coffee makers, A/C, color TV, housekeeping service, cots. Modern structure. Rates: DVOQ $14. TDY, PCS in/out can make reservations, others Space-A. No pets.

DV/VIP: 49 FW/CC, Bldg 29, D-312-867-5573/74, E9/O6+/GS-15+.

NEW MEXICO
Holloman Air Force Base, continued

TML Availability: Good, Nov-Jan. Difficult, other times.

CREDIT CARDS ACCEPTED: Visa, MasterCard and American Express.

Locator 475-7510   Medical 475-7768   Police 475-7171

Kirtland Air Force Base (NM03R3)
377th Service Squadron/SVML
2000 Wyoming Blvd SE, Suite 5661
Kirtland AFB, NM 87117-5661

TELEPHONE NUMBER INFORMATION: Main installation numbers: C-505-846-0011, D-312-246-0011.

Location: From I-40 east, exit on Wyoming Blvd, south for 2 miles to Wyoming Blvd. gate to AFB. *USMRA: Page 114 (D-4).* NMC: Albuquerque, 1 mile southeast.

Lodging Office: Kirtland Inn, Box 5418, Kirtland AFB, NM 87185, Bldg 22016, Club Drive, **C-505-846-9653, D-312-246-9653,** 24 hours, Fax 505-846-4142, D-312-246-4142. Check in billeting, check out 1200 hours daily. Government civilian employee billeting.

TML: TLF. Bldg 23227, all ranks, leave or official duty. Separate bedroom suites, private bath (24). Kitchen, A/C, color TV, housekeeping service, cots, ice vending, washer/dryer. Renovated 1992. Rates: $24 per suite, per day. PCS in/out can make reservations, others Space-A. No pets.

TML: Cottages. All ranks, leave or official duty. Two bedroom, private bath (16); Kitchen, A/C, color TV, housekeeping service, cots, washer/dryer. Older structure, renovated. Rates: $24 per cottage, per day. PCS in/out can make reservations, others Space-A. No pets.

TML: VOQ. Bldgs 1911, 22001, 22003, 22010, 22011, 22012, 23225, officers all ranks, official duty and Space-A. Suites, living room, bedroom, private bath (140). Refrigerator, A/C, color TV, housekeeping service, washer/dryer, ice vending. Older structure. Rates: $10 per person per night. Duty on orders can make reservations, others Space-A. No pets.

TML: VAQ. Bldgs 22002, 20101, 23226. Enlisted all ranks, official duty, Space-A. SNCO suites, living room, bedroom, kitchenettes, private bath (22). Super Chief Suites (2) (reserve through Protocol); bedrooms, semi private bath and private bath (144). All buildings have washer/dryers, color TV, A/C, housekeeping service, ice vending. Rates: $10 per person per night; Chief Suites $16. Duty makes reservations, others Space-A. No pets.

TML: DV/VIP. Bldgs 22000, 22011. Suites "top of the line" (25). Rates: $16 per person, per night, leave or official duty. No pets.

DV/VIP: 377 ABW/Protocol Office, reservations C-505-846-4119, D-312-246-4119, O6+, civilian equivalents.

TML Availability: Best, late fall and winter. Fri and Sat nights always better than during the week. Worst, June-Oct.

Temporary Military Lodging Around the World - 169

NEW MEXICO
Kirtland Air Force Base, continued

Take the tram to the Sandia Mountains, investigate the National Atomic Museum, and Old Town Albuquerque, founded in 1706. Enjoy local skiing, the State Fair in September, the International Hot Air Balloon Fiesta each October.

Locator 846-0011   **Medical 846-3730**   **Police 846-7926**

White Sands Missile Range (NM04R3)
WSMR Billeting Office
P.O. Box 37
White Sands Missile Range, NM 88002-0037

TELEPHONE NUMBER INFORMATION: Main installation numbers: C-505-678-2121, D-312-258-2121.

Location: From Las Cruces, east on US-70, 30 miles to WSMR. From Alamogordo west on US-70, 45 miles to WSMR. *USMRA: Page 114 (D-6,7,8)*. NMC: El Paso, TX 45 miles south.

Lodging Office: ATTN: WSMR Billeting Office, P.O. Box 37, **C-505-678-4559**, Fax: C-505-678-2367, 0745-1615 hours daily. Other hours SDO, Bldg 100, C-505-678-2031. Check out 1200 hours daily. Charge for late checkouts.

TML: VOQ/DVQ. Bldgs 501, 502. All military and DoD civilians on official duty. Bedroom, private bath (3); suites, private bath (43); three bedroom houses, private bath (8). Refrigerator, microwave, community kitchen, complete utensils, A/C, color TV, housekeeping service, cribs, washer/dryer, soda/snack vending. Rates: TDY $25, spouse $2 additional. Reservations confirmed only for TDY or PCS military families in/out. No pets. Three bedroom houses at $30-$45 per night depending upon number of beds used are also available.

TML: Guest House. Bldg 506. All ranks, PCS/TDY, official duty, leave and retired military. Reservations confirmed only for military in PCS/TDY status. Bedroom, 2 double beds, sofa bed, private bath, kitchen units, complete utensils, A/C, color TV, cribs, washer/dryer. Modern structure. Rates: $25.

DV/VIP: CG, WSMR, ATTN: STEWS-PC, Bldg 100, room 227, C-505-678-1028, O6/GS-15+.

TML Availability: Very good.

CREDIT CARDS ACCEPTED: Visa, MasterCard, American Express and Discover.

Las Cruces' blending of three cultures, and New Mexico State University supply much entertainment locally. Visit the International Space Hall of Fame in Alamogordo, White Sands National Monument, and El Paso, gateway to the Southwest and Mexico.

Locator 678-1630   **Medical 678-2882**   **Police 678-1234**

170 - *Temporary Military Lodging Around the World*

NEW YORK

Fort Drum (NY06R1)
Lodging Office
Bldg T-2227, Officers' Loop
Fort Drum, NY 13602-5097

TELEPHONE NUMBER INFORMATION: Main installation numbers: C-315-772-6900, D-312-341-6011.

Location: From Syracuse, take I-81 north to exit 48, past Watertown, and follow signs to Fort Drum. *USMRA: Page 21 (J-3,4)*. NMC: Watertown, 8 miles southwest.

Lodging Office: Bldg T-2227, Officers' Loop, 24 hours, **C-315-772-5435**. Check in billeting, check out 1100 hours daily. Government civilian employee billeting.

TML: Guest House. Bldg 2340, all ranks, leave or official duty. Fax 315-773-2566. Separate bedrooms, private bath (9); two bedroom, private bath (5). Kitchen, complete utensils, color TV, housekeeping service, cribs/cots, washer/dryer. Older structure. Rates: $24, each additional person $5. All categories may make reservations.

TML: VOQ. Cottages (9), 1 and 2 bedroom (2), private bath. Fax 315-772-9647. All ranks, leave or official duty. Kitchens, complete utensils, color TV, housekeeping service, cribs/cots, washer/dryer. Rates $15, each additional person $5.

TML: TLF. **The Inn**. Civilian funded motel operated by the Army, all ranks, leave or official duty, C-315-773-7777. Rooms (111), 64 with kitchenettes and microwaves. Queen size beds, remote control CATV, room telephones, individual A/C and heating. Rates: This facility is included under Guest House rates, as above.

DV/VIP: Protocol Office, Bldg P-10000, C-315-772-5010, Fax 315-772-9647 O6+. Retirees and lower ranks Space-A.

TML Availability: Good, Oct-Apr. Difficult, other times.

CREDIT CARDS ACCEPTED: Visa, MasterCard, American Express, Diners' Club and Discover.

Sackets Harbor Battle Ground, site of war of 1812 battle. Nearby is the fascinating area called 1,000 Islands, rich in water recreation. Canada is 45 minutes away.

Locator 772-5869   Medical 772-5236   Police 772-5156

Fort Hamilton (NY02R1)
Adams Guest House
109 Schum Ave
Brooklyn, NY 11252-5330

TELEPHONE NUMBER INFORMATION: Main installation numbers: C-718-630-4101, D-312-232-1110.

NEW YORK
Fort Hamilton, continued

Location: From Belt Parkway, exit 2 (Fort Hamilton Parkway) to 100th Street, right to Fort Hamilton Parkway, right to main gate. *USMRA: Page 26 (D-7)*. NMC: New York, in the city.

Lodging Office: Adams Guest House, Bldg 109, Schum Ave, **C-718-630-4564, D-312-232-4564/4052/4892,** 24 hours. Check in facility after 1400 hours daily. Check out 1000 hours daily. Government civilian employee billeting (on orders).

TML: Adams Guest House. Bldg 109. All ranks, leave or official duty. Bedroom, private bath (39). Kitchen, microwave, A/C, color/cable TV in room and lounge, coin washer/dryer, ice vending. Older structure, renovated 1991. Rates: single $45, two people $50, maximum $50. Special rates for PCS military personnel. All can make reservations.

TML: Transient quarters. Bldg 110, C-630-4348, D-312-232-4348. All ranks, leave or official duty. Bedrooms, shared bath (48). Above amenities. Rates: one person $35; two people $40. TDY has priority, others Space-A.

TML: DV/VIP. Bldg 109, officers O6+, leave or official duty, C-718-630-4892/4052. Separate bedrooms, private bath (2). Refrigerator, color /cable TV, coffee/bar set up, A/C, housekeeping service. Rates: single $50, maximum $55. Duty and retirees can make reservations.

DV/VIP: Liaison and Protocol Office, Bldg 302, room 13, C-718-630-4324, O6+. Retirees Space-A.

TML Availability: Good, winter months. Difficult, summer months.

Locator 630-4958   **Medical** 630-4615   **Police** 630-4456

Niagara Falls Air Reserve Station (NY12R1)
914th AW/SVML
10780 Kinross Street
Niagara Falls IAP/ARS, NY 14304-5058

TELEPHONE NUMBER INFORMATION: Main installation numbers: C-716-236-2000, D-312-238-3011.

Location: Take I-190 to Niagara Falls, exit #23 Packard Road and turn right - straight through to Lockport Road. Approximately 4 miles from the exit. From US-62 West to Walmore Road, North to AFB. *USMRA: Page 20 (D-6)*. NMC: Niagara Falls, 6 miles west.

Lodging Office: Bldg 312, 10780, Kinross Street. Reservations **1-800-456-4990, C-716-236-2014, D-312-238-2014,** Fax: C-716-236-6348, D-312-238-6348, hours of operation 0700-2300. Checkout 1000 hours daily. Government civilian employee lodging.

TML: VOQ. Bldg 312, officers all ranks, leave or official duty. Bedroom, private bath (43), telephone, refrigerator, AC, color TV and other essentials. Housekeeping service, washer/dryers, soda/snack vending, ice vending, crib and cots. Lounge with microwave. Meeting/conference rooms and exercise room available. Rates: $8 per person. Duty can make reservations, others Space-A.

TML: VOQ/VIP. Bldg 312, officers O5+, GS/GM 13+, leave or duty. Living room/bedroom suites, private bath (6). A/C, telephone, color TV, refrigerator microwave and other essentials. Housekeeping service, soda/snack vending. Meeting/conference rooms and exercise room available. Rates: $10 per person. Duty can make reservations, others Space-A.

NEW YORK
Niagara Falls Air Reserve Station, continued

TML: VAQ. Bldgs 502 and 504, enlisted, all ranks, leave or official duty. Bedroom, 2 beds per room each building, common bath (34), TV, A/C refrigerator, essentials, housekeeping service, washer/dryer, soda/snack vending, ice vending. Meeting/conference rooms and exercise room available. Rates: $8 per person. Duty can make reservations, others Space-A.

TML: VAQ. Bldg 508, enlisted all ranks. Bedroom, semi-private bath (36). Housekeeping service, washer/dryer, soda/snack vending, ice vending. Meeting/conference rooms and exercise room available. Rates: $8 per person. SNCO: living/bedroom suites, private bath (2). TV, A/C refrigerator telephone and other essentials. Rates: $10 per person.

TML: VOQ/VIP. DV Suites (4). Bldgs 304E, 304W, 306E, 306W. Three bedrooms, queen size bed, private bath, shared living room. A/C, telephones, color TV, refrigerators, microwave, washer/dryers, housekeeping service, soda/snack vending. Meeting/conference rooms and exercise room available. Rates: $8 per person.

TML: VOQ/VIP. Bldg 308. Bedrooms, king size bed, private bath (2). A/C, telephone, color TV, refrigerator. Shared living room, and dining area. Washer/Dryer, housekeeping service, soda/snack vending. Meeting/conference rooms and exercise room available. Rates: $10 per person.

TML Availability: Good, Oct-Mar. Difficult, Apr-Sep. Avoid weekends.

CREDIT CARDS ACCEPTED: Visa, MasterCard and American Express.

Niagara Falls, Winter Gardens, Niagara Power Vista, Old Fort Niagara, Our Lady of Fatima Shrine, Native American Center for the Living Arts, Art Park, and the Aquarium are all attractions in this area. Also visit the amusement parks and scenic area surrounding the Niagara frontier.

Locator 236-2002   Medical 236-2086/7   Police 236-2278

Soldiers', Sailors', Marines' and Airmen's Club (NY17R1)
283 Lexington Ave
New York, NY 10016-3540

TELEPHONE NUMBER INFORMATION: Main installation numbers: C-212-683-4353, Fax: C-212-683-4174. In US toll free **1-800-678-TGIF (8443)**.

Location: From Lincoln Tunnel, E. on 34th Street, to 3rd Ave., left to 37th Street. (1 block), left on Lexington Ave, club on left mid-block. *USMRA: Page 26 (E-4)*. NMC: New York, in the city.

Author's Note: The **Soldiers', Sailors' and Airmen's Club** is a tax exempt, not-for-profit organization founded in 1919 to serve the needs of service personnel while visiting New York City. **This club is not US Military/Government lodging.**

Office: Check in and out at the lobby desk, 24 hours. Check in 1430 hours, check out 1030 hours. Call the numbers listed above for reservations and information on lodging and related club activities.

DoD Conference Center

Conference Section

table of contents

The Mologne House Hotel at Walter Reed Army Medical Center, DC..................2-3

Seward Military Resort, AK..4

Fort Myer Five Star Catering, VA..5

The Inn at Schofield Barracks, HI...6

Marine Memorial Club, CA...7

Dragon Hill, Korea; Garmisch & Chiemsee, Germany......................inside front cover

Hale Koa Hotel, HI..back cover

--- Military Travel Information from <u>Off Duty Publications</u> ---

Off Duty..8

MILITARY Living PUBLICATIONS

For more information on advertising with Military Living, please contact R.J. Crawford at:
*P.O. Box 2347, Falls Church, VA 22042-0347 • Phone: **703-237-0203** • Fax: 703-237-2233*
E-mail: milliving@aol.com • Homepage: http://militaryliving.com

There's A New House *near* the White House

Mologne House
HOTEL

Walter Reed Army Medical Center
Washington, D.C.

MWR

We welcome Active Duty Military, Retirees, Guard & Reserve and Active and Retired Government Civilians for Official Duty or Leisure Travel. Eligible Family Members, to include Unaccompanied and Visitors of Patients, are also welcome.

- ★ THE ARMY'S NEWEST HOTEL
- ★ 200 LUXURY ROOMS AND SUITES
- ★ RESTAURANT
- ★ MEETING & BANQUET SPACE
- ★ STATE-OF-THE-ART SECURITY
- ★ 15 MINUTES TO DOWNTOWN ATTRACTIONS
- ★ 5 MINUTES TO METRO
- ★ COURTESY VAN
- ★ 50% HANDICAP ACCESSIBLE

- ★ FREE PARKING
- ★ TOTAL CONVENTION SERVICES
- ★ WEDDINGS
- ★ MEETINGS FROM 2-200
- ★ OUTDOOR RECREATION FACILITIES FOR PICNICS, ATHLETICS, ETC.
- ★ TOTAL BUSINESS CENTER SUPPORT
- ★ ADJACENT TO CHAPEL
- ★ FITNESS CENTER ACCESS

Phone: 202-726-8700   **Fax: 202-782-4665**

Yes! *I would like more information on the Mologne House. Check all that apply:*
❏ Groups/Meetings ❏ TDY ❏ Vacation ❏ Other _____

Name:_____

Address:_____

_____

Phone:_____ Fax:_____

Mail to: **Mologne House**, P.O. Box 59728, Washington D.C. 20012
Military Living TML 1997

Seminars • Conventions • Conferences • Reunions

Seward Resort
Experience Alaska Year 'Round
Special Winter Rates Available

Summer:
1 May to 15 September

Winter:
16 September to 30 April

- Luxury cabins and resort facilities in a picturesque atmosphere

- Local transportation: air, railroad, car rental

- Special summer group Charter Fishing, Boat, & Bus Tours

- Special winter group Boat Tours and Dog Sled Rides

- Conference facilities for up to 100 guests

- Full audio visual equipment

- Local catering available

- Only 1 mile from downtown Seward

- Complementary bus service to local restaurants and shops

1-800-770-1858

DSN: 384-FISH (3474)
384-LINE (5463)
Fax DSN: 384-0248

Seward Resort
P.O. Box 329
Seward, Alaska
99664

Web page address:
http://143.213.12.254/mwr/seward.htm

FIVE STAR CATERING

Five Star Catering

CONFERENCES · MEETINGS · ELEGANT WEDDINGS

Your choice in the national capital region...

- **Convenient location**
- **Ideal break-out rooms**
- **Conference space totaling more than 26,000 square feet**
- **Prestigious facilities**
- **Excellent service**

Five Star Catering is the catering service of the Fort Myer Military Community. Call 703-524-0200 today!

Conferencing in Hawaii at. . .

THE INN AT SCHOFIELD BARRACKS

The Inn at Schofield Barracks is the official temporary lodging for all Army personnel on Oahu and is the only facility authorized to issue a Room Status Certificate. For all personnel located in the Fort Shafter area or other areas on Oahu, the Tripler Billeting Facility should be the first choice of transient lodging. If space is not available there, the soldier must process through the Inn at Schofield Barracks to qualify for per diem entitlements. We have 192 guest rooms, tastefully decorated and appointed to cater to the special needs of the military traveler.

- Conference Room
- 24-hour Convenience/ Video store
- Full Service Deli
- Near Golf Course & Swimming Pool

- Free Cable TV and Local Calls
- Relocation-area information
- Package and Fax service
- One day Dry Cleaning & Laundry Service

563 Kolekole Ave • Wahiawa, Hawaii 96786
Phone: **808-624-9650** • Fax: 808-624-5606
Reservations: **800-490-9638** • DSN 315-455-5036
Internet: //www.innatschofield.com
E-mail: theinn@aloha.com

Reunions & Banquets

Why not meet at the "Crossroads of the Corps?"

at the **Marines' Memorial Club & Hotel**
San Francisco

The Regimental Room

The Crystal Ballroom

Just Right

The Marines' Memorial Club and hotel in San Francisco offers five elegant meeting rooms which accommodate groups of 10 to 400, plus 137 luxurious yet affordable rooms and suites. Group hotel bookings are available in conjunction with banquet room rentals.

Reservations
(415) 673-6672
ext. 264 or 277

PCS?

TDY?

VACATION?

You're Ready For Travel With the Handy OFF DUTY Welcome Guide!

With up-to-date base directories and valuable tips on local customs, climate, shopping and much more, an OFF DUTY Welcome Guide is the essential 'survival guide' for service people on the move!

The Welcome Guides of your choice are available at $2.50 per copy, postage paid*.

*U.S. and APO/FPO address only. For non-APO/FPO address outside the U.S., please add $1.00 per copy for airmail postage.

Title of Guide	No. of Copies	Title of Guide	No. of Copies
Welcome to Florida	_____	*Welcome to Germany*	_____
Welcome to Guam	_____	*Welcome to Hawaii*	_____
Welcome to Hong Kong	_____	*Welcome to Japan*	_____
Welcome to Korea	_____	*Welcome to Okinaw*	_____
Welcome to Singapore	_____	*Welcome to Texas*	_____

Total Number of Guides _____   *I have enclosed a payment of $*_____

Please send a check or money order. We cannot be responsible for cash sent through the mail

Name _____

Address ____ _____

_____

Tel. # ____ _____

Mail to: OFF DUTY, Dept. W, 3303 Harbor Blvd. Suite C-2, Costa Mesa, CA 92626

NEW YORK
Soldiers', Sailors', Marines' and Airmen's Club, continued

The USO of Metropolitan New York is now located at the Soldiers', Sailors', Marines' and Airmen's club.

Staten Island Navy Lodge (NY07R1)
Bldg 408, North Pass Road
Staten Island, NY 11251-5000

TELEPHONE NUMBER INFORMATION: Main installation numbers: C-718-442-0413. Police 718-816-1709.

Location: I-95 N to Elizabeth, NJ, I-278 to Staten Island. Last exit before Verrazano bridge, Bay Street exit, follow signs. *USMRA: Page 26 (C-7).* NMC: New York.

Lodging Office: Navy Lodge. Call **1-800-NAVY-INN**, 24 hours, or **C-718-442-0413**, Fax: C-718-816-0830. Check in 1500-1800 (after hours guaranteed reservations pick up room key at front gate pass office), check out 1200 daily. Notify Lodge of late check in, out. Eligibility: check Appendix C.

TML: Navy Lodge. All ranks. Bedrooms, 2 double beds, private bath, dining area (50). Three sets interconnecting, two handicap accessible, 30 non-smoking. Kitchenette, microwave, utensils, A/C, CATV, phone, iron/ironing board, cribs, washer/dryer, housekeeping service, soda/snack vending, ice vending, parking, playground, mini-mart with video rentals. No pets (nearby kennel). Rates: $54.50. All categories can make reservations.

TML Availability: Good all year, weekends difficult.

CREDIT CARDS ACCEPTED: Visa, MasterCard, American Express and Discover

Transportation: Off base taxi 442-4242.

National Park Service has opened Fort Wadsworth. For information call 718-354-4500. While visiting, take a 30 minute ferry ride to Manhattan, or see sites such as the Statue of Liberty, the Empire State Building, Times Square or Rockefeller center.

Stewart Army Sub-Post (NY09R1)
Five Star Inn, Bldg 2605
P.O. Box 9000
New Windsor, NY 12553-9000

TELEPHONE NUMBER INFORMATION: Main installation numbers: C-914-564-6309, D-312-247-3524.

Location: From I-87 take Newburgh exit to Union Ave, south to NY-207. Stewart is approximately 15-20 minutes north of West Point. Follow signs to Stewart Airport. *USMRA: Page 21 (M-10).* NMC: Newburgh, 4 miles northeast.

174 - Temporary Military Lodging Around the World

NEW YORK
Stewart Army Sub-Post

Lodging Office: Five Star Inn. The West Point and STAS Guest House, Bldg 2605, New Windsor, NY, **C-914-563-3311**, Fax: C-914-564-6328, D-312-688-3009, 24 hours. Check out 1000 hours daily. Active duty and family, PCS, visiting relatives and guests of hospital patients, active, reservist and retired military personnel, civilians sponsored by military personnel; military and DoD civilians on TDY. Reservation taken daily 0800-2200.

TML: Guest House. Bldg 2605, **Five Star Inn**, all ranks, leave or official duty. Bedroom, private bath (18); bedrooms, semi-private bath (34); apartments (8). A/C, laundry, CATV, direct dial telephones, auto wake-up service, complimentary coffee, lounge, refrigerator, cribs, snack vending, ice vending. Older structure, redecorated 1992. Rates: $30-$45, each additional person $5. PCS rates charged by BAQ/VHA. Maximum three per room. Children under two free. Reservations 30 days prior for Space-A, 60 days PCS. Reservations confirmed with credit card or advance deposit.

TML Availability: Fairly good, Oct-Mar. Difficult, other times.

CREDIT CARDS ACCEPTED: Visa, MasterCard, and American Express.

Visit the Crawford House in Newburgh, try antique shopping near Millbrook, tour a local winery, or try a balloon tour near Port Jervis. Visit Sugar Loaf Crafts Village - the Hudson River Valley is full of interesting things to do.

Locator 564-6309   **Medical 563-3430**   **Police 564-0580**

United States Military Academy, West Point (NY16R1)
Housing Division
Bldg 620, Thomas Hall
ATTN: MAEN-H (CHRRS)
West Point, NY 10996-5000

Hotel Thayer — West Point — Center of the Scenic Hudson Valley

TELEPHONE NUMBER INFORMATION: Main installation numbers: C-914-938-4011, D-312-688-1110, Fax: C-914-564-6328.

Location: Off I-87 or US-9 west. Clearly marked. *USMRA: Page 21 (M,N-10) and Page 28 (D-3).* NMC: New York City, 36 miles south.

Lodging Office: Bldg 674, **C-914-446-4731**, or toll free **1-800-247-5047**, 24 hours. Check in facility, check out 1200 hours daily. No government civilian employee billeting.

TML: Hotel Thayer. C-914-446-4731, or toll free 1-800-247-5047, D-312-688-2632. Bedroom, private bath (189), A/C, color TV in room and lounge, housekeeping service, cribs/cots $10 each, ice vending, soda/snack vending. Older structure, renovated. Government rates: 10% discount off rack rates with ID card. TDY rates available upon request/orders, includes continental breakfast. Open to the public. Reservations accepted 1 year in advance.

DV/VIP: Protocol Office, Bldg 600, C-914-938-4315/4316, O7/GS-16+. Retirees Space-A.

TML Availability: Good, except during special holiday events at USMA.

Temporary Military Lodging Around the World - 175

NEW YORK
United States Military Academy, West Point, continued

CREDIT CARDS ACCEPTED: Visa, MasterCard, American Express, Discover and Diners' Club.

Part of the US Armed Forces Recreation System, the history of the Military Academy, sporting events, and special vacation packages are available at this castle-like hotel rising above the Hudson River.

Locator 938-4412   Medical 938-3637   Police 938-3333

NORTH CAROLINA

Camp Lejeune Marine Corps Base (NC10R1)
ATTN: AC/S Facilities, Bachelor Housing
PSC Box 20004
Camp Lejeune, NC 28542-0004

TELEPHONE NUMBER INFORMATION: Main installation numbers: C-910-451-1113, D-312-484-1113.

Location: Main gate is 6 miles east of junction of US-17 and NC-24. *USMRA: Page 45 (M-5).* NMC: Jacksonville, three miles northwest.

Lodging Office: Bldg 2617, **Seth-Williams**. C-910-451-1385/2146, Fax: C-910-451-1755, 24 hours. Check in 1400, check out 1100 hours daily. Government civilian employee billeting.

TML: Hostess House. Bldg 896, off Holcomb Ave near MCX, four miles from main gate. C-910-451-3041. Check in after 1400 hours daily, 24 hour desk. All ranks. Leave or official duty. Bedroom, 2 double beds, semi-private bath, fold-out couch, sleeps 5 persons (90). Kitchen, utensils, A/C, color TV, housekeeping service, porta cribs, cots ($1), coin washer/dryer, video players, soda/snack vending, many extras. Exercise room available. Modern structure, motel type. Across street from Burger King and Dominos Pizza. Rates: $26 per unit. Duty can make reservations, others Space-A.

TML: BOQ/BEQ. Bldg 2617 (BOQ), C-910-451-1385/2146. Officer all ranks. Bldg HP-53 (BEQ), C-910-451-5262. Enlisted E6-E9. Leave or official duty. Efficiencies, private bath, kitchenette (18); Suites, living room, bedroom, private bath, kitchenette, refrigerator w/ice maker (53); bedroom SNCO transient billeting (21). Utensils, AC, color TV in room and lounge, housekeeping service, cribs/cots, washer/dryer, soda/snack vending, facilities for DAVs, coffee and coffee maker. Exercise room available. Older structure, renovated. Rates: $10-$20. Duty can make reservations, others Space-A.

TML: DG/VIP. Bldg 2601: two bedroom suite, private bath, kitchen (1); bedroom suites, private bath, kitchen (2). Bldg 2607: separate bedroom suites, private bath, kitchenettes (6). All have A/C, housekeeping service, washer/dryer, cribs, soda/snack vending. Exercise room available. Rates: DV $15-$26 per unit. Bldg HP53, C-910-451-5262: SNCO bedroom, private bath (2). All categories can make reservations.

DG/VIP: Protocol Office, C-910-451-2523. O6+. Retirees and lower ranks Space-A.

NORTH CAROLINA
Camp Lejeune Marine Corps Base, continued

TML Availability: Limited, year round.

CREDIT CARDS ACCEPTED: Visa, MasterCard and American Express.

Transportation: On base taxi 451-3674.

Nearby Onslow Beach offers swimming, surfing and picnicking, and local marinas offer boat rentals. Two 18 hole golf courses are also nearby.

Locator-451-3074   Medical-451-4372   Police-451-2555

Cape Hatteras Recreational Quarters (NC09R1)
Lodging Office, P.O. Box 604
Buxton, NC 27920-0604

TELEPHONE NUMBER INFORMATION: Main installation numbers: C-919-995-6435.

Location: From the North. Follow Route 12 from Nags Head about 50 miles to Buxton. In Buxton, turn left at Red Drum Texaco (Old Lighthouse Road). Road leads to Group Office and Recreation Quarters. From the South. Follow Route 70 East from Morehead City 45 miles to Cedar Island. Board Ocracoke Ferry (1.5 hour ride w/toll charge). Follow Route 12 to Hatteras Island Ferry (no charge). On Hatteras proceed North Route 12 to Buxton. Turn right at Red Drum Texaco (Old Lighthouse Road) Road leads to Group Office and Recreation Quarters. *USMRA: Page 45 (P-3)*. NMC: Elizabeth City, 110 miles northwest.

Billeting Office: None. Reservations required with advance payment 30-90 days by mail. Summer months **C-919-995-6435**. Address: Cape Hatteras Recreational Quarters, Group Cape Hatteras, P.O. Box 604, Buxton, NC 27920-0604.

TML: Rooms that sleep 5 (6), rollaway available. Private bath, portable refrigerator, TV. Rates: $25-$32. Suite sleeps seven, private bath, kitchen, TV. Rate: $37-$52. VIP suite, O4+, sleeps five, private bath, kitchen area, TV. Rates: $55. Winter rates available. All categories can make reservations. All rooms non-smoking, no pets.

TML Availability: Limited. Book early.

Within walking distance of historic Cape Hatteras Lighthouse. Famous for fishing, a mecca for wind surfers - "the best surfing on the east coast". For those with less strenuous interest, peaceful, clean beaches, and solitude (off season).

Cherry Point Marine Corps Air Station (NC02R1)
Billeting Fund
Bldg 487, BOQ 1 Madison Drive
Cherry Point MCAS, NC 28533-5079

TELEPHONE NUMBER INFORMATION: Main installation numbers: C-919-466-2811, D-312-582-1110.

Location: On NC-101 between New Bern and Morehead City, NC. US-70 south connects with NC-101 at Havelock, NC. *USMRA: Page 45 (M,N-4)*. NMC: Morehead City, 18 miles southeast.

NORTH CAROLINA
Cherry Point Marine Corps Air Station, continued

Lodging Office: Bldg 487 (Officer) **C-919-466-5169**; Bldg 3673 (enlisted ranks E1-E9). **C-919-466-3060**, Fax: C-919-466-5221, 24 hours. Check in facility, check out 1200 hours daily. Government civilian employee billeting.

TML: Guest House (DGQ). Bldg 487, O6+ leave or official duty. Commander, C-919-466-2848, D-312-582-2848. Four bedroom, private bath (1). One bedroom suites, private bath (4). Kitchenette, microwave, complete utensils, A/C, color TV, VCR, telephone in room, housekeeping service, washer/dryer. Rates: four bedroom $30; suites $19. O6+ may make reservations, others Space-A.

TML: BOQ/TOQ. Bldgs 487, 496, officers all ranks. Leave or official duty. C-919-466-5169. D-312-582-5169. Check out 1200 hours. Bedroom, private bath (47); separate bedroom suites, private bath (29). Refrigerator, A/C, color TV telephone in room, housekeeping service, washer/dryer, ice vending. Older structure, renovated. Rates: single $14, suite $17. Duty can make reservations, others Space-A.

TML: BEQ/TEQ. Bldg 3673. Enlisted, leave or official duty. 104 total spaces, E1-E5 two man rooms, private bath. SNCO bedroom, private bath (40). A/C, color TV (E5+/SNCO), telephone in room, housekeeping service, washer/dryer, ice vending. Older structure, renovated. Rates: $7 per person. TAD/PCS have priority, others Space-A.

DV/VIP: Commander's Office. C-919-466-2848, D-312-582-2848.

TML Availability: Limited, book early.

CREDIT CARDS ACCEPTED: Visa, MasterCard and American Express.

New Bern museums, shopping and dining, area historical attractions, the sailing center at Oriental, where you can catch Neuse River blue crabs, the nearby Outer Banks, and Cape Lookout National Seashore - don't miss them!

Locator 466-2109   Medical 466-4410   Police 466-3615

Elizabeth City Coast Guard Support Center (NC03R1)
MWR, Bldg 5
Elizabeth City CGSC, NC 27909-5006

TELEPHONE NUMBER INFORMATION: Main installation numbers: C-919-335-6379.

Location: Take I-64 east to VA-104S to US-17 south to Elizabeth City, left on Halstead Blvd, three miles to main gate of Center. *USMRA: Page 45 (O-1)*. NMC: Elizabeth City, in the city.

Lodging Office: Bldg 5, **C-919-335-6397**, 0800-1630 hours daily. Reservations accepted up to two months in advance, 90 days if on PCS orders. Check in facility, check out 0800-1000 hours daily. No government civilian employee billeting.

TML: Mobile homes. 16A-F, all ranks, leave or official duty. Two bedroom, private bath (6). Kitchen, limited utensils, A/C, color TV, coin washer/dryer. Modern structure. Rates: $20-$35 per night depending on pay grade, sleeps 6. All categories may make reservations.

TML Availability: Good, Oct-Apr. Difficult, other times.

178 - Temporary Military Lodging Around the World

NORTH CAROLINA
Elizabeth City Coast Guard Support Center, continued

Visit Kitty Hawk and the Outer Banks. Read *Military RV, Camping and Rec Areas Around the World* for more information on this area.

Locator 335-6379   Medical 335-6460   Police 335-6398

Fort Bragg (NC05R1)
Lodging Office (Airborne Inn)
Bldg D-3601, Room 101
Fort Bragg, NC 28307-5000

TELEPHONE NUMBER INFORMATION: Main installation numbers: C-910-396-0011, D-312-236-0011.

Location: From I-95 exit to NC-24 west which runs through post as Bragg Blvd. From US-401 (Fayetteville Bypass) exit to All American Expressway, 5 miles to Fort. *USMRA: Page 45 (I,J-4)*. NMC: Fayetteville, 15 miles southeast.

Lodging Office: Airborne Inn, Bldg D-3601 (**Moon Hall**), room 101, off Bastogne Drive, **C-910-396-9574/7700, D-312-236-9574/7700,** Fax: C-910-396-2025, D-312-236-2025. Front desk check-in 24 hours daily, C-910-436-1669. Check in facility, check out 1100 hours daily. Government civilian employee billeting.

TML: Airborne Inn Guest Houses. All ranks, leave or official duty. **Delmont House**, Bastogne Drive, Bldg D-4215, C-910-436-2211. **Normandy House**, Totten and Armistead Street, Bldg 1-4428, C-910-436-2250. **Leal House**, Reilly Road, behind NCO Club, check in at Delmont or Moon Hall, C-910-436-3033. Bedroom/private bath (111), separate bedroom suites, private bath (8). Kitchen (some), microfridge or refrigerator, A/C, color TV in room and lounge, housekeeping service, cribs/cots, washer/dryer, ice vending, facilities for DAVs (Delmont House). Modern structures. Rates: E1-E6 $23, E7+ $25. PCS can make reservations, UVs and all others Space-A.

TML: Airborne Inn Transient (TDY) Bldgs D-3601, D-3705, 1-1939. All ranks, leave or official duty. C-910-396-7700-9574. Bedroom, private bath (520); separate bedroom suites; private bath (27). Kitchen (suites), refrigerator, A/C, color TV, housekeeping service, washer/dryer, ice vending, facilities for DAVs. Modern structures. Rates: $19 all ranks, $25 suites. Maximum 2 per unit. Duty can make reservations, UVs and all others Space-A.

TML: DV/VIP. Bldg 1-4425. Officer O7+, leave or official duty. C-910-396-2804. Three-bedroom suite, private bath (1). Kitchen, complete utensils, A/C, color TV, housekeeping service, cribs/cots, washer/dryer. Modern structure. Rate: $25. All categories can make reservations.

TML: Fisher House. Note: Appendix B has the definition of this facility. C-910-432-1486.

DV/VIP: Protocol Office. C-910-396-2804. O7+. Retirees Space-A.

TML Availability: Good, Sep-Apr. Difficult, other times.

CREDIT CARDS ACCEPTED: Visa, MasterCard, American Express and Espirit.

NORTH CAROLINA
Fort Bragg, continued

The Airborne Inn Guest House is the winner of the 1995 Lodging of the Year Award competition in the super category. The 82nd Airborne Division War Memorial Museum has over 3,000 objects on view. The Historic Fayetteville Foundation gives walking tours of historical sites, and Sandhills area golf resorts are world famous.

Locator 396-1461   **Medical 432-0301**   **Police 396-0391**

Fort Fisher Air Force Recreation Area (NC13R1)
P.O. Box 380
Kure Beach, NC 28449-3321

TELEPHONE NUMBER INFORMATION: Main installation numbers: C-910-458-6723.

Location: From the north, take I-40 south to Wilmington. Follow Hwy 132 south to Hwy 421 to Kure Beach. From I-95 travelling north from SC, take Hwy 75/76 into Wilmington, then south on Hwy 421 to Kure Beach. *USMRA: Page 45 (L-6)*. NMC: Wilmington.

Lodging Office: Bldg 118, Reception Center. **C-910-458-6549**, 0800 to 1900 daily. Check in reception center, 1600 to 1900 daily. Check out 1100. Late check outs call reservations. Rooms may not be ready before 1600, but use of resort facilities allowed until check in.

TML: One of the Air Force's beachside resorts. Operated by Seymour Johnson Air Force Base MWRSS Division, year round. All ranks. Beach cottages, private bath, color cable TV, washer/dryer (22), executive cottages, private bath, color cable TV, washer/dryer (4), mobile homes, private bath (6), executive suites (8), lodge rooms, shared bath (27), lodges suites, shared bath (13). A/C in rooms, suites, cottages, some kitchenettes, refrigerators, housekeeping service, CATV, complete utensils, linens, washer/dryer (cottages only), coin washer/dryer other facilities. Convenience store, gift and beach shop, restaurant, basketball and tennis courts, dock, boat ramp, petting zoo. Access to beach, sailing, boating, fishing, swimming. Bicycle, pontoon boat and sail boat rentals. No pets allowed in cottages. Pets permitted on leash in designated areas, owners must clean up after pet, kennel available $5 per night.

Summer Rates: (1 Apr-31 Oct) Cottages (sleeps 6-12) $90-110/weekday, $115-$135/weekend day, $560-660/week; executive cottages (sleep six) $110/weekday, $135/weekend day, $560/week; mobile homes (sleeps eight) $100/weekday, $125/weekend day, $610/week; executive suites (sleeps four) $65/weekday, $75/weekend day, $385/week; executive rooms (no children under 12) (sleeps two) $50/weekday, $60/weekend day, $310/week; lodge suites (sleeps four to six) $40-$50/weekday, $50-$60/weekend day, $225-$305/week; lodge rooms (sleeps two) $25/weekday, $30/weekend day, $160/week.

Winter Rates: (1 Nov-31 Mar). Cottages $50-$70/weekday, $65-$85/weekend day, $340-$460/weekend; Mobile home $60/weekday, $75/weekend day, $410/week; executive suites $40/weekday, $50/weekend day, $260/week; executive rooms $30/weekday, $40/weekend day, $215/week; lodge suites $30-35/weekday, $40-$45/weekend day, $180-$205/week; lodge rooms $15/weekday, $20/weekend day, $125/week.

Additional persons in all units charged extra. Weekdays are Sun through Thurs, weekends are Fri, Sat, and nights prior to a holiday. (linens and towels available, $5 per person).

NORTH CAROLINA
Fort Fisher Air Force Recreation Area, continued

Reservations: All categories. Active duty Air Force 90 days ahead. All other active duty 85 days ahead. Retirees 75 days ahead. All others, 60 days ahead. Confirmed with Visa, MasterCard, American Express, Seymour Johnson AFB Club Card, or advance payment. Limits to number of rooms reserved during Memorial Day to Labor Day. Cancellations 15 days prior, or one night fee.

TML Availability: Very good. Best, 1 November-31 March.

CREDIT CARDS ACCEPTED: Visa, MasterCard, American Express and Seymour Johnson AFB Club Card.

Aside from all the recreational activities at this resort, the North Carolina Aquarium at Fort Fisher, the Fort Fisher State Historic Site Civil War Museum, and USS NC Battleship Memorial, Orton and Poplar Grove Plantations are worth visiting.

New River Marine Corps Air Station (NC06R1)
Bldg 705, Flounder Road
Jacksonville, NC 28545-5079

TELEPHONE NUMBER INFORMATION: Main installation numbers: C-910-451-1113, D-312-484-1113.

Location: Off US-17, two miles south of Jacksonville. Clearly marked. *USMRA: Page 45 (L,M-5)*. NMC: Jacksonville, two miles northeast.

Lodging Office: Bldg 705, Flounder Road. **C-910-451-6621/6903**, Fax: C-910-455-0997, 24 hours. Check in at facility, check out 1200 hours daily. Government civilian employee billeting.

TML: BOQ. Bldg 705. Officers, all ranks; E6+, leave or official duty. Bedroom, private bath (50). Refrigerator, A/C, VCR, color TV in room and lounge, housekeeping service, cribs/cots, essentials, washer/dryer, snack vending, ice vending, coffee makers, microwave, telephones. Modern structure, remodeled. Rates: (leave status) single room $12, two room suite $18, each additional person $4. Maximum four persons per unit. Duty can make reservations, others Space-A.

TML Availability: Difficult. Best, Sep-Mar.

CREDIT CARDS ACCEPTED: Visa, MasterCard and American Express.

Some area interests include Fort Macon, Hammocks Beach, Hanging Rock, Jones Lake, and Cape Hatteras National Seashore. North Carolina National forests and local festivals are all drawing cards for visitors.

Locator-451-6568   Medical-451-6500   Police-451-6111

Pope Air Force Base (NC01R1)
Carolina Inn, 23 SVS/SVML
302 Ethridge Street
Pope AFB, NC 28308-2310

TELEPHONE NUMBER INFORMATION: Main installation numbers: C-910-394-0001, D-312-424-1110.

NORTH CAROLINA
Pope Air Force Base, continued

Location: Take I-95, exit to NC-87/24 W. Signs point the direction to AFB and Fort Bragg. *USMRA: Page 45 (J-4)*. NMC: Fayetteville, 12 miles southeast.

Lodging Office: Carolina Inn, 302 Ethridge Street, **C-910-394-4131, D-312-424-4131,** Fax: C-910-394-4912, D-312-424-4912, 24 hours. Check in billeting, check out 1200 hours daily. Government civilian employee billeting with reservations.

TML: VOQ. Bldgs 229-247, all ranks, leave or official duty. Bedroom, private bath (96); separate bedroom, private bath (12); eight bedroom units (8). Community kitchen, refrigerator, A/C, color TV, housekeeping service, cribs, washer/dryer, ice vending. Older structure. Rates: $10. TDY can make reservations, others Space-A.

TML: VAQ. Bldg 287, enlisted all ranks, leave or official duty. Bedroom, shared bath (68); separate bedroom, private bath (4). Refrigerator, A/C, color TV, housekeeping service, washer/dryer, ice vending. Older structure, renovated 1991. Rates: $10. TDY can make reservations, others Space-A.

TML: DV/VIP. Bldg 295, officer O6+, leave or official duty. C-910-394-4739. Bedroom, private bath (4). Kitchen, utensils, A/C, color TV, housekeeping service, washer/dryer, ice vending. Older structure. Rates: $16 per person. All categories can make reservations.

TML: TLF. Bldg 229, all ranks, PCS in/out. Bedroom, private bath (8), kitchenette, utensils, A/C, color TV, housekeeping service, washer/dryer. Rates: E1-E2 and O1 $15; E3-E6 $22; E7+ $24. PCS can make reservations, all others Space-A.

DV/VIP: Protocol Office. 259 Maynard Street, Suite C, C 910-394-4739. O6+. Retirees Space-A.

TML Availability: Good, winter. Difficult, other times.

CREDIT CARDS ACCEPTED: Visa, MasterCard and American Express.

Near Goldsboro, Cliffs of the Neuse River, picnicking, refreshments, fishing swimming and rental rowboats, museum. Also visit historic Fort Macon, the Cape Hatteras National Seashore, and Fayetteville.

Locator 394-4822   Medical 394-2778   Police 394-2800

Seymour Johnson Air Force Base (NC11R1)
Southern Pines Inn
4 SVS/SVML
1235 Wright Ave
Seymour Johnson AFB, NC 27531-2468

TELEPHONE NUMBER INFORMATION: Main installation numbers: C-919-736-5400, D-312-488-1110.

Location: From US-70 in Goldsboro take Seymour Johnson exit onto Berkeley Blvd to main gate. Clearly marked. *USMRA: Page 45 (L-3)*. NMC: Raleigh, 50 miles northwest.

182 - Temporary Military Lodging Around the World

NORTH CAROLINA
Seymour Johnson Air Force Base, continued

Lodging Office: Southern Pines Inn. ATTN: 4 SVS/SVML. Bldg 3804, 1235 Wright Ave; from main gate, go left on Wright Brothers Ave, located on left past the Officers' Club. **C-919-736-6705, D-312-488-6705,** Fax: C-919-736-5643, D-312-488-5643, 24 hours daily. Check in 1500, check out 1200 daily. Government civilian employee billeting VOQ.

TML: TLF. Bldg 3802. All ranks. PCS families priority one. Retirees, leave, or TDY Space-A basis. Bedroom, private bath (3); separate bedroom, private bath (25); two bedroom, private bath (1). Kitchen, limited utensils, A/C, color TV/VCR, housekeeping service, washer/dryer, ice vending. Newly renovated structure. Rates: (For PCS) E1-E2 and O1 $13.50; E3-E6 $20.50; E7+ $24; all Space-A $24 per unit. Priority one can make reservations anytime, Space-A can make reservations 24 hours in advance. No pets.

TML: VAQ. Bldg 3803. Enlisted all ranks. Official duty priority one. Retirees or leave Space-A basis. Bedroom, private bath (6); bedroom, semi-private bath (28); SNCO suite, separate bedroom, private bath (5); Chief suite, separate bedroom, private bath (1). A/C, color TV/VCR, housekeeping service, washer/dryer, ice vending, soda/snack vending. Exercise room available. Older structure. Rates: single $10, double $23. Priority one can make reservations anytime, Space-A can make reservations 24 hours in advance. No pets.

TML: VOQ. Bldg 3804. Officers all ranks. Official duty priority one. Retirees or leave Space-A basis. Suite, kitchen, separate bedroom, private bath (5); bedroom, private bath (38). A/C, color TV/VCR, conference room, housekeeping service, washer/dryer, ice vending. Sundry items sold at front desk: snacks, sodas, juices, alcoholic beverages, frozen entrees, personal hygiene items, military clothing items. Meeting/conference room available. Modern structure. Rates: single $10, double $14; suites, single $16, double $23. Priority one can make reservations anytime, Space-A can make reservations 24 hours in advance. No pets.

TML: DV/VIP. Bldg 2820. Officer O6+. Retirees, leave or official duty. Separate bedroom suites, private bath (10). Kitchen, color TV/VCR, housekeeping service, washer/dryer. Modern structure. Rates: single $16, double $23. Reservations: call protocol C-919-736-6483, D-312-488-6483.

TML Availability: Good, Nov-Apr. Difficult, other times.

CREDIT CARDS ACCEPTED: Visa, MasterCard and American Express.

Transportation: On base taxi 736-6622, off base taxi City Cab Company 735-2202, East Side Taxi 735-4711, Webb Town Taxi 734-8444, car rental agencies: American Auto Rental 736-8077, Enterprise Rent-A-Car 778-4828, U-Save Auto Rental 778-4889.

Nearby Ashville is good for rafting, hiking and skiing, while Carowinds, in Charlotte, is a large family entertainment center. Ashboro's zoological park, and Raleigh, the state capital, are well worth visits.

Locator 736-5584   **Medical 736-5577**   **Police 736-6413**

NORTH DAKOTA

Camp Gilbert C. Grafton (ND03R3)
A.T.S. Billeting Office
Route 5, Box 278A Building 6010
Devils Lake, ND 58301-9235

TELEPHONE NUMBER INFORMATION: Main installation numbers: C-701-662-0200, D-312-344-5226.

Location: From the intersection of US-2 and 20 in the city of Devil's Lake, turn south on US 20 and proceed for five miles. Gate entrance will be on the right side. *USMRA: Page 83 (G-3)*. NMC: Devils Lake, five miles north.

Lodging Office: Route 5, Box 278A, Bldg 6010, Devils Lake, ND 58301-9235. **C-701-662-0239, D-312-344-5226 ext 239,** Fax: C-701-662-04448, 0700 to 1630 hours daily. Follow signs from the front gate to the information center. After hours use phone in information center, Bldg 6010. Check in at billeting office after 1430 hours, check out 1000 hours. Late checkout pays extra day.

TML: BOQ/BEQ. Bldg 3600 and 3800, all ranks, leave or official duty, C-701-662-0239. Bedroom, two beds, shared bath (80). Refrigerator (40), kitchenette (2), color TV, A/C, housekeeping service, washer/dryer in separate building, soda/snack vending, mini-mart. Modern structure. Rates: Official duty $5, unofficial duty and dependents $6 per unit, maximum $20. Maximum six per unit. Reservations required for duty, others Space-A. No pets.

TML: Guesthouse. Double wide trailers (19), 3 bedrooms, 2 baths. Kitchen, refrigerator, stove, A/C, color TV, daily housekeeping service, washer/dryer (10), living/dining room, soda/snack vending, mini-mart. Rates: Same as above. Reservations required for duty, others Space-A. No pets.

TML: DV/VIP. One House, 2 bedrooms, private bath, fully equipped kitchen, A/C, color TV, daily housekeeping service, living/dining room, soda/snack vending, mini-mart. Rates: Same as above. Reservations required for duty, all others Space-A. No pets.

TML Availability: Good. Best, Sep-May. Difficult, May to Sep.

CREDIT CARDS ACCEPTED: Visa, MasterCard and American Express.

Transportation: Off base taxi 662-7812/1192, car rental agencies 662-1144/5346/2124.

This area is known for its Summer and Winter fishing and seasonal waterfowl hunting (must have ND license). At certain times of the year the skies are black with migrating ducks and geese. Enjoy boating, snowmobiling, historical sites and casinos. Only 90 miles from the Canadian border, an outdoor paradise.

Locator 662-0200   **Medical 662-5323**   **Police 662-5323**

NORTH DAKOTA

Grand Forks Air Force Base (ND04R3)
ATTN: 319 SVS/SVML
Lodging Office, Warrior Inn (Bldg 117)
Grand Forks AFB, ND 58205-0001

TELEPHONE NUMBER INFORMATION: Main installation numbers: C-701-747-3000, D-312-362-3000.

Location: From I-29 take US-2 W exit for 14 miles to Grand Forks, County Rd B-3 (Emerado/Air Base) one mile to AFB. *USMRA: Page 83 (I-3)*. NMC: Grand Forks, 15 miles east.

Lodging Office: Warrior Inn, Bldg 117, Holzapple and 6th Ave. **C-701-747-7051/7048**, Fax: C-701-747-3069, D-312-362-3069, 24 hours. Check out 1200 hours daily. Government civilian employee lodging.

TML: TLF. Across street from billeting, all ranks, leave or official duty. Efficiency apartments, private bath (40). Kitchen, limited utensils, A/C, color TV, housekeeping service, washer/dryer, ice vending. Modern structure. Rates: $24 per unit. PCS in/out reservations required. Duty can make reservations, others Space-A.

TML: VOQ. Bldg 117, officers all ranks, leave or official duty. Two-bedroom suites, private bath (12); bedroom, semi-private bath (6). Refrigerator, A/C, color TV, housekeeping service, washer/dryer, ice vending. Rates: $10 per person. PCS in/out reservations required, duty can make reservations, others Space-A.

TML: VAQ. Bldg 117, enlisted all ranks, leave or official duty. Bedroom, semi-private bath (12); 2-bedroom suites, private bath (10). Refrigerator, color TV, housekeeping service, washer/dryer, ice. Rates: $10 per person. PCS in/out reservations required. Duty can make reservations, others Space-A.

TML: DV/VIP. Bldg 132, officers O7+, leave or official duty. Four-bedroom house, private bath, kitchen, living room, dining room, washer/dryer (1). Rates: $16 per person. For reservations contact Protocol (see below).

TML: DV/VIP. Bldg 117, Officer 06+, leave or official duty. Suites, one bedroom, private bath, living room, refrigerator, color TV, A/C, housekeeping service, washer dryer, ice vending. Rates: $16 per person. For reservations call Protocol.

TML: DV/VIP. Bldg 117, enlisted E9, leave or official duty. Two-bedroom suites, private bath (2). Living room, refrigerator, color TV, A/C, housekeeping service, washer/dryer, ice vending. Rates: $146 per person. For reservations contact Protocol.

DV/VIP: 319 AD Protocol Office, Bldg 307, C-701-747-5055, E9. C-312-362-5055. O6+. Retirees and lower ranks Space-A.

TML Availability: Good, winter. Difficult, spring and summer.

CREDIT CARDS ACCEPTED: Visa, MasterCard and American Express.

Locator 747-3344   **Medical 747-5600**   **Police 747-5351**

NORTH DAKOTA

Minot Air Force Base (ND02R3)
Sakakawea Inn
5 SVS/SVML
201 Summit Drive, Unit 5
Minot AFB, ND 58705-5049

TELEPHONE NUMBER INFORMATION: Main installation numbers: C-701-723-1110, D-312-453-1110.

Location: On US-83, north of Minot. *USMRA: Page 83 (D-2).* NMC: Minot, 12 miles south.

Lodging Office: Sakakawea Inn, 14 Summit Drive. **C-701-723-6161, D-312-453-6161,** Fax: C-701-723-1844, D-312-453-1844, 24 hours. Check out 1200 hours.

TML: TLF. Bldgs 221, 223, 227, 229, Missile Avenue, all ranks, leave or official duty, C-701-723-6161. Separate bedroom apartments, private bath (39). Kitchen, complete utensils, A/C, microwave, color TV/VCR, housekeeping service, washer/dryer, ice vending. All non-smoking units. One unit meeting all ADA (Americans with Disabilities Act) requirements. Modern structure. Rates: $23 per unit. Space-A reservations accepted 24 hours in advance; confirmation based on availability.

TML: VOQ. Bldg 16, Summit Drive, officers all ranks, leave or official duty, C-701-723-6161. Bedrooms, private and semi-private bath (40). Refrigerator and/or complete kitchen, A/C, microwave, color TV/VCR, housekeeping service, washer/dryer, ice vending, all non-smoking rooms. Modern structure. Rates: $10-$16 per person, $14-$23 per couple. Space-A reservations accepted 24 hours in advance, confirmation based on availability.

TML: VAQ. Bldg 14, Summit Drive, enlisted all ranks, leave or official duty, C-701-723-6161. Bedroom, private and semi-private bath (32). Refrigerator and/or complete kitchen, A/C, microwave, color TV, housekeeping service, washer/dryer, all non-smoking rooms. Chief suites. Modern structure. Rates: $10-$16 per person, $14-$23 per couple. Space-A reservations accepted 24 hours in advance, confirmation based on availability.

TML: DVQ. Bldg 12, Summit Drive (Rough Rider Suite and Magic City Suite), officers O6+, C-701-723-6161. Suites, private bath (4); bedroom suite with office (2). Kitchen, A/C, microwave, color TV/VCR, housekeeping service, washer/dryer. Rates: $16-$27 per person, $23-$39.50 per couple. Space-A reservations accepted 24 hours in advance, confirmation based on availability.

DV/VIP: Protocol Office 201 Summit Drive. C-701-723-3474, D-312-453-3474. Rates: $10-$39.50.

TML Availability: Generally good. Difficult, Jul and Oct.

CREDIT CARDS ACCEPTED: Visa, MasterCard and American Express.

Swimming pools, tennis courts, city zoo are in Roosevelt Park. Visit General Custer's command post at Fort Lincoln State Park, and the International Peace Garden on the Manitoba/North Dakota border. Lake fishing, abundant hunting for deer and fowl.

Locator 723-1841   **Medical 723-5633**   **Police 723-3096**

OHIO

Camp Perry Clubhouse (OH06R2)
Bldg 600
Port Clinton, OH 43452-9578

TELEPHONE NUMBER INFORMATION: Main installation numbers: C-419-635-4114, D-312-346-4114.

LOCATION: On post. On OH-2, five miles west of Port Clinton. *USMRA: Page 67 (D-3)*. NMC: Sandusky, 25 miles southeast.

RESERVATIONS: Preferred, up to one year in advance. Write to: Clubhouse Manager, Bldg 600, Camp Perry Military Training Site, Port Clinton, OH 43452-9578. **C-419-635-4114, D-312-346-4114**, check in 1400-2200 hours. Open to the public. Military discount.

TML: Cottages, Bldgs 501-527, one- and two-bedroom, private bath, A/C (27). Sofa-bed, telephone upon request, utensils, dishes, toaster, coffeepot, snack vending. Rates: $27-$80 daily.

TML: Motel, Bldgs 120, 150, 160, 170, 529, 530, units with kitchen, one double bed, sofa bed, private bath, A/C (20). Utensils, dishes, toaster, coffeepot. Rates: $27-$40 daily. Motel units without kitchen, private bath, A/C (207) Rates: $16-$35 daily. Snack vending, coin-op laundry.

Note: Daily housekeeping service is not provided. Cleaning and trash removal is a personal responsibility. Cleaning materials provided upon request. Linen exchange: towels exchange daily, bed linens exchange bi-weekly. No pets allowed.

TML Availability: Good, Jan-Mar. Difficult, other times.

CREDIT CARDS ACCEPTED: Visa, MasterCard and American Express.

Situated along Lake Erie approximately 30 miles from the Canadian border. Limited support facilities available on post. Fishing/license, swimming, fishing pier, grills, picnic area.

Locator 635-4114   Medical 9-911   Police 9-911

Defense Supply Center (OH05R2)
Bldg 1/1, 2nd floor
3990 E. Broad Street
Columbus, OH 43216-5000

TELEPHONE NUMBER INFORMATION: Main installation numbers C-614-692-3131, D-312-850-3131.

Location: From I-270 (Beltway) take exit 39 to Broad Street W, main gate at 4990 Broad Street. *USMRA: Page 67 (D-6)*, NMC: Columbus, in city limits.

Lodging Office: Bldg 1/1, 3990 E. Broad Street. **C-614-692-4756, D-312-850-4758,** Fax: C-614-692-3390, D-312-850-3390, 0730-1530 hours Mon-Fri. After hours, weekends and holidays, check security at Broad Street gate for vacancy list, C-614-692-3608. Check in billeting 1400 hours, check out 1100 hours daily.

OHIO
Defense Supply Center, continued

TML: TLQ. Bldg 201, C-614-692-4758. Bedroom, private bath (6); suite, private bath (2); apartment (2). All have kitchenette, refrigerator, utensils, color TV, housekeeping service, washer/dryer, soda/snack vending. Meeting/conference rooms, exercise room and mini-mart available. Reservations required. Rates: $17-$35.

DV/VIP: Protocol, C-614-692-2167, D-312-850-2167. O6+. Retirees and lower ranks Space-A. Rates: PCS $20; all others $30.

CREDIT CARDS ACCEPTED: Visa and MasterCard.

Transportation: On/off base shuttle bus 692-2350, on/off base taxi 692-2350.

Locator 692-3131   **Medical** 692-2227   **Police** 692-2111

Wright-Patterson Air Force Base (OH01R2)
88 SPTG/SVML
2439 Schlatter Drive
Wright-Patterson AFB, OH 45433-5519

TELEPHONE NUMBER INFORMATION: Main installation numbers: C-513-257-1110, D-312-787-1110.

Location: South of I-70, off I-675 at Fairborn. Also, access from OH-4, AFB clearly marked. *USMRA: Page 67 (B-7).* NMC: Dayton, 10 miles northwest.

Lodging Office: Bldg 825, 2439 Schlatter Drive. C-513-257-3451, D-312-787-3451, Fax: C-513-257-2787, D-312-787-2787, 24 hours. Check in billeting, check out 1200 hours daily. Government civilian employee billeting.

TML: TLQ. Bldg 825, all ranks, leave or official duty, C-513-257-3810. Bedroom, bath (40). Kitchen, complete utensils, microwaves, A/C, color TV, housekeeping service, cribs, washer/dryer, ice vending. Exercise room and mini-mart available on base. Modern structure, renovated. Rates: $24 per unit. Sleeps five. Duty can make reservations, others Space-A.

TML: VOQ. Bldg 825, all ranks, leave or official duty. Bedroom, private bath (108); bedroom, semi-private bath (492). Refrigerator, microwave, beverage, snacks, microwavable dinners, coffee maker, A/C, color TV, housekeeping service, washer/dryer, ice vending. Exercise room and mini-mart available on base. Fax service available at no charge for VOQ/VAQ quests. Rates: $10 per person, maximum $14 per family. Maximum three per room. Duty can make reservations, others Space-A.

TML: DV/VIP. Bldgs 825/826, call about eligibility, leave or official duty, C-513-257-3810. Two-bedroom suites, private bath (22); top three suites, private bath (11). Refrigerator, A/C, color TV, housekeeping service, cribs/cots, washer/dryer, ice vending, microwaves, microwave dinners, beverage, snacks. Exercise room and mini-mart available on base. Rates: $16 per person, maximum $23 per family. Maximum five per suite. Duty can make reservations.

TML: Hope Hotel and Conference Center, the Air Force's first private sector financed hotel. Bldg 823, all ranks, leave or official duty. DoD Civilian lodging. One- and two-bedroom (doubles), private bath (260). A/C, CATV, ice vending, iron/ironing board, handicap accessible. Seven full service conference rooms available, catering available from on site restaurant. Exercise room and mini-mart

OHIO
Wright-Patterson Air Force Base, continued

available on base. Call for rates. Official duty reservations call billeting at C-513-257-3810, D-312-787-3810. Others, C-513-257-1285, D-213-787-1285. Major credit cards accepted.

TML: Fisher House. Note: Appendix B has the definition of this facility. C-513-257-8762/0855.

DV/VIP: Protocol, 645 ABW/CCP, Bldg 10, C-513-257-3110. O7/GS-16+. Retirees and lower ranks Space-A.

TML Availability: Good, late Nov, early Jan. Difficult, other times.

CREDIT CARDS ACCEPTED: Visa, Mastercard and American Express.

Transportation: On base shuttle/bus/taxi 257-3755, 0600-2300 hours Mon-Fri.

The Air Force museum on base, and the city of Dayton with its art and natural history museums, local arts and the Nutter Sports Center all make this area an interesting place to visit.

Locator 257-3231   **Medical 257-2968**   **Police 257-6841**

Other Installations in Ohio

Gentile Air Force Station, Dayton DESC, Kettering, OH 45444-5000, C-614-692-2418. Limited lodging, call for more information, 0700-1530 Mon-Fri.
Youngstown Air Reserve Station, Eagles Nest Inn, 3976 King Graves Road, Vienna, OH 44473-0910, C-330-609-1268, D-312-346-1268, Fax: C-330-609-1120, D-312-346-1120. BEQ/BOQ. Meeting/conference room and exercise room available. Rates: single $6, each additional person $3 ($2 surcharge on sponsor with guest). Credit cards accepted.

OKLAHOMA

Altus Air Force Base (OK02R3)
Red River Inn Lodging
97 SVS/SVML
308 North First Street
Altus AFB, OK 73523-5146

TELEPHONE NUMBER INFORMATION: Main installation numbers: C-405-481/482-8100, D-312-866-1110.

Location: Off US-62, south of I-40 and west of I-44. From US-62 traveling west from Lawton, turn right at first traffic light in Altus and follow road to main gate northeast of Falcon Road. *USMRA: Page 84 (E-5)*. NMC: Lawton, 56 miles east.

Lodging Office: Red River Inn, Bldg 82. **C-405-481-7356, D-312-866-7356,** Fax: C-405-481-5704, D-312-866-5704, 24 hours. Check in lodging, check out 1200 hours daily. Government civilian employee billeting.

OKLAHOMA
Altus Air Force Base, continued

TML: VOQ. Bldgs 81-85, officers all ranks. Bedroom, private bath (128); separate bedrooms, private bath (24). Kitchen, A/C, color TV, housekeeping service, washer/dryer. Modern structure, hotel type lodging. Rates: $8.50 per person. Duty can make reservations. Space-A can make reservations within 72 hours.

TML: Temporary VOQ. Bldg 82, officers all ranks. Bedroom, common bath (49). A/C, color TV in room and lounge, housekeeping service. Modern structure. Rates: $8.50 per person. Duty can make reservations. Space-A can make reservations within 72 hours.

TML: VAQ. Bldg 313, 314, enlisted all ranks. Bedroom, central latrine (144). Bldg 327, bedroom, common bath (76). Rates: $8.50 per person. Call for reservation information.

TML: TLF. One-bedroom units (8); three-bedroom duplexes (2). Call for rates, eligibility and reservation information.

TML: DV/VIP. Bldg 81, 84, 85, officer O4+, leave or official duty. Separate bedrooms private bath (8). Kitchen, A/C, color TV, housekeeping service, washer/dryer. Modern structure, hotel type lodging. Rates: $16 per person. Duty can make reservations, others Space-A.

DV/VIP: Wing EXO, Bldg 1, C-405-481-7044. O6+. Retirees and lower ranks Space-A.

TML Availability: Good, Dec. Difficult, other times.

CREDIT CARDS ACCEPTED: Visa, MasterCard and American Express.

Visit the Museum of the Western Prairie for the saga of the area's wild west roots. Quartz Mountain State Park hosts the county fairs, rodeos and roundups that are part of life here.

Locator 481-7250   **Medical** 481-5213   **Police** 481-7444

Camp Gruber Training Site (OK03R3)
ATTN: OKCG-L-H
P.O. Box 29
Braggs, OK 74423-0029

TELEPHONE NUMBER INFORMATION: Main installation numbers: C-918-487-6001, D-312-487-6057.

Location: Exit I-40 at Webber Falls (exit 287), take Hwy 62 to Gore, OK, take state Hwy 10 to Braggs. First entrance to camp after passing through Braggs. *USMRA: Page 84 (I-4).* NMC: Muskogee, 20 miles northwest.

Lodging Office: Bldg 155, 4th Street and Anzio Drive. **C-918-487-6067**, Fax: C-918-487-6135, 0730-1600 hours. Check in, check out 1000 hours. Late arrivals OK with reservation.

TML: BOQ/BEQ. All ranks, leave or official duty. Two-bedroom mobile home (11). Kitchen, refrigerator, A/C, color TV, housekeeping service. Rates: AD $10; all others (includes AD on leave) $15. No pets. No tobacco products.

OKLAHOMA
Camp Gruber Training Site, continued

TML: BOQ/BEQ. E9, WO3, O3+, leave or official duty. Three-bedroom mobile home (1); 2-bedroom mobile home (6). Kitchen, refrigerator, microwave, A/C, color TV, housekeeping service. Rates: AD $10; all others (includes AD on leave) $15. No pets. No tobacco products.

TML: BOQ/BEQ. Bldg 232. E9, WO3, O3+, leave or official duty. Refrigerator, microwave, A/C, color TV, housekeeping service. Rates: AD $7; all others (includes AD on leave) $10. No pets. No tobacco products.

TML: BOQ/BEQ. Bldgs 226, 227, 228, all ranks, leave or official duty. Semi-private bedroom, shared bath (30). Refrigerator, microwave, color TV, housekeeping service. Rates: AD $5; all others (includes AD on leave) $7. No pets. No tobacco products.

DV/VIP: General officer. Three-bedroom, double-wide mobile home. Refrigerator, microwave, A/C, color TV, housekeeping service. Rates: AD $10; all others (includes AD on leave) $15. No pets. No tobacco products.

TML Availability: Best, Sep-Apr. Difficult, May-Aug.

Located in the heart of Green Country, next to Greenleaf Lake, Arkansas River, twenty minutes from lake Tenkiller, twenty minutes from lake Fort Gibson.

Locator 487-6002   **Medical** 911   **Police** 487-6021

Fort Sill (OK01R3)
ATTN; ATZR-EHB
P.O. Box 33334
Fort Sill, OK 73503-5100

TELEPHONE NUMBER INFORMATION: Main installation numbers: C-405-442-8111, D-312-639-7090.

Location: From I-44 at Lawton take US-62/277, four miles northwest to post. Clearly marked. *USMRA*: Page 84 (E,F-5). NMC: Lawton, adjacent to city.

Lodging Office: Bldg 5676, Fergusson Road. **C-405-353-5007/442-5000, D-312-639-5000,** Fax: C-405-442-7033, 24 hours. Check in building, check out 1200 hours daily.

TML: Guest House. Office in Bldg 5690, Geronimo Road, C-405-442-3214, D-312-639-3214, 24 hours. Check in Bldg 5690, all ranks, leave or official duty. Rooms (75). Refrigerator, microwave, kitchen, A/C, color TV in room and lounge, housekeeping service, cribs/cots, washer/dryer, ice vending. Rates: E1-E4 $22 per room; E5- E6, W1, and O1 $27 per room; E7-E9, WO2-WO4, O2-O3 $32 per room; O4-O5, guests $36 per room. PCS can make reservations, others Space-A.

TML: BOQ/BEQ. E7+. Official duty only, reservations not taken, waiting list maintained. Must be signed into unit to get on waiting list. Spaces in BOQ (97); spaces in BEQ (8). Modern structure, renovated. Rates: no charge for room; maid fee $3-$4 per day. Maximum one per room. Dependents not authorized.

OKLAHOMA
Fort Sill, continued

TML: VOQ/VEQ. Both take overflow from Guest House. All ranks, official duty only. Spaces in VOQ (690); spaces in VEQ (130); VIP suites (25). Modern structure, renovated. Rates: sponsor $18, adult $7; VIP suites $21. No children. Billeting recommends that children stay in guest house with spouse. Duty can make reservations, others Space-A.

TML: DVQ. Bldg 460, officer O6/GS-15+, leave or official duty, C-405-442-5511. Dining room. Modern structure, renovated. Rates: sponsor $32 at Comanche House (Bldg 460); all other DVQs $32, additional adult $7. Duty can make reservations, others Space-A.

DV/VIP: Protocol Office, Bldg 455, C-405-442-2436. O7/GS-15+. Retirees Space-A.

TML Availability: Fairly good, fall, winter, spring. Difficult, summer.

CREDIT CARDS ACCEPTED: Visa, MasterCard, American Express and Discover.

Don't miss the original stone buildings constructed by the "Buffalo Soldiers" of the 10th Calvary, the Guardhouse where Geronimo was confined, the large museum on post, and the Museum of the Great Plains in Lawton.

Locator 442-3924   Medical 458-2500   Police 442-2101

Tinker Air Force Base (OK04R3)
Indian Hills Inn
ATTN: 72 SPTG/SVML
Tinker AFB, OK 73145-3010

TELEPHONE NUMBER INFORMATION: Main installation numbers: C-405-732-7321, D-312-884-1110.

Location: Southeast Oklahoma City, off I-40. Use gate 1 off Air Depot Blvd. Clearly marked. *USMRA: Page 84 (G-4)*. NMC: Oklahoma City, 12 miles northwest.

Lodging Office: Indian Hills Inn. 4002 Mitchell Street. **C-405-734-2822**, Fax: C-405-734-7426, 24 hours. Check in billeting, check out 1100 hours daily for DV, VOQ, VAQ, and TLQ. Government civilian employee billeting.

TML: TLF. Bldgs 5824, 5826, 5828, 5830, 5832, all ranks, leave or official duty. Rooms (39). Kitchen, A/C, color TV, housekeeping service, washer/dryer, playground. Rates: $21 per unit. Duty can make reservations, others Space-A.

TML: VOQ. Bldgs 5604, 5605, 5606, officers, all ranks, leave or official duty. Rooms, private and semi-private baths (100). Refrigerator, A/C, color CATV/ VCR, housekeeping service, washer/dryer. Rates: $10 per person. Duty can make reservations, others Space-A.

TML: VAQ. Bldg 5915, enlisted, leave or official duty. Bedrooms, private and semi-private (50). Refrigerator, A/C, color CATV/VCR housekeeping service, washer/dryer. Rates: $10 per person. Duty can make reservations, others Space-A.

DV/VIP: OC-ALC/CCP, Bldg 3001, C-405-734-5511. O6/GS-15+. Retirees and lower ranks Space-A.

OKLAHOMA
Tinker Air Force Base, continued

TML Availability: Limited in summer.

CREDIT CARDS ACCEPTED: Visa, MasterCard and American Express.

In Oklahoma City visit Remington Park, the National Cowboy Hall of Fame and Western Heritage Center, the city Zoo, tour the mansions of Heritage Hills. Five municipal golf courses, four lakes, and many sports events are available.

Locator 734-2456   Medical 734-8249   Police 734-2151

Vance Air Force Base (OK05R3)
71 FTW/NW-SL
426 Goad Street, Suite 131
Vance AFB, OK 73705-5116

TELEPHONE NUMBER INFORMATION: Main installation numbers: C-405-213-5000, D-312-940-7110.

Location: Off US-81, south of Enid. Clearly marked. *USMRA: Page 84 (F-3)*. NMC: Oklahoma City, 90 miles southeast.

Lodging Office: Bldg 714, Goad St. **C-405-213-7358, D-312-940-7358,** Fax: C-405-213-6278, 24 hours. Check in billeting, check out 1200 hours daily. Government civilian employee billeting.

TML: TLF. Bldg 790, all ranks, leave or official duty. Separate bedrooms, private bath (10). Kitchen, utensils, A/C, color TV, housekeeping service, cribs, washer/dryer, ice vending. Rates: E6 $18 per unit; E7+ $22 per unit. Duty can make reservations, others Space-A.

TML: VOQ/TAQ. Bldgs 713, 714, all ranks, leave or official duty. Bedroom, private bath (48); separate bedroom suite, private bath (DV/VIP) (1); 2-bedroom suites, private bath (DV/VIP) (2). Kitchen, microwave, A/C, color TV in room and lounge, housekeeping service, washer/dryer, ice vending, facilities for DAVs. Modern structure. Rates: $8.50 per person; DV/VIP $16, maximum $11.75 per family; DV/VIP $46. Duty can make reservations, others Space-A.

DV/VIP: Retirees Space-A, duty reservations as above.

TML Availability: Difficult. Best, Dec, Jan.

CREDIT CARDS ACCEPTED: Visa, Mastercard and American Express.

In Enid visit Government Springs Park where cowboys watered cattle 75 years ago - swimming pool, waterfall and lake for boating; and Meadowlake Park has an 18-hole golf course, amusement park, and a 14-acre lake.

Locator 249-7791   Medical 249-7416   Police 249-7200

OREGON

Kingsley Field (OR03R4)
Kingsley Dormitory
Bldg 208, McConnell Circle
Klamath Falls, OR 97603-0949

TELEPHONE NUMBER INFORMATION: Main installation numbers: C-541-885-6350, D-312-830-6350.

Location: On Hwy 140. *USMRA: Page 100 (D-8)*. NMC: Klamath Falls, three miles west.

Lodging Office: Kingsley Dormitory. Bldg 208, McConnell Circle. **C-541-885-6365**, 0700-1600 hours Mon-Fri. After hours extra keys at Security Gate.

TML: VOQ. All ranks, official duty. Suites, private bath (16); bedrooms, two beds, semi-private bath (40). Wood frame structure. All categories may make reservations.

TML Availability: Very good. **Note: Lodging available to personnel on official business only.**

There is a clinic and small BX on base. Experience top notch fishing, bald eagles that winter nearby, world class skiing, golf, horseback riding, camping, hunting. Then there's Crater Lake and Mt. Shasta within an hour's drive.

Locator 885-6308   Medical 885-6308   Police 885-6647

Rilea Armed Forces Training Center (OR07R4)
Route 2, Box 497-E
Warrenton, OR 97146-9711

TELEPHONE NUMBER INFORMATION: Main installation numbers: C-503-861-4018, D-312-355-3974.

Location: From Portland, Oregon take Highway 26 to oregon Coast, approximately 65 miles. When you reach Highway 101, proceed north 12 miles. Located between Seaside and Astoria. *USMRA: Page 100 (B-1)*. NMC: Astoria, five miles north.

Lodging Office: Bldg 7404. **C-503-861-4018**, Fax: C-503-861-4049, 0830-1630 hours daily. Check in billeting. Reservations accepted. E-mail: snikkila@aol.com.

TML: BOQ. E7+, leave or official duty. Rooms (18). Refrigerator, kitchenette, utensils, CATV, housekeeping service, soda/snack vending. Meeting/conference rooms, fitness center, and mini-mart available. Rates: $15 per night.

TML: BEQ. All ranks, leave or official duty. Bedrooms (53). Refrigerator, kitchenette, utensils, CATV in lounge, housekeeping service, soda/snack vending. Meeting conference rooms, fitness center, and mini-mart available. Rates: $10 per night.

TML: State homes. O6+, Chateau; E8+, Cottage; O4/CW4+, Hilltop. Call for more information.

194 - Temporary Military Lodging Around the World

OREGON
Rilea Armed Forces Training Center, continued

TML Availability: Good.

CREDIT CARDS ACCEPTED: None at this time, but will allow Visa and MasterCard by September 1997; call for verification.

Visit the many National Forests and State Parks that dot the coastline and state.

Locator 861-4018   **Medical 911**   **Police 911**

PENNSYLVANIA

Carlisle Barracks (PA08R1)
ATZE-DPW-GH
Bldg 7 Washington Hall
Ashburn Street, Carlisle Barracks
Carlisle, PA 17013-5002

TELEPHONE NUMBER INFORMATION: Main installation numbers: C-717-245-3131, D-312-242-4141.

Location: From I-81 exit 17 to US-11, two miles southwest to Carlisle, signs clearly marked to Barracks and Army War College. *USMRA: Page 22 (F-6)*. NMC: Harrisburg, 18 miles north.

Lodging Office: Washington Hall, 7 Ashburn Drive. **C-717-245-4245,** Fax: C-717-245-3757, 0700-1800 hours weekdays, 0800-1600 hours weekends. Other hours Bldg 400, pick up key at MP desk. Check in 1400-1800 hours daily, check out 1100 hours daily. Government civilian employee billeting. Note: only family members with valid ID card can stay at this facility. E-mail: richardp@carlisle-emh2.army.mil.

TML: Guest House. Bldgs 7, 37, all ranks, leave or official duty. Bedrooms, private bath (14); bedrooms, shared bath (4); bedrooms, community bath (6); VIP suites, private bath (one, night only) (4). Community kitchen, A/C, color TV in room and lounge, iron/ironing board, refrigerator, hair dryer, coffee pot/coffee, toilet amenities, housekeeping service, cribs/cots ($2), ice vending. Rates: single, private bath, $12-$30, shared bath, $8-$20, community bath, $6-$15, extra person $5, each additional person $3. Suites $20-$35. Rates vary according to rank, status and/or type of room. PCS and guests of USAWC have priority. All categories can make reservations.

TML Availability: Good, Jan-Mar. Difficult, other times.

CREDIT CARDS ACCEPTED: Visa, MasterCard and American Express.

An arsenal during the Revolutionary War, near the Gettysburg Battlefields, site of the Military History Institute, home of the Army War College, Carlisle Barracks has an illustrious history worth tracing.

Locator 245-3131   **Medical 245-3915/3400**   **Police 245-4315**

PENNSYLVANIA

Defense Distribution Region East (PA06R1)
**ATTN: WNSH
Bldg 268, J Ave
New Cumberland, PA 17070-5001**

TELEPHONE NUMBER INFORMATION: Main installation numbers: C-717-770-6011, D-312-977-6011.

Location: From I-83 take exit 18 to PA 114. East for one mile to Old York Road, left .75 miles to Ross Ave, right for one mile to main gate. *USMRA: Page 22 (G-6).* NMC: Harrisburg, seven miles northeast.

Lodging Office: ATTN: WNSH, Bldg 268, J Ave, New Cumberland, PA 17070-5001. **C-717-770-7035,** Fax: C-717-770-4579, 0800-1630 hours daily. Government civilian employee billeting in BOQ.

TML: VOQ/DV/VIP. Bldg 268, all ranks, leave or official duty. Bedroom, shared bath (18); separate bedroom, private bath (1); 2-bedroom, private bath (1). Refrigerator, community kitchen, A/C, color TV, housekeeping service, cribs/cots, washer/dryer. Older structure, renovated. Rates: VOQ $30, DVQ $30. Duty with TDY, PCS orders can make reservations, others Space-A. Maximum two adults and one child per unit.

DV/VIP: Protocol Office, Bldg 81, C-717-770-7192. O6/GS-15+, retirees and lower ranks Space-A.

TML Availability: Good, Nov-Feb. Difficult, other times.

CREDIT CARDS ACCEPTED: Visa, MasterCard, American Express and MAC debit card.

Visit Hershey Park, famous Pennsylvania Dutch Country, Gettysburg National Military Park, and General Lee's Headquarters and Museum.

Locator 770-6011   Medical 770-7281   Police 770-6222

Fort Indiantown Gap (PA04R1)
**Housing Division
1 Garrsison Road, Room 28
Annville, PA 17003-5033
*Scheduled to close October 1998.***

TELEPHONE NUMBER INFORMATION: Main installation numbers: C-717-861-2000, D-312-491-2000.

Location: From I-81 take exit 29 W, north on PA-934 to facility. *USMRA: Page 22 (G-6).* NMC: Harrisburg, 20 miles southwest.

Lodging Office: 1 Garrison Road, Room 28. **C-717-861-2512/2540, D-312-491-2512/2540,** Fax: C-717-861-2821, D-312-491-2821, 0800-2330 hours daily. Check in billeting 1500 hours, check out 1100 hours daily.

PENNSYLVANIA
Fort Indiantown Gap, continued

TML: Reserve/National Guard post. VOQ/BEQ. All ranks, official duty. Bedroom, common bath (26); separate bedroom, private bath (5); Cottages (13). A/C, CATV, housekeeping service, washer/dryer, facilities for DAVs. Older structure, renovated. Rates: rooms $5.50; suites $10; cottages $20, each additional person in suites/cottages over age eight $4. Dependents allowed. Space-A walk in only; unable to take reservations.

TML Availability: Difficult, most of the time. Best, Nov-Mar.

CREDIT CARDS ACCEPTED: Visa, MasterCard and American Express.

Hershey Park, Museum and Chocolate World, Indian Echo Caverns with a spectacular underground display, and local Pennsylvania German farm and village festivals and crafts demonstrations are "must sees."

Locator 861-2000   **Medical 861-2091**   **Police 861-2727**

Letterkenny Army Depot (PA03R1)
Lodging Office
ATTN: SDSLE-EH
Chambersburg, PA 17201-4150

TELEPHONE NUMBER INFORMATION: Main installation numbers: C-717-267-8111, D-312-570-5110.

Location: From I-81 exit 8 W on PA-997 to PA-433 on left and enter depot at Gate 6. *USMRA: Page 22 (E-7).* NMC: Harrisburg, 45 miles northeast.

Lodging Office: ATTN: SDSLE-EH, Bldg 663. **C-717-267-8890,** 0730-1600 hours Mon-Fri. Other hours call security C-717-267-8800. Check in billeting 1300 hours, check out 1100 hours daily. Government civilian employee billeting.

TML: Guest House. Bldg 539, all ranks, leave or official duty. One-bedroom, private bath (1); 1-bedroom, private bath, kitchen (1); 2-bedroom, private bath, kitchen (1). Limited utensils, A/C, color TV, housekeeping service, cribs/cots, washer/dryer. Older structure, renovated. Rates: 1-bedroom $12; separate bedroom, kitchen $14; 2-bedroom $17. Reservations required, others Space-A.

TML: VOQ. Bldg 503, officers and government service ranks, leave, PCS or official duty. Two-bedroom, private bath, kitchen (1); 1-bedroom, private bath (5). A/C, color TV, housekeeping service, washer/dryer. Rates: 1-bedroom $8; 2-bedroom $15. Reservations required, others Space-A.

DV/VIP: ATTN: SDSLE-CA, Bldg 500, C-717-267-8659. DV/VIP determined by CO. Retirees Space-A.

TML Availability: Best, Sep-Mar.

Tour famous Gettysburg Battlefield, try local bass and trout fishing in Rocky Springs Reservoir, local hunting is very good.

Locator 264-1413   **Medical 267-8416**   **Police 267-8800**

PENNSYLVANIA

Pittsburgh Air Reserve Station (PA15R1)
Bldg 206, 2275 Defense Ave.
Corapolis, PA 15108-4463

TELEPHONE NUMBER INFORMATION: Main installation numbers: C-412-474-8000, D-312-277-8000.

Location: Take I-279W which merges into PA-60 (Airport Pkwy), take Exit 3 Business Route 60 to Thorn Run Interchange to Air Force Reserve Station. *USMRA: Page 22 (A-5,6)*. NMC: Pittsburgh, 15 miles southeast.

Lodging Office: Bldg 206, 2275 Defense Ave, Corapolis, PA 15108-4463. **C-412-474-8229/8230,** D-312-277-8230, Fax: C-412-474-8752, D-312-277-8752, 0700-2300 hours daily, check out 1200 hours.

TML: VOQ/DV. Bldg 206, officers, all ranks. Bedroom, semi-private bath (20), bedroom, private bath (2); 2-room DV suite, private bath (2). Telephone, refrigerator, color TV/VCR, A/C, housekeeping service, ice vending, microwave in lounge. Rates: $10 per night.

TML: VAQ/SNCO. Bldg 209, 216, 217, 218, 219, enlisted, all ranks. Bedroom, two beds per room, common bath (72); bedroom, private bath (44),; 2-room SNCO suite, private bath (10). Telephone, refrigerator, color TV/VCR, A/C, housekeeping service, ice vending, microwave in lounge. Rates: rooms $8 per night; SNCO suites $10 per night.

CREDIT CARDS ACCEPTED: Visa, MasterCard and American Express.

Locator 474-8000   Medical 474-8117   Police 474-8250/8255

Tobyhanna Army Depot (PA05R1)
Housing Office
11 Hap Arnold Blvd
Tobyhanna, PA 18466-5090

TELEPHONE NUMBER INFORMATION: Main installation numbers: C-717-895-7000, D-312-795-7110.

Location: I-80E or W to I-380N, exit 7 to depot. *USMRA: Page 22 (I-4)*. NMC: Scranton, 24 miles northwest.

Lodging Office: Bldg 1001, **C-717-895-7970**, Fax: C-717-895-6984, D-312 795-6984, 0730-1600 hours Mon-Fri. Other hours Security, Bldg 20, C-717-895-7550. Check in billeting 1400 hours, check out 1000 hours daily.

TML: Guest House, Bldgs 1013,1014, all ranks, leave or official duty. Two-bedroom, private bath (3); 3-bedroom, private bath (1). Kitchen, limited utensils, color TV, housekeeping service, cribs, washer/dryer. One older structure, two newly renovated. Rates: $30 per day, each additional person over 2-years old $5. Reservations can be made 30 days in advance.

DV/VIP: ATTN: Protocol Office, Bldg 11-2, C-717-895-6223. O6+. No DV/VIP quarters.

198 - Temporary Military Lodging Around the World

PENNSYLVANIA
Tobyhanna Army Depot, continued

TML Availability: Good, Apr-Nov. Difficult, other times.

In the Pocono Mountains Resort Area. Nearby lakes and streams provide fishing and water sports. Skiing and winter sports Jan-Mar. State parks and forest picnic areas in the immediate area will lure visitors.

Locator 895-7000　　　　　**Medical 895-7121**　　　　　**Police 895-7550**

Willow Grove Naval Air Station/ Joint Reserve Base (PA01R1)
CBQ Bldg 609
NAS/JRB Willow Grove
Willow Grove, PA 19090-5000

TELEPHONE NUMBER INFORMATION: Main installation numbers: C-215-443-1000, D-312-991-1000.

Location: Take PA Turnpike (I-276), exit 27N on PA 611, five miles to NAS/JRB. *USMRA: Page 22 (I,J-6)*. NMC: Philadelphia, 21 miles south.

Lodging Office: Bldg 609. **C-215-442-5800/5801**, D-312-991-5800, Fax: C-215-442-5817, 24 hours. Toll-Free Reservations 1-800-227-9472. Check in facility 1500 hours, check out 1100 hours daily.

TML: BOQ. Bldg 5, officers all ranks, leave or official duty. Single bedroom, common bath (20); suites, private bath, window A/C (10). Refrigerator, microwave, color CATV, vending machines, housekeeping service, washer/dryer. Older structure, renovated. Rates: single $10; suite $18; each additional person $3. PCS with family, TDY, AD can make reservations, retirees and others Space-A.

TML: BEQ. Bldg 172, enlisted E6 and below, leave or official duty. E5/6: Bedroom, private bath (14); E4 and below: double rooms, private bath (20). A/C, refrigerator, microwave, color CATV, iron/ironing board, alarm clock, coffee pot, vending machines, washer/dryer, housekeeping service. Rates: single $12; double $6 per person. PCS, TDY active duty and reservists can make reservations, retirees and others Space-A.

TML: BEQ. Bldg 609, enlisted E9 and below, leave and official duty. Bedroom/living room suites, queen bed, private bath (3); 2-bedroom (one queen bed, two singles), private bath (7). A/C, refrigerator, microwave, color CATV, iron/ironing board, alarm clock, coffee pot, vending machines, washer/dryer, housekeeping services. Rates: suite $15, each additional person $3. PCS with family, TDY active duty and reservists can make reservations, retirees and others Space-A.

DV/VIP: Contact the CBQ directly.

TML Availability: Fair. Except weekends when extremely limited due to ASW Training School and Reserve Unit training.

CREDIT CARDS ACCEPTED: Visa, MasterCard and American Express.

Temporary Military Lodging Around the World - 199

PENNSYLVANIA
Willow Grove Naval Air Station/Joint Reserve Base, continued

See Philadelphia's Liberty Bell, Art Museum and Zoo. Visit the 9th Street Market in Little Italy (Rocky Balboa made his famous run here). A short drive to Washington's crossing, Valley Forge, Sesame Place, Six Flags, Dorney Park, Poconos, Crystal Cave and the Amish Country. Society Hill, New Market, summer open air concerts along the Parkway and at Robin Hood Dell.

Locator 443-1000   Medical 443-1600   Police 443-6067

RHODE ISLAND

Newport Naval Education and Training Center (RI01R1)
Newport, RI 02845-5001

TELEPHONE NUMBER INFORMATION: Main installation numbers: C-401-841-1341, D-312-948-1110.

Location: From I-95S take the East Greenwich/Route 4 exit, continue for approximately 20 minutes. Take exit for 138 East/Newport. Continue on 138E over Newport Bridge. Once past bridge, continue until stoplight (Jai Alai will be directly in front of you). Turn right, you will approach a rotary, go half way around and continue straight. NETC Gate 1 will be directly in front of you. Also accessible from US-1. *USMRA: Page 17 (J-8); Page 25 (B,C-1,2,3).* NMC: Newport, two miles south.

Lodging Office: No central billeting office. Officers, Bldg 684. **C-401-841-3156,** Fax: C-401-841-3906. Enlisted, Bldg 1315, **C-401-841-7900,** both 24 hours. Check in facility 1300 hours. Check out 1100 hours daily. Government civilian employee billeting in BOQ.

TML: BOQ/BEQ. E-4 and below are transient status. Bedroom, private/shared bath (575); separate bedrooms, private bath (4). Full facility. Rates: moderate, no families. Duty can make reservations, others Space-A.

TML: Navy Lodge. Bldg 685, all ranks, leave or official duty. Reservations: **1-800-NAVY-INN.** Lodge number is C-401-849-4500, Fax: C-401-841-1807, 0700-2300 hours daily. Check in 1500-1800 hours, check out 1200 hours. Bedroom, two double beds, private bath (39); bedroom, two double beds, studio couch (28). Kitchenette, utensils, coffee/tea, A/C, clocks, color TV, housekeeping service, cribs, phones, high chairs, game room, snack vending, ice vending, irons/ironing board, lounge, coin washer/dryer. Modern structure. Rates: Dec-Apr, apartments $52; room $40; Apr-Dec, apartments $64; room $51. All categories can make reservations. *Runner-up of the 1996 Edward E. Carlson Award for Navy Lodge excellence in the medium category.*

DV/VIP: Contact CO, C-401-841-3715 or C-401-841-6464, NWC War College, President's office.

TML Availability: Good, winter. Difficult, summer.

CREDIT CARDS ACCEPTED: Visa, MasterCard and American Express.

RHODE ISLAND
Newport Naval Education and Training Center, continued

Stroll along cobblestone streets, or ocean front walks; admire turn-of-the-Century mansions; visit many national historic landmarks, and the Naval War College Museum. Admire the wonderful sailing vessels - this is Newport!

Locator 841-1341   **Medical 841-3111/2222**   **Police 841-3241**

SOUTH CAROLINA

Beaufort Marine Corps Air Station (SC01R1)
BOQ, Bldg 431
Beaufort MCAS, SC 29904-5001

TELEPHONE NUMBER INFORMATION: Main installation numbers: C-803-522-7100, D-312-832-7100.

Location: From I-95 exit at Pocataligo to SC-21, four miles to MCAS. Clearly marked. *USMRA: Page 44 (G-9)*. NMC: Savannah, 40 miles south.

Lodging Office: BOQ, Bldg 431. **C-803-522-7676**, Fax: C-803-522-7674, 24 hours. Check in facility, check out 1200 hours daily. Government civilian employee billeting.

TML: de Treville House. Bldg 1108, C-803-522-1663, all ranks, leave or official duty. Bedroom, private bath (21); separate bedroom, private bath (21). Kitchen (in separate bedroom), A/C, cots ($5); cribs, ice vending. housekeeping service, special facilities for DAVs, color TV, complete utensils, washer/dryer, playground, picnic area with grills. handicap accessible. Staff NCO Club adjacent. Modern structure. Rates: one person $30; two people $35; kitchen $40. Maximum five adults per unit. Make reservations. Non-military personnel visiting relatives stationed at Beaufort may stay on a Space-A basis.

TML: BOQ. Bldg 431, all ranks, leave or official duty. Bedrooms (officers) (39); suites, private bath (officers) (5); bedroom, private/shared bath (enlisted) (17). Refrigerator, microwave, community kitchen, limited utensils, A/C, color TV room and lounge, iron/ironing board, housekeeping service, washer/dryer, ice vending. Modern structure, renovated. Rates: duty: rooms $10-$15; suites $15-$20; each adult family member $3, no children. No pets. Duty can make reservations, others Space-A.

DV/VIP: Contact CO, Bldg 601, C-803-522-7158. Retirees and lower ranks Space-A.

TML Availability: Very good, most of the year. Best, Sep-Apr.

CREDIT CARDS ACCEPTED: Visa, MasterCard, American Express, Diners Club and Discover.

Locator 522-7188   **Medical 522-7311**   **Police 522-7373**

Temporary Military Lodging Around the World - 201

SOUTH CAROLINA

Beaufort Naval Hospital (SC07R1)
ATTN: Billeting Office
1 Pinckney Blvd
Beaufort, SC 29902-6148

TELEPHONE NUMBER INFORMATION: Main installation numbers: C-803-525-5600, D-312-832-5600.

Location: From I-95 exit take any Beaufort exit and follow signs. *USMRA: Page 44 (G-9).* NMC: Savannah, GA, 40 miles south.

Lodging Office: BEQ. **C-803-525-5418/9, D-312-832-5419,** Fax: C-803-525-5320. Check in facility after 1200 hours, check out 1100 hours.

TML: BEQ. Rooms (187). Color TV, washer/dryer, game room. Exercise room, All Hands Club, Navy Federal Credit Union, exchange, mini-mart, pool and picnic areas available. Call for rates and more information.

Bubba Gump Shrimp Festival, Parris Island, Hilton Head, casinos, golf courses, fishing and beaches are easily accessible from Hospital.

Locator 525-5608   Medical 525-5600   Police 525-5600

Charleston Air Force Base (SC06R1)
Inns of Charleston
102 N Davis Drive
Charleston AFB, SC 29404-4825

TELEPHONE NUMBER INFORMATION: Main installation numbers: C-803-566-6000, D-312-673-2100.

Location: From I-26 E exit to West Aviation Ave to traffic light, continue through light to second light on right, follow road around end of runway to Gate 2 (River Gate). *USMRA: Page 44 (H-8,9).* NMC: Charleston, five miles southeast.

Lodging Office: The Inns of Charleston, 102 N. Davis Drive. **C-803-552-9900, D-312-673-2100 ext 860.** Reservations: Mon-Fri 0800-1700 hours, **C-803-566-3806, D-312-673-3806,** Fax: C-803-566-3394. Check in facility, check out 1200 hours daily. Government civilian employee billeting in contract quarters.

TML: VOQ/DV/VIP. Bldgs 343, 344, 362, officers, all ranks, leave or official duty. Bedroom, shared bath (102); bedroom suites, private bath (O6+) (4). Kitchen (suites only), micro-refrigerator, A/C, housekeeping service, cribs/cots, washer/dryer, ice vending. Modern structure. Rates: DV/VIP (suites) single occupancy $16, accompanied $23; DV Mini-Suites and VOQ, single occupancy $10, accompanied $14. Maximum five per room. Duty can make reservations, others Space-A. No pets.

TML: VAQ. Senior enlisted (E7+), Bldg 346, leave or official duty. Bedroom, private bath (4); bedroom, shared bath (40). A/C, color TV, housekeeping service, washer/dryer, ice vending. Rates: suites, single occupancy $16, accompanied $23; rooms, single occupancy $10, accompanied $14. Duty can make reservations, others space A. No pets.

SOUTH CAROLINA
Charleston Air Force Base, continued

TML: Junior enlisted (E1-E6), Bldg 346, leave or official duty. Bedroom, shared bath (44). A/C, color TV, housekeeping service, washer/dryer, ice vending. Rates: $10 per person. Duty can make reservations, others Space-A. No dependents, no pets.

TML: TLF. Bldg 330, all ranks. Bedroom suites, private bath, kitchen, sleeps five (18). A/C color TV, housekeeping service, washer/dryer, ice vending. Rates: $24 per family. Duty can make reservations, others Space-A.

DV/VIP: Lodging office 24 hour operation 803-566-386. O6+. Retirees Space-A. No pets.

TML Availability: Good, Nov-Dec. Difficult, other times because of duty traffic.

CREDIT CARDS ACCEPTED: Visa, MasterCard and American Express.

Visit stately mansions along the Battery, and Boone Hall, where scenes from "Gone With the Wind" and "North and South" were filmed. Take a water tour, and visit historic Fort Sumter and Charleston Harbor.

Locator 566-3282   Medical 566-2775   Police 566-3600

Charleston Naval Weapons Station (SC11R1)
1A Hickory Hall
1 Mahan Circle
Goose Creek, SC 29445-8601

TELEPHONE NUMBER INFORMATION: Main installation numbers: C-803-764-7901, D-312-794-7901.

Location: I-26 to I-526 to North Rhett, North Rhett to Red Bank Road, take a right on Red Bank Road, at third light, take a left, follow signs to station. *USMRA: Page 44 (H-8)*. NMC: Charleston, 25 miles south.

Lodging Office: C-803-764-7218, D-312-794-7218.

TML: DVOQ. O5-O10. A/C, refrigerator, kitchenette, utensils, color TV in lounge and room, housekeeping, soda/snack vending, mini-mart, washer/dryer. Exercise room available. Call for rates and more information. No pets. **Winner of the 1996 Elmo R. Zumwalt Award for Excellence in Housing.**

Visit Charleston for excellent historical and shopping experiences.

Locator 764-7218   Medical 743-7000   Police 764-7205

Fort Jackson (SC09R1)
Bldg 3499 Jackson Blvd
Fort Jackson, SC 29207-5000

TELEPHONE NUMBER INFORMATION: Main installation number: C-803-751-7511, D-312-734-1110.

SOUTH CAROLINA
Fort Jackson, continued

Location: Exit from I-77 at Fort Jackson Blvd, turn right to enter Gate 1 or exit I-77 at Strom Thurmond Blvd, turn left to enter Gate 2. *USMRA: Page 54 (G-6).* NMC: Columbia, 12 miles southwest.

Lodging Office: Bldg 2785, corner Semmes Road and Lee Road. **C-803-751-6223, D-312-734-6223.** Toll free reservations for government official duty personnel (on post) and local hotels **1-800-261-1950 (subject to change)**, 24 hours. Check in billeting, check out 1000 hours daily. Government civilian employee billeting.

TML: Guest House, **Palmetto Lodge**. Bldg 6000, all ranks, leave or official duty, C-803-751-4779. Bedroom, private bath, sleeps six (70). Kitchen, limited utensils, A/C, telephone, color TV in room and lounge, housekeeping service, washer/dryer, ice vending. Rates: vary, call for more information. No pets. Duty can make reservations, others Space-A.

TML: Kennedy Hall. Bldg 2785, all ranks, leave or official duty. Bedroom, one bed, private bath (transient units) (142). Refrigerator, microwave, A/C, color TV, housekeeping service, washer/dryer. Modern structure, remodeled. Rates: vary, call for information. Maximum two per unit. No pets. Duty can make reservations, others Space-A.

TML: VEQ. Bldg 2464, enlisted all ranks, official duty. Bedroom, one bed, private bath (76). Refrigerator, microwave, color TV, housekeeping service. Rates: vary, call for more information. No pets. Duty can make reservations, others Space-A.

TML: DV/VIP. Cottages, Bldgs 3640-3645, 4416, Legion Landing and Dozier House. Officers O6+, official duty. Check out 1100 hours. Bedroom, private bath (2), 2-bedroom, private bath (4), 3-bedroom, private bath suite (1). Kitchen, utensils, A/C, color TV, telephone, housekeeping service. Remodeled. Rates: vary, call for information. No children, no pets. Duty can make reservations, others Space-A.

TML: Weston Lake Recreation Area and Travel Camp. C-803-751-LAKE, D-312-734-LAKE. Cabins: 4-bedroom (1), 3-bedroom (2), 2-bedroom (2), 2-bedroom log (1), 1-bedroom duplex; private bath, kitchen, furnished, color TV, dishes, pots and pans, microwave, stove, linens available for fee. Lakefront cabins come with use of a rowboat. Rates: $30-$50 daily. See *Military Living's Military RV, Camping and Rec Areas Around the World* for additional information and directions.

DV/VIP: Protocol Office, HQ Bldg, C-803-751-6618, D-312-734-5218. O6+.

TML Availability: Very good, Oct-May.

Riverbanks Zoological Park, Town Theater amateur productions, and a carriage ride along historic Broad Street compete with local golf courses, Lake Murray and numerous public recreation areas as local popular pastimes.

Locator 751-7671   Medical 911   Police 751-3113

Parris Island Marine Corps Recruit Depot (SC08R1)
Billeting Office, Bldg 330
Parris Island MCRD, SC 29905-0059

TELEPHONE NUMBER INFORMATION: Main installation numbers: C-803-525-2111, D-312-832-1110.

SOUTH CAROLINA
Parris Island Marine Corps Recruit Depot, continued

Location: From I-95 S take exit 5 to Beaufort via SC-170; from I-95 N take exit 33 via US 17 t r US-21, east to SC-280 to SC-802 which leads to main gate of depot. *USMRA: Page 44 (G-10).* NMC: Savannah, 45 miles southwest.

Lodging Office: Billeting office, Bldg 330, for information/reservations call **C-803-525-2976/3460, D-312-832-2976/3460,** Fax: C-803-525-3815, D-312-832-3815. Check in facility after 1400 hours, check out no later than 1100 hours. Government civilian employee billeting in Hostess House. Reservations accepted 90 days in advance. **All Space-A required to confirm 72 hours in advance.**

TML: Hostess House. Bldg 200, two miles from main gate, all ranks, leave or official duty, C-803-525-2976. Bedroom, two beds, sleep sofa, private bath (30). Kitchenettes, A/C, color TV/VCR in room, housekeeping service, cribs, washer/dryer, ice vending, facilities for DAVs. Western Union, video rental and snacks in lobby. Modern structure, renovated. Rates: officer/enlisted $25, with kitchen $35. Golf course villa, two bedrooms, private bath. Rates: $50 per night. All categories can make reservations.

TML: VOQ. Beaufort River Inn. Bldg 254, officers all ranks, leave or official duty, retired, DAVs, military widows, accompanied dependents, government civilians GS7+ on official duty. C-803-525-2567. Bedroom, private bath, kitchen, complete utensils(4). Bedroom, private bath (2). Refrigerator, A/C, color TV in room and lounge, housekeeping service, cots, washer/dryer, ice vending. Older structure, renovated. Rates: $8-$15 per room, each additional person $3; civilian $20-$25, each additional person $3. Maximum four per unit. All categories can make reservations.

TML: BOQ. Osprey Inn I. Bldg 289, officers all ranks leave or official duty, civilian government employees, retired, DAVs, military widows, C-803-525-2744. Bedroom, private bath (19); bedrooms, common bath (4). A/C, color TV, washer/dryer, ice vending. Older structure. Rates: O1-O3 $8-$12 per room; O4+ $12-$15 per room, each additional person $3; GS7-GS10 $12-$16 per room; GS11+ $17-$20 per room, each additional person $3. Maximum four per room. All categories can make reservations.

TML: BEQ. Osprey Inn II. Bldg 330, enlisted, all ranks, leave or official duty, civilian government employees, retired, DAVs, military widows. Bedroom, hotel style with all amenities (1); bedroom, hotel style with private bath (5); bedroom, college style, shared bath (64). Refrigerator, microwave, A/C, color CATV, housekeeping service, washer/dryer, ice vending. Modern structure. Rates: E7-E9 (Hotel style w/amenities) $8-$12, each additional person $3; all other rooms $6-$10 for military, $8-$12 for civilians, each additional person $3.

DV/VIP: VOQ. **Beaufort River Inn.** Bldg 254, contact staff secretary for reservation at C-803-525-2567/2594 active and retired officers O6+, leave or official duty, distinguished guests. Two-bedroom suite, sitting room, and dining area, kitchen and private bath, completely furnished with all amenities. Older structure, renovated. Rates: AD $15-$20 per room, each additional person $3; civilian $20-$25, each additional person $3. Maximum four per unit.

TML Availability: Good except graduation days.

CREDIT CARDS ACCEPTED: Visa, MasterCard and (Government) American Express.

Locator 525-3358   **Medical 525-3315**   **Police 525-3444**

SOUTH CAROLINA

Shaw Air Force Base (SC10R1)
Carolina Pines Inn
471 Myers Street
Shaw AFB, SC 29152-5000

TELEPHONE NUMBER INFORMATION: Main installation numbers: C-803-668-8110, D-312-965-1110.

Location: Off US-76/378 eight miles west of Sumter. Clearly marked. *USMRA: Page 44 (H-6).* NMC: Columbia, 35 miles west.

Lodging Office: Carolina Pines Inn, Bldg 471, Myers Street. **C-803-668-3210, 1-800-769-7429, D-312-965-5125/5124,** Fax: C-803-668-5756, D-312-965-5756, 24 hours. Check in facility, check out 1100 hours daily. Advanced Space-A reservations accepted. Space-A, can request availability 24 hours in advance.

TML: TLF. Bldgs 931-934, all ranks, leave or official duty. Handicap accessible. Separate bedrooms, sleeper sofa, private bath (40). Kitchenette, A/C, color TV, housekeeping service, cribs/cots, washer/dryer. Modern structure. Rates: $24 per unit. Maximum five per apartment. Duty can make reservations, others Space-A.

TML: VAQ. Bldg 900, enlisted all ranks, leave or official duty. Bedroom, one bed, shared bath (44). A/C, color TV, housekeeping service, washer/dryer, ice vending. Modern structure. Rates: $10 per person; chief suites, $16. Duty can make reservations, others Space-A.

TML: VOQ. Bldgs 911, 924, 927, officers all ranks, leave or official duty. Bedroom, private bath (68); separate bedroom suites, private bath (14). Kitchen, limited utensils, A/C, color TV, housekeeping service, washer/dryer, ice vending. Modern structure. Rates: $10 per person. Maximum two per room. Duty can make reservations, others Space-A.

TML: DV/VIP. Bldg 924, officer O6+, leave or official duty. Bedroom, private bath (6). Kitchen, utensils, A/C, color TV, housekeeping service, washer/dryer, ice vending. Older structure, remodeled. Rates: $16 per person. Maximum two per room. Duty can make reservations, others Space-A.

TML: Wateree Recreation Area. C-803-668-3245/2204, D-312-965-3245/2204. Cabins: 2-bedroom (11), 3-bedroom (1); handicap accessible, fully equipped, including TV/VCR, linens, dishes, pots and pans, microwave. Rates: $50-$75 daily. See *Military Living's Military RV, Camping and Rec Areas Around the World* **for additional information and directions.**

DV/VIP: Protocol Office, C-803-668-2156/2311, D-312-965-2156/2311. O6+. Retirees Space-A.

TML Availability: Good. Best, Dec-Mar.

CREDIT CARDS ACCEPTED: Visa, MasterCard and American Express.

An 18-hole golf course, three swimming pools, tennis courts and fitness center on base, and Columbia, the state capital, and Charleston, not to mention Myrtle Beach, the Blue Ridge and Smokey Mountains.

Locator 668-2811   **Medical** 668-2778   **Police** 668-2493

SOUTH CAROLINA

Short Stay (SC02R1)
211 Short Stay Road
Moncks Corner, SC 29461-5000

TELEPHONE NUMBER INFORMATION: Main installation numbers: C-803-761-8353.

Location: Take I-26 to US 17-A toward Moncks Corner (15 miles). Left on US 52 for three miles. Follow signs to Navy Recreation Area. *USMRA: Page 44 (H-8).* NMC: Charleston, 35 miles South.

Lodging Office: 211 Short Stay Road, Moncks Corner, SC 29461. **C-803-761-8353/743-5608,** 24 hours. Office hours: 0715-1830 hours Sun-Thu, 0715-1930 hours Fri-Sat. Check in at facility 1500 hours, check out 1100 hours. Late checkout call C-803-761-8353. Security at front gate when office is closed.

TML: Six cabins, five log cabins, 24 two-bedroom villas, 12 three-bedroom villas. Cabins and 2-bedroom villas sleep four; 3-bedroom villa sleeps six. Three units handicap accessible. Cabins and villas: kitchenette, private bath, deck, color CATV, picnic tables, grills. Four reservable pavilions. Log cabins: A/C, heat, outdoor cooking grill and picnic table. Public bath and restrooms. Recreation center, convenience store, snack bar, boat rental, bait and tackle, swimming beach, miniature golf, game room, laundry, gas. Rates: villas $40-$62 per day (low, mid, high seasons, military, civilian rates); cabins $55-$66, log cabins $18-$22. Write for brochure. Cancellations OK three days prior to check-in date (later, $15 fee). One unit per ID per time period. Minimum age to reserve 21. Pets permitted in campground only. Restrictions apply.

DV/VIP: None.

TML Availability: Good. Best, Sep-May. Difficult, Jun-Aug.

CREDIT CARDS ACCEPTED: Visa, MasterCard and American Express.

Located on Lake Moultrie (60,000 acres), fishing, watersports, Charleston offers beaches, golf, historic sites. Read Military Living's *Military RV, Camping and Rec Areas Around the World* for more information.

Locator 761-8353   Medical 911   Police 911

SOUTH DAKOTA

Ellsworth Air Force Base (SD01R3)
Pine Tree Inn
2349 Risner Drive
Ellsworth AFB, SD 57706-4708

TELEPHONE NUMBER INFORMATION: Main installation numbers: C-605-385-1000, D-312-625-1110.

Location: Off I-90 (exit 66), 10 miles east of Rapid City. Clearly marked. *USMRA: Page 85 (B-5).* NMC: Rapid City, 10 miles west.

SOUTH DAKOTA
Ellsworth Air Force Base, continued

Lodging Office: Pine Tree Inn, 2349 Risner Drive. **C-605-385-2844, D-312-675-2844,** Fax: C-605-385-2718, 24 hours. Check in facility 1500 hours, check out 1000 hours daily (TLF 1000 hours). All rooms are no smoking and no pets.

TML: TLF. **Aspen Inn**. Bldg 8008, all ranks, leave or official duty, C-605-385-2844. One-bedroom, two hide-a-beds, full kitchen, A/C, color CATV, housekeeping service, washer.dryer, ice vending. Rates: On orders to Ellsworth AFB, E-1, E-2 or O-1 $14.50; all other ranks and Space-A $24.

TML: VOQ/VAQ. **Pine Tree Inn**. Bldg 1103, all ranks, leave or official duty. Two-bedroom, private bath (VOQ) (34); **Oak Inn**. Bldg 110, bedroom, private bath (VOQ) (38); **Cedar Inn**. Bldg 5907, bedroom, private bath (VOQ) (48); **Juniper Inn**. Bldg 109, bedroom, private bath (15), bedroom, shared bath (42) (VAQ) (57). Refrigerator, A/C, color CATV, housekeeping service, washer/dryer, ice vending. Older structure. Rates: $10 per person, $14 per couple. Space-A reservations confirmed 24 hours prior to arrival.

DV/VIP: Protocol, C-605-385-1205, D-312-675-1205. O6+. Retirees and active duty. Rates :$10 per person, $23 per couple.

TML Availability: Good, Oct-Apr. Difficult, other times.

CREDIT CARDS ACCEPTED: Visa, MasterCard and American Express.

While you're here visit the Air and Space Museum, Mount Rushmore, the Badlands, Crazy Horse Monument, Deadwood and the Black Hills.

Locator 385-1379   Medical 385-3534   Police 399-4001

TENNESSEE

Arnold Air Force Station (TN02R2)
Forest Inn
4176 Westover Road
Tullahoma, TN 37388-2213

TELEPHONE NUMBER INFORMATION: Main installation numbers: C-615-454-3000, D-312-340-3000.

Location: From Tullahoma, take Arnold Engineering Development Center access highway. From I-24 take AEDC exit 117, four miles south of Manchester. Clearly marked. *USMRA: Page 41 (I-9)*. NMC: Chattanooga, 65 miles southeast; Nashville, 65 miles northwest.

Lodging Office: Forest Inn, 4176 Westover Road. **C-615-454-3099, D-312-340-3099,** 0600-2200 hours Mon-Fri, 1000-2000 hours Sat-Sun, 1000-1800 hours holidays. After hours, Security C-615-454-5662. Check in billeting 1400 hours, check out 1200 hours.

TML: VOQ. Bldg 3027, all ranks, leave or official duty. Bedroom, shared bath (36); bedroom, private bath(4); bedroom (DV/VIP) (5). Refrigerator, microwave, coffee maker, community kitchen, limited

208 - Temporary Military Lodging Around the World

TENNESSEE
Arnold Air Force Station, continued

utensils, A/C, color TV in room and lounge, housekeeping service, cribs, washer/dryer, ice vending. Older structure. Rates: $10 per person, $14 per couple, DV/VIP $16 per person, $23 per couple. Duty can make reservations, Space-A up to 24 hours in advance.

DV/VIP: Billeting Office. O6+. Retirees, Space-A.

TML Availability: Good, all year.

CREDIT CARDS ACCEPTED: Visa, MasterCard and American Express.

On this 44,000 acre installation, Woods Reservoir has a 75 miles shoreline for fishing and all water sports. Visit the Grand Ole Opry, Music Row, the Parthenon, the Hermitage in Nashville, Jack Daniels Distillery, Rock City, Look-out Mountain, and NASA Space Center in Huntsville, AL. Civil War buffs: lots to see.

Locator 454-3000   Medical 454-5351   Police 454-5662

Memphis Naval Support Activity (TN01R2)
Bachelor Quarters Dept.
Millington, TN 38054-6024

TELEPHONE NUMBER INFORMATION: Main installation numbers: C-901-874-5111, D-312-966-5111.

Location: From US-51 N at Millington, exit to Navy Road, right to first gate on right, main gate. *USMRA: Page 40 (B-9,10).* NMC: Memphis, 20 miles southwest.

Lodging Office: Bachelor Quarters Dept. **C-901-874-7082, D-312-966-7082.** BOQ reservations **C-901-874-5345 or 901-872-6317,** BEQ **C-901-874-5459**, 24 hours. Check in facility, check out 1200 hours daily.

TML: Navy Lodge. Bldgs N-931, all ranks, leave or official duty, and NEX associates. Reservations: **1-800-NAVY-INN.** Lodge number is C-901-872-0121, Fax: C-901-873-1695. Check in 1500-1800 hours, check out 1200 hours. Bedroom, one queen size and a sleeper sofa , private bath (22); bedroom, two extra-long double beds, private bath (27). Four interconnecting units, 23 non-smoking. Kitchenette, microwave, dining table, utensils, VCPs, direct dial AT&T service, A/C, CATV, BBQ, clock radio, hair dryers, coffee, vending automat, on-site laundry facilities playgrounds, cribs, phones, high chairs, ice vending, iron/ironing board, picnic grounds, playground, rollaways, housekeeping service, coin washer/dryer. Rates: $. All categories can make reservations. No Pets, kennel nearby. Tennis, NEX mini-mart, golf, Navy Lake, stables nearby.

TML: BOQ/BEQ. All ranks, leave or official duty. Check in at facility. Officers: bedroom, private bath (82); enlisted: bedroom, private bath (some shared bath) (163). Refrigerator, A/C, TV in lounge, housekeeping service, washer/dryer, ice vending, special facilities for DAVs. Modern structure. Rates: BOQ $9-$21 per person, BEQ $5-$17 per person. Dependents must use Navy Lodge. Duty can make reservations, others Space-A.

DV/VIP: Commander, C-901-874-5101. O6+. Retirees Space-A.

TENNESSEE
Memphis Naval Support Activity, continued

TML Availability: Good, Dec. Difficult, other times.

CREDIT CARDS ACCEPTED: Visa, MasterCard, American Express and Discover are accepted at the Navy Lodge.

Check out the nearby attractions of Graceland, Beale Street (Home of the Blues), Shelby Forest State Park provides thousands of acres of native woodlands for walking, riding, picnicking and boating. The Memphis area is famous for bird and duck hunting.

Locator 874-5111   Medical 911   Police 874-5533

TEXAS

Armed Services YMCA (TX50R3)
7060 Comington Street
El Paso, TX 79930-4239

TELEPHONE NUMBER INFORMATION: Main installation numbers: C-915-562-8461.

Location: From I-10 take Alamagordo exit to left at Fred Wilson exit, turn left. At Dyer Street turn left, right on Hayes Street, to Fort Bliss gate. Residence center straight ahead. *USMRA: Page 86 (B-6)*. NMC: El Paso, in city limits.

Lodging Office: Bldg 7060, Comington Street. **C-915-562-8461**, Fax: C-915-565-0306, 24 hours. Check in front desk, check out 1100 hours daily. **Note: This facility is on Fort Bliss. For additional TML see Fort Bliss listing.**

TML: Motel-style ASYMCA, residence, all ranks, leave, retirees or official duty. King-size room, private bath (16); doubles, private bath (36). Color CATV, refrigerator (all), kitchenette (30 units), lounge area with food service and color CATV, housekeeping service, essentials, cots, coin washer/dryer, handicap accessible units, snack vending, ice vending. Rates: AD $29; retired $30; civilian personnel $32 (all per room, per night). Maximum four per room, arrangements can be made to adjust. All categories may make reservations. Pets allowed.

TML Availability: Good. Best, Sep-May. Difficult, Jul-Aug and Jan.

CREDIT CARDS ACCEPTED: Visa, MasterCard, American Express and Diners Club.

Visit old Juarez and the Tiqua Indian Reservation. There are numerous military museums on post.

Locator 568-1113   Medical 569-2331   Police 568-2115

TEXAS

Belton Lake Recreation Area (TX07R3)
Reservations Office
ATTN: AFZF-CA-CRD-OR-BLORA
Fort Hood, TX 76544-5056

TELEPHONE NUMBER INFORMATION: Main installation numbers: C-817-287/ 288-1110, D-312-737/738-1110.

Location: From I-35 take Loop 121 N to Sparta Road. Stay on Sparta, turn right on Cottage Road, area marked. *USMRA: Page 87 (K-4,5).* NMC: Austin, 60 miles south.

Lodging Office: Reservations: Business Operations Division, AFZF-GA-BOD-OR-BLORA, Fort Hood, TX 76544-5056. **C-817-287-2523, D-312-737-2523,** Fax: C-817-287-3722. Check in cottages after 1500 hours, check out 0730-1200 hours.

TML: Cottages. All ranks, leave or official duty. Bedroom, private bath, sleeps four (10). Kitchen, kitchen appliances, dishwasher, A/C, color TV, fully equipped. Rates: E1-E4 $25 per day, all other authorized users $30 per day. One day deposit required within 72 hours of reservation. All categories can make reservations. No Pets.

TML Availability: Good, winter. Difficult, May-Sep.

CREDIT CARDS ACCEPTED: Visa, MasterCard, American Express and Espirit.

A full round of recreational opportunities is offered here: jet skiing, sailing, windsurfing, deck boats, fishing, paddle and ski boats can be rented; the picnic areas, RV camp sites, tent camping sites and party pavilions are fun, fun, fun.

Locator 287-2137   Medical 288-8000   Police 287-2176

Brooks Air Force Base (TX26R3)
Brooks Inn
2804 5th Street
Brooks AFB, TX 78235-5120

TELEPHONE NUMBER INFORMATION: Main installation numbers: C-210-536-1110, D-312-240-1110.

Location: At intersection of I-37 and Loop 13 (Military Drive). *Page 91 (C-4).* NMC: San Antonio, five miles northwest.

Lodging Office: Brooks Inn, Bldg 214, 2804 5th Street. **C-210-536-1844, D-312-240-1844,** Fax: C-210-536-2327, D-312-240-2327, 24 hours. Check in facility, check out 1200 hours daily. Government civilian employee billeting.

TML: TLF. Bldg 211, all ranks, leave or official duty. Handicap accessible. Bedroom, private bath (8). Kitchen, living room, cribs, A/C, utensils, linen, housekeeping service, washer/dryer. Rates: $22. Duty can make reservations. PCS in 30 day limit. PCS out seven day limit. PCS have priority, others Space-A.

TEXAS
Brooks Air Force Base, continued

TML: VAQ. Bldg 718, C-210-536-3031, enlisted all ranks, leave or official duty. Separate bedrooms, private bath (2); 1-bedroom, shared bath (52). A/C, ice vending, housekeeping service, refrigerator, color TV, washer/dryer. Modern structure. Rates: $10-$16 per person, accompanied $23 maximum. Duty can make reservations, others Space-A.

TML: VOQ. Bldgs 212, 214, 218, 220, officers all ranks, leave or official duty. Separate bedrooms, private bath (109); 2-bedroom, shared bath (50). A/C, cribs/cots, ice vending, housekeeping service, refrigerator, color TV, washer/dryer. Modern structure. Rates: sponsor $10-$16, maximum $14-$23 per family. Duty can make reservations, others Space-A.

TML: DV/VIP. Officer O6+, leave or official duty, C-210-536-3238. Separate bedrooms, living room, private bath (6). Housekeeping service, washer/dryer. Rates: $16 per person, accompanied $23 maximum. Duty can make reservations, others Space-A.

DV/VIP: PAO Office, C-210-536-3238. O6+. Retirees Space-A.

TML Availability: Limited. Base has contract hotel/motel lodging. Contact Lodging Office, C-210-536-1844.

CREDIT CARDS ACCEPTED: Visa, MasterCard and American Express.

Popular with Brooks' people are the recreation areas at Canyon Lake, on the Guadalupe River northwest of New Braunfels, San Antonio Riverwalk and the Alamo.

Locator 536-1841   **Medical 536-3278**   **Police 536-2851**

Corpus Christi Naval Air Station (TX10R3)
Combined Bachelor Quarters
Corpus Christi, TX 78419-9999

TELEPHONE NUMBER INFORMATION: Main installation numbers: C-512-939-2811, D-312-861-2811.

Location: On TX-358, on southeast side of Corpus Christi. The south gate is on NAS Dr. *USMRA: Page 87 (K-8,9).* NMC: Corpus Christi, 10 miles northwest.

Lodging Office: 11801 Ocean Drive. **C-512-939-2388/89, D-312-861-2388/89,** Fax: C-512-939-3275, D-312-861-3275. CBQ 24 hours.

TML: CBQ. Bldg 1281, all ranks, leave or official duty. Bedroom, private bath (205). Refrigerator, microwave, A/C, color TV/VCR in room and lounge, housekeeping service, washer/dryer. Modern structure, renovated. Rates: E1-E9 $11.00, each additional person $2.75; W1-O5 suite $16, each additional person $4; O6, GS15 and above DV Suite $24, each additional person $6. Maximum three per unit. Duty can make reservations, others Space-A.

TML: Navy Lodge. Bldg 1281, all ranks, leave or official duty. Reservations: **1-800-NAVY-INN**. Lodge number is C-512-937-6361, Fax: 512-937-7854, 0800-1800 hours Mon-Fri, 0900-1800 hours Sat-Sun, holidays. Suites, one queen bed, sleeper sofa, private bath (10); bedroom, queen bed,

TEXAS
Corpus Christi Naval Air Station, continued

private bath (11). One handicap accessible unit, 12 non-smoking. Kitchenette, microwave, utensils, A/C, CATV, clocks, coffee/tea, cribs highchairs, hair dryers, iron/ironing board, housekeeping service, rollaways, coin washer/dryer, snack vending, ice vending. Modern structure. Rates: $31-$39 per unit. All categories can make reservations. PCS on orders can make reservations anytime.

DV/VIP: Protocol Office. Bldg 1281, Admin Office, C-512-939-2388/z89, D-312-861-2388/89. Commander's discretion. Retirees and lower ranks Space-A.

TML Availability: Very Good, Jan-Mar and Jun-Dec. Difficult, Apr-May.

CREDIT CARDS ACCEPTED: The Navy Lodge accepts Visa, MasterCard, American Express, Diners Club and Discover.

The Padre Island National Seashore, the famous King Ranch, the Confederate Air Force Flying Museum, and the Texas State Aquarium are all local sights worth seeing.

Locator 939-2383   Medical 939-3735/3839   Police 939-3460

Dallas Naval Air Station (TX12R3)
Combined Bachelors Quarters
8100 West Jefferson Blvd
Dallas, TX 75211-5000-9501

Currently in the process of moving to Fort Worth NAS/Joint Reserve Base; completion expected in 1998. Dallas NAS will close after the move is complete.
Call ahead to ensure TML is still available.

TELEPHONE NUMBER INFORMATION: Main installation numbers: C-214-266-6111, D-312-874-6111.

Location: Exit from I-30 at loop 12 west of Dallas, go south on loop 12 to Jefferson Ave exit. NAS on left, south side of ave. Near Grand Prairie. *USMRA: Page 88 (E-3)*. NMC: Dallas, 15 miles northeast.

Lodging Office: Bldg 209, 8100 West Jefferson Blvd, **C-972-266-6155**, 24 hours. Check in facility, check out 1100 hours daily. Government civilian employee billeting.

TML: BOQ. VIP $20, each additional person $5. Duty can make reservations, others Space-A.

TML: BEQ. Bldgs 209, 231, enlisted all ranks, leave or official duty. Beds, hall bath (564). Rates: private room $5 per day; E5+ $8, each additional person $2. Duty can make reservations, others Space-A.

DV/VIP: Administrative Officer, C-972-266-6103/6104. Commander's discretion.

TML Availability: Difficult and unpredictable.

CREDIT CARDS ACCEPTED: Visa, MasterCard and American Express.

TEXAS
Dallas Naval Air Station, continued

Texas is "another country" and Dallas is big city Texas. Don't miss the museums, the shopping and especially Texas Barbecue! Also, checkout Wet n' Wild Water Park and Six Flags Over Texas.

Locator 266-6111   Medical 266-6284   Police 266-6139

Dyess Air Force Base (TX14R3)
Dyess Inn
441 5th Street
Dyess AFB, TX 79607-1244

TELEPHONE NUMBER INFORMATION: Main installation numbers: C-915-696-3113, D-312-461-1110.

Location: Six miles southwest of Abilene. Main gate is three miles east of I-20. Accessible from I-20 and US-277. *USMRA: Page 87 (I-3)*. NMC: Abilene, six miles northeast.

Lodging Office: Dyess Inn, Bldg 441, 5th Street. **C-915-696-8610, D-312-461-2681,** Fax: D-312-461-2836, 24 hours. Check in facility, check out 1200 hours daily. Government civilian employee lodging.

TML: TLF. Bldg 325, Fourth Street, all ranks, leave or official duty, handicap accessible. Separate bedroom, private bath (sleeps five)(39). Kitchen (with utensils), A/C, color TV, cribs/cots, washer/dryer, ice vending. Modern structure. Rates: $12.50-$24. Duty can make reservations, others Space-A.

TML: VAQ. Bldg 313 Fifth Street, enlisted all ranks, leave or official duty. Single rooms, shared bath (52); Bldg 398, suites (40). Refrigerator, A/C, color TV, housekeeping service, washer/dryer, ice vending. Rates: $10-$14. Duty can make reservations, others Space-A.

TML: VOQ. Bldgs 225, 233, 241, 249, 441, officers all ranks, senior enlisted only. Handicap accessible, leave or official duty. One-bedroom, private bath (79), separate bedroom DV/VIP suites (8), private bath. Kitchen (suites only), refrigerator, A/C, color TV, housekeeping service, washer/dryer, ice vending. Older structure, remodeled. Rates: $10-$27 per person. Maximum two per room. Duty can make reservations, others Space-A.

DV/VIP: 7 WG. Protocol Office, C-915-696-5610. O6+. Retirees and lower ranks Space-A.

TML Availability: Very good all year.

CREDIT CARDS ACCEPTED: Visa, MasterCard and American Express.

Abilene has an award winning Zoo, a collection of vintage aircraft on display at the base Air Park, boating, fishing and sailing at Lake Fort Phantom Hill, and a visit to Buffalo Gap Historic Village a "must".

Locator 696-3098   Medical 696-4677   Police 696-2131

TEXAS

Fort Bliss (TX06R3)
Fort Bliss Billeting
P.O. Box 16150
Bldg 251, Club Road
Fort Bliss, TX 79906-1150

TELEPHONE NUMBER INFORMATION: Main installation numbers: C-915-568-2121, D-312-978-2121.

Location: From I-10 take Airway Blvd El Paso International Airport exit to Robert E Lee gate (open 24 hours). Follow directional signs to front desk. *USMRA: Page 86 (B,C-5,6)*. NMC: El Paso, Fort Bliss, in city limits.

Lodging Office: Bldg 251, Club Road. **C-915-568-4888/2703, D-312-978-4888/2703,** Fax: C-915-568-7078, D-312-978-7078, 24 hours. Check in billeting after 1500 hours, check out 1100 hours daily. **Note: see Armed Services YMCA for additional TML on Fort Bliss.**

TML: Guest House. **The Inn at Fort Bliss.** All ranks, leave or official duty, C-915-565-7777. Deluxe kitchenette units with microwave, coffee maker and additional standard units. CATV, A/C, cribs ($2), housekeeping service, ice vending. Rates: standard rooms: single $31.75; double $37.50, each additional person $5; deluxe rooms: single $34.25; double $41, each additional person $5. Call for reservation information.

TML:VQ. Visitors Quarters, Front Desk, Bldg 251, all ranks leave or official duty, C-915-568-4888/2703, D-312-978-4888/2703, Fax: C-915-568-7078, D-312-978-7078. Club Road for check in. Several large apartments, bedroom, living room, study rooms, full kitchen, coffee maker, private bath, telephone with voice mail and wake up service, color TV, HBO, soda/snack vending, ice vending, limited rollaway beds, iron/ironing board, washer/dryer. Bedroom, shared bath (180). Microfridge, telephone, TV/HBO. Full breakfast service in Pace Hall, 0630-0830 hours Mon-Fri. Indoor heated swimming pool near quarters. Rates: $9.50-$26, additional person $5.

TML: DV/VIP. Four houses, 12 suites, officers O6+ (active duty or retired) and equivalent civilian grade, leave or official duty, C-915-568-5319/5330, D-312-978-5319/5330. Completely furnished DV/VIP facility. Rates:$ 35 per day, each additional person $5.

TML: Fisher House. Located at William Beaumont Army Medical Center. C-915-569-1860. Note: Appendix B has the definition of this facility.

DV/VIP: Protocol Office, C-915-568-5319/5330, D-312-978-5319/5330. O6+ (active) and equivalent civilian grade, leave or official duty. Retirees and lower ranks Space-A.

TML Availability: Good.

CREDIT CARDS ACCEPTED: Visa, MasterCard, American Express and Diners Club.

Transportation: Off base taxi 915-533-3433, car rental agency 915-772-4255.

Visit old Juarez and the Tiqua Indian Reservation, check out the Scenic Drive that gives you a view of all of El Paso and old Mexico. There are numerous military museums on post.

TEXAS
Fort Bliss, continued

Locator 568-1113   **Medical 569-2331**   **Police 568-2115**

Fort Hood (TX02R3)
Transient Billeting, Bldg 108
Fort Hood, TX 76544-5057

TELEPHONE NUMBER INFORMATION: Main installation numbers: C-817-288-1110, 287-1110, D-312-738-1110.

Location: From I-35 N exit to US-190 W, nine miles to Killeen. Main gate is clearly marked. *USMRA: Page 87 (K-4,5)*. NMC: Killeen, at main entrance.

Lodging Office: Bldg 36006, Wratten Drive. **C-817-287-0422,** Fax: C-817-288-7604, 24 hours. Check in facility, check out 1100 hours daily. Reservations: **C-817-287-3815/2700,** 0730-1630 hours Mon-Fri. Government civilian employee billeting.

TML: Poxon Guest House. Bldg 111, all ranks, leave or official duty, C-817-287-3067. Bedroom, private bath (45). Handicap accessible. Refrigerator, community kitchen, A/C, color TV in room and lounge, housekeeping service, cribs/cots, washer/dryer, ice vending. Older structure, renovated. Rates: $29. Duty can make reservations, others Space-A.

TML: VQ. Bldg 36006, all ranks, leave or official duty. Bedroom, private bath (225). Refrigerator, A/C, color TV, housekeeping service, washer/dryer, ice vending. Older structure renovated. Rates: TDY $28.50; PCS $33.50. Duty can make reservations, others Space-A.

TML: VQ. Bldgs 5790/92, all ranks, leave or official duty. Bedroom, (60). Refrigerator, community kitchen, A/C, color TV, housekeeping service, washer/dryer, ice vending. Older structure, renovated. Rates: TDY $28.50, PCS $33.50. Duty can make reservations, others Space-A.

TML: Junior Guest Quarters. Bldgs 2305/06/07, enlisted E1-E4, leave or official duty, C-817-288-3067. Bedroom, shared bath (48). Refrigerator, community kitchen, A/C, color TV in room and lounge, housekeeping service, cribs/cots, washer/dryer. Older structure. Rates: $10. Duty can make reservations, others Space-A.

TML: DV/VIP. Bldg 36006, officers O6+, leave or official duty. Two-bedroom, private bath (10). Kitchen, utensils, A/C, color TV, housekeeping service, cribs/cots, washer/dryer, ice vending. Older structure, remodeled. Rates: TDY/PCS $30. Duty can make reservations, others Space-A.

DV/VIP: Bldg 36006. Reservations: C-817-287-3815/2700.

TML Availability: Good, winter. Difficult, May-Sep.

CREDIT CARDS ACCEPTED: Visa, MasterCard and American Express.

Visitors should tour Lake Belton, and other lakes in the regions where boating, fishing, swimming and camping are main pursuits for residents.

Locator 287-2137   **Medical 288-8133**   **Police 287-2176**

216 - Temporary Military Lodging Around the World

TEXAS

Fort Sam Houston (TX18R3)
Billeting Office
Bldg 592, Dickman Road
Fort Sam Houston, TX 78234-5000

TELEPHONE NUMBER INFORMATION: Main installation numbers: C-210-221-1110, D-312-471-1110.

Location: Take the Fort Sam Houston exit off of I-35. *USMRA: Page 91 (C,D-2,3).* NMC: San Antonio, northeast section of city.

Billeting Office: Bldg 592, Dickman Road. **C-210-221-6125/6262, D-312-471-6125/6262,** Fax: C-210-221-6275, D-312-471-6275, 24 hours. Check in facility 1300 hours, check out 1100 hours daily. Government civilian employee billeting.

TML: Guest House. Bldg 1002, Gorgas Circle, all ranks, leave or official duty, C-210-221-8744. Rooms, private bath (110); 2-bedroom suites, refrigerator, microwave, A/C, color TV, housekeeping service, cribs, coin washer/dryer, rollaway. Rates: $22; suites, $26. Duty can make reservations, others Space-A.

TML: VOQ. Bldgs 592 and 1384, officers all ranks, leave or official duty. Bedrooms, private bath (499). Kitchenette with microwave, refrigerator, A/C, color TV, housekeeping service, washer/dryer. Rates: $20, second guest $10.00. Duty can make reservations, others Space-A.

TML: VEQ. Bldgs 590/591. TDY enlisted students only. Units, shared bath (114). Refrigerator, microwave, A/C, color TV, housekeeping service, washer/dryer. Rates $20.

TML: DV/VIP. Bldgs 48 (Staff Post Road), 107 (Artillery Post), officers O6+ and comparable grade DoD civilian, leave or official duty. Two-bedroom suite, private bath (2); 1-bedroom suite, private bath (22). Continental breakfast served (Mon-Fri) Bldg 48 only. Refrigerator, A/C, color TV, honor bar, housekeeping service. Recently renovated. Rates: $30, second guest $15. All categories can make reservations. All except TDY subject to bump.

TML: Canyon Lake Recreation Area. C-888-882-9878, 210-964-3318, D-312-471-3318. Mobile homes (32); 3-bedroom, furnished except for towels and soap. See *Military Living's Military RV, Camping and Rec Areas Around the World* for additional information and directions.

TML: Fisher House. Located at Brooke Army Medical Center. Note: Appendix B has the definition of this facility. C-210-225-4855 ext 101.

DV/VIP: PROTOCOL. C-210-221-2231. O6+. Retirees and lower ranks Space-A.

TML Availability: Good. Best, Oct-Mar.

CREDIT CARDS ACCEPTED: Visa, MasterCard and American Express.

In December 1996, Fort Sam Houston broke ground for a new 150-room guest house. Completion is expected in mid-1998. Keep up to date with *Military Living's R&R Space-A Report®*, **published six times a year.**

Temporary Military Lodging Around the World - 217

TEXAS
Fort Sam Houston, continued

Surrounded by San Antonio, this historic post has seen much colorful military history, from its namesake to the "Rough Riders" and Teddy Roosevelt, and key roles in WWI and WWII, to today's role as a medical training center. While you're here why not visit The Alamo, Retama Horse Racing Park and Sea World. Also visit the Quadrangle Military Museum.

Locator 221-2302   Medical 221-6141   Police 221-2222

Fort Worth Naval Air Station/Joint Reserve Base (TX21R3)
1324 Military Parkway
Fort Worth NAS/JRB, TX 76127-5000

TELEPHONE NUMBER INFORMATION: Main installation numbers: C-817-782-5000, D-312-739-1110.

Location: On TX-183. From Fort Worth, west on I-30, exit at Camp Bowie Blvd., then turn right onto Horne Street. Follow signs to main gate. *USMRA: Page 88 (A-3)*. NMC: Fort Worth, seven miles east.

Lodging Office: 1324 Military Parkway. **C-817-782-5393**, Fax: C-817-782-5391, 24 hours daily. Check in facility 1400 hours, check out 1100 hours daily. Government civilian employee billeting.

TML: VAQ/VOQ. Bldgs 1522,1520, 1565, 1566, officers all ranks, leave or official duty. Bedroom, shared bath. All rooms have a shared bath, refrigerator, microwave, A/C, color TV, housekeeping service, laundry room in building, ice. Modern structure. Rates: $8, each additional person $2. Maximum two per unit. TDY can make reservations, others Space-A.

TML: DV. Bldg 1324, officer O6+, leave or official duty. Chief suites (15), Officer suites (24). One-bedroom suites, private bath. Sitting room, refrigerator, microwave and limited utensils, A/C, color TV, housekeeping service, washer/dryer, ice. Modern structure. Rates: $25, each additional person $3. Duty can make reservations, others Space-A.

DV/VIP: Protocol, C-817-782-7614.

TML Availability: Limited space due to rehabilitation of many buildings. It's best to make reservations 30-45 days in advance.

CREDIT CARDS ACCEPTED: Visa, MasterCard and American Express.

Visit the historic Stockyard District, and then world renowned art museums. How about Southfork? Or the Water Gardens? Or Six Flags Over Texas, and the Opera? Fort Worth has come a long way since 1841!

Locator 782-5000   Medical 266-6282   Police 782-5200

Goodfellow Air Force Base (TX24R3)
Angelo Inn, Bldg 3305
313 E Kearney Blvd E
Goodfellow AFB, TX 76908-4410

TELEPHONE NUMBER INFORMATION: Main installation numbers: C-915-654-3231, D-312-477-3217.

TEXAS
Goodfellow Air Force Base, continued

Location: Off US-87 or US-277, clearly marked, *USMRA: Page 86 (H-6,7)*. NMC: San Angelo, two miles northwest.

Lodging Office: Angelo Inn, Bldg 3305, Kearney Blvd. **C-915-654-3332, D-312-477-3332,** Fax: C-915-654-5177, D-312-477-5177, 24 hours. Check in facility, check out 1200 hours daily. Government civilian employee billeting.

TML: TLF. Bldgs 910, 920, 922, 924, all ranks, leave or official duty. Handicap accessible. Separate bedrooms, private bath (29). Kitchen, complete utensils, color TV, housekeeping service, cribs, washer/dryer, ice vending. Modern structure. Rates: E1-E6 $18; E7-O6 $22. PCS can make reservations, others Space-A.

TML: VAQ. Bldgs 3307, 3311, enlisted all ranks, leave or official duty. Handicap accessible. Bedroom, shared bath (100); room with two beds, shared bath (270). Bldg 239 - NCO Academy, bedroom, shared bath (60). Refrigerator, microwave, A/C, color TV, housekeeping service, washer/dryer. Modern structure. Rates: $7 per person; second person, 50% of the rate. Duty can make reservations, others Space-A.

TML: VOQ. Bldgs 702, 711, officers all ranks, leave or official duty. Separate bedrooms, private bath (115). Kitchenette, microwave, A/C, color TV, housekeeping service, washer/dryer, microwave. Modern structure. Rates: $7-$8 per person; second person, 50% of the rate. TDY can make reservations, others Space-A.

TML: DV/EV. Bldg 910 (DV), Bldg 3307 (EV), officers O6+, enlisted E7, leave or official duty. Separate bedrooms, private bath (10). Kitchen, complete utensils, A/C, color TV, housekeeping service, washer/dryer, ice vending. Modern structure. Rates: $16 per person; second person, 50% of the rate. Duty can make reservations, others Space-A.

TML Availability: Fairly good all year.

CREDIT CARDS ACCEPTED: Visa, MasterCard and American Express.

Visit historic Fort Concho, a preserved Indian fort, and home of the "Buffalo Soldiers", the Concho River Walk and Plaza, and three lakes within 20 minutes of downtown feature camping, boating and fishing.

Locator 654-3410   Medical 654-3135   Police 654-3304

INGLESIDE NAVAL STATION (TX30R3)
1455 Ticonderoga Road, Suite W123
Ingleside, TX 78362-5001

TELEPHONE NUMBER INFORMATION: Main installation numbers: C-512-776-4200, D-312-776-4201.

Location: From Corpus Christi, take Highway 181N through Portland to Highway 361 to Main Street. Turn right on Main Street, NSI is 4.5 miles. I-37S to Route 361 to Route 58 to I-77 into Gregory, follow signs to Naval Station. *USMRA: Page 87 (K,L-8)*. NMC: Corpus Christi, 37 miles south.

TEXAS
INGLESIDE NAVAL STATION, continued

Lodging Office: Bldg 130. C-512-776-4420, D-312-776-4420, Fax: C-512-776-4620, D-312-776-4620, 24 hours daily. Check in billeting office.

TML: BEQ. Bldg 134, 138, all ranks, leave or official duty. Bedroom (20); CPO suites (3). Refrigerator, microwave, color TV/VCR in room and lounge, housekeeping service, essentials, washer/dryer, ice vending, soda/snack vending. Meeting/conference room and fitness center available. Modern structure. Rates: E1-6 $10 per person per night, each additional person $2.50; CPO E7-9 $15 per person per night, each additional person $3.75. Maximum four per unit. Duty can make reservations, others Space-A. No pets.

TML Availability: Fair. All months limited due to facility size.

CREDIT CARDS ACCEPTED: Visa, MasterCard and American Express.

Transportation: On/off base shuttle/bus 776-4299, off base taxi 758-5858, car rental agency (USO) 776-4777.

Visit the USS Lexington, Texas State Aquarium, Mustang Island Beach, Corpus Christi Beach, Greyhound Race Track, King ranch, Harbor Playhouse or the Corpus Christi Botanical Gardens during your stay!

Locator 776-4200   **Medical** 776-4575   **Police** 776-4454/4238

Kelly Air Force Base (TX03R3)
Bldg 1650 Goodrich Road
Kelly AFB, TX 78241-5000
Scheduled to close July 2001.

TELEPHONE NUMBER INFORMATION: Main installation numbers: C-210-925-1110, D-312-945-1110.

Location: All of the following: I-10, I-35, I-37, I-410 intersect with US-90. From US-90 take either the Gen Hudnell or Gen McMullen exit and go south to Kelly AFB. *USMRA: Page 91 (B-3,4)*. NMC: San Antonio, seven miles northeast.

Lodging Office: Bldg 1650, Goodrich Road. **C-210-925-1844/924-7201, D-312-945-1844,** 24 hours. Check in 1400 hours, check out 1200 hours daily.

TML: VOQ. Bldg 1676, officers all ranks, leave or official duty. Bedroom, private bath. Kitchen, microwave, A/C, CATV, housekeeping service, washer/dryer, ice vending. Older structure. Rates: $10 per person.

TML: VAQ. Bldg 1650, enlisted all ranks, leave or official duty. Refrigerator, microwave, A/C, CATV, housekeeping service, washer/dryer, ice vending. Older structure. Rates $10 per person.

TML: DV/VIP. Bldg 1676. Rates: $16 per person.

TML Availability: Limited all year.

TEXAS
Kelly Air Force Base, continued

Your trip to San Antonio will be well remembered if you visit Sea World, Fiesta Texas, the Alamo and the historic mission sites.

Locator 925-1841   Medical 925-4544   Police 925-6811

Kingsville Naval Air Station (TX22R3)
CBQ, Bldg 2700
1140 Moffett Ave
Kingsville NAS, TX 78363-5054

TELEPHONE NUMBER INFORMATION: Main installation numbers: C-512-516-6136.

Location: Off US-77 S, exit to TX-425 SE to main gate. *USMRA: Page 87 (K-9).* NMC: Corpus Christi, 40 miles northeast.

Lodging Office: Bldg 2700, 1140 Moffett Ave. **C-512-516-6321, D-312-861-6591,** Fax: C-512-516-6428, 24 hours. Check in facility after 1200 hours, check out by 1200 hours daily. Government civilian employee billeting.

TML: BOQ/BEQ. Bldgs 2700, 3729, 3730, 3730A, 3730W, all ranks. Bedrooms, private bath, shared lounge (36); bedrooms, private bath, shared lounge (16). CATV, refrigerator, amenities, microwaves, A/C, laundry facilities, snack vending, housekeeping service. Thirty-five upgraded rooms, new carpet, furniture. Rates: single $12.60 per day, each additional person $3; DoD civilian $22, each additional person $5. PCS in/out personnel should make reservations, others Space-A.

TML: Escondido Ranch. C-210-373-4419. Seventeen-room lodge with an adjacent cook house containing four BBQ pits, electric stove and electric grill. The lodge also has a huge lounge with tables, TV/VCR, sofas, pool table, electronic darts, and microwave. Rooms are furnished, but limited water prevents linen service. Rates: $10-$50.

DV/VIP: Protocol Office, Bldg 3730W, C-512-595-6481. O6+. VIP 3-bedroom suites (6). Retirees Space-A.

TML Availability: Excellent, Dec-Jan. Good, other months.

CREDIT CARDS ACCEPTED: Visa, MasterCard, American Express and Diners'.

Home of the King Ranch, for Santa Gertrudis cattle, beautiful thoroughbred and quarter horses, the historic ranch house, and other interesting sites. Texas A&I University is located here.

Locator 516-6136   Medical 516-6305   Police 516-6217

Lackland Air Force Base (TX25R3)
37 SVS/SVML
1750 Femoyer Street
Lackland AFB, TX 78236-5431

TELEPHONE NUMBER INFORMATION: Main installation numbers: C-210-671-1110, D-312-473-1110.

TEXAS
Lackland Air Force Base, continued

Location: Off US-90 S. Loop 13 (Military Drive) bisects Lackland AFB. *USMRA: Page 87 (J-6,7); Page 91 (A,B-3,4).* NMC: San Antonio, six miles northeast.

Lodging Office: Bldg 10203, 1750 Femoyer Street. **C-210-671-2523/2296, D-312-473-2523,** Fax: C-210-671-4822, D-312-473-4822, 0730-1630 hours Mon-Fri.

TML: VAQ. Bldg 10203, west side of base, Femoyer Street, 24 hours, all ranks, C-210-671-4277/2556. Check in facility, check out 1200 hours daily. Two-person rooms, semi-private baths (770); one-person rooms, semi-private baths; SNCO rooms, semi-private baths (78); suites with bedrooms, private baths. A/C, color TV, housekeeping service, washer/dryer, snack vending, ice vending. Modern structure. Rates: $7-$23 per unit. Duty can make reservations, all others Space-A.

TML: VOQ/DV/VIP: Bldg 2604, 24 hours, C-210-671-3622, officers all ranks, leave or official duty. Separate bedrooms, shared bath (32); separate bedrooms, private bath (96). Microwave, refrigerator, A/C, color TV, housekeeping service, washer/dryer, snack vending, ice vending. Bedroom suites, private bath (DV/VIP) (13) Two bedroom suites, private bath (DV/VIP) (4). Refrigerator, A/C, color TV, housekeeping service, washer/dryer, ice vending. Older structure, remodeled. Rates: $5-$10 per person. Air Force policy requires advance payment. Duty can make reservations, others Space-A.

TML: Fisher House. Note: Appendix B has the definition of this facility. C-210-678-3000. There are two houses at Lackland AFB.

DV/VIP: Protocol Office, C-210-671-2423. O6+.

TML Availability: Difficult, Jan-Nov.

San Antonio takes its name from Mission San Antonio de Valero or, the Alamo. Visiting the local Missions, and brushing up on the long history of this gracious city, is only one of a number of activities for visitors here.

| Locator 671-1110 | Medical 670-7100 | Police 671-2018 |

Laughlin Air Force Base (TX05R3)
Laughlin Manor
47 SVS/SVML
416 Liberty Drive
Laughlin AFB, TX 78843-5227

TELEPHONE NUMBER INFORMATION: Main installation numbers: C-210-298-3511, D-312-732-1110.

Location: Take US-90 W from San Antonio, 150 miles or US-277 S from San Angelo, 150 miles to Del Rio area. The AFB is clearly marked off US-90. *USMRA: Page 86 (H-9).* NMC: Del Rio, eight miles northwest.

Lodging Office: Laughlin Manor, 416 Liberty Drive. **C-210-298-5731, D-312-732-5731,** Fax: C-210-298-5272, D-312-732-5272, 24 hours. Check in billeting, check out 1200 hours daily. No government civilian employee billeting.

TEXAS
Laughlin Air Force Base, continued

TML: TLF. Bldgs 460-463, all ranks, leave or official duty. Separate bedroom, private bath (20). Kitchen, utensils, A/C, color TV, limited housekeeping service, cribs, washer/dryer (Bldg 463), ice vending. Modern structure. Rates: E1-E6 $18-$20 per unit; E7+ $22-$24 per unit. Duty can make reservations, others Space-A.

TML: VOQ/VAQ. Bldg 470, all ranks, leave or official duty. Bedroom, shared bath (officers all ranks) (16); bedroom, shared bath (enlisted all ranks) (14). Refrigerator, A/C, color TV in room and lounge, housekeeping service, cribs/cots, washer/dryer, ice vending. Older structure, renovated. Rates: VOQ/VAQ $8.50 per person. Duty can make reservations, others Space-A.

TML: DV/VIP. Bldg 470, officers O6+, leave or official duty. Separate bedroom, private bath (2); 3-bedroom, private bath (4). Kitchen, utensils, color TV, housekeeping service, washer/dryer, ice vending. Older structure, renovated. Rates: $16-$23 per person. Duty can make reservations, others Space-A.

DV/VIP: 47 FTW/CCP, Bldg 338, room 1, C-210-298-5041. O6+.

TML Availability: Good, Nov-Jan. Difficult, other times.

CREDIT CARDS ACCEPTED: Visa, MasterCard and American Express.

Visit the historical district in Brown Plaza, particularly for Cinco de Mayo and Diez Y Seis de Septiembre celebrations. The Brinkley Mansion, Valverde Winery, and the visitor's center at Lake Amistad, are all worthwhile to visit.

Locator 298-3511   **Medical 911**   **Police 911**

Randolph Air Force Base (TX19R3)
12 SPTG/SVML
415 B Street East
Randolph AFB, TX 78150-4424

TELEPHONE NUMBER INFORMATION: Main installation numbers: C-210-652-1110, D-312-487-1110.

Location: From I-35 take exit 172, Pat Booker Road. From I-10 take exit 587, TX FM-1604. *USMRA: Page 91 (E-2).* NMC: San Antonio, six miles south.

Lodging Office: Bldg 118. **C-210-652-1844**, Fax: C-210-652-2616, 24 hours. Check in billeting, check out 1200 hours daily. Government civilian employee billeting in TDY status.

TML: TLF. Bldgs 152-155, all ranks, PCS in/out, leave or official duty. Handicap accessible (1). Bedroom, private bath (30). Living room, full kitchen, utensils, A/C, color TV, housekeeping service, iron/ironing board, hair dryer, cribs/cots, washer/dryer, ice vending. Older structure, renovated. Rates $18-$22 per person, depending on rank. PCS in/out can make reservations, Space-A up to 24 hours in advance.

TML: VOQ. Bldgs 110, 111, 120, 121, 161, 162, 381, officers all ranks, leave or official duty. Bedroom, living room, private bath (100), 76 with stocked bar and snacks; bedroom, private bath (256), 160 with stocked bar and snacks; 2-bedroom, 2-private bath, living room, kitchen with stocked

TEXAS
Randolph Air Force Base, continued

bar and snacks (2). A/C, refrigerator, microwave, color TV, utensils for two, iron/ironing board, hair dryer, housekeeping service, washer/dryer, cribs/cots, ice vending. Some modern, some older structures. Rates: $8.50-$16 per person. Duty can make reservations, Space-A up to 24 hours in advance.

TML: VAQ. Bldgs 861, 862, enlisted all ranks, leave or official duty. Bedroom, living room, kitchen, stocked bar and snacks, private bath (5); bedroom, queen bed, private bath, stocked bar and snacks (68); bedroom, queen bed, shared bath (46). Bedroom, single bed, shared bath (48). A/C, color TV, housekeeping service, refrigerator, microwave, utensils for two, iron/ironing board, hair dryer, cribs/cots, ice vending, washer/dryer. Modern structure. Rates: $8.50-$16 per person. TDY can make reservations, Space-A up to 24 hours in advance.

DV/VIP: Protocol. Bldg 900, room 306, C-210-652-4126. O7+/SES. All retirees Space-A up to 24 hours in advance.

TML Availability: Good, Nov-Feb. Fair, other times.

CREDIT CARDS ACCEPTED: Visa, MasterCard and American Express.

San Antonio is nestled between the Texas Hill Country and the coast, and there are a wealth of local things to do. Visit New Braunfels to the north, for a fascinating look at Texas' German pas,t and Sequin to the east.

Locator 652-1110   **Medical** 652-2734   **Police** 652-5700

Red River Army Depot (TX09R3)
Housing Office
ATTN; SIORR-O
100 Main Drive
Texarkana, TX 75507-5000
Lodging facility is scheduled to close July 1998.

TELEPHONE NUMBER INFORMATION: Main installation numbers: C-903-334-2141, D-312-829-4110.

Location: From I-30 E or W, take Red River Army Depot exit #206 south .5 miles. Route clearly marked. *USMRA: Page 87 (N-2).* NMC: Texarkana, 20 miles east.

Lodging Office: Bldg 228, Texas Ave, half mile east of the main gate. **C-903-334-3976, D-312-829-3976,** Fax: C-903-334-2494, 0700-1700 hours Mon-Thur. Check in billeting, check out 1100 hours. No after hours check in .Duty/ TDY can make reservations, other Space A (confirmed two days). E-mail: renteria@redriverad-emhl.army.mil.

TML: BOQ. Bldg 40, all ranks, leave or official duty, retired. Bedroom, private bath (1), refrigerator, microwave, coffee service, A/C, CATV, HBO; separate living room/bedrooms, private bath (5), kitchenette, microwave, coffee service, A/C, CATV, HBO. TV room, housekeeping service (Mon-Fri), washer/dryer, cribs/rollaways. New building and furnishings. Rates: sponsor $7, each additional adult, child, infant $1, maximum $9 per family. Maximum five per room. Must make arrangements for after hours check-in. Small pets OK if leashed outside.

TEXAS
Red River Army Depot, continued

TML: DV/VIP. Bldg 40, officers O6+, leave or official duty. Report to Protocol Office, C-903-334-2316. Separate rooms, private bath (2), one with bedroom, refrigerator/microwave, coffee service; one with bedroom, living room, kitchenette/microwave, limited utensils. Rooms adjoin and may be used as a single, 2-bedroom unit. A/C, CATV, HBO, TV room, housekeeping service, laundry and TV room, cribs/rollaways. New building and furnishings. Rates: same. Duty can make reservations, others Space-A. DV/VIP are designated non-smoking rooms.

DV/VIP: Protocol Office, Bldg 15, C-903-334-2316, during normal business hours (0700-1700 hours Mon-Thurs). O6+, GS-14+. Retirees, lower ranks, DoD civilians Space-A but will not be confirmed until two days prior to arrival (no earlier than Thurs for a Sun arrival).

TML Availability: Extremely limited. Best, Nov-Mar. Difficult, Apr-Oct.

CREDIT CARDS ACCEPTED: American Express.

Lake Texarkana, nine miles southwest of the city, offers all water sports. Many local golf courses, and September's Four States Fair and Rodeo are the pride of local residents. There's a 9-hole golf course, tennis courts, and a swimming pool all within walking distance of BOQ.

Locator 334-2141   Medical 911   Police 334-2911

Sheppard Air Force Base (TX37R3)
82 SVS/SVML
400 J Ave
Sheppard AFB, TX 76311-2613

TELEPHONE NUMBER INFORMATION: Main installation numbers: C-817-676-2511, D-312-736-1001.

Location: Take US-281 N from Wichita Falls, exit to TX-325 which leads to main gate, clearly marked. *USMRA: Page 87 (J-1)*. NMC: Wichita Falls, five miles southwest.

Lodging Office: Sheppard Inn, 400 J Ave. **C-817-855-7370, D-312-736-1844/4538,** Fax: C-817-676-7434, DSN Fax-312-736-7434, 24 hours. Check in lodging, check out 1200 hours daily (TLFs 1000 hours). Government civilian employee lodging.

TML: TLF. Bldgs 127-134, 160-165, 1511, all ranks, leave or official duty, C-817-676-2707. Separate bedrooms, private bath (73). Four-bedroom, two bath (8). Kitchen (23 with microwave only), utensils, A/C, color TV, housekeeping service, cribs/cots, washer/dryer, ice vending. Modern structure. Rates: E1-E6 $18 (small), $20 (large); E7+ $22 (small), $24 (large). Maximum four to eight per unit. Duty can make reservations, others Space-A.

TML: VAQ. Bldgs 632, 633, 1601, 1602, 1603, 1604, enlisted all ranks, leave or official duty, C-817-676-2707, D-312-736-1844. Bedroom, two beds, shared bath (1524); separate bedrooms, private bath (12); bedroom, one bed, shared bath (282). Refrigerator, A/C, color TV, ice vending, housekeeping service, washer/dryer, microwaves. Modern structure. Rates: standard room $7 per person, $9 with guest; suites $16 per person, $23 with guest. Maximum two per room. Duty can make reservations, others Space-A.

TEXAS
Sheppard Air Force Base, continued

TML: VOQ. Bldgs 240, 260, 331, 332, 333, 370, officer all ranks, leave or official duty, C-817-676-2707, D-312-736-1844. Bedroom, kitchenette, private bath (407); separate bedrooms, kitchenette, private bath (12). Refrigerator, A/C, color TV, washer/dryer. Rates: standard room $8 per person, $11 with guest; suites $16 per person, $23 with guest. Maximum two per room. Duty can make reservations, others Space-A.

TML: DV/VIP. Bldg 332, officer O6+, leave or official duty, C-817-855-2123. D-312-736-2123. Separate bedroom suites (8), private bath. A/C, kitchenette, housekeeping service, color TV, utensils, washer/dryer. Modern structure. Rates: $16 per person, $23 with guest. Maximum two per room. Duty can make reservations, others Space-A.

TML: Sheppard AFB Recreation Annex, C-903-523-4613. Cabin, 2-bedroom, sleeps four (1), Cabins, sleeps four to six (41), Mobile Home, sleeps six (1); AC, private bath, TV, furnished except for towels and personal items. Rates: $25-$40 daily. See *Military Living's Military RV, Camping and Rec Areas Around the World* **for additional information and directions.**

TML Availability: Good, winter. Difficult, Apr-Sep.

CREDIT CARDS ACCEPTED: Visa, MasterCard and American Express.

Visit the Wichita Falls Museum and Art Center, Lucy Park, and the 3.5 miles drive to Wichita Falls' waterfall (the original washed away 100 years ago, and this one is man made!).

Locator 676-1841   Medical 676-2333   Police 676-6302

UTAH

Camp Williams (UT11R4)
Camp Williams Billeting
17800 S. Camp Williams Road
Riverton, UT 84065-4999

TELEPHONE NUMBER INFORMATION: Main installation numbers: C-801-253-5455, D-312-766-5455.

Location: From I-15 take exit 296 (Draper./Riverton), turn west onto Hwy 111. Turn left at third traffic light, drive approximately seven miles, Camp Williams is on the left. *USMRA: Page 112 (D-4)*. NMC: Salt Lake City, 25 miles north.

Lodging Office: Bldg 802, 17800 S. Camp Williams Road. **C-801-253-5410, D-312-766-5410,** Fax: C-801-253-9543, 1000-1600 hours daily. Check in at billeting office, check out 1200 hours.

TML: TLF. Bldg 820, officers, all ranks, enlisted E7-E9. Bedrooms, semi-private bath (60); Bedroom, private bath (5). Refrigerator, color TV, housekeeping service, washer/dryer, soda/snack vending. Rates: $6-$12. AD/reserve may make reservations, others Space-A.

TML Availability: Difficult. Best, fall and winter.

226 - Temporary Military Lodging Around the World

UTAH
CAMP WILLIAMS, continued

CREDIT CARDS ACCEPTED: Visa, MasterCard and American Express.

While you're here visit Salt Lake City's Temple Square, planetarium, Hogle Zoo, Trolley Square for shopping, Salt Palace for pro sports. Close to skiing and hiking.

Locator 253-5455   Medical 911   Police 253-5455

Dugway Proving Ground (UT04R4)
Billeting Office, PO Box 128
Dugway, UT 84022-5000

TELEPHONE NUMBER INFORMATION: Main installation numbers: C-801-831-2151, D-312-789-2151.

Location: Isolated but can be reached from I-80. Take Skull Valley Rd (exit 77) for 40 miles south. *USMRA: Page 112 (B,C-4,5).* NMC: Salt Lake City, 80 miles northeast.

Lodging Office: Bldg 5228, Valdez Circle. **C-801-831-2333**, Fax: C-801-831-2669, D-312-789-2669, 0630-1730 hours Mon-Thur, 0730-1130 hours Fri, closed weekends and holidays. After hours, Main Gate, 801-831-2718. Check in billeting 1800 hours, check out 1100 hours daily. Government civilian employee billeting.

TML: DVQ/VOQ/Houses. Bldgs 5226, 5228, 5218, officer and enlisted, all ranks, leave or official duty. Bedroom, semi-private bath (18); Private bath (5); separate bedroom suites (32); houses with two to three bedrooms (6). Refrigerator, A/C, color TV/VCR in room and lounge, housekeeping service (weekdays only), essentials, cribs/cots, washer/dryer, ice vending, soda vending, exercise room, microwave in lobby. Handicap accessible. Older structures, remodeled. Rates: $22-$25 per room, $37 per suite or house, each additional family member $3. Duty can make reservations, others including contractors and social guests Space-A.

DV/VIP: C-801-831-3707, D-312-789-3707.

TML Availability: Good. Best, fall and winter.

CREDIT CARDS ACCEPTED: Visa, MasterCard and American Express.

Pristine alpine mountains, vast deserts, the mysterious Great Salt Lake - this area offers many outdoor activities without entry fees or hype, and is only minutes away from metropolitan Salt Lake City!

Locator 831-2151   Medical 831-2222   Police 831-2933

Hill Air Force Base (UT02R4)
5847 D Ave
Hill AFB, UT 84056-5206

TELEPHONE NUMBER INFORMATION: Main installation numbers: C-801-777-7221, D-312-777-1100.

UTAH
Hill Air Force Base, continued

Location: Adjacent to I-15 between Ogden and Salt Lake City. Take exit 336, east on UT-193 to south gate. *USMRA: Page 112 (D-3)*. NMC: Ogden, eight miles north.

Lodging Office: Mountain View Inn, Bldg 146, D Ave. **C-801-777-1844**, Fax: C-801-775-2014, 24 hours. Check in lodging office, check out 1200 hours daily. Government civilian employee billeting.

TML: DV/VIP. Bldg 1118, officers O6+, official duty, leave or space-A. Separate bedroom suites, private bath (6). Kitchen (no stove), microwave, refrigerator, coffee pot, limited utensils, A/C, essentials, two color TVs, VCR, housekeeping service, washer/dryer, ice vending. Older structure, renovated. Rates: single $14; double $28. Duty can make reservations, others Space-A.

TML: DV-VOQ. Bldg 134. Three-bedroom, dining, living, complete kitchen, 1 1/2 private baths (5). Laundry room, small yard. Two color TVs, A/C, VCR, essentials, ice vending, housekeeping service. Older structure, renovated. Rates: single $16; family $23. Official duty, leave or Space-A.

TML: DV-VOQ. Bldg 150. Separate bedroom suites, private bath (8); bedroom, private bath (1). Two color TV/s (suites), A/C, microwave, refrigerator, coffee pot, essentials, housekeeping service. Older structure, renovated. Rates: single $16; double $23. Official duty or Space-A.

TML: VOQ. Bldgs 141, 142, officers all ranks, leave or official duty. Bedroom, private bath (40). Microwave, A/C, refrigerator, coffee pot, color TV, washer/dryer, ice vending, housekeeping service, essentials. Older structure, renovated. Rates: single $10; double $14. Duty can make reservations, others Space-A.

TML: VAQ. Bldgs 350, 351, enlisted all ranks, leave or official duty. Bldg 351: separate bedroom suites, private bath (76); Bldg 350: (Prime Knight quarters) separate bedroom suites (25) (38 enlisted, six SNCO). Microfridge, A/C, TV, coffee pot. Older structures, renovated. Rates: $10; Chief suites, $14. No families. Official duty may make reservations, others Space-A.

TML: VOQ-Chief Suites. Bldg 480. Separate bedroom suites, kitchen, bath; bedroom, shared living, kitchen and bath (16); bedroom, shared kitchen and bath (8). Two color TVs, A/C, complete utensils, ice vending, laundry room. Rates: single $16; double $23. Official duty or Space-A.

TML: Bldg 472, all ranks. Separate bedroom, private bath, kitchen (40). A/C, complete utensils, two color TVs, cribs/rollaways. Washer/dryer, ice vending, limited housekeeping service. Older structure, renovated. Rates: $22 per night. PCS/TDY can make reservations, others Space-A.

TML: Hillhaus Lodge, C-801-621-2202, D-312-458-3525. This lodge is now open to the public, reservations are highly recommended. Reservations no longer handled by Hill AFB. Bedrooms, private bath (3); suites, private bath (4); loft, sleeps seven (1). Lounge, sun deck, gas fireplace, snack bar, kitchen, dining area. A-frame, renovated. Sleep and ski packages. Rates: $45-$98 daily; entire lodge rental $450 per day. Breakfast, lunch and dinner offered. **Note: check *Military RV, Camping and Rec Areas Around the World* for more information.**

DV/VIP: Protocol ALC/CCP, Bldg 1118, C-801-777-5565. O6+. Retirees Space-A.

TML Availability: Good.

CREDIT CARDS ACCEPTED: Visa and MasterCard. Hillhaus Lodge accepts Visa, MasterCard and American Express.

UTAH
Hill Air Force Base, continued

Locator 777-1844   Medical 777-1100   Police 777-3056

Tooele Army Depot (UT05R4)
ATTN: SDSTE-PWH
Tooele, UT 84074-5008

TELEPHONE NUMBER INFORMATION: Main installation numbers: C-801-833- 3211, D-312-790-3211.

Location: From west I-80, exit 99 to UT-36 S for 15 miles to main entrance. *USMRA: Page 112 (C-4)*. NMC: Salt Lake City, 40 miles northeast.

Lodging Office: Bldg 1, HQ Loop. **C-801-833-2124**, Fax: C-801-833-2810, 0630-1700 hours Mon-Thur, closed Fri. Other hours, SDO, Bldg 8, C-801-833-2304. Check in billeting 1300 hours, check out 1100 hours daily. Government civilian employee billeting. E-mail: sculley@tooele-emhl.army.mil

TML: VOQ/DVQ. Bldg 35, all ranks, leave or official duty. Two-bedroom apartments, private bath (9). One-bedroom apartments, private bath (3). Kitchen with utensils, A/C, CATV, housekeeping service, building washer/dryer, soda/snack vending, exercise room. PX, Eagles Nest Community Club and Arts and Crafts shop. Rates: sponsor $11, each additional adult $2. No charge for children. All categories may make reservations, unofficial duty may make reservations seven days in advance of arrival date for a period of three days. No pets.

Military Discount Lodging: Comfort Inn, 491 S Main, Tooele, C-801-882-6100. Best Western Inn, 365 N Main, Tooele, C-801-882-5010.

TML Availability: Good. Fair, Dec-Mar.

CREDIT CARDS ACCEPTED: American Express.

Transportation: Off base shuttle/bus (UTA) 882-9031, off base taxi (Green Top Taxi Cab) 882-3100.

Some special sights in Salt Lake City: the Mormon Temple and Temple Square, the Pioneer Memorial museum. There are several local ski resorts within reach of Tooele.

Locator 833-2094   Medical 833-2572 or 911   Police 882-5600 or 911

VIRGINIA

Camp Pendleton
Virginia National Guard (VA50R1)
Virginia Beach, VA 23461-5000

TELEPHONE NUMBER INFORMATION: Main installation numbers: C-804-491-5140.

VIRGINIA
Camp Pendleton/Virginia National Guard, continued

Location: Camp Pendleton is north of Dam Neck Fleet Combat Training Center, and south of Virginia Beach. Going south across the bridge from Virginia Beach on General Booth Blvd, watch for gate on the left. *USMRA: Page 52 (J-7)*. NMC: Virginia Beach, in city limits.

Lodging Office: C-804-775-9102, Fax: C-804-775-9338. Write to: Adjutant Gen. Office, Dept. Military Affairs, 600 E Broad Street, Richmond, VA, 23219-1832. Government civilian employee lodging.

TML: Cottages and trailers. All ranks, leave or official duty. Two- and three-bedroom cottages, private bath (5); 2-bedroom trailers (5). A/C, color TV, screened porch, full kitchen, utensils, no housekeeping service (renters leave quarters clean), linens provided except for towels (bath and kitchen) cribs must be brought by renters. Rates: cottages $45-$60; trailers $35. One mile from beach. Write to above address for reservations. Reservations open 15 Mar. Cottages rent year round, trailers close 1 Nov. $100 deposit required. Two week notice for cancellation. After 1 April one week stay mandatory. National Guard has priority, others Space-A.

TML Availability: Best, Sep-Mar. Difficult, summer.

Its closeness to the eastern shore makes this place a find for visitors lucky enough to be able to rent one of the cottages or trailers.

Locator 491-5140   Medical 911   Police 491-5140

Cheatham Annex Fleet and Industrial Supply Center (VA02R1)
Morale, Welfare and Recreation
108 Sanda Ave
Williamsburg, VA 23187-8792

TELEPHONE NUMBER INFORMATION: Main installation numbers: C-757-887-4000, D-312-953-4000.

Location: From I-64 take exit 242-B on US-199 east to main gate of Cheatham Annex. *USMRA: Page 47 (N-8)*. NMC: Williamsburg, six miles west.

Lodging Office: MWR, Bldg 284, 108 Sanda Ave. **C-757-887-7224/7101/7102**, 0800-1530 hours week days. After duty hours, Bldg 295, C-757-887-7418. No government civilian employee billeting.

TML: Recreation Cabins. Cabins 161, 163-165, 167-170, 261, 262, AD, retirees and reservists, handicap accessible. **C-757-887-7224.** Reservations required 90 days advance. Twelve cabins, private bath: each sleeps four to ten, furnished, color CATV, phone, refrigerator, kitchen, utensils, dishes, linens, and a boat (with motor, battery and charger, paddles, cushions). Eleven cabins: each has AC and central heat, wood burning stove or fireplace (wood furnished). Rates: winter, 1 Nov thru 31 Mar $45-$65 daily, $270-$390 weekly; summer, 1 Apr thru 31 Oct $50-$70 daily, $300-$420 weekly. See Military Living's *Military RV, Camping and Rec Areas Around the World* for more information.

DV/VIP: Cabins 261, 161, reserved O6+. Commander's Office, C-757-887-7108.

TML Availability: Good, Nov-Mar, Mon-Fri. Difficult, other months, Fri-Sun.

VIRGINIA
Cheatham Annex Fleet and Industrial Supply Center, continued

CREDIT CARDS ACCEPTED: Visa, MasterCard and American Express.

Near Colonial Williamsburg/Jamestown, many museums. Busch Gardens. Great deer hunting, contact Special Services. Fitness Center, pool, racquetball and tennis courts, bowling alley, Snack Bar.

Locator 887-4000   Medical 887-7222   Police 887-7222

Dahlgren Naval Surface Warfare Center (VA06R1)
Lodging Office, Bldg 960
Dahlgren, VA 22448-5000

TELEPHONE NUMBER INFORMATION: Main installation numbers: C-540-653-8531, D-312-249-1110.

Location: From I-95 in Fredericksburg, VA, east on VA-3 to VA-206 (17 miles), left at VA-206, east to Dahlgren (11 miles). Also, US-301 S to VA-206, east to main gate. *USMRA: Page 47 (M-6)*. NMC: Washington, DC, 38 miles north.

Lodging Office: Bldg 960. C-540-653-7671/72, D-312-249-7671/72, Fax: C-540-653-4274, 24 hours. Check in billeting, check out 1100 hours daily. Government civilian employee billeting.

TML: BOQ. Bldgs 215, 217, officers, all ranks, leave or official duty. Bedroom, private bath (12); separate bedrooms, private bath (20); 2-bedroom, private bath suite (DV/VIP) (1). Community kitchen, limited utensils, refrigerator, A/C, essentials, ice vending, color TV in room and lounge, housekeeping service, washer/dryer, soda/snack vending. Meeting/conference room and exercise room available. Older structures, renovated. Rates: $16 for officer transients, slightly higher for DV/VIP. Duty can make reservations, others Space-A.

TML: BEQ. Bldg 959, E5-E9, leave or official duty. Bedroom, private bath (4). A/C, essentials, ice vending, housekeeping service, refrigerator, color TV in room and lounge, washer/dryer, soda/snack vending. Meeting/conference room and exercise room available. Rates: E5-E6 $10; E7-E9 $16. Duty can make reservations, others Space-A.

TML: TLQ. Bldg 909, all ranks, leave or official duty, PCS in/out have priority. Two-bedroom, private bath (4). Kitchen with utensils, housekeeping service, color TV, soda/snack vending. Meeting/conference room and exercise room available. Older structure, renovated. Rates: E4 and below $10; E5-E6 $12; E7+ $15. Duty can make reservations, others Space-A.

DV/VIP: Public Affairs Office, C-540-653-815. O6+/SES equivalent. Retirees Space-A.

TML Availability: Difficult. Best, Nov-Feb.

CREDIT CARDS ACCEPTED: Visa, MasterCard and American Express.

Take a walk through Dahlgren's Beaver Pond Nature Trail, and then savor the history of Washington's and Lee's birthplace in historic Fredericksburg. The area is full of interesting historic sites.

Locator 653-8216/8701   Medical 911   Police 653-8500

VIRGINIA

Dam Neck Fleet Combat Training Center Atlantic (VA25R1)
CBQ Billeting
FCTCLANT
1912 Regulas Ave
Virginia Beach, VA 23461-2098

TELEPHONE NUMBER INFORMATION: Main installation numbers: C-757-433-2000, D-312-433-2000.

Location: On the ocean front, "Dam Neck at the Dunes" is two miles southeast of Oceana NAS, off Dam Neck Road. *USMRA: Page 47 (O-9,10); Page 52 (J-7,8).* NMC: Virginia Beach, three miles south of the resort strip.

Lodging Office: "Dam Neck at the Dunes," enlisted Bldg 566C. **C-757-491-2449** (BEQ). Check in facility 1400 hours, check out 1000 hours daily. Officers Bldg 241. **C-757-433-7013**, Fax: C-757-433-6228/6854. Check in and out same. Government civilian employee billeting.

TML: BOQ. Bldgs 225, 241, officers all, leave or official duty. Bedroom, private bath (96); bedroom, living room, private bath (53); VIP suites, private bath, living room (13); DV rooms, kitchenette, private bath (4). Refrigerators, coffee makers, A/C, CATV/VCR, housekeeping service, cots, washer/dryer, ice vending. Sun deck, hot tub and sauna. Modern structures. Rates: standard room, $17.50 per person; suites, $23.50 per person; DV rooms, $37 per person. Under five no charge. Duty on orders can make reservations, others Space-A.

TML: BEQ. Bldgs 532, 550, 566, enlisted all ranks. Total 1,336 rooms including 56 Chief's rooms. Refrigerator, A/C, color TV/VCR, housekeeping service, washer/dryer, lounges. Modern structures. Others: Sun deck, BBQ, phone, CATV, washer/dryer and housekeeping service. Rates: E5+ $15.50, E1-E4 $8.50. Reservations accepted for official orders, others Space-A.

DV/VIP: Protocol Office, Taylor Hall, C-757-433-6542. For O7+/civilian equivalent. Reservations: C-757-433-7718, D-312-433-7718, retirees space A.

TML Availability: Because this is a training command, availability is usually poor and only fair at best.

CREDIT CARDS ACCEPTED: Visa, MasterCard and American Express.

Some rooms have ocean views. Bldg 241 and 225 are on the beach. Lake with boat rentals and fishing. Dam Neck is two miles from Ocean Breeze Water Park and the Marine Science Museum. A new 50-room Navy Lodge is under construction, with completion date expected in early 1998.

Locator 433-6211   Medical 677-7200   Police 433-6929

Defense Supply Center Richmond (VA30R1)
8000 Jefferson Davis Highway
Richmond, VA 23297-5100

TELEPHONE NUMBER INFORMATION: Main installation number: C-804-279-3861, D-312-695-3861.

VIRGINIA
Defense Supply Center Richmond, continued

Location: From I-95 (Richmond-Petersburg Turnpike) exit 64 or 67 to US-1/301. Clearly marked. *USMRA: Page 47 (L-8).* NMC: Richmond, eight miles north.

Lodging Office: 8000 Jefferson Davis Hwy. **C-804-279-3371, D-312-695-4198,** Fax: C-804-279-6419, D-312-695-6419.

TML: VOQ. Rates: PCS, AD, Reserves, Civilian on leave or duty: single $22, family $30 per night; TDY: single $28, family $35 per night.

Locator 279-3861   Medical 279-3821   Police 279-4888

Fort A.P. Hill (VA17R1)
Housing Division
Bldg TT0114
2nd and Burke Street
Bowling Green, VA 22427-5000

TELEPHONE NUMBER INFORMATION: Main installation numbers: C-804-633-8710, D-312-578-8760.

Location: From I-95 S, take Fort A.P. Hill exit, US-17 (bypass) E to VA-2 S to Bowling Green, take VA-301 NE to main gate. Also, exit I-95 N to VA-207 N to VA-301 N and to main gate. *USMRA: Page 47 (L,M-6,7).* NMC: Fredericksburg, 14 miles northwest.

Lodging Office: Bldg TT0142, corner 2nd and Burke Streets. **C-804-633-8335, D-312-578-8335,** Fax: C-804-633-8418, D-312-578-8418, 0800-2100 hours daily. SDO, Bldg TT-0101, C-804-633-8201. Check in 1500 hours, check out 1200 hours. Government civilian employee billeting.

TML: Guest House. **Dolly's House.** All ranks, leave or official duty. Bedroom, private bath (two rooms make a suite) (6); handicap accessible (1). Same amenities as DV/VIP. New structure 1990. Rates: $20 per person, each additional person $4. Reservations at 804-633-8219. Rates subject to change.

TML: VOQ/VEQ. Bldgs TT-0117, TT-119, TT-0146, all ranks, leave or official duty. Bedroom, semi-private bath (23). Community kitchen, limited utensils, A/C, color TV, housekeeping service, ice vending. Older structures. TT0118, four suites with bedroom, private bath, and livingroom. Rates: $15 per person; suites $30 per person. TDY can make reservations, others Space-A.

TML: VOQ/VEQ. Cottages, five each, all ranks, leave or official duty. Bedroom, private bath (2); 2-bedroom, private bath (2); 3-bedroom, private bath (1). Kitchen, complete utensils, A/C, color TV, housekeeping service. Older structures. Rates: $30 per person, $40 per couple. TDY can make reservations, others Space-A.

TML: DV/VIP. Recreation Bldgs SS-0252-0254, PO-0290, officer O6+, C-804-633-8367. Separate bedrooms, private bath (2); 2-bedroom, private bath (2); 3-bedroom, private bath (1). Kitchen, complete utensils, A/C, color TV, housekeeping service. Rates: $20 per person, family rates available. TDY can make reservations, others Space-A.

Temporary Military Lodging Around the World - 233

VIRGINIA
Fort A.P. Hill, continued

TML: Recreation Lodge. Bldg SS-0251, all ranks, leave or official duty, C-804-633-8219. Nine-bedroom, (sleeps 18) semi-private bath (1). Kitchen, complete utensils, freezer, ice vending, color TV, two woodburning fireplaces, lounge chairs. Rates: $150 per day for groups of six (minimum) or $25 per person. All categories can make reservations.

TML: Recreation Cabins. Bldgs PO-0292/93/94, all ranks, report to Bldg TT-0106, C-804-633-8219. Check out 1100 hours. Three-bedroom, private bath (3). Kitchen, complete utensils, A/C, color TV, washer/dryer. Modern structures. Rates: $25 per person, family rates available. Maximum six per family. All categories can make reservations.

DV/VIP: Commander's Office, Bldg TT-0101, C-804-633-8205. O6+.

TML Availability: Good, Oct-Mar. Difficult, other times.

CREDIT CARDS ACCEPTED: Visa, MasterCard and American Express.

This is a <u>very</u> rustic area with good hunting and fishing in season. Dolly's House is named for Kitty "Dolly" Hill, wife of Gen. A.P. Hill, for whom the Fort is named. Support facilities: snack bar, exchange and theater on base. Limited facilities off base. Good variety in Fredericksburg, 30 minutes northeast.

Locator 633-8324   **Medical** 833-8216   **Police** 633-8239

Fort Belvoir (VA12R1)
Transient Billeting Branch
9775 Gaillard Road, Suite 144
Fort Belvoir, VA 22060-5905

TELEPHONE NUMBER INFORMATION: Main installation numbers: C-540-545-6700, D-312-227-0101.

Location: From I-95 S or US-1 S take Fort Belvoir exits. Clearly marked. *USMRA: Page 47 (L,M-5); Page 55 (B,C-8).* NMC: Washington, DC, 10 miles northeast.

Lodging Office: Bldg 470, 9775 Gaillard Road. **C-800-295-9750 or 703-805-2333, D-312-655-2333,** Fax: C-703-805-3566, D-312-655-3566, 24 hours. Billeting Manager, C-703-805-2005. Check in 1700 hours, check out 1200 hours daily. Government civilian employee billeting VOQ.

TML: VOQ/VEQ. Various buildings, officers all ranks, leave or official duty. Bedroom, private bath (VOQ) (321); bedroom, semi-private bath (VOQ) (122); separate bedroom, private bath (VOQ)(50); 2-bedroom, private bath (VEQ) (13); double rooms for E1-E6, shared bath (VEQ) (8); single rooms for E7-E9, private bath (VEQ) (8). Color TV, housekeeping service, telephones, microwave/refrigerator, utensils, washer/dryer, cribs/rollaways. Meeting/conference room available (seats 12, overhead projector, podium, TV/VCR). Modern structure. Rates: standard room, sponsor $34, two room suite, $40; spouse $5, child $3, maximum $48 per family. TDY and PCS can make reservations. No pets.

DV/VIP: C-703-805-2640. Bldgs 20 (O'Club), 470, officers O6+, leave or official duty. Separate bedroom suites, private bath (4); (470) bedroom, double bed, private bath (7). Kitchen, complete utensils, A/C, color TV, housekeeping service, cribs/cots, ice vending. Meeting/conference room

VIRGINIA
Fort Belvoir, continued

available (seats 12, overhead projector, podium, TV/VCR). Modern structure, renovated 1997. Rates: sponsor $43.50, spouse $5, child $3, maximum $51.50 per family. Duty can make reservations. No pets.

TML Availability: Good, Dec. Difficult, May-Sep.

CREDIT CARDS ACCEPTED: Visa, MasterCard and American Express.

Transportation: On base shuttle/bus 1-800-295-9750, 1600-2210 hours Mon, Wed, Fri, car rental agency 1-800-FOR-CARS.

Exit Walker Gate to see George Washington's Mill, and visit nearby Mount Vernon, Woodlawn Plantation, and Gunston Hall. See the Smithsonian Museums and Capitol Hill in downtown Washington, DC; northern Virginia is rich in colonial and Civil War history.

Locator 805-2043   Medical 805-1106   Police 805-1104

Fort Eustis (VA10R1)
P.O. Box 4278
Fort Eustis, VA 23604-5200

TELEPHONE NUMBER INFORMATION: Main installation numbers: C-757-878-1110, 312-927-1110.

Location: From I-64, exit 60A to VA-105, west to fort. *USMRA: Page 47 (N-9); Page 52 (B,C-2,3).* NMC: Newport News, 13 miles southwest.

Lodging Office: 2110 Pershing Ave. **C-757-878-5807, D-312-927-5807,** Fax: C-757-878-3251, D-312-927-3251, 24 hours. Check in 1600 hours, check out 1100 hours daily. Government civilian employee billeting.

TML: VOQ/VEQ/DVQ/TLQ. Bldg 2110, all ranks, leave or official duty. Suites (29) and four cottages for transient persons; VOQ: bedrooms (236); VEQ: bedrooms (302); DVQ suites (9). Refrigerator, community kitchen, kitchen (cottages and DVQ only), A/C, essentials, color TV in room and lounge, housekeeping service, cribs/cots, washer/ dryer, snack vending, ice vending, handicap accessible. Rates: DVQ $34, each additional person $7; VOQ $28-$30; VOQ/VEQ $28, each additional person $7; VEQ $28 $30; cottages $ 28-$34, each additional person $7. Priority for VOQ: officers attending Transportation Office Basic Course. Priority for VEQ: enlisted personnel attending Advanced Non-commissioned Officer Course and Basic Non-commissioned Officer Course. Duty can make reservations, others Space-A. Space-A check in 1800 hours. Pets allowed in cottages, $5 per day.

DV/VIP: Protocol Office. Bldg 210, Room 207, C-757-878-6010/30. O6+. Retirees and lower ranks Space-A.

TML Availability: Good. Best, Oct-May.

CREDIT CARDS ACCEPTED: Visa, MasterCard and American Express.

Temporary Military Lodging Around the World - 235

VIRGINIA
Fort Eustis, continued

Visit Busch Gardens, the Army Transportation Museum, tour historic Yorktown Battlefield, and Colonial Williamsburg for a crash course in United States' early history.

Locator 878-5215   Medical 878-7765   Police 878-4555

Fort Lee (VA15R1)
Fort Lee Lodging Operation
P.O. Box 5019
Fort Lee, VA 23801-1515

TELEPHONE NUMBER INFORMATION: Main installation numbers: C-804-734-1011, D-312-765-3000.

Location: From I-95 take Fort Lee/Hopewell exit, and follow VA-36 to main gate. *USMRA: Page 47 (L-8).* NMC: Petersburg, three miles west.

Lodging Office: Bldg P-8025, Mahone Ave. **C-1-800-403-8533 or 804-733-4100, D-312-687-6698/6694,** Fax: C-804-765-3585, 24 hours daily. Check in lodging 1530-2300, check out 1200 Mon-Sat, 1000 Sun and holidays.

TML: Guest House. Bldg 9056, all ranks, leave or official duty. Bedroom, two beds, sofa bed, living room, private bath (40). Refrigerator, A/C, color TV, iron/ironing board, coffee, housekeeping service, cribs/cots, washer/dryer, ice vending. Meeting/conference room and fax/photocopy service available. Modern structure. Rates: sponsor $25-$38, second person $5. Maximum two per room. Duty can make reservations, others Space-A. Note: primarily for TDY personnel. No pets.

TML: VOQ/VEQ. Bldgs P-8025/26, P-9001, P-9051-55, P-4229, officers all ranks, E4-E9, leave or official duty. Bedroom, private bath (482). Kitchen, A/C, color TV, iron/ironing board, coffee, housekeeping service, washer/dryer, ice vending, handicap accessible (2). Meeting/conference room and fax/photocopy service available. Modern structures. Rates: sponsor $25-$30, second person $5. Maximum two per room. Duty can make reservations, others Space-A. Note: primarily for TDY personnel. No pets.

TML: DVQ. Bldg P-9052, officers O4+, enlisted E7+. Official duty only. Bedroom, private bath (16). Kitchen, A/C, color TV, iron/ironing board, coffee, housekeeper service, washer/dryer, ice vending. Meeting/conference room and fax/photocopy service available. Modern structure. Rate: $30, second person $5. Maximum two per room. Duty can make reservations, others Space-A. Note: primarily for TDY personnel. No pets.

TML: DV/VIP. Davis House, Bldg P-8042, officers O6+, enlisted E9. Official duty only. Two-story, 4-bedroom house (1), living room, dining room, kitchen, complete utensils, microwave, seating room, two private bathrooms, A/C, color TV, housekeeping service, handicap accessible. Meeting/conference room and fax/photocopy service available. Modern structure. Rates: sponsor $30, second person $5. Maximum two per room. Duty can make reservations, others Space-A. Note: primarily for TDY personnel. No pets.

DV/VIP: Protocol Office, Bldg P-105000, room 221, C-804-734-1773, D-312-687-1773. O6/GM-15+. Retirees and lower ranks Space-A. No pets.

TML Availability: Best, Dec and weekends and holidays. Difficult, Jan-Nov.

236 - Temporary Military Lodging Around the World

VIRGINIA
Fort Lee, continued

CREDIT CARDS ACCEPTED: Visa, MasterCard and American Express.

Visit the Quartermaster Museum, and Battlefield Park, which is rich in Civil War history. Wonderful bass and crappie fishing is on the Chickahominy River. Virginia Beach swimming, fishing and boating is 85 miles east.

Locator 734-6855   Medical 734-9000   Police 765-6869

Fort Monroe (VA13R1)
ATTN: ATZG-WH
Bldg 80, Armistead Hall
Fort Monroe, VA 23651-6000

TELEPHONE NUMBER INFORMATION: Main installation numbers: C-757-727-2111, D-312-680-2111.

Location: From I-64 exit Hampton and follow tour signs through Phoebus to Fort Monroe. *USMRA: Page 47 (N-9); Page 52 (F-4)*. NMC: Hampton, one mile southeast.

Lodging Office: Bldg 80, Armistad Hall. **C-757-727-2128, D-312-680-2128,** 0800-1645 hours Mon-Fri. Check in billeting 1400 hours, check out 1000 hours. No government civilian employee billeting.

TML: VQ. Bldgs 61, 80, 136, 137, all ranks, leave or official duty. Two-bedroom suites, private bath (2); bedroom suites, private bath, kitchen with utensils, A/C, color TV, housekeeping service, cribs/cots, washer/dryer. Older Victorian, renovated. Rates: single $30, maximum $37.50 per family. All categories can make reservations.

TML: DVQ. Bldg 147, 80, officer O6+, leave or official duty, C-757-727-3596, D-680-3596. Check in 1400 hours, check out 1000 hours daily. Two-bedroom suites, private bath (4). Kitchen, complete utensils, A/C, color TV, housekeeping service, washer/dryer. Older Victorian, remodeled. Rates: $37.50, maximum $45 per family. All categories can make reservations, others Space-A.

DVQ: ATTN: Billeting Office, Bldg 80, C-757-727-3596/2128. O6+.

TML Availability: Fairly good, Oct-Apr. Difficult, May-Sep.

CREDIT CARDS ACCEPTED: American Express (Government) for TDY personnel only.

A National Historic Landmark, touring Fort Monroe is a US history lesson. Historic Hampton is also nearby, as well as Williamsburg. This area is a treasure trove for history buffs.

Locator 727-3175   Medical 727-2840   Police 727-2238

Temporary Military Lodging Around the World - 237

VIRGINIA

Fort Myer (VA24R1)
318 Jackson Ave, Bldg 50
Fort Myer, VA 22211-5050

DoD Conference Center

TELEPHONE NUMBER INFORMATION: Main installation numbers: C-703-545-6700, D-312-227-0101.

Location: Adjacent to Arlington National Cemetery. Take Fort Myer exit from Washington Blvd, at 2nd Street, or enter From US-50 (Arlington Blvd) first gate. Also, exit from Boundary Drive to 12th Street north entrance near the Iwo Jima Memorial. *USMRA: Page 54 (E-5)*. NMC: Washington, DC, six miles northeast.

Lodging Office: Bldg 50, Johnson Lane. **C-703-696-3576/77, D-312-226-3576/77**, Fax: C-703-696-3490, 0600-2200 hours Mon-Sun, 0800-1600 hours Sat. Check in 1400 hours, check out 1200 hours daily. Late checkout 697-7051. Government civilian employee billeting. No pets. **This facility is in charge of Fort Lesley J. McNair billeting in Washington, D.C.**

TML: BOQ, Bldg 48, apartment style, kitchenette, private bath. Color TV, A/C, living room, cribs/rollaway, washer/dryer and soda/snack vending machines. Meeting/conference rooms available. Rates: sponsor $30, each additional person $5, child/infant up to 10 free.

TML: DV/VIP. Wainwright Hall, Bldg 50, officers O7+, leave or official duty. Bedroom suites, living room, private bath (18). Refrigerator, bar, A/C, color TV in room and lounge, telephone, housekeeping service. Older structure, remodeled. Rates: sponsor $50, each additional person $5, child/infant up to 10 free. Maximum three per unit. Duty, Reserve and National Guard can make reservations (through DA Protocol), others Space-A. Space-A O4+ after 1700 hours.

DV/VIP: Write to: DA Protocol, Pentagon, Bldg 50, C-703-697-7051, D-312-227-7051, O7+. Retirees and lower ranks Space-A.

TML Availability: Very Good. Difficult Apr-Nov.

CREDIT CARDS ACCEPTED: Visa, MasterCard and American Express.

Transportation: On base shuttle/bus 696-8848, off base taxi 522-2222, car rental agency 524-1863.

Tour Arlington National Cemetery for a fascinating look at military history and traditions. Don't miss the stables of ceremonial horses used in military funerals, the Old Guard Museum. Fort Myer is home to the US Army Band.

Locator 545-6700   **Medical 696-3628**   **Police 696-3525**

Fort Pickett (VA16R1)
ATTN: AFRC-FMP-PW-H
Blackstone, VA 23824-5000
Scheduled to close September 1997.

TELEPHONE NUMBER INFORMATION: Main installation numbers: C-804-292-8621, D-312-438-8621.

VIRGINIA
Fort Pickett, continued

Location: On US-460, one mile from Blackstone. Clearly marked. *USMRA: Page 47 (K-9)*. NMC: Richmond, 60 miles northeast.

Lodging Office: Bldg T-469, Military Road. **C-804-292-2443,** 0730-1600 hours duty days. Other hours, PMO, Bldg T-471. **C-804-292-8444, D-312-438-8444,** Fax: C-804-292-8617, D-312-438-8617. Check in billeting, check out 1000 hours daily. Government civilian employee billeting. Note: confirm all reservations by phone at least 24 hours in advance.

TML: VOQ. Cottages, officers all ranks, E6-E9, leave or official duty. Bedroom, two beds private bath (13). Kitchen, complete utensils, A/C, color TV, housekeeping service, cribs/cots $2 per extra person. Older structures. Rates: $7 per unit. Maximum four per unit. Duty can make reservations, others Space-A. Pets allowed outside.

TML: VOQ. Officers all ranks, leave or official duty. Bedroom, common bath (28); Bedroom suites, two beds, private bath (4). Community kitchen, complete utensils, A/C, color TV in lounge, housekeeping service, cribs, cots $2 per extra person, washer/dryer. Older structures. Rates: $4-$7 per adult. Maximum four per unit. Duty can make reservations, others Space-A. Pets allowed outside.

TML: VEQ. Enlisted all ranks, leave or official duty. Bedroom, common bath (28); Bedroom suites, two beds, private bath (4). Community kitchen, complete utensils, A/C, color TV in lounge, housekeeping service, cribs/cots ($2 extra), washer/dryer. Older structure. Rates: $4-$7 per adult. Maximum four per unit. Duty can make reservations, others Space-A. Pets allowed outside.

TML Availability: Good, Sep-Mar. Difficult, other times.

CREDIT CARDS ACCEPTED: Visa, MasterCard, American Express, Diners Club and Discover.

Some of the best hunting and fishing in the state of Virginia. Charlottesville, Richmond, Williamsburg, the James River Plantations and Washington, DC are within easy reach of this facility.

Locator 292-2266   **Medical** 292-2528   **Police** 292-8444

Fort Story (VA08R1)
Billeting Office
Bldg 727, Atlantic Ave
Fort Story, VA 23459-5010

TELEPHONE NUMBER INFORMATION: Main installation numbers: C-757-422-7305, D-312-438-7305.

Location: From Interstate 64 take exit 79, Northampton Blvd (US-13) for 4.3 miles, take Shore Drive (Route 60) exit. (Sign = East-West Shore Drive, Beaches). Turn right to Shore Drive and after five miles turn left to West Gate, Fort Story (Route 305 North) just after the entrance to Seashore State Park). *USMRA: Page 47 (O-9); Page 52 (I,J-5,6)*. NMC: Virginia Beach, seven miles south.

Lodging Office: Bldg 727, Atlantic. **C-757-422-7322, D-312-927-9321,** 0730-1530 hours Mon-Fri. Check in billeting 1400 hours, check out 1000 hours daily. Government civilian employee billeting.

VIRGINIA
Fort Story, continued

TML: TLQ. Bldgs 526, all ranks, leave or official duty. Bedroom, private bath (1); two separate bedrooms, private bath. Kitchen, refrigerator, community kitchen, limited utensils, A/C, color TV in room and lounge, housekeeping service, essentials, cribs/cots, washer/dryer, handicap accessible (1). Older structures, redecorated. Rates: sponsor $28, each additional person $7. Duty can make reservations, others Space-A.

TML: Cape Henry Inn. Bldg 1116, C-757-422-8818, Fax: C-757-422-6397. **Sandpiper:** Bedroom (10), two full beds, refrigerator, sleeps four. Rates: $29-$45. **Dune:** Bedroom (30), two full beds, separate sitting area with pull-out couch, kitchenette, sleeps six. Rates: $39-$55. **Pelican:** Bedroom (10), queen-sized bed, kitchenette, sleeps two, handicap accessible. **Chesapeake:** Two-bedroom (12), living room with pull-out couch, kitchen, sleeps six. Rates: $60-$70. **Tidewater:** Three-bedroom (6), living room with pull-out couch, kitchen, sleeps eight, one unit is handicap accessible. Rates: $60-$70. Bungalow: Two-bedroom (8), living room with pull-out couch, kitchen. See *Military Living's Military RV, Camping and Rec Areas Around the World* for additional information and directions.

TML: DV/VIP. Cottages for O4, E9 and W4+, Memorial Day-Labor Day. Contact office of the Commanding General, USATCFE, Fort Eustis, VA 23604-5000, C-757-878-4804, D-312-927-4804. Requests for reservations accepted first working day in January. O3 and below C-757-422-7028, D-312-438-7028, first working day of the month for the following month, beginning 0730 hours; during the off-season, day after Labor Day through Thursday before Memorial Day weekend. Summer reservations, Memorial Day weekend through Labor Day, are reserved by "lottery." Cottages are 2-bedroom (12) and 3-bedroom (6). All have kitchens, stove, refrigerator, A/C/heat, CATV, housekeeping service, cribs (upon request), on-post telephone, BBQ and picnic tables available. Sponsor or spouse must accompany group. Inventories taken. Reservations held to 2000 hours. No shows (failure to cancel) counts against future reservations. One reservation per service member, summer season. One reservation per service member per month for winter season. Rates: DVQ, sponsor $34 per day, each additional person $7 (12+); $5 per pet, two pet limit. Leave only, all categories can make reservations. Cottages on Chesapeake Bay/Atlantic Ocean. Swimming, Recreation Center, Gym, Bowling, Fishing/equipment available, golf.

TML: Cape Henry Travel Camp. C-757-422-7601, D-312-438-7601. Log Cabins (13); Kamping Kabins (3), one 12x12 room, sleeps four. Rates: $30-$55 daily. See *Military Living's Military RV, Camping and Rec Areas Around the World* for additional information and directions.

DV/VIP: Handled by Fort Story/Fort Eustis as indicated above, C-757-878-5206.

TML Availability: Good, Oct-Mar. Difficult, other times.

CREDIT CARDS ACCEPTED: Visa, MasterCard and American Express.

See the Old Cape Henry Lighthouse, Douglas MacArthur Memorial, Virginia Beach Science Museum, Williamsburg Pottery Factory. Busch Gardens, Ocean Breeze Park and Norfolk Naval Base nearby.

Locator 422-7682   **Medical 422-7802**   **Police 422-7141**

240 - Temporary Military Lodging Around the World

VIRGINIA

Judge Advocate General's School (VA01R1)
ATTN: SSL-H
600 Massie Road
Charlottesville, VA 22903-1781

TELEPHONE NUMBER INFORMATION: Main installation numbers: C-804-972-6300, D-312-934-7115 ext 450.

Location: On the North grounds of the University of Virginia in Charlottesville. Take the 250 bypass off I-64 to the Barracks Road exit, turn right at light onto Millmont, right onto Arlington Blvd, then right at the top of the hill to the school. *USMRA: Page 47 (J-7).* NMC: Charlottesville, in city limits.

Lodging Office: 600 Massie Road. **C-804-972-6450**, Fax: C-804-972-6328, 0750-1650 hours Mon-Fri, Room 156 in TJAGSA, adjacent to Hall of Flags. Other hours, SDO front desk. Check in 1500 hours, check out 1200 hours. Government civilian employee billeting only on orders to TJAGS. E-mail: giddinno@otjag.army.mil.

TML: BOQ/BEQ. All ranks, leave or official duty. Handicap accessible. Bedroom, one bed, private bath (72). A/C, community kitchen, cots ($2), ice vending, housekeeping service, refrigerator, color TV, washer/dryer, soda vending. Meeting/conference rooms and exercise room available. Modern structure. Rates: TDY, sponsor $8, family members $5; AD on leave and retirees $20, family members $5. Most space reserved for TJAGS students.

DV/VIP: ATTN: JAGS-ZA, C-804-972-6301. O6+. Retirees and leave Space-A. Rates: TDY, sponsor $10, family members $5; retirees $25, family members $5.

TML Availability: Very limited, last two weeks in Dec. Difficult, other times.

CREDIT CARDS ACCEPTED: American Express.

Transportation: Off base taxi 295-4131, car rental agency 973-3336, Hertz 973-6040.

Visit historic Monticello, Ash Lawn and the Michie Tavern. For outdoor activities, try Wintergreen, Shenandoah National Park, Barboursville Vineyard, Montfair Camp Grounds, Lake Albemarle.

Locator 972-6400   **Medical 924-2231**   **Police 911**

Langley Air Force Base (VA07R1)
Langley Inns
1 SVS/SVML
66 Nealy Ave
Langley AFB, VA 23665-5528

TELEPHONE NUMBER INFORMATION: Main installation numbers: C-757-764-9990, D-312-574-9990.

Location: From I-64 E in Hampton take Armistead Ave exit, go right to stop light; right onto La Salle Ave and enter AFB. *USMRA: Page 47 (N-9); Page 52 (E-3).* NMC: Hampton, one mile west.

VIRGINIA
Langley Air Force Base, continued

Lodging Office: 66 Nealy Ave. **C-757-764-4667, D-312-574-4667,** Fax: C-757-764-3038, D-312-574-3038, 24 hours. Check in 1500 hours, check out 1200 hours daily. Government civilian employee billeting.

TML: TLQ. North and South, all ranks, leave or official duty. Separate bedrooms, private bath (39). Kitchen, utensils, A/C, color TV, housekeeping service, cribs/cots, washer/dryer, ice vending. Sleeps five. Modern structures, renovated. Rates: PCS, AB, AMN, 2 Lt $15.50 per unit, all others $24. Duty can make reservations, others Space-A.

TML: VOQ. Bldgs 14, 16, officers, leave or official duty. Bedroom, private bath (78). Kitchen, A/C, color TV, housekeeping service, cots, washer/dryer, ice vending. Modern structures. Rates: $10 per person. Duty can make reservations, others Space-A.

TML: VAQ. Bldg 66, 45 enlisted all ranks, leave or official duty. Bedroom, 1- and 2-bed units, common bath (92); separate bedrooms, private bath for SNCOs (5). Refrigerator, A/C, color TV, housekeeping service, washer/dryer, ice vending. Modern structure, renovated. Rates: $10 per person, maximum two per room; SNCO suites $16 per person, $23 per couple. Duty can make reservations, others Space-A.

TML: VAQ. Boots Hall, Bldg 45, enlisted, E4+ leave or official duty. Bedroom, shared bath (123). Refrigerator, A/C, color TV, housekeeping service, washer/dryer, ice vending. Modern structure. Renovated. Rates: $10 per person, maximum one per room. Duty can make reservations, all others Space-A.

TML: DV/VIP. Bldgs 132 (Lawson Hall), 141 (Dodd Hall), officers O6+/GS-15+, leave or official duty. Lawson: separate bedroom suites, private bath (11). Dodd: separate bedroom suites, private bath (10). Kitchen, limited utensils, A/C, color TV, housekeeping service, cribs/cots, washer/dryer, ice vending. Older structures, renovated. Rates: $16 per person, $23 per couple; Super Suites $27 per person, $39.50 per couple. Duty can make reservations, others Space-A.

DV/VIP: Protocol Office, Bldg 205, C-757-764-5044. O6+. Retirees and lower ranks Space-A.

TML Availability: Good, winter. Difficult, summer.

CREDIT CARDS ACCEPTED: Visa, MasterCard and American Express.

Historic Colonial Williamsburg, Busch Gardens, beautiful Virginia beach, and the Mariner's Museum are all close by and worth a visit.

Locator 764-5615   Medical 764-6833   Police 764-5092

Little Creek Naval Amphibious Base (VA19R1)
Combined Bachelor Quarters
Norfolk, VA 23521-2698

TELEPHONE NUMBER INFORMATION: Main installation numbers: C-757-444-0000, D-312-564-0111.

Location: From I-64 S through Hampton Roads Bridge Tunnel take Northampton Blvd exit, five miles to base, exit VA-225. From Chesapeake Bay Bridge Tunnel proceed west on US-60 to base. *USMRA: Page 47 (N,O-9); Page 52 (G,H-5,6).* NMC: Norfolk, 11 miles southwest.

VIRGINIA
Little Creek Naval Amphibious Base, continued

Lodging Office: Officers: Drexler Manor, Bldg 3408, 1120 A Street. **C-757-464-7522**, Fax: C-757-464-8635, D-312-680-8635. Enlisted: Shields Hall, Bldg 3601, 1350 Gator Blvd. **C-757-464-7577**, Fax: C-757-464-7149, D-312-680-7149. Check in facility, check out 1330. Government civilian employee billeting.

NAVY LODGE

TML: Navy Lodge. Bldg 3531, all ranks, leave or official duty. Reservations: **1-800-NAVY-INN.** Lodge number is C-757-464-6215, Fax: C-757-464-1194. Check in prior to 1800 hours to avoid cancellation. Check out 1200 hours daily. Bedroom, two beds, private bath (72); queen bed and sofa bed, private bath (18). Kitchen, complete utensils, A/C, color CATV/VCP, housekeeping service, coin washer/dryer, ice vending. Handicap accessible rooms. Conference rooms can be reserved (2). Modern structure, renovated. Rates: $44 per night (Sep-May), $43 (May-Sep). All categories can make reservations. No pets except birds in cages, fish in tanks.

TML: BOQ. Drexler Manor, Bldg 3408, 1120 A Street, NAB Little Creek, Norfolk, VA 23521-2230. Officers all ranks, leave or official duty, C-757-464-7522. Check out 1330 hours daily. Bedroom, private bath (230); separate bedroom suites, private bath (14). Microwaves, A/C, CATV, housekeeping service, washer/dryer, ice vending. Modern structure, renovated. Rates: $15 per person; suites $25. Duty on orders can make reservations, others, one day basis, Space-A.

TML: BEQ. Shields Hall, Bldg 3601, 1350 Gator Blvd, NAB, Little Creek, Norfolk, VA 23521-2698. Enlisted all ranks, on official duty, C-757-464-1183, D-312-680-7577. Check out 1330 hours daily.; bedroom, two beds, private bath (140); single rooms, private bath (E5-E9) (195). Micro-frig, A/C, CATV, housekeeping service, washer/dryer, ice vending. Modern structure, renovated. Rates: E1-E9 $8 per person; VIP $20. Dependents not authorized. Duty can make reservations 90 days advance, others Space-A.

TML: DV/VIP. Bldg 3186, officer O6+, leave or official duty, C-757-444-5901, D-312-564-5901. Check out 1200 hours daily. Separate bedroom suites, private bath (4). Queen beds, refrigerator, community kitchen, limited utensils, A/C, CATV, housekeeping service, cots, ice vending. Older structure, remodeled. Rates: AD, $35 per person.

DV/VIP: SURFLANT-planetarium. C-757-322-3007. O6+. Retirees Space-A.

TML Availability: Good, Oct-Dec. Difficult, Jun-Aug.

CREDIT CARDS ACCEPTED: Visa, MasterCard and American Express. The Navy Lodge accepts Visa, MasterCard, American Express and Discover.

Winner of the 1996 Elmo R. Zumwalt Award for Excellence in Housing. History is all around Little Creek, with Jamestown and Williamsburg one hour north. Nearby beautiful Virginia beaches beckon, and check out Norfolk.

Locator 444-0000   Medical 363-4444   Police 363-4444

VIRGINIA

Norfolk Naval Base (VA18R1)
Billeting Code N46
Norfolk, VA 23511-2995

TELEPHONE NUMBER INFORMATION: Main installation numbers: C-757-396-3000, D-312-964-3000.

Location: From north or south I-64, take naval base exit, follow signs. *USMRA: Page 52 (F-5,6).* NMC: Norfolk, in city limits.

Lodging Office: BEH: Billeting Code N46, Bldg I-A, Pocahontas and Bacon Streets. **C-757-444-2839,** Fax:-757-444-0797, 0730-1530 hours daily. Other hours, Central Assignments, Bldg R-63, C-757-444-4425. BOH: BOH Billeting Fund, Bldg A128, Powhattan Street off Maryland Avenue, C-757-402-4444, Fax 757-445-9888, 24 hours. Check in anytime daily, check out 1200 hours daily. Government civilian employee billeting. Reservations (BEH) C-757-444-4425, (BOH) C-757-404-4444.

TML: Navy Lodge. Bldg SDA-314 (take I-64 to 564 exit to Terminal Blvd., right on Hampton Blvd. Lodge on left), all ranks, leave or official duty. Reservations: **1-800-NAVY-INN.** Lodge number is C-757-489-2656, Fax: C-757-489-9621 (for large groups only!), 24 hours. Check in 1500-1800 hours, check out 1200 hours. Bedroom, two double beds, private bath (156, four handicap accessible); bedroom, two queen beds, private bath (64); bedroom, queen bed (24); bedroom double bed (40). Kitchenette, microwave, utensils, A/C, CATV, clocks, coffeepot, housekeeping service, cribs, phones, fax service, hair dryers, high chairs, snack vending, ice vending, mini-mart, picnic area, playground, coin washer/dryer. Smoking or non-smoking rooms available. Modern structure. Rates: $46 per unit. All categories can make reservations. **This is the largest Navy Lodge in the world with 294 rooms!**

TML: BOH. Bldgs A125, A128, officers all ranks, leave or official duty. Bedroom, private bath (274); separate bedrooms, kitchen, private bath (3). Refrigerator, microwave, A/C, CATV in room and lounge, housekeeping service, washer/dryer, ice vending, sauna/exercise room, jacuzzi, sun deck. Modern structures. Rates: $12 per unit, each additional person $3. Duty can make reservations, others Space-A.

TML: BEH. Bldgs R63, (NAVSTA), U-16 (NAS), enlisted all ranks (no E7+ at NAS), leave or official duty. NAVSTA C-757-444-4425, NAS C-757-444-4983. Bedroom, hall bath (NAVSTA)(125); five buildings, hall bath (NAS). Check out NAVSTA 1200 hours daily, NAS 1000 hours daily. Both: Refrigerator, A/C, color TV room, housekeeping service, washer/ dryer, ice vending. Modern structures. Rates: $6 per person. Duty can make reservations, others Space-A.

DV/VIP: Naval Station, C-757-402-4401. CINCLANTFLT **Camp Elmore,** C-757-444-6323. O7+. Retirees Space-A. Suites used for O6+ with BOH manager's permission (4). Rates: VIP suites $27; single $22.

TML Availability: Good, fall and winter. Difficult, other times.

CREDIT CARDS ACCEPTED: Visa, MasterCard and American Express. The Navy Lodge accepts Visa, MasterCard, American Express and Discover.

VIRGINIA
Norfolk Naval Base, continued

Winner of the 1996 Elmo R. Zumwalt Award for Excellence in Housing. This is the largest naval base in the world. There is an interesting tour given daily. If you can see a ship launching, do so! Also, visit Hampton Roads Naval Museum, and the MacArthur Memorial. Nearby are Williamsburg, Yorktown and Jamestown.

Locator 444-0000   Medical 677-6291   Police 444-2324

Norfolk Naval Shipyard (VA26R1)
Combined Bachelor's Quarters
Bldg 1504A, Code 834
Portsmouth, VA 23709-5000

TELEPHONE NUMBER INFORMATION: Main installation numbers: C-757-396-3000, D-312-961-3000.

Location: Take I-64 to I-264 through the tunnel. First exit turn left on Effington Street. Follow signs to shipyard. *USMRA: Page 52 (F-7)*. NMC: Virginia Beach, 15 miles northeast.

Lodging Office: Bldg 1504A. **C-757-396-4449, D-312-961-4449**, Fax: C-757-396-4968. Check in at the facility, 24 hours, check out 1200 hours. Late checkout C-757-396-4562. Government civilian employee billeting.

TML: BEQ. **Seamarks Inn**. Bldgs 1531, 1503 enlisted (E1-E9), 1439 (ships in overhaul, official duty only), all ranks, leave or official duty. Reservations accepted. Check out 1200 hours daily. Rooms, semi-private bath (200); rooms, private bath (158); rooms for official ship overhaul duty only (Bldg 1439)(242). Essentials, snack vending, refrigerator, microwave, housekeeping service, color TV in room and lounge, washer/dryer. Modern structure, remodeled 1994. Rates. May-Sep: transient $8.25; suite $12.75; guest $4. Oct-Apr: transient $6; suite $8.50; guest, $4. Family members not allowed to stay in facility. AD can make reservations, others Space-A. No pets. TAD personnel must make reservations through local SATO.

TML: The Cheaspeake Inn. Bldg 1530, C-757-398-8500, D-312-961-1030, all ranks, leave or official duty. Bedroom, private bath (78). Suites, VIP. Essentials, snack vending, kitchenette, utensils, no stove, color TV/VCR in room and lounge, housekeeping service, cots, washer/dryer. Rates. May-Sep: transient $9.2; suite $13.50; VIP $21.25. Oct-Apr: transient $12.50; suite $18.25; VIP $29; guest $4; guest VIP $5. Maximum three per unit. No pets. All categories can make reservations, AD, reserve and national guard on orders have priority, others Space-A. TAD personnel must make reservations through local SATO.

TML: DV/VIP. Code 800, Bldg 1500, Portsmouth Naval Shipyard, Portsmouth, VA 23709, C-757-396-8605, D-312-961-8605. Bldg 1530, O7+. Suites are retiree eligible.

TML: Fisher House. Note: Appendix B has the definition of this facility. (Portsmouth Naval Hospital) C-757-398-6889. There are two houses in Portsmouth. The second can be reached at C-757-399-5461.

TML Availability: Good. Best, Dec. Difficult, Sep.

CREDIT CARDS ACCEPTED: American Express.

Temporary Military Lodging Around the World - 245

VIRGINIA
Norfolk Naval Shipyard, continued

Virginia Beach's famed boardwalk and beaches will tempt summer visitors. See the Portsmouth Naval Shipyard museum, attend a play, dine on excellent seafood, or take in a ballgame at Harbor Park.

Locator 396-3000   **Medical 396-3268**   **Police 396-7266**

Oceana Naval Air Station (VA09R1)
Lodging Office
Bldg 460, G Street
Virginia Beach, VA 23460-5120

TELEPHONE NUMBER INFORMATION: Main installation numbers: C-757-444-0000, D-312-564-0111.

Location: From I-64 exit to Norfolk-Virginia Beach Expressway (VA-44 east), east on Virginia Beach Blvd. Bordered by Oceana Blvd (VA-615) and London Bridge Road. Also, bordered by Potters and Harper Roads. *USMRA: Page 47 (O-9); Page 52 (I,J-7).* NMC: Virginia Beach, in city limits.

Lodging Office: Bldg 460, G Street across from O'Club. **C-757-425-0500 ext 168/71/72, D-312-433-3293,** Fax: C-757-422-0173, 24 hours. Check in billeting, check out 1300 hours daily. Government civilian employee billeting.

TML: BOQ. Bldg 460, officer all ranks, leave or official duty. VIP suites (9); suites, private bath (88); bedroom, private bath (105). Essentials, snack vending, ice vending, housekeeping service, refrigerator, color TV/VCR in room and lounge, HBO, hair dryer, coffee pot, washer/dryer. Hotel type telephone systems. Meeting/conference room available. Golf, bowling, and gym on base; riding stables, beaches, exchange and commissary nearby. Rates: single $12; suite $15; VIP suite $22; VIP flag $25; dependents $3-$6. Reservations limited during summer months.

TML Availability: Good, winter. Difficult, summer.

CREDIT CARDS ACCEPTED: Visa, MasterCard and American Express.

Transportation: Off base taxi 486-6585, Airport Express 467-5756.

Great beaches at Virginia Beach.

Locator 491-4260   **Medical 433-2221/22**   **Police 433-9111**

Quantico Marine Corps Base (VA11R1)
Bachelor Housing Branch
15 Liversedge Drive
Quantico, VA 22134-5013

TELEPHONE NUMBER INFORMATION: Main installation numbers: C-703-784-2121, D-312-278-2121.

Location: From I-95 N or S take Quantico/Triangle exit 150A. US-1 N/S is adjacent to base. Clearly marked. *USMRA: Page 47 (L-5,6).* NMC: Washington, DC, 40 miles north.

VIRGINIA
Quantico Marine Corps Base, continued

Lodging Office: Bldg 15, Liversedge Hall (BOQ/SNCO). **C-703-784-3148, D-312-278-3148/9**, Fax: C-703-784-5940, 24 hours. Housing Office, 0800-1630 hours Mon-Fri, C-703-784-2711. Check in billeting, check out 1000 hours (1200 hours Hostess House). Government civilian employee billeting.

TML: Crossroads Inn. C-800-965-9511, 703-630-4444. Bedroom, private bath (78), two double beds, TV/VCR, refrigerator, microwave. Suites, private bath (18), two double beds, sleeper sofa, table with four chairs, TV/VCR (2), refrigerator, microwave, dishwasher, coffee maker, toaster, stove, wet bar. For both, washer/dryer, soda/snack vending, cribs, rollaway beds. Meeting/conference rooms available. Handicap accessible. Rates: rooms $40; suites $50. Reservations: PCS up to 60 days in advance, other Space-A. Maximum 30-day stay.

TML: BOQ. Bldg 15, Liversedge Hall, officers all ranks, official or non-official duty, C-703-748-3148/9, D-278-3148/9. Bedroom, semi-private bath (transient duty)(72); guest suites/visitor's suites, private bath (TAD/TDY) (18). Micro/fridge (six units), limited utensils, A/C, CATV, in room and lounge, housekeeping service, washer/dryer, ice vending. Older structure. Rates: TAD/TDY $14-$18; suites $20-$30. TAD/TDY Group reservations 90 days in advance. Names submitted 30 days prior to arrival. Non TAD/TDY 30 days in advance, others Space-A.

TML: SNCO Quarters. Bldg 3229, Shuck Hall, enlisted E6-E9, official duty (TAD/TDY) or non-official duty, C-703-748-3148/9. D-312-278-3148/9. Bedroom, semi-private bath (TAD/TDY) (22); separate bedroom suite, private bath, A/C, CATV, housekeeping service, washer/dryer. Older structure. Rates: room $8-$12; suites $18-$25. Duty on orders, may make reservations 30 days in advance, others Space-A.

DV/VIP. DGQ, Crossroads Cottage (Guest House), 3300 Russell Road, C-703-784-4477, D-312-278-4477. O7+. Rates: $23-$30. Duty on orders or leave, retirees, and dependents Space-A.

TML Availability: Good, Oct-Apr. Difficult, summer.

CREDIT CARDS ACCEPTED: Visa, MasterCard and American Express.

Located on the Potomac River, near Washington, DC. Woodbridge is the major shopping and recreation district close by, but the battlefield of Manassas, Occoquan (craft shops and marinas) is also near.

Locator 748-2141   **Medical 911**   **Police 911**

Wallops Island AEGIS Combat Systems Center (VA46R1)
Combined Bachelor Quarters
Wallops Island, VA 23337-5000

TELEPHONE NUMBER INFORMATION: Main installation numbers: C-757-824-2355. HP: http://www.navy.mil.

Location: From south: take Chesapeake Bay Bridge-Tunnel N. Stay on US Route 13 to Route 175 (a right at T's Corner) for five miles, a left at Route 798 (Ocean Deli). BQ facilities will be on the right. From north: take Route 13 S, five miles over MD/VA line to Route 175, same directions as above. *USMRA: Page 47 (P-7).* NMC: Salisbury, MD, 40 miles north.

VIRGINIA
Wallops Island AEGIS Combat Systems Center, continued

Lodging Office: Bldg R-20. **C-757-824-2064**, Fax: C-757-824-1764, 24 hours. Write to: CBQ, ACSC Wallops Island, VA 23337-5000. Check in billeting, check out 1100 hours. Late check out call OD C-804-824-2068. Government civilian employee billeting.

TML: BOQ. Osprey Manor Bldg Officers, all ranks, leave or official duty. Bedroom, private bath (16). Kitchenette, limited utensils, A/C, CATV in room and lounge, ice machine, housekeeping service, essentials, snack vending, cribs, rollaways, washer/dryer, award winning modern stick-built structure. Handicap accessible. All non-smoking rooms. Outdoor screened gazebo. Rates: $10, each additional person $3. Duty, Reserves and National Guard on orders, military widows can make reservations, others Space-A. No pets.

TML: BEQ. Eagles Nest Building, enlisted, all ranks, leave or official duty. Bedroom, private bath (25); bedroom, shared bath (30); suites, private bath (7) (E7+). Kitchenette, limited utensils (suites), essentials, snack vending, housekeeping service, refrigerator, microwave, cribs, rollaways, VCR, CATV in room and lounge, washer/dryer, training trailer (weights etc.). Recreation room, pool table, ping pong and large screen TV. Screened in deck. Modern structure. Handicap accessible. Some non-smoking rooms. Galley next door. Bicycles available for residents. Rates $7-$8, depending upon rank; each additional person $3.50. Duty, Reserves and National Guard on orders, military widows can make reservations, others Space-A. No pets.

TML Availability: Very Good. Best, Sep-Mar. Difficult, Apr-Aug.

CREDIT CARDS ACCEPTED: American Express.

Close to Chincoteague National Wildlife Refuge and Assateague National Seashore Park, where wild ponies are auctioned each May. A variety of outdoor activities abound - boating, crabbing. This is the Eastern Shore!

Locator 384-0306   Medical 552-5555   Police 384-0823

Yorktown Naval Weapons Station (VA14R1)
Nelson House
P.O. Box 32
Lackey, VA 23694-0032

TELEPHONE NUMBER INFORMATION: Main installation numbers: C-757-887-4545, D-312-953-4545.

Location: From I-64 exit to 249 W, .5 miles to gate 3, Skiffes Creek. *USMRA: Page 47 (N-8); Page 52 (B,C-1).* NMC: Newport News, 15 miles southeast.

Lodging Office: Nelson House, Bldg 704. **C-757-887-7621**, Fax: 887-7627, 24 hours. Check in facility, check out 1100 hours. Government civilian employee billeting if GS-7+ with advance reservations.

TML: BOQ. Bldg 704, officers all ranks, leave or official duty, C-757-887-7621. Bedroom, private bath, suite (DV/VIP) (2); separate bedroom suites, private bath (10). Community kitchen, A/C, color CATV in room and lounge, housekeeping service, cots, washer/dryer, ice vending, exercise room, micro-fridge. Modern structure. Rates: sponsor $23 maximum per family; VIP $25 maximum per family. Duty can make reservations, others Space-A.

248 - Temporary Military Lodging Around the World

VIRGINIA
Yorktown Naval Weapons Station, continued

DV/VIP: MWR Director, Bldg 2011, C-757-887-4234. O6+/GS-15+.

TML Availability: Good, winter. Limited, summer.

CREDIT CARDS ACCEPTED: Visa, MasterCard and American Express.

The Battlefield at Yorktown, restored Colonial Williamsburg, and the first permanent English settlement in America, are all within a 20 mile radius of the station. Also check out Busch Gardens and WIlliamsburg Pottery. Stop by the MWR Department for special tickets to events and parks.

Locator 887-4000   Medical 887-7404   Police 887-4676

Other Installations in Virginia

Yorktown Coast Guard Reserve Training Center. Main installation numbers: C-757-898-3500. Location: From I-64 exit to US-238E and follow to CG base entrance. *USMRA: Page 47 (N-8,9), Page 52 (D-1).* NMC: Newport News, 15 miles southeast. Lodging office: C-757-898-2378, D-312-827-2378, Fax C-757-890-0406, 24 hours daily. Check in Cain Hall, Bldg 235. TML: BOQ, all ranks, leave or official duty. Private bedroom, private bath (8), refrigerator, microwave, color TV. Rates: $13 per night. DV/VIP, Captain's Office, C-757-898-2212, D-312-827-2212. Reservations for PCS-TDY, others Space-A. No pets.

WASHINGTON

Bangor Naval Submarine Base (WA08R4)
Evergreen Lodge
Bldg 1101, Room 122
Bangor Submarine Base, WA 98315-5000

TELEPHONE NUMBER INFORMATION: Main installation numbers: C-360-396-1110, D-312-744-1110.

Location: From Bremerton, on WA-3, follow signs "Hood Canal," bypassing Bremerton and Silverdale. Follow SUBASE signs to main gate. *USMRA: Page 103 (A-1,2).* NMC: Bremerton, 12 miles south.

Billeting Office: Evergreen Lodge, Bldg 2750. **C-360-396-6581, D-312-744-6581**(BOQ); **C-360-396-4034/4035/4036, D-312-744-4035** (BEQ east and west). 24 hours, seven days a week. Check in facility, check out 1200 hours daily. Government civilian employee billeting.

NAVY LODGE TML: Navy Lodge. Bldg 2906, Trigger Ave., NSB Bangor, Silverdale, WA 98315. Reservations: **1-800-NAVY-INN.** Lodge number is C-360-779-9100, Fax: 360-779-9117. Check in 1500-1800 hours, check out 1200 hours. Bedroom, two queen beds, private bath (45); bedroom, one queen bed, sleeper sofa, private bath (5). Six sets interconnecting, two handicap accessible, 32 non-smoking. Kitchenette, microwave, utensils, A/C,

WASHINGTON
Bangor Naval Submarine Base, continued

CATV/VCP, coffee/tea, hair dryers, cribs, high chairs, soda/snack vending, ice vending, housekeeping service, phones, irons/ironing board, coin washer/dryer, playground, rollaways. Rates: $45. Maximum five per room. Seeing eye dogs, fish, caged birds OK. *Runner-up of the 1996 Edward E. Carlson Award for Navy Lodge excellence in the medium category.*

TML: BOQ. Evergreen Lodge, Bldg 2750, officers all ranks, leave or official duty. Bedroom, private bath, (66); suites, two with kitchen (VIP)(6). Micro refrigerator, color TV in room and lounge, cribs/cots, housekeeping service, washer/dryer, snack vending, ice vending, computer, jacuzzi. Modern structure. Rates: sponsor $16 adult, $4 child under 12; suites $12-$28, each additional person $4. PCS are confirmed, duty, reservists can make reservations, others Space-A.

TML: BEQ. Bldg 2200, enlisted all ranks, leave or official duty. Rooms undergoing renovation. When completed, all rooms will have 1-2 beds (depending on rank), private bath, refrigerator, microwave and TV (56). Housekeeping service, cribs/cots, washer/dryer, snack vending, ice vending. Modern structure. Rates: single $12; double $7; each additional person $3. Duty can make reservations, others Space-A.

TML: VIP Cottage. Bldg 4189, officer O6+, leave or official duty. Bedroom cottage, private bath (1). Kitchen, complete utensils, housekeeping service, cribs/cots, color TV. Renovated and remodeled. Rates: sponsor $28 adult, $5 child. Maximum four persons. Duty can make reservations, others Space-A.

DV/VIP: PAO, Bldg 1100, room 213, C-360-396-5514. O6+. Civilians determined by commander, retirees Space-A.

TML Availability: Fairly good. Best. Oct-Apr, Difficult, May-Sep.

CREDIT CARDS ACCEPTED: Visa, MasterCard and American Express. The Navy Lodge accepts Visa, MasterCard, American Express and Discover.

Transportation: Off base shuttle/bus 1-800-562-7948.

Visit Poulsbo, known as "Little Norway", and stroll the boardwalk along Liberty Bay. Try Bremerton's Naval Shipyard Museum (Ferry Terminal on First Street). For picnicking and boating visit Silverdale Waterfront Park.

Locator 396-6111   **Medical 396-4222**   **Police 396-4444**

Everett Naval Station (WA10R4)
2000 West Marine View Drive
Everett, WA 98207-5001

TELEPHONE NUMBER INFORMATION: Main installation numbers: C-206-304-3000, D-312-727-3000.

Location: From I-5 take exit 193, west on Pacific Avenue, turn right on Marine View Drive, base is on the left. *USMRA: Page 101 (D-3)*. NMC: Seattle, 25 miles south.

Lodging Office: BEQ C-206-304-3111/2, Fax: C-206-304-3119.

250 - Temporary Military Lodging Around the World

WASHINGTON
Everett Naval Station, continued

TML: BEQ. Rates: E4 and below $6; E5+ $10. Call for description of lodging and more information. **Winner of the 1996 Elmo R. Zumwalt Award for Excellence in Housing.**

TML: Navy Lodge. All ranks, leave or official duty. Reservations: **1-800-NAVY-INN**. Lodge number is C-360-653-6390, Fax C-360-659-2062. Two queen-sized beds, private bath (48); one double bed, sleeper sofa, private bath, handicap accessible (2). Interconnecting and non-smoking rooms available. Kitchenette with microwave, utensils, A/C, cable TV/VCPs, telephone, hair dryer, cribs/rollaways, iron/ironing board, snack vending, playground, laundry facility available.

Locator 304-3000   Medical 304-4062   Police 304-3262

Fairchild Air Force Base (WA02R4)
ATTN: 92 SVS/SVML
Bldg 2392, Short Street
Fairchild AFB, WA 99011-5000

TELEPHONE NUMBER INFORMATION: Main installation numbers: C-509-247-1212, D-312-657-1110.

Location: Take US-2 exit from I-90 west of Spokane. Follow US-2 through Airway Heights, after two miles left to base main gate and Visitors' Control Center. *USMRA: Page 101 (I-4)*. NMC: Spokane, 12 miles east.

Lodging Office: Bldg 2392, Short Street. **C-509-247-5519**, Fax-509-247-2307, 24 hours. Reservations: C-509-244-2290 ext 2120. Check in lodging, check out 1200 hours daily. Government civilian employee lodging official duty only.

TML: VOQ. Bldgs 2392, all ranks, leave or official duty. Bedroom, shared bath (25). Cots, washer/dryer, ice vending, soda/snack vending, ironing boards, exercise room. Renovated structures. Rates: $10 per person; $14 couple; DV/VIP/SNCO $16 per person, $23 couple. Duty can make reservations, others Space-A.

TML: VAQ. Bldg 2272, enlisted all ranks, leave or official duty. Bedroom, semi-private bath (47). Refrigerator, A/C, color TV, housekeeping service, washer/dryer, soda/snack vending, exercise room. Modern structure. Rates: $10 per person, $14 couple. Maximum two per room. TDY can make reservations, others Space-A.

TML: TLF. Bldg 2399, all ranks, leave or official duty. One-bedroom suites, private bath (18). Kitchen, complete utensils, color TV, housekeeping service, cribs/cots, washer/dryer, soda/snack vending, ice vending., exercise room. New structure. Rates: E1-E2 $14; O1 $19; all others $24.

DV/VIP: Bldg 2393, C-509-247-2127. Only O6+ call 509-247-2127. Retirees and lower ranks Space-A.

TML Availability: Good, Sep-Mar. Difficult, other times.

CREDIT CARDS ACCEPTED: Visa, MasterCard and American Express.

Temporary Military Lodging Around the World - 251

WASHINGTON
Fairchild Air Force Base, continued

Transportation: Off base shuttle/bus 328-7433, off base taxi 535-2535, car rental agency 838-8223.

Visit Manito Park and Botanical Gardens, while there look at the local pottery, the Cheney Cowles Museum and historic Campbell House. Try Factory Outlet shopping in Post Falls, Greyhound racing in Coeur D'Alene.

Locator 247-5875   Medical 247-5661   Police 247-5493

Fort Lewis (WA09R4)
Fort Lewis Billeting
P.O. Box 33085
Fort Lewis, WA 98433-0085

TELEPHONE NUMBER INFORMATION: Main installation numbers: C-253-967-1110, D-312-357-1110.

Location: On I-5, exit 120 in Puget Sound area, 14 miles north of Olympia, 12 miles south of Tacoma. Clearly marked. *USMRA: Page 101 (C-5); Page 103 (A,B-7)*. NMC: Tacoma, 12 miles north.

Lodging Office: Bldg 2111, between Utah and Pendleton Avenues. **C-253-967-2815/7862/6754, D-312-357-2815/357-7862,** Fax: C-253-967-2955, D-312-357-2253, 24 hours. Check in facility, check out 1000 hours. Government civilian employee billeting.

TML: Fort Lewis Lodge. Guest house, all ranks, leave or official duty, C-253-964-0211. Bedroom, private bath (74); bedroom, private bath cottages, fully furnished for enlisted PCS families (9). Community kitchen on each floor (some units have kitchenettes), CATV, housekeeping service, recreation room, lounge, cribs/cots, coin washer/dryer, ice vending. Modern structure. Rates: based on rank of military member $17-$34, each additional person $3. Maximum five per room. TDY can make reservations, others Space-A.

TML: VOQ/VEQ. Main Post, two buildings all ranks, leave or official duty. Bedroom, private bath suites (16); bedroom private bath suites (27); single rooms (3). At Madigan Army Medical Center (MAMC) two buildings with suites (40) and single rooms (3). Some suites and singles share bath. Community kitchen on each floor, limited utensils, CATV, housekeeping service, washer/dryer, cribs/cots available. Older structures. Rates: $26, each additional person $5. TDY can make reservations, others Space-A.

TML: DVQ. Bldg 1020, **Bronson Hall**, officer O4+, leave or official duty. VIP suites, private bath (3); main post cabins (2). Rates: $30 per night, each additional person $5. Cabins have kitchen. Refrigerator, in-room fee beverage service, CATV, housekeeping service, washer/dryer. Older structure. Rates: sponsor $26, each additional person $5. Duty can make reservations, others Space-A.

TML: Klatawa Village, officer cabins. Main Post, family units (6). Small kitchen, limited utensils, color TV, housekeeping service. Enlisted Cabins. PCS in/out families may make reservations, others Space-A. Family units (10). Rates: call.

TML: Fisher House. Located at Madigan Army Medical Center. Note: Appendix B has the definition of this facility. C-206-964-9283.

WASHINGTON
Fort Lewis, continued

DV/VIP: Protocol Office, Bldg 2025, C-253-967-5834, D-312-357-5834, O7+.

TML Availability: Fair, Oct-Apr. Difficult, other times.

From majestic Mount Rainier, to the inland sea waters of Puget Sound, perfection for the outdoorsman. Tacoma, Olympia and Seattle are nearby.

Locator 385-2350   Medical 911   Police 911

Madigan Army Medical Center (WA15R4)
Lodging Office, Bldg 2110
Tacoma, WA 98431-0001
This is part of Fort Lewis Lodging Services.

TELEPHONE NUMBER INFORMATION: Main installation numbers: C-253-967-5051, D-312-357-5151.

Location: From I-5 N or S take the Madigan exit. Clearly marked. *USMRA: Page 103 (A-7).* NMC: Tacoma, 12 miles north.

Lodging Office: Bldg 211. **C-253-964-0211**, 24 hours. Check in billeting, check out 1000 hours daily. Government civilian employee billeting.

TML: Guest House. Bldg 9901, all ranks, leave or official duty. Bedroom, shared bath (6); separate bedrooms, semi-private bath (14). Community kitchen, refrigerator, limited utensils, housekeeping service, cribs/cots, washer/dryer. Older structure. Rates: sponsor $16-$26, each additional person $5. Maximum three per unit. MEDEVAC priority.

TML: VOQ/VEQ. Bldg 9906, all ranks, leave or official duty. Bedroom, private bath (7). Bedroom, semi-private bath (16). Community kitchen, refrigerator, limited utensils, housekeeping service, washer/dryer. Older structure. Rates: $16-$26, each additional person $5. TDY/med student reservations, others Space-A.

TML Availability: Fairly good. Best, Oct-May.

Locator 967-6221   Medical 968-1110   Police 967-3107

McChord Air Force Base (WA05R4)
Evergreen Inn
P.O. Box 4118
McChord AFB, WA 98438-1109

TELEPHONE NUMBER INFORMATION: Main installation numbers: C-253-984-1910, D-312-976-1110.

Location: From I-5 exit 125. You come in front gate on Main Street, go straight through the traffic light, lodging is the last building on the left hand side. Clearly marked. *USMRA: Page 101 (C-5); Page 103 (B-7).* NMC: Tacoma, eight miles north.

WASHINGTON
McChord Air Force Base, continued

Lodging Office: Evergreen Inn, Bldg 166, Main Street. **C-253-984-5613**, D-312-984-5613, Fax: D-312-984-3596, 24 hours. Check in facility, check out 1100 hours daily. No government civilian employee billeting.

TML: VOQ. Bedroom, private bath (48); Color TV, mini-kitchens, microfridge, limited utensils, house keeping, cribs/cots, washer/dryer. Rates: single $10; double $14. Duty can make reservations, others Space-A.

TML: VAQ. Bedroom, private bath (108); shared bath (22). Two bedrooms, private bath (72). Microfridge, limited utensils, color TV, housekeeping service, cribs/cots, washer/dryer. SNCO Rooms: Bedroom, private bath (11); living area. Rates: single $10; double $14. Duty can make reservations, others Space-A.

TML: DV/VIP. O6+, leave or official duty, C-253-584-3591. One-bedroom suites, private bath (22 O6+ and 1 CMS), queen size bed, full kitchen, living, dining area, honor bar, color TV/VCR cribs/cots, washer/dryer. One-bedroom suites (4 CMS), wet bar, microfridge, living area. Rates: single $16; double $23. Duty can make reservations, others Space-A.

DV/VIP: EXO 62/MAW/CCE, Bldg 100, C-253-584-2621. O6/GS-15+. Call billeting for reservations. Retirees and lower ranks Space-A.

TML Availability: Good, Nov-Feb. Difficult, Mar-Oct. Very limited on family units.

CREDIT CARDS ACCEPTED: Visa, MasterCard and American Express.

Transportation: On base shuttle/bus, Mon-Fri only, direct line to Budget Rent-A-Car located in lobby.

Washington has lots to do: hiking, biking, canoeing, kayaking and skiing. Visit tacoma attractions such as the Seattle Waterfront & Aquarium, Seattle center, Pikes Place Market, Woodland Park Zoo, Ballard locks & Fish Ladder and other national treasures such as Mt. Rainier National Park, Mt. St. Helen's and Snoqualmie Falls!

Locator 984-2474   **Medical 911**   **Police 714-5777**

Pacific Beach Resort and Conference Center (WA16R4)
P.O. Box 0
Pacific Beach, WA 98571-1700

TELEPHONE NUMBER INFORMATION: Main numbers: 1-800-626-4414.

Location: Located on the coast in Pacific Beach, WA, 150 miles southwest of Seattle. Accessible from US-101 (Coastal Highway) and US-12 from Yakima. *USMRA: Page 101 (A-4,5)*. NMC: Seattle, 150 miles northeast.

Lodging Office: Send information requests to: PACIFIC BEACH RESORT, P.O. Box 0, Pacific Beach, WA 98571. **C-1-800-626-4414,** 0800-1600 hours. Check in 1600 hours, check out 1100

WASHINGTON
Pacific Beach Resort and Conference Center, continued

hours. Reservations made over the phone are confirmed when made. Make checks payable to: Pacific Beach. Cancellations must be received 10 days prior (A $15 cancellation fee will be assessed). Notices received less than 10 working days will be assessed one day's rental. Reservations not paid within 10 working days are subject to cancellation. Reservation Priority: (one reservation per family) AD 90 days, other military personnel 60 days, all other authorized personnel 30 days. Note: A new Conference Center is now open.

TML: Cabin, suites, family (13) and studio units (13). Cabin, 3- and 4-bedrooms (28); suites, one bedroom, sitting room, private bath (adults only) (6); family and motel units. Each cabin sleeps two people per bedroom. The suite and the studios can accommodate two adults. The family units sleep two adults and two children. Oceanside cabin with fireplace add $10 per day, tent sites add $5 per day. See Military Living's *Military RV, Camping and Rec Areas Around the World* for more information on camping and RV information. Crib linens not provided. Lodging can be reserved from one night in the suites, studios and family units and a minimum of two nights in the cabins. Maximum stay, except for the RV park, is two weeks. Extensions granted when space is available. Holiday weekends minimum of three nights (Fri-Mon). All other requests on a Space-A basis. Note: sponsor must accompany civilian guests during stay. All military ID card holders welcome. There are both pet and no-pet accommodations.

TML Availability: Fairly good. Best, winter.

CREDIT CARDS ACCEPTED: Visa, MasterCard and American Express.

Seasonal Rates - (Off Peak Oct 1-Mar 31/Peak Season Apr 1-Sep 30)

Type of Lodging	E1-E6				E7-O9 & DoD Civilians			
	Off Peak		Peak		Off Peak		Peak	
RV	$7	$7	$9	$10	$7	$7	$9	$10
Studios	$15	$25	$25	$30	$15	$25	$25	$30
Family	$20	$30	$30	$35	$20	$30	$30	$35
Suites	$35	$45	$50	$55	$35	$55	$50	$55
*3-Bedroom House	$40	$50	$55	$60	$40	$60	$60	$70
*4-Bedroom House	$45	$55	$60	$65	$45	$65	$65	$75

RATES PER DAY PER UNIT
*Add $10 for oceanfront accommodations and $5 for pet house rental

"May be the Navy's best kept vacation secret"! Social room with activities weekends off-season, and daily in spring, summer and fall. Bowling, exercise room, spa, restaurant and lounge, ball field, horseshoe pits, picnicking, and whale watching platform, for what else? Watching whales!

Locator 276-4414   Medical 911   Police 276-4414

Puget Sound Naval Shipyard (WA11R4)
Lodging Office, Bldg 865
Bremerton, WA 98314-5001

TELEPHONE NUMBER INFORMATION: Main installation numbers: C-360-476-3711, D-312-439-3711.

WASHINGTON
Puget Sound Naval Shipyard, continued

Location: Take WA-16 W to end of freeway, NS clearly visible three miles north. *USMRA: Page 101 (C-4); Page 103 (A-3).* NMC: Seattle, 60 miles southeast.

Lodging Office: C-360-476-2840 (BOQ), C-360-476-7619/7627 (BEQ), Fax: C-360-476-0045 (BOQ), C-360-476-6895 (BEQ). Check in facility 24 hours, check out 1300 hours daily. Government civilian employee billeting.

TML: BEQ. Underwood Hall, Keppler Hall, Nibbe Hall. Bldgs 865, 885, 942, enlisted all ranks, leave or official duty, C-360-476-7619, D-312-439-7627 (Fax also). Bedroom, shared bath (447); family rooms (6). Refrigerator in room, community kitchen 1st floor, color TV in room and lounge, housekeeping service, washer/dryer, snack vending, ice vending, hot tub, mini gym, washer/dryer, microwave each floor, picnic facilities. Modern structure. Rates: $3.75 per person; couple $9, with one child $10.75, with two children $12.50. AD and retired can make reservations, others Space-A.

TML: BOQ. Bldg 847, officers all ranks and GS-7+, leave or official duty, C-360-476-2840, D-312-476-2840, Fax: C-360-476-0045. Bedroom, private bath (70); VIP/family suites, private bath (5). Refrigerators, cooking facility 1st floor, essentials, CATV in room and lounge, housekeeping service, washer/dryer, snack vending, ice vending, complimentary coffee/doughnuts weekdays, telephones, sauna/spa, mini-gym, library and reading room, conference/meeting room, children's playground. Rates: $8 per person; VIP $15.50 per person. Maximum four per room. Reservation services 24 hours.

DV/VIP: BOQ, Bldg 847. O6+. Retirees Space-A, D-312-439-2840.

TML Availability: Fairly good, Nov-Mar. Difficult, Jun-Sep.

CREDIT CARDS ACCEPTED: Visa and American Express.

A beautiful Northwest location is supplemented by these lodging facilities.

Locator 476-3711   Medical 911   Police 476-3393

Whidbey Island Naval Air Station (WA06R4)
CBQ Billeting
Bldg 973, McCormick Lodge
Midway Ave
Oak Harbor, WA 98278-5200

TELEPHONE NUMBER INFORMATION: Main installation numbers: C-360-257-2211, D-312-820-0111.

Location: Take WA-20 to Whidbey Island, three miles west of WA-20 on Ault Field Road. *USMRA: Page 101 (C-2,3).* NMC: Seattle, 90 miles southeast.

Lodging Office: Bldg 973, McCormick Lodger, Midway Blvd. **C-360-257-2529,** all ranks. Check in facility, check out 1100 hours daily. Government civilian employee billeting (on orders). Reservations will be held no later than 2300 hours on day of arrival.

WASHINGTON
Whidbey Island Naval Air Station, continued

NAVY LODGE

TML: Navy Lodge. Bldg 2125 N Coral Sea Avenue, Oak Harbor, WA 98278. Take WA-20 to Whidbey Island, make a left onto Midway Blvd and a left onto Pioneer Way. A seaplane will take you to base. Reservations: **1-800-NAVY INN**. Lodge number is C-360-675-0633, 0700-2300 hours daily. Check in 1500-1800 hours, check out 1200 hours. Two-bedroom modular units, kitchen, full bath (23). A/C, TV, hairdryers, iron/ironing board, rollaways, housekeeping service, washer/dryer, playground. Rates: $48. Maximum six per room. Seeing eye dogs, fish and caged birds OK. *Winner of the 1996 Edward E. Carlson Award for Navy Lodge excellence in the small category.*

TML: Bldg 973 and 2527, all ranks, leave or official duty. Bedroom, private bath. Refrigerator, housekeeping service, essentials, snack vending, ice vending, color CATV/VCR in room and lounge, telephone in room, washer/dryer. Recently renovated. Rates: single occupancy $9.75; multiple occupancy $5.75. Maximum two per unit. Navy funded TAD orders personal can make reservation through SATO, 1-800-576-9327, or through command transportation office. Other duty personal may call 1-800-576-9327. Non-duty personnel are Space-A.

DV/VIP: CO Secretary, Bldg 108, C-360-257-2037 or CBQ manager, C-360-257-3205/6550, O6+.

TML Availability: Best, winter. Difficult, weekends due to Reserve Training.

CREDIT CARDS ACCEPTED: Visa, MasterCard and American Express. Navy Lodge accepts Visa, MasterCard, American Express and Discover.

Whidbey Island can also be reached by ferry from Mukilteo (north of Seattle) to Clinton, in South Whidbey. Visit the hamlet of Langley then take a two hour drive north to Oak Harbor and beautiful Puget Sound scenery.

Locator 257-2211   Medical 257-9500   Police 257-3122

Other Installations in Washington

Bremerton Naval Hospital. Bremerton, WA 98312-5000. BEQ C-360-478-9334, Fax: C-360-478-9577. E1-E4: two beds per room, shared bath. E5-E6: private room, shared bath. TV lounges, laundry rooms, barbecue pit, sun deck, game room.

Jim Creek Regional Outdoor Recreation Area. Jim Creek Naval Radio Station (T), WA 98223-8599. C-360-435-7335 or 1-800-734-1123 (WA state only), D-312-727-3715, Fax C-360-435-7433. Two log cabins. Rates: $20 daily. See *Military Living's Military RV, Camping and Rec Areas Around the World* for additional information and directions.

WEST VIRGINIA

Camp Dawson Army Training Site (WV03R1)
Billeting
240 Army Road, Box 1, Route 2
Kingwood, WV 26537-1077

TELEPHONE NUMBER INFORMATION: Main installation numbers: C-304-329-4334, D-312-366-6552 ext 4334.

Location: From I-68 E to Bruceton Mills exit. Route 26 S to Albright WV, approximately 12 miles, turn left onto the St Joe Road (WV State Route 7/12), go 4.5 miles to the "Y" intersection. Take a right at the "Y" onto Camp Dawson Road (WV Route 7/26), follow to camp, approximately one mile. From I-68 W to Sabraton exit (Route 7), turn left at traffic light. Follow Route y through Kingwood. At bottom of hill, cross bridge, make a left, then another immediate left (under bridge) to Camp Dawson. *USMRA: Page .46 (H-3).* NMC: Morgantown, 24 miles northwest.

Lodging Office: Bldg 301. C-304-341-6591, D-312-366-6552, ext 420/4415, Fax: C-304-341-6591, D-312-366-6591, 0730-1600 hours Sat-Thur, 0730-2200 hours Fri. Check in billeting office, check out. After duty hours check in Post Security, Bldg 100. E-mail: atswy@wy-ngnet.army.mil.

TML: BOQ/BEQ. Bldg 106, all ranks, leave or official duty, C-304-329-4420, D-312-366-6552, ext 420. Bedroom (26). Refrigerator, color TV in room and lounge, housekeeping, washer/dryer, ice vending, soda/snack vending. Handicap accessible rooms available. Meeting/conference rooms and exercise room available. Rates: $10.50 per person per night, each additional person $5.25, maximum $15.75 per family; PCS/TDY $9.00 per person per night, each additional person $4.50, maximum $13.50 per family. Maximum two per room. Duty can make reservations, others Space-A. No pets.

TML: BOQ/BEQ. Bldg 301, all ranks, leave or official duty, C-304-329-4420, D-312-366-6552, ext 420. Bedroom (12). Refrigerator, color TV, washer/dryer, ice vending. Handicap accessible rooms available (6). Meeting/conference rooms and exercise room available. Rates: $9.50 per person per night, each additional person $4.75, maximum $23.75 per family; PCS/TDY $8 per person per night, each additional person $4, maximum $20 per family. Maximum four per room. Duty can make reservations, others Space-A. No pets.

TML: BOQ/BEQ. Bldg 302, 303,304, all ranks, leave or official duty, C-304-329-4420, D-312-366-6552 ext 420. Cottages (3). Refrigerator, kitchenette, complete utensils, color TV, housekeeping service. Meeting/conference rooms and exercise room available. Rates: $11.50 per person per night, $5.75 each additional person, maximum $34.50 per family; PCS/TDY: $10 per person per night, $5 each additional person, maximum $30 per family . Maximum four per unit (five if sponsor is couple). Duty can make reservations, others Space-A. No pets.

TML: BOQ. Bldg 104, all ranks, leave or official duty. C-304-329-4420, D-312-366-6552, ext 420. Cottages (1). Refrigerator, kitchenette, complete utensils, color TV, housekeeping service. Meeting/conference rooms and exercise room available, handicap accessible. Rates: $11.50 per person per night, $5.75 each additional person, maximum $40.25 per family; PCS/TDY $10 per person per night, $5 each additional person, maximum $35 per family. Maximum five per unit (six if sponsor is couple). Duty can make reservations, others Space-A. No pets.

TML: BEQ. Bldg 305, all ranks, leave or official duty, C-304-329-4420, D-312-366-6552 ext 420. Bedroom (9). Refrigerator, handicap accessible. Meeting/conference rooms and exercise room

WEST VIRGINIA
Camp Dawson Army Training Site, continued

available. Rates: $6.50 per person per night, each additional person $3.25, maximum $9.75 per family; PCS/TDY $5 per person per night, each additional person $2.50, maximum $7.50 per family. Maximum two per unit (one room has the capacity for one female). Duty can make reservations, others Space-A. No pets.

TML: DV. Bldg 101, E9/O6+, leave or official duty, C-304-329-4420, D-312-366-6552 ext 420. Cottages: three bedrooms, private bath (1); two bedrooms, private bath (1); one bedroom, private bath (1). Refrigerator, kitchenette, complete utensils, color TV in lounge, housekeeping service, washer/dryer. Meeting/conference rooms and exercise room available. Rates: $15.50 per person per night, each additional person $7.75, maximum $65 per family; PCS/TDY $14.00 per person per night, each additional person $7.00, maximum $60 per family. Maximum five per unit (six if sponsor is couple). Duty can make reservations, others Space-A. No pets.

DV: Contact billing office. E9/O6+. C-304-341-6591, D-312-366-6552 ext 420/4415, Fax: C-304-341-6591, D-312-366-6591.

TML Availability: Fairly Good, Dec-Feb. Difficult, Mar-Nov.

CREDIT CARDS ACCEPTED: Visa, MasterCard, American Express and Diners Club.

Transportation: Car rental agencies: Hertz 842-4554, 296-2331 or AMS Rental 291-5867.

While you are here, catch a sporting event live at West Virginia University!

Locator 329-4334   Medical 329-1400   Police 329-1611

Sugar Grove Naval Security Group Activity (WV06R1)
MWR Department
Building 64
Sugar Grove, WV 26815-9700

TELEPHONE NUMBER INFORMATION: Main installation numbers: C-304-249-6309, D-312-564-7276 ext 6309.

Location: Traveling North or South on Route 81, take exit 287 to Route 33. Travel 37 miles west on Route 33 to Brandywine. Take a left at the stop sign and travel south on Highway 21 for approximately five miles, NSGA is on the right side of the highway. *USMRA: Page 47 (I-6)*. NMC: Harrisonburg, 36 miles east.

Lodging Office: Bldg 26. C-304-249-6309, Fax: C-304-249-6385, 0730-1600 hours Mon-Fri. Check in facility. After 1600 hours, check in at security.

TML: Rec Cottages. MWR Department, Bldg 20, all ranks, leave or official duty. Cottages: two bedrooms, private bath, sofa bed (4); log cabin: one bed, private bath (1). Refrigerator, microwave, kitchenette, complete utensils, CATV, essentials, cribs/cot, iron/ironing board, BBQ, handicap accessible (1). Meeting/conference room, exercise room, soda/snack vending and mini-mart available. Modern structure, renovated. All structures are non-smoking facilities. Rates: Five persons $35, each additional person $5. Maximum five per cabin, seven per cottage. All ranks, reservations. No pets.

WEST VIRGINIA
Sugar Grove Naval Security Group Activity, continued

DV/VIP: Contact MWR office. O7+.

TML Availability: Good, Sep-Feb. Difficult, Mar-Aug.

CREDIT CARDS ACCEPTED: Visa, MasterCard and American Express.

New Market Civil War Battlefield and Museum, Massanutten and Season Resort, Grand Caverns, Shenandoah Caverns, Shenandoa Canaan Valley Resort and white water rafting are all within a short driving distance.

Locator 249-6309   Medical 249-6381   Police 249-6310

Sugar Grove Cabins . . .
Your Military Lodging Getaway
- 4 brand new 2 bedroom units sleeps seven
- Rustic one-room log cabin sleeps four

Things to Do
Boat Rental, Cabin Rental, Fishing, Hunting, Swimming Pool, Tennis Courts, Hiking, Gym, Library, Softball and much more!

For Reservations: 304-249-6309

Other Installations in West Virginia

Eastern West Virginia Regional Airport. Martinsburg, WV 25401-0204. Very limited TML, **C-304-267-5174.**

WISCONSIN

Fort McCoy (WI02R2)
Director of Public Works
ATTN: AFRC-FM-DLH-B
2171 South 8th Ave
Fort McCoy, WI 54656-5163

TELEPHONE NUMBER INFORMATION: Main installation numbers: C-608-388-2222, D-312-280-1110.

Location: From west on I-90 to north on WI-27 to northeast on WI-21 to fort. From east on I-90, to west on WI-21 to fort. *USMRA: Page 68 (C,D-7).* NMC: La Crosse, 35 miles southwest.

Lodging Office: Bldg 2168, 8th Street. **C-608-388-2107, D-312-280-2107,** Fax: C-608-388-3946, D-312-280-3946, 24 hours. Check in billeting 1200 hours, check out 1100 hours daily. Government civilian employee billeting.

WISCONSIN
Fort McCoy, continued

TML: TLQ. All ranks, leave or official duty. Bedroom, shared bath (230); bedroom, private bath (70); bedroom (2) 2-bedroom (5) and 3-bedroom (2), private bath (4 units are trailers). Kitchen, utensils, A/C, CATV, cribs/cots ($3), essentials, washer/ dryer. Older structure, new trailers. Rates: vary according to rank/grade of guest/type quarters occupied, call for details. All categories can make reservations.

TML: Pine View Recreation Area. DPCA, 1439 South "M" Street, ATTN: Pine View Recreation Area, Fort McCoy, WI 54656-5141, C-608-388-3517, D-312-280-3517. One-room cabins (2), 1-bedroom duplex (2). Rates: cabins $30; duplex $35. **See** *Military Living's Military RV, Camping and Rec Areas Around the World* **for additional information and directions.**

DV/VIP: Protocol, Bldg 100, C-608-388-3607. O6+. Retirees and lower ranks Space-A.

TML Availability: Fairly good, Jan-May and Sep-Dec. Difficult, other times.

CREDIT CARDS ACCEPTED: Visa, MasterCard and American Express.

Transportation: On base shuttle/bus C-388-3652, D-280-3652, car rental agencies 269-7692.

Mid December - February the installation ski hill has good cross country and downhill snow skiing. Visit the cheese factories, brewery, Amish shops and Cranberry Expo Museum. Equipment rental, C ext 4498/3360. See *Military RV, Camping and Rec Areas Around the World* for more information.

Locator 388-2225   **Medical 338-2444**   **Police 115**

Other Installations in Wisconsin

Sherwood Point Cottage. Commander, Coast Guard Group Morale Fund, 2420 South Lincoln Memorial Drive, Milwaukee, WI 53207-1997, C-414-747-7185. One cottage, bedroom, sleeps eight adults; furnished, except bed linens; toilet items; community kitchen, microwave, color TV/VCR, washer/dryer, pots/pans, dishes. Blankets provided. Rates: $35 daily. **See** *Military Living's Military RV, Camping and Rec Areas Around the World* **for additional information and directions.**

WYOMING

Francis E. Warren Air Force Base (WY01R4)
Crow Creek Inn
7103 Randall Street
Francis E. Warren AFB, WY 82005-2987

TELEPHONE NUMBER INFORMATION: Main installation numbers: C-307-773-1110, D-312-481-1110.

Location: Off I-25, two miles north of I-80, clearly marked. *USMRA: Page 102 (I-8)*. NMC: Cheyenne, adjacent to the city (west side).

Temporary Military Lodging Around the World - 261

WYOMING
Francis E. Warren Air Force Base, continued

Lodging Office: Crow Creek Inn, 7103 Randall Street. **C-307-773-1844, D-312-481-1844,** Fax: C-307-773-4450, D-312-481-4450, 24 hours. Check in 1500-1800 hours, after 1800 hours, credit card hold required. Check out 1200 hours daily. All lodging rooms are non-smoking and pets are not authorized in, on or around lodging facility. Base does not authorize pets to be kept in vehicles..

TML: Guest Lodging. Bldgs 1454, 238, 241, all ranks, leave or official duty. Two- or three-bedroom apartments. Kitchen, living room, housekeeping service, cribs and high chairs, washer/dryer, CATV/VCR. Older structures, renovated. Rates: $26.50 per night. PCS can make reservations. Space-A can make reservations up to 24 hours prior to check in.

TML: VOQ. Bldgs 44, 79, 129, officers and civilians, leave or official duty. One- or two-bedroom suites, private bath, some with kitchen. Refrigerator, CATV, housekeeping service, washer/dryer. Older structure, renovated. Rates: $15.50 per person per night, $31 for two persons on duty or $25.25 for one person accompanied by another who is not on duty.

TML: VAQ. Bldgs 21, 224.. SNCO suites. E6 and below: single rooms, some with private bath. Refrigerator, microwave, CATV, housekeeping service, washer/dryer. Older structure, renovated. Rates: SNCO $16 per person per night, $32 for two person on duty/orders or $23 if accompanied by another who is not on duty/orders; AMN and NCO $13 per person per night, $26 for two persons on duty/orders or $19.25 if accompanied by another who is not on duty/orders.

DV/VIP: Please call PAO, C-307-773-2137/3052. E9/O6+. Historic rooms and houses. Rates: SNCO $16 per person per night, $32 for two persons on duty/orders or $23 if accompanied by another who is not on duty/orders; O6+ $27 per person per night, $54 for two or more on duty/orders or $39.50 if accompanied by another who is not on duty/orders.

TML Availability: Good, except last week of July for Cheyenne Frontier Day Rodeo.

CREDIT CARDS ACCEPTED: Visa, MasterCard, American Express and NCO/Officer Club Card.

This base was once a frontier Army post, and many of its buildings are on the National Historic Register. Cowboy and Indian lore abound, and nearby Colorado skiing draws many visitors. Visit Fort Collins' Old Town nearer by.

Locator 775-1841   Medical 775-3461   Police 775-3501/911

Other Installations in Wyoming

Grant's Village, Yellowstone National Park, Mountain Home AFB, ID 83648-5000. C-208-282-6333, D-312-728-6333. Travel Trailers, 24-foot (6), self contained, sleeps six. **See** *Military Living's Military RV, Camping and Rec Areas Around the World* **for additional information and directions.**

UNITED STATES POSSESSIONS

GUAM

Andersen Air Force Base (GU01R8)
Lodging Office
Bldg 27006, 4th and Caroline Ave
APO AP 96543-4004

TELEPHONE NUMBER INFORMATION: Main installation numbers: C-(USA) 011-671-366-1110, D-315-366-1110.

Location: On the north end of the island, accessible from Marine Drive which extends entire length of the island of Guam. *USMRA: Page 130 (E,F-1,2)*. NMC: Agana, 15 miles south.

Lodging Office: Bldg 27006, 4th and Caroline Ave. **C-(USA) 011-671-366-8201/8144, D-315-366-8144,** Fax: C-(USA) 011-671-366-6264, 24 hours. Check in billeting 1400 hours, check out 1200 hours daily. Government civilian employee billeting.

TML: VOQ. Bldgs 25003, 27006, officers all ranks, leave or official duty. Bedroom (18), shared bath (100). Refrigerator, A/C, CATV, housekeeping service, washer/dryer, ice vending. Older structure. Rates: $12. Duty can make reservations, others Space-A.

TML: VAQ. Bldg 25003, enlisted all ranks, leave or official duty. Two-bedrooms, shared bath (60). Refrigerator, A/C, CATV, washer/dryer. Older structure. Rates: $12 per person. Duty can make reservations, others Space-A.

TML: TLF. Bldg 1656, officer, enlisted, all ranks, PCS move or leave. Bedrooms, private bath, (18). Kitchenette, A/C, CATV, housekeeping service, washer/dryer. Rates: $32. PCS can make reservations, others Space-A.

TML: DV/VIP. Bldg 27006, officer O6+, leave or official duty. Bedroom, private bath (6); separate bedroom, private bath suites (5). A/C, CATV, housekeeping service, washer/dryer. Rates: rooms $17: suites $22. Duty can make reservations, others Space-A.

DV/VIP: Protocol Office, 36 ABW, C-(USA) 011-671-351-4228. O7+, retirees Space-A.

TML Availability: Good, year round.

CREDIT CARDS ACCEPTED: Visa, MasterCard and American Express.

Lots of sunshine, beaches, coral reefs, exciting WWII shipwrecks to explore for scuba enthusiasts. Hikers enjoy tropical mountains and jungles.

Locator 351-1110   Medical-366-2978   Police 366-2913

Guam Naval Computer & Telecommunications Area Master Station, WESTPAC (GU05R8)
FPO AP 96540-1099

TELEPHONE NUMBER INFORMATION: Main installation numbers: C-(USA) 011-671-355-1110, D-315-322-1110.

Location: From Route 10A, right onto Route 1. Follow Route 1 until you see a Pizza Hut, take a left at the next traffic light onto Route 3. Take a left right before the McDonald's and you will see the front gate.

Lodging Office: BOQ/BEQ: C-(USA) 011-671-355-5731/5749, D-315-322-5731/5749, Fax: C-011-671-355-5610. Check in after 1200 hours, check out 1300 hours.

TML: BOQ. Bedroom, private bath; VIP suites. A/C, iron/ironing board, clock radio, refrigerator. Mini-mart, NEX, galley, swimming pool and Reef Club also available. Call for rate information.

TML: BEQ. E1-E4 two to a bedroom, shared bath; E5-E6 private bedroom, shared bath. A/C, iron/ironing board, clock radio, refrigerator. Mini-mart, NEX, galley, swimming pool and Reef Club also available. Call for rate information.

DV/VIP: C-(USA) 011-671-355-5731/5749.

TML Availability: Fairly good. Best, Dec. Difficult, Jul-Aug.

Enjoy the many beaches, SCUBA diving, swimming, boating and sailing that is abundant in Guam.

Guam Naval Station (GU02R8)
Combined Bachelor Quarters
PSC 455, Box 169
FPO AP 96540-1099

TELEPHONE NUMBER INFORMATION: Main installation numbers: C-(USA) 011-671-351-1110, D-315-322-1110.

Location: South on Marine Drive, through main gate, clearly marked. *USMRA: Page 130 (C-3)*. NMC: Agana, 10 miles north.

Lodging Office: Centralized, contact CBQ Barracks 18 lower, on Chapel Road off Marine Drive. **C-(USA) 011-671-339-5259**, D-315-339-5259, Fax: C-(USA) 011-671-339-6250, D-315-339-6250, 24 hours. Check in facility after 1200 hours, check out 1200 hours daily. TLA approved. Government civilian employee billeting.

TML: CBQ. Barracks 7, 22, officers, enlisted, government civilian employees (stateside hire), all ranks, leave or official duty. Bedroom, private bath (12); suites, private bath (52). Refrigerator, CATV/VCR, A/C, housekeeping service, washer/dryer, ice, coffee maker. Rates: Barracks 22 $4 per person. Duty can make reservations, others Space-A.

GUAM
Guam Naval Station, continued

TML: BOQ. Bldgs 2000, 179, officers and equivalent civilians, all ranks. Bedroom, private bath (58). Refrigerator, A/C, CATV and VCR, housekeeping service, washer/dryer, ice and coffee maker. Rates: $8 per person, $4 per family member over eight years old. Duty can make reservations, others Space-A.

DV/VIP: Flag Lt, C-(USA) 011-671-339-5202. O7+.

TML Availability: Fairly good. Best, December. Difficult, Jul-Aug.

These quarters are within walking distance of all base support facilities. Scuba diving and other beach related activities are popular.

| Locator 351-1110 | Medical 344-9369 | Police 333-2989 |

PUERTO RICO

Borinquen Coast Guard Air Station (PR03R1)
La Plaza, Room 26
Aquadilla, PR 00604-5000

TELEPHONE NUMBER INFORMATION: Main installation numbers: C-787-890-8400.

Location: At old Ramey AFB, north of Aquadilla. Take PR-2 from San Juan or north from Mayaguez to PR-110 N to CGAS. *USMRA: Page 130 (B,C-2)*. NMC: San Juan, 65 miles east.

Lodging Office: La Plaza, room 227A. **C-787-890-8492**, 0930-1600 hours Mon-Fri. Check in 1400 hours, check out 1100 hours daily.

TML: Guest House. All ranks, leave or official duty. Bedroom, private bath, A/C, shared living room and fully equipped kitchen area, CATV, washer/dryer (5). Rate: $15-$25 per night. Three-bedroom, one bath houses (7), fully furnished, kitchen, cable TV, A/C, washer/dryer, linens, housekeeping Mon-Fri. Rate: $40-$55 per night. Maximum capacity six per unit. Reservations a must. PCS have priority; AD may reserve 45 days in advance, all others 30 days. Sponsor must make reservations (Military widows make their own.) No pets.

TML: Lighthouse (located behind Punta Borinquen Lighthouse). Two-bedroom apartment suites, private bath, fully furnished, kitchen, CATV, A/C, washer/dryer, housekeeping Mon-Fri (2). Rates: $40-$65 per day. Maximum capacity four per unit. Reservations a must. PCS have priority; AD may reserve 45 days in advance, all others 30 days. Sponsor must make reservations (military widows make their own). No pets.

TML Availability: Very limited. Best, Sep-May.

Recreation gear available for rent, theater, swimming pool, Exchange/Mini Mart/Package Store, picnic areas, several beaches surrounding area. Water sports, golf, horseback riding nearby. Contact MWR for information: 787-890-8492.

| Locator 882-3500 | Medical 882-1500 | Police 890-5201 |

PUERTO RICO

Fort Buchanan (PR01R1)
Lodging Office, Bldg 119
P.O. Box 34192
Fort Buchanan, PR 00934-5042

TELEPHONE NUMBER INFORMATION: Main installation numbers: C-787-273-3401, D-313-740-1110.

Location: From Munoz Rivera International Airport take highway 26 west toward Bayamon to highway 22 to the Fort Buchanan sign. *USMRA: Page 130 (E-2).* NMC: San Juan, six miles southwest.

Lodging Office: Bldg 119. **C-787-792-7977, D-313-740-3821,** Fax: C-787-273-3273, 0630-1800 hours daily. Other hours SDO, MP Station, Bldg 212, C ext 3723. Check in facility 1300 hours, check out 1100 hours daily. No government civilian employee billeting.

TML: Su Casa Guest House. Bldgs 119 and 1315, all ranks, leave or official duty. Handicap accessible. Bedroom, private bath (each with queen bed) (28). Refrigerator, microwave, coffee pot, A/C, CATV, housekeeping service, cribs/cots, facilities for DAVs. Older structure, remodeled. Rates: $18-$36, each additional person $5. PCS may make reservations with orders. Other AD 14 days in advance, others Space-A.

DV/VIP: Headquarters Command, Bldg 399, C-787-792-3340. O6+. Reservations through Protocol Officer.

TML Availability: Good, Nov-Apr. Difficult, Jun-Oct.

CREDIT CARDS ACCEPTED: Visa, MasterCard and American Express.

This is the capital of Puerto Rico. Visit El Morro Castle, Plaza las Americas Shopping Center, Pawo la Princessa, El Condado, local Bacardi Rum Distillers, and beautiful beaches. Post facilities include a gym swimming pool, bowling alley and fitness center, PX and Commissary.

Locator 273-3400   Medical 793-5593   Police 273-3913

Roosevelt Roads Naval Station (PR02R1)
P.O. Box 3010
FPO AA 34051-5000

TELEPHONE NUMBER INFORMATION: Main installation numbers: C-787-865-2000, D-313-831-2000.

Location: From San Juan International Airport, turn right onto PR-26 for 20 minutes, turn left onto PR-3 (Carolina exit) for 30 minutes, then turn left after Puerto Del Rey Marina into NS. *USMRA: Page 130 (F-2,3).* NMC: San Juan, 50 miles northwest.

Lodging Office: Bldg 1688 (officers), Bldg 1708 (enlisted). **C-787-865-3490 ext 4334/3364 (officers), 787-865-2000 ext 4145/4147 (enlisted),** Fax: C-787-865-5378, 24 hours. Check in billeting, check out 1100 hours daily. Government civilian employee billeting.

PUERTO RICO
Roosevelt Roads Naval Station, continued

TML: CBQ. Officers, all ranks, leave or official duty. Handicap accessible. Two-bedrooms, private bath (8); three-bedrooms, private bath (4). Microwave, refrigerator, limited utensils, A/C, color TV/VCR, movies, phones, fax, housekeeping service, cots ($2). Modern structure. Rates: rooms (BEQ) $6; (VIP) $15; (BOQ) $10; (VIP) $20. AD on orders, PCS/TAD/TDY have priority for reservations, others Space-A. Rates subject to change.

TML: Guest House. Two-bedroom houses (O6+) (2). Kitchen, complete utensils, microwave, A/C, CATV, phone, housekeeping service, washer/dryer. Rates: $25, each additional person per night $10. Duty can make reservations, others Space-A.

TML: Navy Lodge. All ranks, leave or official duty. Reservations: **C-1-800-NAVY-INN**. Lodge number is C-787-865-8281/8282, Fax: C-787-865-8283. Bedrooms, 2 double beds, private bath (72) (interconnecting units for large families, two handicap accessible). Kitchenette, complete utensils, microwave, A/C, CATV/VCP, refrigerator, phone, hair dryers, housekeeping service, coin washer/dryer, mini-mart, children's playground. Rates: $52.50 per night. All categories can make reservations. Check in 1500-1600 hours, check out by 1200 hours. *Winner of the 1996 Edward E. Carlson Award for Navy Lodge excellence in the large category.*

TML: TVQ. Naval Reserve Station, downtown San Juan, stop 7 1/2. Naval Reserve Bldgs 441, 448, enlisted E7+. Suites, private baths (2); guest house apartments, two bedrooms, private bath, full kitchen, patio (6). Rates: suites $20 per day, each additional person $10; apartments $25 per day, each additional person $10.

DV/VIP: C-809-865-3364. O7+, retirees Space-A.

TML Availability: Good, Oct-Mar. Difficult, Apr-Sep.

CREDIT CARDS ACCEPTED: Visa, MasterCard and American Express. (Discover accepted at the Navy Lodge.)

Don't miss El Yuunque (L-EE-UN-KEE) rain forest with its magnificent water falls, hiking trails, and restaurant.

Locator 865-2000   **Medical** 865-5700   **Police** 865-4011

Sabana Seca Naval Security Group Activity (PR04R1)
Bldg 3, PSC 1009, Box 1
FPO AA 34053-1000

TELEPHONE NUMBER INFORMATION: Main installation numbers: C-787-261-8300.

Location: Route 3 W to Bayamon exit to PR-22 W to PR-886 N to base. *USMRA: Page 130(D,E-2)*. NMC: San Juan, 14 miles east.

Lodging Office: BOQ, Bldg 3, **C-787-261-2611**. BOQ, Bldg A-C, **C-313-787-8413**. Contact Quarterdeck after hours.

PUERTO RICO
Sabana Seca Naval Security Group Activity, continued

TML: Very limited TML available. Extremely tight security; be prepared to show proper military ID and state your purpose of visiting the base. Plan to arrive only during daylight hours. This TML is not recommend for "leisure travelers" but is listed in the event of a need for lodging in the immediate area.

Visit the great beaches, El Yunque Rain Forest, El Morro Fort and Casinos.

Locator 795-2255/2399 **Medical 795-8755** **Police 785-8310**

FOREIGN COUNTRIES

BAHRAIN

Bahrain Naval Support Unit (BA01R9)
Administrative Support Unit
FWA Bahrain
PSC 451, Box 95
FPO AE 09834-2800

TELEPHONE NUMBER INFORMATION: Main installation numbers: C-(USA) 011-973-724-XXX, D-318-439-XXXX.

Location: A group of islands off the coast of Saudi Arabia in the Persian Gulf. A 15 mile causeway connects the main island city of Manana with Saudi Arabia. NMC: Dhahran, Saudi Arabia, 30 miles northwest.

Lodging Office: Mannai Plaza, **C-(USA) 011-973-727-762/318, (BA) 973-727-762,** Fax: C-(USA) 011-973-727-291 (BA) 973-727-291, 24 hours daily. Reservations accepted here.

TML: CBQ, Mannai Plaza. Rates: enlisted $2 per person per night; officers $4 per person per night. Call for more information.

TML: Andalous Bldg, C-(USA) 011-973-715-060. Call for accommodations, rates and more information.

TML: Female bunkhouse, C-(USA) 011-973-724-312. Call for accommodations, rates and more information.

TML: Male bunkhouse, C-(USA) 011-973-724-485. Call for accommodations, rates and more information.

Transportation: On base shuttle 727-762/318

Bahrain is an island off the coast of Saudi Arabia. The State of Bahrain requires a visa for all personnel entering the country.

BAHRAIN
Bahrain Naval Support Unit, continued

Locator 973-724   Medical 724-260   Police 724-257

BELGIUM

NATO/SHAPE Support Group (US) (BE01R7)
Hotel Raymond Billeting
80th ASG (NSSG), CMR #451
APO AE 09708-5000

TELEPHONE NUMBER INFORMATION: Main installation numbers: C-(USA) 011-32-65-32-75-11, ask operator to connect you, (BE) 065-31-1131/32, D-314-361-1110 (Chieveres Air Base - ask operator to connect you).

Location: From Bruxelles Airport take E-10 toward Paris, exit at Mons, Belgium and follow signs to "GARE" (train station). Hotel is across from GARE. NMC: Brussels, 50 miles north.

Lodging Office: Write to: Hotel Raymond, 80th ASG (NSSG), CMR #451, APO AE 09708-5000. Priority I - TDY military and civilians, PCS military personnel and their families. Priority II - Space-A personnel to include military/civilian personnel on leave, retirees and AAFES/DODDS personnel on PCS orders. **C-(USA) 011-32-65-32-75-11, (BE) 065-31-1131/32**, D-314-361-5248, Fax C-(USA) 011-32-65-32-75-01. Check in 1300 hours, check out 1000 hours daily, Government civilian employee billeting. This hotel was renovated in 1993.

TML: Hotel Raymond. All ranks, leave or official duty. Bedroom, private bath (67). Refrigerator, color TV, full custodial service (except Sunday/holidays), cribs/cots, washer/dryer, buffet breakfast at nominal cost ($2.50), snack vending, ice vending. Rates: $35, each additional person $5. Space-A may check availability same day as arrival, above number.

TML Availability: Fairly good. Best, Oct-mid May.

CREDIT CARDS ACCEPTED: Visa, MasterCard, American Express, Diners Club and Discover.

In Mons visit the Church of St. Waudru. "The Belfry" is accessible by elevator. Then visit the main square, town hall, and Van Gogh's house. To contact the Tourist Office, Grand-Place, 7000 Mons, call C-(BE) **065-33-55-80.**

Locator 44-7111   Medical 44-3321   Police 27-5301

Note: Hotel Raymond is moving!!! Hotel Raymond is moving to a larger facility closer to SHAPE and will now be called Hotel Maisiers. The new facility is scheduled to open in September 1997. Information may be obtained through the Chievres operator at C(USA) 011-32-6827-5111. The DSN and address will remain the same: D-314-361-5248, Hotel Maisiers, 80th ASG (NSSG), CMR #451, APO AE 09708-5000. Watch for more details in Military Living's R&R Space-A Report®.

BELGIUM

Tri-Mission Association (BE02R7)
c/o American Embassy
APO AE 09724-5000
(U.S. State Department Billeting)

TELEPHONE NUMBER INFORMATION: Main installation number: C-(USA) 011-32-2-502481.

Location: In Centrum Brussels, follow signs to "Centrum," a large avenue with tunnels. Look for #28 Boulevard Du Regent.

Lodging Office: 28 Blvd Du Regent. **C-(USA) 011-32-2-5082481**, Fax: C-(USA) 011-32-25-11-1626, 0800-1600 hours Mon-Fri. After duty hours report to American Embassy. Check in at facility (after hours at Embassy), check out 1000 hours. No government civilian employee billeting.

TML: All ranks, leave or official duty. Ten apartments, private bath, kitchenette, utensils, color TV weekly housekeeping service, cribs/cots, washer/dryer. Apartments are 2 and 4-bedroom that sleep up to seven. Rates: AD $135; PCS/TDY on leave $85. AD may make reservations, all others Space-A. Pets allowed ($20 cleaning fee).

TML Availability: Fairly good. Best, Nov-May. Difficult, Jun-Oct.

Other Installations in Belgium

SHAPE/Chievres Air Base Community. SHAPE Inn, Bldg 904, Room 108, PSC 79, Box 3, APO AE 09724-5000. **C-(USA) 011-32-65-44-5323**. To reach NATO/SHAPE Headquarters, take the E-10 north from Paris or take the A-15/E-42 from Liege West to the Mons exit and follow signs. Chievres Air Base is located off BE-56 in the village of Chievres.

CANADA

8th Wing Trenton (CN04R1)
Yukon Lodge
8th Wing, Trenton
PO Box 1000 STN Forces
Astra, Ontario CN, KOK 3W0
(Canadian Forces Billeting)

TELEPHONE NUMBER INFORMATION: Main installation numbers: C-613-392-2811 (recording, then press 1, then 3402), D-312-827-7011, ext 3402.

Location: From Toronto take Highway 401 east approximately 100 miles. May also be reached by crossing Canada/USA border at 1000 Islands, NY and proceeding west 70 miles on Highway 401. NMC: Toronto, 100 miles west.

Lodging Office: Bldg 76. **C-613-392-2811, ext 3402, D-312-827-7011, ext 3402**, Fax: C-613-965-7550. Write to: **Yukon Lodge**, 8th Wing Trenton, Astra, Ontario CN KOK 3W0. From 401 take

CANADA
8th Wing Trenton, continued

Glenn Miller exit, follow RCAF signs; Yukon Lodge. Reservations accepted for leave personnel and their family members. Check in at Bldg 23 (Accommodations) for keys 24 hours, check out 1200 hours, late checkout can be arranged.

TML: Yukon Lodge. All ranks, leave or official duty. Bedrooms, one to five beds each, private and semi private baths. Cribs, snack vending, color TV in room and lounge, A/C, refrigerator, washer/dryer, telephones, iron/ironing boards, ice vending, mini-mart. Older structure. Rates: $12 adults, $2 child (6-12), $10 AD (Canadian). Verification of military/family member status required. No pets. Space-A lodging only.

DV/VIP: Base Protocol, CFB Trenton, Astra, Ontario, CN KOK 1BO. Bldg 22. O6+. C-613-965-3379, D-312-827-3379. Limited number of accommodations.

TML Availability: Difficult. Best, Oct-May. Difficult, Jun-Sep.

CREDIT CARDS ACCEPTED: Visa, MasterCard, American Express and Interac (debit card).

Transportation: Off base taxi 392-3525, car rental agency 392-3300.

The Bay of Quinte Region is filled with wonderful fishing, camping, sailing and historical landmarks. Write to: Central Ontario Travel Association, P.O. Box 1566, Peterborough, Ontario K9J 7H7, or call C-1-800-461-1912 for more information.

Locator 392-2811   Medical 392-3480   Police 392-3385

CUBA

Guantanamo Bay Naval Station (CU01R1)
PSC 1005, Box 53
FPO AE 09593-5000

TELEPHONE NUMBER INFORMATION: Main installation numbers: C-(USA) 011-53-99-4063, D-313-564-8877 ext 4063.

Location: In the southeast corner of the Republic of Cuba. Guantanamo Bay Naval Station is accessible only by air. NMC: Miami, FL, 525 air miles northwest. Note: All personnel not assigned must have the permission of the Commander to visit Guantanamo Bay Naval Station.

Lodging Office: ATTN: Billeting, PSC 1005, Box 53. **C-(USA) 011-53-99-2400/01, D-313-564-8877 ext 2400/01,** Fax: C-(USA) 011-53-99-2154, 24 hours. Check in facility, check out 1200 hours daily.

TML: Navy Lodge. PSC 1005, Box 38, FPO AE 09593-0003, all ranks, leave or official duty. Reservations: **C-(USA)011-53-99-3103**, Fax: 011-53-99-3414, 0800-1900 hours Mon-Sun and holidays. Check in 1500-1800 hours, check out 1200 hours daily. Bedroom, two double beds, studio couch, private bath (26). Kitchen, A/C, color TV/VCP, in room telephones, coin washer/dryer. Rates: $40 per unit.

CUBA
Guantanamo Bay Naval Station, continued

TML: BOQ. Bldg 2147. E7+, leave or official duty. Bedroom, private bath (35). Refrigerator, A/C, color TV in room and lounge, cable, housekeeping service, washer/dryer, snack vending machines, ice. Modern structure. Rates: enlisted $7 per person; officer $12 per person.

DV/VIP: BOQ. Bldg 2147. O6 +. Rates: $25. C-011-53-99-4400, D-313-564-8877 ext 4400. Reservations must be made through the CO's office.

Chief VIP: BOQ Bldg 2147. E8- E9. Rates: $15. Reservations: C-011-53-99-2400/2401, D-313-564-8877 ext 2400/2401.

TML Availability: Good most of the year except holidays.

CREDIT CARDS ACCEPTED: American Express.

Transportation: On base taxi 011-53-99-4497, car rental 011-53-99-4564.

Locator 4453/4366   **Medical 72360**   **Police 4105/3813/4145**

DENMARK
(GREENLAND)

Other Installations in Denmark

Thule Air Base (Greenland). Bldg 97, APO AE 09704-5000. C-(USA) 011-299-50-636 ext 2270, D-314-268-1110 ext 3276, Fax: C-(USA) 011-299-50-636 ext 2270, D-314-268-1110 ext 2270. Rates: single $10 per night; suites $16 per night. **Base Commander's written permission is required to visit Thule AB.**

FRANCE

Cercle National Des Armées (FR01R7)
(National Officers' Club of the Armies)
Vice-President, Director of the Officers' Club
#8, Place Saint-Augustin
75008 Paris, France

NOTE: FOR OFFICERS ONLY.

TELEPHONE NUMBER INFORMATION: Main information numbers: C-011-33-1-4490-26-26, ext. Ask for Reservations or Front Desk. Fax: C-011-33-1-4522-24-05, Telegraph Address: "MILICERCLE-PARIS," Account Number 643-638 F.

LOCATION: In Paris Center, at #8, Place Saint-Augustin, across from the Church of Saint-Augustin. It is a short (4.5 city blocks) walk to des Champs Elysées. Paris Metro one block away and taxi service at the front entrance.

FRANCE
Cercle National Des Armées, continued

LODGING/RESERVATION OFFICE: The hotel is open to all members of the Officers' Club, their wives, children and parents accompanying them. The hotel is not open to other relatives of members' families. As a rule the maximum length of stay in the hotel is eight 8 days. After this time, the occupant may be requested to leave the room within 24 hours after being notified. Officers must provide written proof stating the relation of family members accompanying them (ID cards/passports are adequate). To secure a room, it is best to write 30 days in advance indicating the exact date of arrival and length of stay; the administration, however, cannot promise rooms in any special category. Moreover, reservations made over the telephone must be confirmed in writing with deposit (one day's lodging). Payment is required upon reply. Reserved rooms are only held until 1700 hours unless the occupant has notified the hotel of his/her exact arrival in the evening. Those who have reserved rooms which remain unoccupied, and have failed to cancel their reservations at least 24 hours in advance, will be billed accordingly.

ACCOMMODATION (ROOM) RATES: Appartement (Suite, bedroom, living room and bath) 610-795 F ($122.50-$159.65); Chambre avec bains et w.c. (Double room with tub) 420-450 F ($84.35-$90.35); Chambre avec douche et w. c. (Double room with shower) 385 F ($77.30); Chambre avec lavabo et w.c., Grand lit, (Double room, no bath) 240-270 F ($48.20-$54.20); Chambre avec lavabo et w.c., Un lit une personne (Room, one person, no bath) 190-240 F ($38.15-$48.20); Chambre avec lavabo, un lit une personne (Room, one person, no bath) 175-190 F ($35.15-$38.15). The above rates were effective 1 January 1996. Rates are subject to change at anytime; however, rates are normally changed on the first day of each year.

RESTAURANTS/CAFE-BAR: The Officers' Club Restaurant provides "Mess Hall" Service, "Small Menu" Restaurant, "A La Carte" Service and a "Large Lunch, Dinner and Banquet" Service. "Small Menu" Service is offered exclusively to Officers' Club members and their families. "Big Menu" Service is open to Officers' Club members, their families and guests, as well as to visiting officers. "Large Lunch, Dinner and Banquet" Service is reserved for Officers' Club members, their families and guests. The Cafe-bar opens every day from 1130-2200 hours.

OTHER CLUB FACILITIES/SERVICES: The Club reading rooms open every day, 0900-2200 hours; library-study room is open daily, except Saturdays, Sundays and Holidays, 1100 to 1200 and 1300-1700 hours; the game room is open every day, 1200-2200 hours; the barbershop is open Monday through Friday 0930-1100 hours and 1200-1800 hours; closed Saturdays, Sundays and Holidays. Fencing and

CERCLE NATIONAL DES ARMÉES
8, place Saint-Augustin
75008 PARIS

FRANCE
Cercle National Des Armées, continued

Physical Culture room is open daily 1600-2000 hours except Saturdays, Sundays and Holidays (three Fencing Masters-one Physical Culture Teacher). Theater and show ticket reservation service is available at the Reception Desk. Bulletin board service is available through the Reception Desk. Also, upon presentation of membership cards, members are given discounts on merchandise at numerous retail goods shops in Paris. Please inquire about membership at the Reception Desk.

Editor's Notes: The French Officers' Club has allowed the use of its facilities by American active duty and retired military officers, and their families for many years. Deceased officers' widows have also written us about their stay in this beautiful hotel which is so conveniently located in Paris.

Quite a few impressive American "military" clubs can also assist their members in obtaining accommodations. These clubs offering reciprocal benefits are not a part of the U.S. military establishment, however. If you belong to an association or club which serves the military, ask if they can assist you in getting reservations.

There has been some inconsistency in whether or not some of our readers have been able to obtain reservations. The courtesy of extending accommodations has always been on a space-A basis after the needs of their Armed Forces are met.

At times, our readers have received letters written in French which state that the club is not available to them. And, in that regard, we must say that the French Officers' Club is under no obligation to accept reservations from our United States officers. It is our belief, however, that some have been turned away simply because the hotel was full at the time of the reservation's request. When some of our readers have called us and told us this, we have often replied, "It must be April." Most hotels in Paris are booked solid during the pleasant months of April and May.

We suggest that if you are calling to inquire about reservations, that you call when it is late evening or early morning in Paris. The desk is less busy at that time, and you will probably find that the person answering the call speaks English and will gladly answer your questions. They may, however, advise you to contact the Reception Manager during the day for final reservations. If you speak French or know someone who does, who can compose a letter or telefax for you, a written inquiry or telefax might also work well.

If accommodations are not available to you at the time you desire, let the Paris USO (see info below this listing) help you find suitable accommodations at another civilian hotel. You may use the restaurants in the French Officers' Club even if not staying there. The club lounge is also a big $aver on drinks and is very pleasant.

Please see letters from our readers in the latter part of this book. You will find some good information which our readers have sent us on the French Officers' Club in Paris.

United Service Organizations (USO) - Paris (FR02R7)
20 Rue de La Tremille
75008 Paris, France

TELEPHONE NUMBER INFORMATION: C-011-33-1-40-70-99-68, Fax: C-011-33-1-40-70-99-53.

Location: 20 Rue de La Tremille, 75008 Paris, France. One block south of des Champs Elysées, near the Arc de Triomphe.

Mail Address: AMEMBASSY, Paris (USO) PSC 116, APO AE 09777-5000.

274 - Temporary Military Lodging Around the World

FRANCE
United Service Organizations (USO) - Paris, continued

Services/Facilities: The Paris USO provides the following facilities/services: **Hotel Reservations,** Night Club Reservations, English-speaking Baby Sitters, APO Letter Drop, Lounge-Free Coffee, Storage Lockers, Discount Tours, Souvenir Shop, Directions for Shopping/Free Fashion Shows, Assistance in Translations and Travel Information, and more!!!

GERMANY

Ansbach Base Support Battalion (GE60R7)
Katterbach BOQ Office
APO AE 09177-5000

TELEPHONE NUMBER INFORMATION: Main installation numbers: C-(USA) 011-49-981-83-1110 (Ansbach), C-(USA) 011-49-9802-832-1110 (Katterbach), C-(GE) 0981-83-1110, 09802-832-1110; ETS-468-7/8-1110 (Ansbach), 467-1110 (Katterbach); D-314-460-1110 (Ask for ANS).

Location: Exit from A6 Autobahn E or W to B-14 or B-13 N, four miles. Follow US Forces signs to Katterbach Kaserne. NMC: Nürnberg, 26 miles northeast.

Lodging Office: Katterbach transient facility office, **C-(USA) 011-49-9802-83-2812, (GE) 09802-83-1700, D-314-468-2812,** ETS-468-1700, Fax: C-(USA) 011-49-9802-1701, Mon-Fri 0600-2200 hours, Sat 0900-1700 hours, Sun 1000-1800 hours. Check in 1300 hours daily, check out 1000 hours.

TML: TLF, **Franconian Inn,** Bldg 5908, all ranks, leave or official duty. Single rooms, private bath, shared kitchenette (28); family rooms, living room, private bath, private kitchenette (5). Kitchenettes have stove, refrigerator, microwave, toaster, coffee maker, utensils, color TV/VCR, cribs/cots available, housekeeping service, washer/dryer, soda/snack vending. Rates: first person $28, second person $15, each additional person $9. PCS in 60 days, PCS out /TDY 30 days. Space-A often available 24 hours in advance.

DV/VIP: 235th BSB, ETS-468-1500, O6+, retirees Space-A.

TML Availability: Good. Best in Feb-Apr, and Sep-Oct.

CREDIT CARDS ACCEPTED: Visa, MasterCard and American Express.

Transportation: On base shuttle/bus, off base taxi 0981-5005.

Internationally famous for its yearly "Bach Week Ansbach", this Franconian capital also offers gourmet specialties, try "Schlotengeli", or "Pressack" with a cool Ansbach beer. Visit Orangerie Park at the "Hofgarten" afterwards.

Locator 4672-541/542   Medical 4672-717   Police 114

Temporary Military Lodging Around the World - 275

GERMANY
Ansbach Base Support Battalion, continued

Augsburg Base Support Battalion (GE39R7)
Augsburg Guest House
Bldg 184
Unit 250001
APO AE 09178-5000
Scheduled to close November 1998.

TELEPHONE NUMBER INFORMATION: Main installation numbers: C-(USA) 011-49-821-540-1700, (GE) 0821-540-1700, ETS-435-1700, D-314-435-1700.

Location: From Munich-Stuttgart, Autobahn E-8, exit at "Augsburg West" and follow "US Military Facilities Augsburg" signs to Sheridan Kasernes. NMC: Augsburg, in the city.

Lodging Office: Augsburg Guesthouse, Bldg 184, Sheridan Kaserne, 86157 Augsburg. **C-(USA) 011-49-821-521540, (GE) 0821-540-1700, D-314-435-1700,** Fax:C-(USA) 011-49-821-52154105, (GE)-0821-441529, 24 hours. Reservations accepted, PCS up to 90 days, TDY up to 60 days, all others up to 30 days. Check in 1300, check out 1000 hours. Government civilian employee billeting. E-mail: jacksonr@email.augsburg.army.mil

TML: Guest House. Bldg 184, Sheridan Kaserne, all ranks, leave or official duty. VIP Suites, private bath (2); long term suites with private bath, queen size bed, living room, kitchenettes, color TV/VCR, coffee maker, housekeeping service Mon-Sat, cribs/cots ($6), washer/dryer, soda/snack vending. Meeting/conference rooms, mini-mart, exercise room and tanning available ($5 per half hour). Older structure, remodeled. No pets.

TML: Bldgs 180, 182, Sheridan Kaserne, all ranks, leave or official duty. Bedroom, hall bath (17); VIP suites, private bath (3); Bldg 182: suites, queen bed, private bath, living room (16). All rooms have refrigerator, microwave, color TV/VCR, housekeeping service Mon-Sat, washer/dryer, soda/snack vending. Meeting/conference rooms, mini-mart, exercise room and tanning available ($5 per half hour). Older structure. Rates: single $35, double $43, each additional $6; suites single $55, double $70, each additional $6; VIP suite, single $60, double $75, each additional $6. Older structure, remodeled. No pets. **PX, Cafeteria, Pizza Hut, Kentucky Fried Chicken in walking distance.**

TML Availability: Good, Oct-Mar. Difficult, Apr-Sep.

CREDIT CARDS ACCEPTED: Visa, MasterCard and American Express

Transportation: Bus line front of guest house, local taxi service available 35025.

German history is mirrored in the 2,000 year story of Augsburg. Visit imperial Maximilianstrasse, and the romantic alleys of the Lech area.

Locator 435-113   Medical 435-4132   Police 435-114

Babenhausen Kaserne (GE90R7)
Railgunner's Arms, Bldg 4502
APO AE 09089-5000

TELEPHONE NUMBER INFORMATION: Main installation numbers: C-(USA) 011-49-6073-72-880, (GE) 06073-72-880, D-314-348-3655.

276 - Temporary Military Lodging Around the World

GERMANY
Babenhausen Kaserne, continued

Location: Located midway between Darmstadt and Aschaffenburg. Take route B26 E toward Babenhausen. The Kaserne is clearly marked and is on B26. NMC Darmstadt, approximately 10 miles southwest.

Lodging Office: Railgunner's Arms, Bldg 4502. **C-(USA) 011-49-6073-72-880, (GE) 06073-72-880, D-314-348-3655,** Fax: C-(GE) 06073-72-869, 0800-1700 hours Mon-Fri. Mail can be sent to the Patriot Inn Guest House. Check in lodging office 0800-1700 hours, check out 1100 hours. After hours SDO, Bldg 4508. Government civilian employee billeting.

TML: Guest House. Bldg 4502, all ranks, leave or official duty. Bedroom, hall bath (17); suites, private bath (2). Refrigerator, utensils (loan closet kitchen packages), color TV, VCR, housekeeping service, essentials, cribs/cots, washer/dryer, ice vending, , iron/ironing board, alarm clock radios. Modern building, renovated. Rates: sponsor $30, additional adult $10, children under 16 $5. PCS in/out have priority, all categories may make reservations.

DV/VIP: Protocol Office, C-(USA) 011-49-6073-38-621. O1+, WO1. Retirees and lower ranks Space-A.

TML Availability: Good.

CREDIT CARDS ACCEPTED: Visa, Mastercard and American Express.

Babenhausen traces its history to year 1236, and possibly even earlier. A walled city with castle, it was largely destroyed during the 30 Years War and Plague. The late 19th century crossing of two railway lines revitalized the town, and today it has a population of more than 15,000.

Locator 38-655   Medical 8376   Police 696233

Bad Aibling Station (GE91R7)
MWR Customer Service Center
APO AE 09098-5000

TELEPHONE NUMBER INFORMATION: Main installation numbers: C-(USA) 011-49-8061-385-778/779, (GE) 08061-385-778/779, ETS-441-3893.

Location: From Autobahn A-8 (Munich-Salzburg) take Bad Aibling exit and follow signs through Bad Aibling to Munich on secondary road. Station is one mile out of Bad Aibling. NMC: Munich, 30 miles west.

Lodging Office: WildBor Hof. MWR Customer Service Center, Bldg 352. **C-(USA) 011-49-8061-385-778/779, (GE) 08061-385-778/779,** Fax: C-(USA) 011-49-8061-385-731, 0700-2100 Mon-Fri, 0800-1600 Sat-Sun. Check in 1400-2100, check out 1000 hours. Government civilian employee billeting.

TML: Visitors Quarters. Bldgs 359, 361, all ranks, leave or official duty. Bedroom, living room, private bath (24); Family suites, living room, private bath (2); VIP suites (2). Refrigerator, microwave, iron/ironing board, color TV, VCP, alarm clock radio, housekeeping service. Community kitchen and washer/dryer located in each building. Older structure. Rates: standard room $42, family suite $54; VIP $60 per night, $12 per additional guest, with commander approval 18 years old and up, children under 18 free. Duty, reservists and national guard on orders can make reservations, others Space-A.

GERMANY
Bad Aibling Station, continued

DV/VIP: Chief of Staff, Bldg 302. O6+, GS15+. C-011-49-8061-38-5745, ETS-441-3827. Duty may make reservations, others Space-A.

TML Availability: Very good. Best, Dec-Jan. Difficult, Feb-Nov.

Bad Aibling is a picturesque health resort near the Alpine mountains, excellent skiing opportunities are 20 minutes away in Austria. This location is only 50 miles from Salzburg on the crossroad to Italy and only 30 miles from historic Munich.

Locator 441-3893   Medical 441-3781   Police 441-3822

Bad Kreuznach Community (GE01R7)
ATTN: American Guest House, Bldg 5649
410th Base Support Battalion (BSB)
APO AE 09252-5000

TELEPHONE NUMBER INFORMATION: Main installation numbers: C-(USA) 011-49-671-1110, (GE) 0671-1110, ETS-490-1110, D-314-490-1110.

Location: Approximately 50 miles south from Frankfurt am Main, via Mainz to Bad Kreuznach Autobahn A-66 and A-60. Take B-41, at the east outskirts of the city, go south on Bosenheimer Street, left on Alzyer Street, to Nahe Club on the right, billeting next to club. NMC: Bad Kreuznach, in city limits.

Lodging Office: ATTN: American Guest House, Dept. of Army 410th BSB Bldg 5649, Attn: Guest House, APO AE 09252, **C-(USA) 011-49-671-77122, (GE) 0671-77122,** D-314-490-1700, ETS-490-1700, 0700-2300 hours Mon-Fri, Sat-Sun 0700-1500. Check in facility, check out 1100 hours daily.

TML: American Guest House, all ranks, leave or official duty. Bedroom, shared bath (30); bedroom private bath (1); suites, private bath (DV/VIP) (3). Refrigerator, community kitchen, color TV, VCR, housekeeping service, cribs ($5), cots ($4), washer/dryer. All refrigerator, TV, VCR, clock radio, private telephone. Older structure. Rates: sponsor $33, additional occupant $10. DV/VIP $55, additional occupant $15. Duty can make reservations, others Space-A. Pets OK for $5 per night.

TML Availability: Good.

Visit the spa park on the slopes of the Hardt, the Oranienpark, Rose Island and the open air inhaling area with the Radon grading galleries for an interesting trip into German health care. Then take a sip of the local wine.

Locator 490-6274   Medical 490-116   Police 490-114

Bamberg Base Support Battalion (GE34R7)
Bamberg Inn
ATTN: AETV-WG-BA
APO AE 09139-5000

TELEPHONE NUMBER INFORMATION: Main installation numbers: C-(USA) 011-49-951-300-1110, (GE) 0951-300-1110, ETS-469-1110, D-314-460-1110, ask for Bamberg.

GERMANY
Bamberg Base Support Battalion, continued

Location: On GE 26/505. Warner Barracks, the main installation, is on the east side of the city between Zollner and Pödeldorter Streets. Follow signs. NMC: Nürnberg, 30 miles southeast.

Lodging Office: Bamberg Inn. Guest House Office, Bldg 7678, room 4, 1st floor, **C-(USA) 011-49-951-300-1700, (GE) 0951-300-1700, D-314-469-1700/8604,** ETS-469-8700, Fax: C-(USA) 011-49-951-37957, 0800-1730 Mon-Fri, 1030-1430 Sat-Sun. Other hours, Military Police, Bldg 7108. Check in facility 1400, check out 1100 hours daily. Government civilian employee billeting.

TML: Bamberg Inn. Guest Houses, Bldg 7678, annex Bldg 7070, 1st floor, O'Club, Zollnerstrasse. All ranks, PCS, ETS, TDY. Bedrooms, shared baths (40); suite, private bath (VIP-O1+)(3); DV/VIP suite (O3+)(1). Refrigerator, color TV, alarm clock/radios in all rooms, vending rooms (2 microwaves, snack coffee and coke machines), laundry room, housekeeping Mon-Fri, cribs, irons, ironing boards available, hall phones. Older structure, renovated. Rates: standard, first person $35, each additional person $5; mini suite, first person $45, each additional person $10; VIP suite, first person $55, each additional person $15. PCS, TDY and Space-A may make reservations. No pets.

DV/VIP: Deputy Community Commander. O5+. Call (USA) 011-49-951-300-1700. Retirees and lower ranks Space-A.

TML Availability: Limited.

CREDIT CARDS ACCEPTED: Visa, American Express and Diners.

Bamberg's streets are a Gothic tapestry, wander them and you'll find St. Michaels Church, the Old Town Hall, and a Baroque castle-the Concordia. Don't miss "Little Venice".

Locator 469-7738   Medical 469-8741/97   Police 469-8700

Baumholder Annex (Bieuenfeld) (GE54R7)
Guest House, Bldg 9961
APO AE 09260-4675

TELEPHONE NUMBER INFORMATION: Main installation numbers: C-(USA) 011-49-6782-13-1110, (GE) 06782-13-1110, ETS-493-7-1110, D-314-485-1110, ask for NEU.

Location: On GE-41, about 90 miles southwest from Rhein-Main Airport (Frankfurt), about 25 miles northwest from Ramstein Air Base, near Baumholder. Follow signs to Neubruecke Hospital. NMC: Baumholder, 9 miles east.

TML: Guest House. Bldg 9961, C-(USA) 011-49-6782-13-287, ETS-493-7287, all ranks, leave or official duty. Handicap accessible. Two bedroom, shared bath (30); two bedroom, private bath (2). Refrigerator, community kitchen, limited utensils, color TV, housekeeping service, cribs, washer/dryer. Older structure, remodeled. Rates for PCS/TDY on leave/vacation; sponsor $28, second person $15, additional person $10.

TML Availability: Best, Sep-Apr. Difficult, May-Aug.

CREDIT CARDS ACCEPTED: Visa, MasterCard, American Express, and EuroCard

Temporary Military Lodging Around the World - 279

GERMANY
Baumholder Annex (Bieuenfeld), continued

The Rheinland Pflaz is full of colorful villages that preserve many German traditional customs.

Locator 06782-13-1110   Medical 116   Police 114

Baumholder Base Support Battalion (GE03R7)
Hotel Lagehof Inn
Ivy Street, Bldg 8076
APO AE 09034-5000

TELEPHONE NUMBER INFORMATION: Main installation numbers: C-(USA) 011-49-6783-6-1700, (GE) 06783-6-1700, ETS-485-113 ask for Baumholder and ext, D-314-485-113 ask for Baumholder and ext.

Location: From Kaiserslautern, take Autobahn 62 toward Trier, exit north at Freisen and follow signs to Baumholder and Smith Barracks. NMC: Kaiserslautern, 35 miles southeast.

Lodging Office: Hotel Lagerhof, Ivy Street, Bldg 8076, **C-(USA) 011-49-6783-5182, (GE) 06783-5182, D-314-485-1700,** Fax C-(USA) 011-49-6738-6-6960, 0730-2000 Mon-Fri, 1000-1800 Sat-Sun, 0730-1600 Holidays, C ext 1700. Check in 1300-2000, check out 1100 hours daily. Government civilian employee billeting.

TML: Lagerhof Transient Billeting. Bldg 8076, all ranks, leave or official duty. Bedroom, private bath (10); two bedroom, private bath (8); Doll House, four bedroom, private bath (1); Chalet, one bedroom, bath (1). Community kitchen, limited utensils, refrigerator, color TV lounge, housekeeping service, cribs/cots, washer/dryer, color TVs, soda/snack vending. Older structure. Rates for PCS, TDY and Space-A: first person $30, second person $17, third person and each additional $12; DVQ $28, third person $14. Doll House $32, third person $17. Chalet $30, third person $16. Duty can make reservations, others Space-A. Pets allowed, fee still pending, call for more information.

Note: An annex will be added to the existing Lagerhof. Construction is projected for late 1997, early 1998.

DV/VIP: Commander, C-(USA) 011-49-6783-6300, O6/GS-12+.

TML Availability: Very good.

CREDIT CARDS ACCEPTED: Visa, MasterCard, American Express, Euro and Access.

Transportation: On base shuttle/bus 485-6475, on base taxi 485-6100.

Visit nearby Idar Oberstein for precious gems and stones, Trier's Roman ruins, the Mosel Valley's, castles and vineyards.

Locator 485-6446   Medical-485-1750   Police-485-7265

This area will be greatly reduced in the future. Keep posted on the latest developments with Military Living's *R&R Space-A Report*®.

GERMANY

Chiemsee AFRC (GE08R7)
Reservations, Unit 24604
APO AE 09098-5000

TELEPHONE NUMBER INFORMATION: Main installation numbers: C-(USA) 011-49-8051-803172, (GE) 08051-803172, Fax: C-(USA) 011-49-8051-803158.

Location: Located directly off Munich-Salzburg Autobahn A-9 southeast of Munich. Buses use Felden exit; automobiles continue for 800 meters and exit when you see the sign for AFRC Chiemsee Campground. NMC: Bad Aibling, 20 miles northwest.

TML: Two hotels; the Chiemsee Lake Hotel and the Park Hotel have accommodations for more than 300 guests.

Reservations: Accepted six months in advance. Write to: AFRC Chiemsee Reservations, Unit 24604, APO AE 09098-5000, or Rasthuas am Chiemsee, Felden 25, 83233, Bernau, C-(USA) 011-49-8051-803172, (GE) 080501-803172, Fax: C-(GE) 08051-803-158, 0800-1900 hours daily, closed American holidays.

Eligibility: AD/Retired/DoD civilian assigned overseas. See Garmisch listing for details.

Facilities: Cafeteria, laundromat, Lake Hotel restaurant and bar, AAFES, camp store, check cashing, sports equipment rental, boat rental, ESSO station nearby, ice, recreation room, campground.

Rates: Park Hotel, double occupancy, E1-E5 $50; E6-O3 $54; O4-06 $58; 07+ $62. Lake Hotel, double, E1-E5 $54; E6-O3 $58; O4-O6 $62, O7+ $66. Small suite, all ranks, $77. Large suite $92. Children 15 and under stay free in parent's room on existing bed space, with cot $6 daily. Cribs $3 daily. For more than two adults in one room, add $9 per adult per night. Handicapped rooms available. Prices subject to change.

CREDIT CARDS ACCEPTED: Visa, MasterCard, American Express, Diners Club and Discover.

AFRC Chiemsee is situated on the shores of Germany's largest lake - Chiemsee. Enjoy water sports such as canoeing, paddleboats, sailing and windsurfing. At the nearby Chiemgauer Alps you can hike, hang glide and take in the panoramic scenery.

Locator 440-355   Medical 116   Police 114

Darmstadt Base Support Battalion (GE37R7)
Patriot Inn Guest House
Cambrai Fritsch Kaserne
233d BSB; CMR 431
APO AE 09175-5000

TELEPHONE NUMBER INFORMATION: Main installation numbers: C-(USA) 011-49-6151-69-1700 or 011-49-6151-96430, (GE) 06151-69-1700, or 06151-96430, D-314-348-1700.

GERMANY
Darmstadt Base Support Battalion, continued

Location: Accessible from the A-5 and A-67 autobahns. One mile south of downtown Darmstadt (Cambrai Fritsch Kaserne). NMC: Darmstadt, one mile north.

Lodging Office: Patriot Inn, CMR 431, APO AE 09175. **C-(USA) 011-49-6151-96430, Fax: (GE) 06151-964336, D-348-1700,** 0730-2100 Mon-Fri, Sat-Sun 1300-2100. Check in 1300, check out 1100. Call before 1800 for late check-in. Government civilian employee billeting.

TML: Patriot Inn. Bldg 4090, 4091, Jefferson Village, all ranks, leave or official duty. Single rooms, shared bath (20); suites, private bath (33). Refrigerator, community kitchen, utensils, color TV, housekeeping service, cribs/cots, lending closet, washer/dryer, ice vending. Older structure, remodeled. Rates: shared bath $30, suites $40 per night, each additional person $15, children under 16, $7. Duty and DAVs can make reservations, others Space-A.

DV/VIP: VIP suites (2) recently renovated.

TML Availability: Good, Jan-Apr. Difficult, May-Dec.

CREDIT CARDS ACCEPTED: Visa, MasterCard and American Express.

Downtown Darmstadt has a great "walkplatz" for shopping, hike to the Odenwald from the railroad station, or tour the Mathildenhöhe, and the Kranichstein hunting palace on the city's outskirts.

Locator 348-6229   **Medical 116**   **Police 348-7777**

Freidberg Community (GE68R7)
ATTN: Freidberg Guest House
Bldg 3635
APO AE 09074-5000

TELEPHONE NUMBER INFORMATION: Main installation information: C-(USA) 011-49-6031-81-113, D-314-324-3113.

Location: Friedberg is 20 miles northeast of Frankfurt, 5 miles east of the Frankfurt-Giessen #5/E-4 Autobahn on GE-3. Follow signs to Ray Barracks. NMC: Frankfurt, 20 miles southeast.

Lodging Office: Friedberg Guest House, Bldg 3635, C-(USA) 011-49-6031-81-1700, D-314-324-1700, Fax C-(USA) 011-49-6031-13-736.

TML: Call for room descriptions, rates and availability.

Visit the many historic structures, rich in medieval architecture. One of these is the Judische Bad which extends some 25 meters underground. Jewish women used the Bad, or bath, for centuries and is one of only four existing Hebrew baths in all of Germany.

GERMANY

Garmisch AFRC (GE10R7)
Vacation Planning Center
Unit 24501
APO AE 09053-5000

TELEPHONE NUMBER INFORMATION: Main installation numbers: C-(USA) 011-49-8821-72981, (GE) 08821-72981, D-314-440-2575.

Location: Take Autobahn A-95 south from Munich to Garmisch-Partenkirchen. From Austria take national roads numbered 2 or 187. NMC: Munich, 60 miles north.

Description of Area: Garmisch has been Germany's leading winter recreation and sports area for over 50 years. Located 60 miles south of Munich, Garmisch sits at the foot of Germany's highest mountain, the Zugspitze. A $3 million renovation project was underway at press time at both the General Patton and General Von Steuben Hotels to increase room size and amenities, including new balconies, private baths, and entertainment systems. Kitchen, dining room, and lounge renovations will also upgrade guest services. Full range of ski programs, beginner to expert. Golf opportunities, tennis, kayaking, white-water rafting, windsurfing, mountaineering, arts and crafts. For more than 45 years AFRC Garmisch has provided the means for quality economy vacations.

TML: Two hotels: **General Patton, General Von Steuben and guest house Haus Flora.** Accommodations for about 540 guests per night. Off site apartments also available.

Reservations: Accepted up to six months in advance. One year for groups of 25 or more. Deposits required within 30 days after booking. Write to: AFRC Garmisch Reservations Office, Unit 24501, APO AE 09053 or Osterfelderstr. 2, 8100 Garmisch-Partenkirchen. **C-(USA) 011-49-8821-750575, (GE) 08821-750575,** Fax: C-(USA) 49-8821-3942, (GE) 08821-3942. Office open 0800-1900 hours Mon-Fri, 0900-1700 Sat, 0900-1700 Sun. Note: Call **early** morning - 6 hours ahead of Eastern Standard Time.

Season of Operation: Year round.

Eligibility: In general: US military forces and family members assigned in the USEUCOM area (permanently or temporarily); Reserve in training in Europe; US DoD civilian employees working full time in USEUCOM and family members residing with them (Red Cross, USO, certain US embassy personnel; US citizen consultant and technical representatives; personnel with USAREUR ID Card AE Form 600-700); retired US military personnel residing in or visiting Europe (Army, Navy, Marines and Air Force); PHS/NOAA not authorized; EUCOM Coast Guard; British Forces of the Rhein/Canadian Forces w/family members residing with them stationed in Germany; certain NATO forces/liaison personnel authorized to purchase in commissary/PX; those on official duty to AFRC or NATO/SHAPE School; unaccompanied widows/ers, and dependents retired with appropriate ID. Certain authorized guests, accompanied.

Facilities: APO, Merchants Bank, beauty/barber shop, commissary, chapel, Snack-O-Mat, library, sports shop, gym, Bavarian Shop, class VI (Package Store), Foodland, PX, Stars and Stripes AAFES Bookmark, child care center, hotel restaurants and bars, TV room and much more. (Note: No U.S. medical support in Garmisch). **AFRC Garmisch Room Rates:** Double with bath E1-E5 $55, E6-O3 $59, O4-O6 $63, O7+ $67. Hotel suites, all ranks, $87. Haus Flora Suites, all ranks, $97. Children

GERMANY
Garmisch AFRC, continued

15 and under free in parent's room on existing bed space, add $6 daily for cot. Cribs $3 daily. More than two adult occupants, add $9 to double rate. Group rates available on request. No pets. Recreation prices in May. Special rates may be available during non-peak seasons: April and November.

TML Availability: Good except Jun-Aug and Christmas/New Year periods. Loisach Inn difficult Dec-Sept. Good Oct-Nov.

CREDIT CARDS ACCEPTED: Visa, MasterCard, American Express, Diners Club and Discover.

Garmisch Community (GE62R7)
Loisach Inn
Garmisch Billeting
Unit 24515
ZCFHGGP82
APO AE 09053-5000

TELEPHONE NUMBER INFORMATION: Main installation numbers: C-(USA) 011-49-8821-53396/750873, D-314-440-2873/76/92/1700.

Location: From Munich: Autobahn A95 to Oberau. Priority (Main) Road from Oberau to Garmisch Statmitte (City Center) thru Farchant. Located 3/4 mile from Garmisch Statmitte off Zugspitzster, at the corner of Zugspitzster and Gernackerster. NMC: Munich, 65 miles northeast.

Lodging Office: Bldg 104, Room 334, C-(USA) 011-49-8821-53396/750873, D-314-440-2873/76/92/1700, Fax C-(USA) 011-49-8821-53401, 0630-2230 Mon-Fri, 0800-1700 Sat-Sun and holidays. Check in billeting office after 1400 Mon-Fri/1300 Sat-Sun, military police station after hours. Check out 1000 hours, late check out request D-314-440-2873/76.

TML: Loisach Inn. All ranks, leave or official duty. Bedroom, private bath (16); suite, private bath (4). Refrigerator, microwave, color TV/VCR, housekeeping service, essentials, cribs/cots available ($4), washer/dryer, ice-vending. Rates: room, first person $35; suite, first person $45; each additional person $4. Maximum $43 per family room; $57 suite. Maximum three per unit, three to four per suite. Duty can make reservations, all others Space-A. Space-A reservations seven days prior; can be bumped by official duty. Pets allowed for PCS in/out only. Charge: one night extra basic room fee and $2 per day in addition to regular cost, inform when making reservation.

TML Availability: Good, Mar-Apr and Sep-Oct (except during Oktoberfest). Difficult, May-Aug and Nov-Feb.

Locator D 370-7571   **Medical 19222**   **Police (MP) 440-2801**

Giessen Base Support Battalion (GE23R7)
Guesthouse, Bldg 63
414th BSB - North - Unit 20911
APO AE 09169-5000

TELEPHONE NUMBER INFORMATION: Main installation numbers: C-(USA) 011-49-641-402-1110, (GE) 0641-402-1110, ETS-343-1110, D-314-343-1110.

284 - Temporary Military Lodging Around the World

GERMANY
Giessen Base Support Battalion, continued

Location: Autobahn E-5 to Gambach Kreuz, take 45 to Giessen then 485 to Giessen. Turn off Ursulun exit, follow signs to HHQ Giessen. NMC: Giessen, in the city.

Lodging Office: Guest House, Bldg 63, C-(USA) 011-49-641-402-1700 (GE) 0641-402-1700, D-314-343-1700, 0800-1930 Mon-Fri, 0900-1630 weekends and holidays. Check in facility 1300, check out 1000 hours daily.

TML: Guest House. Bldg 63, Giessen General Depot, all ranks, leave or official duty. Bedroom suite, private bath (8); bedroom, private bath (6); bedroom, shared bath (8). In room cooking facilities, color TV, housekeeping service, cribs/cots, washer/dryer, soda/snack vending. Older structure, newly renovated. Rates: private bath $39, shared bath $25, each additional person $15. $60 non-refundable pet deposit for a suite. $50 non-refundable pet deposit for a regular room. $6 per day pet fee. Duty can make reservations, others Space-A.

DV/VIP: Cmdr. ETS-343-8434. Determined by Cmdr.

TML Availability: Good.

CREDIT CARDS ACCEPTED: Visa, MasterCard, and American Express.

Locator 343-8307   Medical 346-7701   Police 346-8601

Grafenwöhr Community (GE11R7)
Tower Inn
Bldg 213, Argonne Ave
APO AE 09114-5000

TELEPHONE NUMBER INFORMATION: Main installation numbers: C-(USA) 011-49-9641-83-113, (GE) 09641-83-113, ETS-475-XXXX, D-314-475-1110.

Location: From Autobahn A-9 (Nürnberg-Berlin) exit at Pegnitz/Grafenwöhr, follow signs to training area. NMC: Nürnberg, 56 miles southwest.

Lodging Office: Tower Inn, Bldg 213, Argonne Ave, opposite Community Club, **C-(USA) 011-49-9641-83-1700/6182, (GE) 09641-83-1700/6182,** E-mail: towerinn@email.grafenwoehr.army.mil, 0700-2200 Mon-Fri, 0700-1700, Sat and Sun. After Duty hours see SDO 7th ATC Bldg 621, or call ETS-475-8302 for confirmed reservations or open rooms. Check in 1300, check out 1100.

TML: Total of 83 rooms located in 9 buildings. All ranks, leave or official duty. Single and double rooms with private bath, family rooms with kitchen, refrigerator, microwave, color TV, VCR, mini bar, housekeeping service, cribs, rollaway beds, washers/dryers. Older structure renovated. Rates: private bath and living room$42, each additional person $6; private bath $34, each additional person $4. Reservations accepted 30 days prior for TDY and three days prior for visiting.

DV/VIP: Protocol Office, 7th Army Training Command, O6+, ETS-475-7145/6221, 3 DVQ suites. Rates $42, each additional occupant $6. Retirees and lower ranks Space-A.

TML Availability: Best, Nov-Jan.

GERMANY
Grafenwöhr Community, continued

The Tower Inn is the winner of the 1995 Lodging of the Year Award competition in the large category. Attractions available near Grafenwöhr include Crystal, Porcelain and Nutcracker factories. Call Army Community Service for a list of local Castles, Churches and other sightseeing areas near the Grafenwöhr community, ETS-475-8433.

Locator 475-6128   Medical-116   Police 114

Hanau Community (GE13R7)
414th BSB CMR470
New Argonner Kaserne, Bldg 203
APO AE 09165-5000

TELEPHONE NUMBER INFORMATION: Main installation numbers: C-(USA) 011-49-6181-88-1700, (GE) 06181-88-1700, ETS-322-1700, D-314-322-1700.

Location: From Autobahn 66 to Highway 8 or 40 to Hanau, New Argonner and Pioneer Housing Area south of Highway 8. Clearly marked. NMC: Frankfurt, 15 miles west.

Lodging Office: Bldg 203, New Argonner Kaserne, APO AE 09165, **C-(USA) 011-49-6181-88-1700, (GE) 06181-88-1730 (ask for billeting)**, Fax: C-(USA)011-49-6181-955230, 0730-2130 Mon-Fri; 0730-1600 Sat-Sun. Check in billeting 1400, check out 1000 hours daily. Government civilian employee billeting.

TML: Guest House. Bldg 318, Pioneer Housing, all ranks, leave or official duty. Two bedroom, private bath (6); three bedroom, private bath (8); four bedroom, private bath (7). Cribs/cots, housekeeping service, refrigerator, microwave, color TV, VCR washer/dryer. Older structure. Rates: sponsor $39, each additional person $15. Duty can make reservations, others Space-A. Pets OK with $60 non-refundable fumigation fee and $6 per pet per night.

TML: Guest House. **New Argonner**, Bldg 203, all ranks, leave or official duty. Bedroom, two beds, private bath (30). Cribs/cots, refrigerator, community microwaves, color TV, VCR, housekeeping service, washer/dryer. Older structure, renovated. Rates: same as Guest House above. Maximum two per room. Duty can make reservations, others Space-A. Pets OK with $50 non-refundable cleaning fee + $6 per night.

TML: VOQ. Bldg 204, O6+ and civilian equivalents. One bedroom suites, 2 beds, living room, private bath (2). Refrigerator, kitchenette with microwave, cribs/cots, color TV, VCR, housekeeping service, washer/dryer. Older structure, renovated 1991. Rates: $45, each additional person $15. Maximum two per room. Duty can make reservations, others Space-A.

TML: Copper Top Inn. Bldg 1617, Gelnhausen (30K from Hanau). Rooms with two beds, private bath, refrigerator, TV/VCR, microwave, laundry facilities (15). Reservations are made through Hanau Billeting. Rates: same as Guest House.

TML Availability: Difficult.

CREDIT CARDS ACCEPTED: Visa, MasterCard and American Express.

Remember Hansel and Gretel, Snow White and Little Red Riding Hood? Visit the monument to native sons, the Grimm Brothers on the Marktplatz in the center of town. Many other attractions are located in Hanau.

GERMANY
Hanau Community, continued

Locator 113 Medical 116 Police 110

Heidelberg Community (GE33R7)
US Army Guesthouse, Heidelberg
411th BSB-Hospitality Management Group
APO AE 09102-5000

TELEPHONE NUMBER INFORMATION: Main installation numbers: C-(USA) 011-49-6221-57-100, (GE) 06221-57-1700, D-314-370-1700.

Location: South from Frankfurt direction Basel/Karlsruhe, approximately one hour drive. Take Schwetzingen/Patrick Henry Village exit and continue on main road bearing left at the fork and straight to Bldg 4527 (hotel) on left side. NMC: Heidelberg, in the city.

Lodging Office: Patrick Henry Village, Bldg 4527, North Lexington Ave, 24 hours. Reservations 0730-1630 Mon-Fri. **C-(USA) 011-49-6221-795100, (GE) 06221-795100, D-341-370-6941,** Fax: C-(USA) 011-49-6221-795600, Check in facility, check out 1100 hours daily. Government civilian employee billeting. **Note: This facility received the USAREUR Lodging Operation of the Year Award for medium-size billets for 1995.**

TML: Guest house. Bldg 4527, all ranks, leave or official duty. Bedroom, private bath (162), Rates: single $50, double $80; suites (21), Rates: single without kitchen $60, double $90; single with kitchen $70, double $100; "Key Quarter Apartments" with all amenities (40), Rates: $51.50 per day. Refrigerator, community kitchen, color TV/VCR, housekeeping service, cribs/cots, washer/dryer, international direct dial phone, handicap accessible facilities, fitness room/sauna, non-smoking rooms available. Older structure, renovated. Rates: varies according to status and type of room, call for information. PCS reservations, 60 days ahead, TDY 14 days ahead, others Space-A. Firm reservation two weeks ahead for Weekend Getaway special w/credit card. $/DM conversion available for in-house guests. Pets allowed with one day single room charge and $4 per day service charge. Cots and cribs available for $8 each, per night.

DV/VIP: SGS, HQ USAREUR, D-314-370-8707/6502, O6/GS-15+. Suites, private bath (21). Retirees and lower ranks Space-A.

TML Availability: Good over Christmas holiday. Difficult all other times.

CREDIT CARDS ACCEPTED: Visa, MasterCard, American Express and Diners.

Visit famous University of Heidelberg, and its Students' Inns - Roten Ochsen (Red Ox) and Zum Sepp' are adjacent on the Hauptstrasse. The Castle above the city, and bridge across the Neckar River also should not be missed.

Locator 370-7571 Medical 371-2891 Police 370-6400

Hohenfels Community (GE71R7)
Guesthouse, Bldg 63
APO AE 09173-5000

TELEPHONE NUMBER INFORMATION: Main installation numbers: C-(USA) 011-49-9472-83-113, D-314-466-1110.

GERMANY
Hohenfels Community, continued

Location: Take the #3/E-5 Autobahn southeast from Nurnberg and exit at Parsberg then drive seven miles east to Hohenfels. follow the American installation signs. NMC: Nurnberg, 35 miles northwest.

Lodging Office: Guesthouse, Bldg 63, C-(USA) 011-49-9472-950155/2 or C-(USA) 011-49-9472-83-1700, D-314-466-1700/2219, Fax: C-(USA) 011-49-9472-95-0154, Mon-Fri 0600-2200 hours, Sat and Sun 0730-1630 hours. Reservations C-(USA) 1-800-462-7691, Fax C-(USA) 011-49-69-699-6309.

TML: Guesthouse. Singles, doubles and suites, private bath (50). Kitchen, laundry facility, ice vending, telephones. Rates: single $22-$32, each additional person $4; suite $38, each additional person $6; DV/VIP $42, each additional person $6, reservations through Protocol.

TML: Bldgs 70, 71, 6, 7, 1177, 1173, and 1172. Call for more information.

Hohenfels is located in the mountains on the edge of a US Army Training Area neat the confluence of the Vils and Naab rivers.

Medical 09472-83-116

Illesheim Community (GE72R7)
Illesheim Army Community Services
CMR 416 Box I
APO AE 09140-5000

TELEPHONE NUMBER INFORMATION: Main installation numbers: C-(USA) 011-49-9841-83-113, D-314-467-1110.

Location: From the #7/E-70 Autobahn south or Wuerzburg exit to GE-13 north or south exit GE-470 northeast in the direction of Bad Windwheim. Follow the U.S. signs marked Storck Barracks. NMC: Nurnberg, 38 miles east.

Lodging Office: Bldg 6624, BOQ C-(USA) 011-49-9841-83-550/650, D-314-467-4550/4650.

TML: Limited transient officer billeting.

Located on the Aisch River and settle in the 8th century, Illesheim was once the site of four castles, three of which were destroyed during the 15th century. A 14th century castle however, remains. Illesheim is only 12 miles from the ancient walled city of Rothenburg on the Tauber River.

Kaiserslautern Community, Ramstein Air Base (GE30R7)
Ramstein Inns Vogelweh
86 SVS/SVMLR
Unit 3250 Box 500
APO AE 09054-0500

TELEPHONE NUMBER INFORMATION: Main installation numbers: C-(USA) 011-49-631-536-1110, D-314-489-1110, (GE) 0631-536-1110.

GERMANY
Kaiserslautern Community, Ramstein Air Base, continued

Location: Off the A-6 Mannheim-Saarbruecken Autobahn, take the Kaiserslautern exit for Vogelweh Housing Area. Follow signs to housing area or Kapaun Barracks (AS). NMC: Kaiserslautern, 3 miles northeast.

Lodging Office: Bldg 305, C-(USA) 011-49-6371-47-7345/7864/2445/2614, (GE) 06371-42589, Fax C-(USA) 011-49-6371-42589, 0730-1700 Mon-Thu, 0730-1630 Fri. Check in facility, check out 1100 hours daily. Government civilian employee billeting. **Note: See Ramstein Inns: North, South, Sembach and Landstuhl listing for more lodging.** Building 305 on Ramstein AB manages all reservations for Kaiserslautern Community which includes Ramstein AB, Sembach AB, Vogelweh AS and Landstuhl Medical Center lodging facilities.

TML: Guest House, Bldg 1002, 1003 and 1004, C-(USA) 011-49-6371-47-7190/7621, D-314-489-7190/7621, Fax C-(USA) 011-49-6371-47-7659, D-314-489-7659, all ranks, leave or official duty. Check in Bldg 1002. Bedrooms, shared bath (98); family units, bedrooms, private bath (33); Suites (DV/VIP) (16). All have color TV, VCR, microwave, ironing board/iron, telephone, clock radio, free washers and dryers. Rates: $12-$17 per person, family units $27.50. Duty can make reservations, others Space-A.

DV/VIP: PAO. Ramstein AB, C-(USA) 011-49-6371-47-6854, O6+, retirees Space-A.

TML Availability: Difficult. Best Dec-Jan.

CREDIT CARDS ACCEPTED: Visa, MasterCard and American Express.

Transportation: On base shuttle/bus/taxi 480-5961, off base shuttle/bus 011-49-631-316670, off base taxi 06371-50510/58326, car rental agency 06371-44202.

The city hall (Rathaus), is the highest in Germany. There is an elegant restaurant in the penthouse. Visit the Pfalztheater for opera, operetta, plays and ballet. Harry's gift shop, known around the world by military families, is at 5-11 Manheimer Strasse (C-(USA) 011-49-631-67081). TelePassport® Service is now available; call home in privacy/receive calls in your room.

Locator 480-6120   Medical 116   Police 114

Kitzingen Community (GE75R7)
Woodland Inn Rod & Gun Club
417th BSB Unit 26124
APO AE 09031-5000

TELEPHONE NUMBER INFORMATION: Main installation numbers: C-(USA) 011-49-9321-305-113, D-314-355-8113.

Location: Take A7 from Frankfurt to Wuerzburg, follow signs to Biebelreid, Kitzingen exit. Follow signs to Kitzingen, you will be on B8. Stay on the main/Priority road through Kitzingen. Turn right at green and yellow E Center, follow to end of the street, turn left. Turn right at 2nd light, follow to Woodland Inn Rod & Gun Club.

Lodging Office: Bldg 166, C-(USA) 011-49-9321-305-600, D-314-355-8600, Fax- C-(USA) 011-49-9321-31836, 0830-1600 M-F, Bar other hours. Reservations recommended.

GERMANY
Kitzingen Community, continued

TML: Guest House, all ranks and civilians, leave or official duty. C-011-49-9321-305-600, D-314-355-8600. Rooms with refrigerator, color TV, housekeeping service, washer/dryer, restaurant. Rates: all categories, sponsor $25, each additional person $10, children under 2 free.

CREDIT CARDS ACCEPTED: Visa, MasterCard, American Express, Wed-Sun only, $50 minimum.

Transportation: On/off base shuttle bus 0931-889-1800-7368, car rental 0931-708475, off base taxi 09321-8088, train station (Bahnhof) 09321-5100

The Woodland Inn was built in 1934 as a club for officers of the German Luftwaffe. The art and architecture is typical of the era, the setting is a Bavarian hunting lodge.

Landstuhl Medical Center (GE40R7)
Ramstein Inn-Landstuhl
86 SVS/SVMLL
Unit 3250, Box 500
APO AE 09094-5000

TELEPHONE NUMBER INFORMATION: Main installation numbers: C-(USA) 011-49-6371-86-1110, (GE) 06371-86-1110, ETS-486-1110, D-314-486-1110.

Location: Take the Landstuhl exit from the A-6 Mannheim-Saarbrücken Autobahn. Follow signs for "US Hospital". NMC: Kaiserslautern, 10 miles northeast.

Lodging Office: Bldg 305, **C-(USA) 011-49-6371-47-7345/7864/2445/2614,** **(GE) 06371-42589,** Fax C-(USA) 011-49-6371-42589, 0730-1700 Mon-Thu, 0730-1630 Fri. Check in facility, check out 1100 hours daily. Government civilian employee billeting. **Note:** See Ramstein Inns: North, South, Vegelweh, and Sembach listing for more lodging. Building 305 on Ramstein AB manages all reservations for Kaiserslautern Community which includes Ramstein AB, Sembach AB, Vogelweh AS and Landstuhl Medical Center lodging facilities.

TML: VOQ/VAQ. **Ramstein Inn-Landstuhl,** Bldg 3752, **C-(USA) 011-49-6371-47-8128/8342, D-314-486-8128/8342**, Fax C-(USA) 011-49-6371-47-7627, D-314-486-7627, all ranks, leave or official duty. Check in Bldg 3752. Bedroom, shared bath (230). Refrigerator, color TV, housekeeping service, washer/dryer, microwave, VCR, video rental, irons, ceiling fan. Older structure, remodeled. Rates: $12 per person, maximum $24 per room. Duty can make reservations, others Space-A.

DV/VIP: Community Commander, C-(USA) 011-49-6371-486-7183, O6+.

TML Availability: Good, Nov-Feb. Difficult, summer months.

CREDIT CARDS ACCEPTED: Visa, MasterCard and American Express.

Transportation: On base shuttle/bus/taxi D-480-5961, off base shuttle/bus 011-49-631-316670, off base taxi 06371-50510/58626, car rental agency 011-49-710-6219407.

Visit the Marktplatz in Kaiserslautern for a traditional German farmer's market. Also, ask at USO Kaiserslautern for directions to local fests and sights -they have a wealth of information to share! TelePassport® Service is now available; call home in privacy/receive calls in your room.

290 - Temporary Military Lodging Around the World

GERMANY
Landstuhl Medical Center, continued

Locator 486-8342   Medical 116   Police 114

Mannheim Base Support Battalion (GE43R7)
HHD 293 BSB
Unit 29901, Box 3
APO AE 09086-5000

TELEPHONE NUMBER INFORMATION: Main installation numbers: C-(USA) 011-49-621-730-1110, (GE) 0621-730-1110, ETS-380-1110, D-314-380-1110.

Location: Accessible from the E12/A6 Autobahns. Take the Viernheim exit, follow B38 to Benjamin Franklin Village Housing Area on Fürther Strasse. NMC: Mannheim, 8 miles southwest.

Lodging Office: Bldg 312, Benjamin Franklin Village Housing Area, Fürtherstrasse, 0600-2400 daily. **C-(USA) 011-49-621-730-6118/6547/1700, (GE) 0621-730-6118/1700,** Fax: C-(GE) 0621-738607. Mon-Fri 0600-2400, Sat-Sun and holidays, 0800-2400, closed Christmas and New Years. Check in 1200, check out 1000.

TML: Guest house. **Franklin House**, Bldg 312, Benjamin Franklin Village Housing Area, Fuertherstrasse, all ranks, leave or official duty, C-(USA) 011-49-621-730-1700/8118/6547, (GE) 0621-730-1700/8118/6547. Two bedroom, private bath (39); suites, private bath (DV/VIP) (3). Housekeeping service, cribs/cots, ice vending, kitchenette, CATV, washer/dryer, VIP suites have honor bars. Older structure, renovated. No pets. Rates: single $40, double $40, each additional person $20; VIP suites $50, second person $20, each additional person $8. Duty can make reservations, others Space-A. *Winner of the USAREUR Lodging of the Year Award for small lodging facilities and first runner-up in the Army worldwide lodging competition.*

TML: Sub-standard quarters (previously maids quarters) on the fourth floor of family apartment buildings. There are 5, 4, and 3 bedroom units. Rates: $52 per day regardless of size. Pets allowed.

DV/VIP: C-(USA) 011-49-621-730-6118/6547/1700.

TML Availability: Good, Dec-Jun. Difficult, May-Sep.

CREDIT CARDS ACCEPTED: Visa, MasterCard, American Express and Diners.

Visit the National Theater, Observatory and Mannheim Castle. A good area for a Volksmarch.

Locator 730-1110   Medical 730-116   Police 730-114

Oberammergau Community (GE36R7)
NATO Community Club
Hotel & Restaurant
82487 Oberammergau-Am Anger 3, Germany

TELEPHONE NUMBER INFORMATION: C- (USA) 011-49-8822-916-0.

Location: Munich-Garmisch Highway 196 to B23 to pass Oberau, follow signs to direction Oberammergau. After 6 km, go through Ettal, after 4 km take the first exit to Oberammergau. Take

GERMANY
Oberammergau Community, continued

first right onto Am Rainenbichel, go one km (past NATO school (Shape)), and take first right onto Am Anger. NMC: Garmisch-Partenkirchen, 20 km.

Lodging Office: NATO Community Club, C- (USA) 011-49-8822-916-0, Fax C- (USA) 011-49-8822-916-0-252, e-mail: aurrammer.klaus@t-online.dc, Mon-Tue and Thu-Fri 0730-2000, Wed 0700-1400, Sat 0730-1030 and 1500-2000, and Sun 0730-2300. Check in facility.

TML: Standard class hotel, Bldg 763, all ranks, leave and official duty. Bedrooms, private bath 965). Refrigerator, color TV, housekeeping service, cribs/cot, washer/dryer, ice vending, soda/snack vending, restaurant with German and International menus. Modern structure. Meeting/conference room, exercise room, mini mart (PX, NEC) available. Rates: *DM 49,50 per person per night, DM 37,50 each additional person, DM 23,50 for a rollaway bed; TDY DM 5,00 less. Maximum charge per family: DM 49,50 single, DM 87 double, DM 110,50 three or more. Maximum four per unit. All rates include Breakfast Buffet at NCC restaurant. Reservations accepted, direct request is also possible, space allowing. Small pets allowed.

TML Availability: Good, year round.

CREDIT CARDS ACCEPTED: Visa (cash advance). Other options: US cash, travellers cheques and personal checks; DM cash, travellers cheques and Eurocheques.

* $1 US = 1.65 DM
Note: This is a private hotel and is not government/military billeting.

Visit the famous King Ludwig II castles, "Neuschwanstein" and "Linderhof" or traditional "Weis-Church" in the nearer surrounding Oberammergau. Oberammergau offers to all visitors a traditional village with the famous "Passion Play," world famous woodcarvings or take your family for a day to "Wellenberg Alpenbad" Swimming Pool and Sport Center. Enjoy mountain climbing, tours through one of the most beautiful areas of Southern Bavaria.

Ramstein Air Base (GE24R7)
Ramstein Inns North and South
86th SVS/SVH
Bldg 305, Washington Ave
APO AE 09094-5000

TELEPHONE NUMBER INFORMATION: Main installation numbers: C-(USA) 011-49-6371-47-1110, (GE) 06371-47-1110, D-314-480-1110.

Location: Two exits from Mannheim-Saarbrücken E-6 Autobahn, exit Landstuhl, turn left, follow signs to Ramstein. Also, west on B-40 to Landstuhl Street, turn right follow signs to Flugplatz Ramstein. NMC: Kaiserslautern, 12 miles east.

Lodging Office: Bldg 305, C-(USA) 011-49-6371-47-7345/7864/2445/2614, (GE) 06371-42589, Fax C-(USA) 011-49-6371-42589, 0730-1700 Mon-Thu, 0730-1630 Fri. Check in facility, check out 1100 hours daily. Government civilian employee billeting. **Note:** See Ramstein Inns: Vegelweh, Sembach and Landstuhl listing for more lodging. Building 305 on Ramstein AB manages all reservations for Kaiserslautern Community which includes Ramstein AB, Sembach AB, Vogelweh and Landstuhl lodging facilities.

GERMANY
Ramstein Air Base, continued

TML: Ramstein Inns North. Guest house, Bldg 202, 304, 305, 306 and 908, **C-(USA) 011-49-6371-47-2228/6652, D-314-480-2228/6652,** Fax C-(USA) 011-49-6371-47-9749, **D-314-480-9749,** 24 hours daily, all ranks, leave or official duty. Check in Bldg 305. Bedrooms, shared bath (185); family units, bedrooms, private bath (83); suites (DV/VIP) (22). Washer/dryer, color TV, radio, microwaves, telephones. Older structure. Rates: $12-$17.50 per person, family units $27.50-$35. Duty can make reservations, others Space-A.

TML: Ramstein Inns South. Guest house, Bldg 2408 and 2409, **C-(USA) 011-49-6371-47-2382/5529, D-314-480-2382/5529,** Fax C-(USA) 011-49-6371-47-9749, **D-314-480-5800,** 24 hours daily, all ranks, leave or official duty. Check in Bldg 2408. Bedrooms, shared bath (150); suites (DV/VIP) (10). Washer/dryer, color TV, radio, telephone, VCR, irons/ironing boards. Older structure. Rates: $12-$17 per person, suites $17.50-$25.25. Duty can make reservations, others Space-A.

TML: TLF. Bldgs 303, 908, 1004, all ranks, leave or official duty. Bedroom, private bath (2); two bedroom, private bath (77). Kitchen (some), limited utensils, color TV in room and lounge, housekeeping service, washer/dryer, ice vending. Modern structure. Rates: $32.50 per unit. Maximum six per unit. Duty can make reservations, others Space-A.

TML: VAQ. Bldgs 1003, 2408, 2409, 3752, 3756, enlisted all ranks, leave or official duty. Bedroom, shared bath (674); separate bedroom suites, private bath (2). Refrigerator, limited utensils, color TV in room and lounge, housekeeping service, cribs/cots, washer/dryer, ice vending. Modern structure. Rates: $8 per person. Duty can make reservations, others Space-A.

TML: VOQ. Bldgs 304-306,1002,3751,3754. Officers all ranks. Bedroom, shared bath, private bath (533); separate bedrooms, private bath (27). Refrigerator, limited utensils, color TV in room and lounge, housekeeping service, washer/dryer, ice vending. Modern structure. Rates: $12 per person. Duty can make reservations, others Space-A.

TML: General Cannon Hotel. DV/VIP. Bldg 1018, officers O6+, leave or official duty. See numbers under Protocol below. Separate bedroom suites, private bath (11). Refrigerator, limited utensils, color TV, washer/dryer, ice vending. Modern structure, renovated. Rates: $22 per person. Duty can make reservations, others Space-A.

DV/VIP: Protocol, Bldg 201. C-(USA) 011-49-6371-47-4851, (GE) 06371-43856, D-314-480-7558/7411, Fax: C-(GE) 06371-477109, D-314-480-7109, O6+. Retirees Space-A.

TML Availability: Very good all year. Best, winter months.

CREDIT CARDS ACCEPTED: Visa, MasterCard and American Express.

Transportation: On base shuttle/bus/taxi 480-5961,off base shuttle/bus 011-49-631-316670, off base taxi 06371-50510/58626, car rental agency 011-49-710-6219407.

Small villages surround Ramstein, it's fun to just drive through them. People here are friendly and helpful, and many speak English. Kaiserslautern, and Landstuhl are nearby. TelePassport® Service is now available; call home in privacy/receive calls in your room.

Locator 480-6120/6989   **Medical 116**   **Police 114**

Temporary Military Lodging Around the World - 293

GERMANY

Rhein-Main Air Base (GE16R7)
Bldg 600
APO AE 09050-5000

TELEPHONE NUMBER INFORMATION: Main installation numbers: C-(USA) 011-49-69-699-1110, (GE) 069-699-1110, ETS-330-1110, D-314-330-1110.

Location: Adjacent to Frankfurt International Airport off E-5 Autobahn to Darmstadt. NMC: Frankfurt, 10 miles north.

Lodging Office: Bldg 600, C-(USA) **011-49-69-699-6843**, (GE) **069-699-6843, D-314-330-6843**, (for reservations) daily. Fax: C-(USA) 011-49-69-699-7440, D-314-330-7440, 24 hours. Check in at front desk, check out 1000 hours daily. Government civilian employee billeting on official duty.

TML: Rhein-Main Hotel, VQ, Bldg 600, all ranks, leave or official duty. Bedroom with one double bed and shared bath (126), bedroom with one double bed equipped for handicapped with shared bath (2), bedroom with double bed, sitting room and private bath (15), DV bedroom with queen bed, sitting room and private bath (5). Refrigerator, microwave, color TV, housekeeping service, cribs, washer/dryer, ice vending, picnic area and playground. Rates: $12 per night per person, $17 per night per two persons; $36 per night per person, $53 per night per two persons. Duty can make reservations, others Space-A. No pets, all rooms are no smoking.

TML: TLF, Bldg 634, all ranks, leave or official duty. Living/dining room, kitchen, bath, and two bedrooms (6), living/dining room, kitchen, bath, and three bedrooms (6). Refrigerator, microwave, color TV, housekeeping service, cribs, washer/dryer, ice vending, picnic area and playground. Rates: $33-$35 per night per family. Duty can make reservations, others Space-A. Priority to families PCS to Rhein-Main AB. No pets, all rooms are no smoking.

TML Availability: Good, Dec-Feb. Difficult, other times.

CREDIT CARDS ACCEPTED: Visa, MasterCard and American Express.

Transportation: On base shuttle/bus, on base taxi 2304, car rental agencies 2188.

Don't miss Frankfurt's famous Fairgrounds (Messa), for exhibits of all types, and the Frankfurt Zoo. The southern part of the city is a forest with deer, hiking and bicycling paths. Watch for special seasonal "fests".

Locator 7691/7348   Medical 7307   Police 114/7177

Schweinfurt Base Support Battalion (GE48R7)
Bradley Inn Guest house, Bldg 89
280th Base Support Battalion
APO AE 09033-5000

TELEPHONE NUMBER INFORMATION: Main installation numbers: C-(USA) 011-49-9721-96-1700, (GE) 09721-96-1700, ETS-354-1700, D-314-350-1110, ask for Schweinfurt.

Location: 9 miles east of Kassel-Würzburg, E-70 autobahn. On GE-303, 2 miles past GE-B19. Follow US Forces signs. NMC: Schweinfurt, in the city.

GERMANY
Schweinfurt Base Support Battalion, continued

Lodging Office: Bldg 89, 0800-2300 hours daily, C-(USA) 011-49-9721-7940, (GE) 09721-7940, ETS-354-1700. After hours contact SDO, Bldg 1, Conn Barracks, C-09721-96-6288, D-314-354-6288. Check in facility between 1300-1800 hours Mon-Fri, check out 1000 hours daily. Government civilian employee billeting.

TML: Guest House. **Bradley Inn**, Bldg 89, Conn Barracks. All ranks, leave or official duty. DV/VIP suites, private bath (2); large-family room units, private bath (20); small-family room units, private bath (14); single rooms, private bath (6); bedroom, double bed, private bath (2); bedroom, 2 single beds, private bath (8). Community kitchens, utensils, housekeeping service, cribs/cots, washer/dryer, snack vending. Older structure, renovated. Rates: Suites, single occupancy $98, each additional family member $10; large family room $49, each additional family member up to six $10; small family room $44, each additional family member up to three $10; single room $29; bedroom, double or two single beds $29, with family member $39, two family members $49. Duty may make reservations, others Space-A. No pets. Schweinfurt is only 1 1/2 hours from Frankfurt International Airport. Travel to and from airport may be coordinated upon request.

DV/VIP: Chief, Business Operations, Bldg 206, C-(USA) 011-49-9721-803834, ETS-354-6715, O3/GS-13/14+. Retirees and lower ranks Space-A. VIP for **Bradley Inn**: C-(USA) 011-49-9721-803834.

TML Availability: Good, all year.

CREDIT CARDS ACCEPTED: Visa, MasterCard and American Express.

Wednesday and Saturday morning, and Tuesday and Friday afternoon, the Schweinfurt Marktplatz hums with activity. Don't miss a colorful sight. Then stroll down to the Stadtpark and the Tiergehege near the Main River.

Locator 354-6748   Medical 09721-82397   Police 09721-802160

Sembach Air Base Annex (Ramstein AB)(GE18R7)
Ramstein Inn-Sembach
86 SVS/SVMLB
Unit 3250 Box 500
APO AE 09094-5000

TELEPHONE NUMBER INFORMATION: Main installation numbers: C-(USA) 011-49-6371-47-1110, (GE) 06371-47-1110, D-314-496-1110.

Location: From the E-12 Autobahn exit A-6 marked Enkenbach-Alsenborn and follow B-48 in the direction of Bad Kruznach. Immediately past town of Munchweiler right to Sembach AB. Also, accessible from B-40 North. NMC: Kaiserslautern 9 miles west.

Lodging Office: Bldg 305, C-(USA) 011-49-6371-47-7345/7864/2445/2614, (GE) 06371-42589, Fax C-(USA) 011-49-6371-42589, 0730-1700 Mon-Thu, 0730-1630 Fri. Check in facility, check out 1100 hours daily. Government civilian employee billeting. **Note:** See Ramstein Inns: North, South, Vegelweh, and Landstuhl listing for more lodging. Building 305 on Ramstein AB manages all reservations for Kaiserslautern Community which includes Ramstein AB, Sembach AB, Vogelweh and Landstuhl lodging facilities.

GERMANY
Sembach Air Base Annex (Ramstein AB), continued

TML: VOQ/DV/VIP. **Ramstein Inn-Sembach** Bldg 110, first, second and third floors, **C-(USA) 011-49-6371-47-7588, D-314-496-7588,** Fax C-(USA) 011-49-6371-47-4948, D-314-06302-4948. Officers all ranks, leave or official duty. Check in Bldg 216. Handicap accessible. Bedroom, shared bath (60); family units, bedrooms, private bath (30); separate bedroom suites, (DV/VIP) (20). Refrigerator, community kitchen, limited utensils, color TV, housekeeping service, washer/dryer, ice vending. Older structure. Rates: rooms $12 per person, family $27.50 per person, suites $17.50 per person. Duty and Space-A can make reservations.

TML: VAQ. Bldgs 210, 216, enlisted all ranks, leave or official duty. Bldg 210: new structure, bedroom, 2 beds, shared bath (221); separate bedroom suites, private bath (Chiefs) (4). Bldg 216: bedroom, 2 beds, hall bath (55). Housekeeping service, color TV, washer/dryer. Older structures, renovated. Rates: rooms $12 per person, suites $17.50. Duty and Space A can make reservations.

TML: TLF. All ranks, PCS families. Two bedroom, private bath (6); three bedroom, private bath (3); 4 bedroom, private bath (3). Cribs, housekeeping service, color TV, laundry.

DV/VIP: 601 SW/CCE, Bldg 112, C-(USA) 011-49-6302-67-7960, O6+, retirees Space-A.

TML Availability: Difficult. Best, Dec-Jan.

CREDIT CARDS ACCEPTED: Visa, MasterCard and American Express.

Transportation: On base shuttle/bus/taxi 480-5961, off base shuttle/bus 011-49-631-316670, off base taxi 06371-50510/58626, car rental agency 011-49-710-6219407.

Sembach has been greatly reduced in size. The runway is closed and there is limited base support but Ramstein AB is within easy reach. Keep updated with Military Living's *R&R Space-A Report*®. The city hall (Rathaus), is the highest in Germany. There is an elegant restaurant in the penthouse. Visit the Pfalztheater for opera, operetta, plays and ballet. TelePassport ® Service is now available; call home in privacy/receive calls in your room.

Locator 480-6120   **Medical 116**   **Police 114**

Spangdahlem Air Base (GE19R7)
52nd Services Squadron
Unit 3670, Box 170
APO AE 09126-5000

TELEPHONE NUMBER INFORMATION: Main installation numbers: C-(USA) 011-49-6565-61-1110, (GE) 06565-61-1110, ETS-452-1110, D-314-452-1110.

Location: From the Koblenz-Trier Autobahn E-1 exit at Wittlich, to B-50 west toward Bitburg. The AB is near Binsfeld 24 km west of Wittlich. Signs mark the AB entrance. NMC: Trier, 21 miles southeast.

Lodging Office: Eifel Arms Inn, Bldg 38, **C-(USA) 011-49-6565-61-6504, (GE) 06565-61-6504,** D-314-452-6504, Fax C-011-49-6565-95-4444, D-314-452-7684, 24 hours. Check in facility 1800, check out 1100 hours daily. No government civilian employee billeting.

GERMANY
Spangdahlem Air Base, continued

TML: VOQ/VAQ. Bldg 38, all ranks, leave or official duty. VOQ: bedrooms, private bath (60); suites, private bath (6); DV/VIP (12). Kitchenette, microwave, color TV, housekeeping service, washer/dryer, ice vending. Older structure, renovated. Rates: suites $25.50, maximum $38.25 for two persons. VOQ/VAQ: regular rooms $12, maximum $17 for two persons. Duty/official travel can make reservations, others Space-A.

TML: TLF. Facility is located 12 miles from the base (Bitburg AB Annex). Check in at Bldg 38, on main base. All ranks, PCS families, leave or official duty. Two bedroom, private bath (6); three bedroom, private bath (21); four bedroom, private bath (12). Kitchen, refrigerator, microwave, color/cable TV, housekeeping service. Modern structure. Rates $35 per unit. Duty can make reservations.

DV/VIP: Bldg 38 (6 suites). During duty hours reservations controlled by base protocol, C-(USA) 011-49-6565-61-6434. After duty hours check with front desk at C-(USA) 011-49-6565-61-6504.

TML Availability: Limited all year. Best, Nov-Dec.

Trier lies where the Saar and Mosel rivers meet, and is Germany's oldest city, dating from the second century. Don't miss lunch in the shadow of the Porta Nigra, and a stroll past renaissance half-timbered houses in the Hauptmarkt.

Locator 452-7227   Medical 116   Police 114

Stuttgart Community (GE20R7)
Swabian Inn, Patch Barracks
Unit 30401, Box 4010
APO AE 09131-5000

TELEPHONE NUMBER INFORMATION: Main installation numbers: C-(USA) 011-49-711-680-1110, (GE) 0711-680-1110, D-314-430-1110.

Location: Situated next to A-8, exit at Stuttgarter-krewz continue in direction of Stuttgart and take first exit and follow signs to Patch Barracks. NMC: Stuttgart, in city limits.

Lodging Office: Swabian Inn, Bldg 2506, **C-(USA) 011-49-711-67840, (GE) 0711-67840, D-314-430-1700,** Fax C-(USA) 011-49-711-6784199, 24 hours daily. Check in at facility, check out 1000 hours.

TML: VOQ **Swabian Inn**, Bldg 2506, Patch Barracks, all ranks, leave or official duty. Bedroom, shared bath (54); O6+/GS15+ separate bedroom suites, private bath (VIP) (7). Refrigerator, microwave, color TV/VCP, housekeeping service, cribs/cots, washer/dryer, ice vending, full kitchen on each floor. Older structure, renovated. Rates: room $35, suite $46.50, each additional person $4. All Ranks Community Club, D-420-6129. Maximum capacity/charge depends on lodging and number in party. Duty can make reservations, others Space-A.

TML: Hilltop Hotel, Robinson Barracks. **Note: Hilltop Hotel is currently under renovation and will reopen in February 1998.** Watch for more details in Military Living's R&R Space-A Report®.

Temporary Military Lodging Around the World - 297

GERMANY
Stuttgart Community, continued

TML: Guest House, Panzer Kaserne, Panzer Community Club, Bldg 2916, C-(USA) 011-49-7031-15-401, D-314-4312-401. Kelly Barracks, Kelly Community Club, Bldg 3308,C-(USA) 011-49-711-7292-811/568, D-314-4212-811/568. Rooms and suites available. Rates: single $35, suite $85, each additional person $15. Call lodging office above for more information.

DV/VIP: HQ USEUCOM, Patch Barracks, Unit 30400, APO AE 09131-5000, C-(USA) 011-49-711-680-8763, D-314-430-8763. O6/GS-15+. Retirees Space-A.

TML Availability: Swabian Inn: Good, Dec-Mar. Difficult, May-Aug.

CREDIT CARDS ACCEPTED: Swabian Inn: Visa, MasterCard, American Express and Diners'.

Starting the end of April the Stuttgarter Frülingsfest, with carnival attractions and beer tents is a must for visitors. Also don't miss the Cannstatter Volksfest, at Bad Cannstatt at the end of September.

Locator 113   Medical 116   Police 114

Vilseck Base Support Battalion (GE85R7)
AST Vilseck
CMR 411, Box 917
APO AE 09112-5000

TELEPHONE NUMBER INFORMATION: Main installation numbers: C-(USA) 011-49-9662-83-4100, (GE) 09662-83-4100, ETS: 476-2555.

Location: From Nürnberg take Hwy 14 east to Hahnbach, turn north to Vilseck. Also E9 Autobahn north of Nürnburg to E85 south, Vilseck is east 3-5 miles. NMC: Nürnburg, 38 miles southwest.

Lodging Office: 100th ASG. Rose Barracks, Bldg 275, **C-(USA) 011-49-9662-83-2555/1700, (GE) 09662-83-2555/1700,** Fax: C-(USA) 011-49-9662-83-4140. 0700-2300. Check in at facility, check out 1100 hours. Government civilian employee lodging.

TML: TLQ. Kristall Inn. Bldgs: 233, 241, 252, 253 ,254, 255, 256. All ranks, leave or official duty. Rooms, private bath. color TV, refrigerator, housekeeping service, cribs/cots, washer/dryer. Modern structure, renovated. Rates: sponsor $34, each additional person $4. Pets allowed (PCS), fee $3 per day (spray fee $20). All categories may make reservations.

TML: Big Mike Travel Camp. C-(USA) 011-49-9662-83-2563. Two-bedroom apartment (2) and three-bedroom apartment (2), furnished, living room, kitchen, utensils. Rates: $60-$70 daily. **See** *Military Living's Military RV, Camping and Rec Areas Around the World* **for additional information and directions.**

DV/VIP: C-(USA) 011-49-9662-414-100, O6+, GS12+.

TML Availability: Good. Best in winter, difficult Aug/Sep.

CREDIT CARDS ACCEPTED: Visa, MasterCard, American Express and Diners.

GERMANY
Vilseck Base Support Battalion, continued

Vilseck is near Grafenwöehr. Army Community Service (VM 2650/2733) has a wonderful list of "points of interest" in the area put together by the Oberpfalz area women's clubs.

Locator 113   Medical 116   Police 287

Wiesbaden Base Support Battalion (GE27R7)
American Arms Hotel
221st Base Support Battalion (Wiesbaden)
APO AE 09096-5000

TELEPHONE NUMBER INFORMATION: Main installation numbers: C-(USA) 011-49-611-705-1110, (GE) 0611-705-1110, D-314-337/338-1110.

Location: Accessible from Autobahns E-3, E-5, connect to E-66. Take exit WI-Erbenheim (This will be B455). Stay straight on B455 (Do not take 2nd Erbenheim exit). Coming into Wiesbaden, you will come to an underpass. Stay in right lane, following signs to STADMITTE Kurhaus/Casino. When you come out of the underpass you will be on Frankfurter Strasse. Go through one traffic light. Hotel will be on the left. NMC: Wiesbaden, in the city.

Lodging Office: American Arms Hotel, 17 Frankfurterstrasse, 24 hours, **C- (USA) 011-49-611-343664, (GE) 0611-343664, D-314-338-7493,** Fax: C-(USA) 011-49-611-304522. E-mail- aah@wiesbaden.army.mil. Check in at front desk, check out 1100 hours daily. Government civilian employee billeting.

TML: American Arms Hotel, 17 Frankfurterstrasse, all ranks, leave or official duty. Suites, private bath, living room bedroom, mini-bar refrigerator, coffee pot, TV and complementary bottle of wine (70); Bedroom, standard room , shared bath (133). Refrigerator, phone, TV. Housekeeping service (all rooms), cribs/cots, washer/dryer, ice/vending machines. Modern structure, renovated. Restaurant, bar, weinstube, meeting/conference room, ATM machine . Rates: standard room, single $49.50, double $35(each person), each additional person (over age 11) $20, (age 5-11) $12, (under age 5) $8; standard suite, $59.50, each additional person (over age 11) $25, (age 5-11) $15, (under age 5) $10; DV/VIP suite, $69.50, each additional person (over age 11) $25, (age 5-11) $15, (under age 5) $10. Duty can make reservations, others Space-A.
Complimentary breakfast and Sunday Brunch included.

TML: On Wiesbaden Air Base there are 92 Transient Officer billets, and 172 Enlisted billets, call ETS-339-6525 for information and accommodations.

DV/VIP: Contact the Conference Sales Office of the American Arms Hotel at C-(USA) 011-49-611-343350, (GE) 0611-343350 D 314-338-7496, O5,+, GS14+. All other grades and retirees are Space-A.

TML Availability: Good.

CREDIT CARDS ACCEPTED: Visa, MasterCard, American Express and Diners.

Transportation: On/off base shuttle/bus, off base taxi 0611-333333, car rental 0611-713031.

GERMANY
Wiesbaden Base Support Battalion, continued

The American Arms Hotel is conveniently located in historic downtown Wiesbaden. In addition to other amenities, it also has 24-hour slot machines. Hainerberg Shopping Center is 3 blocks away from lodging and is "shop till you drop" country! In the center of Wiesbaden, you are also within walking distance of wonderful architectural and cultural treasures (Wiesbaden had little damage during WWII).

Locator WBNC-705-5055   Medical 705-5237   Police 705-114

Worms Community (GE31R7)
Thomas Jefferson Inn
Bldg 5032, Liebenauer Strasse
APO AE 09056-3879

TELEPHONE NUMBER INFORMATION: Main installation numbers: C-(USA) 011-49-6241-48-1110, (GE) 06241-48-1110, ETS-383-1110, D-314-383-1110.

Location: Take the Worms exit from the Mannheim-Saarbrücken E-6 Autobahn. Follow the signs to Thomas Jefferson Village. NMC: Worms, in the city.

Lodging Office: Thomas Jefferson Inn, Bldg 5032, Liebenauer Strasse, **C-(USA) 011-49-6241-955-414/273, (GE) 06241-955-414/273,** D-314-383-5414/5273, 0600-2200 Mon-Fri, 0800-2200 Sat, Sun, and holidays. Check out 1000 hours daily. Government civilian employee billeting.

TML: TLF. All ranks, leave or official duty. Bedroom, shared bath (16); VIP suites (4), family suites, separate bedroom, living room, private bath, bar (14). Refrigerator, color TV, VCR, cribs/cots ($2). Older structure. Rates: $40 single, $20 second, $8 each additional, suites $50 single, $20 second, $8 each additional. TDY can make reservations, others Space-A.

TML Availability: Good.

Astonishing antiquity is everyday reality in Worms Cathedral, completed in 1184. Just outside the city visit Liebfrauen kirche, from where the famous Liebfraunmilch wine was born.

Locator 383-92   Medical 116   Police 114

Würzburg Community (GE21R7)
American Guesthouse
Bldg 2, Leighton Barracks
APO AE 09036-5000

TELEPHONE NUMBER INFORMATION: Main installation numbers: C-(USA) 011-49-931-889-1110, (GE) 0931-889-1110, ETS-350-1110, D-314-350-1110.

Location: From west on Autobahn E-3 take Heidingsfeld/Stadtmitte exit to Rottendorfer Street north to Leighton Barracks. Take first right after HQ, Bldg 6, third right to Bldg 2. NMC: Würzburg, one mile south.

Lodging Office: American Guesthouse. Bldg 2, Leighton Barracks, **C-(USA) 011-49-931-889-1700, (GE) 0931-889-1700,** D-314-350-1700, 24 hours. Check in 1200 hours, check out 1000 hours daily. Government civilian employee billeting.

GERMANY
Würzburg Community, continued

TML: American Guesthouse, Bldg 2, all ranks, leave or official duty. Bedrooms, shared bath (42); separate bedroom suite (VIP) (2). Kitchen (suites), refrigerator, color TV, VCR microwave, coffeepot, housekeeping service (7 days/week), washer/dryer, vending machines. Older structure. Rooms refurbished in December 1996. Rates: single $40, each additional person $10; suites $60, each additional person $15. Duty can make reservations, others Space-A.

TML: Leighton Country Club, Leighton Barracks (across from American Guest House), **C-0931-709097**. Bedrooms, doubles and singles, basin, hall shower (5); separate bedroom suite (VIP) (1). Color TV, housekeeping service, washer/dryer. Older structure. Rates: bedrooms $30; suites $40 per day, each additional person $10. Duty can make reservations, others Space-A.

TML: Kitzengen Officer's Club, Kitzengen, Harvey Barracks, **C-09321-31836.** Bedrooms, hall bath (10); separate bedroom suite, private bath (VIP) (1), two bedroom suite, private bath (VIP) (1). Refrigerator, housekeeping service, color TV, washer/dryer. Duty can make reservations, others Space-A.

DV/VIP: SGS, Protocol, Bldg 6, C-(USA) 011-49-931-889-7241, O6/GS-15+. Retirees Space-A.

TML Availability: Good, Oct-Mar. Difficult, other times.

The Annual Mozart Festival in summer, famous Franken wine in the light of a thousand candles at Würzburg Castle, the old walled city of Rothenburg on the Tauber, and the Marienberg Castle.

Locator 350-98   Medical 116   Police 114

Other Installations in Germany

Geilenkirchen Air Base. Bldg 80, **C-(USA) 011-49-2451-63-4962/0**, D-314-453-4962. Lodging for O1+, single military on a Space-A basis only. Shared bath, no TV, no phone.

GREECE

Other Installations in Greece

Souda Bay Naval Support Activity/Air Facility (Crete), FPO AE 09865-0007, C-(USA) 011-30-821-63388/63340 ext 1110, D-314-661-3388/3340. Limited BEQ facilities are available.

HONG KONG

Hong Kong Community (HK02R8)
11 Middle Road, Kowloon
FPO AP 96659-2200

TELEPHONE NUMBER INFORMATION: Main installation number: C-(USA) 011-852-2-861-0063 (USN Contracting Department).

HONG KONG
Hong Kong Community, continued

Location: Fenwick Pier is on Lung King Street, Wanchai District, Hong Kong. It is located off Convention Avenue across from the Hong Kong Academy for Performing Arts. There are MTR (Underground Rail) entrances nearby on Hardcourt Road. NMC: Hong Kong, in city limits.

Lodging Office: Mariners' Club, 11 Middle Road, Kowloon, **C-(USA) 011-852-2-368-8261**, (HK) 2368-8261Fax C-(USA) 011-852-2-366-2928. Both clubs are operated by the Mission to Seamen, an Anglican missionary society which provides churches, clubs and chaplains in two hundred of the world's largest ports.

TML: Hong Kong Mariners' Club, 11 Middle Road, Kowloon, all ranks, leave or official duty. Facility includes en-suite family rooms, bedroom, private bath. TV, laundry service, bar, dining, darts, video/lazer films, pool and Ten Pin Bowling Alley. Rates: single $67, double $89. *Note: This site has plans for renovations slated for early 1998; call in advance to verify that lodging is available.*

TML: Kwai Chung Mariners' Club, 2 Container Port Road, Kwaichung, C-(USA) 011852-2-410-8240, (HK) 2410-8240, all ranks, leave or official duty. Call for information on rooms and rates.

Note: This is not a military installation, but a Seafarer's Club primarily for the use of Merchant Seaman, however they do welcome the Allied Armed Forces. These facilities are operated by the Mission to Seamen, an Anglican missionary society.

Be sure to visit all the sights in Hong Kong.

ICELAND

Keflavik Naval Station (IC01R7)
Combined Bachelor's Quarters
U.S. Naval Air Station
PSC 1003 Box 34
FPO AE 09728-0334

TELEPHONE NUMBER INFORMATION: Main installation numbers: C-(USA) 011-354-425-0111 (IC) 425-0111, D-(USA) 312-450-0111 (Europe) D-314-228-0111.

Location: IAP shares landing facilities with Naval Station. From Reykjavik seaport take Hwy S follow signs to Keflavik. Well marked. Naval Station is 2.5 miles before town of Keflavik. NMC: Reykjavik, 35 miles north.

Lodging Office: Bldg 761, **C-(USA) 011-354-425-4333, (IC) 425-4333,** 24 hours. Check in at billeting, check out 1200 hours daily. Government civilian employee billeting.

NAVY LODGE TML: Navy Lodge. Naval Station, Box 10, Bldg 786. All ranks, leave or official duty. **C-(USA) 011-354-425-2210, (IC) 425-2000 ext 7594/2210,** Fax: C-(USA) 011-354-425-2091. One and two bedroom units, private bath (27). Kitchens, color TV in room and lounge, housekeeping service, cribs/cots, coin washer/dryer, ice vending. Newly renovated structure. Rates: $51-$86. Maximum six persons. All categories can make reservations. Trivia: Reykjavik McDonald's takes credit cards.

302 - Temporary Military Lodging Around the World

ICELAND
Keflavik Naval Station, continued

TML: CBQ. Bldgs 761, all ranks, leave or official duty. Bedroom, private bath (27). Refrigerator, color TV, housekeeping service, washer/dryer, soda/snack vending, community kitchen. Older structure. Rates: enlisted $8, officer and equivalent $9 per person. Sponsors for duty personnel can make reservations, others Space-A.

DV/VIP: Commander, C-(USA) 011-354-425-4414. O5+, retirees Space-A.

TML Availability: Lodge, good in winter months; billeting, fair. Lodge, difficult, Apr-Aug; billeting, poor.

CREDIT CARDS ACCEPTED: Visa, MasterCard and American Express at the Navy Lodge.

Transportation: On base taxi/off base taxi 421-2525, car rental 421-3357, other 425-7596.

Into summer skiing? Visit the Kerlingarfjoll area. Fishing? July and August are best for brown trout, char and salmon. Also try sightseeing.

Locator ext 2100   Medical ext 3300   Police ext 2211

ITALY

Admiral Carney Park (IT03R7)
ATTN: MWR
PSC 810, Box 13
FPO AE 09619-1013

TELEPHONE NUMBER INFORMATION: Main installation numbers: C-(USA) 011-39-81-724-1110, (IT) 081-526-1579.

Location: On the west coast of Italy in Admiral Carney Park, 7 miles from Naples and 5 miles from US Naval Support Activity, Naples. NMC: Naples, 7 miles south.

Lodging Office: Admiral Carney Park, Morale, Welfare and Recreation building, **C-(USA) 011-39-81-526-3396/1579, (IT) 081-526-3396/1579,** Fax: C-(USA) 011-39-81-526-4813. Reservations required. Check in facility 1300, check out 1030 hours daily. No pets. Operates year round.

TML: The 54 acre recreational and sports complex is contained within the walls of a crater. All ranks. Bedroom cabins (13); two bedroom cabins (13). Bath house and laundromat separate, kitchenette, refrigerator, no utensils, grill and picnic area, linens, blankets, no towels. Rates: $30-$45 per night per cabin, weekly rates available. Maximum four to six per cabin. All categories can make reservations up to 90 days in advance.

TML Availability: Good, winter. Difficult, summer.

Visit historic Pompeii, Herculanum, the popular beaches on Capri, and Ischia. In Naples the National Museum, the Art Gallery of Capodimonte are nearby. This is a full rec park - for more details see *Military RV, Camping and Rec Areas Around The World.*

Temporary Military Lodging Around the World - 303

ITALY
Admiral Carney Park, continued

Locator 724-4367   **Medical 724-4872**   **Police 724-4686**

Aviano Air Base (IT04R7)
Aviano Lodging
31 SVS/SVML
Unit 6122, Box 45
APO AE 09601-2245

TELEPHONE NUMBER INFORMATION: Main installation numbers: C-(USA) 011-39-434-66-7111, (IT) 0434-66-7111.

Location: Adjacent to town of Aviano in Pordenone province. Thirty miles east of Udine, IT and 50 miles northeast of Venice. From A-28 North exit Pordenone to IT-159 for 8 miles to Aviano AB. NMC: Pordenone, 8 miles south.

Lodging Office: Bldg 256, Pedemonte Street, **C-(USA) 011-39-434-66-7262/7722**, (IT) 0434-66-7262/7722, D-314-632-7262/7722, Fax: C-(USA) 011-39-434-66-7581, 24 hours. Check in facility, check out 1100 hours daily. Government civilian employee billeting.

TML: VOQ/VAQ. Bldgs 230, 232, 255, 273, 274. All ranks, leave or official duty. Room, private bath (17); bedroom suites, private bath,(DV/VIP-Officer) (3); bedroom, private bath suites (DV/VIP Chiefs) (2). Family members OK. No TLF. Rates: VAQ $8 per night, VOQ $9 per night, DV suites $24 per night.

DV/VIP: PAO, CCP, Bldg 1360, room 4, D-314-632-7604. O6+.

TML Availability: Good, Dec-Jan. More difficult, other times.

CREDIT CARDS ACCEPTED: Visa, MasterCard and American Express.

Don't miss the Castello di Aviano, Aviano's castle ruins. Pordenone (eight miles south) for shopping, strolling and cappuccino. Many other sights are nearby.

Locator 66-7111   **Medical 66-116**   **Police 66-7200**

Camp Darby (IT10R7)
AESE BSL EH
Unit 31314, Box 60
APO AE 09613-5000

TELEPHONE NUMBER INFORMATION: Main installation numbers: C-(USA) 011-39-50-54-7111, (IT) 050-54-7111, ETS-633-7111.

Location: Located midway between Livorno and Pisa. From Autostrada A-12 take Pisa Central exit. Turn right and continue to end of road, right onto Via Aurelia (SS 1), right to S Piero A Grado and follow Camp Darby signs. NMC: Pisa, 6 miles north.

Lodging Office: Guest house, Bldg 202, C-(USA) 011-39-50-54-7448/7791/7478, 0800-1800 Mon-Fri, 0900-1500 Sat, Sun, after duty hours, w/prior reservations, Bldg 731, MP Desk. Check in billeting, check out 1000 hours daily. Rec area open year round.

ITALY
Camp Darby, continued

TML: Sea Pines Lodge, outdoor recreation, Bldg 836. C-(USA) 011-39-50-54-7225, (IT) 050-54-7225 reservation desk, ETS 633-7225/7221/7791/7616, Fax: C-(USA) 011-39-50-54-7758, (IT) 050-54-7758, ETS 633-7758, 0700-2100 hours daily (winter), 24 hours (summer). All ranks, leave or official duty. Bedrooms (24). Cabins, 2-bedroom, one double bed and one bunk bed (sleeps 4), no linens, heated, close to showers (20). Community dining and microwave, housekeeping service, cribs ($3). Color TV, VCR, slot machines in recreation room (motel). Swimming pool in season. Modern structures. Rates: one person $41; two persons $51; three persons $56; four persons $61. Pets allowed $3.50 per night and $50 damage deposit. Government civilian employee billeting (official duty). All categories may make reservations for summer beginning 1 Feb. Written requests mailed to: Sea Pines Lodge, 219 BSB CMR 426, MWR 31314, Box 20, APO AE 09613-5000.

TML: Casa Toscana, Guest house, Bldg 202, HQ Livorno AST, AESE-BSL-EH, Unit 31314, Box 20 MWR, APO AE 09613. E-mail: aese-bsl-eh-04livorno,emh1.army.mil. Reservations: C-(USA) 011-39-50-54-7448/7580, (IT) 050-54-7448/7580, Fax: C-(USA) 011-39-50-54-7373. Check in Billeting, above building, hours. Rooms, suites and apartments. Bedroom, shared bath (3); separate bedroom, private bath (22); suite (1). Kitchenette, utensils (apartments only), refrigerator, essentials, cribs, housekeeping service (Mon-Fri), DAVs (ground floor), color TV/VCR. New A/C, carpeting, TVs, renovation 1991. Rates: rooms $40, each additional person $10; apartments $60 (one to two persons), each additional person $10; DVOQ (one to two persons) $60, each additional person $10. Pets allowed $5 per pet per day and $50 damage deposit. Government civilian employee billeting. PCS in/out may make reservations. others Space-A.

DV/VIP: Commander, 8th TASG, APO AE 09613, Bldg 302, C-(USA) 011-39-50-54-7505/7506, O6+/GS-13+, retirees Space-A.

TML Availability: Best, Oct-Ma., Difficult, Apr-Sep.

Located in the choice Tuscany region of Italy, one hour from Florence. Camp Darby even has its own stretch of Mediterranean beach at the resort town of Tirrenia. The famous Leaning Tower of Pisa is 6 miles north.

Locator 112   Medical 116   Police 114

La Maddalena Naval Support Activity (IT13R7)
Calabro Hall, Paradiso Complex
PSC 816 Box 1795
FPO AE 09612-0006

TELEPHONE NUMBER INFORMATION: Main installation numbers: C-(USA) 011-39-789-798130, (IT) 0789-798130, D-314-623-8113.

Location: Located off the northern tip of the island of Sardinia. Take the main road (IT-125) north from Olbia to Palau (45 minute drive), then take a 20 minute ferry ride to La Maddalena and follow signs to the installation. NMC: Olbia, 28 miles southeast.

Lodging Office: Calabro Hall, C-(USA) 011-39-789-798297/416/417/418/419, (IT) 0789-798297/416/417/418/419, D-314-623-8297/416/417/418/419, Fax: C-(USA) 011-39-789-798294, (IT) 0789-798249, D-314-623-8249, 24 hours. Check in facility, check out anytime. **Note:** No TML available for personnel on leave or temporary duty. PCS facilities only. There is no BOQ.

ITALY
La Maddalena Naval Support Activity, continued

TML: BEQ (Paradiso Complex (71) and Santo Stefano (36)). Bldg 300, all ranks, PCS personnel only. Bedroom, one bed, shared bath (10); bedroom, one bed, shared bath (51); two bedrooms, private bath (5). A/C, soda/snack vending, ice vending, housekeeping service, refrigerator, microwave, washer/dryer. Modern structure. Rates: no charge. Maximum two per room.

DV/VIP: Write to: Supply Officer, NSA La Maddalena, FPO AE 09612. Bldg 13. Bedroom, two beds, private bath (1). Kitchenette, limited utensils, color TV, housekeeping service, washer/dryer, ice vending. Rates: N/A. Officers and GS on official orders. Reservations required. No pets.

TML Availability: Extremely difficult, especially in summer.

Facilities Available: Meeting/conference rooms, exercise room, small NEX/Commissary, swimming pool, gazebo with barbeque patio.

CREDIT CARDS ACCEPTED: Visa.

Transportation: Off base shuttle, off base taxi, car rental agencies.

A very historical area. Hotel rooms are limited during the summer months due to the large number of tourists.

Locator 789-798-244   Medical 798-275   Police 798-244

Naples Naval Support Activity (IT05R7)
BEQ Office
PSC 817, Box 5
FPO AE 09619-0003

TELEPHONE NUMBER INFORMATION: Main installation numbers: C-(USA) 011-39-81-724-1110, (IT) 081-724-1110, D-314-625-1110.

Location: In Naples, a large port city south of Rome on the N-S Autostrada (toll road) and IT-1. NMC: Naples, in the city.

Lodging Office: BEQ. Bldg 71, **C-(USA) 011-39-81-724-4842, (IT) 081-724-4842, D-314-625-4842,** Fax C-(USA) 011-39-81-724-3512, (IT) 081-124-3512, D-314-625-3512. Check in facility, check out 1200 hours daily. Enlisted military billeting only.

TML: BEQ. Bldg 71, enlisted all ranks, leave or official duty. Single rooms, hall and common bath. Refrigerator, color TV lounge, essentials, housekeeping service, washer/dryer, snack vending, ice vending, microwaves in lounges. Older structure, upgraded 1989. New quarters complex anticipated late 1995. Rates: $12 per person; E7-E9 $20. Dependents not authorized. Duty can make reservations, others Space-A.

NAVY LODGE **TML:** Navy Lodge. **Hotel Costa Bleu,** PSC 810 Box 30, FPO AE 09619. All ranks, leave or official duty, **C-(USA) 011-39-81-509-7120, (IT) 081-509-7120/21/22/23,** Fax: C-(USA) 011-39-81-509-7124, (IT) 081-509-7124. E-mail-navylodge-naples@nexmail. Apartments: bedroom/sitting room, private bath (14); two bedroom, 2 bath (75); three bedroom, 2 bath (8); four bedroom, 3 bath (4). Full kitchen, utensils, microwave, color TV w/military channel, ceiling fans, hair dryers, patio furniture, ironing board, housekeeping,

ITALY
Naples Naval Support Activity, continued

washer. Irons, bed rails, strollers, cribs, shopping carts available on request. Free daily shuttle bus to the Pinetamare NEXmart located approximately one mile from the Lodge. Services provided within the Lodge are a full service restaurant (room service provided), a snack bar, movie theater, slot machine room, beauty salon, fax service, parking garage, free summer swim park, private beach access, play area for children, video rental photo studio, ITT travel, souvenirs, and conference room. Nearby; medical support, mini-mart one mile, Naval Support Activity, 19 miles. No pets, kennel available. Rates: Based on number of occupants/fluctuating per diem (i.e. around $69 for one person, each additional person $25). PCS have priority, others may make reservations. Availability: May-Sep difficult, other times good.

DV/VIP: Bldg 71, C-(USA) 011-39-81-568-3161, NSA Protocol Office.

TML Availability: Extremely limited. Best, winter.

CREDIT CARDS ACCEPTED: Visa, MasterCard, American Express and Discover.

The Navy Lodge is located in the Italian beach resort of Pinetamare, which is approximately 20 miles from NSA Naples. From the Navy Lodge, visit the Caserta palace, the Amalfi Coast, Sorrento, Capri, Pompeii, Vesuvius and the magnificent city of Naples. Tours can be arranged through ITT which operates a satellite office in the Navy Lodge lobby on Tuesday and Thursdays.

Locator 4556   Medical 300/301   Police 4686

Sigonella Naval Air Station (IT01R7)
PSC 812, NASII BOQ
FPO AE 09627-2650

TELEPHONE NUMBER INFORMATION: Main installation numbers: C-(USA) 011-39-95-86-1111, C-(IT) 095-86-1111, D-314-624-1113.

Location: On the east coast of the Island of Sicily. From Autostrada Messina-Cantania (A18), follow direction for Austrada Cantania-Pacermo (A19), exit Motta Street Anastadia, take SS192-Cantania, NAS is approximately one mile. NMC: Catania, IT, 10 miles northeast.

Lodging Office: CBQ. Air Terminal Billeting Office **C-(USA) 011-39-95-86-5467/5575, (IT) 095-86-5467/5575,** Fax: C-(USA) 011-39-95-86-6143, 24 hours. E-Mail:1downing@nassig.navy.mil Check in facility, check out 1000 hours daily. Government civilian employee billeting.

TML: BOQ. Officers, all ranks, leave or official duty, C-(USA) 011-39-95-86-2300. Bedroom, private bath (42); A/C, color TV, VCRs, housekeeping service, washer/dryer, ice vending. Available gymnasium, fitness center, bar, non-alcohol/non-smoking club, on-base restaurants, meeting rooms, mini-mart, soft drink/snack vending machines.Older structure. Rates: $10 per person, maximum $25 per family. Maximum three per unit. Duty can make reservations, others Space-A.

TML: BEQ. Enlisted, all ranks, leave or official duty, C ext 5467. Bedroom, private bath (42); VIP suites, private bath (11). A/C, TV in lounge, washer/dryer, ice vending, housekeeping service. Older structure. Rates: E1-E8 $5 per day; suites $15. Duty can make reservations, others Space-A.

ITALY
Sigonella Naval Air Station, continued

TML: Navy Lodge, Bldg 313. All ranks, leave or official duty, **C-1-800-NAVY-INN.** Lodge number is C-(USA) 011-39-95-7130190, (IT) 095-713-0190, D-314-624-4082, Fax: C-(USA) 011-39-95-7190206, (IT) 095-713-0206, 24 hours. Rates: $61 per night. Soda/snack vending. All categories can make reservations. PSC 824 Box 2620, FPO AE 09627-2620. *Winner of the 1996 Edward E. Carlson Award for Navy Lodge excellence in the medium category.*

DV/VIP: Protocol, Bldg 632, C-(USA) 011-39-95-86-2300. O6+. Separate bedroom suites, private bath, VCR, honor bar (DV/VIP) (16). Rates: $25 per person. Retirees Space-A. No dependents under age 15.

TML Availability: Good, Oct-Nov. Difficult, May-Sep.

CREDIT CARDS ACCEPTED: American Express.

Transportation: On-base shuttle bus, personnel on orders only, 624-5355; car rental (Hertz) toll-free 1678-2209.

Mount Edna, beaches, local markets, wonderful Italian cuisine, and old world charm of Sicily at its best.

Locator 113   **Medical 114**   **Police 114**

Vicenza Community (IT06R7)
HQ 22nd ASG
Unit 31401, Box 15
Attn: Ederle Inn
APO AE 09630-5000

TELEPHONE NUMBER INFORMATION: Main installation numbers: C-(USA) 011-39-444-515190/518034/158035, (IT) 0444-515109/518034, D-314-634-8034/8035/8036.

Location: Take the Vicenza (east) exit from the Number 4 Autostrada which runs from Trieste to Milano. Follow signs to Caserma Carlo Ederle or SETAF HQs. NMC: Vicenza, in city limits.

Lodging Office: Bldg 345. **C-(USA) 011-39-444-518034/35, (IT) 0444-51-8034/35, D-314-634-8034/35, Fax-0444-515380,** 24 hours. Check in 1500 hours, check out 1100 hours daily. Government civilian employee billeting.

TML: Guest House/DVGH. Bldg 345, all ranks, official duty, PCS in/out and MTDY, TDY and leave Space-A. Handicap accessible. Bedroom w/double beds, sofa sleeper, private bath, adjoining bedroom capability (25); three bedroom suites (subject to change) (4) (subject to change). A/C, color TV, microwave, mini-refrigerator, housekeeping service, cribs, soda/snack vending, meeting/conference rooms. Modern structure, remodeled. Rates: Guest House PCS/TDY $48, additional person $11, DV PCS/TDY $58, additional person $11. Space-A $48, additional person $11. Limited pet space.

DV/VIP: Protocol, HQ SETAF, Bldg 1, D-634-7712, O5/GS-15+, Retirees Space-A.

ITALY
Vicenza Community, continued

TML Availability: Good, Oct-Nov. Difficult, May-Sep.

CREDIT CARDS ACCEPTED: Visa, American Express and Discover.

Transportation: Off base taxi (Bruno Taxi) 500-461, car rental agencies (Eurocar) 505-916 .

The Guest House is the winner of the 1995 Lodging of the Year Award competition in the medium category. Verona, the city of Romeo and Juliet, is rich in monuments of every period and a modern and hospitable city. Don't miss the Roman Arena, which is still an active entertainment site. Venice, Florence, Pisa, and many others are close.

Locator 634-7430   Medical 634-7297 or 113   Police 634-7626

Other Installations in Italy

Gaeta Naval Support Activity, ATTN: Billeting, Gaeta Family Service Center, PSC 811, FPO AE 09609-1001. BEQ, D-314-7677/7679.

JAPAN

Atsugi Naval Air Facility (JA14R8)
BQ Housing Manager
NAF Atsugi, Japan
PSC 477, Box 19
FPO AP 96306-1219

TELEPHONE NUMBER INFORMATION: Main installation numbers: C-(USA) 011-81-3117-64-3698, D-315-264-3698, (JA) 0467-78-5015 ext 264-3698.

Location: In central Japan off Tokyo Bay. Yokohama is 15 miles east and Tokyo is 28 miles northeast. From Narita Airport, use bus or train service - information provided by the Northwest Military Counter at the airport. Camp Zama is 5 miles north. NMC: Tokyo, 28 miles northeast.

Lodging Office: BEQ, Bldg 1290, BOQ Bldg 482, C-(USA) **BOQ-011-81-3117-64-3698, BEQ-011-81-3117-64-3698, D-BOQ-315-264-3698, BEQ-315-264-3698, (JA) BOQ-0467-77-5321 BEQ-0467-70-4948**, Fax: BOQ-011-81-467-77-5321, BEQ-011-81-3117-64-3256,. 24 hours. Write to: BOQ, PSC 477, Box 19, FPO AP 96306-1219. DoD Civilian employee billeting. Check in billeting. Check out 1200 hours.

NAVY LODGE **TML:** Navy Lodge: Bldg 946, Navy Lodge, PSC 477, Box 10, FPO AP 96306-0003. All ranks, leave or official duty. Handicap accessible. **C-(USA) 011-81-311-764-6880,** Fax: C-(USA) 011-81-311-764-6882, D-315-264-6882, (JA) 0467-78-5015 ext 264-6880, D-315-264-6880, 24 hours. Check in 1500, check out 1200 hours. Bedroom, 2 double beds, private bath, no kitchen (30); Bedroom, 2 double beds, private bath, kitchen units w/ complete utensils (58). Refrigerator, cribs, essentials, ice vending, housekeeping service, washer/dryer. Modern structure. Rates: $40-$48 per unit. Maximum five per unit. All categories can make reservations. No pets, kennels at Camp Zama.

JAPAN
Atsugi Naval Air Facility, continued

TML: BOQ. Bldg 480, 482 and 483. Officers, all ranks, leave or official duty and civilian employees on orders, others Space-A. Separate bedroom, double bed, private bath (269). Kitchenette, complete utensils, coffee pot, toaster, microwave, color TV, VCR, hair dryer, housekeeping service, essentials (toiletries), washer/dryer, ice vending, snack vending, closed circuit movie channel, video checkout, ping pong table and recently renovated rooms. Rates: $8, each additional person $2; VIP rooms (O-6) (6) $10, each additional person $2; Guest Quarters. (O7 and above) (2) $20, each additional person $5. AD, Reservists and National guard on orders may make reservations others Space-A. No pets, kennels at Camp Zama (15 minutes by car).

TML: BEQ, Bldg 484, enlisted E-7 to E-9, on leave or official duty. Separate bedroom, double bed, private bath (40). Kitchenette, complete utensils, toaster, coffee pot, microwave, TV, VCR, housekeeping service, essentials (toiletries), washer/dryer, snack vending, ice vending, closed circuit movie channel, sauna, pool table. Active duty, reservist and Nation Guard on orders may make reservations others Space-A. Rates: E7+ $7, each additional person $1. Used to billet permanent party and transient enlisted on orders.

TML: BEQ, Bldg 979, enlisted, all ranks, leave or official duty. (E1-E4) Bedroom, single bed, 2 beds per room, private bath (54). (E5-E6) bedroom, single bed, private bath. (E7-E9) Separate bedroom, double bed, private bath (51). Refrigerator, color TV in lounge and room, housekeeping service, essentials (toiletries), washer/dryer, snack vending, ice vending, closed circuit movie channel, pool and ping pong tables. Central kitchen. Rates: E7+ $5, each additional person $1; E1-E6, $3. AD, Reservists and National Guard on orders may make reservations, others Space-A.

TML: BEQ, Bldg 985 and 986, enlisted, all ranks leave or official duty, Bedroom, shared bath (258). Refrigerator, color TV in lounge and room, closed circuit movie channel, pool and ping pong tables. Recently renovated. AD, Reservists and National Guard on orders may make reservations, others Space-A.

TML: BEQ, Bldgs 980, 981, 982, enlisted, all ranks, leave or official duty. Bedroom, shared bath (80). Refrigerator, color TV in room and lounge, housekeeping service, essentials (toiletries), washer/dryer, snack vending, ice vending, closed circuit movie channel, recently renovated. Active duty, Reservists and National Guard may make reservations, others Space-A.

TML: BEQ, Bldg 47, enlisted, E1-E3, leave or official duty. No female personnel. Bedrooms, 2 beds, communal bath (68). Refrigerator, color TV in room and lounge, housekeeping service, essentials (toiletries), washer/dryer, snack vending, ice vending, VCR in rooms. Renovated. Building built in 1942, General MacArthur stayed here! Active duty, Reservists, National Guard may make reservations, others Space-A.

TML: BEQ, Bldg 984, all ranks. PCS families into NAF Atsugi, limited space for Space-A families. Bedroom, 2 beds, private bath (12). Refrigerator, color TV, housekeeping service, essentials (toiletries), cribs/cots, VCR, coffee pot, recently renovated. Reservations required.

TML: DV/VIP: Commanding Officer's Office, C-(USA) 011-81-3117-64-3104, D-315-264-3104 or through BOQ office. O6+, others Space-A. Off-base hotels located in front of main gate.

NOTE: All rooms in BEQ/BOQ have irons, ironing board, coffee makers (except Bldg 47). All buildings have outdoor BBQ shelters, bicycle, motorcycle, sheds, and large screen TVs in the lounges. Overnight guests are not permitted, unless they are dependents of a valid military/civilian ID card holder and registered at check-in.

JAPAN
Atsugi Naval Air Facility, continued

TML Availability: Difficult, best when CVW-5 is deployed, worst when in port or in the local area.

CREDIT CARDS ACCEPTED: American Express. The Navy Lodge accepts Visa, MasterCard and American Express.

Book a one day tour of Tokyo through MWR at Atsugi, or just ask the friendly Navy Lodge people to provide you with maps, directions and info, but don't miss seeing as much as you can of this marvelous city! Note: Expected to open BEQ 989 (266 rooms) 30 July 95.

Locator 264-3698   Medical 264-3951   Police 264-3200

Camp S. D. Butler Marine Corps Base (JA07R8)
Transient Billeting Fund
PSC 557, Box 935
FPO AP 96379-0935

TELEPHONE NUMBER INFORMATION: Main installation numbers: C-(USA) 011-81-98-892-5111 or 011-81-6117-40-110, (JA) 098-892-5111, D-315-640-1110.

Location: Four miles south of Okinawa City on Hwy 330 at Camp Foster 2 miles north of Futenma. NMC: Naha, 7 miles south.

Lodging Office: ATTN: FACS, Billeting/Housing Director, **C-(USA) 011-81-98-892-2459, (JA) 098892-2191, D-315-635-2191,** Fax: C-(USA) 011-81-6117-45-7549, D-315-645-7549, 0700-1630 daily. Other hours, Bldg 1, OD, D-315-635-7218/2644. Check in facility, check out 1200 hours daily. Government civilian employee billeting.

TML: TLF. **Courtney Lodge**, Bldg 2540, **Camp Courtney**, all ranks, leave or official duty, C-(USA) 011-81-98-972-9578, D-315-622-9578. Suites, private bath (16). Refrigerator, A/C, CATV in room and lounge, housekeeping service, cribs/cots, coin washer/dryer. .25 miles to 7 day store, 1.25 miles to commissary and exchange. Modern structure. Rates: $30 per unit, each additional person $5. Maximum three per unit. No pets.

TML: Hansen Lodge, Bldg 2540, **Camp Hansen**, all ranks, leave or official duty. C-(USA) 011-81-98-972-7159/4511, D-315-623-4511. Same as Courtney except bedroom, shared bath (18). Older structure. Rates: $10 per room. Maximum two per room. Reservations accepted. No pets. BOQ/BEQ. $10-$12 per person, each additional person $10. Reservations up to 24 hours in advance.

TML: TLF. **Kuwae Lodge**, Bldg 400, **Camp Lester**, all ranks, leave or official duty. C-(USA) 011-81-98-892-9102/9106, D-315-645-9103/9106. Rooms with kitchen (165). Washer/dryer, playroom, rec rooms. Rates: $32,each additional person $5. Double adjoining rooms, $66-$70, 3 room suite. Reservations accepted 30 days in advance. Free shuttle bus service. No pets.

TML: WESTPAC Inn. Camp Foster, C-(USA) 011-81-98-892-2459/2660, D-315-635-2459/2191, Fax C-(USA) 011-81-61175-7549, D-315-645-7549, 0730-1630 hours. (TQ) all ranks, leave or official duty. Futenma, C-(USA) 011-81-92-2112, (VOQ) officers, all ranks, leave or official duty. Separate bedroom, living room, private bath (20); (Futenma) bedroom, private bath (10); separate bedroom, private bath (2); suites, private bath (2). Maximum 2 per suite, 2 per room. Kitchen, A/C, color TV, housekeeping service, washer/dryer, video cassette reception in room. Older structure, renovated. Rates: $10, $12, $19 according to rank and status. Duty can make reservations, others Space-A. No pets.

Temporary Military Lodging Around the World - 311

JAPAN
Camp S. D. Butler Marine Corps Base, continued

TML: White Beach Recreation Services (NAVY), Commander, Fleet Activities Okinawa, PSC 480, MWR Department, FPO AP 96370-0057, C-(USA) 011-81-634-6952/6954. Cabins. Bedroom, living room, private bath (4); Studio, private bath (8). Fully furnished, kitchen, TV/VCR. Rates: with living room $50; studio $40. Reservations required with full payment up to 10 days in advance.

TML: DV/VIP. Day House, Awase House, Bldgs 4205, 4515. Same as above. Rates: $30.

DV/VIP: Protocol Office, Bldg 1, **Camp SD Butler MCB,** C-(USA) 011-81-98-892-7274, D-315-645-7274. Protocol Office, Bldg 4225, III MEF, Camp Courtney, C-(USA) 011-81-98-2972-7749, D-315-645-7749. Protocol Office, Bldg 1, 1st MAW, Camp SD Butler MCB, C-(USA) 011-81-98-892-2901, D-315-635-2901.

TML Availability: Good. Best, Aug-Mar. More difficult, other times.

Direct dialing from the US to Okinawa
011-81-6117+ last six digit extension number
Example: MCB locator service 645-7218, from the US 011-81-6117-45-7218

Miscellaneous Lodging in Okinawa

BASE	USMC MAIN NUMBER	BILLETS
Camp Foster	645-7558	CBOQ-640-1113
Camp Hansen	622-1131	BOQ-623-4711/BEQ-623-7159
MCAS Futenma	622-1131	BOQ-636-3443/BEQ-636-3748
Camp Courtney	622-1131	CBOQ-622-9602
Camp Schwab	622-1131	BOQ-625-2738/BEQ-625-2230
Camp Kinser	640-1113	CBOQ-637-3748

CREDIT CARDS ACCEPTED: American Express (for TAD/TDY personnel only).

Transportation: Camp-to-camp shuttle busses are available; inquire at each lodging desk for details.

Don't miss seeing Nakagusuku Castle, left over from Okinawa's feudal period, and the Nakamura House, which displays Okinawan lifestyle of yesteryear. Check with the USO for locations and possible tours.

Locator 645-7218 (USMC)   Medical 634-1756   Police 635-7441
        632-7653 (USN)
        644-4300 (USA)
        634-3374 (USAF)

Camp Zama (JA06R8)
Commander
17th ASG-CM
ATTN: APAJ-GH-EH-HB (Billeting)
APO AP 96343-0068

TELEPHONE NUMBER INFORMATION: Main installation numbers: C-(USA) 011-81-311-7-63-1110, (JA) 03117-63-1110, D-315-263-1110.

Location: 25 miles south of Tokyo or north of Yokohama. Excellent rail service. NMC: Tokyo, 25 miles north.

JAPAN
Camp Zama, continued

Lodging Office: ATTN: APAJ-GH-EH-HB, Bldg 563, Sand Street, C-(USA) **011-81-311-763-4474** (ask for 263-3830/4474), (JA) **04062-51-5344** (ask for 263-3830/4474), D-315-263-4474/3830, Fax: C-(USA) 011-81-311-763-3598, D-315-263-3598, 24 hours. Check in 1500 hours, check out 1200 hours daily. Government civilian employee billeting.

TML: VOQ/VEQ. Bldg 742, all ranks, official duty, or leave. Bedroom, private bath (38). Refrigerator, microwave, stocked bar, community kitchen, A/C, color TV and VCR, housekeeping service, washer/dryer, snack vending, ice vending. Modern structure. Rates: single $15, double $20, each additional person $5. Duty can make reservations, others Space-A.

TML: Guest House. Bldg 552, all ranks, PCS in and out, or official duty. Handicap accessible first floor. Separate bedroom, private bath (56). Kitchenettes, complete utensils, housekeeping service, color TV and VCR, A/C, ice vending, washer/dryer. New structure, furnishings 1992. Rates: single $25, double $30, each additional person $5. Duty can make reservations, others Space-A.

TML: Guest House. Bldg 780, all ranks, PCS in/out. Bedroom, hall bath (5); two bedroom, hall bath (14); three bedroom, private bath (2). A/C, refrigerator, microwave, complete utensils, community kitchen, color TV and VCR, housekeeping service, washer/dryer, ice vending. Older structure, refurbished 1991. Rates: sponsor $16, each additional person $5 . Duty can make reservations, others Space-A.

TML: DVQ. Bldg 550, officer O6+, official duty or leave. Separate bedroom, private bath (12). A/C, community kitchen, cots/cribs ($5), housekeeping service, refrigerator, stocked bar, microwaves, TV and VCR, ice vending, washer/dryer. Modern structure, refurbished 1991. Rates: sponsor $25, each additional person $5. Duty can make reservations, others Space-A. Pets boarded at clinic for $4 per day.

DV/VIP: USARJ Protocol Office, Bldg 101. C-(USA) 011-81-311-763-4019/4134, D-315-263-4134, O7+, retirees Space-A.

TML Availability: Guest House: good, DVQ: good, Jan-Feb difficult. VOQ/VEQ: good, Jan-Feb difficult.

CREDIT CARDS ACCEPTED: Visa, MasterCard and American Express.

Check with the ITT office on base for local tours. A round trip shuttle bus to Tokyo (the New Sanno Hotel) is available, as are trips to Disneyland, Kamakura, Hakone, Mount Fuji, Kyoto, Nikko and Seto.

Locator 263-5344   Medical 263-4127   Police 263-3002

Iwakuni Marine Corps Air Station (JA12R8)
Morale, Welfare and Recreation
ATTN: Temporary Lodging Facility
PSC 561, P.O. Box 1867
FPO AP 96310-1867

TELEPHONE NUMBER INFORMATION: Main installation numbers: C-(USA) 011-81-827-21-4171, (JA) 0827-21-4171, D-315-253-5409. Direct dial from U.S. 011-81-6117-53-3181.

JAPAN
Iwakuni Marine Corps Air Station, continued

Location: Facing the Inland Sea on the south portion of the island of Honshu, 450 miles southwest of Tokyo, .5 miles off JA-188 on JA-189. NMC: Hiroshima, 25 miles north.

Lodging Office: Bldg 444, C-(USA) 011-81-6117-53-3221, (JA) 0827-21-4171 ext 3221, D-315-253-3221, 0800-2200 hours daily. Check in Bldg 444, check out 1000 hours daily. Government civilian employee billeting.

TML: Transient Billeting. Bldgs 203, 606, 1189, all ranks, leave or official duty, C ext 3181. Some facilities handicap accessible. Bedroom, private bath (enlisted) (73); separate bedroom, private bath (SNCOs and officers) (51); two bedroom, private bath (DV-Shogun House) (1); Kitchenette (Bldg 606), refrigerator, utensils, A/C, color TV, housekeeping service, ice vending. Essentials on sale front desk. Modern structure. Rates: sponsor/spouse and adult dependents over age 12 $7, officers $15, SNCOs $12, E-5 and below $10. Duty can make reservations, others Space-A.

TML: Lodge Facility. Bldgs 444 and 1188, .5 miles from gate. Single room, private bath, kitchenette (24); two room suites, private bath, kitchenette (24). 3/4 miles from commissary, exchange, seven day store and clubs. Rates: $30-$40 for one or two persons, each additional person $2. A priority system rather than a reservation system is used. PCS on station, command sponsored accompanied (Priority 1A); PCS off station, command sponsored (Priority 1B); all others Space-A.

DV/VIP: DGR, Bldg 511, D-315-253-4211.

TML Availability: Good.

CREDIT CARDS ACCEPTED: American Express.

See the famous Kintai Bridge, and view the Iwakuni Castle Ropeway. Hiroshima is 50 minutes by train, and visitors should see the Peace Memorial Park, Atomic Bomb Memorial Dome, and reconstructed Hiroshima Castle. Don't miss the cherry blossoms in bloom, Mar-Apr.

Locator 113   **Medical** 253-5571   **Police** 253-3222

Kadena Air Base (JA08R8)
ATTN: 18 SVS/SVML
APO AP 96368-5134

TELEPHONE NUMBER INFORMATION: Main installation numbers: C-(USA) 011-81-611-938-1111, (JA) 0611-938-1111, D-315-630-1110.

Location: Take Hwy 58 North from Naha to Kadena's Gate 1 on the right immediately north of USMC Camp Lester. NMC: Naha, 12 miles south.

Lodging Office: Bldg 332, Beeson Ave, C-(USA) 011-81-611-732-1000, D-315-632-1100, 24 hours. Check in 1500 hours at billeting, check out 1000 hours daily. Government civilian employee billeting.

TML: TLF. Family Quarters. Bldg 322, 437, 507, all ranks, leave or official duty. Handicap accessible. Apartments (122). A/C, refrigerator, kitchen, complete utensils, color TV, VCR, housekeeping service, cribs, rollaway, washer/dryer, exercise room and mini-mart available. Modern structure. Rates: $35 per unit. Maximum six persons per unit. Duty can make reservations, others Space-A.

JAPAN
Kadena Air Base, continued

TML: VAQ. Bldgs 317, 332, 504, 506, 509, 510, enlisted all ranks. Bedroom, private bath (124); shared bedrooms, semi-private bath (60). A/C, housekeeping service, refrigerator, color TV/VCR, washer/dryer, exercise room and mini-mart available. Rates: $12 per person per night, each additional person $5. Maximum two per unit. Duty can make reservations, others Space-A.

TML: VOQ. Bldgs 306, 311, 314, 316, 318, 502, 508, officers all ranks. Bedroom, private bath (109); separate bedroom, semi-private bath (20). A/C, housekeeping service, refrigerator, color TV, VCR, washer/dryer, exercise room and mini-mart available. Rates: $12 per person per night, each additional person $5. Maximum two persons. Duty can make reservations, others Space-A.

TML: DVQ. Bldgs 78, 85, 315, 2024, officers O6+, leave or official duty. Bedroom, living area private bath (24); two bedroom, private bath, living area, dining area (2); bedroom, private bath, living area, dining area (1). A/C, essentials, kitchen, complete utensils, housekeeping service, color TV, VCR, washer/dryer, exercise room and mini-mart available. Rates: $22.00 per person per night, each additional person $10. DV Houses: $27 per person per night, each additional person $12.50. Duty can make reservations, others Space-A.

DV/VIP: Protocol Office, Bldg 10, D-315-634-3548, O6+.

TML Availability: Good, Dec-Jan. Difficult, spring and summer.

CREDIT CARDS ACCEPTED: Visa, MasterCard and American Express.

Transportation: On/off base taxi 937-2467, military taxi: 634 4505, car rental agencies 632-1880, 633-0007.

This is the cross roads of the Pacific, and a great Space-A departure point, but don't miss seeing the Children's Park Zoo in Okinawa City, the Ryukyuan Village and Takoyama Habu Center. Near Nenoko see the Shell house, visited by shell collectors.

Locator 634-1110   Medical 634-1922   Police 634-2475

Misawa Air Base (JA03R8)
Misawa Inn
35 SVS/SVML
Unit 5019
APO AP 96319-5021

TELEPHONE NUMBER INFORMATION: Main installation numbers: C-(USA) 011-81-176-53-5181, (JA) 0176-53-5181, D-315-226-3526/4294.

Location: On the northeast portion of the Island of Honshu, 400 miles north of Tokyo. NMC: Hachinohe City, 17 miles southeast.

Lodging Office: Misawa Inn, 35 SVS/SVML, Unit 5019, APO AP 96319-5000, **C-(USA) 011-81-176-53-5181 ext 3526, (JA) 0176-53-5181 ext 3526, D-315-226-3526,** Fax: C-(USA) 011-81-176-53-2165, D-315-226-2165, 24 hours. Check in billeting, check out 1200 hours daily.

TML: TLF. Bldg 670, all ranks, leave or official duty. Single family units (40). Private bath, living room, kitchen, utensils, soda/snack vending. Meeting/conference room and exercise rooms available. Rates: $35 per unit.

JAPAN
Misawa Air Base, continued

TML: VOQ. Bldgs 662, 664, officers O1-O6, leave or official duty. Bedroom, private bath (56). Kitchen, utensils, refrigerator, color TV, VCR, housekeeping service, washer/dryer., soda/snack vending. Meeting/conference room and exercise rooms available. Older structure. Rates: $12 per person. Duty can make reservations, others Space-A.

TML: VAQ. Bldg 669, enlisted all ranks, leave or official duty. Bedroom, private bath (28). Prime Knight Aircrew Quarters, (top three suites, 10); suites, private bath (E9) (2). Refrigerator, color TV, VCR, housekeeping service, washer/dryer, ice vending, soda/snack vending. Meeting/conference room and exercise rooms available. Rates: $12 per person. Duty and civilians on official duty can make reservations, others Space-A.

TML: DV/VIP. Bldg 17, officer O6+ (Mon and Fri), leave or official duty. Bedroom, private bath, suites (4). Kitchen, utensils, refrigerator, A/C, color TV, VCR, housekeeping service, soda/snack vending. Meeting/conference room and exercise rooms available. Modern structure. Rates: $9.50 per person. Duty can make reservations, others Space-A.

TML: BOQ/BEQ, Misawa Naval Air Facility, C-(USA) 011-81-3117-66-3131/4483, Fax C-(USA) 011-81-3117-66-9312. BOQ, Bedroom, private bath, mini music system (122); BEQ, E1-E4 double room, shared bath; E5+ single, private bath, iron/ironing board, clock radio, refrigerator, microwave (325). Rates: enlisted $4, officers $8. Duty can make reservations, others Space-A. **Winner of the 1996 Elmo R. Zumwalt Award for Excellence in Housing.**

DV/VIP: 35th FW/CCP. C-(USA) 011-81-176-53-5181 ext 4804, O6+. Retirees Space-A.

TML Availability: Good, Nov-Mar. Difficult, other times.

CREDIT CARDS ACCEPTED: Visa, MasterCard, and American Express.

Enjoy the excellent eating establishments in downtown Misawa, and try a hot bath at Komakis. Explore the Komaki Onsen, Komaki Grand and the Second Grand Hotels. Get hints from Services (Bldg 1044) for trips farther afield.

Locator 0176-53-5181   **Medical 226-2985**   **Police 226-4358**

THE NEW SANNO
U.S. FORCES CENTER

The New Sanno
US Forces Center (JA01R8)
Tokyo
APO AP 96337-5003

TELEPHONE NUMBER INFORMATION: Main installation numbers: C-(USA) 011-81-3-3440-7871, (JA) 03-3440-7871.

Location: At 4-12-20 Minami Azabu, Minato-ku, Tokyo 106, a five minute walk from nearest subway station, Hiroo (Hibiya line). NMI: Tokyo Administrative Facility/Hardy Barracks, one mile. NMC: Tokyo, in city limits.

JAPAN
The New Sanno US Forces Center, continued

Description: Located in a quiet residential area not far from downtown Tokyo, only a five-minute walk from the nearest subway station, Hiroo. Offers guests commercial hotel quality, newly renovated accommodations and food service at affordable prices. Each of 149 guest rooms features private bath or shower, and central heating and air conditioning. Rental videos are available. Two traditional Japanese-style suites for guests to enjoy the full flavor of the Orient.

    A family dining room, Japanese-style restaurant, fine dining restaurant, lounge and snack bar are available to guests of The New Sanno. Entertainment and special events are scheduled on a regular basis in The New Sanno's main ballroom which can seat up to 350 guests, and banquet and conference facilities are available.

    There is a rooftop pool (seasonal), an exercise room and video game room, first and second floor arcades with a Navy Exchange, bookstore, convenience store and concessionaires. An APO, military banking facility, pack and wrap service, barber shop, beauty salon, flower shop and laundry and dry cleaning, plus public rest rooms (handicap accessible) on the lobby level, and other American-style conveniences make The New Sanno a meeting place for military personnel and their families touring Tokyo.

    Tours, theater, concert and sporting event tickets are available through the Information and Tours Desk. They can also book airline reservations, C-03-3440-7871 ext 7200. If you are arriving at Narita International Airport, an economical airport express bus is available to The New Sanno's front door. Daily buses run to and from Yokota Air Base (schedule available at AMC terminal). The New Sanno is a Joint Services, all ranks facility managed by the US Navy as Executive Agent.

Room Rates for the New Sanno U S Forces Center

Room Type	No.	I*	II*	III*	IV*
Single (Queen bed)	43	$29	$38	$44	$63
Double (Queen + single bed)	78	$40	$47	$55	$77
King Suite (King + sofa)	50	$56	$61	$68	$95
Twin Suite (2 twins + sofa)	3	$56	$61	$68	$95
Family Suite (sgl room + bunk)	2	$56	$61	$76	$100
Japanese Suite	2	$70	$76	$84	$111

*I: E1-E5; **II:** E6-O3, WO1-WO4; **III:** O4-O10; **IV:** retired/non-DoD. I, II and III include comparable DoD Civilian grades. II includes DAVs, Unremarried Widows and Orphans (all with DD1173).

ALL RATES SUBJECT TO CHANGE.

Season of Operation: Year round.

Eligibility: Active/Retired/US Embassy Tokyo/UN Command(Rear), Active Reserves, DoD and other SOFA recognized Federal Civilian Employees on official orders to or through Japan.

Reservations: Reservations may be made up to 365 days in advance, recommended at least 45 days in advance with one nights deposit for each room reserved. Deposits by check, money order, American Express, Diners' Club, MasterCard, Visa. Address: The New Sanno Hotel, APO AP 96337-5003, Attn: Reservations. C-(USA) 011-81-3-3440-7871 ext 7121, (JA) 03-3440-7871 ext 7121, D-315-229-7121, Fax: C-(USA) 011-81-3-3440-7824, D-315-229-7102; E-Mail: navjntservact@zama-emh1.army.mil.

Restrictions: No pets.

Temporary Military Lodging Around the World - 317

JAPAN

Okuma Joint Services Rec Facility - Okinawa (JA09R8)
Schilling Leisure Resource Center
Okuma Reservation
18th SVS/SVMR
Unit 5135, Box 10
APO AP 96368-5135

TELEPHONE NUMBER INFORMATION: Main installation numbers: C-(USA) 011-81-98-041-5164 (JA) 0980-41-5164, D-315-634-4601, Fax C-(USA) 011-81-98-041-5165, (JA) 098-041-5165.

Location: On Hwy 58, 50 miles north of Kadena AB, Okinawa. Left off Hwy 58 before Hentona. NMC: Naha, JA 62 miles south.

Lodging Office: Schilling Tours, 18 SVS/SVMR, Unit 5135 Box 10, APO AP 96368-3135. Duty, retired, DoD civilians assigned overseas. May make reservation up to 90 days in advance, **C-(USA) 011-81-611-734-4322, (JA) 098938-1110 ext 634-4322, D-315-634-4322,** 0800-1700 hours M-F (summer), W-M (winter). Reception Center Bldg 116, check in 1500 hours, check out 1100 hours daily. Operates year round.

TML: Rec Cabanas. All ranks, leave or official duty. Bedroom, 2 double beds, shared bath, (30); bedroom, 2 double beds, private bath (10); bedrooms, double bed, private bath, dry bar, couples only (12); suites, 4 double beds, private bath (9); VIP suite (1). Refrigerator, microwave, A/C, color TV/VCR, housekeeping service, cribs/rollaways ($3), washer/dryer. Meeting/conference rooms, Mini Shoppette, Restaurant & lounge. Rates: $25-$55 daily. All categories can make reservations.

DV/VIP: 18th Wing/Protocol, Bldg 10, Kadena AB, Okinawa, D-315-634-0106, O6+. Retirees and lower ranks Space-A.

TML Availability: Good, Nov-Feb. Difficult, other times.

CREDIT CARDS ACCEPTED: Visa and MasterCard.

Great beach rec area. For full details and camping opportunities, see Military Living's *Military RV, Camping and Rec Areas Around The World.*

Sasebo Fleet Activities (JA15R8)
Combined Bachelor Quarters
U.S. Fleet Activities, Sasebo
PSC 476, Box 1
FPO AP 96322-1100

TELEPHONE NUMBER INFORMATION: Main installation numbers: C-(USA) 011-81-956-24-6111, (JA) 0956-24-6111, D-315-252-1110.

Location: From either Nagasaki or Fukuoka. take the Nishi-Kyushu Expressway to Sasebo exit (both in Japanese and English). Follow Route 35 to downtown SASEBO, ask directions to naval base. Far southwestern Japan, on the Korean Strait, NMC: Fukuoka, 50 miles northeast.

JAPAN
Sasebo Fleet Activities, continued

Lodging Office: ATTN: CBQ Officer, U.S. Fleet Activities, Sasebo, PSC 476, Box 1, FPO AP 96322-1100. C-(USA) 011-81-956-24-6111 (BOQ ext 3794) (BEQ ext 3413), (JA) 095624-6111 (BOQ ext 3794) (BEQ ext 3413), D-315-252-3794 (BOQ), D-315-252-3413 (BEQ), Fax: C-(USA) 011-81-956-24-6111 (BOQ/BEQ ext 3530), D-315-252-3530 (BOQ/BEQ), 24 hours. Check in BOQ/BEQ office after 1200 hours, check out 1200 daily. Government Civilian Employee billeting.

TML: BOQ. Bldgs 1455, 1603, all ranks leave or official duty. Bedrooms (145). Kitchenette, utensils, refrigerator, microwave, essentials, color TV/VCR in room and lounge, housekeeping service, snack vending, ice vending, cribs, washer/dryer. Modern structure. Rates: $7 per person per unit, maximum $12 per family. Maximum two per unit. Active duty PCS and TAD/TDY (civilians GS7+) on orders to FLEACT Sasebo may make reservations up to 45 days in advance, all others Space-A. No pets.

TML: BEQ. Bldgs 1604, 1663, all ranks leave or official duty. Shared bedrooms, private bath (140). Refrigerator, color TV/VCR in room/lounge, microwave, phone, snack vending, ice vending machines, washer/dryer. Modern structure. Rates: $4 per person per unit, maximum $8. Maximum two per unit. Active duty PCS and TAD/TDY (civilians GS7+) on orders to FLEACT Sasebo may make reservations up to 45 days in advance, all others Space-A. No pets.

TML: Navy Lodge, ATTN: Navy Fleet Activities Sasebo, PSC 476, Box 30, FPO AP 96322-0003. Reservations: C-(USA) 011-81-956-24-6111 ext 3608, D-315-252-3608, Fax: C-(USA) 011-81-956-24-0173, D-312-252-3602, 0700-2300 hours daily. All ranks, leave or official duty. Bedroom, 2 double beds, private bath (26). A/C, color TV, housekeeping service, coin washer/dryer, ice vending. Near MWR, All Hands Club, Snack Bar, Swimming pool, Base Galley, NEX 10 minute walk. Modern structure. Rates: $48. All categories can make reservations.

TML: DV/VIP. Bldg 80, C-(USA) 011-81-956-24-3401, leave or official duty. Duty can make reservations, others Space-A.

DV/VIP: Commander, Fleet Activities Sasebo, Attn: Protocol Officer, PSC 476, Box 1, FPO AP 96322-1100, BOQ O6+, BEQ E9+.

TML Availability: Fairly good, Apr-Aug. Difficult, Sep-Dec.

CREDIT CARDS ACCEPTED: American Express. The Navy Lodge accepts Discover.

Winner of the 1996 Elmo R. Zumwalt Award for Excellence in Housing. Mount Yumihari has an excellent view. Take a 99 Islands boat cruise, from nearby Kashimae Pier (15 minutes from base by car). Hachiman Shrine is a 20 minute walk from base. Nagasaki and Fukuoka are one hour drives. Don't miss the Fukagawa/Noritake Chinaware Factory, the finest bone china in the world! Don't forget to see Huis Ten Bosch and Holland Village.

Locator 1110   Medical 3624/3625   Police 3446/3447

JAPAN

Tama Outdoor Recreation Area (JA10R8)
374 SPTG/SVBL
APO AP 96328-5119

TELEPHONE NUMBER INFORMATION: Main installation numbers: C-(USA) 011-81-423-77-7009, (JA) 0423-77-7009, D-315-224-3421/3422.

Location: Fifteen miles southeast of Yokota AB. NMC: Tokyo, 45 minute train ride.

Lodging Office: 374 SPTG/SVBL. Yokota AB, APO AP 96328-5000, **C-(USA) 011-81-423-77-7009, (JA) 0423-77-7009, D-315-224-3421/3422,** 24 hours. Check in at facility 1400, check out 1100 hours daily. Operates year round. Reservations required with first days rent.

TML: Rec Lodge and cabins. All ranks, leave or official duty. Reservations required (60 days in advance for weekends, 90 days for weekdays). Suites, private bath (6); double rooms, private bath (14); executive and single cabins, private bath (18). Refrigerator, A/C, color TV, housekeeping service, washer/dryer, soda/snack vending, ice vending. Meeting/conference rooms, exercise room, and mini-mart available. Rates: $25-$50. All categories can make reservations. Pets allowed in cabins.

TML Availability: Good, Oct-Mar. Difficult, other times.

CREDIT CARDS ACCEPTED: Visa, MasterCard and American Express.

Transportation: Off base taxi.

This is a 500 acre retreat west of Tokyo. Its a quiet getaway offering many facilities, such as a golf course. See Military Living's *Military RV, Camping and Rec Areas Around The World* for more details.

Locator 0423-77-7009   Medical 225-9111   Police 224-3421 ext 40

Tokyo Administration Facility (JA02R8)
Akasaka Press Center (Hardy Barracks)
Bldg 1, Room 413-A
APO AP 96337-0007

TELEPHONE NUMBER INFORMATION: Main installation numbers: C-(USA) 011-81-3117-29-3270 (JA) 03-3402-6024, touchtone 229-3270, D-315-229-3270/3345.

Location: At #7-23-17 Roppongi, Minato-ku, Tokyo. Near Imperial Palace and 2 miles by taxi from New Sanno Hotel. Nogizaka subway station, left out of exit #5. NMC: Tokyo, in the city.

Lodging Office: Hardy Barracks, Bldg 1, Room 413-A, **C-(USA) 011-81-3-3440-7871 ext 229-3270, (JA) 03-3440-7871 ext 229-3270,** 0730-2230 daily. Check in at facility 1600, check out 1200 hours daily. Government civilian employee billeting.

TML: VOQ/VEQ. All ranks, leave or official duty. Bedroom, shared bath (19); separate bedroom suites, private bath (2). Refrigerator, community kitchen, A/C, color TV, VCR, micro-fridge, coffee, travel kit, housekeeping service, cribs, washer/dryer. Remodeled March 1994. Rates: sponsor $20,

JAPAN
Tokyo Administration Facility, continued

each additional person $5, suites $30 for two people. Reservations may be made up to 15 days in advance by telephone or in person for Space-A. Pets not allowed. **Note: Tokyo city bus 97 runs between the New Sanno Hotel and Hardy Barracks.**

DV/VIP: Call Camp Zama, Bldg 101, room W-223, D-315-263-4474, for assistance.

TML Availability: Good. Best months Jan-Mar.

CREDIT CARDS ACCEPTED: Visa, MasterCard and American Express.

Check with the New Sanno Hotel for guided tours, or just pick up some city maps. Then visit the Ginza, Kabuki theater, Akasaka/Roppongi (the entertainment district), Ueno Park, Zoo, and shopping are musts.

Locator 3117-29-3270   Medical 225-9111   Police 3117-29-3270

Torii Station (JA11R8)
Unit 35115
APO AP 96376-5115

TELEPHONE NUMBER INFORMATION: Main installation numbers: C-(USA) 011-81-6117-44-1000, D-315-644-1000.

Location: Located in Okinawa. Off Hwy 58, north on Hwy 6, 11 miles north of Naha and three miles northwest of Kadena City an the East China Sea. Enter gates from Hwy 6. NMC: Naha, 11 miles south.

Lodging Office: C-(USA) **011-81-6117-44-1000, D-315-644-1000.**

TML: BOQ: Bedroom, private bath (30). Limited availability for Space-A.

TML: Shogun Inn at Kadena AB, six miles away. C-(USA) 011-81-6117-1000/1100, D-315-632-1000/1100.

Yokosuka Fleet Activities (JA05R8)
Combined Bachelor's Quarters
PSC 473, Box 40
FPO AP 96349-1110

TELEPHONE NUMBER INFORMATION: Main installation numbers: C-(USA) 011-81-468-211-911, (JA) 0465-211-911, D-315-243-1110.

Location: About 23 miles south of Tokyo and 25 miles north of Yokohama. NMC: Tokyo, 23 miles north. Excellent train service.

Lodging Office: C-(USA) **011-81-3117-43-7317** (BOQ), C-(USA) **011-81-3117-43-5569/7777** (BEQ), D-315-243-7317 (BOQ), D-315-243-5088 (BEQ), Fax: C-(USA) 011-81-3117-43-8990 (BOQ), C-(USA) 011-81-3117-43-5088 (BEQ), 24 hours. Check in facility after 1200 hours, check out before 1200 hours daily. Government civilian employee billeting.

JAPAN
Yokosuka Fleet Activities, continued

NAVY LODGE

TML: Navy Lodge. Bldg J-4807, all ranks, leave or official duty, Reservations: **C-(USA) 011-81-311-743-6708, (JA) 0-468-27-0080, D-315-243-6708,** Fax: C- (USA) 011-81-311-743-6759 Write to: Navy Lodge, PSC 473, Box 70, FPO AP 96349-0003. Two double beds, kitchenette with microwave, private bath (99); one double bed with sofa sleeper, private bath, handicap accessible (2); one bed and a sofa sleeper, private bath (1); two double beds, kitchenette, private bath (7); two double beds, micro-fridge, private bath (56). A/C, cable TV/VCPs, movie rental, clock, cribs, dining table, futons, hairdryers, ice vending, soda/snack vending, iron/ironing boards, lounge, mini-mart, picnic grounds, playground, restaurant, coffee, coin washer/dryer. Rates: $44 (the $44 units were under renovation and were not available at press time, call for more information), kitchen units $48. Four handicap accessible. Pets kept overnight in lounge until kennel opens.

TML: BEQ. Bldg 1492, enlisted, all ranks, leave or official duty. Bedroom, 3 beds, private bath (232). Refrigerator, A/C, color TV in room and lounge, housekeeping service, washer/dryer. Modern structure. Rates: $6 per person. Maximum two per room. Duty can make reservations, others Space-A.

TML: BOQ. Bldgs 1556, 1723, officer all ranks, leave or official duty. Bedroom, private bath (95). Kitchen, A/C, color TV in room and lounge, housekeeping service, washer/dryer, barber shop. Modern structure. Rates: $12 per person; VIP suite $20; Togo Room (O7+) $25. Duty can make reservations, others Space-A. Note: most rooms have only one single bed.

TML: CPOQ. Bldg 1475, enlisted E7-E9, leave or official duty. Bedroom, private bath (26). Refrigerator, community kitchen, A/C, color TV in room and lounge, housekeeping service, washer/dryer, ice vending. Modern structure. Rates: $8 per person; VIP $8; DV (Command) $10. Duty can make reservations, others Space-A. Note: all beds are singles.

TML: Other. NASU Lodge. 100 miles north of Tokyo. Rec Service Office. C ext 5613/ 7306. Two-story wood-frame building accommodates up to 26 persons. Japanese style floor and bath. Kitchen and lodging requirements. Near many rec areas for skiing, fishing, hiking, horseback riding. Reservations taken one month in advance. Call for rates. Group rates available. All ranks.

DV/VIP: Protocol Office, C-(USA) 011-81-468-21-1911-EX-5685, D-315-243-7317, O7+. Retirees Space-A.

TML Availability: Good. Somewhat difficult, Jun-Sep.

CREDIT CARDS ACCEPTED: American Express. The Navy Lodge accepts Visa, MasterCard and American Express.

Located close to Tokyo, near many historic Japanese shrines, beautiful beaches, a 10 minute walk to a shopping mall, and two hours from Disneyland Tokyo, Yokosuka boasts "the best MWR facility in the Pacific."

Locator 113   **Medical 116**   **Police 243-5000/5001**

JAPAN

Yokota Air Base (JA04R8)
Kanto Lodge
374 SPTG/SVML
APO AP 96328-5119

TELEPHONE NUMBER INFORMATION: Main installation numbers: C-(USA) 011-81-3117-55-1110 (JA) 0428-52-25-10, D-315-225-1101.

Location: Take JA-16 South from Tokyo. AB is one mile west of Fussa. Clearly marked. NMC: Tokyo, 35 miles northeast.

Lodging Office: Bldg 10, Bobzien Ave and 1st Street, C-(USA) **011-81-425-52-2511 ext 5-7712**, (JA) **0425-52-2511 ext 5-7712, D-315-225-9270,** Fax: C-(USA) 011-81-425-52-3499, D-315-225-3499, 24 hours. Check in billeting, check out 1000 hours daily. Government lodging.

TML: TLF. Bldg 10, all ranks, leave or official duty, C ext 5-9270. Four bedroom, shared bath (31). Kitchen, utensils, A/C, color TV in room and lounge, housekeeping service, cribs, washer/dryer, handicap accessible. Modern structure. Rates: $35 per room. Duty can make reservations, others Space-A. Limited pet care available on base.

TML: VOQ. Bldgs 14, 120, 131-133, officers all ranks, leave or official duty, C ext 5-9270. Bedroom, private bath (136); suites, separate bedroom, private bath, (15). Refrigerator, A/C, color TV, housekeeping service, washer/dryer. Older structure. Rates: $12 per person. Duty can make reservations, others Space-A.

TML: VAQ. Bldg 16, 690, 134, enlisted all ranks, leave or official duty, C ext 5-9270. Bedroom, common bath (80); two bedroom (22). Refrigerator, A/C, color TV, housekeeping service, washer/dryer. Older structure. Rates: $12 per person. Maximum four per unit. Duty can make reservations, others Space-A.

TML: DV/VIP. SNCO, Bldg 32, enlisted E7-E9, leave/official duty, C ext 5-9270. Suites, bedroom, private bath, (3). Refrigerator, A/C, TV, housekeeping service, washer/dryer. Modern structure. Rates:$15 per person. Duty can make reservations, others Space-A.

TML: DV/VIP. Bldgs 13, 17, 32, officers O6+ (Mon and Fri), leave or official duty, C ext 5-9270. Separate bedroom, private bath, suites (9); two bedroom, private bath, suites (4). Kitchen, utensils, A/C, color TV, housekeeping service, cribs, washer/dryer. Older structure. Rates: $15 per person. Duty can make reservations, others Space-A.

DV/VIP: 5th AF/CSP, C-(USA) 011-81-425-52-2511 ext 5-4141, O6+. Retirees and lower ranks Space-A.

TML Availability: Good, Oct-Mar. Difficult, other times.

CREDIT CARDS ACCEPTED: American Express.

Locator 225-8390   **Medical** 911   **Police** 911

# KOREA

Camp Casey (RK01R8)
Unit 15543
APO AP 96224-0453

TELEPHONE NUMBER INFORMATION: Main installation numbers: C-(USA) 011-82-351-869-1110, (RK) 351-869-1110, D-315-730-1110.

Location: Located in northwestern South Korea. Take Hwy 3 north from Seoul for 25 miles to Tongduchon and follow signs to Camp Casey, gate 2 and Kelly Bird. NMC: Tongduchon, one mile south.

Lodging Office: Casey Lodge. Bldg 2626, C-(USA) **011-82-351-869-4247, D-315-730-4247**, Fax: C-(USA) 011-82-351-869-4247, D-315-730-4247, E-mail: caseylodge@iname.com.

TML: Bldg 2626, all ranks leave or official duty. Bedroom, twin bed (24); Deluxe room, queen-size bed (2), private bath, cable TV, VCR, mini-refrigerator, soda/snack vending. Rates: standard room $35-$49 based on double occupancy; deluxe room $50.

CREDIT CARDS ACCEPTED: Visa, MasterCard, and American Express.

Camp Henry (RK02R8)
Billeting Office, Taegu Housing Div
DPW-Taegu, 20th Area Support Group
Unit 15494
APO AP 96218-0562

TELEPHONE NUMBER INFORMATION: Main installation numbers: C-(USA) 011-82-53-470-7440/59, (RK) 53-470-7440/59, D-315-768-7440/59.

Location: NMC: Taegu, in city limits.

Lodging Office: Bldg 1712. **C-(USA) 011-82-53-470-7459, D-315-768-7459,** Fax: C-(USA) 011-82-053-470-8948, D-315-768-8948, 24 hours daily.

TML: BEQ/BOQ. Bldg 1712, all ranks, leave or official duty. Single bedroom, private bath (24). Kitchenette, refrigerator, color TV in room and lounge, housekeeping service, washer/dryer. Rates: $26; each additional person $5.

TML: VOQ. Bldg 1712, all ranks, TDY and PCS. Single bedroom, private bath (28). Refrigerator, Kitchenette, color TV in room, lounge, housekeeping service, washer/dryer. Rates: first person $33, each additional person $5.

TML: DVQ. Bldg 565, C- (USA) 011-82-53-470-8949, officers O5+, TDY or PCS. Queen bed, private bath (3); Twin bed, private bath (2). Refrigerator, kitchenette, color TV, lounge and housekeeping service. Rates: first person $43, each additional person $10.

TML: DV/VIP. Bldg 1712, all ranks, leave or official duty. Bedroom, private bath (5). Kitchenette, refrigerator, color TV in room and lounge, housekeeping service, washer/dryer. Rates: $35, maximum $45. Maximum two per room.

KOREA
Camp Henry, continued

TML Availability: Very good. Best, Nov-Dec. Difficult, May-Oct.

Camp Hialeah (RK10R8)
20th Support Group
Unit 15181
APO AP 96259-0270

TELEPHONE NUMBER INFORMATION: Main installation numbers: C-(USA) 011-82-51-801-3668, (RK) 51-801-3668, D-315-763-3668/7562

Location: Driving Directions: Camp Hialeah is located 100 miles south of Taegu and about eight miles north of Pusan (second largest city in Korea).Exit from the Seoul-Pusan Hwy 1, follow signs to Camp Hialeah. There is a subway stop 10 minutes (walking) from Camp Hialeah. NMC: Pusan, eight miles south.

TML: Bldg 508 BOQ: Bedroom (31), no kitchen, some have private bath. Bedroom (32), kitchen, private bath. Rates: $18-$25.

TML: DV/VIP: 06+. Bedroom (2), living room, kitchen, private bath. Rates: $35.

Camp Humphreys (RK08R8)
Housing Division
DPW, USASA Area III
Unit 15716
APO AP 96271-0716

TELEPHONE NUMBER INFORMATION: Main installation numbers: C-(USA) 011-82-333-690-7355,(RK) 333-690-7355, D-315-753-7355.

Location: Fifty (50) miles south of Seoul via Highway I, take Pyongtaek exit. Camp Humphreys is located 8 miles south of Pyongtaek. NMC: Pyongtaek, eight miles north.

Lodging Office: Bldg S-247. **C-(USA) 011-82-333-690-7355, D-315-753-7355,** Fax: C-(USA) 011-82-333-690-7357, D-315-753-7357, Mon-Fri 0800-1700, Sat 0800-1200. After hours report to EOC, Bldg 251. Check in billeting, check out 1200.

TML: BEQ. Bldgs 727, 728, 738, all ranks, leave or official duty. Single bedroom, private bath (6); single bedroom, hall bath (46). Refrigerator, color TV, housekeeping service, washer/dryer. Rates: $20 with bath, $18 without bath. AD can make reservations, all others Space-A

TML: BOQ. Bldgs 203, 206, 254, all ranks, leave or official duty. Bedroom, private bath (5). Kitchenette, refrigerator, color TV, housekeeping service, washer/dryer (in Bldg 206). Rates: $25.

TML Availability: Fairly good. Difficult, Dec-Feb.

Don't miss seeing the Secret Garden and Puyong Pavilion in Seoul.

Locator 690-7355   **Medical 116**   **Police 110**

Temporary Military Lodging Around the World - 325

KOREA

Camp Page (RK03R8)
DEH USAG
ATTN: Billeting
APO AP 96208-0210

TELEPHONE NUMBER INFORMATION: Main installation numbers: C-(USA) 011-82-279-13-1110, (RK) 279-13-1110, D-315-721-1110.

Location: From Seoul, take MSR#46 northeast into Chunchon City. NMC: Chunchon City, in city limits.

Lodging Office: Bldg T-452. **C-(USA) 011-82-361-59-5331**, D-315-721-5331/5691, 24 hours. Reservations through Installation Commanders Office, C-(USA) 011-82-361-59-5316, D-315-721-5316.

TML: BEQ. Bldgs S-1304, S-1306, S-1307, E1-E9, leave or official duty. Combination of single shared bedrooms, and single private bedrooms, private bath (48). Kitchenette, refrigerator, Rates: Primarily used by permanent party members; with shared bath $3 per night; with private bath $5 per night.

TML: BOQ. Bldgs S-1416, S-1129, officers, leave or official duty. Bedroom, private bath (48). Kitchenette, refrigerator. Rates: Primarily used by permanent party members, no rates furnished.

TML Availability: Good. Best, December. Difficult, June.

Locator 720-5820/5819   **Medical 721-5318**   **Police 721-5410**

Chinhae Fleet Activities (RK06R8)
Combined Bachelor Quarters, PSC 479
FPO AP 96269-1100

TELEPHONE NUMBER INFORMATION: Main installation numbers: C-(USA) 011-82-553-40-5110, (RK) 553-40-5110 D-315-762-5110, Chinhae OOD (Officer of the Day).

Location: On the east coast of Korea, south of Pusan. Take the Seoul-Pusan expressway to Pusan, exit and continue along the coast for 25 miles south.

Lodging Office: Billeting Office, duty hours. **C-(USA) 011-82-553-40-5336, D-315-762-5336.** After hours, C-(USA) 011-82-553-40-5110, D-315-762-5110. Fax: C-(USA) 011-82-553-40-5526, D-315-762-5526. Check in facility, check out 1200 hours daily.

TML: BOQ/BEQ. Bldg 794 all ranks, leave or official duty. BOQ: bedroom, private bath (2); BEQ: bedroom, shared bath. A/C, telephone, housekeeping service. Older structure, renovated. Rates: BOQ $23 per night; BEQ $21 per night. Duty can make reservations, others Space-A.

TML: DV/VIP. Bldg 710, DV suite (2), A/C telephone, housekeeping service. Rates: $23.

TML Availability: Very limited.

If you are lucky enough to be in Chinhae in April (1-15) you will see the city covered in cherry blossoms, folk dances, and visit fascinating street markets, plus many other activities. This is a very interesting port city.

KOREA
Chinhae Fleet Activities, continued

Locator 791-3110   Medical 762-5415   Police 791-3110

DRAGON HILL LODGE

DoD Conference Center

Dragon Hill Lodge (RK09R8)
Unit 15335
APO AP 96205-0427

TELEPHONE NUMBER INFORMATION: Main installation number: C-(USA) 011-82-2-790-0016, (RK) 2-790-0016.

Location: Located on South Post, Yongsan, in Seoul. From Kimpo International Airport, enter the Olympic Stadium Expressway 88 for approximately 15 miles, then take the Panpo Bridge exit and cross the bridge. Look for the Capital Hotel on the right side as you come off the bridge. Stay on the right side of the road and do not go under ground where the road splits. Go to the major intersection and turn left (one mile from bridge), enter the second gate on the left side (gate 10) and proceed to the Lodge. NMC: Seoul, in the city.

Lodging Office: None. Check in at front desk. C-(USA) 011-82-2-790-0016, (RK) 790-0016, D-315-738-2222, Fax: C-(USA) 011-82-2-790-1576 (RK) 792-1576.

TML: Dragon Hill Lodge, all ranks, leave or official duty. Handicap accessible. Bedroom, double bed, double sleeper sofa, private bath (289); 9th floor family rooms - bedroom, 2 double beds, living room w/sleeper sofa, private bath (10). Family rooms may be expanded as a three bedroom accommodation (additional charge). Non-smoking rooms on 7th and 8th floors. Five handicap accessible rooms (partial ambulatory). Even numbered rooms face front of hotel, odd numbers face garden. A/C, kitchenette, microwave (in 277 of the 289 rooms), refrigerator, utensils, color TV, VCR, clock radio, phone, housekeeping service, cots ($10), cribs, ice vending, washer/dryer, recreation facilities, Oasis coffee shop/Mexican restaurant, Greenstreet restaurant, (breakfast, lunch, dinner, Sunday brunch) Sables fine dining restaurant, Bentleys Pub, Whispers Lounge, Anthony's pizza, deli/bakery. Other services: bank, ATM, hair care center, tailor shop, post exchange, bookstore, shopping arcade, fitness and health club. Eligibility: Active duty, retired military, dependents, DoD civilians and all foreign non-Korean military with orders to USFK. All must present either DD form 1173 or DD form 2. Rates: TDY $105-$110 per room all ranks and grades; leave/pass status BG-Gen SES $75 per room; SW4, Maj-Col, DoD Civilian, retired military $65 per room; leave/pass status SSG-CSM, WO1-CW3, 2Lt-Cpt. Pvt-Sgt. $55 per room; leave/pass status Pvt.-Sgt $45; each additional person $10. Maximum four persons. All categories can make reservations. Pets can be boarded at vet clinic near Gate 17, South Post.

TML Availability: Good. Best, Oct-May.

CREDIT CARDS ACCEPTED: Visa, MasterCard and American Express.

Temporary Military Lodging Around the World - 327

KOREA
Dragon Hill Lodge, continued

See Myong-Dong (Seoul's Ginza), Korea House, Duksoo Palace. The National Museum and Folk Museum on Kyongbok Palace grounds acquaint visitors with Korean culture. Don't miss Walker Hill tourist complex twenty minutes away.

Locator 724-6830   Medical 737-5545   Police 724-8177

Kunsan Air Base (RK05R8)
Kunsan Lodging
Bldg 392, Unit 2105
APO AP 96264-2101

TELEPHONE NUMBER INFORMATION: Main installation numbers: C-(USA) 011-82-654-470-1110, (RK) 654-470-4604, D-315-782-1110.

Location: On the west central coast of RK. Exit from Seoul-Pusan expressway, directions to AB clearly marked. NMC: Kunsan City, seven miles north.

Lodging Office: Bldg 392, C-(USA) 011-82-654-470-4604, (RK) 654-470-4604, D-315-782-4604, Fax: C-(USA) 011-82-654-472-5275, 24 hours. Check in billeting. Check out 1200 hours daily.

TML: VOQ. Bldg 391, all ranks, leave or official duty, C ext 4604. Bedroom, common bath (28). Refrigerator, A/C, color TV, housekeeping service, washer/dryer. Older structure. Rates: DVQ Large $27; DVQ Small $22; VOQ/VAQ $12. Reservations accepted.

TML Availability: Limited.

CREDIT CARDS ACCEPTED: Visa, MasterCard and American Express.

Kunsan is a deep water port on the Yellow Sea, and a major fishing port. The mountainous areas of Korea are dotted with temples and shrines of both Japanese and Korean influence and are set in magnificent natural scenery.

Locator 782-4604   Medical 782-4333   Police 782-4944

Osan Air Base (RK04R8)
51 SVS/SVML
Unit 2065, Bldg 771
APO AP 96278-2065

TELEPHONE NUMBER INFORMATION: Main installation numbers: C-(USA) 011-82-333-661-4110, (RK) 333-661-4110, D-315-784-4110.

Location: Exit the Seoul-Pusan expressway 38 miles south of Seoul. Directions to Osan AB clearly marked. Adjacent to Song Tan City. NMC: Seoul, 38 miles north.

Lodging Office: Bldg 771, C-(USA) 011-82-331-661-1844/4597, D-315-784-1844/4597, Fax: C-(USA) 011-82-331-661-4872, D-315-784-4872, 24 hours. Check in billeting 1500, check out 1200 hours. Government civilian employee billeting.

328 - Temporary Military Lodging Around the World

KOREA
Osan Air Base, continued

TML: TLF. Bldg 1007, all ranks, leave or official duty. Separate bedroom, sleeps five, private bath (17). Kitchen, fully equipped, A/C, color TV, housekeeping service, cribs, washer/ dryer. Modern structure. Rates: $35 per unit; officer DVQs $22-$27; enlisted DVQs $22. Maximum five per unit. Duty can make reservations, others Space-A.

TML: VOQ. Bldgs 1001, 1093, 1094, officers, all ranks, leave or official duty. Bedroom, private bath (65). Kitchen, limited utensils, A/C, color TV, housekeeping service, cribs, washer/ dryer. Modern structure. Rates: $12 per person, maximum $18 per room (maximum two per room); officer DVQs $22-$27; enlisted DVQs $22. Duty can make reservations, others Space-A.

TML: VOQ/VAQ. Officers, Bldg 745, 746, all ranks, leave or official duty. Bedroom with 2 beds, common bath (258). Refrigerator, community kitchen, limited utensils, A/C, color TV, housekeeping service, washer/dryer. Modern structure. Rates: $12 per person, maximum $12 per room; officer DVQs $22-$27; enlisted DVQs $22. Duty can make reservations, others Space-A.

TML: DV/VIP. On Hill 180. Officer O6+, leave or official duty. Bedroom, private and semi-private baths (20); One separate bedroom suite, private bath. Refrigerator, A/C, color TV, housekeeping service, cribs/cots, washer/dryer. Modern structure. Rates: $10 per person. Maximum two persons. Duty can make reservations, others Space-A.

DV/VIP: Protocol Officer, 7th AF, C-(USA) 011-82-333-661-6020. O6+. Rates: $10. Retirees and lower ranks Space-A.

TML Availability: Best, Nov-Feb. Difficult, other times.

CREDIT CARDS ACCEPTED: Visa, MasterCard, American Express and Services Club Card.

Transportation: On base taxi 784-4121/4122/4123.

Don't miss seeing Duksoo Palace (home of the National Museum), Kyonbok and Changduk Palaces, and the Secret Garden and Puyong Pavilion in Seoul. Onyang (a hot spring resort), and Walker Hill resort shouldn't be missed.

Locator 784-1841   **Medical 911**   **Police 911**

Seoul House (RK11R8)
181, 2 KA, Chung Jong Ro
Sudae Mooku
Seoul, Korea

TELEPHONE NUMBER INFORMATION: Main installation numbers: C-(USA) 011-82-2-363-3491, (RK) 2-363-3491, D-315-723-6151.

Location: In downtown Seoul, across from Kyonggi University. On the metro green line, short walk from city hall.

Lodging Office: Co-located with USAF Seoul House Officers' Club, write to Osan O'Club, Bldg 910, Unit 2097, APO AP 96278-2097, **C-(USA) 011-82-2-363-3491, D-315-723-6151.** 0700-1600 daily.

TML: Luxury suites (3) and individual rooms (2). Rates: $45 per room, $50 per suite. Officers' Club serves lunch and dinner. This facility is an annex of Osan AB Officers' Club.

KOREA

Yongsan Army Garrison (RK07R8)
Lodging Office, Bldg 1112
APO AP 96205-0177

TELEPHONE NUMBER INFORMATION: Main installation numbers: C-(USA) 011-82-2-7913-1110, (RK) 2-7914-8205/8184, D-315-724-8205/8184.

Location: In the Yongsan district of Seoul. NMC: Seoul, in the city.

Lodging Office: Billeting Office, Bldg 1112, **C-(USA) 011-82-2-7918-3220/4446, (RK) 2-7918-3220, D-315-738-4446**, 0800-1700 daily. Check in facility, check out 1200 hours daily. No government civilian employee billeting.

TML: VOQ. Bldgs 8102, 8103, 8104, officers all ranks, enlisted E7-E9, C-(USA) 011-82-2-7918-4249, Official duty only. 571 total units: separate bedroom suites, private bath (3); two bedroom, shared bath (1). Refrigerator, A/C, cribs, color TV, housekeeping service, washer/dryer. Modern structure. Rates: $15 per person, maximum $20 per family. Duty can make reservations, others Space-A.

TML: VEQ. Bldgs 4110, enlisted E1-E6, leave or official duty, C-(USA) 011-82-2-7918-2222. 413 total units: separate bedroom, common bath (29). Refrigerator, community kitchen, A/C, color TV, housekeeping service, washer/dryer. Modern structure. Rates: $4 per room. Duty can make reservations, others Space-A.

TML: DVQ. Bldgs 3723, 4436, 4464, 4468, officer O7+ or civilian equivalent, leave or official duty. C-EX-7913-3315. Separate bedroom, private bath. Community kitchen, kitchenette, complete utensils, cribs, color TV, A/C, housekeeping service. Modern structure. Rates: sponsor $25, adults $12.50, children $5. Duty can make reservations, others Space-A.

DV/VIP: Sec Joint Staff, Protocol Branch, SJS-P, HHC, EUSA, Bldg 2472. C-(USA) 011-82-2--7913-3315, D-315-723-3315, O7+ or civilian equivalent. Lower ranks Space-A.

TML Availability: Good, but reserve early.

Locator 2-7912-87404*   Medical 737-3045/5545   Police D-724-8177

*Must have individual SSAN to locate.

Other Installations in Korea

Camp Carroll. C-(USA) 011-82-53-970-7721/7722. Call for more information.
Cheju-Do Airport. C-(USA) 011-82-641-2471/649-3330. There is a 2nd Infantry Division Training Area on Cheju-Do island which has a lodge. Also used as a rest and recreation location in the winter from Nov-Feb.

330 - Temporary Military Lodging Around the World

NETHERLANDS

Brunssum International Inn (NT02R7)
Lodging Office, Bldg H105
APO AE 09703-5000

TELEPHONE NUMBER INFORMATION: Main installation numbers: C-(USA) 011-31-45-526-2984, (NT) 045-526-2984.

Location: Take Autobahn A-2, A-76 or E-9. Also NE-39, exit at Nuth, follow signs to Brunssum. NMC: Heerlen, NT, 10 miles southwest.

Lodging Office: International Inn, or US Protocol Office, Bldg H105. **C-(USA) 011-31-45-526-2230 ext 3188, (NT) 045-526-2230, D-314-360-2406**, 0800-2230 hours duty days. Call C-045-26-3188 (Schinnen) after hours. Check in facility, check out 1200 hours daily. Government civilian employee billeting in local hotels.

TML: International Inn, above number for information. Officers all ranks, leave or official duty. Suites, private bath (20); bedroom suites, private bath suites (DV/VIP) (2). Rates: 50 guilders single/$30 US, 82 guilders double $49 US, extra bed 17 guilders. No pets. Support facilities at Schinnen Community, 54th Area Support Group, 10 miles. This is NATO Allied and not U.S. government billeting. Brunssum AFCENT BX available to U.S. Forces.

DV/VIP: PAO, Bldg T-8, room 204, C-04493-7-331, O6+.

TML Availability: Limited.

Locator 04493-7-199   **Medical-04526-3-177**   **Police 04493-7-323**

PANAMA

Fort Clayton (PN02R3)
Bldg 518, Hospital Road
APO AA 34004-5000

TELEPHONE NUMBER INFORMATION: Main installation numbers: C-(USA) 011-507-281-1212, (PN) 281-1212, D-313-281-1212/287-3105 (after hours).

Location: Near the Pacific Ocean entrance to the Panama Canal. Take Gaillard Hwy toward the Miraflores Locks. NMC: Panama City, 8 miles southwest.

Lodging Office: Bldg 518, Hospital Road, **C-(USA) 011-507-287-4451/3251, D-313-287-4202, (PN) 287-4451-3251**, Fax: C-(USA) 011-507-287-5609, D-313-287-5609, 0700-1530 Mon-Fri. Check in billeting 1400, check out 1100 hours daily.

TML: Clayton Guest House. Bldg 518, all ranks, leave or official duty. Bedroom, private bath (34); separate bedroom, private bath (5). Refrigerator, A/C, color cable TV, recreation room and lounge, housekeeping service, cribs, washer/dryer, ice vending, La Mola restaurant. Older structure. Rates: $29 per person, maximum $34; suites $33 per person, maximum $38 per family. Official duty and hospital visits can make reservations, others Space-A.

PANAMA
Fort Clayton, continued

TML: Gold Coast Suites, Fort Sherman. All ranks, C-(USA) 011-507-287-4451/3251, D-313-287-4202. Check in from the Clayton Guest house in Bldg 518, 24 hours, Houses fully furnished with two separate bedrooms and private bath (2). Kitchenette, microwave, cooking utensils, A/C, refrigerator, color TV, housekeeping service, washer/dryer, outdoor picnic tables with grills. Rates: $36 per person, maximum $55. Reservations on first come basis.

TML: Quarry Heights VOQ, in Panama City, Bldg 119, enlisted E7+officers, all ranks, leave or official duty. C-(USA) 011-507-282-4899, D-313-282-4899, 24 hours. Separate bedroom, private bath (13). Refrigerator, A/C, CATV, housekeeping service, snack vending. Older structure. Rates: $29-$36. Duty can make reservations, others Space-A.

TML: DV/VIP. Inn of the Americas, Bldgs 91 and 92, enlisted E9/O6+, leave or official duty. Protocol: C-(USA) 011-507-288-3116/3117. Bedroom, private bath (3); separate bedroom with private bath (3). Refrigerator, A/C, color cable TV, housekeeping service, washer/dryer. Breakfast served 0630-0900 hours Mon-Fri. Rates: regular room $21, maximum $25; suite $28, maximum $33. Duty can make reservations, others Space-A.

TML: VEQ. Bldg 130, E6 and below, leave or official duty, C-(USA) 011-507-287-4451/3251, D-313-287-4202. Check in from the Clayton Guest house in Bldg 518, 24 hours, Shared room, common bath (36 rooms, 72 beds); Refrigerator, A/C color cable TV, housekeeping service, washer/dryer, snack vending. Rates: regular room $14 per person. Duty can make reservations, others Space-A.

TML: VOQ. Green Valley Inns, Bldgs 600 A, B, C & D, 602 A, B, C and D, 604 A, B, C & D, all ranks, leave or official duty. C-(USA) 011-507-287-4451/3251. Fully furnished houses w/kitchenette, cooking utensils, refrigerator, microwave, coffee maker, A/C. washer/dryer, cable TV. Rates: $36 - $61. Duty can make reservations, others Space-A.

DV/VIP: Protocol Office, Bldg 95, room 171. C-(USA) 011-507-288-3116/3117. E9/O6+. Retirees and lower ranks Space-A.

TML Availability: Good, Nov-Jan. Difficult, other times.

CREDIT CARDS ACCEPTED: Visa, MasterCard and American Express.

Transportation: On base shuttle/bus 285-6241/5541,off base shuttle/bus 262-7333, car rental 364-8733, on base taxi 232-4046, off base taxi 232-4046.

Panama City is a shoppers paradise - see the Via España - and if you have time don't miss Bias Islands, and the forts of Portobelo and Ft. San Lorenzo.

Locator 285-3139   Medical 282-5400/5111   Police 287-4401

Howard Air Force Base (PN01R3)
24th SVS/SVML
APO AA 34001-5000

TELEPHONE NUMBER INFORMATION: Main installation numbers: C-(USA) 011-507-284-9805, (PN) 284-84-9805, D-313-284-9805.

Location: Adjacent to Thatcher Hwy (K-2) on Pacific side of Panama. NMC: Panama City, 10 miles west.

PANAMA
Howard Air Force Base, continued

Lodging Office: Bldg 708, C-(USA) 011-507-284-6411/5306, (PN) 284-284-4914/5306, Fax: C-(USA) 011-507-284-4589 (for those on official orders only), 24 hours. Check in billeting 1300, check out 1200 hours daily. No government civilian employee billeting.

TML: TLF. Bldg 1511, all ranks, official duty. C ext 4914/4556. Two bedroom apartments (6). Kitchen, complete utensils, A/C, color TV, housekeeping service, cribs/cots, washer/dryer. Older structure, refurbished. Rates: $35 per room per night. Maximum six per room. Duty can make reservations, others Space-A.

TML: VOQ. Bldgs 13, 14, 117, 119, 174, officers all ranks, leave or official duty. Bedroom, private bath (2); separate bedroom, private bath (32). Refrigerator, A/C, color TV, housekeeping service, washer/dryer, ice vending. Older structure, remodeled. Rates: $12 per person, each additional person $5. Maximum two per room. Duty can make reservations, others Space-A.

TML: DV/VIP. Bldgs 16, 118 A&B, officers O6+, leave or official duty. Separate bedroom suite, private bedroom (1); two bedroom suite, private bath (1); three bedroom suite, private bedroom (1). Kitchen, utensils, A/C, color TV, housekeeping service, washer/dryer, ice vending. Rates: single $27.50, double $39.50. Maximum two per room. Duty can make reservations, others Space-A.

TML: DV/VIP. Bldg 519, E9 only, leave or official duty. Two-bedroom suite, private bath (1). Kitchen, utensils, A/C, color TV, housekeeping service, washer/dryer, ice vending. Rate: $17 per night.

DV/VIP: USAFSO/CCP, Howard, C-(USA) 011-507-284-4601. O6+. Retirees and lower ranks Space-A.

TML Availability: Difficult at all times.

In Panama City visit the Avenida de los Martires and Avenida Central for shopping. Don't miss the church on Santa Ana Plaza, and San Jose church in Old Panama. Casco Viejo is quaint with Spanish and French architecture.

Locator 284-5306/6411   Medical 284-3014   Police 284-4711

Panama Canal (Rodman) Naval Station (PN09R3)
Combined Bachelor Quarters, Bldg 77
Unit 6262
FPO AA 34061-1000
Scheduled to close 1999.

TELEPHONE NUMBER INFORMATION: Main installation numbers: C-(USA) 011-507-283-4440/4619/5240/4460, (PN) 283-4440/4619/5260/4590, D-313-221-4440/4619/5240/4460, Fax C-(USA) 011-507-283-4440/4619/5240/4460.

Location: On the west bank of the Panama Canal, one mile left of Tatcher Perry Bridge (Bridge of the Americas). Panama City, 18 miles northwest.

Lodging Office: Bldg 77, C-(USA) 011-507-283-4440/4619/5240/4460, (PN) 283-4440/4619/5240/4460, 24 hours daily. Check in billeting 1300, check out 1100 hours daily. Government Civilian Employee billeting.

PANAMA
Panama Canal (Rodman) Naval Station, continued

TML: BOQ. E7+. Private trailer unit/bath. A/C, Iron, ironing board, clock radio, refrigerator, microwave, TV, VCR, housekeeping service, washers/dryers, ice machine/vending machine (72). No pets. Rates: E7+ $12. Duty can make reservations, others Space-A.

TML: BEQ. E1-E6. Trailer unit separated in half, shared bath E1-E6, A/C, iron/ironing board, clock radio, refrigerator, microwave, TV, VCR, housekeeping service, washer/dryers. ice machine. (150). No pets. Rate: E1-E6 $6. Duty can make reservations, others Space-A.

DV/VIP: Two-bedroom suites, shared bath, clock radio, refrigerator, microwave, TV, VCR, Iron/ironing board, kitchen. Rate: $25 per bed space.

TML Availability: Difficult. Best Nov-Feb, difficult Mar-Sep.

ATTRACTIONS: Bridge of Americas, Miraflores Locks, Portobelo, Beaches; Coronado, Isla Grane, Taboga, Rio Mar, Presidential Palace. Duty Free shopping at the International Airport, and Colon Free Zone, Tinaja Restaurant (Folklore nights and Panamanian cuisine) are favorite pastimes here. Fishing, both lake and ocean, the canal itself and historic sites are also popular.

Locator 283-3300   Medical 284-3014   Police 283-5611/12

PORTUGAL

Lajes Field (Azores) (PO01R7)
Mid-Atlantic Lodge
65 SVS/SVML
Unit 8010
APO AE 09720-8010

TELEPHONE NUMBER INFORMATION: Main installation numbers: C-(USA) 011-351-95-540100 ext 25178/23683, (Europe) 245-5178, D-314-535-5178 (CONUS direct). Contact: 65th MWRS/MWMH, unit 8010, APO AE 09720.

Location: On Terceira Island (Azores PO) 20 miles long and 12 miles wide. Lajes Field is 2 miles west of Praia da Vitoria, PO, on Mason Hwy. NMC: Lisbon, 850 miles east.

Lodging Office: Mid-Atlantic Lodge, Bldg T-166, **C-(USA) 011-351-95-540100, ext 25178/23683 DSN (USA)-314-535-5178**, Fax: C-(USA) 011-35-95-53009, DSN (USA)-535-3790, (Europe) 245-3790, 24 hours for check in at facility, check out 1200 hours. Government civilian employee billeting. Note: Kennel available on base (fee).

TML: TLF. Bldg T-306, all ranks, leave or official duty. Handicap accessible. Bedroom apartments, living room, private bath (30). Kitchenette, color TV, cribs/cots, washer/dryer. Modern structure. Gift Shop in Guest Reception Center open 24 hours daily, exercise room available. Vending/soda machines readily accessible. Rate: $35 per night, $27 for additional unit. Maximum 5 per room. Active duty PCS with family can make reservations, others Space-A.

334 - Temporary Military Lodging Around the World

PORTUGAL
Lajes Field (Azores), continued

TML: VOQ, VAQ: $12 per night, reservations TDY, PCS only, Space-A can make reservations 24 hours in advance.

DV/VIP: Contact lodging office, O6+. Retirees Space-A, $16 per night.

TML Availability: Best, Nov-Apr. Difficult, May-Oct.

CREDIT CARDS ACCEPTED: Visa, MasterCard and American Express.

Each island is unique, visit them all, if you can. Attend a formal bullfight, or a street bullfight (the bull is not killed here!), or listen to one of many village bands perform during a colorful religious holiday procession.

Locator 113   **Medical 911**   **Police 911**

NOTE: Contract Quarters are not available at Lajes Field. There are several hotels in the local area that accept credit cards, prices range from $50-$75 during peak periods.

SAUDI ARABIA

Other Installations in Saudi Arabia

Dhahran Community. DET 1-621 AMSG PSC 1258, Box 878, Unit 66803, APO AE 09858-0878. C-(USA) 011-966-3-899-1119 ext 431-4018, Fax: C-(USA) 011-966-3-899-1119 ext 431-7312. Rates: $4-$15.
Riyadh Community. ATTN: Billeting, USMTM, AFX, AMEM B, Unit 61307, APO AE 09803-1307. Main installation numbers: C-(USA) 011-966-1-891-119, D-318-435-1110. Located in the Province of Riyadh. Call for more information. Note: Only personnel on orders or with country (VISA) approval may travel to Saudi Arabia.

SINGAPORE

Sembawang (SI01R1)
497th Combat Training Squadron/Lodging
PSC 470, BOX 3018
FPO AP 96534-5000

Location: The United States Navy and United States Air Force elements in Singapore are located in the Sembawang area of Singapore and at the RSAF Paya Lebar. The Sembawang area is located in the north central section of the island of Singapore on the Johore Strait. It is approximately 12 miles north of the city (center) of Singapore. The RSAF Paya Lebar is located on Airport Road off Paya Lebar Road.

Lodging Office: 247 Bermuda Road, Sembawang Singapore 759819. **C-(USA) 011-65-750-2309, 758-0677, 750-2504, 711-6848, D-257-6257**, Fax D-257-9597, 0900-1700 Mon-Fri, 0900-1300 Sat.

SINGAPORE
Sembawang, continued

TML: TLQ. Lodging has approximately 100 rooms, Space-A. Rates: $40 per room. For more information call **C-(USA) 011-65-711-6848**.

DV/VIP Information: Two flats available.

Locator 724-2387   Medical 257-4233 or 995   Police 999

SPAIN

Moron Air Base (SP01R7)
496 ABS/SVCH, Unit 6585
APO AE 09643-5000
(This is a contingency base)

TELEPHONE NUMBER INFORMATION: Main installation numbers: C-(USA) 011-34-55-848111, (SP) 95-58-48111, D-314-722-1110. Fax: C-(USA) 011-34-55-848009.

Location: Sevilla, Spain to Alcala, Spain on N-334, pass Alcala to SE-333. At intersection of SE-342 and B-333 proceed on SE-342 to Moron AB. Base well marked. NMC: Sevilla, 40 miles northwest.

Lodging Office: Hotel Frontera. ATTN: 496 ABS, Bldg 303, 1st Street, **C-(USA) 011-34-55-848098, (SP) 95-5-848098, D-314-722-8098,** Fax C-(USA) 011-34-55-848009 24 hours. Check in facility, check out 1200 hours daily. Government civilian employee lodging. **ATTENTION: AD not assigned in Spain, retired personnel, widow(ers), government civilian employees not assigned in Spain, dependents of all groups, are not permitted to purchase any articles free of Spanish taxes on any military installation, i.e. Foodland. Military ID card holder visitors to Spain are permitted to make purchases in open messes, lodging and NEX Mart. Also, personnel arriving by military air at Rota NAS are advised to contact security or passenger service for immigration clearance. This notice applies to other Spanish listings.**

TML: VOQ/VAQ/DV/VIP. **Hotel Frontera**, Bldg 303, all ranks, leave or official duty. Separate bedroom, shared bath (55). Some DV suites, private bath. Refrigerator, community kitchen, A/C, color TV in lounge, housekeeping service, washer/dryer. Modern structure, meeting/conference room, Mini Mart. Rates: $12 per person; DV/VIP $14. Maximum two plus one crib per unit. Duty can make reservations, others Space-A.

DV/VIP: Lodging, C-and D- ext 8098 or 8172. Determined by Commander, retirees Space-A.

TML Availability: Good Nov-Mar, fairly good Apr-Oct.

CREDIT CARDS ACCEPTED: American Express.

Transportation: On Base Shuttle/Bus-ext 8063

Soak up the light and landscape of Sevilla along the Guadalquivir (Great River), and then visit the Cathedral (third largest in the world) and the Giralda Tower. Don't miss the gardens of the Alazar and the many others in the city.

Locator 55848111   Medical 8068   Police 8132

336 - Temporary Military Lodging Around the World

SPAIN

Rota Naval Air Station (SP02R7)
Box 2, FPO AE 09645-5500

TELEPHONE NUMBER INFORMATION: Main installation numbers: C-(USA) 011-34-56-82-2643, (From Spain but outside the province of Cadiz dial 956-822-643), D-314-727-0111.

Location: On Spain's South Atlantic Coast. Accessible from E-25 South and SP-342 West. NMC: Cadiz, 22 miles south.

Lodging Office: No central billeting office. C-(USA) 011-34-56-82-1750/51 (BOQ), 2460/2680, (SP) 821-750 (outside province of Cadiz) 956-82-2643, D-314-727-1751/2460, Fax: C-(USA) 011-34-56-82-1754/1748, D-314-727-1754/1748 hours: 0730-1930 daily. Check in at facility, check out 1200. Government civilian employee billeting.

NAVY LODGE

TML: Navy Lodge. Naval Station, Box 17, Bldg 1674, check-in 1500-1800, check-out 1200, all ranks, leave or official duty. C-(USA) 011-34-56-82-2643, (SP) 956-82-2643, Fax C-(USA) 011-34-56-82-2078. Bedroom, private bath (48). Kitchen, microwave, utensils, A/C, color TV in room and lounge, housekeeping service, cribs/cots, coin washer/dryer. Modern structure. Rates: $53.50 per unit. Maximum five per unit. All categories can make reservations.

TML: BOQ. Bldg 39, officers and enlisted, all ranks, leave or official duty, C-(USA) 011-34-56-82-1750/51. Bedroom, private bath (43); suites, (VIP) (21). Refrigerator, A/C, color TV, VCR, housekeeping service, two laundry rooms, TV lounge, Jacuzzi and sauna. Modern structure. Rates: $12 per person; DV/VIP $18-$25 per person, each additional person $4. Maximum one per bedroom, two per suite. Duty can make reservations, others Space-A.

TML: BEQ. Bldgs 36-39, currently under renovation, most enlisted transients housed in BOQ during renovation, C-(USA) 011-34-56-82-2460/2680. Suites (DV) (2), color TV, VCR, refrigerator, housekeeping service, washer/dryer. Rates: suites $25 per night, each additional person $4, maximum two guests. Duty can make reservations, others Space-A.

DV/VIP: Protocol Office. Bldg 1, 2nd floor, C-(USA) 011-34-56-82-2795/2440, O6+. Retirees Space-A.

TML Availability: All bachelor housing undergoing renovation, expected completion date early 2001. During renovation, Space-A rooms limited, especially May-Sept.

CREDIT CARDS ACCEPTED: The Navy Lodge accepts Visa, MasterCard and American Express.

Gate security is strict (administered by Spanish Military Police). Commissary and NEX unavailable to retirees. Inquire at Navy Family Services about tours of Cadiz, a shopper's delight. Inquire at Osborne and Terry Bodegas for a tour of sherry facilities.

Locator 2222   Medical 3305   Police 2000/1

TURKEY

Incirlik Air Base (TU03R9)
39 SVS/SVML
Unit 8915, Box 165
APO AE 09824-5165

TELEPHONE NUMBER INFORMATION: Main installation numbers: C-(USA) 011-90-322-316-1110, (TU) 322-316-1110, D-314-676-1110.

Location: From Adana Airport, east on E-5 for 12 miles, left at sign for Incirlik. Base is clearly marked. NMC: Adana, 3 miles west.

Lodging Office: Bldg 1081, 7th Street, 24 hours. Check in facility 1300, check out 1100 (Space-A), 1200 hours (all others) daily. **C-(USA) 011-90-322-316-6786, (TU) 322-316-6786. D-314-676-9357,** Fax: D-314-676-9341. E-mail: nolted@bnccl.incirlik.af.mil. Government civilian employee billeting.

TML: TLF. Bldg 1066. All ranks, leave or official duty. Separate bedroom, living room, dining room, private bath (49). Kitchen, complete utensils, microwave, A/C, color TV/VCR in room and lounge, housekeeping service, cribs/cots, washer/dryer, ice vending, soda/snack vending, irons, clock-radios. Modern structure. Rates: $31 per unit; $53 double. TDY/PCS can make reservations, others Space-A.

TML: TLF. Bldgs 1075,1076,1077. All ranks, leave or official duty. Two bedrooms, living room, dining room, private bath (49). Kitchen, complete utensils, microwave, A/C, color TV/VCR in room and lounge, housekeeping service, cribs/cots, washer/dryer, ice vending, soda/snack vending, irons, clock-radios. Modern structure. Rates: $31 per unit; $53 double. TDY/PCS can make reservations, others Space-A.

TML: VQ. Bldgs 1080/82, 934/36. All ranks, leave or official duty. Bedroom, shared bath (24). Refrigerator, A/C, color TV in room and lounge, housekeeping service, washer/dryer (1080/82), soda/snack vending. Meeting/conference rooms and exercise room available. Modern structure (1080/82), Older structure, renovated (934/36). Rates: $12 per person. Duty can make reservations, others Space-A.

TML: VQ. Bldg 952: Prime Knight Program. All ranks, official duty. Bedroom, private bath, refrigerator, A/C, color TV/VCR in room and lounge, housekeeping service, laundry room, soda/snack vending. Meeting/conference rooms and exercise room available. Older structure, renovated. Rates: $12 per person.

TML: DV/VIP. Bldg 1072, officer O6+, leave or official duty. Separate bedroom suites, private bath (6); bedroom, private bath, contract quarters for TDY, funded travel orders only (95). Kitchen, limited utensils, A/C, color TV, housekeeping service, washer/dryer, ice vending, soda/snack vending alcoholic beverages and soft drinks stocked in room on "Honor System." Meeting/conference rooms and exercise room available. Older structure. Rates: $22 per person. Duty can make reservations, others Space-A.

DV/VIP: Protocol Office, 39 WG/CCP, DSN: 676-8352, O6/GS-15+. Retirees and lower ranks Space-A.

TML Availability: Fair.

TURKEY
Incirlik Air Base, continued

CREDIT CARDS ACCEPTED: Visa, MasterCard and American Express.

Transportation: On Base Shuttle/Bus; On/Off Base Taxi DSN: 676-6461.

Historic sites near Adana include Misis (Roman), Yilanlikale (Castle of Snakes), Karatepe (Hittite) and Payas (16th Century and Alexander the Great). There's much more to see and do. A tour here is "no turkey"!

Locator 6289   Medical 6666   Police 3200

Izmir Air Station (TU04R9)
Military Lodging Office
Izmir Air Station
Facility 77, Room 104
APO AE 09824-5000

TELEPHONE NUMBER INFORMATION: Main installation numbers: C-(USA) 011-90-232-484-5360, (TU) 232-484-5360, D-314-675-1110 ext 3579, Fax: C-(USA) 011-90-232-484-5564.

Location: In the center of Izmir on the central west coast of Turkey. NMC: Izmir, in the city.

Lodging Office: Pullman Hotel. C-(USA) **011-90-232-489-4090**, **D-314-675-1110 ext 3379**, C-(USA) 011-90-232-489-4089, 0700-2300 daily. Check in facility, check out 1200 hours daily. Government civilian employee billeting.

TML: TLF. **Pullman Hotel**, all ranks, leave or official duty, handicap accessible. Bedroom, private bath (63). Refrigerator, A/C, color TV in room and lounge, housekeeping service, cribs/cots, washer/dryer, ice vending (The 63 rooms are leased in a 5 Star commercial hotel). Rates: single $125, double $160. Maximum three per unit. Duty can make reservations. TDY/PCS have priority, others Space-A.

DV/VIP: Protocol Office, 7241 ABG/CCE, facility #48, room 603. D-314-675-1110 ext 3341, O6+/E9. Retirees and lower ranks Space-A.

TML Availability: Good, except May-Oct.

CREDIT CARDS ACCEPTED: Visa, MasterCard, American Express and Diners.

Visit the tours desk, MWR for one day, overnight and multi-day excursions to Ephesus, Pergamon, Pamukkale, Aphrodisias, Istanbul, and the Greek Islands. East and west meet here, don't miss the fascinating consequences!

Locator 3431   Medical 3357   Police 3222

UNITED KINGDOM

RAF Alconbury (UK01R7)
423rd SVS/SVMH
Bldg 639, Texas Street
APO AE 09470-5000

TELEPHONE NUMBER INFORMATION: Main installation numbers: C-(USA) 011-44-1480-82-3000, (UK) 01480-82-3000, D-314-268-3000.

Location: From London, take A-1 North to A-14, exit marked RAF Alconbury, follow signs. Approximately 65 miles north of London. NMC: Huntingdon, 4 miles east.

Lodging Office: Bldg 639, Texas Street, **C-(USA) 011-44-1480-6000, D-(USA) 314-236-6000, (UK) 01480-82-6000,** Fax: C-(USA) 011-44-1480-45-4127, 24 hours. Check in facility 1400, check out 1000 hours daily. Government civilian employee billeting.

TML: VOQ. Bldgs 639, 640, officers all ranks, leave or official duty. Bedroom, shared bath (44); suites, private bath (DV/VIP) (7). Refrigerator, color TV in room and lounge, housekeeping service, cribs/cots, washer/dryer, telephone. Modern structure. Rates: room $10 per person; suite $14.50 per person. Maximum two per suite. Duty can make reservations, others Space-A.

TML: VAQ. Bldg 652, 692, enlisted all ranks. Two bedroom, shared bath (38); bedroom suites, shared bath (4); separate bedroom suites, private bath (3). Bldg 692: two per room, central bathroom (22). Refrigerator, color TV/cable, housekeeping service, washer/dryer. Modern structure. Rates: rooms $10 per person; suites $15-$21 per person. Duty can make reservations, others Space-A.

TML: All ranks TLF also available. Suites, private bath (20). Rates: $21 per unit.

DV/VIP: Hq 423rd ABW, C ext 3111/3112, O6+. Retirees and lower ranks Space-A.

TML Availability: Good, Aug-Mar. Difficult, other times.

CREDIT CARDS ACCEPTED: Visa, MasterCard and American Express.

East Anglia, Essex, Suffolk and Norfolk is full of historical sights. Start with the village of Little Stukeley (interesting church with carvings), and pass on to Huntingdon, where Romans first settled.

Locator 2565   Medical 116   Police 114

Diego Garcia Atoll, U.S. Navy Support Facility (UK05R7)
Combined Bachelor Quarters
Air Terminal Officer, Box 20
FPO AP 96595-0020

TELEPHONE NUMBER INFORMATION: C-011-246-370-0111, D-315-370-0111.

Location: In the Chagos Archipelago, approximately 1000 miles off the southern tip of India in the Indian Ocean. NMC: Colombo, Sri Lanka, 900 air miles northeast.

340 - Temporary Military Lodging Around the World

UNITED KINGDOM
Diego Garcia Atoll, U.S. Navy Support Facility, continued

Lodging Office: NSF Billeting, FPO AP 96595-0031. Office located 3 miles north of island airport across from base swimming pool. C-011-246-370-4830, D-315-370-4830, Fax-011-246-370-3972. 24 hours. Check in billeting, check out 1200 hours.

TML: BOQ/BEQ, DV/VIP. Located downtown within walking distance of billeting office. All ranks, active duty/contractors on official business only. Shared room, private bath (150). Refrigerator, TV in lounge and rooms, housekeeping service, essentials, washer/dryer, ice vending. Meeting and conference rooms, mini-mart, exercise room available. Rates: enlisted $4; officers $8; senior officers (flag grade) $10.

DV/VIP: D-315-370-4415, O6+. Bob Hope Suite, two bedroom suite with dining area.

TML Availability: Not Available.

CREDIT CARDS ACCEPTED: American Express.

Transportation: On base shuttle or taxi 370-2771.

ALL PERSONNEL MUST APPLY FOR "AREA CLEARANCE A MINIMUM OF 30 DAYS PRIOR TO TRAVEL TO DIEGO GARCIA. ACCESS IS AVAILABLE ONLY VIA AMC OUT OF NORFOLK, VA OR YOKOTA, JAPAN. SPACE-A PASSENGERS MUST BE STATIONED AT OR EMPLOYED AT DIEGO GARCIA IN ORDER TO FLY INTO, OUT OF OR THROUGH DIEGO GARCIA; NO FAMILIES ARE PERMITTED ON THE ISLAND - NO EXCEPTIONS. Attractions include East Pointe Plantation, deep sea fishing, Snorkeling.

Locator 4830   Medical 4748   Police 95

RAF Fairford (UK11R7)
Gloucestershire
Bldg 551
424 ABS/SVL
APO AE 09456-5000
(This is a contingency base)

TELEPHONE NUMBER INFORMATION: Main installation numbers: C-01285-714272, D-314-247-4272.

Location: Eighty miles west of London. Take the M4 to junction 15, then the A419 to Cirencester. After approximately 10 miles, RAF Fairford signs will be posted on right. NMC: Oxford 18 miles east.

Lodging Office: Bldg 551, **C-(USA) 011-44-285-712784, (UK) 0285-712784 or 0285-714962,** D-314-247-4272, Fax: C-(USA) 011-44-285-714150, Due to being in care-taker status, call ahead to check availability for Space available. Mon-Fri 0700-2000. Sat-Sun 0800-1400. Check-in 1400, check out 1100 hours daily. After duty hours, keys are left at main gate for late check-ins. Government civilian employee billeting.

TML: TLF. Bldg 551. All ranks, leave or official duty. Bedroom, private bath (8). Refrigerator, color TV/VCR in room and lounge. Housekeeping. Cribs, cots and high chairs upon request. Washer/dryer

UNITED KINGDOM
RAF Fairford, continued

available. Modern structure. Rates: $26.50 per person per night. Duty can make reservations. Space A reservations accepted three days in advance.

TML: VOQ. Bldg 551. Officers and E7-E9. Bedroom, private bath (51). Refrigerator, color TV/VCR and housekeeping. Washer/dryer available. Modern structure. Rates: $12 per night for one person; $17 per night for two. Space A reservations accepted three days in advance.

TML: VAQ. Bldg 552. E1-E6, leave or official duty. Bedroom, two single beds with shared bath (86). Refrigerator, color TV/VCR and housekeeping service. Washer/dryer available. Rates $12 per night per person. Space-A reservations accepted three days in advance.

TML: DV/VIP: Bldg 551. E9 and O6+, Call extension 247-4200 for reservations. Suites, private bath (5) Semi-suite (1) Rates $14.50/ one person & $20.75/two. Washers/dryers available.

TML Availability: Fairly good. Best Nov-Mar. Difficult other times.

The Cotswolds is one of the most beautiful parts of England. Fairford boasts a 15th century church with magnificent stained glass windows, Cirencester, 10 miles west offers shops and services, a sports center and the Cornium Museum.

Locator 247-4000   **Medical D-314-263-5224**   **Police 4477**

RAF Lakenheath (UK07R7)
SVS/SVML
Unit 5185, Box 70
APO AE 09464-0105

TELEPHONE NUMBER INFORMATION: Main installation numbers: C-(USA) 011-44-1638-52-1110, (UK) 1638-52-1110, D-314-226-1110.

Location: From London, go north on the M-11 to the A-11 to A-1065. NMC: Cambridge, 30 miles south.

Lodging Office: Liberty Lodge, Bldg 955, **C-(USA) 011-44-1638-52-1844/2172, (UK) 0638-52-1844/2172, D-314-226-6700/2172,** Fax: C-(USA) 011-44-1638-52-6717, D-314-226-6717, 24 hours. Check in facility 1300 hours, check out 1000 hours daily. Some rooms with kitchen, complete utensils, color TV, housekeeping service, cribs/cots, washer/dryer. Modern structure. Rates: $28-436.50 per unit per night. Duty can make reservations, others Space-A. No pets.

TML: VOQ. Bldg 978, all ranks, leave or official duty. Bedroom, private bath (56). Shared kitchen, housekeeping service, color TV, washer/dryer. Rates: $8 per person. Maximum two per unit. Duty can make reservations, others Space-A. No pets.

TML: VAQ. Bldgs 955, 957, 980, all ranks. Shared bedroom (E1-E4), shared bath (39); shared bedrooms (E5-E6), private bath, some rooms with shared kitchen (30); SNCO suites (E7-E9) with private bath, private kitchen, (9), color TV, housekeeping service, washer/dryer. Rates: shared rooms $8 per person; SNCO suites $17.50 per person. Maximum two persons. Duty can make reservations, others Space-A. No pets.

UNITED KINGDOM
RAF Lakenheath, continued

TML: DV/VIP. Various buildings, officers O6+, enlisted E9, leave or official duty. C-0638-52-3500, D-314-226-3500. Enlisted separate bedroom, private bath (3); officer separate bedroom, private bath (4). Kitchenette, cribs, color TV, housekeeping service, washer/dryer. Older structure. Rates: $18.50 per person, each additional person $9.25, maximum $27.75. No pets. Duty can make reservations thru 48 FW/Protocol, ext 2444, others Space-A.

DV/VIP: 48 TFW/CCP, Bldg 1156. C-EX-3500, O6+ and E9. Retirees and lower ranks Space-A.
Note: All numbers are C- or D- extensions.

TML Availability: Very limited.

Don't miss seeing Cambridge College, which attracts thousands of tourists each year. Visit the ITT Travel office for information on the many attractions of London. Lakenheath is the largest US Air Force operated facility in England. Shuttle bus to Mildenhall departs 50 minutes after the hour 0650-1450.

Locator 1841   Medical 116   Police 114

London Service Clubs (UK13R7)

Union Jack Club
Sandell Street, Waterloo
London, SE1 8UJ, United Kingdom
(Not US Government Lodging)

TELEPHONE NUMBER INFORMATION: C-(USA) 011-44-171-928-6401, (UK) 0171-928-6401, Fax: C-(USA) 011-44-171-620-0565.

Location: Opposite Waterloo Station (train), central London. NMC: London, in the city, opposite Waterloo Train Station.

Lodging Office: Address as above. Advance booking office **C-(USA) 011-44-171-928-4814, (UK) 0171-928-4814,** Fax: C-(USA) 011-44-171-620-0565, 0900-1700 daily, the club embodies the original Women's Services and Families Club. *Allied Forces are welcomed and granted Temporary Honorary Membership, 24 hours.* Check in 1300 hours, check out 1000 hours daily.

TML: Club/Hotel. All ranks, leave/vacation only. 335 bedrooms, continuously being improved; 60% now include own bath/shower, WC, and TV. Room types range from simple single rooms to suites. Restaurant, bar, color TV, souvenir shop, snooker/billiards, read, writing and library, soda/snack vending, mini mart, meeting/conference rooms, local gym available. Older structure, renovated. Rates: single *£25.20-£36.90, double £43.50-£66.20, family suite £81.00-86.00. Reservations accepted above number. All charges include VAT. Meals paid for when taken, 10% discount for seven days booking or more, deposit of one night when booking, refundable if canceled 48 hours in advance of arrival.

Other: Club, used by over 6,000 American Service men and women in 1996, will provide rates and other information on request. Reciprocal arrangements with The Marines Memorial Club, San Francisco, CA. **Active and Reserves equally welcome.**

* $1 US = £.63

UNITED KINGDOM
London Service Clubs, continued

Note: This is a private club and is not government/military billeting.

TML Availability: Good, but book early.

CREDIT CARDS ACCEPTED: Visa, MasterCard, Access and Switch cards, checks accepted when supported by cheque card.

A ten minute walk takes you to the West End, Theaterland and the Savoy (for high tea - necktie and jacket required!). All of London is easily accessible by bus or train. Don't miss a trip to Buckingham Palace, the Tower of London and all the history of London!

Victory Services Club
63/79 Seymour Street
London W2 2HF, United Kingdom
(Not US Government Lodging)

TELEPHONE NUMBER INFORMATION: C-(USA) 011-44-171-723-4474, (UK) 0171-723-4474, Fax: C-(USA) 011-44-171-724-1134.

Location: Two blocks from the Marble Arch station, easy walking distance to the American Embassy, Navy Annex, Mayfair and Oxford Streets. NMC: London, in the city.

Lodging Office: Same as above, reservations as above, 24 hours daily. **This is a members only club.** The following are eligible to join. A) serving and ex-service personnel of all ranks of the Armed Forces of the Crown, including those of the Commonwealth and members of NATO Forces; B) spouses of members of the club; C) widows and widowers of ex-service personnel. **The membership year is from 1 April and 31 March. Membership Fees: *£12 annually, £240 lifetime.** Write to the club for an application and further details. **Serving personnel are not required to pay membership fees.**

TML: Club/hotel. All ranks. Bedroom accommodations for 300 members with 80 twin/double bedrooms, some with private bath. Checks accepted when supported by a cheque card. Club facilities include a modern buttery, grill room, bar lounge, game room, television rooms and library. Rates: twin rooms £43; single rooms from £20:10. Twin rooms with private baths available at £59:60. All categories can make reservations.

* $1 US = £.63

TML Availability: Good, but book early.

CREDIT CARDS ACCEPTED: Visa and MasterCard.

Founded in 1907, the present magnificent site was opened in 1948. In WWII it was the site of the American Red Cross Columbia Club - the largest in Great Britain.

344 - Temporary Military Lodging Around the World

UNITED KINGDOM

RAF Mildenhall (UK08R7)
100 SVS/SVML
Unit 4905, Box 400
APO AE 09459-5000

TELEPHONE NUMBER INFORMATION: Main installation numbers: C-(USA) 011-44-1-638-54-1110, (UK) 01638-54-1110 D-314-238-1110.

Location: From London, follow the M11 to the A11, to the A14 Newmarket exit. Follow the A14 for a short distance to the A11 exit (Norwich/Thetford) At 5-ways roundabout, take the A1101 for 2.5 miles through Mildenhall and Beck Row to RAF Mildenhall. NMC: Cambridge, 30 miles southwest.

Lodging Office: Bldg 459, Reservations: **C-(USA) 011-44-1-638-54-2655, (UK) 01638-54-2655,** Fax: C-(USA) 011-44-1-638-54-3688, D-314-238-2655. Open 24 hours. Check in facility 1500, check out 1100 hours daily. Government civilian employee billeting. Lodging manager, Bldg 450, 100 SVS/SVML, C-(USA) 011-44-1-638-54-3044, (UK) (01638) 54-3044, D-314-238-3044, open Mon-Fri 0730-1630 hours.

TML: Gateway Inn, Bldg 459

TML: TLF. Bldg 104, all ranks. Bedroom apartments, private bath (40). Kitchen, microwave, complete utensils, CATV/VCR, complimentary video rental, housekeeping service, cribs, washer/dryer. Modern structure. Rates: $35 per unit. Maximum four per room. Duty can make reservations, others Space-A.

TML: VAQ. 200 and 400 area, enlisted all ranks, leave or official duty. Shared rooms with open bay rest rooms, some bedrooms, private bath (46). CATV, housekeeping service, washer/dryer. Rates: $12 per person. Duty can make reservations, others Space-A.

TML: VOQ. 200 and 400 area. Officers all ranks, leave or official duty. Bedroom, private bath (42). CATV, housekeeping service, washer/dryer. Rates: $12 per person. Duty can make reservations, others 24 hours an advance when space ia available.

TML: DV/VIP. Officer O6+, leave or official duty. Bedroom suites, private bath (3). Rates: $19. Duty can make reservations, others Space-A.

DV/VIP: Protocol Office, 3rd AF, Bldg 239. C-(USA) 011-44-1-638-54-2777, O7+. Retirees and lower ranks (O6) Space-A.

TML Availability: Extremely limited. Best, Nov-Dec. **Note: All numbers C- or D-extensions.**

CREDIT CARDS ACCEPTED: Visa, MasterCard and American Express.

Transportation: On/off base shuttle.

Shopping and antique hunting is popular in the area. Discover the story of Mildenhall Treasure in the Mildenhall Museum on High Street. Most active Space-A airport in the UK. Daily Bus to RAF Lakenheath and AMC Terminal.

Locator 2669   **Medical 2657**   **Police 2667**

UNITED KINGDOM

Portsmouth Royal Sailors' Home Club (UK10R7)
Queen Street
Portsmouth Hampshire
PO1 3HS
United Kingdom 01705 824231
(Not US Government Lodging)

TELEPHONE NUMBER INFORMATION: C-(USA) 011-44-170-582-4231.

Location: The club is conveniently located near the Portsmouth Naval Base and Naval Heritage area. Take Motorway M27 to M275 West, follow signs to Portsmouth HM Naval Base.

Lodging Office: Queen Street, Portsmouth, PO1, 3HS. **C-(USA) 011-44-170-582-4231, D-(USA) 314-238-2655**, Fax: (USA) 011-44-170-529-3496, 24 hours.

TML: Residency club. All ranks. This club has Twin/Double/Single/Family rooms (130), most with in suite bathrooms, color TV, tea/coffee making facilities. Some room handicap accessible. Rates: twin/double *£47, single £22.25, includes breakfast. Choice of bars, restaurant offering carvery style menu, fully equipped leisure center with swimming pool, darts, table tennis, modern gym, skittles alley. There is a £5 membership fee and the Value Added Tax is 17.5%. Payment in cash or with an English bank traveler cheque.

* $1 US = £.63

CREDIT CARDS ACCEPTED: Visa.

Visit Nelson's flagship HMS Victory, Henry VIII's favorite warship Mary Rose, the first ironclad warship in the world, HMS Warrior and D-Day Museum.

Royal Fleet Club (UK14R7)
9-12 Morice Square
Devonport, Plymouth, Devon PL1 4PG, United Kingdom
(Not US Government Lodging)

TELEPHONE NUMBER INFORMATION: C-(USA) 011-44-752-562723.

Location: Arriving from the Exeter direction on the A-38, descent to the larger Marsh Mills. Turn left at sign posted A-374 and Plymouth City Centre. Keep on the A-374 along the Embankment, Royal Parade and Union Street, pass over the Stonehouse Bridge and in about half a mile turn left (first road past traffic lights) into St. Aubyn Road; the Royal Fleet Club will be clearly seen in a short distance in front of you. NMC: Plymouth, 1/2 a mile.

Lodging Office: The Royal Fleet Club, C- (USA) **011-44-752-562723**, Fax C-(USA) 011-44-752-550725, 24 hours daily.

TML: Servicemans Club and Hotel, all ranks, leave and official duty. Bedroom, private bath (60). Color TV in rooms and lounge, housekeeping service, cribs/cot, washer/dryer, ice vending, soda/snack vending. Meeting/conference room available. Modern structure, renovated. Rates: $35 per adult per night, $12 per child (12+). Maximum four per room. Reservations required. No pets.

CREDIT CARDS ACCEPTED: None. Travelers Cheques or cash only.

UNITED KINGDOM

Other Installations in the United Kingdom

London Naval Activity. ATTN: Billeting Manager, COMNAVCTUK, PSC 821, Box 116 A74, FPO AE 09421-0116. Main installation number: C-(USA) 011-44-171-514-1110, D-314-235-1110. Located in London, England, across from the American Embassy. BEQ only (no BOQ), **C-(USA) 011-44-171-514-4717/4140.**
Menwith Hill Station. APO AE 09468-5000,20 miles northwest of Leeds **C-(USA) 011-44-1423-77-7895/7897.** Limited lodging.
RAF Croughton. ATTN: Billeting Manager, APO AE 09494-5000. **C-(USA) 011-44-1280-708-394/055, D-314-263-4394.**
St Mawgan Joint Maritime Facility. FPO AE 09409-5000, 48 miles west of Plymouth, C-011-44-16373-2201/2775, D-314-231-4612. At press time, plans were in the works to convert several TAF facilities to TML. Keep an eye out for updates in the *R&R Space-A Report*®. Limited BEQ/BOQ lodging.

• •

ANOTHER TYPE OF MILITARY LODGING

Military RV, Camping and Rec Areas Around the World often have permanent-type lodging such as cottages, log cabins, A-frames, mobile homes, and small hotels.

These facilities, which are non-appropriated and self-supporting, are usually managed by Morale, Welfare and Recreation (MWR) or Services and are dependent on user support to stay open.

Only a few of the larger MWR facilities are listed in *Temporary Military Lodging Around the World*. Next time you are shopping at your military exchange, look for *Military RV, Camping and Rec Areas Around the World* and see if this lodging can help you to travel on less per day... the military way!™ Remember, you don't have to sleep in a pup tent, unless **YOU** want to!

APPENDIX A

GENERAL ABBREVIATIONS USED IN THIS BOOK

The general abbreviations used in this book are listed below. Commonly understood abbreviates (e.g., Mon-Fri for Monday through Friday) and standard abbreviations found in addresses have not been included in order to save space.

A
AAF-Army Airfield
AAFES-Army & Air Force Exchange Service
AB-Air Base
A/C-Air Conditioning
ACS-Army Community Services
AD-Active Duty
ADT-Active Duty for Training
AE-Army Europe
AF-Air Force
AFAF-Air Force Auxiliary Field
AFB-Air Force Base
AFCENT-Allied Forces Central Europe
AFRB-Air Force Reserve Base
AFRC-Armed Forces Recreation Center
AFRES-Air Force Reserve
AFS-Air Force Station
APG-Army Proving Ground
AIRVAC-Air Evacuation
AMC-Army Medical Center
AMC-Air Mobility Command
ANGB-Air National guard Base
AP-Army Pacific
APO-Army Post Office
ARB-Air Reserve Base
ARNG-
AST-Area Support Team
ATM-Automatic Teller Machine
ATTN-Attention

B
BAQ-Bachelor Airmen's quarters
BBQ-Barbecue
BEQ-Bachelor Enlisted Quarters
BOQ-Bachelor Officers' Quarters
BQ-Bachelor Quarters (Navy)
BSB-Base Support Battalion
BX-Base Exchange

C
C-Commercial phone number
CATV-Cable television
CBQ-Combined Bachelors Quarters
CG-Coast Guard
CGAS-Coast Guard Air Station
CGES-Coast Guard Exchange Service
CGG-Coast Guard Group
CIV-Civilian
CO-Commanding Officer
CONUS-Continental United States
CP-Command Post
CPO-Chief Petty Officer
CPOQ-Chief Petty Officer Quarters
CSM-Command Sergeant Major
CTV-Color TV
CW-Chief Warrant Officer

D
D-Defense Switched Network
DAV-Disabled American Veterans
DD-Defense Department
DEPT-Department
DIV-Division
DM-Deutsche Mark
DoD-Department of Defense
DSN-Defense Switched Network
DV-Distinguished Visitor
DVOQ-Distinguished Visiting Officers' Quarters
DVQ-Distinguished Visitor Quarters

E
EFQ-Enlisted Family Quarters
ETS-European Telephone System
Ext-Extension

F
Fax-Fax telephone number
FPO-Fleet Post Office
FY-Fiscal Year

G
GH-Guest House
GM-General manager
GS-General Schedule

H
HQ-Headquarters
HWY-Highway

I
I-Interstate
IAP-International Airport
ID-Identification
ITR-Information, Ticketing and Registration
ITT-Information, Tickets and Tours

APPENDIX A, continued

J
JRB-Joint Reserve Base

M
MCB-Marine Corps Base
MCAS-Marine Corps Air Station
MCLB-Marine Corps Logistics Base
MCPO-
MCRD-Marine Corps Recruit Depot
MCX-Marine Corps Exchange
MP-Military Police
MWR-Morale, Welfare and Recreation

N
NAF-Naval Air Facility
NAS-Naval Air Station
NAVSTA-Natal Station
NAWC-Naval Air Warfare Center
NB-Naval Base
NCO-Noncommissioned Officer
NEX-Navy Exchange
NG-National Guard
NMC-Nearest Major City
NMI-Nearest Major Installation
NOAA-National Oceanic & Atmospheric Administration
NS-Naval Shipyard
NS-Naval Station
NSA-Naval Support Activity
NSB-Naval Submarine Base
NSCS-Navy Supply Corps School
NSGA-Naval Security Group Activity
NSO-Naval Security Office
NSWC-Naval Surface Weapons Center
NTC-Naval Training Center
NWC-Naval Weapons Center
NWS-Naval Weapons Station

O
O'Club-Officers' Club
OD-Officer of the Day
OIC-Officer in Charge
OOD-Officer of the Day

P
PAO-Public Affairs Office
PCS-Permanent Change of Station
PMO-Provost Marshall's Office
PX-Post Exchange

R
RAF-Royal Air Force

S
SATO-Scheduled Airlines Ticket Office
SDNCO-Senior Duty Noncommissioned Officer
SDO-Staff Duty Officer
SES-Senior Executive Service
SNCO-Senior Noncommissioned Officer
SNCOQ-Senior Noncommissioned Officers' Quarters
Space-A-Space Available

T
TAD-Temporary Attached Duty
TAQ-Temporary Airmen's Quarters
TC-Travel Camp
TDY-Temporary Duty
TEQ-Temporary Enlisted Quarters
TFL-Temporary Family Lodging
TLA-Temporary Lodging Allowance
TLF-Transient Lodging Facility
TLQ-Temporary Living Quarters
TML-Temporary Military Lodging
Tnpk-Turnpike
TOQ-Transient Officers' Quarters
TQ-Temporary Quarters
TV-Television
TVEQ-Temporary Visiting Enlisted Quarters
TVOQ-Temporary Visiting Officers' Quarters
TVQ-Temporary Visiting Quarters

U
USAF-United States Air Force
USCG-United States Coast Guard
USEUCOM-US European Command
USMC-United States Marine Corps
USMRA-United States Military Road Atlas
USN-United States Navy
USNCOQ-Unaccompanied Senior Noncommissioned Officers' Quarters
USPHS-United States Public Health Service
USS-United States Ship

V
VA-Veterans' Administration
VAQ-Visiting Airman's Quarters
VCP-Video Cassette Player
VCR-Video Cassette Recorder
VEQ-Visiting Enlisted Quarters
VFQ-Visiting Female Quarters
VHA-Variable Housing Allowance
VIP-Very Important Person
VOQ-Visiting Officer Quarters
VQ-Visiting Quarters, all ranks

W
WG-Wing
WO-Warrant Officer

APPENDIX B

TEMPORARY MILITARY LODGING QUESTIONS AND ANSWERS

Editors Note: The answers below are based on information available to us at press time. Due to the fact that there is not a uniform DoD temporary military lodging policy, the reader will find that policies differ between and among the Uniformed Services and in some cases also differ from installation to installation within a Uniformed Service. Also policies differ between CONUS and overseas and among the various types of temporary military lodging. For these reasons among others, these general answers must be accepted only as guides—not rules. Specific questions should be directed to each individual installation at the time of your visit. **Policies do often change.**

1. What type of lodging are available on military installations? There are numerous types of lodging available on military installations. They range from very modern, modular-construction, complete housekeeping units which will sleep a family of five with all amenities found in a good motel (plus a furnished kitchenette) such as found in Navy Lodges, to the old faithful guest houses—relics of World War II, which are often barracks-type buildings. Some may have been improved while others are definitely sub-standard. Some are the modern low rise to high rise hotel types such as the Shades of Green, Florida; Hale Koa Hotel AFRC, Hawaii; The New Sanno U. S. Forces Center, Japan and the Dragon Hill Lodge, Korea. There is also the modern motel type lodging such as the Inn at Schofield Barracks, Hawaii and motel chain operations at Fort Bliss, Texas. Somewhere in between, you will find VEQ/VOQ type accommodations that usually consist of private rooms with a shared bath between rooms. Also, there are the DV/VIP facilities which have in most cases a bedroom, sitting room and kitchen/dining facility. If you are the "picky" type, we suggest you take a look before signing in, if possible or talk with the lodging management.

2. Were the units mentioned above constructed with tax dollars? According to information given TML, the answer on most of the lodging is an emphatic "NO". The newer construction was built from non-appropriated funds or grants from welfare funds, generated from profits from military exchanges, etc. The exception to this is in cases where old unused family housing, initially built with appropriated funds, has been converted into temporary military lodging facilities. Also, TML is frequently available in bachelor officer's, NCO and enlisted grade quarters which have been constructed with appropriated funds.

3. What does space-available (Space-A) mean? The purpose of having lodging on military installations is to accommodate duty personnel and those arriving or departing an installation on Temporary Duty orders (TDY)/TAD) or permanent change of station (PCS) orders. Those on orders generally have first priority on all lodging. After these needs have been met, if there is any space left over, leave personnel (including retirees, reservists and their families) may utilize the facilities on a Space-A basis. During the summer months, Space-A lodging may be more difficult to obtain than during the spring, fall and winter.

4. How about advance reservations? While most installations will accept reservations from those on duty; leave, reservist and retired travelers will generally find that they cannot make reservations in advance but are accepted on a Space-A basis on arrival at the billeting office. The USAF is an important exception as they will provide reservations 24 hours in advance of arrival for a stay of up to three days. Also, Navy Lodges do accept reservations from all categories. As we are listing the lodging of five Uniformed Services (USA, USN, USMC, USCG and USAF) in this book, the rules may vary greatly from installation to installation. Please check each listing in this book or call in advance to check on specific policies on making reservations at the time of your trip. You may be surprised and find that the place you want to visit will accept your reservation.

APPENDIX B, continued

5. Can retirees use military lodging? Definitely—usually on the same Space-A basis as active duty on leave. Retirees will also find that they are welcome to use the lodging on most installations overseas, even though they may be restricted from using the commissary and exchange in most overseas areas due to the local Status of Forces Agreement (SOFA). The rules are different for the use of support facilities in each foreign country. Complete details on "Support Authorized United States Uniformed Services Personnel and Their Dependent Family Members Visiting Foreign Countries" is published in our book, **U. S. Forces Travel Guide To Overseas U. S. Military Installations, ISBN 0-914862-43-X.** See Central Order Coupon on the last page of this book.

6. Are Reservists eligible for TML? Many favorable changes have occurred for reservist as a result of the DoD "One Force Policy". Reservist now have the same eligibility for TML as Active Duty personnel. There is one notable exception in that Reservist cannot use TML in foreign countries or facilities in foreign countries where their use is not provided for in the SOFA, i.e. Reservist are not permitted to use the AFRCs in Germany and The New Sanno U S Forces Center in Japan. See Appendix D, "National Guard and Reserve Components Personnel Are Eligible For Temporary Military Lodging".

7. Your book often refers to Defense Switched Network (DSN, or D-) telephone/telefax numbers. What are they? The Defense Switched Network numbers are military telephone/telefax numbers which are to be used only by those on official business. Such numbers can normally be dialed only from a military installation and are monitored to assure their use is not violated. As many of our readers use military lodging and other facilities while traveling on duty, and many government offices use our book as a reference guide, we publish the DSN numbers, when available, as a service to them. **The DSN requires area codes to facilitate dialing to and through different areas of the DSN system. In the DSN system these area codes are called "Area Voice Codes" which are: Alaska=317; Caribbean=313; CONUS=312; Europe=314 and Pacific=315.**

8. What is DV/VIP lodging? It is lodging for distinguished official visitors. Some installations will have a few rooms or a small guest house available for them. If these facilities are not being used by official visitors, many installations will often extend the courtesy of their use to qualified active duty and reservists personnel on leave status or retirees on a day-to-day Space-A basis. Most military installations we surveyed referred to DV/VIP as pay grades 06 and above of all Services. Just a few lodging facilities included lower officer grades (05) and senior NCO (E-8/9) in this category. The Marine Corps calls their distinguished visitors lodging, Distinguished Guest Quarters (DGQ). Since 1977, we have noted that many more Air Force bases are providing DV/VIP lodging for their senior NCOs. Personnel in the DV/VIP category should check our listings in this book for more complete information and inquire at each installation upon arrival. Distinguished visitors will usually find that it is best to make advance reservations through the Protocol Office or Visitor's Bureau of the installation concerned. In some cases, the billeting office has authority to place personnel in the DV/VIP lodging and coordinate the visit for the traveler.

9. My husband is enlisted. What chance do we have at staying in military lodging? Better than ever. In the past few years, concentrated efforts have been made to provide more temporary lodging for enlisted members. Please notice in our listing the numerous references to quarters for all ranks. In the newer Air Force Transient Living Quarters, Navy Lodges, and Army Guest Houses, rank has absolutely no privileges. All ranks are accommodated on an equal basis. Policies may vary on other types of lodging. At some facilities, enlisted have priority.

10. May 100% DAV use TML? Most military lodging units accept 100% DAV (Disabled American Veterans) on a Space-A basis if it is possible. In fact the Hale Koa Hotel, AFRC specifically mentions 100% DAV in their brochure as being eligible. One problem that 100% DAV have encountered has been caused by the color of their ID Card (DD-1173). It is the same color (buff or butterscotch) as carried by family members. Many times 100% DAV are turned away from facilities which require

APPENDIX B, continued

family members to be accompanied by their sponsor. The "ID card-checking authority" assumes this 100% DAV is not a military member but a "dependent" or family member. Watch for more info on this subject in Military Living's R & R Space-A Report®.

11. How about Navy—Bachelor Quarters (BQ)? We are told that a few Bachelor Enlisted Quarters (BEQ) locations are unsuitable facilities for family members—central baths (latrines), ect. However, most Bachelor Enlisted Quarters (BEQ) have suitable facilities. Also, Bachelor Officers' Quarters (BOQ) are almost always suitable. They will generally accept family members accompanying their sponsor. Rules can vary from installation to installation. If a Navy Lodge is not available, always ask about the possible use of BEQ/BOQ.

12. What about widows, widowers, and unaccompanied dependents? The news gets better each time we report in our new TML book. dependents of active duty personnel who are involved in a PCS move may now use TML and make reservations at the installation they are leaving and at the new one to which they are assigned. They may also use TML en route on a Space-A basis. This includes TML in TLF and in VEQ or VOQ.

Unaccompanied dependents of service members on leave and also widows/ers of deceased members may use TML on a Space-A basis in VEQ or VOQ if this policy has been approved by the base commander. Therefore, this may NOT be in effect at all Air Force installations. This does not include the use of TLF.

Uniformed Services other than the USAF generally have always allowed unaccompanied service family members to use TML on a Space-A basis. This, of course, has and will continue to differ from installation to installation. Navy Lodges, however, welcome dependent children, and non-ID card holders when accompanied by a parent or guardian authorized to utilize Navy Lodges.

13. What's a Fisher House? Overview: A Fisher House is "a home away from home" for families of patients receiving medical care at major military and VA medical centers. The houses are normally located within walking distance of the treatment facility or have transportation available. There are 26 Fisher Houses located on 16 military installations and four VA medical centers, including two in design and planning.

Description: Fisher Houses are comfortably furnished homes donated by Zachary and Elizabeth M. Fisher of New York. Each house is designed to provide eight suites, two of which are handicap accessible. The houses can accommodate up to 16 family members. They feature a common kitchen, laundry facilities, spacious dining room and an inviting living room and library, and toys for children. A Fisher House is a temporary residence and is not a treatment facility, hospice or counseling center.

Responsibilities: Fisher Houses are give to the U. S. Government as gifts from Mr. and Mrs. Fisher. The military service secretaries and the Secretary of Veterans Affairs are responsible for the operation and maintenance of the homes. The Fisher House Foundation, Inc., a not-for-profit organization, assists in the coordination of private support and encourages public support for the homes.

Eligibility and Cost: Criteria established locally by hospital or installation commanders. Cost varies by location. The average charge for lodging in 1996 was $8.20 per family per day. Several of the houses offer free lodging.

Editors Note: Families may stay while visiting patients requiring treatment, and are referred by physicians or social workers based on a variety of priorities. Generally priorities are: lack of family in the immediate area; severity of illness; and financial need. Different hospitals may have varying criteria. **The Fisher Houses addresses and telephone numbers are contained in each listing in this book which has one or more Fisher Houses.**

APPENDIX C

BILLETING REGULATIONS AND NAVY LODGE POLICIES

The Department of Defense has issued several instructions which outline for the Military Departments the broad guidance for the organization, operation, management and reporting for several broad categories of Temporary Military Lodging (TML). **(Please see: DoD Instruction 1100.16 and 4165.63 and DoD Manual 4165.63-M).** The Military Departments within the Department of Defense and the United States Coast Guard within the Department of Transportation have issued more specific policy and procedure directives covering the organization, management, and reporting for their respective categories of TML. **There are some consistencies among these Military Department directives but they are not identical or uniform in their content.** As a special service to our readers, we have synthesized each Military Department and Navy Lodge directive below. In each case we have selected the items from the directives which we believe would provide the greatest benefit to our readers. We have provided the reference for each directive and the reader may request to see the complete directive at the respective Military Department lodging facilities or at their personnel offices.

ARMY INSTALLATION HOUSING MANAGEMENT

This regulation condenses regulations in the 210-series that govern the management and operation of the Army's family, unaccompanied personnel and guest housing programs and their related furnishing programs. This regulation **Installation Housing Management-AR-210-50** is effective **24 May 1990** and has several changes since that date. The regulation is applicable to the Active Army, Army National Guard and U. S. Army Reserve.

The primary consideration in the management of billeting activities is to promote the use of housing assets. This must be done to ensure that housing that is available is used for its intended purpose, and meets the housing needs of authorized personnel in the performance of their duties.

Billeting activities include the following:

1-Unaccompanied Personnel Housing (UPH) (PP) (Permanent Party). **2**-Officers Quarters (OQ). **3**-Senior Officer Quarters (SOQ). **4**-Enlisted Quarters (EQ). **5**-Senior Enlisted Quarters (SEQ). **6**-UPH (TDY). **7**-Visiting Officers Quarters (VOQ). **8**-Visiting Enlisted Quarters (VEQ). **9**-Distinguished Visitor Quarters (DVQ). **10**-Guest House (GH).

Authority to occupy Transient Facilities:

A-Personnel authorized to occupy TDY housing.

1-The following personnel with a confirmed reservation:

a-TDY military and TDY DoD civilians. **b**-PCS military personnel when GH not available. **c**-U. S. and foreign guest of the Military Services. **d**-USAR, ARNG and ROTC on Active Duty Training. **e**-Foreign military personnel TDY. **f**-Military family members on medical TDY orders. **g**-Guest of Armed Forces as determined by installation commander.

2-When space is available, the following personnel may occupy TDY housing:

a-Retirees (including Reserve Grey Area), military personnel on leave, family members and guest of military personnel assigned to the installation if GH space is not available.
b-Non-military uniformed personnel of USPHS, NOAA, USCG personnel traveling on official business and foreign military personnel.
c-Within the categories listed in 1 and 2 above, personnel will compete on an equal basis for TDY facilities.
d-Members in promotable status may be assigned to housing of the next higher grade upon presentation of proof of pending promotion.
e-Personnel listed in 2 above will pay the fair market rental rate.

B-Personnel Authorized to Occupy GH Facilities.

1-The following personnel with a confirmed reservation may occupy Guest House (GH) facilities.

a-PCS service members and their families accompanied or alone. **b**-PCS DoD civilian personnel and their families accompanied or alone in an overseas area. **c**-Families, relatives and guests of hospitalized service members or their families. **d**-Active and retired military personnel and family members undergoing outpatient treatment at a medical facility and must remain overnight (RON). **e**-Official guest of the installation. **f**-Families of a soldier visiting an installation incident to internment of the soldier or family members.

2-When space is available, the following personnel may occupy GH facilities.

a-TDY service members and TDY DoD civilian personnel when UPH(TDY) facilities are not available. **b**-Retired service members (including Reserve Grey Area) with or without family members. **c**-Members of USPHS, NOAA and USCG. **d**-PCS DoD civilians with or without family members in CONUS. **e**-Service members on leave not incident to PCS with or without family members, relatives and guest of service members assigned to the installation.

3-Within the categories listed above, personnel may compete on an equal basis or the installation commander may establish priorities within the categories to meet the needs of the installation.

Medal of Honor recipients of all services are authorized transient facilities at the discretion of the installation commander. Medal of Honor recipients may receive priority placement and confirmed reservations in the VOQ, VEQ, DVQ or GH. A DVQ may be assigned regardless of military pay grade.

Reservation System

A-TDY Housing

1-Billeting offices will establish a reservation system that will enable TDY travelers to confirm reservations at least 15 days prior to actual travel. A reservation number will be provided to the traveler.

2-TDY travelers who receive confirmation of non availability of housing may live off the installation.

3-TDY students who have confirmed reservations must reside in transient facilities.

4-Reservations should not be held beyond 1800 hours unless the TDY traveler notifies the billeting office of late arrival.

354 - Temporary Military Lodging Around the World

APPENDIX C, continued

B-GH Facilities

1-Reservations will be on a first-come basis without regard to rank, race, color, religion, gender, national origin or handicap. Reservations should be accepted up to 30 days in advance of requested date. Confirmation should be provided as early as possible.

2-Reservations should not be held beyond 1800 hours unless the billeting office is notified of late arrival. The normal duration of occupancy for all lodging categories is 30 days unless a hardship extension is approved by the installation commander.

NOTE: The Army will begin operation of a worldwide access reservation system by March 1994, located in Huntsville, AL. This central reservation system will serve Army Temporary Military Lodging worldwide. **The toll free reservation number is 1-800-GO-ARMY-1 or 1-800-462-7691.** This central reservation number does not serve all Army Temporary Military Lodging locations.

NAVY BACHELOR HOUSING

The Navy operates bachelor housing and Navy Lodges as Temporary Lodging Facilities. The bachelor housing facilities are operated for both permanent party and TDY/TAD personnel. The Navy Lodge program is administered by the Navy Exchange Service and provides Temporary Lodging Facilities for a wide category of personnel (See below).

The Navy bachelor housing program is covered in **BUPERS Instruction 11103.1B, Activities With Bachelor Quarters, (to be issued Sep 1993)** which promulgates the basic Navy policy covering among other things, the utilization and occupancy of BQ and the related management of this program. This instruction applies to the Navy worldwide.

The instruction applies to active duty and reserve personnel, DoD civilians, civilians authorized by SECNAV, National Guard personnel on active duty for training or active duty, retirees and dependent personnel.

This instruction applies to the following quarters:

1-Bachelor Enlisted Quarters (BEQ). **2**-Bachelor Officers' Quarters (BOQ). **3**-Bachelor Civilian Quarters (BCQ). **4**-Recruit Training Quarters (RTQ). **5**-Reserve Component Quarters (RCQ). **6**-Quarters for duty personnel. **7**-Discipline and legal hold quarters. **8**-Medical holding units. **9**-Ashore Quarters for Afloat Staffs. **10**-United States Marine Corps Barracks. **11**-Leased or contract Quarters. **12**-Temporary Lodging Facilities (TLF Navy Lodges). **13**-Transient Visiting Officers Quarters (TVOQ). **14**-Transient Personnel Unit Quarters (TPU).

The Navy has a new program to assign bachelor quarters to their "geographic bachelors" for the entire length of their tour of duty. The implementation of this program **may considerably reduce the availability of bachelor quarters to active duty (TDY/TAD), leave, retirees and Reserve personnel.**

The Navy has priority for use of quarters and reservation systems similar to the other services. When the new instruction is available we will publish this information in later changes to this TML book and in **Military Living's *R and R Space-A Report*®**. Please see the Central Order Coupon in the back of this book.

APPENDIX C, continued

NAVY LODGES

Navy Lodge Mission. The Navy Lodge mission is to provide United States Uniformed Services personnel accompanied by dependents under Permanent Change of Station (PCS) orders with temporary lodging accommodation, and to provide lodging for all other authorized quests.

Reservations

WHO MAY STAY?

Reservations are accepted for all eligible personnel on an as-received basis. **Once a reservation is made it will be firm and you cannot be bumped.** Reservations and room assignments are made without regard to rank or rate.

CATEGORY	DATE
PCS with family	Anytime
Active Duty on TDY orders	Anytime
Active Duty leave, TAD, Rest & Relaxation, Widows/Widowers/dependents of Active Duty Military Personnel	60 days
Single PCS	60 days
Retirees, Widows/Widowers/Dependents of Retired Military Personnel, Retired Reservists	30 days
Foreign Military	60 days
DoD and DN (Department of Navy) (on orders), DoD and DN (not on orders with Navy Exchange Privileges), U. S. Public Health Service and American Red Cross (on orders)	30 days
Medical in-patients and family of seriously ill	Anytime
Medical out-patients	60 days
Weekend Reservist	60 days

Official guest and visitors of the command may stay at Navy Lodges, but must be checked in by their sponsors.

Family members and guests of military personnel may stay at Navy Lodges provided the military member is present at check-in.

FOR RESERVATIONS CALL: 1-800-NAVY INN (1-800-628-9466)

HOW DO I MAKE A RESERVATION? CALL 1-800-NAVY INN or you may call the lodge directly at the numbers found in each Navy Lodge listing in this book.

APPENDIX C, continued

HOW DO I GUARANTEE MY ROOM FOR LATE ARRIVAL? Reservations are held until 1800 hours at most Navy Lodges. Your reservations can be guaranteed for late arrival with either a major credit card or an advance cash deposit (one night's lodging directly to the lodge). For more information call 1-800-NAVY INN.

HOW DO I CANCEL MY RESERVATION? If you have guaranteed your reservation for late arrival with a credit card or advance deposit it is essential that you call to cancel your reservation before check-in time. **If your reservation is not canceled prior to check-in your credit card will be charged for the first night.** Call 1-800 NAVY INN prior to day of arrival or the Lodge directly on the scheduled day of arrival prior to check-in time to cancel your reservation.

WHEN IS CHECK-INN? Check-in time at most lodges is between 1500 and 1800 hours (call 1-800-NAVY INN for more information). Early arrivals will be accommodated according to room availability.

WHAT TIME IS CHECK-OUT? Check-out time at all Navy Lodges is Noon.

IS MY PET ALLOWED? Unfortunately pets are not allowed in the Navy Lodges. Please ask for local kennel information at the time of your reservation.

Navy Lodge Renovations

In a continuing effort to provide Navy Lodge guest with comfortable accommodations, the Navy Lodge System renovates all Navy Lodge guest rooms on a continuing schedule. Each guest room is scheduled for renovations on a five-year cycle.

The Navy Lodge System pledges to each guest, that every effort is made to ensure your stay with us is a pleasant and comfortable experience. If you have any suggestions on how we can improve our service, please complete a comment card or call our Guest Assistance number, 1-888-24-SERVE.

MARINE CORPS HOUSING MANAGEMENT MANUAL

The following has been extracted from the **Marine Corps Housing Management Manual, MCO P11000.22, dated 14 February 1991, with changes.**

Transient Quarters Management. Transient quarters are operated primarily to provide a service to duty transient personnel and TAD students. Adequate quarters shall be set aside to accommodate TAD transient personnel. When designated transient quarters are fully occupied, transients may voluntarily occupy permanent party quarters.

The following personnel are entitled to designated TAD transient quarters on a confirmed reservation basis: **a**-Military personnel and DoD civilians on TAD orders. **b**-American Red Cross and Navy Relief Society on official business. **c**-U. S. and Foreign civilians traveling as guest of Armed Forces. **d**-Reserve personnel in TAD status, unit training status, and annual trainees on individual orders. **e**-TAD foreign nationals or foreign military trainees engaged in or sponsored by military assistance or similar training programs unless prohibited by the Status of Forces Agreement (SOFA). **f**-Family members on medical TAD orders. **g**-Military personnel with or without family members, arriving or departing for overseas installations on PCS when TLF or permanent housing is not immediately available. **h**-Official guests of the activity commander.

APPENDIX C, continued

The following personnel may occupy designated transient quarters on a space-available basis: **a**-Retirees, military personnel on leave, family members, or guests of military personnel assigned to the activity if TLF space is not available. **b**-DoD civilian employees and their families arriving or departing incident to PCS when TLFs are not available. **c**-Guests of the activity commander.

Non-duty transients shall be advised at the time of registration that occupancy is strictly on a day-to-day, space-available basis and that they must vacate not later than the following day if the quarters are required for duty transients.

Distinguished Guest Quarters (DGQ) are also available to accommodate the frequent travel of high ranking officials, both civilian and military. DGQs are under the control of the installation commander.

COAST GUARD TEMPORARY GUEST HOUSING FACILITY POLICIES

The following has been extracted from **Coast Guard Recreation Areas and Temporary Guest Housing Facilities Guide, Publication P1710.14 dated 18 January 1989, with changes.**

Most large Coast Guard installations have developed guest housing in response to the need for temporary lodging for Coast Guard members and their families. These facilities are operated and managed by the Coast Guard Exchange System (CGES). Since each installation manages its own GH, each has its own rules and regulations regarding usage.

Guest housing was developed mainly for use by active duty Coast Guard members and their families traveling under PCS orders; however, Coast Guard personnel in other than PCS status and members of the other uniformed services are allowed to use some Coast Guard guest housing facilities. It is always advisable to call the facility you intend to visit to determine your eligibility and reservation policy. Most of this essential information is listed in each Coast Guard listing in this book.

RECENT AIR FORCE LODGING POLICY

Reservations Confirmed for Space-A Lodging

The USAF has implemented a confirmed reservations policy for Space-A customers (worldwide). Since 1 December 1995 the following policy has been in effect at all Air Force bases:

1. Lodging will accept and confirm reservations for Space-A customers 24 hours in advance of their arrival.

2. Reservations may be confirmed for up to a 72-hour (three-day) stay, space permitting.

3. Duty travelers will not "bump" Space-A guest with confirmed reservations, nor will they bump them once they have been assigned quarters for a special period of time, generally three days.

4. Lodging should attempt to negotiate reduced rates for their Space-A guests under their commercial lodging contracts.

The Air Force Services Agency noted that "Not only are we sending a clear message that we value Space-A customers, we're increasing the financial benefits to the Services organizations by maximizing the investment in our lodging operations and opening additional avenues for our community-services activities."

APPENDIX C, continued

Surcharge for Visiting Airmen and Officer Quarters (VAQ/VOQ)

The Air Force Services Agency who is responsible for Air Force Lodging worldwide announced in late 1996 that they would begin to collect an approved surcharge of $2 per night worldwide for visiting airmen and officers quarters (VAQ/VOQ). This surcharge would be used to finance temporary lodging facility construction to include communications systems such as telephone, television, cable television and related.

BEST AIR FORCE LODGING FOR 1996

The Air Force selected for the 1996 Innkeeper Award, Eglin Air Force Base, FL and Malmstrom Air Force Base, MT. The award recognizes lodging facilities with exemplary customer service, facilities, equipment,and procedures. This is the second year in a row the Eglin Inn was selected for this award.

All customers of Air Force Lodging may send comments regarding Air Force Lodging and Customer Service to: Hq AFSVA/SVOHL, 10100 Reunion Place, Suite 401, San Antonio, TX 78216-4138.

AIR FORCE LODGING REQUIRES GUEST TO PAY AT CHECK IN

All Air Force lodging guests, must provide a valid credit card at check in or pay in advance with cash or check for anticipated room charges. This new policy does not apply to agency billings. Advance payment will allow credit cards guest to check out without visiting the front desk. Not only is this a convenient time saver, it reduces lobby congestion. Also, it allows a lodging facility to provide the same standard of customer service as its commercial counterparts. Most guest can't check in to a commercial hotel without first identifying how they are going to pay their bill. In conclusion, it should be noted that delinquent accounts decrease lodging revenue and ultimately increase room rates for everyone.

Air Force Billeting Operations Regulations

The following has been extracted from **Air Force Regulation 34-601, Air Force Lodging, dated 24 May 1993.**

Transient Quarters Operation. Transient Quarters are operated to provide a service to duty transient personnel and TDY students. The operation of transient quarters is based on the need of the services and the availability of quarters at an installation.

Personnel Eligible for Transient Quarters: The following personnel are eligible to occupy Visiting Officer Quarters (VOQ) and Visiting Enlisted Quarters (VEQ) **commensurate with their grade on a space-confirmed basis. The order in which the following are listed does not indicate a priority:** **a**-TDY personnel, including crew members. **b**-TDY U.S. civilian employees, and civilians traveling under competent authority. **c**-Members of the Air National Guard and Air Force Reserve on annual tours, school tours, special tours of active duty, or active duty for training. **d**-Members of the Air National Guard and Air Force Reserve on inactive duty training. **e**-TDY or TDY student, foreign military, or civilian personnel sponsored through security assistance, allied exchange, or foreign liaison programs. **f**-USAFA and AFROTC cadets traveling on official orders. **g**-Aircraft passengers on official orders or emergency leave at aerial ports of embarkation, if aerial port quarters are not available. **h**-Dependents on medical TDY orders. **i**-Military and civilian personnel using military aircraft in TDY or PCS status who, for reasons beyond their control, remain overnight (RON) at

APPENDIX C, continued

locations other than their TDY or PCS location. **j**-Contract engineering and technical services personnel (CETSP). **k**-Guests of the armed forces as determined by the installation commander. **l**-Applicants for an Air Force commission. **m**-Active duty personnel on emergency leave. **n**-Unaccompanied personnel, including civilians, entitled to permanent quarters who are temporarily without permanent housing due to PCS travel orders. **o**-Military and civilian personnel and their families arriving or departing an overseas location incident to PCS, if no other government temporary lodging is available. **p**-Military and civilian personnel in a TDY status to nearby locations who desire government quarters in lieu of commercial quarters. **q**-Personnel on permissive TDY orders.

The following personnel are eligible to occupy VOQ/VEQ on a space-available basis. Maximum stay is 30 days during any one visit. Extensions must be approved by the installation commander. The order in which the following are listed does not indicate a priority: **a**-Dependents accompanying official TDY personnel. **b**-Married military and civilian personnel with their families in CONUS who are temporarily without permanent housing due to PCS orders, only when TLFs (see below) are not available. **c**-Unaccompanied personnel entitled to permanent quarters who arrive or depart incident to PCS and are temporarily without permanent housing. **d**-Dependents of members who are patients in Air Force hospitals, only if TLF not available. **e**-Retirees and retirement eligible Reservists in a non duty status (who have DD Form 2 AFRES with a copy of ARPC certificate of retirement eligibility) and their dependents. **f**-Active duty members and their dependents on ordinary leave, environmental and morale leave (EML), or travel status. **g**-U.S. civilians and their dependents on EML orders from overseas duty assignments, only if TLF is not available. **h**-Active status and/or in training Air National Guard and Air Force Reserve members and their dependents. **i**-Space-available passengers aboard military aircraft interrupted short of destination, or passengers arriving at ports for space-available travel on departing military flights. **j**-AFROTC cadets, organizations, and youth groups when approved by the installation commander. **k**-Civil Air Patrol (CAP) members on official visits.

Note: transient dependents of deceased military members and dependents unaccompanied by their active or retired military sponsor, or U.S. civilian sponsor in overseas areas, may occupy transient quarters when approved by the installation commander.

Personnel requesting space-available lodging will be assigned lodging upon arrival, unless all rooms are occupied or reserved by priority 1 personnel.

Temporary Lodging Facility Operations. Temporary Lodging Facilities (TLFs) are operated to provide temporary housing to authorized personnel at the lowest possible cost consistent with giving good service.

Eligibility for and Assignment to TLFs. Personnel listed below are eligible to occupy TLFs. Assignments are made without regard to rank and on a first-come-first-served basis. Following personnel have priority 1 status: **a**-Active duty military members accompanied by their dependents or their dependents alone, incident to PCS, separation, or retirement. **b**-Civilian and military friends and relatives of patients in Air Force hospitals. **c**-Hospital outpatients. **d**-Personnel who are accompanied by dependents and in permissive TDY, ordinary leave, or terminal leave status, and traveling for the purpose of house hunting in conjunction with PCS, retirement, or separation. **e**-Displaced Military Family Housing occupants required to temporarily vacate their assigned lodging. **f**-Official guest of the installation commander.

Following personnel have priority 2 status: a-Military members and dependents on leave or delay en route. **b**-Military and civilian personnel, whether or not accompanied by dependents, on TDY when VOQ or VAQ facilities are fully occupied. **c**-Retired military members and dependents. **d**-Unaccompanied married personnel and unmarried members being joined by or acquiring dependents. **e**-Unaccompanied married personnel and unmarried members incident to PCS, if neither transient nor

APPENDIX C, continued

permanent party government quarters are available. **f-**Civilians accompanied by their dependents incident to PCS, active status Air National Guard and Air Force Reserve not in a duty status and their dependents. **g-**Air National Guard and Air Force Reserve members not in a duty status. **h-**Members of USCG, USPHS and NOAA.

Following personnel have priority 3 status: a-Friends and relatives of assigned military personnel. Note: Personnel in priorities 2 and 3 are accommodated on a space-available basis and are required to vacate quarters no later than the next day after quarters are required by personnel in priority 1.

Reservations. Only personnel in priority 1 may request advance reservations. Reservation request should include expected arrival time and date. Reservations will not be held beyond 1700 hours unless the billeting office is notified in advance of personal needs for a later arrival time. Normal check out time is 1200 hours.

Recent change to chapter 4, Transient Quarters. 4-1c(2) ------- Travelers requesting quarters on a space-available basis should be assigned quarters upon arrival and should not wait until 1800 hours in the event of "no-shows." Upon assignment, travelers desiring space-available quarters for more than one night's stay must be advised to check at the billeting desk prior to check-out time the following day. If known requirements indicate that quarters are not needed for priority 1 personnel, the traveler should be confirmed for another night's stay at that time.

NATIONAL GUARD AND RESERVE COMPONENTS PERSONNEL ARE NOW ELIGIBLE FOR TEMPORARY MILITARY LODGING

Temporary Military Lodging on military installations is now open to all National Guard and Reserve Component Personnel with an ID card, on a Space-A basis. Previously, only Reserve Component members on orders or on inactive duty for training at the installation could stay in transient unaccompanied personnel housing (UPH) or temporary lodging facilities (TLF). This change was directed by the Deputy Assistant Secretary of Defense, Installations in a Memorandum to the Services Deputy Assistant Secretaries, dated 04 August 1995.

This memorandum states that in addition to Reserve Component personnel on duty for training, all other Reserve Component members shall be eligible to use temporary lodging facilities (TLF), and transient unaccompanied personnel housing (UPH) on a Space-A basis, in accordance with the following guidelines.

To support the total force concept, Reserve Component members not addressed by DoD 4165.63-M are eligible to use TLF and transient UPH as follows:

1. TLF: All Reserve Component members (including members not under orders, paid retirees, and grey area retirees*) may occupy TLF on a Space-A basis.

2. Transient UPH, on a Space-A basis, when TLF are not available: If TLF are not available, Reserve Component members not otherwise addressed by DoD 4165.63-M shall be accommodated on a Space-A basis. These include members not under orders, paid retirees, and grey area retirees. A service fee, instead of a rental rate, may be charged if the Reserve Component member's status is the same as other military members paying service fees under DoD 4165.63-M.

Reserve Component personnel shall be accommodated in TLF on the same basis as members on active duty. Heads of Components shall supplement the TLF reservation-eligible list if they determine that Space-A access does not provide "same basis" accommodation.

APPENDIX C, continued

* A "grey area retiree" is a Reserve Component member with an ID card (red, marked Ret-2, and issued per DoDI-1000.13), who would be eligible for retired pay under Chapter 67 of Title 10, U. S. C. but for the fact the member is under 60 years of age.

Editors Note: Reserve Component personnel temporary military lodging is not authorized in countries/lodging facilities which are not provided for in the Status of Forces Treaty for the country. Examples are the AFRCs in Germany and the New Sanno U. S. Forces Center in Japan. Reserve Component personnel are authorized AFRC lodging in CONUS, Hawaii and Korea.

EXPANDED USE AND ELIGIBILITY OF AFRCs

Expanded DoD instruction 1015.10 patronage policy allows currently employed and retired DoD civilians (both non-appropriated fund and appropriated fund) patronage of the Armed Forces Recreation Centers (AFRCs) **where not prohibited by status of forces agreement (SOFA)**.

As a result of the expanded patronage policy, currently employed and retired DoD civilians can visit prime resort AFRCs in Orlando, Florida (Shades of Green); Hawaii (Hale Koa Hotel; and Seoul, Korea (Dragon Hill Lodge). SOFA agreement precludes DoD civilian patronage at AFRC-Europe (Garmisch and Chiemsee, Germany)—unless the DoD civilian employee is stationed outside the United States.

ANOTHER TYPE OF MILITARY LODGING

Military RV, Camping and Rec Areas Around the World often have permanent-type lodging such as cottages, log cabins, A-frames, mobile homes, and small hotels.

These facilities, which are non-appropriated and self-supporting, are usually managed by Morale, Welfare and Recreation (MWR) or Services and are dependent on user support to stay open.

Only a few of the larger MWR facilities are listed in *Temporary Military Lodging Around the World*. Next time you are shopping at your military exchange, look for *Military RV, Camping and Rec Areas Around the World* and see if this lodging can help you to travel on less per day... the military way!™ Remember, you don't have to sleep in a pup tent, unless **YOU** want to!

APPENDIX D
TELEPHONE INFORMATION
A Few Words About Telephone Systems in Germany

Each of the commercial/civilian telephone numbers at the top of all listings in Germany follow the same pattern. When dialing from the USA, the first set of digits is the international access, 011, the second set of digits is the country code (49 in Germany), and the third set of digits is the city code (631 - Kaiserslautern). The fourth set of digits is the local area civilian prefix. The next set of digits is the civilian-to-military conversion code. The last set of digits is the line number/extension (or a set of Xs indicating line number/extension). Telephone calls originating on civilian instruments and terminating on military instruments require the conversion code. Telephone calls originating and terminating on civilian instruments do not require the conversion code. Commercial-to-commercial or commercial-to-military telephone calls originating and terminating in the same local area do not generally require the use of the civilian prefix either. Also, local area civilian prefixes all begin with a "0". The "0" is only used in-country. Drop the "0" if dialing from outside the country.

WORLD WIDE AREA VOICE CODES FOR THE DEFENSE SWITCHED NETWORK (DSN) TELEPHONE SYSTEM

ALASKA -	317
CARIBBEAN -	313
CONTINENTAL UNITED STATES -	312
EUROPE -	314
PACIFIC -	315

STANDARD EMERGENCY & SERVICE NUMBERS FROM ALL DEFENSE SWITCHED NETWORK EUROPE TELEPHONE (DSN-E)

DSN EMERGENCY	NUMBER
Ambulance/Hospital/Clinic	116
Engineer	115
Fire	117
Military Police	114

MILITARY SERVICE	NUMBER
Operator	0 or 1110
CONUS DSN	312
Booking	112
Information	113
Civilian Access	133
AFN-TV Trouble	113
Telephone Repair	119

CIVILIAN EMERGENCY NUMBERS
(From Civilian Phone)

COUNTRY	FIRE	MEDICAL	POLICE
Belgium	100	100	101
Germany	112	110	110
Italy	115	-----	112
Netherlands	0611	0611	0611
United Kingdom	999	999	999

NOTE: The United States Army, Europe Telephone Directories list "Civilian to Military prefixes", "Telephone Exchange DSN-E prefixes" and "Numerical Military Dial prefixes" all of which are too numerous to list here!

Note: * The Direct Distance Dial (DDD) system (also known as the Military system) has been replaced with the Defense Switched Network - Europe (DSN-E).

MILITARY R·Y Living™
Where the fun begins™

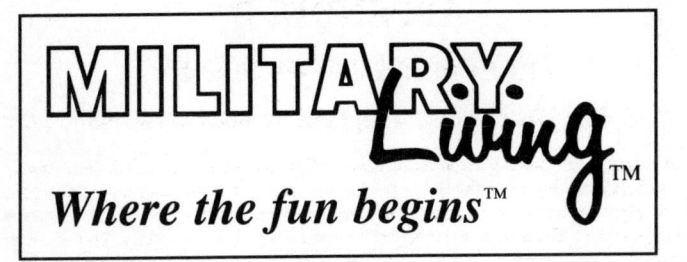

HAVING A RETIREE DAY OR PRE-RETIREMENT BRIEFING?

Let **Military Living** ™ help make your big day a success!

Retirees are anxious to know more about flying Space-A on U.S. military aircraft. Military Living Publications is well-known as being a leading authority on military recreation and Space-A air travel.

Military Living ™ will send your Retiree Activity Office complimentary sample copies of Military Living's *R&R Space-A Report*® and door prizes to give away at the Retiree Day. We can also provide materials for your Pre-Retirement Briefings.

To participate in Military Living's™ **Retiree Day Program**, simply have your Retiree Activity Office write or fax us on the office letterhead giving the date and time of the next retiree day. A name of the Retiree Office contact and phone number are also necessary. We must have a street address of the Retiree Activity office in order to send the publications by United Parcel Service. We also need to know how many people attended last year and the expected number for this year.

It would be greatly appreciated if you would include the participation of Military Living in advance publicity in order to let your retirees know that they should look for our publications at the Retiree Day.

As it is costly for our small business to supply the Retiree Day door prizes and copies of Military Living's *R&R Space-A Report*®, we ask that if there are any leftovers of the newsletter, that you return them to your Retiree Activity Office to give to visitors to your office. Please honor our copyright by **not** making copies of the *R&R Space-A Report*®. We would appreciate your sending us a copy of your retiree newsletter if there is one being published.

Thanks to all of you who help military retirees so much!

Ann, Roy, and RJ Crawford

Publishers, Military Living Publications

P.O. Box 2347, Falls Church, VA 22042-0347

Phone (703) 237-0203; FAX (703) 237-2233

CENTRAL ORDER COUPON
Military Living Publications
P.O. Box 2347, Falls Church, VA 22042-0347
TEL: (703) 237-0203 FAX: (703) 237-2233

Publications (Prices as of 1 June 1997)		QTY
R&R Space-A Report®: *The worldwide travel newsletter. 6 issues per year.* 1 yr/$15.00 - 2 yrs/$24.00 - 3 yrs/$33.00 - 5 yrs/$49.00		
Military Space-A Air Basic Training.	$13.95	
Military Space-A Opportunities Air Route Map. (Folded)	$13.95	
Military Space-A Air Opportunities Around the World.	$18.95	
Temporary Military Lodging Around the World.	$16.95	
Military RV, Camping & Rec Areas Around the World.	$14.95	
U.S. Forces Travel and Transfer Guide.	$14.95	
U.S. Forces Travel Guide to Overseas U.S. Military Installations.	$17.95	
U.S. Military Museums, Historic Sites & Exhibits. (Soft Cover)	$17.95	
United States Military Road Atlas.	$18.95	
U.S. Military Installation Road Map. (Folded)	$7.95	
COLLECTOR'S ITEM! Desert Shield Commemorative Maps. (Folded) (2 flat wall maps in a hard tube)	$8.00 $18.00	
Assignment Washington Military Road Atlas.	$10.95	
California State Military Road Map. (Folded) Florida State Military Road Map. (Folded) Mid-Atlantic States Military Road Map (Folded) Texas State Military Road Map. (Folded)	$5.95 $5.95 $5.95 $5.95	
Military Living Magazine, Camaraderie Washington. *Local Area magazine. 1 year (4 seasonal issues)*	$8.00	
Virginia Addresses add 4.5% sales tax (Books, Maps & Atlases only)		
ALL ORDERS SHIPPED FIRST CLASS MAIL	TOTAL $	

*If you are an R&R Space-A Report subscriber, you may deduct $1.00 per book. (No discount on the R&R Report itself or on the maps or atlas.) Mail Order Prices are for U.S. APO & FPO addresses. Please consult publisher for International Mail Price. Sorry, no billing.

We're as close as your telephone...by using our Telephone Ordering Service. We honor American Express, MasterCard, Visa and Discover. Call us at **703-237-0203** (Voice Mail after hours) or Fax 703-237-2233 and order today! Sorry, no collect calls. Or fill out and mail the order coupon on the next page.

NAME:_____
STREET:_____
CITY/STATE/ZIP:_____
PHONE:_____ SIGNATURE:_____
RANK (or rank of sponsor):_____ Branch of Service:_____
Active Duty:___ Retired:___ Widow/er:___ 100% Disabled Veteran:___ Guard:___ Reservist:___ Other:___
Card #_____ Card Expiration Date:_____

Mail check/money order to Military Living Publications, P.O. Box 2347 Falls Church, VA 22042-0347.
Tel: 703-237-0203, Fax: 703-237-2233.
Save $$$ by purchasing any of our books, Maps, and Atlases at your Military Exchange.
Prices subject to change. Please check here if we may ship and bill the difference........ ☐